THE

PUBLICATIONS

OF THE

Lincoln Record Society

FOUNDED IN THE YEAR
1910

VOLUME 113

ISSN 0267-2634

Interior of Louth St James.

THE LOUTH ST JAMES CHURCHWARDENS' ACCOUNTS:

1527–1570

EDITED BY
DR BRIAN HODGKINSON

The Lincoln Record Society
The Boydell Press

© Lincoln Record Society 2025

All Rights Reserved. Except as permitted under current legislation no part of this work may be photocopied, stored in a retrieval system, published, performed in public, adapted, broadcast, transmitted, recorded or reproduced in any form or by any means, without the prior permission of the copyright owner

First published 2025

A Lincoln Record Society publication
published by The Boydell Press
an imprint of Boydell & Brewer Ltd
PO Box 9, Woodbridge, Suffolk IP12 3DF, UK
and of Boydell & Brewer Inc.
668 Mt Hope Avenue, Rochester, NY 14620-2731, USA
website: www.boydellandbrewer.com

Our Authorised Representative for product safety in the EU is Easy Access System Europe – Mustamäe tee 50, 10621 Tallinn, Estonia, gpsr.requests@easproject.com

ISBN 978 1 910653 16 6

A CIP catalogue record for this book is available
from the British Library

Details of other Lincoln Record Society volumes are available
from Boydell & Brewer Ltd

The publisher has no responsibility for the continued existence or accuracy of URLs for external or third-party internet websites referred to in this book, and does not guarantee that any content on such websites is, or will remain, accurate or appropriate

Printed and bound in Great Britain by
TJ Books, Padstow, Cornwall

CONTENTS

Acknowledgements	vi
Bibliographical Abbreviations	vii
Introduction	1
The Louth St James Churchwardens' Accounts: 1527–60	33
The Louth St James Churchwardens' Accounts: 1560–70	291
Appendix 1. Louth St James Churchwardens: 1500–70	364
Appendix 2. Sunday Collections by Year: 1500/1–70/1	372
Index of Persons and Places	374
Index of Subjects	404

ACKNOWLEDGEMENTS

I would like to acknowledge the support given during the preparation of this volume by Dr Nicholas Bennett, who first suggested the idea to me back in 2013 and gave continuing editorial advice throughout its lengthy period of gestation.

Along with my friend Dr Wendy Atkin, Dr Bennett also helped with sections of Latin translation and the index, with my subsequent editor, Professor Philippa Hoskin correcting and finalising the preparation of the text for publication. Many thanks to you all.

I would also like to acknowledge Jean Howard, Stuart Sizer, Richard Gurnham and Christopher Marshall for their assistance with the history of Louth, which as a 'foreigner' to the town was vital to my understanding of the subject.

My appreciation for the staff at Lincolnshire Archives must not go unexpressed. Their assistance with the various documents, as well as their ability to endure my sometimes-eccentric sense of humour, is much valued.

I would like to convey my heartfelt gratitude to the people of Louth and Lincolnshire as a whole. I have encountered consistent interest in my undertaking and unfailing goodwill from local people.

The story of the church of St James is extensive, but thanks to the work of the churchwardens of Louth five hundred years ago, this volume will hopefully preserve their legacy for future generations.

Brian Hodgkinson
September 2023

BIBLIOGRAPHICAL ABBREVIATIONS

Primary source documents

Accounts II	LAO, Louth St. James Churchwarden's Accounts, PAR, 7/2.
Accounts III	LAO, Louth St. James Churchwarden's Accounts, PAR, 7/3.
Goulding, Papers	LAO, Goulding Papers, 5/1–10. Documents of Richard Goulding deposited at the Lincolnshire Archives.
Inventories	LAO, Inventories, various boxes.

Printed material

Goulding, Papers	LAO, Goulding Papers, 5/1–10. Documents of Richard Goulding deposited at the Lincolnshire Archives.
AASRP	*Associated Architectural Societies Reports and Papers*.
Addy, *Church and Manor*	Sidney Addy, *Church and Manor: A Study in English Economic History* (New York, Rep. 1970).
Alexander, 'Building Stone'	Jenny Alexander, 'Building Stone from the East Midlands Quarries', *Medieval Archaeology*, 39 (1995).
Alford, *Kingship*	Stephen Alford, *Kingship and Politics in the Reign of Edward VI* (Cambridge, 2004).
Bayley, *Notitiæ Ludæ*	Robert Bayley, *Notitiæ Ludæ, Notices of Louth* (Louth, 1834).
Benton, *Early Days*	R. N. Benton, *Louth in the Early Days* (Cheddar, 1985).

Bindoff, *House of Commons*	Stanley Bindoff, *The History of Parliament: The House of Commons, 1509–1558*, 3 Vols (London, 1982).
Bowker, *Henrician Reformation*	Margaret Bowker, *The Henrician Reformation: The Diocese of Lincoln under John Longland, 1521–1547* (Cambridge, 1981).
Brears, *Lincolnshire*	Charles Brears, *Lincolnshire in the 17th and 18th Centuries* (London, 1940).
Bristow, *Glossary*	Joy Bristow, *The Local Historian's Glossary & Vade Mecum* (2nd ed., Nottingham, 1997).
Burgess, *Accounts*	Clive Burgess (ed.), *The Pre-Reformation Records of All Saints' Church, Bristol: Part II, the Churchwardens' Accounts*, Bristol Record Society, 53 (2000).
Burgess, *Church Book*	Clive Burgess (ed.), *The Pre-Reformation Records of All Saints' Church, Bristol: Part I, the All-Saints' Church Book*, Bristol Record Society, 46 (1995).
Burton, *Old Lincolnshire*	George Burton, *Old Lincolnshire: An Antiquarian Magazine*, Vol. I, 1883–5 (Stamford, 1883–5).
CClR	*Calendar of Close Rolls*.
Chambers, *Faculty Office*	David Chambers (ed.), *Faculty Office Registers, 1534–1549* (Oxford, 1966).
Cheney and Jones, *Handbook of Dates*	Christopher Cheney and Michael Jones (eds), *Handbook of Dates for Students of British History, New Edition* (Cambridge, 2000).
Cole, *Chapter Acts*, I	Robert Cole (ed.), *Chapter Acts of the Cathedral Church of St. Mary of Lincoln, A.D. 1520–36*, LRS, Vol. 12 (1915).
Cole, *Chapter Acts*, II	Robert Cole (ed.), *Chapter Acts of the Cathedral Church of St. Mary of Lincoln, A.D. 1536–1547*, LRS, Vol. 13 (1917).
Cole, *Chapter Acts*, III	Robert Cole (ed.), *Chapter Acts of the Cathedral Church of St. Mary of Lincoln, A.D. 1547–1549*, LRS, Vol. 15 (1920).
Cox, *Churchwardens*	John Charles Cox, *Churchwardens' Accounts: From the Fourteenth Century to the Close of the Seventeenth Century* (London, 1913).

Cox, *Parish Registers*	John Charles Cox, *The Parish Registers of England* (London, 1910).
CPR	*Calendar of Patent Rolls.*
Cross, *Christian Church*	Frank Cross (ed.), *The Oxford Dictionary of the Christian Church* (London, 1957).
Davis, *Gravesend*	Francis Davis (ed.), *Rotuli Ricardi Gravesend; Episcopi Lincolniensis A.D. 1258–1279*, LRS, Vol. 20 (1925).
DNB	Oxford Dictionary of National Biography Online. https://www.oxforddnb.com.
Dudding, *Accounts*	Reginald Dudding (ed.), *The First Churchwardens' Book of Louth, 1500–1524* (Oxford, 1941).
Duffy, *Altars*	Eamon Duffy, *Stripping of the Altars: Traditional Religion in England, c1400–c1580* (London, 1992).
Emden, *Biographical Register*	Alfred Emden, *A Biographical Register of the University of Oxford, A.D. 1501 to 1540* (Oxford, 1974).
Everson and Stocker, 'Markitt Stede'	Paul Everson and David Stocker, 'The Cros in the Markitte Stede: The Louth Cross, Its Monastery and Its Town', *Medieval Archaeology*, 61/2 (2017).
Everson and Stocker, 'Wulfwig's Purchase'	Paul Everson and David Stocker, 'A Note on "Wulfwig's Purchase": A Red Herring in Louth's Historiography', *Lincolnshire History and Archaeology*, 49 (2014).
Farmer, *Saints*	David Farmer, *The Oxford Dictionary of Saints* (Oxford, 1996).
Field, *Hidden Town*	Naomi Field, *Louth the Hidden Town* (Lincoln, 1978).
Foster and Longley, *Domesday*	Charles Foster, Thomas Longley (eds), *The Lincolnshire Domesday and Lindsay Survey*, LRS, 19 (1924).
Foster and Thompson, 'Chantry Certificates'	Charles Foster and Alexander Hamilton Thompson (eds), 'The Chantry Certificates for Lincoln and Lincolnshire', *Reports & Papers of the Associated Architectural Societies*, 36 (1921–2), 37 (1923–5).
Foster, 'Certificate'	Charles Foster (ed.), 'Certificate or Return of all Fees, Annuities, Corrodies or Pensions Payable to Religious Persons', *Reports & Papers of the Associated Architectural Societies*, 37 (1923–5).

Foster, *Cambridge*	J. E. Foster (ed.), *Churchwardens' Accounts of St. Mary the Great, Cambridge*, Cambridge Antiquarian Society, 35 (1905).
Foster, *Church Furniture*	Charles Foster, *English Church Furniture*, Lincolnshire Notes & Queries, 14 (1917).
Foster, *Episcopal Records*	Charles Foster (ed.), *Lincoln Episcopal Records in the Time of Thomas Cooper STP, Bishop of Lincoln, 1571–1584*, LRS, Vol. 2 (1912).
Foster, *Lincoln Wills*, III	Charles Foster (ed.), *Lincoln Wills Listed in the District Probate Registry at Lincoln, Vol. III, A.D 1530 to A.D. 1532*, LRS, Vol. 24 (1930).
Freeman, 'Organ Builders'	Andrew Freeman, 'Records of English Organ Builders', 940–1660, in Frederick Thornsby, *Dictionary of Organs and Organists* (2nd ed., London, 1921).
Frere and Kennedy, *Articles*	Walter Frere and William Kennedy (eds), *Visitation Articles and Injunctions*, Vol. II (London, 1910).
Friar, *Parish Church*	Stephen Friar, *The Companion to the English Parish Church* (London, 1996).
Fryde et al., *Handbook*	Edmund Fryde, Diana Greenway, S. Porter and Ian Roy (eds), *Handbook of British Chronology* (3rd ed., Cambridge, 1986).
Gee and Hardy, *Documents*	Henry Gee and William Hardy (eds), *Documents Illustrative of English Church History* (London, 1896).
Gibbons, 'Saxilby'	Alfred Gibbons, 'A Transcript of Old Churchwardens' Accounts of the Parish of Saxilby-cum-Ingleby', *AASRP*, 19 (1888).
Goulding, *Annals*	Richard Goulding, *Annals of Louth: Its Inhabitants and Its Institutions, 1086–1600* (Louth, 1918).
Goulding, *Briefs*	Richard Goulding, *Contributions towards Briefs, Protections and Letter of Request Recorded in the Louth Churchwardens' Accounts* (Louth, 1905).
Goulding, *Cawod*	Richard Goulding, *John Cawod and the First Volume of the Louth Churchwarden's Accounts* (Louth, 1911).

Goulding, *Corporation Records*	Richard Goulding, *Louth Old Corporation Records, Being Extracts from the Accounts, Minutes and Memoranda of the Warden and Six Assistants of the Town of Louth and Free School of King Edward VI in Louth: And Other Ancient Documents Relating to the Town, Compiled by R.W. Goulding* (Louth, 1891).
Goulding, *Court Rolls*	Richard Goulding, *On the Court Rolls of the Manor of Louth* (Louth, 1901).
Goulding, *Customs*	Richard Goulding, *Some Obsolete Louth Customs* (Louth, 1922).
Goulding, *Grammar School*	Richard Goulding, *Notes on the Foundation of the Grammar School and Bedehouses of Louth* (Louth, 1902).
Goulding, *Louth Houses*	Richard Goulding, *Louth Houses and their Former Occupants* (Louth, 1903).
Goulding, *Markets and Fairs*	Richard Goulding, *Notes on the Markets and Fairs of Louth* (Louth, 1898).
Goulding, *Parish Church*	Richard Goulding, *The Parish Church of Louth* (Louth, 1930).
Goulding, *Spire*	Richard Goulding, *The Building of the Louth Spire* (Louth, 1908).
Goulding, *St. Mary's*	Richard Goulding, *St. Mary's Church Louth* (Louth, 1909).
Goulding, *Vicars*	Richard Goulding, *The Vicars and Vicarages of Louth* (Louth, 1906).
Green, *Origins*	Caitlin Green, *The Origins of Louth, Archaeology and History in East Lincolnshire, 400,000BC–AD1086* (Louth, 2011).
Green, *Streets of Louth*	Caitlin Green, *The Streets of Louth: An A–Z history* (Louth, 2014).
Gunn, *Brandon*	Steven Gunn, *Charles Brandon, Henry VIII's Closest Friend* (Stroud, 2016).
Gurnham, *Early Louth*	Richard Gurnham, *The Story of Early Louth from its Origins to the Reformation* (Louth, 2019).
Gurnham, *Free School*	Richard Gurnham, *The Free School of King Edward VI at Louth: A Short History* (Louth, 2006).

Gurnham, *History of Louth*	Richard Gurnham, *A History of Louth* (Andover, 2013).
Haig, 'Introduction'	Christopher Haigh, 'Introduction', in Christopher Haigh (ed.), *The English Reformation Revised* (Cambridge, 1987).
Hamilton, *Wriothesley*	William Hamilton (ed.), *A Chronicle of England during the Reign of the Tudors from 1485 to 1559 by Charles Wriothesley*, Camden Society, n.s., xl (1875).
Harkrider, *Women, Reform and Community*	Melissa Franklin Harkrider, *Women, Reform and Community in Early Modern England: Katherine Willoughby, Duchess of Suffolk, and Lincolnshire's Godly Aristocracy, 1519–1580* (Woodbridge, 2008).
Hodgett, *Ex-Religious*	Gerald Hodgett, *The State of Ex-Religious and Former Chantry Priests in the Diocese of Lincoln, 1547–74*, LRS Vol. 53 (1959).
Hollis, *Church Notes*	Gervase Holles, *Lincolnshire Church Notes*, LRS 1 (Lincoln, 1911, Reprint, 2010).
Hoyle, *Pilgrimage*	Richard W. Hoyle, *The Pilgrimage of Grace and the Politics of the 1530s* (Oxford, 2001).
James, 'Obedience and Descent'	Mervyn James, 'Obedience and Dissent in Henrician England: The Lincolnshire Rebellion 1536', *Past and Present*, 48 (1970).
Kennan, 'Guilds and Society'	Claire Kennan, 'Guilds and Society in Louth, Lincolnshire, c. 1450–1550', Unpublished PhD Thesis, Royal Holloway, University of London (2019).
Ketteringham, *Bells*	John Ketteringham, *Lincolnshire Bells and Bellfounders* (Lincoln, 2004).
Knowles and Hadcock, *Religious Houses*	David Knowles and Richard Hadcock, *Medieval Religious Houses: England and Wales* (Harlow, 1971).
L&P	John Brewer, James Gairdner and Robert Brodie (eds), *Letters and Papers, Foreign and Domestic, of the Reign of Henry VIII, 1509–1547*, 21 Vols. (London, 1862–1932).
LAO	Lincolnshire Archives Office.
LCC	Lincoln Consistory Court.

Le Neve, *Fasti*	John le Neve, *Fasti Ecclesiae Anglicanae, Lincoln Diocese*, 2 Vols, 1066–1300, 1300–1541 (London, 1962, 1977).
Leach, *English Schools*	Arthur Leach, *English Schools at the Reformation: 1546–8* (Westminster, 1896).
Lehmberg, *Cathedrals*	Stanford E. Lehmberg, *The Reformation of Cathedrals: Cathedrals in English Society, 1485–1603* (Guildford, 1988).
Lincs to the Past	https://www.lincstothepast.com.
Lloyd, *St. Lawrence*	David Lloyd, Margaret Clark and Chris Potter, *St. Lawrence's Church, Ludlow* (Eardisley, 2010).
Louthe, 'Reminiscences'	John Louthe, 'Reminiscences of John Louthe', in John Nichols, *Narratives of the Days of the Reformation*, Camden Society, 77 (1859).
LRS	Lincoln Record Society.
MacCulloch, *Thomas Cromwell*	Diarmaid MacCulloch, *Thomas Cromwell: A Life* (London, 2018).
Madden, *Privy Purse*	Frederic Madden, *Privy Purse Expenses of the Princess Mary, Daughter of King Henry the Eighth, afterwards Queen Mary: With a Memoir of the Princess, and Notes* (London, 1831).
Maddison, *Lincolnshire Pedigrees*	Arthur Maddison, *Lincolnshire Pedigrees*, Harleian Society, Vols. 50–2, 55 (1902–4, 1906).
Merriman, *Letters*, II	Roger Merriman, *Life & Letters of Thomas Cromwell*, Vol. II (Oxford, Rep. 2000).
Nichols, *Illustrations*	John Nichols (ed.), *Illustrations of the Manners and Expences of Antient Times in England, in the Fifteenth, Sixteenth, and Seventeenth Centuries, Deduced from the Accompts of Churchwardens, and Other Authentic Documents, ... with Explanatory Notes* (London, 1797). Gale ECCO Print Editions.
OED	*Oxford English Dictionary Online.* https://www.oed.com.
Owen, *Church and Society*	Dorothy Owen, *Church and Society in Medieval Lincolnshire*, History of Lincolnshire, Vol. V (Reprint, Lincoln, 1990).

Paddison, *Charters*	Richard Wilson Paddison (ed.), *The Charters of the Corporation of the Town of Louth and Free Grammar School of King Edward VI* (Louth, 1831).
Peacock, 'Kirton'	Edward Peacock, 'Kirton in Lindsay: Churchwardens' Accounts etc.', *The Antiquary*, 19 (1889).
Peacock, 'Leverton'	Edward Peacock, 'Extracts from the Churchwardens' Accounts of the Parish of Leverton in the County of Lincoln', *Archaeologia*, 41 (1866).
Peacock, 'Sutterton'	Edward Peacock, 'Churchwardens' Accounts of Saint Mary's, Sutterton', *Archaeological Journal* (1882).
Peacock, *Church Furniture*	Edward Peacock, *English Church Furniture, Ornaments and Decorations, at the Period of the Reformation: As Exhibited in a List of Goods Destroyed in Certain Lincolnshire Churches, AD 1566* (London, 1866).
Pevsner, *Buildings of England*	Nikolaus Pevsner, John Harris and Nicholas Antram, *The Buildings of England: Lincolnshire* (2nd ed., London, 2001).
Pillans, *Organs*. J.	Craig Pillans, *A History of the Organs in Louth Parish Church* (Burgh-le-Marsh, 1973).
Platt, *Parish Church*	Colin Platt, *The Parish Churches of Medieval England* (London, 1995).
Raine, *Fabric Rolls*	James Raine, *The Fabric Rolls of York Minster*, Surtees Society, 35 (1859).
Regan, *Advent to Pentecost*	Patrick Regan, *Advent to Pentecost: Comparing the Seasons in the Ordinary and Extraordinary Forms of the Roman Rite* (Collegeville, MN, 2012).
Robinson, *Book of Louth*	David Robinson, *The Book of Louth* (Buckingham, 1979).
Rowson, *Inventories*	Roderick Rowson, *Louth Probate Inventories* (LAO, Unpublished Document, 2010).
Salter, *Subsidy*	Herbert Salter (ed.), *A Subsidy Collected in the Diocese of Lincoln in 1526, Vol. 1, Lincolnshire* (Oxford, 1909).

Smith and London, *Heads*, II	David M. Smith and Vera C. M. London, *The Heads of Religious Houses: England & Wales*, 3 Vols, II, 1216–1377 (Cambridge, 2001).
Smith, 'Suffragan Bishops'	David M. Smith, 'Suffragan Bishops in the Medieval Diocese of Lincoln', *Lincolnshire History and Archaeology*, 17 (1982).
Smith, *Heads*, III	David M. Smith, *The Heads of Religious Houses: England & Wales*, 3 Vols, III, 1377–1540 (Cambridge, 2008).
Statutes III	Alexander Luders et al. (eds), *The Statutes of the Realm: Printed by Command of His Majesty King George the Third, in Pursuance of an Address of the House of Commons of Great Britain; From Original Records and Authentic Manuscripts*, 11 Vols. (London, 1810–22), Vol. III (1817, Reprint, 1963).
Statutes IV (i)	Alexander Luders, et al. (eds), *The Statutes of the Realm: Printed by Command of His Majesty King George the Third, in Pursuance of an Address of the House of Commons of Great Britain; From Original Records and Authentic Manuscripts*, 11 Vols (London, 1810–22), Vol. IV (i) (1819, Reprint, 1975).
Stokes, *Drama*	James Stokes, *Records of Early English Drama: Lincolnshire*, 2 Vols (London, 2009).
Swaby, *History of Louth*	John Swaby, *A History of Louth* (London, 1951).
Tate, *Parish Chest*	William E. Tate, *The Parish Chest: A Study of the Records of Parochial Administration in England* (3rd ed., Cambridge, 1969).
Thompson, *Boston*	Pishey Thompson, *The History and Antiquities of Boston and the Hundred of Skirbeck* (Boston, 1856, Rep. 1997).
TNA	The National Archives.
VCH Lincs	William Page (ed.), *Victoria Country History, Lincolnshire*, Vol. II (London, 1906, Rep. 1988).
VE	J. Caley and J. Hunter (eds), *Valor Ecclesiasticus, temp Henrici VIII, auctorite regia institutus*, 6 Vols. (London, 1810–34).

Ward, *Rising*	Ann Ward, *The Lincolnshire Rising, 1536* (2nd ed., Louth, 1996).
Westlake, *Gilds*	Herbert Westlake, *The Parish Gilds of Medieval England* (London, 1919).
Williams, *Historical Documents*	Charles Williams (ed.), *English Historical Documents*, Vol. V, 1485–1558 (London, 1967).
Williamson, 'Religious Guilds'	Magnus Williamson, 'The Role of Religious Guilds in the Cultivation of Ritual Polyphony in England: The Case of Louth, 1450–1550', in Fiona Kisby (ed.), *Music and Musicians in Renaissance Cities and Towns* (Cambridge, 2001).
Wright, *Churchwardens' Accounts*	Thomas Wright (ed.), *The Churchwardens' Accounts of the Town of Ludlow in Shropshire for 1540 to the End of the Reign of Queen Elizabeth*, Camden Society Old Series, 102 (1869).
Wright, *Ludlow*	Thomas Wright, *The History of Ludlow and Its Neighbourhood, Forming a Popular Sketch of the History of the Welsh Border* (London, 1852).

INTRODUCTION

Item, to Maltby the Smith for mending the clock and chime at the Feast of St Luke, 6s 8d, for the which sum afore paid he hath promised to stand with charge of the said clock and chime to keep them going and to repair them with all such stuff as to his occupation appertaineth, the Clerks doing their duty from this day till the feast of Easter[1] next ensuing and from that time till Easter 12 months after.

Louth Churchwardens' Accounts, 1528/9[2]

This entry from the sixteenth-century churchwardens' accounts of the parish church of St James, situated in the Lincolnshire market town of Louth, is one of many regarding the maintenance of the church's clock along with its peal of bells. The latter were contained within the fifteenth-century steeple, itself crowned with one of the most architecturally impressive spires in the country; Nikolaus Pevsner affirming that St James's was 'one of the most majestic of English parish churches'.[3]

The Louth churchwardens' accounts are some of the county's most comprehensive surviving parish records.[4] These continue in an almost unbroken sequence from the beginning of the sixteenth century, opening a panorama on the financial undertakings of a large and relatively wealthy parish church. The first published transcription, edited by Reginald Dudding, rector of Saleby (1859–1937), covered the years 1500/1 to 1523/4[5] and recounts the construction of the church's spire in considerable detail.[6] The documents transcribed in this

---

[1] Noted as 'Pascha'.
[2] Page 51. Accounts II, *f.* 7r.
[3] Pevsner, *Buildings of England*, p. 538.
[4] Other accounts from Lincolnshire are from Saxilby, Leverton, Wigtoft, Kirton in Lindsey and Market Deeping.
[5] Dudding, *Accounts*. LAO, Louth St James, PAR/7/1. The accounts for the year 1524/5 are fragmentary; those from 1525/6 to 1526/7 are missing.
[6] At 295ft (89.9m), it is the tallest steeple and spire of any medieval parish church in England.

present publication date from 1527/8 to 1570/1 and comprise two volumes.[7] These, alongside the comprehensive parish registers commencing in 1538,[8] illustrate both fiscal and social interactions between a local church and its parishioners. It should however be remembered that although these texts are in hindsight historically significant, to the churchwardens of the period they were primarily a statement of the financial situation of the church; nothing more, nothing less.

Louth

Geographically, Louth nestles in the valley of the River Lud on the eastern edge of the Lincolnshire Wolds, enveloped by hills rising to the north, south and west. Grimsby is 16 miles (25km) to the north and Boston 32 miles (50km) southwards, with Lincoln around 27 miles (43km) to the south-west.[9] To the east, the Lud winds north-easterly across the once regularly flooded marshland towards the coast; in a straight line, a distance of around 10 miles (16km). Here, havens and inlets, notably Saltfleethaven, provided access to the sea. Vessels were also beached at places such as Theddlethorpe and Ingoldmells[10] and other anchorages along the east coast, vital for exporting the town's produce. This largely consisted of woollen products, notably cloth, and leather goods, both originating from livestock farmed on the surrounding Wolds and in the Marsh. The churchwardens' accounts document some of the residents' occupations, reflecting the importance of these resources. Drapers, shoemakers, weavers, fullers, mercers, glovers, barkers and tanners are some of the many trades recorded.

St James's was one of the county's wealthier parish churches, situated in a town with a population in 1524/5 of around one thousand.[11] It was a 'peculiar' jurisdiction,[12] with the largely absent prebendary acting as rector in the name of the dean and chapter of Lincoln cathedral. In the *Taxatio* of 1291, it was assessed at £60, of which the church was £46 13s 4d and the vicarage £13 6s 8d.[13] Two hundred and forty-four years later, the *Valor Ecclesiasticus* of 1535 valued the church at £73 5s, the sum greater than twenty-one of Lincolnshire's

---

[7] Accounts II, 1527/8–1559/60, and Accounts III, 1560/1–1570/1: this volume continues to 1623.

[8] Transcript of Louth Parish Registers, 1538–1681. LAO, Goulding Papers, 5/2.

[9] Distances on modern roads. Retrieved from http://www.theaa.com/route-planner.

[10] In 1509/10, 64 fathoms of rope (384ft, 117m) was purchased from (Bishop's) Lynn and landed at 'Ingomels'. Dudding, *Accounts*, p. 121.

[11] Williamson, 'Religious Guilds', p. 83.

[12] Exempt from or not subject to the jurisdiction of the bishop of the diocese. *OED*.

[13] In comparison, the *Taxatio* records Boston at £51 6s 8d; Grimsby £36 with the two moieties at Grantham totalling £114 13s 4d. https://www.dhi.ac.uk/taxatio (Accessed 13/11/2018).

fifty-two monasteries.[14] The number of clergy in St James's was also considerable, unsurprising when communicants in 1547 totalled about 1,800.[15] The clerical subsidy of 1526 notes twelve priests ranging from the prebendary, Master Robert Shorton (1523–35)[16] with an income of £36 3s 4d; the vicar, Thomas Egiliston (1514–27), earning £13 6s 8d; and the remainder rewarded stipends varying from £5 6s 8d to £8 11s.[17] The most notable incumbent during this period was however Thomas Kendall. He was probably a native of the town, who, after attending Oxford, was subsequently inducted into the vicarage of Louth on Friday, 2 October 1534.[18] Exactly two years later, he would become intimately involved in the Lincolnshire Rising, suffering the consequences of his activities at Tyburn.[19]

The churchwardens

In Louth, the post of churchwarden would be perceived as largely honorific but nevertheless socially significant, the parish clerk generally being responsible for the everyday administration of the church.[20] The churchwarden's primary obligation was to oversee the maintenance of the church building and provide the required finance for ornaments, vestments and liturgical texts intended for the performance of services. The accounts were presented at a visitation to demonstrate financial security, and, importantly, that the overall spiritual prerequisites of parishioners were suitably provided.[21] Additional

---

[14] *VE*, IV, p. 6.

[15] Goulding, *Corporation Records*, p. 174.

[16] Shorton left a will dated 8 October 1535, donating 40s to the poor of Louth. TNA, PROB 11/25/403. He was buried in the College of Stoke by Clare, Suffolk. *DNB* https://doi.org/10.1093/ref:odnb/25469 (Accessed 27/8/2019). Shorton's successor was Henry Williams (1535–54). Le Neve, *Fasti*, Lincoln, 1300–1541, p. 87. Cole, *Chapter Acts*, III, p. 109.

[17] Salter, *Subsidy*, p. 12. For a list of incumbents, see Goulding, *Vicars*. By contrast, Boston had thirty-three clergy, Grantham nineteen, Tattershall College eleven and Barton ten. Salter, *Subsidy*, pp. 6, 27, 66–7, 68–9.

[18] Cole, *Chapter Acts*, I, p. 184.

[19] Kendall fled following the collapse of the Rising, arriving ten days later at the Coventry Charterhouse. *L&P*, XII (i), 19, p. 14, 4 January 1536/7. Goulding, *Vicars*, p. 11. There he was arrested and subsequently hung, drawn and quartered at Tyburn on Thursday, 29 March 1537 for his involvement in the revolt. *L&P*, XII (i), 734, pp. 323–5, 26 March 1537. Hamilton, *Wriothesley*, p. 62. His successor was Geoffrey Bailey, inducted 31 March 1537. Cole, *Chapter Acts*, II, pp. 4–5. For Kendall's earlier appointments, see Emden, *Biographical Register*, pp. 327–8. For the Rising, see Ward, *Rising*; Hoyle, *Pilgrimage*, pp. 98–175; Swaby, *History of Louth*, pp. 114–34; Gurnham, *History of Louth*, pp. 55–62.

[20] Gurnham, *Early Louth*, p. 137.

[21] Burgess, *Accounts*, pp. 20–1.

duties included the presentment of miscreants, including clerics, licensing visiting preachers and in later periods the collection of alms for the poor.[22]

Being unpaid, the position was consequently apportioned to the most affluent, with the town's merchants and numerous tradesmen frequently elected.[23] There may however have been an 'elite' of parishioners, a vestry, who appointed the churchwardens and other church officials.[24] However, the only evidence is in the use on occasions of the term 'parishioners', first recorded in 1538/9: 'Memorandum, that the money pertaining to the Common Cart by the assignment of the parishioners shall remain for the year following in the hands of George Spyllesby & Thomas Provest …'[25] Nevertheless, throughout this period the churchwardens' obligations increased considerably as both church and state loaded substantial responsibilities, both secular and ecclesiastical, on to Louth's four appointed officials.[26] These varied from the upkeep of the local infrastructure, roads, bridges and especially drainage, to the purchase of military equipment and the control of vermin endangering crops.[27]

Comparisons can be made with similar accounts in the county and also from Ludlow in Shropshire, where the large parish church of St Lawrence still dominates the town centre. Ludlow's accounts continue from 1540 through to the reign of Elizabeth, illustrating the workings of the church and its close relationship with both the secular administration and an influential guild.[28] In Lincolnshire, the churchwardens' accounts from the fenland town of Market Deeping survive in part from 1570 but are separate from those of the bailiffs, constables and dikereeves, the latter generally in charge of the local infrastructure.[29] At Saxilby, west of Lincoln, the accounts continue from 1551 until

---

[22] For other duties, see Tate, *Parish Chest*, pp. 95–9. The accounts also detail wages paid per day, giving some idea of the income of the various tradesmen and their servants working on the church building.

[23] See Appendix 1 for the list of churchwardens.

[24] There is no use of the term 'vestry' in this context in the accounts.

[25] Page 134. Accounts II, *f.* 47r.

[26] Most parish churches in the county retained only two churchwardens. Louth's four officials may have originally represented the four 'byrlaws' or quarters of the manor held from the bishop: the Parson's Fee by the Prebendary, Tupholme Fee, formally retained by Tupholme Abbey (Premonstratensian Canons) and the William Malerbe and John Bude Fees. Each possessed its own court, a situation that continued into the early sixteenth century. Swaby, *History of Louth*, p. 47–8. Addy, *Church and Manor*, p. 277. The *OED* notes a 'local custom or "law" of a township, manor, or rural district, whereby disputes as to boundaries, trespass of cattle, etc., were settled without going into the law courts'.

[27] 'An Act to dystroye Choughes, Crowes and Roks', 24 Henry VIII, Chapter X, 1532–3, replicated in 1566 as the 'Act for the Preservation of Grain', 8 Elizabeth, Chapter XV (ii). *Statutes* III, p. 425-6, *ibid.*, IV (i), p. 498.

[28] Wright, *Churchwardens' Accounts*.

[29] LAO, Market Deeping, PAR/10/1. Market Deeping is 12 miles (19km) from Spalding and 8 miles (13km) from Stamford.

1569 and portray similar activities to that of most parish administrations during this period.[30] Documents from Leverton are also extant, giving an insight into the workings of a marshland village church adjacent to the east coast.[31] The market town of Kirton in Lindsey, situated to the west of Ermine Street (A15) in north-west Lincolnshire, was, like Louth, a peculiar jurisdiction. Here the accounts commence in 1484 and continue sporadically until the seventeenth century,[32] as do those from Wigtoft, a small village in Holland on the edge of the fens.[33]

Religious and political context

This volume partly encompasses the reigns of four of the five Tudor monarchs, who, from 1534 onwards, were essentially leaders of a 'state church', with each retaining their individual interpretations of the Christian doctrine. Consequently, this was undoubtedly the most unsettled period the English Church had experienced since the re-foundation of Christianity in the late sixth century.

These fluctuations are reflected in the accounts, outwardly taking the form of a cycle of removal and reinstatement of church furniture, altars and clerical regalia along with liturgical volumes and spiritual texts. However, the documents also subtly reveal parishioners' responses to edicts from the central authorities throughout this period. These suggest at times a measure of dissatisfaction with the prevailing *status quo*. This is principally reflected in a general decline in the amounts detailed in the Sunday collections, along with a fall in the number and quantity of *post-mortem* bequests, suggesting a dwindling reverence for the ever-changing doctrines of the 'established church'.[34]

There were also differing reactions to the changes of sovereign. In 1537, Louth celebrated the birth of Prince Edward; 'for ale, bread & wine spent in the marketsted at the general procession for joy of the Nativity of Prince Edward, 3s 9d'.[35] This was doubtless in celebration for the birth of a male heir and thereby in theory ending the succession crisis. In 1547, however, there were no festivities documented on Edward's accession or indeed a record of his father's death. Nevertheless, in 1553 the churchwardens 'paid for wine

---

[30] Gibbons, 'Saxilby'. Saxilby is 7 miles (11km) west of Lincoln.
[31] LAO, Leverton, PAR/7/1. Peacock, 'Leverton'. Leverton is 6 miles (10km) north-east of Boston.
[32] LAO, Kirton in Lindsey, PAR/7/1. Peacock, E., 'Kirton in Lindsay: churchwardens' accounts etc.', *The Antiquary*, 19 (1889). Kirton is 19 miles (31km) north of Lincoln.
[33] Nichols, *Illustrations*, pp. 77–84, 195–249. Wigtoft is 6 miles (10km) south of Boston.
[34] For the annual collections, see Appendix 2.
[35] Page 125. Accounts II, *f.* 42r.

spent on the day of the Proclamation of Queen Mary, 10s',[36] but her death and the succession of Elizabeth go unrecorded. In comparison, at Ludlow in 1547, bell ropes were repaired for 'ryngynge at kynges Harry dirge' and in 1554 'for mendynge of iij ropes when we dyd rynge at the mariage of the Kynge, vjd'.[37]

Income

Considerable donations to St James's emanated from the town's prosperous merchants, shopkeepers and skilled tradesmen. This notably occurred during the construction of the spire, when cartloads of masonry, weighing around a ton, were individually sponsored. Detailed in the earlier accounts, the stone travelled in stages from quarries at Wilsford, Kelby and Heydour near Ancaster. The cargo then journeyed via the River Slea and the Kyme Eau to Dogdyke on the River Witham, and thence across to Tattershall or Coningsby on the River Bain.[38] Here the stone was doubtless carved to order, thereby lessening the weight when travelling via Horncastle over the Wolds to Louth in carts or wagons or possibly carried on the backs of packhorses.[39] Wealthy testators, such as local merchants Symond Lyncoln[40] and Thomas Bradley,[41] left substantial bequests to the church during this period of construction. In

---

[36] Page 233. Accounts II, *f.* 106r. Allegedly 20 gallons. Gurnham, *History of Louth*, p. 65.

[37] Wright, *Churchwardens' Accounts*, pp. 26, 58. The marriage of Queen Mary and Philip II of Spain (d.1598) in Winchester Cathedral on 25th July 1554, the festival of St James, patron saint of Spain.

[38] Goulding, *Spire*, pp. 4–5. The distance from Wilsford to Louth by modern roads is around 41 miles (66km), but via the route taken during the period of construction, especially on tracks over the Wolds, it was about 62 miles (99km). For details of the route, see Alexander, 'Building Stone', p. 128, n. 107.

[39] Lincolnshire packhorses were noted as being 'fine, strapping, broad chested animals, bearing on either side their packs of merchandise to the weight of half a ton'. Brears, *Lincolnshire*, pp. 92–3. These were probably a variation of the Old English Black, cross-bred during medieval period but now extinct, http://messybeast.com/history/draft-horses.htm (Accessed 24/2/2020).

[40] TNA, PROB 11/14/561, 10 April 1505. Symon (Symond) Lyncoln, churchwarden in 1504, was a prominent local merchant. Dudding, *Accounts*, p. 47. In his will of 10 April 1505, he donated to forty-six Lincolnshire churches and eight of the county's monasteries. He left St James's gifts to the 'works' (20s), a temporary chantry for seven years (c.£35) and guild obits worth 3s 4d p.a. St Mary's and St John's chapel each received 20d. Gervase Hollis recorded a brass in the church, stating: 'Pray for ye Soule of Simon Lincolne, sometime Marchant of the Staple, who dyed 25th April 1505.' Hollis, *Church Notes*, p. 93.

[41] TNA, PROB 11/20/238, 18 June 1519, Codicil 16 June 1521. Thomas Bradley was a merchant of the Staple of Calais, and churchwarden in 1503 and 1514. Dudding, *Accounts*, pp. 47, 165.

1505, Lyncoln gave nearly £37 to various sectors of the church, and in 1519 Bradley donated a total of £35 16s 8d. In 1504, another merchant, Symond Lindesay, bequeathed 6s 8d for 'bulding of the broche of Lowth stepull'.[42]

Regular income also came from burials and the tolling of bells at funerals and commemorations. The cost of interment remained the same throughout the period: 6s 8d for burial in the church (children 3s 4d) and also 3s 4d within the south porch.[43] It was recorded in 1556/7, 'to John Anderson for covering the grave of William Worsley's wife, 4d', although there is no evidence of payment for burials in the churchyard, only the maintenance of the area.[44] The charges for ringing the numerous bells appear to have been relative to their size and consequently the number of ringers required. The Great or James Bell, weighing over 2 tons, cost 12d, the smaller Trinity Bell at 1 ton was 8d and the Lady Bell 6d.[45]

In a relatively prosperous town such as Louth, it might be expected that the church would own a considerable portfolio of property. There is however little evidence of this in the accounts.[46] Indications from the few surviving glebe terriers dating from 1663 onwards show that income was derived from leasing a small number of houses, mostly located in the churchyard.[47] In 1562, it was noted, 'received of the plumber for one year's rent of the house in the churchyard, 6s 8d'.[48] Originally, some of these properties were probably the result of testamentary donations in return for intercessionary prayers. In 1527/8, it was recorded, 'received of John More part of a more sum for the house [of

---

[42] TNA, PROB 11/14/471, 12 September 1504. These wills were deposited in the Prerogative Court of Canterbury, but unfortunately no similar documents survive for this period from town's Prebendal Court. Testaments from the Lincoln Consistory Court mention donations originating from Theddlethorpe St Helen, Saltfleetby All Hallows (All Saints), Utterby, North Somercotes, Grimsby, Trusthorpe and Boston.

[43] The price largely remained the same in later periods and was still 6s 8d at Market Deeping in 1632. LAO, Market Deeping, PAR/10/1, *f.* 32r. At Kirton in Lindsey, the cost was 3s 4d regardless of age or the position of interment. LAO, Kirton in Lindsey, PAR/7/1, *f.* 15v.

[44] Page 269. Accounts II, *f.* 125v. Agnes Worsley was buried 16 August 1556. LAO, Goulding Papers, 5/2. Both she and her husband were interred in the church, and therefore the 'covering' probably relates to a gravestone, see p. 233.

[45] Ketteringham, *Bells*, p. 164.

[46] William Tate suggests an absence of a record of church stock is characteristic of the period. Tate, *Parish Chest*, p. 90. In contrast, the Lady guild owned over 200 acres along with property both in the town and the local hinterland, perhaps leaving little for the church to acquire.

[47] LAO, DIOC/TER BUNDLE/LINCS/LOUTH.

[48] Page 306. Accounts III, *f.* 16v,

the] late John Girdyke[49] as appears by his will, 53s 4d', and in 1544/5, 'paid towards the building of the new house of Thomas Taylor's gift, 26s 8d'.[50]

There are also no entries in the accounts relating to the collection of tithes or church rates.[51] The prebendary, who as rector took the great tithe, possibly retained the details in a separate account, whereas the vicar, holding the small tithe, was probably noted in an Easter or Tithe Book. The later glebe terriers stated that lambs, wool, pigs, poultry, bees, honey, orchards and gardens were 'tithable in kind'. At Easter in lieu of a milk tithe, 3d was taken for every cow, and each communicant paid 2d.[52] The Enclosure Survey of 1801 noted that the prebendary claimed land in compensation for the greater tithes, with the vicar similarly in lieu of the lesser.[53] However, whether the church owned the same quantity of assets in the sixteenth century and similarly took the tithe in lieu is regrettably unknown.

Other churches in Louth

Like Boston, Grantham and Grimsby, Louth today retains a single large parish church, but in the sixteenth century there were two other places of worship: St Mary's, a possible chapel-of-ease, and St John the Baptist chapel in the Market Place. The earliest reference to St Mary's was in 1267, with the election there of Peter de Barton as abbot of Bardney (1267–80).[54] In 1317, Thomas de Luda (d.1329), treasurer of Lincoln, founded a chantry at the altar of the Holy Trinity, later merging into the Trinity guild.[55] The charter notes, 'ordination of a certain chantry in the chapel of the Blessed Mary of Louth depending on the said prebendal church', that is, subordinate to St James's.[56] Being

---

[49] Page 38. Accounts II, f. 2v. In 1501/2, under the heading 'gifts given when the first stone was set of the broach', it was entered 'received of John Gyrdyke, 6s 8d'. He died 1502/3 and gave 20s to the church. Dudding, *Accounts*, pp. 19, 32.

[50] Thomas Taylor, draper and churchwarden in 1501, 1505, 1509 and 1514, left a will dated 12 February 1523/4. Dudding, *Accounts*, pp. 15, 74, 115, 165. In it, he requested the setting up of a chantry in St James's. This appears however never to have come into fruition partly due to expenses occurred in repairing the property left to the chantry. Its value was £4 18s 10d, and the income was later used to finance education. Goulding, *Corporation Records*, pp. 176–7. Swaby, *History of Louth*, p. 67. Taylor also paid for the weathercock atop the new spire. This was purchased in York, having allegedly been fashioned from a copper bowl taken from Flodden Field in 1513. Gurnham, *History of Louth*, p. 52.

[51] For church rates, see Tate, *Parish Chest*, pp. 93–5.

[52] Swaby, *History of Louth*, pp. 199–200. Bayley, *Notitiæ Ludæ*, pp. 158–60.

[53] Swaby, *History of Louth*, p. 263.

[54] Davis, *Gravesend*, p. 23. Smith & London, *Heads*, II, p. 20.

[55] Goulding, *St Mary's*, p. 5. Le Neve, *Fasti*, Lincoln, 1300–1541, p. 21.

[56] Goulding, *St Mary's*, p. 3. A slightly earlier document of 1311 with similar wording is noted in *CClR*, 1307–13, p. 346. St James's had been a prebendal church

the responsibility of the churchwardens, the accounts record donations for maintaining St Mary's, along with requests for burial, the church being used until at least the end of Henry VIII's reign.[57]

When King Edward VI Grammar School was officially refounded in 1551, St Mary's became its first premises until a new building was constructed on what is now Schoolhouse Lane.[58] Repairs were still being carried out as late as 1562 – 'paid for making of a gate at St Mary's church with wood for the same, 20d'.[59] The final reference to the church in the accounts hitherto researched occurred in 1584, when it was noted: 'Paid to Thomas Winter for 3 loads of stones from St Mary's church to this church, 18d.'[60] The building was subsequently employed as a poor house and later a barn and cattle shed.[61]

St John the Baptist chapel was first mentioned in 1317 in the same charter as St Mary's.[62] It was recorded in the accounts in 1501/2 in relation to carrying timber to St James's, and again in 1504/5 connected with a tree 'that lay at Saynt John chappyll'.[63] In 1527/8, John Curtas donated 12d,[64] and in the will of William Gaunce of Theddlethorpe St Helen it was noted, 'to St John chapel in the market place, 6d'.[65] The last mention in the accounts was in 1546/7, when Richard Beverlay bequeathed 12d.[66] The building was demolished in the same year and the site sold.[67] The final known entry is in the Corporation accounts for 1567 – 'paid for the purchase of a piece of land where St John's chapel stood', 76s 8d.[68]

---

since 1146; the vicarage was ordained in 1247. Le Neve, *Fasti*, Lincoln, 1066–1300, p. 84.

[57] Gurnham, *Early Louth*, p. 159.

[58] Goulding, *St Mary's*, p. 9. Construction cost £43 12s 6d. *VCH Lincs*, p. 436. Goulding suggests £34 8s. Goulding, *Corporation Records*, p. 109.

[59] Page 308. Accounts III, *f.* 19v.

[60] Accounts III, *f.* 120v.

[61] In 1638, it was noted 'payd to 2 men in St Mary's church for 1 hole [*sic*] year, 6d a week'. Goulding, Papers, 5/9.

[62] Goulding, *Corporation Records*, p. 164.

[63] Dudding, *Accounts*, pp. 27, 63.

[64] Page 38. Accounts II, *f.* 2v.

[65] Foster, *Lincoln Wills*, III, p. 219. 12 March 1531/2.

[66] Page 182. Accounts II, *f.* 75v.

[67] Goulding, *Corporation Records*, pp. 149–50. Map, Everson & Stocker, 'Wulfwig's Purchase', p. 60, Fig. 1. Naomi Field suggests that the chapel was owned by St Catherine's chantry at Saltfleethaven. Field, *Hidden Town*, p. 17. The site was granted by Edward VI to Sir Ralph Sadler and Laurence Wynnyngton, 15 December 1550. It was sold 26 November 1551 to Laurence Eresbie and the newly knighted Sir William Cecil. They in turn traded the land to William Kinge of Louth, mercer, and from thence to the Corporation. Goulding, *Annals*, p. 34.

[68] Goulding, *Corporation Records*, p. 150.

Manor and Corporation

The manor of Louth had been retained first by the See of Dorchester (on Thames), then following the Conquest relocated to Lincoln.[69] Because the town never acquired borough status, the manorial system was the primary form of local government until the Corporation was established in 1551.[70] The manor court was presided over by the steward, aided by an elected reeve along with a bailiff appointed by the bishop.[71] It adjudicated on criminal cases, the management of animals and crops, disputes over tenancies, actions against debtors and rogue traders along with the regular 'defilement of Aswell Spring', the town's main water source.[72] By the sixteenth century, the criminal aspect was much reduced, with major offences tried at Lincoln and the churchwardens held responsible for delivering the accused into custody. Recorded in 1545/6, 'to the constables for the charges of a prisoner to Lincoln, 4s 3d'.[73]

In 1547, Bishop Henry Holbeach (1547–51) was 'persuaded' to grant the manor to the king.[74] It then passed to Edward Fiennes, Lord Clinton, but in 1560 again reverted to the Crown.[75] In 1564, the Corporation purchased the manor from Queen Elizabeth for £223 7s 6d,[76] of which the parish contributed £79 8s 2d, including a provision of £9 6s 6d for 'loss by fall of money'.[77] This gives an indication of the close working relationship between the parish and the Corporation, with some of the latter's records relating to the church being integrated into the churchwardens' accounts.[78]

Louth Corporation was essentially a self-perpetuating oligarchy consisting of the 'Warden and Six Assistants'.[79] Some of its meetings were held in the

---

[69] The Domesday value rose from £12 pre-Conquest to £22 in 1086. Foster & Longley, *Domesday*, 7:56, p. 53.

[70] There is no mention of the manor court in the accounts.

[71] Hoyle, *Pilgrimage*, p. 98. Gurnham, *Early Louth*, p. 72.

[72] Goulding, *Court Rolls*, n.p. Gurnham, *Early Louth*, pp. 72, 93–7.

[73] Page 175. Accounts II, *f*. 72r.

[74] *CPR*, Edward VI, 1547–8, p. 153, 2 September 1547. This was part of a 'deal' confirming his bishopric, by which the duke of Somerset (ex.1552) as Lord Protector received thirty manors in the name of the Crown, one of which was Louth. *DNB* https://doi.org/10.1093/ref:odnb/13477 (Accessed 1/2/2020).

[75] Edward Fiennes (1512–85), 9th Baron Clinton and Saye and 1st earl of Lincoln. Clinton had obtained the Manor of Louth in 1551, held in fealty of the king, but surrendered it to the Crown in exchange in 1560. *CPR*, 1549–51, pp. 425–6, 1 December 1551: *ibid.*, 1560–63, p. 103, 5 November 1561. Swaby, *History of Louth*, p. 155. Clinton is mentioned three times in the accounts: pp. 241, 263, 289. Accounts II, *f*. 129r: Accounts III, *f*. 8r, 35r.

[76] Goulding, *Corporation Records*, p. 80. *CPR*, 1563–6, p. 106–7, 29 May 1564.

[77] Page 282. Accounts II, *f*. 136v. Inflation was a considerable problem throughout the Tudor period.

[78] Pages 300–3. Accounts III, *ff*. 12v–14v.

[79] Known locally as the 'Warden and Six'. *CPR*, Edward VI, 1550–3, pp. 119–22, 21 September 1551. The Corporation continued until 1835, a total of 284 years, when

library room situated above the south porch, no doubt attended by church officials.[80] A number of churchwardens also held the post of warden or assistant, although not simultaneously. Consequently, the names of the same wealthy and influential families appear regularly in both accounts. Amongst those frequently recorded were Bradley,[81] Chapman, Blanchard, White, Bailey and Grey. John Chapman, gentleman, was churchwarden in 1547/8 and warden in 1557, with Gilbert Blanchard elected churchwarden in 1553/4 and becoming warden in 1558.

In Ludlow, the town's infrastructure was administered by the local authority.[82] This consisted of the 'Twelve' (aldermen) and the 'Twenty-Five' (common councillors). This functioned in a similar manner to the 'Warden and Six' in Louth, interlacing its activities with the other local bodies, notably the influential Palmers' guild. The authority's leading officials were the bailiffs, effectively the mayors of the town. These were elected by the town's burgesses and also appear to have had some administrative control over the church, especially concerning the purchase and sale of private pews and possibly the appointment of churchwardens.[83] In comparison with Louth, in Ludlow the position of churchwarden was largely seen as an 'apprenticeship' on the first rung of the administrative 'ladder', gradually rising to senior positions within the town's ruling elite.[84] Permissions also had to be solicited from the bailiffs for the most mundane activities. In 1548, the deacons were paid 12d 'for ryngyng [the] day belle after Easter at Mr Baylifes commaundyment'.[85]

The guilds

From the fifteenth century, Louth's two foremost incorporated guilds, St Mary's and the Holy Trinity, were major property owners in the town, their income varying from £80 to £100 per annum.[86] The two entities closely collaborated

---

the Municipal Reform Act established a mayor, six aldermen and eighteen councillors. Swaby, *History of Louth*, p. 249. Goulding, Papers, 5/10.

[80] Swaby, *History of Louth*, p. 52. This chamber was removed during the reordering of the church by James Fowler in 1868–9. Pevsner, *Buildings of England*, p. 539.

[81] For the Bradley family, see Swaby, *History of Louth*, pp. 180–3; Maddison, *Pedigrees*, I, pp. 169–71. Goulding, *Louth Houses*, n.p.

[82] For a comparison with the Ludlow bailiffs, see Lloyd, *St Lawrence*, p. 76.

[83] Bindoff, *House of Commons*, I, p. 176. Wright, *Ludlow*, pp. 314–17. From the outset, pew sales were a major feature in the Ludlow accounts. From 1550, the names of the bailiffs are noted when new churchwardens are elected. Wright, *Churchwardens' Accounts*, pp. 6, 42, 121–2. Lloyd, *St Lawrence*, pp. 75–6.

[84] Lloyd, *St Lawrence*, p. 75.

[85] Wright, *Churchwardens' Accounts*, p. 35.

[86] The St Mary guild was the wealthier of the two. In 1476, it acquired 218 acres, cottages and messuages through a petition to the king by the vicar and two guild priests. Williamson, 'Religious Guilds', p. 84. For the location of guild property and their cooperation, see Kennan, 'Guilds and Society', Chapter 5, pp. 6–9, 11–13, map,

to the benefit of the church by providing chantry priests, and also to the lay community, notably its members, both men and women. This cooperation is further illustrated through the guild's financial assistance in the construction of the spire between 1500 and 1515.[87] The following year, 1516, witnessed the cementing of this relationship by placing the guild's financial records consisting of the accounts of St Mary's and those of the various lights in a chest in the Rood loft.[88] In 1531, the Lady guild was instrumental in purchasing an organ, constructed by the king's later organ builder William Betton. This cost £22, of which the guild paid half.[89] Earlier in 1508/9, a smaller instrument, imported from Flanders, had been acquired via a loan from the Trinity guild, both organs being placed on the Rood loft.[90]

Along with supporting the two bedehouses, the guilds were also active in maintaining the town's infrastructure.[91] In 1488–9, repairs were carried out on the roads in Westgate, Gospelgate, the Market Place and Upgate, all places where St Mary's guild held property.[92] In 1499, the manor court instructed the same guild to repair a causeway in Maiden Row and also paid 10s 5½d for 'cleaning the common sewers and dyking'.[93] A lease of 1529 refers to a tenement in the Sheep Market granted to Thomas Jackson, a paver, in return for paving any place belonging to the guild at a groat per day.[94] The guilds even contributed to the 'fire brigade'. In 1533/4, the accounts note:

> Item it is agreed by the parishioners assembled at this account that to the buying of scale ladders, making iron hooks & other things necessary for resing[95] about scathe fires[96] in times of need there shall be taken of Our Lady Guild, 6s 8d, of the Trinity Guild, 6s 8½d, of Corpus Christi Guild 3s 4d, of St Peter's Guild, 3s 4d and of the Plough Light 23d.[97]

---

p. 10. My thanks to Dr Clair Kennan for material concerning the guilds. For gifts of property, see Gurnham, *Early Louth*, p. 150. For details of guild assets conveyed to the Corporation, see Paddison, *Charters*, pp. 5–11.

[87] Kennan, 'Guilds and Society', Chapter 5, p. 3. The guilds lent approximately £74. Goulding, *Spire*, p. 3.

[88] Dudding, *Accounts*, p. 182.

[89] Page 79. Accounts II, f. 19v. Whether this was a gift or a loan is unknown.

[90] Williamson, 'Religious Guilds', pp. 85, 87–8.

[91] Unlike Ludlow, there were no craft guilds recorded in Louth.

[92] Kennan, 'Guilds and Society', Chapter 5, p. 33.

[93] *Ibid*.

[94] Swaby, *History of Louth*, p. 74. A Groat was 4d.

[95] To attack or assault (the fire), *OED*. Goulding suggests 'refuge'. Goulding, Papers, 5/3.

[96] A destructive fire or conflagration, *OED*.

[97] Page 96. Accounts II, f. 27r.

Clearly, the guilds took an active part in undertakings beneficial to the town as a whole, not just those of a spiritual nature exclusive to their influential members.

Replicating the construction of the steeple in Louth, in the fifteenth century the dominant Ludlow Palmers' guild purchased stone for the building of a new tower.[98] Similarly, when interior fittings were renewed, it was principally the guild that the churchwardens approached for funding. This situation was also comparable to the Louth guilds in the provision of an organist and choristers for the church along with a number of clergy. Similarly, the guild also financed a schoolmaster to the free grammar school and maintained over thirty alms-folk.[99]

Infrastructure

During the mid to late sixteenth century, obligations towards the maintenance of local infrastructure, along with many other secular activities, had been increasingly transferred to the local parishes.[100] The first entry of many in these accounts was in 1532/3, when 2d was paid 'to Fawer for leading[101] down a spout to Stewton Gate',[102] and also 14d 'to 2 labourers for feying[103] the sewer & working there by the space of 2 days to meat & wages'.[104] Thirty-five years later, in 1567, it was noted: 'Item paid for leading of 6 loads of stone from Louth Park[105] to Haregarths Corner[106] to the new bridge, 4s 4d.'

---

[98] Lloyd, *St Lawrence*, p. 41.

[99] Westlake, *Gilds*, p. 19, https://www.stlaurences.org.uk/history (Accessed 18/11/2019).

[100] Cox, *Churchwardens*, pp. 2–3. Tate, *Parish Chest*, p. 90.

[101] Carrying.

[102] Page 85. Accounts II, *f.* 22r. Probably the present Stewton Lane.

[103] To fit, adapt or join, *OED*.

[104] Page 85. Accounts II, *f.* 22r. This may relate to an act of 1531, whereby 'walles, diches, bankes, guttuers [gutters], calceis [causeways], bridges, stremes [streams] and other defences by the costs [coasts] of the See and Marsshe grounde …' 23 Henry VIII, Chapter V. Statutes III, pp. 368–72. Similar entries are also noted in the first volume of accounts. Dudding, *Accounts*, pp. 10, 111, 112, 131, 168, 190, 213.

[105] Page 311. Accounts III, *f.* 54r. The Cistercian abbey of Louth Park, 2 miles east of Louth, was founded in 1139 by Bishop Alexander of Lincoln (1123–48). In 1535, its gross value was £169 5s 6½d. It was dissolved on Friday, 8 September 1536, three weeks prior to the Rising. The site was still being used thirty years later as a source of stone. *VE*, iv, p. 58. *VCH Lincs*, pp. 138–41. A similar situation occurred at Wigtoft in 1543 in connection with Swineshead Abbey, also belonging to the Cistercian order. The accounts relate that 2d was paid to Henri Dayl, 'for caring ye bell to ye abbay, & bryngyng ye other home', and the same amount for 'drynke wan we were at Swynshed to change ye bell'. Nichols, *Illustrations*, p. 230.

[106] 'Haregarths', with various spellings, is regularly mentioned in the accounts. It was probably situated within the South Field, but its exact location is open to

This situation appears to have continued on an ad-hoc basis until 1555, when the Highways Act stipulated that roads were to be regularly maintained.[107] The churchwardens acknowledged this legislation in the accounts:

> Memorandum, also that the forty shillings charged for the Common Cart is now delivered to the hands of the new churchwardens to remain in their hands to the use of the church for the space of seven years *videlicet* during the time of the statute for the amendment of the highways.[108]

In 1556/7, it was recorded: 'The election of the surveyors of the highways to Gilbert Blancherd & John Brown.'[109] This was typically followed by a list of four 'Boon Days', generally in spring, when work was performed.[110] In Market Deeping, repairs were recorded in the dikereeves' accounts, and at Kirton 6s 8d was 'paid to Thomas Croxton for the dyking of part of our meadow'.[111]

Periods of uncertainty

As noted earlier, the accounts record a variable decline in Sunday offerings. This decrease shadowed the Lincolnshire Rising of October 1536. In July of that year, a programme of monastic suppression had commenced in the county, along with unsubstantiated rumours that the county's numerous parish churches were possibly the next target. Those with considerable assets, along with many in close proximity to each other, initiating rumours of closure or amalgamation, were consequently perceived to be under threat.[112] Although St

---

speculation. Caitlin Green suggests that it lay off Legbourne Road, around 1½ miles (2.5km) south-east of Louth. David Robinson noted that a nearby farm is called 'Agarth', and there is an 'Aygarth House' opposite 'Southfield Farm', both on Legbourne Road. Green, *Streets of Louth*, pp. 145–6. Robinson, *Book of Louth*, p. 80.

[107] 'An Act for Mending the Highways', 2 & 3 Philip & Mary, Chapter VIII. *Statutes* IV (i), pp. 284–5. For details, see Tate, *Parish Chest*, pp. 243–50.

[108] 1555/6. Page 264. Accounts II, *f.* 123r. The term 'Common Cart' probably refers to a fund (common account), in this case to finance highway maintenance.

[109] Page 265. Accounts II, *f.* 123v.

[110] Boon Day. Doing boon-work, in this case repairing of public roads without remuneration. This was increased to six days from 1565.

[111] Kirton, PAR/7/1, *f.* 17v.

[112] There was possibly an unsuccessful Bill concerning the merger of parish churches placed before Parliament in 1536, although the *L&P* records this as 1539. It states: 'Draft Act of Parliament providing that when parsonages, vicarages, etc. are not worth more than £8 per annum, over and above the King's tenth, the King's Vicegerent may upon suit made therefor [*sic*] amalgamate two or more such churches.' *L&P*, XIV (i), 868 (15). There is however no mention of the confiscation of assets. A letter from the king to the commissioners of the subsidy in Lincolnshire states, 'as to the taking away of the goods of parish churches, it was never intended'. *L&P*, XI, 569, p. 226, 6 October 1536.

James's as the primary church of the deanery was in little danger of closure, there was still considerable local unease regarding the church's treasures and also the future spiritual direction of the English Church following the Act of Supremacy of 1534.[113]

Suspicions were further aroused by the publication in the summer of 1536 of the 'Ten Articles', closely followed by 'First Book of the King's Injunctions', both works challenging existing religious doctrines and traditions. Partly because of these edicts, Louth's parishioners probably became reluctant to donate as liberally to the king's ever depleting treasury as they had before. Margaret Bowker's suggestion that 'it would be a dull man indeed who did not recognise ... that an offering to the church might rapidly become Henry VIII's pocket money', would appear to have been a well-founded proposition.[114] The contents of the collection plate therefore may have reflected this uncertainty; Christopher Haigh's submission that Thomas Cromwell instituted, 'if not a reign of terror, at least a reign of nervousness', surely reflected the feelings of several Ludensian parishioners.[115]

Some may also have been wary of donating to a Church with whom they may have theologically disagreed, when the needy could benefit from their largess. As a result, money possibly destined for the collection plate may have increasingly been deposited in the 'poor man's box', no doubt strategically positioned at the church entrance.[116] There was also an overall decline in testamentary bequests, perhaps reflecting a gradual theological rejection of intercessionary prayers. However, this decline could also have signalled shifting generational attitudes towards financing the ever-changing doctrines, or possibly a gradual disconnection from a 'state church' of whichever religious persuasion. This suspicion and distrust of the central authorities, particularly the escalating power and influence of Thomas Cromwell as the Vice-Gerent in Spirituals, led ultimately to the Lincolnshire Rising, commencing in Louth on Sunday, 1 October 1536.

The Lincolnshire Rising

On that eventful day, the vicar, Thomas Kendall, preached a sermon touching on a visitation to be carried out the following day.[117] However, the collection

---

[113] Henry VIII, Chapter I. *Statutes* III, p. 492. An inventory of the church's assets was taken in 1486 and is recorded in Dudding, *Accounts*, pp. 150–8, 169–74.

[114] Bowker, *Henrician Reformation*, p. 93.

[115] Haigh, 'Introduction', p. 12.

[116] This box is first mentioned as such in 1548/9. Page 194. Accounts II, *f.* 82v. Saxilby accounts note in 1551, 'ij lockes for ye porre manys chest'. Gibbons, 'Saxilby', p. 351.

[117] William Moreland, a former monk of Louth Park, stated in his deposition that the vicar 'told his parishioners that next day they should have a visitation, and advised

only amounted to 2s 10d, despite usually ranging from 3 to 4 shillings during this period. This decrease was possibly due to an intervention by the townsfolk during the offertory. Directed by one Nicholas Melton,[118] they entered the building to secure the church's valuables, before John Frankish, the bishop's registrar, arrived the following morning (Monday, 2 October) to administer the visitation.[119]

During a violent altercation in the Cornmarket following Frankish's appearance, volumes denounced by the assembled crowd as profane were burnt. A later deposition noted:

> [Nicholas] Melton and his company then fetched Mr. Franke [Frankish], the Bishop's officer, from the Saracen's Head, with his books, which they burned on the Corn Hill, together with all English books of the New Testament, and other new books they could get by proclamation. Arthur Graye brought a book called Frythe his book, and Thomas Spencer, Robert Walleys and many others also brought books.[120]

If these men were indeed the owners of the volumes, this suggests a degree of curiosity concerning the new translations by a number of educated individuals such as Graye and Spencer, both leading members of the community.[121] Possession of commentaries by evangelical theologians such as John Frith (ex.1533) also shows the reformist programme retained a number of interested parties, even in a 'conservative' town such as Louth.[122]

Despite the momentous events unfolding, only a single line was recorded in the accounts specifically mentioning the Rising. Noted in the Sunday collections

---

them to go together and look well upon such things as should be required of them'. *L&P*, XII (i), 481, p. 228, 22 February 1536/7.

[118] Melton was a shoemaker, later acquiring the sobriquet 'Captain Cobbler'.

[119] Ward, *Rising*, pp. 13–14. Richard Hoyle suggests Frankish was also there to collect the 'First Fruits and Tenths' from the clergy. One of his 'reckoning' books saved from the fire by William Moreland may have contained a record of these assessments. Some priests from outlying villages attending the visitation possessed sums of cash, possibly to pay the commissioner, which were later donated to the rebels. Hoyle, *Pilgrimage*, p. 103, note 26. *L&P*, XI, 968, p. 390, *ibid.*, XI, 972, p. 397, 3 November 1536. Frankish was a public notary holding numerous positions within the diocese, notably in the south. He died c.1556. Cole, *Chapter Acts*, III, p. 137.

[120] Deposition of Thomas Foster, yeoman and singingman. *L&P*, XI, 828, 2 (iii), (1), p. 323, 23 October 1536.

[121] For Gray, see p. 66, note 407. Thomas Spencer, draper, was churchwarden in 1527/8 and 1539/40. Page 1, note 3.

[122] John Frith (1503–ex.1533) was a reformist theologian. The volume burned was possibly his *Disputacion of Purgatorye* (Antwerp, 1531). *DNB*, https://doi.org/10.1093/ref:odnb/10188 (Accessed 3/2/2020).

on 8 October are the words *nihil propter tumultum populi* (nothing because of the rising of the people).[123] Although a service was probably performed, many parishioners had taken up arms and were subsequently absent.[124] Church services were however resumed on 15 October, when 2s 8d was collected. People were gradually drifting back from Lincoln following the collapse of the revolt, doubtless fearing retribution by the advancing royal army but probably also to sow their winter crops. Nevertheless, the two following Sundays, 22 and 29 October, the collection was again registered as *nihil* (nothing). With the king's forces approaching, fear of arrest was probably a major factor. The accounts later note, 'for coals occupied in the Marketsted when my Lord Admiral was here, 2s'.[125] This was William Fitzwilliam, 1st earl of Southampton (1490–1542), and the entry was probably connected with the occupation of Louth on Friday, 27 October.[126] As a footnote to the Rising, on Saturday, 10 March 1537, six men from Louth were due to be hanged in the Market Place.[127] However, at least one may have been reprieved. In charge of the proceedings was Sir William Parr (c.1480–1547),[128] who possibly released one Robert Hudson – a man of that name was buried 8 September 1541.[129]

Submission

Following the Rising, Lincolnshire appears to have deferred to the inevitable, with Parr commenting, 'thinks the people are sorry for their late ill demeanour ... no shire is in better quietness'.[130] In 1536/7, an entry in the accounts notes, 'for making and writing the supplication sent by the town to the Lord Privy Seal, 20d'.[131] In 1538, Thomas Cromwell published the 'Second Royal Injunctions'. One clause involved the keeping of 'one boke or registre ... wherein ye shall write of every weddyng, christeying and burying'.[132] In 1538/9, the

---

[123] Page 112. Accounts, II, *f.* 36r. My thanks to Dr Nicholas Bennett for the translation.

[124] 'Since the twelfth century canon law declared that a priest must in general content himself with one daily Mass.' Catholic Encyclopaedia Online, https://www.newadvent.org/cathen/10006a.htm (Accessed 11/8/2020).

[125] Page 123. Accounts, II, *f.* 41v.

[126] Gunn, *Brandon*, p. 161 and note 32. *DNB*, https://doi.org/10.1093/ref:odnb/9663 (Accessed 27/12/2019). Hoyle suggests the 28th. Hoyle, *Pilgrimage*, p. 174.

[127] *L&P*, XII (i), 639, p. 286, 12 March 1537. Ward, *Rising*, p. 36.

[128] William Parr was the uncle of Katherine Parr, later queen. *DNB*, https://doi.org/10.1093/ref:odnb/58528 (Accessed 3/11/2019).

[129] Page 154. Accounts, II, *f.* 60r. LAO, Goulding Papers, 5/2.

[130] *L&P*, XII (i), 639, p. 286, 12 March 1537.

[131] Thomas Cromwell. Page 126. Accounts, II, *f.* 42v.

[132] Merriman, *Letters*, II, p. 154.

churchwardens obediently purchased a parish register: 'Item for the register book of burials & weddings, 6d.'[133]

The injunctions also relate to a 'travaill for the abolishing of suche images ... as might be of so greate an offence to god'.[134] The churchwardens recorded, 'to the labourers for bearing away the image of St George after it was taken down, 3d'.[135] This equestrian statue had been a prominent feature in St James's, with much expended on gilding the figure.[136] In 1534, Wigtoft also purchased an image of George complete with dragon.[137] Ludlow retained a similar statue, which was sold in 1548 to Thomas Hony for 18d, and 7d was paid by Walter Rosse for 'the dragon that the image of saynt George stode upon'.[138] The figures on Louth's Rood screen however remained standing until 1547/8, when 9s 4d was 'paid to Robert Odlyng & J[ohn] Rede for 3 days labouring taking down of the Rood, Mary & John'.[139] The injunctions also made compulsory 'one boke of the hole [sic] bible of the largest volume in English ... as your parishioners may most commodiously resorte to the same and reade yt'.[140] In 1539/40, 22s was paid 'for a new Bible of the largest volume'.[141] Evidence therefore suggests that the people of Louth were conforming to decrees initiated by the government, however unpopular in certain quarters.

New doctrines

With the accession of Edward VI in January 1547, the first fundamental doctrinal changes were instigated by the new administration. Consequently, throughout Edward's reign the accounts record an ongoing programme of alterations to church fittings and religious texts. Valuable plate was sold, seen as irrelevant within the confines of the new liturgy. In 1550/1, the accounts

---

[133] Page 131. Accounts II, f. 46r. Williams, *Historical Documents*, V, p. 813. Diarmaid MacCulloch has suggested that the introduction of registers was also a move against the Anabaptists, a sixteenth-century sect largely centred on Münster that denounced the baptism of children. Therefore, if baptisms were not registered, those concerned could be under suspicion. MacCulloch, *Thomas Cromwell*, pp. 287–8.

[134] Merriman, *Letters*, II, pp. 153.

[135] Page 133. Accounts II, f. 46v. Recorded in 1550/1, 'delivered to the hands of the new churchwardens for St George's sword sold to William Worseldy, 3s 4d'. Page 212. Accounts II, f. 92v.

[136] Gurnham, *Early Louth*, p. 149.

[137] 'Payd to William Bulle, carver, for makyng the gorge & the dragonne, 8s 8d.' Nichols, *Illustrations*, p. 225.

[138] Wright, *Churchwardens' Accounts*, pp. 36–7.

[139] Page 192. Accounts II, f. 81r. The number of days taken to remove the figures suggests they were of considerable size.

[140] Merriman, *Letters*, II, pp. 151–2.

[141] Page 139. Accounts II, f. 50v. The cost was shared between the clergy and parishioners; a smaller volume was purchased in 1541/2 for 9s 8d. Page 147. Accounts II, f. 55v.

state: 'The copy of the bill indentured betwixt Mr. Goodryk & Arthur Gray, William Whyte & others made to them upon the receipt of the town's plate; of gilt 543 ounces, parcel gilt 162 ounces ... total sum 705 ounces [20kg].'[142]

Similarly, at Saxilby in 1552, candlesticks, bells, basins and a 'holy water stocke', weighing 132lbs (59.8kg), were sold to one 'Lyones, ye pewterer of Lincolln', raising 38s 8d.[143] At Leverton in 1549, the churchwardens sold two candlesticks for 13s 8d, the sale of images raised 12d, and two cross cloths and a veil realised 4s 8d.[144] The following year, the same church paid 8s for 'taking up the Rood', 10d 'for taking down images' and £1 5s 10d 'for painting over the Rood', finally paying John Watson 5s 'for making the pulpitt'.[145]

In Louth, a communion table was purchased: 'Item paid for the table that is set in the high choir, 11s.'[146] Two shillings was expended on 'making a lectern above the pulpit', and 8d was paid 'for taking down the altars'.[147] Earlier, in 1547/8, wall paintings had been obliterated with lime-wash: 'Item paid to Thomas Tyllar of a bargain that he took of the churchwardens for wyting of the church, 3s 4d.'[148] All these actions were in abeyance with the Royal Injunctions of 1547, which state 'that they shall take away, utterly extinct and destroy all shrines, covering of shrines, all tables, candlesticks, trindles or rolls of wax, pictures, paintings, and all other monuments of feigned miracles'.[149]

Similar changes were recorded in Ludlow. In 1548, 'whitymymge the churche', and 'makynge the rode loft playne', along with paying 12d for 'lokes for the pore man chest'. Interestingly, in 1551, 6s 8d was paid to Thomas Dike and Thomas Bold for 'leynge of the aulter stonys in the midle of the churche'.[150] Being placed in this position, thereby repeatedly walked upon, was perhaps seen as disparaging sacred 'papist' artifacts.

Traditional religious texts were substituted with reformist literature. In Louth in 1549/50, it was noted, 'paid for a book of *Homilies* and the *Injunctions*, 2s',[151] along with 3s 8d 'for a book of the new service'.[152] One of the final

---

[142] Page 212. Accounts II, *f.* 93r. The plate was later sold for £95. Swaby, *History of Louth*, p. 139.

[143] Gibbons, 'Saxilby', p. 379.

[144] Peacock, 'Leverton', p. 357.

[145] Thompson, *Boston*, p. 567.

[146] 1550/1. Page 210. Accounts II, *f.* 91r.

[147] Page 190. Accounts II, *f.* 90v. Page 177. Accounts II, *f.* 91r. This suggests at least a 'two decker' pulpit.

[148] Page 190. Accounts II, *f.* 80v. There is no previous evidence of whitewashing.

[149] Frere and Kennedy, *Articles*, p. 126.

[150] Presumably the nave centre aisle. Wright, *Churchwardens' Accounts*, pp. 35, 47.

[151] Page 201. Accounts II, *f.* 87r. The *Homily of Good Works Annexed unto Faith* (1547) was a volume of sermons composed by Archbishop Thomas Cranmer (ex.1556). Frere and Kennedy, *Articles*, pp. 114–30. Cross, *Christian Church*, p. 651.

[152] Page 200. Accounts II, *f.* 86r. First issued in 1549, this initial Book of Common Prayer displeased both reformists and conservatives, and consequently a second

measures implemented in Edward's reign was in 1553/4 – 'received for the overplus of all the ornaments of the church which was sold at Whitsuntide last past, £3 5s 4d'.[153] Clearly, the churchwardens were dutifully enacting the reforms demanded by the Edwardian Church; whether they were wholeheartedly welcomed or sullenly tolerated can only be conjectured.

Throughout Edward's reign, Louth's parishioners must have recognised that their fears concerning the 'desecration' of their church, against which they initially rose in 1536, had finally come to fruition. Some indications of this local unease are revealed in the Sunday collections gathered during the period. The lowest annual total came to only £3 2s 3½d in 1549/50, although this gradually rose to £6 8s 9½d by the end of the reign, a fraction of that collected in the first third of the century.[154] This gradual increase may however indicate a measured acceptance of the religious changes, perhaps influenced by visiting preachers. Noted in 1562, 'paid to one Knyght, a preacher for his sermon given of the benevolence by the township, 6s 8d'.[155] At Wigtoft in 1550, 3s 4d was given to 'a preste for prechyng ye word of god'.[156] An older conservative generation was perhaps being supplanted by younger, more reform-minded parishioners, addressed by university-educated clergy advancing the new theology.

Education

The reformed doctrine was also taught in the grammar school by tutors such as John Goodall. He was master from 1528 to 1541, when he became *Magister scole grammaticalis* at Thornton College, formerly Thornton Abbey (Augustinian Canons). With the closure of the college in 1547, Goodall resumed his former position prior to becoming the first schoolmaster of the refounded King Edward VI Grammar School.[157] The first known reference to a schoolmaster in Louth, *Magister scolarum de Luda*, was in 1276, and in 1433 a Thomas Rydlay was mentioned as *Magister scolarum gramaticalium de*

---

volume was issued in 1552. Cross, *Christian Church*, p. 318. Williams, *Historical Documents*, V, pp. 849–51.

[153] Page 231. Accounts II, *f.* 105r. In 1553, Pentecost (Whitsuntide) was 21 May: Edward died on 19 July.

[154] Pages 198, 230. Accounts II, *ff.* 85r, 104v.

[155] Page 308. Accounts III, *f.* 19v.

[156] Nichols, *Illustrations*, p. 235.

[157] Gurnham, *Free School*, pp. 13–14. *VCH Lincs*, p. 237. Despite today having several schools named in his honour, Edward VI probably only directly founded Christ's Hospital in London, established on the site of the Greyfriars; the remainder were refoundations. Louth Grammar was retained via a Continuance Warrant, the only change being the system of governance. Leach, *English Schools*, pp. 138, 141–2. Benton, *Early Days*, p. 23.

Luda.¹⁵⁸ The guilds were also active in this sphere. Whereas St Mary's guild provided the premises, the Holy Trinity was proactive in administering the grammar school.¹⁵⁹ A licence of 1453 required the Trinity guild to see to 'the maintenance of one chaplain sufficiently learned in grammar who instructed the boys of the town'.¹⁶⁰

Grammar schools, of which in Lincolnshire there were thirty-three by the end of the sixteenth century, were largely instituted to propagate the reformed doctrine.¹⁶¹ Therefore, to be appointed schoolmaster of the Edward VI school, John Goodall must have been of the reformist persuasion to match that of its patrons and royal 'founder'. The school was established by John Bradley, a merchant of the Staple, his half-brother Richard Goodrich¹⁶² and Lawrence Eresby (d.1561/2),¹⁶³ with Eresby's brother-in-law, Sir William Cecil, acting as intermediary at court.¹⁶⁴ Goodrich (c.1508–62) was an attorney at the Court of Augmentations and was recorded in 1546/7, when the parish 'paid for a dinner when Master Goodryke and Master Bellow was here to view the lands of the guilds, 6s 4d'.¹⁶⁵

During the sixteenth century, there were three places of learning in the town: the song and grammar schools and later a petty school for the younger children.¹⁶⁶ Originally, the schoolmaster was supported by the guilds, with the accounts of 1535/6 noting:

---

¹⁵⁸ Goulding, *Grammar School*, p. 7.

¹⁵⁹ Gurnham, *History of Louth*, p. 43.

¹⁶⁰ Goulding, *Grammar School*, p. 4.

¹⁶¹ Harkrider, *Women, Reform and Community*, pp. 92–3.

¹⁶² He was cousin of Thomas Goodrich (d.1554), the reformist bishop of Ely. For Richard Goodrich, see *DNB*, https://doi.org/10.1093/ref:odnb/10979 (Accessed 7/1/2019), and Bindoff, *House of Commons*, II, pp. 231–3.

¹⁶³ Lawrence Eresby was the county's Commissioner of Inquisitions Post-mortem in 1548 and for chantries in Grantham in 1550. In 1551, he became the first warden of Louth Corporation and grammar school. Alford, *Kingship*, pp. 79, 145–6. *CPR*, Edward VI, 1550-1553, pp. 119-22. Will: TNA, PROB 11/45/47, Probate, 13 February 1561/2. Buried 9 January 1561/2. LAO, Goulding Papers, 5/2.

¹⁶⁴ Gurnham, *Free School*, p. 14. Alford, *Kingship*, p. 146.

¹⁶⁵ Page 184, Accounts II, *f.* 76v. No doubt the visit was with a view to suppression and the purchase of property. John Bellow (c.1513–59), a Crown Surveyor for Thomas Cromwell, was captured at Legbourne Priory at the start of the Rising. He later transacted considerable purchases of monastic and chantry landholdings. *L&P*, XII (i), 380, p. 175: XX (i), 1335 (11–12), pp. 655–60. He was mayor of Grimsby on four occasions and in 1547 became the town's MP alongside Richard Goodrich, a position he held six times; Louth was part of the constituency. Bindoff, *House of Commons*, I, pp. 135, 415–16.

¹⁶⁶ Little is known about the petty school, first mentioned in 1553/4, when a John Laycock was paid £6 pa. to teach, therefore it may have been included in the refoundation of the grammar school. Goulding, *Corporation Records*, p. 140. *VCH Lincs*, p. 463. The school building was in Chequergate, donated by John Bradley, with the song

It is agreed by [the] parish that Master John Godeall [Goodall] schoolmaster of grammar shall have yearly toward his living and wages 40s, that is to say 10s of Our Lady guild, 6s 8d which of the pece which he now hath, 13s 4d of St Michael light, 5s of Corpus Christi guild & 5s of St Peter's guild.[167]

With the suppression of the guilds in 1547, a new source of finance was required in order to uphold the town's education system and provide funding to sustain the poor. These factors ultimately led to the creation of the Corporation.[168]

Charity

The 1551 charter inaugurating the Corporation and school also officially sanctioned the bedehouses, bringing them together under the same administrative umbrella. The two were administered by the Trinity and Lady guilds, with the inmates possibly required to wear an emblem, the accounts of 1537/8 noting 'to Overay Paynter for making badges to the poor folks', 6d.[169] When the grammar school was transferred to Schoolhouse Lane around 1558, the new structure incorporated an alms-house on the lower floor.[170] Later, charitable donations were given directly via a poor box administered by the parish. In

---

school situated in the churchyard. Gurnham, *History of Louth*, pp. 80–1. In 1556/7, the accounts state, 'paid for 3 quarters of thatch for the school in the churchyard 12s', and 'for 8 days work in walling the said schoolhouse, 3s 4d'. Page 234. Accounts II, *f.* 124v. Until c.1560, the master was William Man. In Thomas Kendall's deposition following the Rising, he mentioned a William Man 'who sings bass in the choir at Lowthe'. *L&P*, XII (i), 70, p. 33, 12 January 1537. Gurnham, *Free School*, p. 13. Williamson, 'Religious Guilds', pp. 90–1.

[167] Page 184. Accounts II, *f.* 35r. Interestingly, the Trinity guild, usually associated with the school, is not listed. Goodall, John Cawod and Nicholas Parnell were also scribes of the accounts. Cawod similarly compiled those of the Trinity guild (1489/90–1522/3) and the Lady guild (1496/7–1503/4). In addition, he was the parish organist, choirmaster, a lay chorister (singingman), minister and musician from 1476 to his death in 1528/9, a total of at least fifty-three years' service to the church. He received a stipend of 20s, later raised to 30s 4d p.a. Goulding, *Cawod*, pp. 3–4. Gurnham, *Free School*, pp. 10–11. In 1512/13, Cawod transcribed an inventory into the accounts dating from 1486, illustrating the many vestments and other valuable regalia that the church possessed. Dudding, *Accounts*, pp. 150-8, 169-74. A Nicholas Parnell or Pernell had connections with the Lady guild and in 1544 obtained a pension of 20s p.a. He is noted as being married with children. Hodgett, *Ex-Religious*, pp. 53, 68, 112.

[168] 'An Act whereby certain Chantries, Colleges, Free Chapels and the Possessions of the same be given to the King's Majesty', 1 Edward VI, Chapter XIV, 1547. Chapter VIII refers to the foundation of grammar schools using the proceeds from former guild properties. *Statutes* III, pp. 24–33.

[169] Page 124. Accounts II, *f.* 42r. Alternatively, a licence to beg issued under the Vagabonds Act of 1530 (22 Henry VIII c.12). *Statutes* III, pp. 328–32.

[170] Goulding, *Grammar School*, p. 8.

1546/7, an entry recorded 'given in alms to poor people 2s 4d', the first of many in the subsequent pages. In 1555/6, the names of the destitute started to be recorded en masse.[171] There followed extensive lists of recipients, many names repeated, indicating payments at regular intervals.[172] This was unusual during the period, the lowest in society being rarely documented. These records ended in 1562, although mention of a poor man's box continued until 1572.[173]

Money from church funds and practical assistance was also given to outlying settlements. In 1553/4, the accounts relate, 'paid to the relief of sick people in Saltfleethaven ..., 2s'.[174] This village, situated on the east coast, was an important entrepôt; Louth therefore retained an interest in its welfare. Fotherby, to the north, also appears to have succumbed to an epidemic. In 1552/3, 2s was 'paid to Saltmarsh's wife for serving of Fotherby folks when they were sick'.[175] In 1546/7, nearby Welton le Wold also received aid, although not entirely altruistically. 'Item John Bello for serving of Welton town folks when they were visited with plague to keep them out of the town & to buy them victuals, 18d.'[176] A similar entry occurred in 1540/1, when the churchwardens gave 2s as 'a reward to a man in Costragate visited with plague to provide for himself in the country'.[177]

Queen Mary

With Mary's accession in July 1553, there was a speedy response in Louth to directives permitting the return of traditional services. This was illustrated by the prompt reinstatement of church furniture and liturgical volumes outlawed under the previous administration. In 1553/4, there was 'paid to Thomas Mysterchambers for a Manual and a Dirige Book, 4s 6d', and 'to William King for a holy water vat & a pair of censers, 4s'.[178] A new high altar, in total costing £1 5s 11d, was placed into position accompanied by celebrations – 'paid for bread and ale at the raising of the altar stone, 5d'.[179] There followed a close succession of entries noting the purchase of numerous items used in the performance of the re-established services. The churchwardens were apparently more than willing to rapidly restore the church to its former splendour and reintroduce the traditional liturgy.

---

[171] Page 182. Accounts II, *f.* 76r. Page 220. Accounts II, *f.* 116v.

[172] Pages 252–9. Accounts II, *ff.* 116v to 119v.

[173] Accounts III, *f.* 73v. Out of over two thousand burials dating from 1538/9–1570/1 in the Parish Registers, only seventeen 'Paupers' were recorded.

[174] Page 236. Accounts II, *f.* 107v. Twelve further entries suggest a serious outbreak.

[175] Page 227. Accounts II, *f.* 102v.

[176] Page 182. Accounts II, *f.* 76r.

[177] Cisterngate. Page 111. Accounts II, *f.* 54r.

[178] Page 235. Accounts II, *f.* 107r.

[179] Page 236. Accounts II, *f.* 107v.

Similarly, at Saxilby in 1554, 14d was paid 'to Robert Bryd and servaunt for settyng vp ye aulter', and 12d for 'makyng iij lynkes to ye sensers', filled with frankincense purchased for ½d.[180] The Rood figures were renewed in 1557, when 30s was paid for 'the Roodemari, and John and saynt Botulphe'.[181] At Ludlow, 11s was apportioned in 1554 for 'makynge the hie aulter', along with purchasing a holy water vat, a canopy for the pyx, timber for the Pascalle and 4d for setting up the Rood.[182] Leverton also witnessed the reversal of the previous strictures. In 1554, a pyx, a sepulchre house with a painted cloth and 2lbs of wax along with two books were brought from London to Boston, no doubt by sea; the total cost being 9s 7d. A new Rood was not constructed however until 1556, when an order was placed in Lincoln after the churchwardens were cited and fined 6s 4d.[183]

In 1554, the Rood figures were restored in St James's – 'to Peper in part of payment of the making of the Rood, 6s 8d', and 'paid to Robert Babsor [for] painting of the Rood, 7s'.[184] Nevertheless, wall paintings were apparently not re-introduced. Noted in 1554/5 was 6s paid 'to William Dixson and Rauf Robson for whiting the church walls'.[185] This was probably a practical move as mural painters were doubtless expensive and whitewashing would also lighten the church interior.

Via Media

In the eyes of some of Louth's parishioners, 'normal service' had been resumed, at least for the remaining years of Mary's brief reign. Even following the accession of Elizabeth in November 1558, matters appeared outwardly to continue as before. The accounts of 1558/9 recorded, 'paid to William Pelson for 14 pounds of wax to the Sepulchre Light, 10s 6d'; the light being a feature uncharacteristic of reformist liturgy.[186] It was not until 1561 that changes were noted: 'Paid to the vicar for the table and the frame containing

---

[180] Gibbons, 'Saxilby', p. 382. In 1555, Saxilby initially gave 15s and later 9s 3d for 'Rome pens'; presumably 'Peter's Pence', originally paid to the Vatican prior to the Reformation. Gibbons, 'Saxilby', pp. 384–5. In the same year, an 'Act, repealing all Statutes, Articles, and Provisions, made against the See of Rome', reversed the actions taken by the previous administrations including payments to the papacy; 1 & 2 Philip & Mary, Chapter 8, III. *Statutes* IV (i), p. 246.

[181] Gibbons, 'Saxilby', p. 384.

[182] Wright, *Churchwardens' Accounts*, p. 56.

[183] LAO, Leverton, PAR/7/1, f. 60r. Thompson, *Boston*, p. 567.

[184] Page 243. Accounts II, f. 111v. The screen itself, along with the Rood loft, appears to have been retained during Edward's reign, only the figures being removed.

[185] Page 244. Accounts II, f. 111v.

[186] Page 280. Accounts II, f. 134v. This was recorded at the end of the year's accounts, therefore probably in the reign of Elizabeth. Mary died 17 November 1558.

the commandments & other sentences of scripture, 2s 5d.'[187] This board was probably inscribed with the Ten Commandments and the Lord's Prayer along with the order of services, the latter detailed as 'paid for a new calendar set forth by my Lord of Canterbury, 8d'.[188]

Inquiries overseen by the royal commissioners in Lincolnshire recorded the destruction of many 'bookes of papistrie' and the removal of 'monuments of supersticion'.[189] Nevertheless, it took until 1566 before any documented evidence appeared in Louth relating to the removal and sale of church fittings associated with the Marian administration. Listed on a single folio was the sale of a hand bell, censers, cruets, candlesticks, altar cloths and 'one passyon clothe'.[190] Their removal and disposal however probably occurred much earlier. At Bilsby, 'our images of the Rood, Mary and John and all other images were burned *anno quarto* Elizabeth' (1561/2), and at Aswardby 'the Roode lofte [was] taken downe [in] 1562 and broken in peces and burnte'.[191]

In Louth, some features of long-established services were however retained. In 1567/8, it was recorded that 5s was paid to Mr Goodall for '4 prick song books to the choir'; clearly choristers were still performing.[192] In 1569, liturgical items were still being divested. The church received £11 4s 8d 'for 2 challises and one paten gilt weighing 42 ounces and half a quarter, sold by Roger Stute at London for 5s 4d the ounce'.[193] Items were also being purchased for the reordered services: 'Paid for one communion cup [of] parcel gilt in white, 15 ounces, £4 9s 3d.'[194] In 1570, the church disposed of the last items from Mary's reign, twelve years after the accession of her half-sister. 'Received of James Mansell and Richard Riggs for 2 tabernacles taken down in St Peter's

---

[187] Page 298. Accounts III, *f.* 10r.

[188] Page 298. Accounts III, *f.* 10v. Listed in the Book of Common Prayer: 'A Table and Kalender, expressing the ordre of the Psalmes and Lessons.' *OED*. The archbishop was Matthew Parker (1559–75), previously dean of Lincoln (1552–4).

[189] Foster, *Church Furniture*, pp. 115–16. At Saxilby in 1566, Alexander Pereson was paid 20d to travel to Lincoln with the 'Inventory of Superstitious Ornaments'. Gibbons, 'Saxilby', p. 387. Page 335.

[190] Page 335. Accounts III, *f.* 46r. A cloth shrouding the Rood during Lent.

[191] Foster, *Church Furniture*, p. 87. Peacock, *Church Furniture*, p. 33.

[192] Page 345. Accounts III, *f.* 55r. Choirs were sanctioned within the Injunctions of 1559. Gee and Hardy, *Documents*, XLIX, p. 435. When the composer William Byrd (1539/43–1623) was organist and choir master at Lincoln Cathedral (1563–72), he visited Louth in 1562/3 and 1564/5, possibly seeking suitable choristers. Williamson, 'Religious Guilds', p. 91. *DNB*, https://doi.org/10.1093/ref:odnb/4267 (Accessed 15/10/2019).

[193] Page 353. Accounts III, *f.* 61r.

[194] Page 355. Accounts III, *f.* 63r.

choir, 2s.'[195] In the same year, Luke Smith was paid 'for painting scripture on the Rood loft, 11s'.[196]

In 1571/2, it was recorded, 'paid for one book of Articles at the commandment of the Bishop, 8d'.[197] Archbishop Parker had attempted to chart a course of *via media* (middle way), hoping to unite the two opposing religious factions. However, in February 1570, Pope Pius V (1566–72) issued the bull *Regnans in Excelsis* (He that reigneth on high), officially excommunicating Elizabeth as 'the pretended queen and servant of crime'.[198] This shadowed the 'Northern Rebellion' of November 1569, in which Louth played its part in securing the county against the threatened incursion.

In late 1569, as part of the county's defence during the short-lived rebellion, the parish paid for armour and weapons to repel an attack from both land and sea.[199] This ranged from 16s for a gun, to 'mending William Holland's gun, staff and matches, 4d'.[200] Further afield, 2s 6d was 'paid [to] 3 men for carrying the town's harness[201] to Borwell',[202] and 6s 8d for 'the making of Saltfleet Haven fire beacons', no doubt to warn of enemy forces approaching along the coast. Some equipment appears to have come in by sea rather than overland during winter. 'Item paid for a corslet[203] and a coat of plate with other furniture received at Grimsby, 8s 4d', and likewise 'to John Blanchard for the receipt of them at the ship ..., 12d'.[204]

Other parishes also purchased weapons. In 1584, the constables' accounts at Market Deeping record the acquisition of items ranging from corselets, pikes, bullets, matches and girdles to 2 pounds of gunpowder. The Louth churchwardens were likewise responsible for maintaining practice butts in the quarry situated to the south of the town.[205] In 1556/7, 'paid to ... George

---

[195] Page 359. Accounts III, *f.* 65r. Tabernacle – an ornamented receptacle for the pyx containing the consecrated host. *OED*.

[196] Page 362. Accounts III, *f.* 67v. Apparently, the loft was still standing.

[197] Accounts III, *f.* 70v. Bishop Thomas Cooper (1571–84). This was the 'Thirty-Nine Articles', finally promulgated within the Subscription (Thirty-Nine Articles) Act, also known as: 'An Act to Reform Certain Disorders touching Ministers of the Church' (1571); 3 Elizabeth, Chapter XII. *Statutes* IV (i), pp. 546–7. Gee and Hardy, *Documents*, pp. 477–80.

[198] Full text at http://www.papalencyclicals.net/Pius05/p5regnans.htm (Accessed 9/7/2018).

[199] Pages 354–6. Accounts III, *ff.* 62r to 63v.

[200] Probably relating to a matchlock musket.

[201] A generic term for various types of armour.

[202] Burwell.

[203] A piece of armour covering most of the body. *OED*.

[204] Page 355. Accounts III, *f.* 63r

[205] Practising archery had been required by law from at least 1388; 12 Rich II, Chapter VI. *Statutes* III, pp. 25–6. In 1541, within the 'Act for Maintenance of Artillery

Sympson for leading 18 loads of sods to the said butts, 4s 4d', and 'to ... Richard Mawborne & Thomas Wake for 3 days to meat & wages for making the said butts, 3s 4d'.[206]

Additional commissions

Another of the church's responsibilities was the supervision of the common bull, used to service the town's cattle. This was a feature from 1522, when 'Robarde Spencer' was refunded 13s 'for a common bull'.[207] The price varied largely depending on the size and quality of the animal. In 1551/2, it was recorded, 'paid for a common bull going with the town kye, 20s 8d'.[208] The last note was in 1625/6, when an animal, previously costing 45s 6d, was sold for 36s 8d.[209] The Leverton accounts in 1537 also relate to 'the common bull when he was in the Hallgarth', the rent being 8d,[210] and the bailiffs' accounts of Market Deeping record receiving payments for the 'town bull'.[211]

Louth's churchwardens were also accountable for 'jail delivery': transporting prisoners to Lincoln Castle for trial.[212] In 1564, they paid 'Ralf Flower for the carriage of a prisoner to Lincoln, the 19th day of August, 3s 4d.'[213] Earlier, in 1535/6, restraints were purchased – 'to the smith for making a pair of manacles, 10d'.[214] One felon in particular caused the parish considerable trouble. An entry for 1566 notes, 'paid to Thomas Hutchynson for carrying of Robert Swetyng ... to Lincoln Castle, 9s 4d'.[215] In 1570, however, Swetyng appears to have either escaped or was an outlaw. Consequently, there was 'paid to Arthur Hill and Richard Emet for making hue and cry after Robert Swetyng from Louth to Barton and Caister, for their labour and expenses,

---

and for Debarring of Unlawful Games', 'every man who was neither lame, nor decrepit, nor maimed (spiritual men and Justices of the Bench and Assize excepted) should use and exercise shooting with the long bow, and also should have a bow and arrows ready continually in his house'; 33 Henry VIII, Chapter IX. *Statutes* III pp. 837–41. Goulding, *Customs*, p. 6.

[206] Page 271. Accounts II, *f.* 127r.

[207] Dudding, *Accounts*, p. 219.

[208] Page 207. Accounts II, *f.* 90v.

[209] Goulding, *Customs*, p. 8.

[210] Thompson, *Boston*, p. 566.

[211] LAO, Market Deeping, PAR/10/1.

[212] Dating from the medieval period, this was defined as 'the clearing a jail of prisoners by bringing them to trial'. *OED*.

[213] Page 324. Accounts III, *f.* 37r. One of the rare occasions when a date is recorded fully.

[214] Page 108. Accounts II, *f.* 33v. These were probably for detainees in the lockup, the stocks or the pillory.

[215] Page 339. Accounts III, *f.* 50r.

4s 4d, and for the hire of 2 horses, 2s 8d'.[216] He was later recaptured, and accordingly 3s 4d was 'paid to Thomas Leich, smith, for giving evidence at Lincoln against Robert Swetyng'.[217]

Both the parish and the guilds were also accountable for the 'fire brigade' – important when most of the town's buildings were constructed of timber and roofed with thatch. Hooks were used to pull down burning thatch and in extreme cases the demolition of an entire building. An entry for 1534/5 records: 'Item to Thomas Provest for a hook of iron for scathe fires weighing 22 lbs – 3s 8d.'[218] In 1551/2, it was noted, 'there is hung at William Howenys a great hook of iron that is for pulling down houses when there is a scathe fire'.[219] There was paid in 1560 to Thomas Lechman, the smith, for 'the shotting of one great fire hook – 2s'.[220]

These are just a few examples of the wide-ranging secular activities that the parish of St James oversaw. Here was a melding of different aspects of local administration into a cohesive entity, where the church and guilds and later the Corporation were conjoined within their respective responsibilities. This perhaps symbolises the parishioners' desires to acquire a modicum of stability in unstable times, for the well-being of the community as a whole and importantly the security of their souls.

Conclusion

The English Church had largely remained a stable and enduring component throughout the previous centuries of both concord and discord. This was particularly notable within the parish context. Louth's parishioners had worshipped in relative peace, employing a liturgy little altered for nearly a millennium and for the most part remaining remote from conflicts emanating from the political centre. In the sixteenth century, all this would change, largely due to the succession crisis, the king's 'Great Matter'.

The Louth churchwardens' accounts reveal the mechanisms of a parish church during a period of English history that had never before witnessed the parallel challenges of deep-seated alterations to religious doctrine alongside considerable volatility radiating from the Tudor Court. The parish church would no longer be a place of spiritual security but instead become immersed within the conflict between king and pope, secular authority and religious convictions. This struggle left parishioners fearful, not only for their souls but sometimes for their very lives. Additionally, local church administrators

---

[216] Page 361. Accounts III, *f.* 66v.
[217] Page 362. Accounts III, *f.* 67v.
[218] Page 102. Accounts II, *f.* 30v.
[219] Page 214. Accounts II, *f.* 94v.
[220] Page 293. Accounts III, *f* 5r.

became part of this unsolicited confrontation, with incremental responsibilities encumbered upon the parish by an increasingly bureaucratic state – St James's being a striking example.

In his seminal work *The Parish Chest*, William Tate records that churchwardens were 'the proper guardians or keepers of the parish church' and 'the very foundation of democratic local government in England', having later imposed on them 'certain additional civil duties'.[221] Evidence suggests that until the advent of the Corporation in 1551, Louth's churchwardens appear to have gradually become administrators for the town, supplanting the manor court. That four churchwardens were elected each year, as against in Lincolnshire the customary two, may give an indication of their considerable administrative responsibilities. Names such as Beverlay, Lyncoln, Bradley, Chapman, Blanchard and Gyrdike frequently occurred in the position, as they had for the posts of manor court officials, guild officers and later administrators of the Corporation.

With its market and fairs, Louth was undoubtedly perceived as the economic hub for the surrounding area, notably in the marshland and the ports and havens along the ever-shifting coastline. It was recorded that prior to the Rising, rumours of church closures travelled far and wide across the county, the 'bruits' no doubt amplified at the town's fair, in the 'Marketstead' and within the many taverns. Louth's merchants and traders would have travelled extensively, both in England and indeed abroad.[222] A number of parishioners are recorded as journeying to London on ecclesiastical and financial business on behalf of the church and to Lincoln to deposit documents with the bishop's administrators and to transport prisoners to the castle.

The accounts reveal that the many laws and decrees, both secular and religious initiated by an increasingly regulatory Tudor government, were consistently obeyed and, with the notable exception of the Rising, appear to have been devoid of any notable opposition. They also illustrate the churchwardens' competence in overseeing the fiscal prosperity of their place of worship. Skilled tradesmen were employed to maintain the structure: plumbers, glaziers, masons and carpenters, who in turn taught apprentices and employed local workers. Equally, the congregation's wealthier members contributed to providing and later replenishing the vestments, silverware and liturgical volumes relative to the ever-changing doctrines. Similar to the Palmers' guild in Ludlow, the Trinity guild delivered education in the form of the grammar school, while the Lady guild provided bedesmen to accompany the lay choristers, who in turn trained pupils in the song school.[223] Similarly, the

---

[221] Tate, *Parish Chest*, p. 84.

[222] In their testaments, some parishioners were noted as Merchants of the Staple of Calais.

[223] Williamson, 'Religious Guilds', p. 86. Gurnham, *Early Louth*, p. 134.

needy and destitute were not forgotten following the suppression of the guilds. There are regular mentions of 'alms to the poor', money that was doubtless previously deposited in the collection plate, again perhaps reflecting a local disenchantment with the ever-shifting creeds.

The accounts undoubtedly reveal a sense of cooperation between the parish church, the guilds, thence the Corporation. Each of these three entities combined their activities to enhance both their own prosperity and that of the community as a whole. The celebrated spire was financed with contributions from both the churchwardens and the guilds along with donations from the pockets of local parishioners. All sections of society, rich and poor, secular and ecclesiastical, collaborated in the running of this prosperous Lincolnshire market town throughout a period of considerable political and religious instability. As evidence of this, there are few better examples than that of the churchwardens' accounts of the parish church of St James in Louth, providing an invaluable insight into Tudor Lincolnshire.

The documents

Of the two volumes of accounts that cover the period edited, the first comprises seventy-two folios dating from 1527/8 to 1559/60 and the second sixty-seven folios continuing to 1570/1; this volume carries on to 1623/4.[224] The second volume is in better condition, and both were bound and covered by board from an unknown date. The text is written in iron-gall ink on rag paper measuring approximately 16" x 6" (40.6 x 15.2cm) and 11½" x 7" (29.2 x 17.8cm) respectively. The writing is mostly in English in a reasonably executed Secretary Hand, which notably improves during the later years, perhaps through the influence of the grammar school.

Naturally, over such a lengthy period there were a number of different hands. Three scribes are known by name: consecutively John Cawod, Nicholas Parnell or Pernell and John Goodall. The layout is largely formulaic, although with a few variances throughout the period. The preamble naming the churchwardens is followed by precise details of the Sunday collections, witwords (legacies), burials, the ringing of bells, along with the regular payments to the 'Ministers of the Church'. This is followed by detailed specifics of income and expenditure. In the margins are entries both in text and numerals along with manicules and dot calculations. Most items are compiled in considerable detail, and in some cases the daily rate is recorded for the different trades, revealing the income of individual workmen.

---

[224] There are twenty blank pages overall and no discernible watermarks.

Editing

This edition follows the pattern Clive Burgess employed in his work on All Saints, Bristol, in that it uses modern rather than original spelling where possible, to increase clarity.[225] In order to convey the 'feel' of the original text, their arrangement has been retained but with added words [in square brackets] and additional punctuation where deemed necessary. The use of extensive footnotes also allows the text to flow naturally.

Capitalisation has been standardised in this edition, with capitals used only for place and personal names, titles (Bishop, Master etc.) and religious festivals. Although Roman numerals were used in the original, these have been largely substituted for 'Arabic' numbers. Places and people's surnames are transcribed in the original spelling, but with most first names in the modern style unless particularly unusual: for example, Jenet, Jarrat and Auncell. Some were originally written in standard abbreviated forms, such as Ric for Richard, Robt for Robert, and again these are recorded in the extended standard modern form.

The complete text for the period 1527–70 has been transcribed, except where the document is damaged or a word or writing is indecipherable, which is indicated thus [...]. Those words whose meaning is unknown or which are titles of publications mentioned in the accounts are marked in *italics*. The folio numbers note recto and verso, and the dates for the financial years (in the Old Style) are noted in **bold**. The Latin, in the annual preambles and some few other places, is translated. Where Latin is used unusually within the English text – for example where a nun is described as *monialis* – this has been left in Latin with a translation given in a footnote at the first occurrence.

The transcribed text consists of over one hundred thousand words (not including footnotes), so some errors will inevitably transpire. I have of course endeavoured to keep these to a minimum, but for those that do occur, in the words of Burgess, 'I can only ask to be forgiven.'[226]

Brian Hodgkinson (2023).

---

[225] Burgess, *Accounts*.
[226] Burgess, *Accounts*, p. 34.

The Louth St James Churchwardens' Accounts: 1527–60[1]

f. 1r.

[1527–8]

IHS [Jesus]

The account of Robert Browne,[2] draper, Richard Curson, Thomas Spencer[3] & Alex[ander] ... [4], taylor, Proctors[5] of the Church of St James of Louth, all

---

[1] LAO, Louth St James, PAR/7/2 dating from 1527/8 to 1559/60 (hereafter Accounts II). LAO, Louth St James, PAR/7/3 dating from 1560/1 to 1570/1 (hereafter Accounts III). The remaining fragments from the year 1524 record the burial of Thomas Pagge, priest, Alles, wife [of] William Walker, Marion, wife [of] William Pullay (old debt): Isabel wife [of] Robert Proketure: [.......] Fraunchman. LAO, Goulding, Papers, 5/3.

[2] During the Lincolnshire Rising of October 1536, which commenced at Louth, a Robert Brown was assigned to guard John Bellow and John Millicent, Thomas Cromwell's commissioners, following their capture at Legbourne Priory and detention in Louth. Money seized from them totalled £6, which was given to Brown for safe keeping. *L&P*, XII (i), 380, p. 178, 9 February 1536/7. Robert's son, John was also taken at Legbourne by the rebels. Ward, *Rising*, p. 15. In an examination before the King's Council on 6 October 1536, Sir Edward Maddison of Caister, one of the Subsidy Commissioners, stated that Robert Brown was 'one of the ringleaders in the field at Castre [Caister]'. *L&P*, XI, 568, p. 225, 6 October 1536: *ibid.*, 854, p. 343, 24 October 1536. A Robert Brown was buried 23 April 1541. LAO, Goulding Papers, 5/2.

[3] In 1535, Thomas Spencer, draper, was chamberlain of the Lady guild and elected alderman in 1544. Swaby, *History of Louth*, p. 174. He was assessed at 40s in the 1524/5 Lay Subsidy. TNA, E179/138/478. During the Rising, Spencer brought 'undesirable works' to be burnt by the rebels. He was appointed 'Petty Captain' and appears to have urged them to travel to Caister to apprehend the Subsidy Commissioners. Ward, *Rising*, p. 15. *L&P*, XI, 828, 2 (iii), p. 323, 23 October 1536: *ibid.*, 972, p. 398, 3 November 1536. He left a will, leaving money for twenty-one chaldrons (chaldron = 21½ cwt) of coal to the poor, which later formed the basis of a permanent charity. TNA, PROB 11/34/122, probate, 14 April 1551. Goulding, *Corporation Records*, pp. 169, 181. Interred 10 March 1550/1. LAO, Goulding Papers, 5/2.

[4] Surname missing. The name Alexander is recorded six times in the accounts as either Alexander Mychelson, Wallis or Doughty. Mychelson was churchwarden 1539/40 and was noted as a tailor (page 135). However, 'Alexander Taillor, son of Robert' is recorded in the Parish Registers as being buried on 20 November 1540. Transcript of Louth Parish Registers, 1538–1681 (hereafter LAO, Goulding Papers, 5/2).

[5] *Praepositorum[a]*. This can also be translated as *procuratores* (officials), kirkmasters, reeves (*prepositus*), churchreeve or churchgrave. Addy, *Church and Manor*, p. 277. Owen, *Church and Society*, pp. 115–16. For a list of churchwardens, see Appendix 1.

receipts and expenses on Sunday the Octave of Easter 1527 until the Octave of Easter 1528.[1]

Item received of churchwardens year afore of money good & ill – 60s 11d.

Sum.[2]

Item received 2nd Sunday after Easter – 4s 5d.
Item received 3rd Sunday after same – 4s 2d.
Item received 4th Sunday after same – 4s 3d.
Item received 5th Sunday after same – 3s 4d.
Item received Sunday after Ascension of our Lord – 3s 8d.
Item received Sunday Pentecost – 3s 10d.
Item received Trinity Sunday – 5s 5d.
Item received 1st Sunday after – 2s 1d.
Item received 2nd Sunday after – 3s 1d.
Item received 3rd Sunday after – 3s 7d.
Item received 4th Sunday after Relike Sunday[3] – 4s 2d.
Item received 5th Sunday after – 3s 10d.
Item received 6th Sunday after – 3s 3d.
Item received 7th Sunday after – 3s 2d.
Item received 8th Sunday after – 3s 7d.
Item received 9th Sunday after – 3s 11d.[4]
Item received 10th Sunday after – 3s 11d.
Item received 11th Sunday after – 3s 3d.
Item received 12th Sunday after – 5s.[5]
Item received 13th Sunday after – 3s 5d.
Item received 14th Sunday after.[6]
Item received 15th Sunday after.
Item received 16th Sunday after.
Item received 17th Sunday after.
Item received 18th Sunday after.
Item received 19th Sunday after.
Item received 20th Sunday after.
Item received 21st Sunday after.

[1] There were four churchwardens, appointed on the Octave of Easter. The preambles to each year were written in Latin until 1549/50.

[2] No amount stated.

[3] Relic Sunday – when relics were venerated. *OED*. This was a movable feast celebrated in the Sarum Use on the first Sunday following the feast of Thomas of Canterbury (29 December), but in the Lincoln diocese on 10 July. Cheney and Jones, *Handbook of Dates*, p. 83, note 58.

[4] Marginalia – '59s 10d'.

[5] This line is noted as 'xj Sonday' instead of 'xij', with the following line as 'xij' and the total, 3s 1d, crossed through.

[6] Illegible.

Item received 22nd Sunday after.[1]
£5 5s 3d.

f. lv.
Item received 23rd Sunday after – 5s 2d.
Item received 24th Sunday after Heu Day[2] – 2s 10d.
Item received 25th Sunday after – 3s 3d.
Item received 1st Sunday of Advent – 2s 10d.
Item received 2nd Sunday after – 3s 6d.
Item received 3rd Sunday after – 2s 8d.
Item received 4th Sunday after – 2s 11d.
Item received 1st Sunday after the Nativity of Our Lord – 2s 5d.
Item received 2nd Sunday after – 3s 4d.
Item received 1st Sunday after Epiphany – 3s.
Item received 2nd Sunday after same feast – 3s 4d.
Item received 3rd Sunday after same – 3s 2d.
Item received 4th Sunday after same Candlemas Day[3] – 3s 8d.
Item received Sunday of *Septuagesima*[4] – 2s 9d.
Item received Sunday of *Sexagesima*[5] – 2s 10d.
Item received Sunday of *Quinquagesima*[6] – 2s 9d.
Item received 1st Sunday Lent – 3s 1d.
Item received 2nd Sunday Lent – 2s 6d.
Item received 3rd Sunday Lent – 3s 3d.
Item received 4th Sunday Lent – 4s 1d.
Item received Passion Sunday – 3s 2d.
Item received Palm Sunday – 3s 10d.
Item received Easter Day – 3s 7d.[7]
Item received 1st Sunday after – 2s.
Sum – £9 19d.[8]
Item received [for] Cecill, wife of John White 1st Sunday after Easter – 6s 8d.
Item received 7th Sunday after Holy Trinity for Walter Bayos father & mother – 7s 6d.
Item received 9th Sunday after [for] Jane Hobthorn – 6s 8d.[9]

---

[1] Marginalia – '45s 10d'.
[2] St Hugh's Day, 17 November.
[3] 2 February.
[4] The third Sunday before Lent, the ninth Sunday before Easter, traditionally marking the beginning of preparations for Lent. *OED*.
[5] The second Sunday before Lent, the eighth Sunday before Easter. *OED*.
[6] The Sunday immediately preceding Lent and ending on Easter Sunday. *OED*.
[7] Marginalia – '73s 11d'.
[8] £9 1s 7d. For the annual collections, see Appendix 2.
[9] Page stained and damaged.

Item received 12th Sunday after Master Thomas Egleston, vicar[1] – 6s 8d.
Item received same day [for] Elen, wife of John Norman, roper[2] – 6s 8d.
Item received [for] Gylbard Clarke, wright – 6s 8d.
Item received [for the] daughter [of] Robert Baly,[3] mercer[4] – 6s 8d.
Item received 3rd Sunday Lent [for] Jenet Beverlay, widow – 6s 8d.
Item received [for] Garrot, shoemaker – 6s 8d.
Item received 4th Sunday Lent [for] John Curtas[5] – 6s 8d.
              Sum – 67s 6d.
f. 2r.
              Great bell ringing.
Cecill, wife [of] John White – 20d.
Robert Westmold, gentleman – 8d.
Agnes, daughter [of] Thomas Carffare – 8d.
Brethren & sisters of [the] Trinity guild – 20d.[6]
John Gyrdike & wife – 8d.[7]
Jane Hobthorn – 8d.[8]
John Langholme, gentleman – 8d.[9]
Gilbard Clarke, wright – 8d.[10]

---

[1] Egleston was vicar 1514–27 on a stipend of £13 6s 8d. His successor was Master George Thomson, inducted on 17 September 1527. Goulding, *Vicars*, p. 10. Salter, *Subsidy*, p. 12. Cole, *Chapter Acts*, I, pp. 82, 84.

[2] A John Norman is noted in the first accounts as working on the spire. Goulding, *Spire*, p. 6. He was also churchwarden in 1510/11. Dudding, *Accounts*, p. 125. A man of that name was buried 17 November 1541. LAO, Goulding Papers, 5/2.

[3] Robert Baly, Baylye, Balley, mercer, was churchwarden in 1523/4. Dudding, *Accounts*, p. 222. He was assessed at £18 in the 1524/5 Lay Subsidy. TNA, E179/138/478. Baly left a will: TNA, PROB 11/31/44, probate 5 February 1545/6. Buried 27 March 1545. LAO, Goulding Papers, 5/2.

[4] A dealer in textile fabrics, notably silks, velvets and other fine materials. *OED*.

[5] John Curtas, yeoman, was churchwarden in 1523/4. Dudding, *Accounts*, p. 222. He was assessed at £33 13s 4d in the 1524/5 Lay Subsidy. TNA, E179/138/478.

[6] For the Holy Trinity guild, see Introduction.

[7] A John Gyrdyke was buried at St James's in 1502/3. Dudding, *Accounts*, p. 32.

[8] Jane Hobthorn is mentioned twice in the list. This is not unusual and may signify payment for the bells on her '7th' day or 'Month's Mind' services, when the initial requiem is repeated.

[9] In 1442, John Langholme of Conisholme, is mentioned as being steward of the Louth manorial court. Goulding, *Annals*, p. 20. In 1474, Langholme and his wife Anna were granted an obit by the St Mary guild, and the 'Langholme Choir' is mentioned in the accounts. Goulding, *Annals*, p. 23. He died in 1515 (Anna died in 1535/6); both are buried in Conisholme church, and a surviving brass notes their fourteen children. Hollis, *Church Notes*, p. 247. *Post Mortem*, TNA, C142/30/53. His son, also John, was assessed at £60 in the 1524/5 Lay Subsidy. TNA, E179/138/478.

[10] Clarke is noted in the first accounts as working on the spire. Goulding, *Spire*, p. 6. He was also churchwarden in 1519/20, named as 'Gilbard Clarke, carpenter'. Dudding, *Accounts*, p. 200.

Brethren & sisters of Our Lady guild,[1] John White, chaplain and all his kindred – 20d.
Richard Raythby, butcher[2] – 8d.
Thomas Egleston, vicar – 20d.
Elenor, wife [of] John Norman – 20d.
Jane Hobthorn – 8d.
John Louth, gentleman – 20d.[3]
William Wake, husbandman – 20d.
A child at John Okeland – 8d.
Thomas Bradelay, mercer – 20d.[4]
John Chapman, merchant – 8d.[5]
Thomas Alderton – 20d.[6]
Thomas Beverlay, mercer[7] – 20d.
Thomas Parkhous & wife – 8d.
John Gyrdike, mercer – 12d.
Jenet Beverlay, widow [1 day] – 20d.
Garrot […],[8] shoemaker – 20d.
John Curtas, 4th Sunday Lent [1 day] – 20d.
Item of said John Curtas at his 7th day – 20d.
Item received of Passion Day, Robert Beverlay – 20d.[9]
Item received for John Curtas, 30th day – 20d.

[1] For St Mary's guild, see Introduction.
[2] Richard Raythby was churchwarden in 1504/5 and 1509/10. Dudding, *Accounts*, p. 59.
[3] In 1466, a licence was granted to the executors of John Louth of Thorpe Hall (d.1459) for landholdings to be given for the maintenance of the 'John Louth Chantry' in St James's church. A later patron was John Chapman, also of Thorpe Hall. Goulding, *Corporation Records*, pp. 173–5. The chantry priest was Sir Thomas Kyrke, noted in 1526 as having an income of £8 13s 7d, and who was interred 16 June 1541. Foster and Thompson, 'Chantry Certificates', 36, p. 278. Salter, *Subsidy*, p. 12. LAO, Goulding Papers, 5/2.
[4] For Bradley, see Introduction.
[5] John Chapman, merchant of the Staple of Calais, was churchwarden in 1504/5. Dudding, *Accounts*, p. 59. His will is dated 24 June 1499. TNA, PROB 11/14/598, probate, 15 June 1505; *Inq. Post Mortem*, TNA, C142/20/57. For the Chapman family, see Maddison, *Lincolnshire Pedigrees*, 50, pp. 237–8.
[6] A Thomas Alderton, alias Cardmaker, yeoman, was churchwarden in 1500/1, 1504/5 and 1511/12. He was buried in 1519/20. Dudding, *Accounts*, pp. 1, 59, 133, 201.
[7] Thomas Beverlay, mercer, was elected churchwarden in 1520/21 but appears to have died in office. Dudding, *Accounts*, pp. 205, 206. He was dean of the Lady guild, 1480/1. Williamson, 'Religious Guilds', p. 89.
[8] Surname missing. Possibly Richardson.
[9] Robert Beverlay (d.1518/19), mercer, was churchwarden in 1501/2 and 1511/12. Dudding, *Accounts*, pp. 15, 133, 196.

Item received for Symon Lyncoln, merchant – 8d.[1]
Sum – 35s 8d.

f. 2v.

Witwords[2] of St James's church, St Mary's church[3] and St John [the] Baptist chapel[4] for reparations of them.
In the first John Curtas wit[5] to reparations of St James's church – 10s.
Also he witt to St Mary's church – 20d.
Also he witt to the chapel of St John – 20d, 8d.[6]
Also Jenet Beverlay, widow wit to St James's church – 12d.
Also to St Mary's church for reparations – 12d.
Also to chapel [of] St John [the] Baptist for same.[7]
Also received of John More[8] part of a more sum for the house [of the] late John Girdyke[9] as appears by his will – 53s 4d.
Sum – 67s.
Sum of all receipts with arrears[10] – £20 12s 8d.

f. 3r.

These parcels[11] following of allowance.
In the first, paid Robert Mekilbaro, glazier, helping diverse glass windows, 9 days – 4s 6d, and also his servant 4s 8d, also for stone, lead, and for lime 12d, also for wood – 12d.
Same Robert for sauder[12] 4s 4d, for his servant's board 3s 8d, for making bars of iron – 3d, & nails for bearing leads – 3d.
Same Robert & his servant 2 days about glass windows, 2s 5d, for their meat & drink, 8d.
Robert Baly for 4 wisps[13] [of] glass, 4d, for lead & rossell[14] – 13d.
Robert Spencer[15], 5d for lime, watching [the] church, 2d.

---

   1   For Lyncoln, see Introduction.
   2   Witword, whitword, whit, wit – gift, legacy. *OED.*
   3   For St Mary's, see Introduction.
   4   For St John the Baptist chapel, see Introduction.
   5   Gave.
   6   Both amounts crossed through.
   7   '12d' crossed through.
   8   A John More was assessed at £33 6s 8½d in the 1524/5 Lay Subsidy. TNA, E179/138/478.
   9   For Girdyke, see Introduction.
   10 Latin.
   11 Parcel – item of an account. *OED.*
   12 Sauder – solder. *OED.*
   13 'Wispe', Wisp – a bundle or parcel containing a definite quantity. *OED.*
   14 A form of putty made from resin. The York Fabric Rolls of 1579 note 'for rossell to the plumber, 3s'. Raine, *Fabric Rolls*, p. 117.
   15 A Robert Spencer, draper, was churchwarden in 1513/14. Dudding, *Accounts*,

To a man of Conysby[1] of old deete[2] carrying stone – 20d.
Harry Deyn for 1 bell-string – 9d.
To a smith making cochon wither – 4d.[3]
Robert Hareson closyng[4] steeple – 3d.
The players of Gremysby[5] when they spoke their bayn[6] of their play – 2s 8d.
Thomas Carfare[7] & his servant about [the] bells 2 days – 20d.
Matthew Plomare & his servant 2½ days – 22d.
William Foster[8] for rings again Corpus Christi day[9] to hanging clos of haros[10] in [the] High choir – 8d.
Robert Baly for 3 wisps [of] glass & penter[11] – 3s 6d.
Robert Mekilbaro & his servant 14½ days and their meat & drink, 16s 11d, also for solder, 3s, also for coloured glass, 10s.
Robert Browne & Alex[ander] for wood – 10d.
Robert Spencer 1 strike[12] [of] lime – 2d.

---

p. 158. He was assessed at £10 in the 1524/5 Lay Subsidy. TNA, E179/138/478. Will: TNA, PROB 11/35/264, probate, 1 August 1552. Buried as *Paterfamilias* 22 July 1552. LAO, Goulding Papers, 5/2.

   1 Coningsby.

   2 Debt? This may relate to the carriage of stone from Coningsby to Louth during the construction of the spire, 1500–15.

   3 Possibly a weathercock.

   4 Perhaps 'cloying' – the action of nailing. *OED*.

   5 Grimsby.

   6 The prelude of a play, frequently in the plural banes or banns. *OED*. Travelling players came regularly to Louth. The Sutterton churchwardens also noted in 1519 'for ye plaars rewards, 9d', and in 1526 the Leverton accounts record 'payde to Maister Holande of Swynsted [Swineshead] and ye plaers of the same towne, whan thei rood [read] and cryed thar bayne, 3s 4d'. Peacock, 'Sutterton', pp. 61–2. Peacock, 'Leverton', p. 349.

   7 In 1515/16, Thomas Carffare is noted in the first book of accounts as a wright working primarily on the bells and scaffolding for the spire. Dudding, *Accounts*, p. 180.

   8 A William Foster is recorded in 1501 as having sued a John Wake, a husbandman of Stewton, for debt in the Court of Pie Powder, presided over by the Steward of the Fair. 'Pie Powder' meant 'dusty foot', a court of summary jurisdiction largely for prosecuting itinerant travellers attending the fair. Goulding, *Markets and Fairs*, n.p. Goulding, *Corporation Records*, p. 5, note 1. Foster was assessed at £6 in the 1524/5 Lay Subsidy. TNA, E179/138/478.

   9 The Thursday after Trinity Sunday. Cheney and Jones, *Handbook of Dates*, p. 68.

   10 Cloths of Arras, tapestry hangings. Stokes, *Drama*, 2, p. 843.

   11 A colour used in glass-painting. *OED*.

   12 Equivalent to a bushel; a measure containing four pecks or eight gallons. *OED*.

Thomas Spencer 1 strike colis.[1]
Also to a smith making bars with other – 3d.
Robert Hareson claisyng[2] church garth, 2½ days – 10d.
To a smith mending [the] chime – 2d.
Nicholas Mason & his servant about spouts – 10d.
Baly of Steuton[3] for 2 troughs draining forth of the vicarage into the church garth – 10d.
To a labourer bearing timber ordand[4] for Maiden Chapel[5] to St Mary's church – 12d.

     Sum of this page[6] – 76s 4½d.

f. 3v.
William West[7] for timber to a bell wheel – 10d.
Thomas Foster[8] for 1 quire[9] [of] paper riall[10] – 4d.
To a smith working iron – 6d.
Richard Capper for lime – 3d, for wood – 16d.
To Alex[ander] Wailis – 3d, bearing into the steeple – 2d.

[1] 'Colis' – probably charcoal or coal, the latter a rare commodity in Lincolnshire.
[2] Cleansing?
[3] Stewton.
[4] 'Ordand' – ordered?
[5] Situated in St Mary's church. Goulding, *St Mary's*, p. 3. Swaby, *History of Louth*, p. 32. In his will, Thomas Bradley, merchant of the Staple of Calais, donated 40d to the 'works' of the chapel. TNA PROB 11/20/238, probate, 18 June 1519, Codicil – 16 June 1521.
[6] Latin – *pagine*.
[7] A William West, butcher, was churchwarden in 1517/18, 1528/29 and 1540/41. Dudding, *Accounts*, p. 188. He was assessed at £20 in the 1524/5 Lay Subsidy. TNA, E179/138/478. West played a moderating part in the Rising, urging Nicholas Melton of Louth, a shoemaker (given the sobriquet Captain Cobbler), 'to leave going to Castor next day and make no more business'. *L&P*, XI, 828, 2 (iii), p. 323, 23 October 1536. Will: TNA, PROB 11/31/43, probate, 5 February 1545/6. Buried 5 September 1546. LAO, Goulding Papers, 5/2.
[8] Both Thomas Foster and his son William were yeomen and singingmen in the church. Williamson, 'Religious Guilds', p. 89. In 1528/29, Foster is noted as being one of the 'ministers in the choir'. Page 50. Thomas was assessed at £5 in the 1524/5 Lay Subsidy. TNA, E179/138/478. During the inquiry following the Rising, Nicholas Melton suggested that 'Thomas Foster ... of £10 of land, dwelling in Louth ... said to Robert Jonson, smith, "Go we to follow the crosses for and if they be taken from us we be like to follow them no more."' *L&P*, XI, 828, (iii), 1, p. 323, 23 October 1536.
[9] Quire – a set of four sheets of parchment or paper folded in two so as to form eight leaves, also a set of twenty-four or twenty-five sheets of paper; one-twentieth of a ream. *OED*.
[10] Belonging or appropriate to a king. *OED*.

Robert Hareson for 1 bell collar – 2d, cleansing galile[1] & steeple – 4d.
Robert Hareson for making 1 bell collar – 2d.
To a smith making plate for the chime – 4d.
Richard Syll helping[2] Sacre bell[3] – 3d.[4]
Thomas Provest[5] about [the] chime & his servant – 10d.
Robert Hareson slising [the] chime string – 2d.
Parish clerk[6] watching [the] church of nights – 3d.
A smith making 2 keys to [the] Corpus Christi hutch[7] – 6d,
For watching [the] church – 4d.
Robert West & Claxby – 4d.
To a plumber promised at this March to work of the church roof & therefore they paid him – 3s 4d.
John North, plumber, laying down webs[8] of lead 1½ day[s], 9½d, also 4lb solder – 16d.
Thomas Carffare 2 days & his servant carting & hewing timber, 2 days his servant making [a] wheel to the chime, 2 days & his servant making turdyll[9] to Westgate[10], 2 days about bells & his servant – 7s 1d.
Robert Joneson, smith, making 1 hoop to the wheel – 4d.

---

[1] Galilee – a porch or chapel at the entrance to a church; in Louth's case beneath the tower. *OED*.

[2] Mending. Goulding, *Cawod*, p. 8.

[3] Sanctus bell, a hand bell rung at the elevation of the host during Mass. Friar, *Parish Church*, p. 403.

[4] Richard Syll was interred 25 March 1543. LAO, Goulding Papers, 5/2.

[5] Thomas Provest is mentioned no fewer than 111 times in the accounts, mainly with regard to the maintenance of the bells and general ironwork, but especially carpentry. He was churchwarden in 1517/18 and chamberlain of the Lady guild in 1537/8. Provest was assessed at £5 in the 1524/5 Lay Subsidy. TNA, E179/138/478. He is last referenced in 1547/8, but there is no record of his burial. Goulding, *Corporation Records*, pp. 169–70. Dudding, *Accounts*, p. 188. A Joanne Provest, noted as a widow, was interred 8 February 1549/50. LAO, Goulding Papers, 5/2.

[6] The parish clerks had responsibilities generally related to the day-to-day running of the church. These ranged from attending the priest at services, leading the singing, keeping the building clean and secure and maintaining the clock and bells. Despite their apparent importance, parish clerks are only mentioned sixteen times in the accounts. Platt, *Parish Church*, pp. 62–4. Friar, *Parish Church*, pp. 333–4.

[7] A chest or ark, probably containing valuables. *OED*.

[8] Lead sheeting. *OED*.

[9] Hurdle? A rectangular frame, originally having horizontal bars interwoven or wattled with hazel or willow. *OED*.

[10] Westgate, running from the church westwards to the junction with Breakneck Lane, was in the sixteenth century the wealthiest part of the town. The property was largely owned by merchants, gentry and wealthier yeomen.

To 2 sawers about same work – 12d.
A plumber 1 day – 6d, solder – 12d.
Robert Loblay & his fellow sawing 3 quarters of a rod[1] – 2s 6d.
For lead to a bell collar.[2]
Matthew Bellman[3] scouring great candlesticks – 6d.
Robert Hareson for ½ [a] hide for bell collars – 8d.
Thomas Provest gluing the great organs bellows with oder and glue – 9d.[4]
Richard Goderke & his fellow watching [the] church – 12d.
Making a hammer for chime – 6d.
Richard Curson writing 2 obligations & their sureties[5] for their trouth[6] & safety of this church – 10d.[7]
      Sum of the page – 29s 6d.

f. 4r.
Item for watching [the] church of nights – 9d.
Robert West for watching – 18d.
To Richard Goderke for watching – 9d.
Thomas Carfare & his servant about [the] bells – 10d.
To a smith cleansing about of clapper – 6d.
Robert Hareson watching at first beginning[8] – 6d.
Thomas Carfare & his servant about [the] leads – 43d.
Harry Deyn [for] 1 bell-string – 17d.
Thomas Carfare about [the] leads – 6d.
John Burnstall & his servant [for] sawing thatch boards – 6d.

 [1] Rod or rood – also known as a pole or perch, equal to 16½ft. (5.02 m). Bristow, *Glossary*, p. 168.
 [2] No amount stated.
 [3] Whether this was his surname is uncertain. He may well have been Mathew who was employed as the bellman. The bellman also acted as 'town crier', making public announcements such as the mandatory cleansing of the streets before the Corpus Christi procession. He also cleaned the church and the various accoutrements such as candlesticks. He was later noted as an 'undertaker's assistant' in the covering of graves. Gurnham, *History of Louth*, p. 41.
 [4] There were a number of organs in St James's, including at least two on the Rood screen and in some of the numerous side chapels. In 1500–1, the accounts note, 'paid to Jels Kynyerby & his 2 men haffyng [heaving] up the new organs into the Rood loft, xvjd' (16d). Dudding, *Accounts*, p. 9. For the church's organs, see Pillans, *Organs*.
 [5] Seurtes in manuscript, sureties in *OED*.
 [6] Trust, confidence. *OED*.
 [7] '8d', crossed through.
 [8] Harvest festival? 'In þe first bygynnyng of fruytes of þi whete heruest. *1382.*' *OED*

Matthew Belman scouring candlesticks, High choir, Our Lady choir & St Peter – 9d. Also to a smith helping chime wheel – 7d.
A tailor & his man – 8d.
Also paid to the Plough light[1] – 16d.
Also in hill silver[2] for helping sewfurs[3] & shipe[4] – 4s 6d.
Also to Robert Goldsmyth[5] for making same – 2s 8d.
Also Nicholas to meat & drink – 12d.
Item paid to the abbot of Revesby[6] for a ffoder[7] [of] lead & also 49 stone – £5 9s 2d.
Also for carriage of said lead to Louth – 2s.
Also a man about said lead & wayng[8] – 21d.
Also paid to John Northe plumber for raising & shotting[9] the high church roof – 53s 4d.
Also for carrying & winding up the said new webs – 2s 7d.
Also for a rope – 4d.
Master Chapman for lime, also 1 quarter lead[10] – 21s 8d.
For bearing pagents[11] – 4s 4d.
Robert Baly for nails – 3s 4d.

[1] This candle was carried before the sacrament on Corpus Christi Day. Sponsorship for the light came from collections by ploughmen, who paraded through the town on Plough Monday; the first after Twelfth Night (6 January). Following the changes in doctrine when lights were abolished, plough money was still collected and used for charitable purposes. Goulding, *Customs*, p. 9. Gurnham, *History of Louth*, p. 55.

[2] Possibly 'hack silver' – fragments of plate or jewellery. *OED*.

[3] Probably 'servers' – assistants arranging the altar and making responses at Mass. *OED*.

[4] Wages, reward. *OED*.

[5] On Monday, 2 October 1536, Robert Goldsmith met with other leading men at the commencement of the Rising in the shop of Robert Bailey, mercer, to discuss the unfolding events. Ward, *Rising*, p. 14.

[6] The Cistercian abbey of St Mary and St Lawrence. The abbot was Thomas Stickney alias Scotte. Smith, *Heads*, III, p. 323.

[7] Fother, fodder, fudder – a quantity of lead, ranging from 19 cwt to 22½ cwt. Bristow, *Glossary*, p. 75.

[8] Weighing?

[9] Welded metal, working with. *OED*. Also casting or recasting bells. Nichols, *Illustrations*, p. 198, note 3. The York Fabric Rolls note: 'For shootinge and mendinge certeyne barres to the glasse wyndowes, 4d.' Raine, *Fabric Rolls*, p. 116.

[10] A fourth of a hundredweight (112lbs), therefore 28 lbs. *OED*.

[11] Pageant – a cart used to carry performers during the mystery plays. *OED*. The Trinity guild stored the various trappings of the Corpus Christi pageant in a barn in Gulpyn Lane, now Schoolhouse Lane. Green, *Origins*, p. 121. Gurnham, *History of Louth*, p. 44.

Thomas Carffare about [the] leads – 6d.
Thomas Maners helping dyvers copis[1] 3 days – 18d.
Robert Baly for threde (thread) – 11d.
     Sum of this page – £11 3s.
      Left 8s 9d.[2]

f. 4v.
    Ministers within the choir this year.
In the first be the whole year William Foster 3 quarters – 20s[3] – [26s 8d].[4]
Item John Cawod for same 3 quarters – 10s.[5]
Item for blayng[6] organs [3 quarters – 10s – 3s 4d].[7]
Item Thomas Foster the whole year 3 quarters – 20s – [26s 8d].[8]
Item parish clerk keeping [the] clock & chime – 10s.
Belman cleansing [the] church above & beneath – 2s 8d.
Robert Hareson keeping [the] bells – 3s 4d.
Thomas Wayte's wife washing pertaining to the altar – 2s.
Thomas Provest in fee – 6s 8d.
Necolas Upton, mason in fee – 6s 8d.[9]
John Cawod writing this account.[10]
      Sum – £4 16d.
     Sum paid – £20 10s 2½d. [11]
     And he owes clear – 3s 8d.
      To the Feretor.[12]
Memorandum, that Jenet Beverlay, widow, has given one pair [of] beads of silver & coral silver beads, 66 silver beads gilded [with] a crucifix & a button of silver gilt and a knope[13] of silk set with pearl weighing four ounces one

---

 1 Diverse copes.
 2 At bottom left of the page and in a different hand.
 3 This and the following three lines were changed from one year to three-quarters.
 4 [Crossed through].
 5 A John Caywod (Cawood, Cawod) was assessed at £5 in the 1524/5 Lay Subsidy. TNA, E179/138/478. For Cawod, see Introduction.
 6 Blowing.
 7 [Crossed through]. The annual payment for blowing the organs was 3s 4d.
 8 [Crossed through].
 9 Nicholas Upton, sometimes described as a mason, is noted seventy-four times in the accounts and earlier worked on the spire. Goulding, *Spire*, p. 6. Buried 2 October 1545. LAO, Goulding Papers, 5/2.
 10 No amount stated.
 11 Marginalia – '*debent*, 2s 5½d'.
 12 Feretor or feretory – a shrine, containing the relics of saints, deposited in the feretory for security. *OED*.
 13 Knope or Knop – a loop or tuft formed in a strand of yarn for an ornament, e.g. upon the stem of a chalice or a candlestick. *OED*.

quarter & half quarter, and also one gold ring weighing five shillings and also a white vestment with a[n] alb[1] unto St Mary's church and also to the church 4½ stone [of] lead.
Church Masters[2]
Robert Fissher[3]
William West
Thomas Wollarby
Thomas Richerson

f. 5r. [1528–9]

IHUS

The account of Thomas Richardson, glover,[4] William West, Robert Fyssher, tanner, Thomas Wollerby, mercer, Master Proctors of the Church of St James of Lowthe, all receipts and expenses on Sunday the Octave of Easter 1528 until the Octave of Easter 1529.
Item received of the churchwardens the year afore in money good & evil – 3s 8d.
Old debt[s] owing.
Agnes Inglish, widow, for her burial – 12d.
Robert Smyth's wife – 6s 8d.[5]
Nicholas Maryn, taylor, Robert Curson, glover, sureties as apperith by a tayle[6] in the hutch – 2s 8d.

---

[1] A white vestment reaching the feet and enveloping the entire body, worn by clergy, servers and others taking part in church services. *OED*.

[2] Another term for churchwarden, also noted in the Saxilby accounts. Gibbons, 'Saxilby', p. 381.

[3] Robert Fisher, Fyssher or Fysher, tanner, was elected the manor reeve or grave at 6s per annum. In 1535, he was appointed alderman of the Lady guild. Swaby, *History of Louth*, p. 106. Goulding, *Corporation Records*, p. 169. Fisher was assessed at £13 in the 1524/5 Lay Subsidy. TNA, E179/138/478. He was noted in the inquiry into the Rising as being a 'petty captain'. *L&P*, XI, 972, p. 397, 3 November 1536. Will: TNA, PROB 11/31/42, probate, 5 February 1546/7. Interred 26 November 1543 under the alias of Torrenter. LAO, Goulding Papers, 5/2.

[4] Thomas Richardson, glover, was churchwarden in 1521/22 and chamberlain of the Lady guild in 1535. Goulding, *Corporation Records*, p. 169. Dudding, *Accounts*, p. 210. He was assessed at £8 in the 1524/5 Lay Subsidy. TNA, E179/138/478. A Thomas Richardson, tanner, was buried 7 February 1538/9. LAO, Goulding Papers, 5/2.

[5] On 17 April 1503, Smith's wife, along with thirty others, were presented to the assize of bread and ale for brewing weak beer. Goulding, *Court Rolls*, n.p. A Robert Smyth, described as a butcher, was churchwarden in 1512/13. Dudding, *Accounts*, p. 141.

[6] 'Tayle' – Tally, an account, placed in the hutch for safe keeping. *OED*.

Byrt Corves[er] for his wife's burial in the south church porch – 2s 9d.
Item received 2nd Sunday after Easter – 5s.
Item received 3rd Sunday after – 5s.
Item received 4th Sunday after – 2s 8d.
Item received 5th Sunday after – 2s 10d.
Item received 6th Sunday after.[1]
Item received Sunday after Ascension of Our Lord – 3s 8d.
Item received Sunday of Pentecost – 5s.
Item received Trinity Sunday – 4s.
Item received first Sunday after – 3s 6d.
Item received 2nd Sunday after – 3s.
Item received 3rd Sunday after – 3s 8d.
Item received 4th Sunday after – 3s 4d.
Item received 5th Sunday after – 3s 10d.
Item received 6th Sunday after – 4s 3d.
Item received 7th Sunday after – 3s 5d.
Item received 8th Sunday after – 3s 10d.
Item received 9th Sunday after – 3s 9d.
Item received 10th Sunday after – 3s 8d.
Item received 11th Sunday after – 4s 3d.
Item received 12th Sunday after – 4s.
Item received 13th Sunday after – 2s 9d.
Item received 14th Sunday after – 3s 4d.
Item received 15th Sunday after – 3s 2d.
Item received 16th Sunday after – 3s 5d.
Item received 17th Sunday after – 3s 1d.
Item received 18th Sunday after – 3s 3d.
Item received 19th Sunday after – 3s 5d.
Item received 20th Sunday after – 4s.
Item received 21st Sunday All Holy Day[2] – 4s 8d.
Item received 22nd Sunday after – 3s 8d.
Item received 23rd Sunday after – 3s.
Item received 24th[3] Sunday after – 4s.
Item received 1st Sunday Advent – 2s 8d.
Item received 2nd Sunday Advent – 3s 5d.
Item received 3rd Sunday Advent – 3s 4d.
Item received 4th Sunday Advent – 3s 7d.[4]
f. 5v.
Item received the 1st Sunday after Nativity – 3s.

[1] Line crossed through.
[2] All Hallows.
[3] Written as '27'.
[4] The last two lines in a different hand are illegible.

Item received the 1st Sunday after Circumcision[1] – 4s 1d.
Item received the 1st Sunday after Epiphany – 3s 3d.
Item received the 2nd Sunday after – 3s 8d.
Item received the Sunday of *Septuagesima* – 2s 10d.
Item received the Sunday of *Sexagesima* – 3s 8d.
Item received the Sunday of *Quinquagesima* – 3s 9d.
Item received the 1st Sunday of *Quadragesima*[2] – 3s 3d.
Item received the 2nd Sunday of Lent – 3s 2d.
Item received the 3rd Sunday of Lent – 3s 8d.
Item received the 4th Sunday of Lent – 2s 9d.
        37s.
Item received Passion Sunday – 3s 5d.
Item received Palm Sunday – 3s 4d.
Item received Easter Day – 4d.
Item received of Lawe[3] Sunday – 2s 6d.
      Sum – 51s 3d.
     Total sum received – £8 17s 10d.
      Burials within the church.
Elizabeth, wife of John Sysson – 6s 8d.
Matthew, son of William Inglish of London.[4]
Joanne,[5] wife of William Wyngod – 6s 8d.
John Paronell – 6s 8d.
William Wyngod – 6s 8d.
d[6] Edward Otle – 6s 8d.
        33s 4d.
John Sadler – 6s 8d.
Maud, wife of William Worslaw – 3s 4d.
Mathew Inglysshe – 6s 8d.
      Sum – 50s.

 1 Feast of Christ's Circumcision, 1 January.
 2 The first Sunday in Lent. *OED*.
 3 Law or Low Sunday – the Sunday following Easter (Octave).
 4 Line crossed through. Matthew Inglisshe left a will dated 14 May 1508. TNA, PROB 11/22/512, probate, 3 June 1528. It records, 'Memorandum 15 May, 20 Henry VIII [1528], the said Matthew Inglisshe, citizen and ironmonger of London ... being sick at Louth in the diocese of Lincoln ... remembering that his wife [Ellen] ... was then great with child, wherefore ... made and named Master Thomas Kendall, clerk, to be co-executor with his said wife.' Although not as yet vicar of Louth, the ill-fated Kendall, later executed at Tyburn, appears to have been supervisor to the original will, with Sir Richard Daddy, parson of Stewton (d.1540), acting as witness.
 5 'Joha' crossed through.
 6 The letters 'd' or 'dd' are Latin abbreviations for *dimidium* or half, in addition to signifying *denarius*, a penny.

f. 6r.

Great bells ringing.

John Wyllamson, merchant & wife – 20d.
Item of Jenet Beverlay, widow – 12d.
Julian White, Alice Cecill – 20d.
Robert Westmold, gentleman – 8d.
Matthew, son of William Inglish, 1 day.[1]
Barwick's wife – 8d.
Master John Langham – 8d.
Item of the brethren and sisters of Our Lady guild & for the soul of Sir John White[2] – 20d.
Master Lowthe – 20d.
Ellyn Holme – 8d.
Richard Ratheby – 8d.
Joanne, wife of William Wyngod – 20d.
John Talke – 20d.
John Chapman, gentleman – 8d.
John Talke – 8d.
Alice, wife of William Walker[3] – 8d.
Thomas Bradley the elder – 20d.
John Paronell – 20d.
Thomas Beverlay, junior – 20d.
Thomas Allerton – 20d.
William Wyngod – 20d.
John Paronell – 8d.
Stephan Parkns – 8d.
William Wyngod – 20d.
d Edward Otel – 20d.
d John Gyrdyck, Thomas Gyrdyck, priests – 12d.
John Cooper – 8d.

31s.[4]

John Sadler – 20d.
John Curtes – 12d.
Garrard Richardeson – 8d.

---

[1] No amount stated.

[2] The title 'Sir' before the priest's name was customary from about the fifteenth century. Allegedly it was used in contrast to master and denoted that the priest had not graduated from a university. *OED*.

[3] Walker was deputy alderman of the Lady guild in 1525. A William Walker was also churchwarden in 1515/16. Goulding, *Corporation Records*, p. 169. Dudding, *Accounts*, p. 174. He was assessed at £10 in the 1524/5 Lay Subsidy. TNA, E179/138/478.

[4] Crossed through.

34s 4d.
Item received of William Raythby[1] for 200 lead price – 10s 8d.
Item received for the offald[2] of a hedge as apperith be – 12d.
Sum – 11s 9d.
Total sum received this year – £13 13s 11d.[3]

f. 6v.

St John Baptist term.

William Foster – 6s 8d.
John Cawod – 3s 4d.
Thomas Foster – 6s 8d.[4]
Parish clerk keeping clock and chime – 2s 6d.
Bellman cleansing the church – 8d.
Robert Haryson keeping the bells 10d, washing to the altar – 6d.
Thomas Provost in fee – 20d.
Nicholas Upton in fee – 20d.[5]

St Michael's term.

William Foster – 6s 8d.
John Cawod – 3s 4d.
Thomas Foster – 6s 8d.
Parish clerk keeping clock and chime – 2s 6d.
Bellman cleansing the church – 8d.
Robert Haryson keeping the bells 10d, washing to the altar – 6d.
Thomas Provost in fee – 20d.
Nicholas Upton in fee – 20d.

Nativity term.

William Foster – 6s 8d.
John Cawod – 3s 4d.
Thomas Foster – 6s 8d.
Parish clerk keeping clock and chime – 2s 6d.
Bellman cleansing the church – 8d.
Robert Haryson keeping the bells 10d, washing to the altar – 6d.
Thomas Provost in fee – 20d.
Nicholas Upton in fee – 20d.

Annunciation term.

William Foster – 6s 8d.
John Cawod – 3s 4d.

---

[1] William Rathby was assessed at £13 6s 8½d in the 1524/5 Lay Subsidy. TNA, E179/138/478.

[2] Possibly chips from dressing wood. *OED*.

[3] Last approximately four lines of page damaged and illegible.

[4] Two Thomas Fosters, probably father and son, were buried on 16 January 1540/1 and 17 December 1545. LAO, Goulding Papers, 5/2.

[5] Nicholas Upton was interred 2 October 1545. LAO, Goulding Papers, 5/2.

Thomas Foster – 6s 8d.
Parish clerk keeping clock and chime – 2s 6d.
Bellman cleansing the church – 8d.
Robert Haryson keeping the bells 10d, washing to the altar – 6d.
Thomas Provost in fee – 20d.
Nicholas Upton in fee – 20d.
John Gooddall for making this account – 3s 4d.
Witword to St James's church.
Imprimis, William Wyngod – 6s 8d.[1]
Ministers in the choir by year.
Item paid to William Foster – 6s 8d & Thomas Foster – 6s 8d.[2]
Item William Foster by year – 26s 8d.
Item John Cawod by year – 13s 4d.
Item Thomas Foster – 26s 8d.
Item Parish clerk keeping clock & chime – 10s.
Item Belman cleansing the church above and beneath – 2s 8d.
Item Robert Haryson keeping bells – 3s 4d.
Item Wat's wife washing pertaining to the altar – 2s.
Item Thomas Provost in fee – 6s 8d.
Item Nicholas Upton, mason, in fee – 6s 8d.
Item John Goodale writing this account – 3s 4d.[3]

f. 7r.
Reparations about the church.
Item first paid to Maltby, smith, for making 1 plate to the chime & 1 key to the clock house door – 5d.[4]
Item paid to Master Vicar for lead – 6s 8d.
Item paid to Harrison for a bell collar and dressing the bell chamber – 5d.
Item to Matthew Tynckeler for mending the holy water vat – 5d.
Item to Robert West for watching in the church at the feast of Corpus Christi – 3d.
Item paid to William Foster for his wages due to him at the feast of Our Lady in Lent – 6s 8d.
Item to John Cawod for [an] old debt – 6s 8d.
Item paid to Henry Deane for a bell-string – 11d.[5]
Item paid to Haryson for grease to the bells and for sliping[6] of a stang[7] – 3d.
Item to Claksby for coals – 4d.
Item for sawing of boards – 3d.

---

[1] Line crossed through.
[2] Line crossed through.
[3] Rest of page damaged. For John Goodall, see Introduction.
[4] John Maltby, smith, was interred 25 February 1551/2 and his wife, Isabel, on 30 November 1549. LAO, Goulding Papers, 5/2.
[5] Henry Dean was buried 8 December 1540. LAO, Goulding Papers, 5/2.
[6] 'Sliping' – to strip the skin or bark. *OED*.
[7] 'Stang' – a wooden bar or beam. *OED*.

Item for diking & cleansing 110 rods of the Kyrke Dyke – 10s 10d.[1]
Item received of John Sadler for the offalde of the same hedge – 13d.[2]
Item for a key to a chest where the books of this account be laid – 2d.
Item to Thomas Foster for old debt due at the feast of Our Lady in Lent – 6s 8d.
Item to Robert Bornsale for sawing 6 drawght[3] of wainscot[4] – 6d.
Item to Robert Beverlay for the setting on a handle to the holy water vat – 2d.
Item to the same for mending a lock – 2d.
Item to Thomas Provost for wainscot – 2s.
Item to Haryson for a hide of white leather – 6d.
Item for mending the clock – 5s.
Item to the plumber for laying down lead at St Mary's church & moold[5] setting – 8d.
Item to Boston for glazing a window – 6d.
Item wire to the clock – 2d.
Item to Maltby the smith for mending the clock and chime at the feast of St Luke[6] 6s 8d, for the which sum afore paid he hath promised to stand with charge of the said clock and chime to keep them going and to repair them with all such stuff as to his occupation appertaineth the clerks doing their duty from this day till the feast of Easter next ensuing and from that time till Easter 12 months after.
Item to the same Maltby for a key – 2d.
Item to Thomas Provest for 2 days work about the bells – 12d.
Item to Haryson for making 3 collars – 2d.
Item to John Norman for 2 bell-string one to the second bell & the other to the third – 2s.
Item to Haryson for working 2 days about …[7]

f. 7v.
Item paid to Norman for a rope to the chime – 3s.
Item to Thomas Kerver for mending the great pax[8] – 10d.
Item for 5 torches – 21d.[9]

[1] Manicule in margin. An image, symbol or typographic mark depicting a hand with a pointing forefinger (☛), used in writing or printing to draw the reader's attention to something. *OED*. Marginalia – 'Scowring ye church.'
[2] Line crossed through.
[3] 'Draught' – a measure of the sawer's work. *OED*.
[4] 'Wainscot' – a superior type of oak, generally used for fine-quality panel-work. *OED*.
[5] Moulding the lead?
[6] 18 October.
[7] Foot of the page damaged.
[8] Pax, pyx, pix – a vessel or box in which the consecrated wafer of the Eucharist is kept. *OED*.
[9] Line crossed through.

Item to Thomas Spencer for 5 lyncks[1] to search the church with – 2s.
Item to Thomas Provost for mending a stall in St Peter's choir – 6d.
Item for watching 2 nights in the church to 2 men – 8d.
Item to William Fawer[2] for carrying 2 lode of doongs[3] out of the churchyard – 2d.
Item lent to William Farrant 8 stone of lead in gage[4] whereof he hath laid in, 5s 8d to the piece.[5]
Item to the bellman for scouring the great candlesticks at the High altar at Nativity – 5d.
Item to Matthew Brown for mending a spout and the leads of the gallery – 12d.
Item to Richard Goderwyck for watching certain nights in the church – 12d.
Item to Thomas Maners for mending the vestments, 5 days – 20d.
Item to Thomas Wollerby for thread, nails and silk to the same – 6d.
Item to Thomas Provest for a day work of himself about the bells and his servant – 12d.
Item Thomas Maners for 4 days work in mending vestments – 16d.
Item to Thomas Wollerby for silk to the said vestments – 5d.
Item for mending of an alb – 2d.
Item to Haryson for grease to the bells – 1d.
Item to Maltby the smith for a key – 2d.
Item to Robert Beverlay for watching in the church – 8d.
Item to William Ratheby[6] for 5 yards of linen cloth for a rochet,[7] to Sir William the parish priest[8] – 2s 4d.
Item to Thomas Provest for 2 days work for himself and his servant about the lodge for the poor men – 2s.[9]
Item to the plumber for laying lead upon the same lodge – 8d.
Item to Thomas Provest for 5 days work of himself and his servant about the *yockyng*[10] of Our Lady bell – 5s.
Item to John Maltby, smith for iron and workmanship about the same bell – 4s.

[1] Link – a torch made of tow or pitch. *OED*.
[2] William Fawer was interred 18 April 1547. LAO, Goulding Papers, 5/2.
[3] Possibly excrement, dung.
[4] A pledge, offer as a guarantee? *OED*.
[5] Entry crossed through. Manicule in the margin. William Farrand was buried 22 March 1553/4. LAO, Goulding Papers, 5/2.
[6] Following the Rising, a William Ratheby was accused of 'collect[ing] money from priests'; presumably for the rebels. *L&P*, XI, 972, p. 397, 3 November 1536. He was interred 2 December 1541. LAO, Goulding Papers, 5/2.
[7] An ecclesiastical vestment similar to a surplice. *OED*.
[8] Possibly William Barton, vicar, noted in 1526 as having an income of £6. Salter, *Subsidy*, p. 12.
[9] Although Swaby disputes this, Bayley suggests that the lodge was situated on Bridge Street. Swaby, *History of Louth*, pp. 173–4. Bayley, *Notitiæ Ludæ*, pp. 208–9. For other proposals, Gurnham, *Early Louth*, pp. 138–9.
[10] Probably yoking, placing some form of collar on the bell mechanism.

Item to Robert Bayly & John White for nails – 11d.
f. 8r.
Item to the bellman for scouring the great candlesticks at the High altar at Easter – 5d.
Item to Richard Bawesforth for casting lead – 2s 8d.
Item to Christopher Elwold serving [the] plumber – 8d.
Item for wood for casting of the lead – 4d.
£4 16s 7d.
Total £9 17s 11d. And there remains £4 2s 8d and 14 hundred of lead ready cast wanting £7, through debts paid to the aldermen and deacons of the Guild of St Mary and 60s, and remains 22s 8d, besides 5s 7d found? over 3s 8d arrears next year after, and so there remains 26s 6d to whom he is in debt 2s. Owed to John Androse of Brakenbrugh [for] the price of one bull 10s, and 3 pounds? of London coal bought from Joan Cutas widow, 9d, there remains clear 21s 2d and 14 hundreds of lead ready casted, wanting £7.
New Church Masters for the next year.
Thomas Hyll, weaver,[1] John Holdernes,[2] butcher, Richard Hynde, miller[3] & Richard Spencer.[4]
f. 8v. [Blank].

f. 9r.

[1529–30]

The account of Thomas Hyll, weaver, John Holdernes, butcher, Richard Hynde, miller, & Richard Spencer,[5] Proctors of the Church of St James of Lowth, all receipts and expenses on Sunday the Octave of Easter 1529 until the Octave of Easter 1530.

Item received of the churchwardens the year afore in money good & evil – 21s 2d, also 24cwt of lead ready casten wanting 7 lb.

Old debt[s] owing, Agnes Inglys, widow, for her burial – 12d. Robert Smyth's wife – 6s 8d. Nicholas Maryn, taylor – 2s 8d. Robert Curson, glover, surety

---

Alternatively, 'a greasy substance composed of excretions (e.g. suint, lanolin, etc.) from a sheep's skin', used for greasing the machinery. Both *OED*.

1   Hyll was assessed at £3 in the 1524/5 Lay Subsidy. TNA, E179/138/478. Thomas Hill senior was buried 6 May 1539. LAO, Goulding Papers, 5/2.

2   Will: TNA, PROB 11/33/228, probate, 21 May 1550. Registered as *Paterfamilias*, he was interred on 23 April 1550. LAO, Goulding Papers, 5/2.

3   Richard Hynde, miller, was noted as churchwarden in 1519/20. Dudding, *Accounts*, p. 200. Interred 16 September 1546. LAO, Goulding Papers, 5/2.

4   Spencer was assessed at £3 in the 1524/5 Lay Subsidy. TNA, E179/138/478. He was buried 8 November 1541. LAO, Goulding Papers, 5/2.

5   A Richard Spencer was reported to the Star Chamber in 1534 for 'throwing down a gate to certain closes [at Haugham] and putting cattle out to graze'. Swaby, *History of Louth*, p. 82.

as appearith by a taile in the hutch. Byrt Corveser for his wife's burial in [the] south church porch – 2s 9d.
Item received 2nd Sunday after Easter – 4s 11d.
Item 3rd Sunday – 4s 6d.
Item 4th Sunday after – 2s 7½d.
Item 5th Sunday after – 2s 7d.
Item 1st Sunday after Ascension – 3s 7d.
Item received Sunday of Pentecost – 5s.
Item received Trinity Sunday – 4s.
Item received Sunday after Corpus Christi – 2s 3d.
Item received 1st Sunday after Trinity – 3s 1d.
Item received 2nd Sunday after – 3s 9d.
Item received 3rd Sunday after – 4s 4d.
Item received 4th Sunday after – 2s 4d.
Item received 5th Sunday after – 3s 1½d.
Item received 6th Sunday, Relic Sunday – 3s 1d.
Item received 7th Sunday – 3s 10d.
Item received 8th Sunday – 3s 2d.
Item received 9th Sunday – 2s 11d.
Item received 10th Sunday – 3s.
Item received 11th Sunday, Assumption of Mary – 3s 11d.
Item received 12th Sunday – 2s 8d.
Item received 13th Sunday – 3s 7d.
Item received 14th Sunday after – 2s 8d.
Item received 15th Sunday after – 2s 8d.
Item received 16th Sunday after – 2s.
Item received 17th Sunday after – 2s 1d.
Item received 18th Sunday after – 3s 4d.
Item received 19th Sunday after – 3s 1d.
Item received 20th Sunday after – 2s.
Item received 21st Sunday after – 2s 8d.
Item received 22nd Sunday after – 3s.
Item received 23rd Sunday after – 2s 5d.
Item received 24th Sunday after – 2s 8d.
Item received 25th Sunday after – 3s 6d.
f. 9v.
Item received 1st Sunday of Advent – 2s 4d.
Item received 2nd Sunday of Advent – 2s 6d.
Item received 3rd Sunday of Advent – 2s 10d.
Item received 4th Sunday of Advent – 2s 5d.
Item received Sunday after Nativity, feast of St Stephen – 2s 8d.
Item received Sunday after Circumcision – 2s 10d.
Item received Sunday after Epiphany – 2s 8d.
Item received 2nd Sunday after – 3s 2d.

Item received 3rd Sunday after – 3s 2d.
Item received 4th Sunday after – 3s 3d.
Item received 5th Sunday after – 2s 6d.
Item received Sunday *Septuagesima* – 4s 3d.
Item received Sunday of *Sexagesima* – 3s.
Item received Sunday of *Quinquagesima* – 2s 10d.
Item received 1st Sunday of *Quadragesima* – 2s 10d.
Item received 2nd Sunday of *Quadragesima* – 3s.
Item received 3rd Sunday of *Quadragesima* – 3s.
Item received 4th Sunday of *Quadragesima* – 2s 7d.
Item received in Passion – 2s 8d.
Item received Palm Sunday – 2s 11d.
Item received Easter Day – 3s 4d.
Item received Sunday after Easter – 19d.
Sum – £8 5s[1] 7d.
Witwords to St James's church & St Mary's church.
John Cawod – 6s 8d.
John Cawod to St Mary's church – 3s 4d.
Margaret Page – 8d.
d Thomas Smyth – 3s 4d.
Sum – 14s.
Item received – 4s 3d.
Item for bell – 12d.
f. 10r.
Great bells ringing.
Item Robert Beverlay – 20d.
Item Symon Lyncoln, merchant – 8d.
Item John Sadler – 8d.
Item Kathrin Whetely – 8d.
John Wylliamson – 20d.
John Cawod – 20d
Robert Westmold, gentleman – 8d.
John Gyrdycke – 8d.
Margery Moore – 8d.
John Cawod – 20d.
William Ireland – 8d.[2]
John May, *puer*[3] – 8d.
Margaret, wife of Master Thymolby – 20d.
d Thomas Dowghtye – 8d.

---

[1] Written as 'iiiii'.
[2] Ireland was assessed at 40s in the 1524/5 Lay Subsidy. TNA, E179/138/478.
[3] Boy.

d Thomas Smith, parson of Ratheby[1] – 20d.
Thomas Pallmore – 8d.
Margaret Page – 20d.
Margaret Page – 8d.
Alice Hyll – 8d.
William Foster – 8d.
Thomas, son of Thomas Wollerby – 8d.
Margaret Page – 8d.
James, son of Robert Fyssher – 8d.
John Lowth – 20d.
Richard Ratheby – 8d.
John Cocke – 20d.[2]
John Talke – 8d.
Alice, wife of William Walker – 8d.
John Cooke – 8d.
John Chapman, gentleman – 8d.
Thomas Bradley – 20d.
John Puyll – 8d.
Thomas Beverlay – 20d.
Thomas Allerton – 20d.
William Wingod – 12d.
Stephan & John Parcins – 8d.
d Thomas Kyrdyke – 12d.
John Curtes – 12d.
William Browghton – 8d.
Robert Beverlay – 20d.
Anne Wryght – 20d.[3]
Symon Lyncoln – 8d.
John Tompson – 8d.

Sum – 43s 8d.

f. 10v.

St John the Baptist term.

William Foster – 6s 8d.
Thomas Foster – 6s 8d.
Parish clerk keeping clock and chime – 2s 6d.
Belman cleansing the church – 8d.
William White keeping the bells 12d, washing to the altar – 6d.
Thomas Provost in fee – 20d.

[1] Raithby cum Maltby.
[2] A John Coke or Cooke was noted as working on the construction of the spire. Goulding, *Spire*, p. 6. He was assessed at 40s in the 1524/5 Lay Subsidy. TNA, E179/138/478.
[3] Noted above the line – '4s 8d'.

Nicholas Upton in fee – 20d.
St Michaels term.
William Foster – 6s 8d.
Thomas Foster – 6s 8d.
Parish clerk keeping clock and chime – 2s 6d.
Belman cleansing the church – 8d.
William White keeping the bells 12d, washing to the altar – 6d.
Thomas Provost in fee – 20d.
Nicholas Upton in fee – 20d.
Nativity term.
William Foster – 6s 8d.
Thomas Foster – 6s 8d.
Parish clerk keeping clock and chime – 2s 6d.
Belman cleansing the church – 8d.
William White keeping the bells 12d, washing to the altar – 6d.
Thomas Provost in fee – 20d.
Nicholas Upton in fee – 20d.
Annunciation term.
William Foster – 6s 8d.
Thomas Foster – 6s 8d.
Parish clerk keeping clock and chime – 2s 6d.
Belman cleansing the church – 8d.
William White keeping the bells 12d, washing to the altar – 6d.
Thomas Provost in fee – 20d.
Nicholas Upton in fee – 20d.
Ministers in the church by year
William Foster by year – 26s 8d.
Thomas Foster by year – 26s 8d.
Parish clerk for keeping the clock & chime – 10s.
Bellman cleansing the church – 2s 8d.
William White keeping the bells – 3s.
Washing to the altar – 2s
Thomas Provost in fee – 6s 8d.
Nicholas Upton in fee – 6s 8d.
Item John Gooddale for writing this account – 3s 4d.
£4 8s 8d.
Burials in the church.
Margery Moore – 6s 8d.
Margaret, wife of Master Thimelby – 6s 8d.
Thomas Dowghtye – 6s 8d.
Margaret Page, otherwise called Bayly – 6s 8d.
William, son of Thomas Foster in the church porch – 3s 4d.
James, son of Robert Fyssher in *eodem loco*[1] – 3s 4d.

---

[1] 'in the same place'.

John Cooke – 6s 8d.
Anne Wright – 6s 8d.
Jenett, wife of Master Gonbye.[1]
Sum – 46s 8d.
Total sum received – £14 11s 1d.

f. 11r.
Expenses for reparations about the church.

Item to Norman for a bell-string to the third bell – 15d.
Item to a man for fetching the common bull[2] – 1d.
Item to Christopher Elwald for one day work of serving the fyner[3] – 4d.
Item to the fyner for his labour of fynyng the lead – 8s.
Item to Christopher Elwald & Humfray for serving the fyner one day – 8d.
Item to John Smyth for lending his bellows to the said fyner – 4d.
Item for a cart that carried the lead – 2d.
Item to Mathew Bellman for giving warning about the town as to keep their cattle, swine and sheep forth of Haregarth[4] – 1d.
Item to Thomas Spencer for 3 torches – 3s 4d.
Item to Robert Beverlay for 4 girdles for reusing – 2d.
Item for boocles[5] to bell collars – 2d.
Item to Maltby for a staple to the bell – 1d.
Item for bearing tile home that was borrowed to the fyner – 1d.
Item to Henry Deane for a bell-string – 17d.
Item to Norman for a bell-string to the greatest bell called the James – 2s 4d.
Item for white leather – 8d.
Item for watching the church – 3d.
Item for helping of the clock – 3s 5d.
Item for mending the cross staff – 8s 11d.
Item to Master Foster for hanging the choir – 6d.
Item for a heng[6] lock to Boston – 2d.
Item to Thomas Provost for a wainscot – 12d.
Item to the same for making a wheel to the chime – 20d.
Item to the clock mender for osmunds[7] – 10d.
Item to Maltby for 27 nails to the church door – 8d.

---

[1] No amount stated.

[2] For the common bull, see Introduction.

[3] Probably a derivation of 'refining'; the finer extracting lead particles from the ashes. *OED*.

[4] For Haregarth, a part the South Field of Louth. The various spellings have been retained.

[5] Possibly buckles.

[6] Hinge. *OED*.

[7] A type of high-quality iron formerly produced in the Baltic region from bog iron ore. *OED*.

Item to Thomas Provost for mending the church door & other 2 stalls in the church – 20d.
Item to Walter Fyswyck[1] for wire – 8d.
Item to the smith for coals – 9d.
Item to William Cawod[2] for the half quarter wage of John Cawod his father – 20d.
Item paid to William Asheby[3] for iron & clapboard to the chime – 14d.
Item for a barrel to make a sow[4] for the church and the making thereof – 5d.
Item to George Tyler for the wage of a man serving the mason a day and a half about the cross work in the Market Place – 7d.[5]
Item to Master Chapman for lime a bushel[6] – 5d.
43s 11d.

f. 11v.
Item to William Ratheby for great nails to the church door – 4½d.
Item to the smith for mending [the] clock and chime – 23s 4d.
Item to Haryson for cleansing the church walls – 6d.
Item to Robert Spencer for dry wood to the fining of the lead – 3s 8d.
Item to Robert Norman[7] for a bell-string to the Fore bell – 12d.
Item paid to John Haryson for a lock to the clock house door – 3d.

---

[1] Walter Fyswike, Fishwick, mercer, was churchwarden in 1522/3. Dudding, *Accounts*, p. 217. He was assessed at £18 in the 1524/5 Lay Subsidy. TNA, E179/138/478. Fyswike is noted as having taken an oath under pressure to 'support' the Rising. Ward, *Rising*, p. 14. In the royal charter of 1551, setting up the Corporation and grammar school, he is recorded as one of the six assistants to the warden. Goulding, *Corporation Records*, p. 4. A Walter Fisshwyck, Fyshwicke or Fishwick left a will: TNA, PROB 11/36/133, probate, 9 May 1553. Buried 19 March 1552/3. LAO, Goulding Papers, 5/2.

[2] William Cawod, the son of John Cawod, choirmaster and organist at St James's, was previously churchwarden in 1521/2. Dudding, *Accounts*, p. 210. He was assessed at £20 in the 1524/5 Lay Subsidy. TNA, E179/138/478. William was also paid 13s 4d as auditor for Louth Park Abbey. *VE*, IV, p. 57. He died in 1536/7, the year he was elected churchwarden, pp. 79, 81. This entry also rules out suggestions that John Cawod was ordained.

[3] A William Ashby, Asseby, Assheby was the constable. It is noted in the inquiry following the Rising that he had 'collected money from the priests', presumably for the rebels. *L&P*, XI, 972, p. 397, 3 November 1536. Ward, *Rising*, p. 14. A William Asseby was churchwarden in 1537/8 and was interred 30 August 1540. LAO, Goulding Papers, 5/2.

[4] Possibly a sow or sough, a drain. *OED*.

[5] Markets were held on Wednesdays and Saturdays. Goulding, *Markets and Fairs*, n.p.

[6] Also known as a strike containing 4 pecks or 8 gallons. In north Lincolnshire, it equalled one-fourth of a quarter. Bristow, *Glossary*, p. 27.

[7] Robert Norman, a roper, is mentioned in the Rising inquiry as giving to John Wylson (noted as Jocken Sene), a sawer or carpenter, 'a penny or pennyworth of ale to demand the keys of the church jewels from the churchwardens; the general belief [being] that the jewels would be taken' the following day by the bishop's representative. Ward, *Rising*, p. 13. *L&P*, XI, 972, p. 397, 3 November 1536.

Item to Maltby for shotting a bolt to a bell wheel – 2d.
Item to Richard Spencer for 3 days labouring about the plumbers – 12d.
Item to Jackson for sawing a wainscot – 3d.
Item to Robert Bayly for nails – 2d.
Item to Richard Clacksby for watching in the church – 2d.
Item to Robert Bayly for nails – 1d.
Item to Thomas Provost for 2 days work in the steeple among the bells – 20d.
Item to the plumbers for solder – 4s 6d.
Item for their wages for 5 days working – 5s.
Item to Richard Spencer for 2 days labouring about the plumbers – 8d.
Item to the glazier for 8 days working about mending the windows, himself & his servant – 6s 9d.
Item to Syll for mending bars of iron about the windows – 4d.
Item to the glazier for 7lbs of solder – 2s 4d.
Item to same glazier for glass – 2s 8d.
Item to the same glazier for his board & his servant – 3s.
Item to George Tyler for a strike of lime – 3d.
Item to Maltby for a lock & a key to the hutch – 7d.
Item to Richard Couper for a hide [of] white leather – 4d.
Item for mending of the bell wheels – 6d.
Item for a lock to Maltby to the church stile – 2d.
Item for nails – 1d.
Item for cleansing a stall in the church – 1d.
Item to George Tyler for a strike of lime – 3d.
Item to a mason for a day's work about the leads where the plumbers hath been – 5d.[1]
Item to Haryson for serving him – 3d.
Item to John Sysson for his work & his 2 servants about the mending of 2 windows in St Peter choir – 6s 10d.
Item to the glazier for glass, solder & his labour – 4s.
Item for wood to the glazier – 4d.
Item for a strike of lime – 3d.
Item to Mathew Bellman for cleansing the grate at the church stile – 1d.
f. 12r.
Item Robert Beverlay for besums or bromes[2] – ½d.
Item to the tynkler[3] for mending the cross – 7d.
Item to Rafe Page for leading[4] lead to St Mary's church – 2d.
Item to Henry Deane for a bell-string – 23d.

---

[1] Line crossed through.
[2] Besoms or brooms.
[3] Tinkler or tinker – an itinerant worker in metal. *OED*.
[4] To carry or convey, usually in a cart or other vehicle. *OED*.

Item to the bellman's wife for scouring candlesticks against the Feast of Nativity – 6d.
Item to Thomas Provost for himself & his servant for one day work about the bells – 10d.
Item to the masons for mending the *balke foote*[1] beside St George – 6s 2d.[2]
Item to George the mason for 7 days work beside one day work that he gave of his devotion to the church – 3s.
Item to Robert Yonger for a torch to search the church with – 15d.
Item to Maltby for a hesp[3] to a bell wheel – 3d.
Item to John Myller for a piece of timber to the bell wheel – 12d.
Item to John Holdernesse for a bull – 13s 8d.
Item to Robert Smyth for a sneck[4] staple[5] to the gate[6] in the church garth & other work about the bell yoke – 6d.
Item to Jackson the sawer for a piece of wood to the gate & for sawing – 8d.
Item to Robert Baily for nails – 1d.
Item to Thomas Provost for stuff & making of a bell wheel – 8s.
Item to H[enr]y for making the north gate & mending the stall – 16d.
Item to Henry Deane for a bell-string to the little bell – 8d.
Item to Thomas Hyll for wood to the gate on the north side of the church – 20d.
Item to John Holdernes for finding the common bull – 12d.
Item to the glazier for 4 days work about windows in both churches – 5s 5d.
Item to Thomas Hyll for wood to the glazier – 2d.
Item for lime – 1½d.
Item to Norman for a string to the clock – 10d
Item to the clocksmith for dressing [the] clocks & chime to meat and reward – 5s 4d.
Item for shoproom fire & iron to the clock smith – 14d.
Item to Robert Bayly for nails – 2d.
Item to Thomas Provost for mending stools in the church – 9d.
Item for scouring the candlesticks – 6d.
Item for coals to Robert Beverlay – 3d.
Item to Thomas Spencer for torches – 2s 8d.
Item to Nicholas Upton for hewing a stone to the window in Master Langholme's choir – 12d.

---

[1] Precise meaning unknown.
[2] The equestrian statue of St George was a notable feature in St James's. St George's guild was valued in 1545 at 7s 4d. Goulding, *Corporation Records*, p. 175.
[3] Hasp – a hinged clasp. *OED*.
[4] The lever that raises the bar of a latch. *OED*.
[5] A short rod or bar of iron or other metal bent into the form of a 'U'. *OED*.
[6] In the accounts, 'gate' is generally spelt 'yate' or 'yat', an Old English variant. *OED*. See also https://quod.lib.umich.edu/m/middle-english-dictionary/dictionary/MED18275.

Item to Thomas Hill for a plank & a chain – 4d.

f. 12v.

Item to 2 masons for 2 days work about hewing stone for the minyons[1] in Master Langholme's choir – 2s.

Item to Mykelbarowgh for 2 days work, his self & his servant at the same choir – 20d.

Item for their commons[2] – 12d.

Item to the same for glass & solder – 20d.

Item for a strike of lime – 3d.

Item for wood to the same work – 3d.

Item to Mathew Bellman for watching in the church at night – 2d.

Item to Richard Spencer for one day work at Haregarth – 3d.

Item to John Holdrenesse for finding the common bull – 8d.

12s 8d.

Total of all expenses – £13 14s 4d.

And remains 16s 9d thereof paid for the rest of the torches to Philip Whyte 9d, and remains 16d. Finally, 21d in the past year's account and so remains clear 17s 9d to whom 10d received of Richard Beverlay and John White, 5 marks at the same over this year. And so it remains clear 27s 9d.[3]

f. 13r.

[1530–1]

The account of William Browne, miller,[4] William Lawrence, Robert Hartburn, walker[5], William Glene, mercer, Proctors of the Church of St James of Lowthe, all receipts and expenses on Sunday the Octave of Easter 1530 until the Octave of Easter 1531.

Item received of the old churchwardens in money good & evil – 27s 9d.

Item received the 2nd Sunday after Easter – 4s 3d.

Item received the 3rd Sunday after – 4s 5d.

Item received the 4th Sunday after – 3s 1d.

Item received the 5th Sunday after – 2s 9d.

Item received the Sunday after Ascension – 3s 4d.

Item received the Sunday of Pentecost – 5s.

Item received Trinity Sunday – 3s 11d.

Item received the 1st Sunday after – 3s 2d.

---

[1] Mullions?

[2] Provisions or expenses in common. *OED*.

[3] At the foot of the page is a list of churchwardens for the following year, repeated at the top of folio 13r.

[4] William Brown, miller, was churchwarden in 1515/16. Dudding, *Accounts*, p. 174. He was assessed at £20 in the 1524/5 Lay Subsidy. TNA, E179/138/478.

[5] Fuller – a person who cleanses wool. Goulding, *Spire*, p. 4. Hartburn was assessed at £6 in the 1524/5 Lay Subsidy. TNA, E179/138/478.

Item received the 2nd Sunday after – 3s 4d.
Item received the 3rd Sunday after – 3s 5d.
Item received the 4th Sunday after – 3s 4d.
Item received the 5th Sunday after – 3s 8d.
Item received the 6th Sunday after – 3s 1d.
Item received the 7th Sunday after – 3s 7d.
Item received the 8th Sunday after – 3s 8d.
Item received the 9th Sunday after – 3s 3d.
Item received the 10th Sunday after – 3s 11d.
Item received the 11th Sunday after – 3s 6d.
Item received the 12th Sunday after – 3s 8d.
Item received the 13th Sunday after – 2s 5d.
Item received the 14th Sunday after – 2s 10d.
Item received the 15th Sunday after – 2s 10d.
Item received the 16th Sunday after – 3s 4d.
Item received the 17th Sunday after – 2s 8d.
Item received the 18th Sunday after – 2s 10d.
Item received the 19th Sunday after – 3s.
Item received the 20th Sunday after – 3s 2d.
Item received the 21st Sunday after – 2s 6d.
Item received the 22nd Sunday after – 2s 8d.
Item received the 23rd Sunday after – 2s 9d.
Item received the 1st Sunday of Advent – 2s 4d.[1]
Item received the 2nd Sunday of Advent – 2s 4d.[2]
Item received the 3rd Sunday of Advent – 3s 4d.[3]
Item received the 4th Sunday of Advent – 2s 8d.
Item received the Lord's Nativity – 3s 2d.
Item received the Sunday after Circumcision – 3s 4d.
Item received the 1st Sunday after Epiphany – 2s 4d.
Item received the 2nd Sunday after – 2s 4d.
Item received the 3rd Sunday after – 3s.
Item received the 4th Sunday after – 2s 6d.
Item received the Sunday of *Septuagesima* – 2s 10d.
Item received the Sunday of *Sexagesima* – 2s 4d.
Item received the Sunday of *Quinquagesima* – 2s 10d.
Item received the 1st Sunday of *Quadragesima* – 2s 4d.
Item received the 2nd Sunday of Lent – 2s 4d.
Item received the 3rd Sunday of Lent – 3s.
Item received the 4th Sunday of Lent – 3s.

---

[1] '24' crossed through.
[2] '25' crossed through.
[3] '26' crossed through.

Item received Passion Sunday – 3s.¹
Item received Palm Sunday – 3s 10d.
Item received Easter Day – 4s 2d.
Item received the Sunday after Easter – 2s 4d.
£9 5s 14d.²

f. 13v.
Burials in the church.
Imprimis, John Moore – 6s 8d.
John Okeland³ – 6s 8d.
Isabell, wife [of] Roland Mondy – 6s 8d.
Katharine, daughter [of] Robert Bayle – 6s 8d.
Richard Melton – 6s 8d.
d Gregory Pullay – 6s 8d.
Elizabeth Brown, wife [of] Robert Brown – 6s 8d.
Joanne Brown, wife [of] William Brown – 6s 8d.
Thomas Holdrenes – 6s 8d.
Sum – £3.
Witword[s] to St James's church and St Mary's church.
Imprimis, John More to St Mary's church – 3s 4d.
Item Richard Melton thereto – 2d.
Item Joanne Brown, the wife of William Browne gave a small pair of beads of coral with silver gaudes⁴ to the feretor.
Item received for the common bull – 8s 8d.
Item received of Robert Johnson of Spyttell Hyll⁵ for 4 stone of lead – 2s 8d.

f. 14r.
Great bell ringing.
Imprimis, John Moore – 20d.⁶
Item John Williamson – 12d.⁷

---

1 '6d' crossed through.

2 £9 6s 2d.

3 A John Okeland, tailor, was churchwarden in 1507/8. Dudding, *Accounts*, p. 94. He was assessed at 40s in the 1524/5 Lay Subsidy. TNA, E179/138/478.

4 Gauds – ornamental beads placed between the decades of 'aves' in a rosary. *OED*.

5 Spital Hill, off South Street, is a nineteenth-century manifestation; the original was probably the route now taken by the present London Road, then known as 'Spittle Hill Laine'. This was the site of a leper hospital first recorded in 1314, noted as a *domus leprosorm* in 1488, and was also where the town gallows was situated. Its buildings were later used as a poorhouse, having been given to the grammar school by John Bradley in 1556/7. Green, *Streets of Louth*, pp. 156, 236–8: Green, *Origins*, p. 119. Swaby, *History of Louth*, p. 33. Goulding, *Louth Houses*, n.p.

6 'Robert Beverlay' crossed through.

7 In 1476, John Williamson, merchant, and his wife Joan had obits performed by St Mary's guild. Goulding, *Annals*, p. 24.

Robert Westmold, gentleman – 8d.
John Cawod.[1]
John Moore – 20d.
John Okeland – 8d.
John Gyrdyck – 8d.
Isabell, wife [of] Roland Mondy – 20d.
John Okeland – 8d.
John Langham, gentleman – 8d.
Brethren of Our Lady guild – 20d.
Isabell, wife [of] Roland Mondy – 8d.
Isabell Page – 20d.
Mary, daughter [of] Martin Mestchamber – 8d.
George, son of Martin Mestchamber – 8d.
John Lowthe – 20d.
Katharine, daughter [of] Robert Bayle – 8d.
Katharine Robynson – 8d.
Richard Melton – 20d.
John Chapman, gentleman – 8d.
John Parronell – 8d.
Thomas Bradlay – 20d.[2]
Richard Melton – 20d.
Thomas Bradlay, the elder – 20d.
Thomas Haulton – 20d.
John Camolks – 8d.
Isabell Wade – 20d.
d George Pullay – 20d.
Elizabeth Brown – 20d.
Stephan & John Parcens – 8d.
d George Pullay – 12d.
Joanne Brown – 20d.
Robert Beverlay – 20d.
William Hudson – 8d.

38s 8d.

Symon Lyncoln – 8d.
Thomas Holdrenes – 20d.

Sum – 41s.
Total sum received – £15 2s.

[1] No amount stated.

[2] In his extensive will of 18 June 1519 (with a codicil dated 16 June 1521), Thomas Bradley, merchant of the Staple of Calais, donated to five of the county's nunneries, the friars of Lincoln and Grimsby along with thirteen parish churches including Louth. Thomas Egleston, the 'master vicar', was given a satin doublet stocked with velvet, in addition to 40s for tithes, later increased to £5. The church's 'works' received 40s and the Lady guild £26 13s 4d. TNA, PROB 11/20/238, probate, October 1521.

f. 14v.

Ministers in the church by year.

Imprimis, William Foster – 26s 8d.
Thomas Foster – 26s 8d.
Parish clerks keeping clock & chime – 10s.
Bellman cleansing the church – 2s 8d.
Haryson & Tace for keeping the bells – 2s 6d.
Cloble's wife for washing to the altar – 2s.
Thomas Provost in fee – 6s 8d.
Nicholas Upton in fee – 6s 8d.
John Gooddale writing this account – 6s 8d.

Sum – £4 10s 6d.
Expenses about the church.

Item to Forman for a bell-string to the third bell – 13d.
Item to Robert Bayly for 2 heng locks & keys to them to the church garth gates – 7d.
To Robert Forman for slicing a bell-string – 2d.
Item to John Belbow for a hide of white leather – 12d.
Item to Thomas Provost for a day work of himself & his servant about the bells – 10d.
Item to Haryson for paring away the weeds from the church walls at Corpus Christi day – 6d.
Item for leading away the said woods – 2d.
Item to 2 men for watching in the church at Corpus Christi tide – 8d.
Item to the mason for a day work about the church walls – 6d.
Item to George Tyler for a bushel of lime – 5d.
Item to a woman for a day work in mending vestments & albs – 4d.
Item to Robert Beverlay for reusing girdles for children – 1d.
Item to a smith for making 2 stops to the chime wheel – 4d.
Item to Haryson for cleansing the steeple – 4d.
Item to Nicholas Upton for 2 load of stone – 8s.[1]
Item for blowing the organs – 6d.
Item for iron for the chime & working thereof – 4d.
Item to James the painter for gilding of St Rocke[2] – 16s 8d.

Sum – 32s 6d.

f. 15r.

Item to Robert Goldsmythe for half an ounce weight of silver – 21d.
Item for mending the fence – 10d.
Item paid to Robert Cardemaker for mending of the lantern – 6d.
Item to Thomas Provest for a day's work of himself & his servant – 10d.

---

[1] Manicule in margin.
[2] St Roche or Rock (c.1350–c.1380) was the patron saint of plague sufferers. Farmer, *Saints*, pp. 420–1.

Item for a yard of buckram[1] – 5d.
Item for a skeyme[2] of silk, thread & rybane[3] – 5½d.
Item to Thomas Manars for 3 days work – 12d.
Item for grease to the bells – 1d.
Item to John Tace[4] for a piece of wood to a busshe[5] – 2d.
Item to Robert Rowtt[6] for nails – 6½d.
Item to Thomas Ednall[7] for 5½ days working at St Mary's church – 22d.
Item to the plumber – 4d.
Item to Robert Norman for a bell-string – 8d.
Item to Thomas Ednall for a day work at St Mary's church – 4d.
Item to George Raynforthe for half a day's work – 2d.
Item to the plumber – 3s 1d.
Item to George Raynforthe for working 3 days & a half, to meat & wages – 14d.
Item to Henry Colyngwod for half a day's work – 2d.
Item to William Plummar – 20d.
Item to Thomas Preston for mending a covering – 2s.
Item to Robert Norman for a bell-string – 12d.
Item to James the glazier for mending a glass window in St James's church – 16d.
Item for 3 yards & a half of canvas – 14d.
Item to William Haryson for mending of the weathercock shank[8] – 3s 4d.
Item to John Rede for thacking[9] 2 days both to meat & wages – 10d.
Item to Thomas Mossam for serving him at his work – 8d.
Item paid to William Lawrence for 8 thresh[10] of straws – 12d.
Item for scouring the candlesticks at Christmas – 6d.
Item to Thomas Preston for mending harrowes[11] clothes belonging to the church – 3s 8d.
Item to Robert Norman for a bell-string – 20d.
Item to Robert Spencer for lead – 4s 2d.

---

1   A kind of fine linen or cotton fabric or a kind of coarse cloth stiffened with gum or paste. *OED*.
2   Skein – a quantity of thread or yarn, wound to a certain length upon a reel, and usually put up in a kind of loose knot. *OED*.
3   Ribbon.
4   A John Tacye was recorded as being confined in Lincoln Castle following the Rising. *L&P*, XI, 828, iii (1), p. 323, 23 October 1536.
5   Bush – a metal lining of the axle-hole of a wheel, a bearing. *OED*.
6   A Robert Rowtte was assessed at £20 in the 1524/5 Lay Subsidy. TNA, E179/138/478.
7   Thomas Ednall was assessed at 40s in the 1524/5 Lay Subsidy. TNA, E179/138/478.
8   Shank – metal shaft attaching the weathervane to the spire.
9   Thatching.
10 A clump of rushes. *OED*.
11 Herod's clothes. An inventory from Holbeach All Saints' in 1547 records: 'Item to John Thorpe for harod's coate' – 18d. Stokes, *Drama*, 1, p. 97.

Item for making 2 pairs of trestles – 2s.
Item to John Haryson for mending of the chime – 4d.
Item for glass & solder – 6d.
To Mathew Bellman – 1d.
Item for rosell & nails – 2d.
Item for bearing the ladder for St Mary's church – 1d.
Item to Thomas Provest for mending the weathercock – 3s.
Item to William Plummar for working at St Mary's church – 2s 3d.
49s 9½d.

f. 15v.
Item for a leather bag – 1d.
Item to William Peper[1] for working at St Mary's church – 15d.
Item to Thomas Provest for 2 days work of himself & his servant in the steeple – 15d.
Item to George Tyler for a strike of lime – 2½d.
Item for 2 pounds of solder – 8d.
Item for nails – 2d.
Item to John Haryson for mending the chime – 1d.
Item to Barnard Bocher for a quarter & a half of lime – 3s.
Item to William Gray,[2] mason, for working at St Mary's church – 3s 9d.
Item to Robert West for watching in the church – 2d.
Item to William Moore for watching – 8d.
Item to Hyan Parret for watching – 6d.
Item to Robert Dyxson for mending the candlestick – 2s 8d.[3]
Item to Richard Gooderick for watching – 3d.
Item to Robert West for 5 nights – 10d.
Item to Leonard.[4]
Item to George Tyler for 3 bushels of lime – 15d.
Item to John Welborn for mending of a staple – 3d.
Item to John Pynder – 2d.
Item to William Harrison for 2 stops to the chime – 22d.
Item to Thomas Provest for 2 days work of himself & a servant about the bells & other necessaries in the church – 20d.
Item to 2 men for watching 2 nights in the church – 8d.
Item to Robert Johnson, smith,[5] for nails, plates & other things about the church doors – 12d.

---

[1] William Pepper's wife Joanna, his two sons, Henry and Thomas, and his daughter Joanna all predeceased him. LAO, Goulding Papers, 5/2.

[2] William Gray is noted in the first accounts as working on the spire. Goulding, *Spire*, p. 6.

[3] Manicule in margin.

[4] No amount stated.

[5] This Robert Johnson, smith, was probably the same person noted in the deposition of Thomas Foster, singingman, taken following the Rising. He spoke to

Item to John Tace for a day work about the bells – 4d.
Item for scouring the candlesticks – 6d.
Item for cleansing the grate – 1d.
Item to a man for watching 7 nights in the church – 14d.
Item to William Glene for stays[1] to the bell – 1d.
Item to Leonard, William Lawrence's servant, for watching 7 nights in the church – 14d.[2]
Item to William Worslay[3] for cherck coals[4] – 3d.
Item to William Page[5] for a lock & key – 4s 4d.
Item for paper for writing this account – 1d.
Item for 2 pounds of candles to search the church with – 4d.
Item to Robert Johnson, smith for mending of the clock hammer – 2d.
  Sum – 30s 1½d.
Total of the pewter to be paid £10 2s 11d, and there remains £4 19s 1d beyond? 17d in money [and] the 1 pare of Corall beads in addition to 16 pairs of silver beads he attached to the same [as a] the gift of Johanne the wife of W[illiam] Browne.
[The following lines are on the reverse of a flyleaf between folios *f. 15v* and *f. 16r*].
Churchwardens.
Thomas Bowland.[6]
Robert Lawson.
Robert Colynwode.[7]
Robert Richardson.
This said money of 40s is paid again as apperithe by the account of Robert Spencer & his fellows made 1532.
Memorandum, that John Spencer of Louth hath received 40s in ready money for the Common Cart[8] for the year following and he to dig & carry four score

---

Johnson concerning the possible abolition of liturgical processions. *L&P*, XI, 828 (iii), 1, p. 323, 23 October 1536. Buried 17 February 1539/40. LAO, Goulding Papers, 5/2.

[1] A prop, pedestal, buttress or bracket. *OED*.
[2] Line crossed through.
[3] Worsley was assessed at £9 in the 1524/5 Lay Subsidy. TNA, E179/138/478. Interred 30 November 1556. LAO, Goulding Papers, 5/2.
[4] Chark, cherch, cherk – wood or coal charred; charcoal, coke. *OED*.
[5] A William Page was assessed at £3 in the 1524/5 Lay Subsidy. TNA, E179/138/478.
[6] Bowland was assessed at £6 in the 1524/5 Lay Subsidy. TNA, E179/138/478.
[7] Collynwod was assessed at 20s in the 1524/5 Lay Subsidy. TNA, E179/138/478. In 1544, Bishop Longland transferred a tenement previously rented by Robert Collyngwoode, noted as a 'wever', to John Makerith, 'sherman'. Cole, *Chapter Acts*, II, p. 98. Robert Collynwod was interred 25 June 1546 and a John Macrithe on 17 March 1564/5. LAO, Goulding Papers, 5/2.
[8] The term 'Common Cart' probably refers to a fund (common account), in this case to finance road repairs.

load [of] stone to be laid in places necessary sureties is William Walker, William Kynge,[1] William Browne & William Cawode.[2]
        There is delivered to the Church Masters.
There is delivered to William Kyng of Louth of the Plough light gathered at Plough Day, 22 *Anno* H8, 4s 7d, as it appears by a count made of the same pertaining with John Spencer which hath promised to gather the rest and 4d also which was delivered by Alexander ...[3]

f. 16r.

[1531–2]

The account of Thomas Bowland, Robert Lawson, Robert Collingwode, Robert Richardson, Proctors of the Church of St James of Louth, all receipts and expenses on Sunday the Octave of Easter 1531 until the Octave of Easter 1532.
Item received of the old churchwardens in money good and ill, £5 6½d. Whereof delivered to Robert Baly in ill money to be changed 19s 8d, whereof he hath delivered to them again in good money 16s, and so remaineth in good money £4 16s 10½d.
Item received 2nd Sunday after Easter – 5s 3d.
Item received the 3rd Sunday after – 3s 9d.
Item received the 4th Sunday after – 3s 10d.
Item received the 5th Sunday after – 3s 2d.
Item received the 6th Sunday after Ascension – 3s 11d.
Item received the Sunday of Pentecost – 5s 4d.
Item received the Trinity Sunday – 4s 6d.
Item received the 1st Sunday after – 2s 11d.
Item received the 2nd Sunday after – 4s.
Item received the 3rd Sunday after – 4s.
Item received the 4th Sunday after – 4s 2d.
Item received the 5th Sunday after – 3s 6d.
Item received the 6th Sunday after – 4s 6d.
Item received the same day of John Moore's wife in part of payment of a greater sum as apperyth by an indenture in the hutch – 3s 4d.
Item received the 7th Sunday after – 4s 6d.

---

    1 A William Kyng was churchwarden in 1522/3. Dudding, *Accounts*, p. 217. In 1533, he was appointed the manors' bailiff on a retainer of £2 18s 11½d. Kyng also held the position of 'Keeper of the Wood' at Louth Park on 1½d per day. Cole, *Chapter Acts*, II, p. 42. Swaby, *History of Louth*, pp. 104–5. During the Rising, he was noted as 'Bailiff of Louth', a 'Petty Captain' and one of 'the ringleaders in the field at Castre' (Caister). *L&P*, XI, 972, p. 397, 3 November 1536: *ibid.*, 568, p. 225, 6 October 1536. He was buried as William Kyng senior on 27 February 1547/8. LAO, Goulding Papers, 5/2.
    2 Paragraph crossed through.
    3 Paragraph crossed through. The rest of the flyleaf is damaged.

Item received the same day of John Moore's wife – 3s 4d.
Item received the 8th Sunday after – 4s 11d.
Item received the same day of John Moore's wife – 3s 4d.
Item received the 9th Sunday after – 4s 10d.
Item received the same day of John Moore's wife – 3s 4d.
Item received the 10th Sunday after – 4s 7d.
Item received the same day of John Moor's wife – 3s 4d.
Item received the same day of Robert Brown for change of lead – 3s.
Item received the 11th Sunday after – 3s 3d.
Item received the same day of John Moore's wife – 3s 4d.
Item received the 12th Sunday after – 4s 8d.
Item received the same day of John Moore's wife – 3s 4d.
Item received the 13th Sunday after – 4s 4d.
Item received the same day of John Moore's wife for the last payment & full contention of her indenture – 3s 4d.
Item received for change of lead – 2s.
Item received the 14th Sunday after – 4s 4d.
Item received the 15th Sunday after – 5s 10d.
Item received the 16th Sunday after – 4s 5d.
Item received the 17th Sunday after – 4s.
Item received the 18th Sunday after – 3s 5d.
Item received the 19th Sunday after – 4s.
Item received the 20th Sunday after – 4s 8d.
Item received the 21st Sunday after – 3s 8d.
Item received the 22nd Sunday after – 3s 8d.
Item received the 23rd Sunday after – 5s.
Item received the 24th Sunday after – 4s.
Item received the 25th Sunday after – 3s 3d.
£13 3s 1½d.

f. 16v.
Item the first Sunday of Advent – 3s 7d.
Item the 2nd Sunday – 4s 4d.
Item the 3rd Sunday – 3s 10d.
Item the 4th Sunday – 4s.
Item the first Sunday after Nativity of Our Lord – 3s 8d.
Item the first Sunday after Epiphany – 4s 6d.
Item the first Sunday after the Octave of Epiphany – 4s 6d.
Item the 2nd Sunday after – 3s 3d.
Item the Sunday of *Septuagesima* – 3s 5d.
Item the Sunday of *Sexagesima* – 3s 4d.
Item the Sunday of *Quinquagesima* – 3s 1d.
Item the first Sunday of *Quadragesima* – 3s 8d.
Item the 2nd Sunday of *Quadragesima* – 3s 11d.
Item the 3rd Sunday of *Quadragesima* – 3s 11d.

Item the 4th Sunday of *Quadragesima* – 3s 7d.
Item the Sunday in Passion – 3s 10d.
Item Palm Sunday – 4s 9d.
Item received Easter Day – 4s 6d.
Item received the Sunday after Easter – 3s 8d.
£3 13s 4d.

Item received of Master Comyssary[1] for mending the great candlestick in the high choir – 2s 7d.
Item received of the gathering for the Plough light – 11s 1d.
Item received of Robert Bayly for 12lbs & 3 quarters of white lead – 19d.
Sum 15s 3d.

Burials within the church.

Imprimis, James Clarck[2] – 6s 8d.
Item John Halton[3] – 6s 8d.
Item Patrick Molter, chaplain – 6s 8d.
Item Thomas Beverlay, son [of] Richard Beverlay[4] – 6s 8d.
Elizabeth, wife [of] John Chapman, gentleman – 6s 8d.[5]
Rowland Munday – 6s 8d.
Item William Barnard, butcher[6] – 6s 8d.
Item John, son [of] Martin Mesterchamber in south church porch – 3s 4d.
Sum – 50s.

Witwords to both churches.

Imprimis, John Halton to St James's church – 20s.
Item the same John to St Mary's church – 3s 4d.
Item William Howsam to St James's church – 4d.
Item William Fornas of Saltfleetby[7] to St James's church – 12d.
Item Rowland Munday to St Mary's church – 4d.
Item William Barnard to St James's church – 20d.
Item the said William to St Mary's church – 12d.
Sum – 27s 8d.
£8 6s 3d.

---

[1] Commissary. A member of the clergy or other official exercising spiritual or ecclesiastical jurisdiction as the representative of a superior authority. *OED*.

[2] James Clerck was assessed at 40s in the 1524/5 Lay Subsidy. TNA, E179/138/478.

[3] A John Halton was assessed at £10 in the 1524/5 Lay Subsidy. TNA, E179/138/478.

[4] Richard Beverlay, mercer and dean of the Lady guild 1513/14, was assessed at £36 13s 4d in the 1524/5 Lay Subsidy. TNA, E179/138/478. He was also churchwarden in 1503/4, 1509/10 and 1514/15. Dudding, *Accounts*, pp. 47, 115, 165. Williamson, 'Religious Guilds', p. 89.

[5] Elizabeth was the wife of John Chapman of Thorpe Hall (d.1532), daughter of Sir Peter Hildyard of Fulstow. Maddison, *Lincolnshire Pedigrees*, 50, p. 237.

[6] William Barnard, Bernard, butcher, was churchwarden in 1517/18. Dudding, *Accounts*, p. 188. He was assessed at £10 in the 1524/5 Lay Subsidy. TNA, E179/138/478.

[7] Saltfleetby All Saints.

f. 17r.
Great bells ringing.

Imprimis, John Williamson – 12d.
John Moore – 20d.
Robert Otter – 8d.[1]
Robert Westmold, gentleman – 8d.
John Cawod – 8d.
Brethren & sisters of the Trinity guild – 8d.
James Clercke – 20d.
John Halton – 20d.
John Okeland – 8d.
Gylbard Asheball – 20d.
James Clarke – 20d.
John Langham, gentleman – 8d.
James Clarck – 20d.
d Patrick Molter – 20d.
d Patrick Molter – 20d.
d Robert & John White & *Fratres*[2] [of the] guild [of] the blessed Mary – 20d.
Thomas, son [of] Walter Fiswick – 8d.
John Halton – 20d.
William Proctor[3] – 8d.
Gylbard Asheball – 20d.
d Patrick Molter – 20d.
John Lowthe – 20d.
Richard Ratheby – 8d.
Thomas Beverlay, son [of] Richard Beverlay – 20d.
Katheryn Robynson – 8d.
Richard Goderick – 8d.
John Talkes – 8d.
John Chapman, gentleman – 8d.
Thomas Bradley, senior – 20d.
Jenet, wife [of] John Young – 20d.
Elizabeth, wife [of] John Chapman – 20d.
John Parnell[4] – 8d.
Rowland Munday – 20d.
Thomas Beverlay, senior – 20d.
Thomas Allerton – 20d.
d Richard Parcins & *fratres* – 8d.

[1] Robert Otter was assessed at £6 in the 1524/5 Lay Subsidy. TNA, E179/138/478.
[2] Brothers, brethren.
[3] A William Proketure, weaver, was churchwarden in 1518/19. Dudding, *Accounts*, p. 195. He was assessed at £7 in the 1524/5 Lay Subsidy. TNA, E179/138/478.
[4] John Pernall, Parnell, husbandman, was churchwarden in 1518/19. Dudding, *Accounts*, p. 195.

d Thomas Gyrdycke – 12d.
William Barnard, butcher – 20d.
William Barnard, butcher – 20d.
Jonane, wife [of] William Brown – 20d.
John, son [of] Martin Mesterchamber – 8d.
51s.
Total sum received – £24 4½d.

f. 17v.

Ministers in the church by year.

Imprimis, William Foster in fee – 26s 8d.
Thomas Foster[1] in fee – 26s 8d.
Parish clerk keeping clock & chime – 10s.
Cloble's wife for washing clothes to the altar – 2s.
Bellman cleansing the church – 2s 8d.
Tace keeping the bells – 4s.
Nicholas Upton in fee – 6s 8d.
Thomas Provest in fee – 6s 8d.
John Gooddale writing this account – 6s 8d.
John Tace for keeping the bells – 20d.[2]
Nicholas Upton in fee.
Thomas Provest in fee – 6s 8d.
Mathew Bellman for Midsummer[3] cleansing the church – 8d.
John Gooddale writing this account – 3s 4d.
Sum – £4 12s.
Expenses about the church.

Item for mending the lodge wall – 1d.
Item to John Harryson[4] for mending St George's lock – 1d.
Item to Henry Deane for a bell-string – 13d.
Item to John Spencer for a white leather hide – 17d.
Item to Henry Deane for a string to the Morrow Mass[5] bell – 8d.
Item to Robert Bayly for a clog[6] to a sarkyng board[7] – 2s 8d.
Item for mending the copper cross – 12d.

---

1   'Provest' crossed through.
2   This and the following four lines are crossed through.
3   Midsummer quarter day 24 June, feast of St John the Baptist.
4   Harrison was assessed at 20s in the 1524/5 Lay Subsidy. TNA, E179/138/478. Following the Rising, John Harrison, smith, stated that 'they [the rebels] would never have gone forward but for the compulsion of Guy Cayme [Kyme], Robert Bayle, Robert Fysher, Robert and Thomas Spencer, and one Robert Cardemaker who were petty captains'. *L&P*, XI, 972, p. 398, 3 November 1536.
5   First Mass of the day. *OED*.
6   A thick piece of wood. *OED*.
7   Sarking board – covering for a roof. *OED*.

Item to Thomas Provest for a stall mending in the choir – 3d.[1]
Item for a common bull – 9s 4d.
Item to Robert Whallay for a pulley & iron thereto & devising girdles – 8d.
Item for sawing of sarkyng board – 2s 4d.
Item for watching in the church at Corpus Christi day – 4d.
Item to William Foster for hanging the choir then – 9d.
Item to the noterd[2] for fetching home the common bull – 2d.
Item to William Fawer for leading a load of wood and a load of sand to St Mary's church for the casting of the lead – 6d.
Item to William Fawer for leading sand & lead to St James's church from St Mary's church – 10d.
Item to the plumber for his work the first week about the south side of the church – 8s.
Item to William West for a load of wood – 2s 8d.
Item for bringing a load of lead from St Mary's church to St James's church – 2d.
                    33s.
            Total Sum – £6 5s.

f. 18r.
Item to Robert Bayly for nails – 18d.
Item to Robert Whallay for his stuff & labour about the new organs – 7d.
Item for carriage of lead from St Mary's church to the high church[3] – 16d.
Item to William Johnson[4] for helping about the same – 9d.
Item to the aforesaid plumber for part of his labour in covering the south aisle – 22s.
Item to Walter Fyswick for an ympuall[5] – 15d.
Item for leading 2 load of lead to St Mary's church – 4d.
Item to Fawer for leading 2 load[s] of lead to St James's church – 4d.
Item to William Farrand for 5cwt [of] lead (6d a stone), 2 stone wanting – 19s 8d.
Item to the plumber for part of his labour in covering the south aisle – 20s.
Item to Fawer for leading 10 loads of wood & lead from the church to the other[6] – 20d.
Item to 2 masons for 2 days work & a half about the aisle over the south church door – 2s 8d.
Item to 2 wrights for 2 days work & a half about the same work – 2s 6d.

---

   1 There are six surviving medieval stalls in St James's in what is now the Angel Chapel. Gurnham, *Early Louth*, p. 132.
   2 Neatherd, a cowherd. *OED*.
   3 St James's.
   4 A William Jonson is noted in the first accounts as working on the spire. Goulding, *Spire*, p. 6.
   5 Ampul, ampule, ampoule – vessel for holding consecrated oil. *OED*.
   6 Presumably St Mary's.

Item for a piece of timber to the same work – 12d.
Item for 3 strikes of lime – 7½d.
Item for cleansing the church from the dirt which fell by the masons & wrights work – 1d.
Item for bringing 6 webs [of] lead to the church – 1d.
Item paid to the plumber for part of his labour in covering the south aisle – 10s.
Item paid to Robert Whallay for washing a suit of albs – 2d.
Item for parchment for the covering of this book – 3d.
Item to Robert Smyth for mending the lock on the clerk's chamber door – 2d.
Item to William Fawer for bringing a load of sand to St Mary's church – 3d.
Item for wire to the chime – 3d.
Item to Norman for a bell-string – 12d.
Item for carriage of lead & wood – 7d.
Item to William Gray for half a fodder of lead – 44s 8d.
Item to Robert Bayly for nails – 3s 8d.
Item to Johnson for leading 2 load of lead – 4d.
Item for leading 5 loads of lead & a load of wood – 10d.
Item to the plumber – 3s 4d.
Item to Norman for a string to the chime – 2s 8d.
Item for 3 strikes of lime – 7½d.
Item to George Mason for 2 days work about the steeple – 12d.
Item to Richard Cortt for 3 days labour – 11d.
Item to Robert Smyth for his bellows & his labour – 2s.
Item to Richard Fletcher for 2 quarters of cherck coals – 5s.
Item to William Gray, mason, for working about the steeple – 8d.
Item to the plumber for his last labour in covering the south aisle – 20s.
Item to the same plumber for fining lead from the ashes – 9s.
Item to the same plumber for making a spout on the north side of the high aisles – 2s.
Item for 2 pound of pewter to solder – 8d.
£9 6s 5d.

f. 18v.

Item to a glazier for a day & a half work about windows in the bellhouse – 20d.
Item Robert Proctor[1] for riding to Lowth Park[2] & to Mablethorpe by the advice of Master Fytzwylliam – 12d.[3]

---

[1] According to the deposition of William Moreland, a former Cistercian monk of Louth Park Abbey and a key participant in the Rising, it was at Robert Proctor's house that John Heneage (c.1485–1557), the bishop's steward, was staying when the rebels forced him into the church, largely for his own safety. *L&P*, XII (i), 380, p. 174, 9 February 1536/7. Heneage was MP for Grimsby in 1523, 1529 and for the county in 1539. Bindoff, *House of Commons*, II, pp. 334–5.

[2] The site of the abbey is 2 miles east of Louth.

[3] Marginalia – 'required by Robert Brown & Richard Curson'. This is either

Item to John Smyth for his horse – 5d.
Item to George Armestrong[1] for mending the window in the clerk's chamber – 2d.
Item for the carriage of 9 sowes[2] of lead to St Mary's church from the Small Wells[3] – 3d.
Item to George Tyler for a strike of lime – 2½d.
Item to Thomas Provest & his servant for one day's work in the steeple – 10d.
Item to Robert Bayly for 80 tile for to make a fernes[4] to sieve the lead ashes with – 4d.
Item to William Haryson for 2 hoops & a vertafell[5] in the chime wheel – 8d.
Item to John Harryson for making 2 gimmers[6] for a stall door where William Foster's wife sits – 3d.
Item Thomas Provest for a day's work of himself & his servant about the bells – 10d.
Item to the said Thomas for nails to the work – 1d.
Item for mending the stop of the organs – 1d.
Item to William Harryson for 4 wedges to the bells – 4d.
Item for boards & ledges to the lodge door – 6d.
Item for meat & wage to 2 wrights for their labour about the same work of the lodge – 10d.
Item for 2 threaffs[7] of straw to the thatching of the lodge – 3d.
Item to Robert Norman for a string to Our Lady bell – 15d.
Item to Robert Brown for 4 pieces [of] timber to the churchyard & other necessaries about the bells – 16s.
Item to a broderer[8] for his work about the mending of vestments the space of a week – 10s 8d.
Item to the plumber for his labour about the steeple in part of a more sum – 3s 4d.

John Fitzwilliam of Mablethorpe (d.1547), Will: LAO, LCC, 1547–9, *f.* 162, or his son George, who also left a will, TNA, PROB 11/43/90, probate, 28 January 1559/60. Maddison, *Lincolnshire Pedigrees*, 50, pp. 357–8.

1   Armstrong was interred 5 September 1544. LAO, Goulding Papers, 5/2.

2   Possibly a derivation of 'pig of lead', crude lead as first obtained from a smelting furnace. *OED*.

3   The Small Wells were located on Bridge Street to the north of the river Lud, marked on Bayley's map of 1834. Green, *Streets of Louth*, p. 25. Bayley, *Notitiæ Ludæ*, Map, p. 211.

4   Furnace?

5   Vartiwell; part of a hinge to a gate, the eye of a gate in which the crook works. *OED*.

6   Hinges. *OED*.

7   Threshes or thraves, threaves – 'stooks of corn containing twelve sheaves each'. *OED*.

8   Brodierer – embroiderer. *OED*.

Item to the glazier for his work & stuff about mending certain holes in the windows of the church – 6s 8d.
Item to Thomas Provest for his work & one of his servants 3 days & half about making the churchyard gates & mending the steeple floor – 3s 6d.
Item to William Lathes for that space working about the same work – 20d.
Item to Thomas Boland for working that space about that work – 20d.
Item to Johnson for carriage of lead & wood 6 loads – 12d.
Item to 2 sawers for their work one day in sawing the timber to the churchyard gates & other planks – 12d.
Item to Robert Smythe for iron work about the churchyard gates – 5d.

55s 10½d.

f. 19r.

Item to the broderer for mending vestments again certain days the next week – 5s.
Item to the plumber for his whole labour about the steeple & for casting lead to the same work – 20s.
Item to Robert Bayly for nails to the steeple – 2s 4d.
Item to the Belman for covering Master Gunby's grave – 2d.[1]
Item to Robert Johnson for a stone percer[2] – 2d.
Item to William Browghton, cooper, for a garth[3] to the lime soo[4] – 1d.
Item to Robert Norman for a bell-string to the Cope bell[5] – 16d.
Item for a lantern – 18d.
Item to the plumber for his labour in fining of lead ashes & other labour about the gallery – 5s.
Item to Thomas Spencer for 1lb of wax & the making thereof into perchers[6] for the lantern – 8d.
Item to the bellman's wife for scouring the candlesticks – 6d.
Item to Thomas Provest for stuff and his labour about the mending of the stall in Our Lady choir where the old organ stood – 4s.[7]
Item to the said T[homas] for a day's work in the steeple – 6d.
Item to Richard Smythe for a strike of cherck coals to the fining of the ashes – 5d.

---

[1] Possibly William Gunby, assessed 7s 6d in the 1524/5 Lay Subsidy. TNA E179/138/478.
[2] Piercer – tool used for boring holes. *OED*.
[3] Garth – to fit with hoops. *OED*.
[4] A large tub. *OED*.
[5] Also noted as the Coo, Cay and Cove bell, but could be interpreted as 'Key'. Golding, *Cawod*, p. 6. John Ketteringham suggests the bell was rung to warn the clergy that a service was imminent and that they should vest themselves accordingly. Ketteringham, *Bells*, p. 153.
[6] A large candle or tallow. *OED*.
[7] There was an organ in the Lady choir from at least 1475/6, when it was noted in the account book of St Mary's guild. Golding, *Cawod*, p. 3. Pillans, *Organs*, p. 3.

Item for 24lbs wax to Robert Bayly for 4 tapers to bear about the sacrament bought with money gathered over Plough Day & since – 12s.
Item to Thomas Spencer for making them – 12d.
Item to Richard Smythe for cherck coals – 3d.
Item for a strike of lime – 3d.
Item to Thomas Provest for putting a bush in the steeple & mending of a stool in the church – 4d.
Item to Sir Christopher[1] for stuff & binding 2 books, a graile book[2] & the antemp book[3] – 18d.
Item to William West for wood occupied about shotting lead to the bellhouse chamber – 3s 4d.
Item to George Tyler for lime – 4d.
Item to the plumber's servant for gathering it – 4d.
£3 12d.[4]
Total paid £21 8s 3½d, [...] 52s 1d.
The total of the aforesaid to be paid £21 8s 3½d and 52s 1d to which 8d remainith in the above accounts of W[illiam] Walker instead of ringing the bells for Ann his wife deceased, and [......] 52s 9d to which 2s 6d he finds in the number of debtors. And of 4s 11d remaining of W[illiam] Kynge to the Plough Light about last year [......] and comes? 50s 2d in which they looked at the money. John Harryson senior in regards to the old bell clappers, remainder 3s 4d, and to whom? 56s 10d.
The foresaid Church Masters leaves this year in lead to the use and upholding of this church which lies in St Mary's church – 22cwt. 3 quarters.
And in solder which lies in thoche[5] – 2 stone 13 quarters.
And in [...] which lies in the lodge 2 pieces & a shore.[6]

f. 19v.

Memorandum,[7] that the honest men of this town of Lowthe desiring to have a good pair of organs[8] to the laud, praise & honour of God & the whole holy company of Heaven, made an assemble together for this said purpose on a

---

[1] This is probably Christopher Smith, curate of Withcall, who was a former Augustinian canon of Thornton Abbey, later receiving a pension of £6 13s 4d. Hodgett, *Ex-Religious*, pp. 3, 45, 103.
[2] A gradual: an antiphon or anthem sung between the epistle and the gospel during the Eucharist. *OED*.
[3] A volume of antiphons. *OED*.
[4] Marginalia – '61s'.
[5] Possibly 'the hutch'.
[6] Page damaged.
[7] Manicule in margin.
[8] This indicates a pair of bellows, not two separate instruments. Pillans, *Organs*, p. 1.

certain day at which time Master Richard Taylor,[1] priest & bachelor of law, then abiding within the Diocese of Norwich being present and hearing the good devout mind and virtuous intent of the said towns men, of his mere devotion and good natural zeal to this town, wherein he was born & brought up, offered for to cause them have a pair made of a cunning man in Lyn,[2] that should be exampled by a pair of [the same man's making who was then called Mr Bylton][3] at Ely which then had a singular praise, for the sum of 22 pounds, whereof he promised to give thereto 11 pounds, upon which promise they accorded, in so much that the said Master Tailor covenanted and bargained the organs to be made and brought to this town & set up on the north side in the High choir on St Barnabe even[4] in the year of Our Lord 1531 at which time the said 22 pounds was paid, 11 pounds by the officer or alderman of Our Lady guild then being upon the stock of Our Lady, and the other 11 pounds by the above named Master Taylor, which also, considering the goodness of the instrument, and how well it satisfied & contented the minds of the parishioners did give further at that time in reward to the maker of the said instrument for a reward beside his covenant 40s for his good diligence & well acquitting him to the said instrument, for which beneficial act I pray Jesus acquit & reward him in his kingdom of heaven. Amen for charity.
Robert Beverlay – 20d.[5]
Symon Lyncoln – 8d.
Item delivered to the Suffragan[6] in reward for hallowing of copes and albs – 10s.
Church Masters.

[1] Taylor was rector of Feltwell in Norfolk. Williamson, 'Religious Guilds', p. 88.
[2] Bishop's (King's) Lynn, Norfolk.
[3] [Marginalia]. This was William Beton or Betton, organ maker, who worked in Bishop's (King's) Lynn after completing his apprenticeship in 1518/19. In 1542/3, it was noted in the Privy Purse expenses of Princess Mary, 'paid to the servants of Betyn for mending the regals of the Princess, vijs vjd' (7s 6d). He was also organ maker to the king, receiving 5s per quarter from 1539 to 1544. A regal was a small portable organ of a type common in the sixteenth and seventeenth centuries. *OED*. Madden, *Privy Purse*, pp. 101, 212. Pillans, *Organs*, p. 5 note 4, p. 9. Williamson, 'Religious Guilds', pp. 87–8. Freeman, 'Organ Builders', pp. 26–7.
[4] Evening – the day before the feast of St Barnabas, i.e. 10th June. *OED*.
[5] This and the following two lines are crossed through.
[6] Suffragan bishops acted as assistants to the diocesan. Possible holders of the title in the Lincoln Archdeaconry during this period were: William Duffield, a Cambridge Franciscan, titled bishop of Ascalon (modern-day Israel), Robert King, abbot of Thame (Cistercian monks), recorded as bishop of Rheon *Reonensis* (Greece). Alternatively, Thomas Swillington, a Cambridge Augustinian friar titled bishop of Philadelphia (Turkey), who held the held position from 1532 to 1546. The most notable of the Lincoln suffragans was however Matthew Mackerall, abbot of Barlings and from 1535 bishop of Chalcedon (Turkey). He was executed at Tyburn in 1537 for his alleged part in the Lincolnshire Rising. Fryde et al., *Handbook*, pp. 286–7. Smith, *Heads, III*,

Robert Spencer.
William Newton.[1]
Thomas Spenythorne.
George Spillesby.[2]

f. 20r.

[1532–3]

The account of Robert Spencer, William Newton, Thomas Spenethorne & George Spillesby, Proctors of the Church of St James of Lowthe, all receipts and expenses on Sunday the Octave of Easter 1532 until the Octave of Easter 1533.[3]

Imprimis, received of the old Church Masters in money good & ill – 56s 10d.
Item in sowes of lead – 22cwt 3 quarters.
Item in solder – 2 stone 13lbs.
Item 2 long pieces of timber & 1 short piece.
     Sum 56s 10d.
Item received the 2nd Sunday after Easter – 6s.
Item received the 3rd Sunday after – 5s 6d.
Item received the 4th Sunday after – 3s 2d.
Item received the 5th Sunday after – 3s 3d.
Item received the Sunday after Ascension – 4s 7d.
Item received the Sunday of Pentecost – 6s 11d.
Item received the Sunday of Trinity – 4s 8d.
Item received the 1st Sunday after – 3s 8d.
Item received the 2nd Sunday after – 3s 11d.
Item received the 3rd Sunday after – 4s.
Item received the 4th Sunday after – 4s 4d.
Item received the 5th Sunday after – 3s 9d.
Item received the 6th Sunday after – 4s 3d.
Item received the 7th Sunday after – 4s 1d.
Item received the 8th Sunday after – 3s 6d.
Item received the 9th Sunday after – 3s 4d.

---

pp. 339, 490. Smith, 'Suffragan Bishops', pp. 26–7. Cole, *Chapter Acts*, I, pp. xiv–xv, note 2.

 [1] A William Newton is noted in the first accounts as working on the spire and recorded as churchwarden in 1518/19, noted as 'William Neuton, glover'. Goulding, *Spire*, p. 6. Dudding, *Accounts*, p. 195. Following the Rising, a man of the same name is also mentioned by William Moreland, stating that he (Moreland) 'tarried an hour' in his (Newton's) house, avoiding an angry mob. *L&P*, XII (i), 380, p. 175, 9 February 1536/7.

 [2] Spillesby was assessed at 10s in the 1524/5 Lay Subsidy. TNA, E179/138/478.

 [3] Marginalia at the top of the page contains calculations for the sum of £10 14s 6d.

Item received the 10th Sunday after – 4s 8d.
Item received the 11th Sunday after – 4s 6d.
Item received the 12th Sunday after – 4s.
Item received the 13th Sunday after – 3s 10d.
Item received the 14th Sunday after – 4s.
Item received the 15th Sunday after – 3s 4d.[1]
Item received the 16th Sunday after – 4s 8d.
Item received the 17th Sunday after – 3s 11d.
Item received the 18th Sunday after – 3s 5d.
Item received the 19th Sunday after – 3s.
Item received the 20th Sunday after – 4s 9d.
Item received the 21st Sunday after – 3s 8d.
Item received the 22nd Sunday after – 3s 6d.
Item received the 23rd Sunday after – 4s 4d.
Item received the 24th – 4s 8d.
Item received the 25th Sunday after – 3s 10d.
Item received the 26th Sunday after – 4s 4d.
Item received the first Sunday of Advent – 3s.
Item received the 2nd Sunday of Advent – 3s 4d.
Item received the 3rd Sunday of Advent – 2s 11d.
Item received the 4th Sunday of Advent – 4s 4d.
Item received the Sunday after Nativity – 3s 4d.
Item received the Sunday after Circumcision – 4s.[2]

f. 20v.

Burials in the church.[3]

First, Ysabell Ratheby – 6s 8d.[4]
Item received the 1st Sunday after Epiphany – 4s.
Item received the 2nd Sunday after – 3s 9d.
Item received the 3rd Sunday after Epiphany – 3s 8d.
Item received the 4th Sunday after – 3s 8d.
Item received the Sunday of *Septuagesima* – 3s 6d.
Item received the Sunday of *Sexagesima* – 3s 8d.
Item received the Sunday of *Quinquagesima* – 3s.[5]
Item received the first Sunday of *Quadragesima* – 5s.
Item received the 2nd Sunday of *Quadragesima* – 3s 2d.
Item received the 3rd Sunday of *Quadragesima* – 3s 10d.
Item received the 4th Sunday of *Quadragesima* – 3s 8d.

---

1   '14th' crossed through.
2   Marginalia – '£10 15s 1d'.
3   Crossed through.
4   Crossed through. Ysabell – Isabel.
5   Marginalia – '25s 3d'.

Item received the Sunday in Passion – 3s 8d.
Item received Palm Sunday – 4s 8d.
Item received Easter Day – 3s 4d.
Item received the Sunday after Easter – 3s 8d.
56s 3d.
Item received for the bull hide – 20d.
20d.

Witwords to the churches.

Imprimis, William Gaunce[1] of Thedlethorpe to St James's church – 12d.
Item William Baker of Saltfletby to St James's church – 13s 4d. [2]
Item John Taulx to St Mary's church – 4d.
14s 8d.

Burials in the church.

First, Ysabell Ratheby, senior – 6s 8d.
Item Joanne, daughter [of] Martin Mesterchamber in south porch.[3]
Item William Smyth – 6s 8d.[4]
Item Ellen, wife [of] John Forman[5] – 6s 8d.
Item Robert Smythe – 6s 8d.
Item Elizabeth, daughter of Thomas Foster in south church porch – 3s 4d.
Item William Foster – 6s 8d.
36s 8d.
Sum – £5 9s 3d.

f. 21r.

Great bells ringing.

First, Robert Beverlay – 20d.
Item Symon Lyncoln – 8d.
Item Joanna Williamson – 12d.

---

[1] William Gaunce of Theddlethorpe St Helen's left a will dated 12 March 1531/2, in which he donated 'to st Jamys churche at Louthe xijd [12d]', and to 'St John chapel in the market place vjd [6d].' Foster, *Lincoln Wills, III*, pp. 219–20. His inventory showed a possible wealth of at least £67 2s 8d (document damaged). LAO, Inventories, Box 4, p. 38, 7 March 1531/2.

[2] Marginalia – '14s 8d'. William Baker of Saltfleetby All Saints' left a will dated 10 May 1532, in which he donated 'to the reparacions of the paryshe churche of st Jamys in Louthe, xiijs iiijd [13s 4d]'. In his testament, he requests that 'my mansion or dwellyng house with the appurtenances in Louthe, wich I of late bought of William Lincoln merchande be solde be my executors ...' Foster, *Lincoln Wills*, III, pp. 230–1. An inventory records his wealth after debts at £120 3s 4d – a considerable sum for the period. LAO, Inventories, Box 4, p. 67, 16 May 1532.

[3] No amount stated.

[4] A William Smyth was assessed at £15 in the 1524/5 Lay Subsidy. TNA, E179/138/478.

[5] Forman was assessed at £10 in the 1524/5 Lay Subsidy. TNA, E179/138/478.

Item Robert Westmold, Gentleman – 8d.
Item brethren & sisters of [the] Trinity guild – 8d.
Item John Gyrdycke – 8d.
Item John Cawod – 8d.
Item Ysabell Ratheby – 20d.
Item Ysabell Ratheby – 8d.
Item Gylbard Archebold – 20d.
Item John Langholme, gentleman – 8d.
Item John Haulton – 20d.
Item John & *Frater* – 20d.
Item William Procter – 8d.
Item John son [of] Martin Mesterchamber.[1]
Item John Louthe – 20d.
Item William, son [of] Robert Frow[2] – 8d.
Item William Smythe – 8d.
Item John Chapman, gentleman – 20d.
Item John Hareyson, senior – 8d.
Item Thomas Bradley, senior – 20d.
Item John Tauk – 8d.
Item John Parnell – 8d.
Item Rowland Munday – 8d.
Thomas Beverlay, senior – 20d.
Thomas Allerton – 20d.
John Jenkenson – 8d.
Stephan Parcens – 8d.
Ellen, wife [of] John Forman – 20d.
Thomas Gyrdyck & John Moore – 12d.
William Barnard – 20d.[3]
Item Richard Carter, chaplain – 20d.
Item Elizabeth, daughter [of] T[homas] Foster – 8d.
Item Robert Beverlay – 20d.[4]
Item William Foster – 20d.
Item Simond Lyncoln – 8d.

Sum – 39s.
Total sum received – £18 3s 4d.

f. 21v.

Ministers in the church.

First, William Foster by year – 26s 8d.
Item Thomas Foster – 26s 8d.

[1] No amount stated.
[2] A Robert Fro is noted in the first accounts as working on the spire. Goulding, *Spire*, p. 6.
[3] Marginalia – '31s'.
[4] Marginalia – '36s 8d'.

Item the keeper of the clock and chime – 10s.
Item for the blowing of the organs – 3s 4d.
Item Cloble's wife for washing clothes to the altar – 2s.
Item Bellman for cleansing the church – 2s 8d.
Item Tace for keeping the bells – 4s.
Item Nicholas Upton in fee – 6s 8d.
Item Thomas Provest in fee – 6s 8d.
Item for writing this account – 6s 8d.
Sum – £4 15s 4d.
Expenses about the church.
Imprimis, given to my Lord Suffragan for a reward for hallowing of copes & albs – 10s.
Item to John White's wife for washing and mending certain albs – 2d.
Item for 2 bulls – 25s 2d.
Item to the smiths for mending the bell clappers and for 3 men for their labour 2 days in helping them about the said work – 8s 3d.
Item to John Wright for making of the ladder – 3d.
Item to the smith for mending the bell clappers in full contention[1] of his duty & for 2 workmen for helping him 2 days – 7s 4d.
Item to Robert Spencer for 2 quarters of coals to the bell clappers – 3s 6d.
Item to Richard Syll for 2 staples & a sneck to the church yard gates – 2d.
Item to John Tace for bearing bell clappers up & down – 4d.
Item to Thomas Spenythorne for a ladder, stool and steps – 5d.
Item to Richard Smythe for cherck coals to the censers,[2] half a strike – 3d.
Item for hanging the choir at Corpus Christi tide – 6d.
Item for watching in the church at Corpus Christi tide – 4d.
Item to Robert Goldsmyth for stuff to the silver candlestick & the mending thereof – 16d.
To John Tace for fetching a bottell[3] of stayes[4] to the bells from Burwell Wood – 2d.
Item to Thomas Provest for his work one day in the steeple – 6d.
Item to Thomas Atkins for sweeping the aisle windows of the church from spynner webs[5] – 2d.
f. 22r.
Item for the carriage of 2 loads of stone from Marshchapell bought by Nicholas Upton for paving the church as apperits[6] *Anno* 1530 – 3d.
Item to a smith for mending the chime wheel – 2d.
Item to Robert Bayly for iron occupied about the bell clappers – 6s 8d.

---

[1] The action of contenting or satisfying. *OED*.
[2] A thurible – a vessel in which incense is burnt. *OED*.
[3] A bundle of straw weighing 7lbs. *OED*.
[4] Rope generally supporting an upright pole or mast. *OED*.
[5] Spider webs.
[6] Manicule in margin. Apparent – manifest. *OED*.

Item to Robert Smythe for a gogeon[1] to the Trinity bell & for mending a gate – 12d.
Item for a skin for covering a Legend Booke[2] – 8d.
Item to old Father Anthony for watching the church on St James's day – 1d.
Item to Thomas Provest for helping the Trinity bell – 8d.
Item to Sir Christopher for paper (3d), mowth glue (2d),[3] & his labour (3d), in covering the Legend Book & clasps (2d) thereto – 10d.
Item to William Kyng which he laid forth for the church business and suit in seeking out for old Master Bradley's will[4] – 6s 8d.
Item to William Goldsmyth[5] for mending 2 cruets[6] – 2s 8d.
Item for nails to the steeple door – 1d.
Item for 2 staples to the spryncle[7] at the south church door – 1d.
Item for a key to the clock house door – 2d.
Item to Robert Forman for a bell-string to Our Lady bell – 15d.
Item to Henry Deane for 2 strings, one to [the] cope bell & another to the Morrow Mass bell – 2d.
Item for 2 thresse of straw for litter[8] to the lodge – 3d.
Item to Fawer for 2 loads of clay to the lodge – 4d.
Item to Richard Spencer for walling about the same one day and a half – 6d.
Item to John Burrett for his work about the same 2 days – 8d.
Item to John Rede for stowryng[9] there – 5d.
Item for nails to the stowryng thereof – 2d.
Item for a stoth[10] & stores to the same lodge – 11d.

[1] Gudgeon – a pivot, usually of metal, fixed on or let into the end of a beam, spindle, axle, etc., and on which a wheel turns, a bell swings. *OED*.
[2] A book of lessons from the scriptures. Foster, *Cambridge*, p. 480. Alternatively, the *Golden Legend* by Jacobus de Voragine (c.1230–98) or similar containing the lives of the saints. *OED*.
[3] Mouth-glue – a compound of glue and sugar. *OED*.
[4] TNA, PROB 11/20/238, probate, October 1521.
[5] A William Goldsmith was churchwarden in 1512/13. Dudding, *Accounts*, p. 141. At the start of the Rising, it was at Goldsmith's house near the Saracen's Head that the rebels captured John Frankish, the bishop's registrar, who had earlier arrived to oversee the deanery visitation and the enforcement of the 'Ten Articles'. Ward, *Rising*, p. 14.
[6] A small vessel to hold wine or water for use in the celebration of the Eucharist. *OED*.
[7] Brush used in holy water stoup (*OED*).
[8] Probably to scatter the threshes on the floor.
[9] 'Felling willows for the stakes (*le stowryng*)', for a new barn. LRS, vol. 85, p. 55.
[10] Stooth – a post, an upright lath; one of the upright battens in a lath-and-plaster wall. *OED*.

Item to William Graye for a throwgh[1] & the laying over thereof in Our Lady choir – 13s 4d.
Item to Thomas[2] Spencer for 4 torches or lyncks[3] to seke[4] the church with – 3s 8d.
Item to the glazier for glass & solder & workmanship about the steeple windows & the west end – 4s.
Item to William Smyth for bars to the windows & a lock to the steeple door – 12d.
Item to William Graye & a servant of his & [a]other 2 masons for their labour a space of one week about dressing the choirs & the church – 8s 8d.
Item to Nicholas Upton for his labour one week about hewing of stone & another weeks work about the foresaid choirs & middle aisle – 5s 2d.
Item to sawers for one day's work in sawing a piece of timber for the organs that was taken forth of the lodge – 7d.
Item to Newton for wood to the glazier – 5d.
Item to George Tyler for a strike of lime – 2½d.
Item to Newton for a horse hide – 14d.
Item to Fawer for leading down a spout to Stewton Gate – 2d.
Item to 2 labourers for feying[5] the sewer & working there by the space of 2 days to meat & wages – 14d.
Item to Thomas Provest for 3 days work about the bells & mending the stalls in the church – 18d.
Item to George Tyler for a piece of wood for the spout aforesaid – 16d.
Item to Thomas Provest for his work about the bell wheel & removing the new organs – 4s.
Item to a smith for 3 wedges of iron to the bells – 2d.[6]

f. 22v.

Item to John Whyte for to buy 2 quires of paper for to make new books to prick[7] in new masses and antyumes[8] – 8d.
Item to Matthew Bellman for scouring the candlesticks against Christmas – 6d.
Item to the same Matthew for cleansing the grate at the church stile – 1d.
Item to William Smythe for mending a stop of the new organs – 3d.
Item to the same Smythe for making a chain & a pin with a staple to the chime wheel – 2d.
Item to Richard Kychen for a provand of cherkyd coals for the censers – 3d.

---

1. Trough – in this case, a stone coffin or sarcophagus. *OED*.
2. 'Nicholas' crossed through.
3. A torch made of pitch. *OED*.
4. Search?
5. To fit, adapt or join. *OED*.
6. Marginalia – '£3 14s 9½d'.
7. Copying, also a mark or dot used in musical notation – setting to music. *OED*.
8. Antiphon.

Item to the smith for making a key to a lock for the west door & a piece of iron to the chime – 4d.

Item for Master Lytherland's[1] costs when he came after Christmas – 2s 5d.

Item to the plumber & his 2 servants for working 3 days at St Mary's church – 4s.

Item to George Tyler for a strike of lime – 2½d.

Item to a workman at St Mary's church for one day's work there in filling under the lead where the plumber had wrought – 4d.

Item for a string to the clock – 10d.

Item for the mending of certain books pertaining to the choir & covering of them – 7s.

Item to Thomas Provest for 2 boards to the covering of the said books – 4d.

Item to the same Provest for mending a bell wheel – 4d.

Item to Nicholas Upton in allowance for the charge of the stone that he bought that was more than 8s that he received to the buying thereof of William Brown & others being Church Masters with him as apperith more plainly by the charge of their accounts, *Anno Domini* 1530 – 17d.[2]

Item to Robert Bayly for nails taken at diverse times – 10d.

Item to James Glasyer for his work 5 days about mending the windows in the church & for glass & solder to the same – 6s.

Item to William Smythe for making 4 staples & 2 hasps[3] to the pulpit where the chime plumb runs in – 5d.

Item for scouring the candlesticks in the High choir against Easter – 6d.

Item to James Glasyer for glassing & finding stuff thereto at St Mary's church – 2s 4d.

Item to Robert Spencer for finding 2 bulls in the winter – 6s 8d.[4]

Item to Thomas Provest in part of payment of his bargain for the covering of the font – 53s 4d.

Item to Master Lytherland for his coming down to keep the court at after Christmas 13s 4d.

Item to a learned man for his council in the same matter pertaining to Master Bradley – 3s 4d.

Item for mending the bell at St Mary's church – 16s 6d.

Item to Walter Fyshwycke for yncle[5] to reusing girdles – 4d.

---

[1] This is probably Henry Litherland, the last treasurer of Lincoln cathedral (1535–8), who in 1522 was noted as keeper of the altar of St Peter. Cole, *Chapter Acts,* I, p. 28. In 1532, he was appointed parish priest at Newark in Nottinghamshire. Litherland was executed at York in 1538 for his alleged part in the Pilgrimage of Grace. Lehmberg, *Cathedrals,* p. 74.

[2] Marginalia with manicule – '18s 8½d'.

[3] A hinged clasp of metal. *OED.*

[4] Marginalia – '29s, 35s'.

[5] Incle – Linen tape. *OED.*

Item to Richard Kychen for cherkyd coals – 3d.
Item to Atkyn for sweeping spinning webs forth of the aisle windows – 1d.
Item to T[homas] Provest for trussing[1] the Trinity bell & other things doing in the church – 6d.
Item to George Tyler for lime – 2d.
Item to Thomas Provest in more payment of his bargain [......] 6s 8d.[2]
f. 23r.
Total to be paid aforesaid £17 19s 2d, and ... 4s 2d, and to certain ... 2s .... 10d. And there remains 3s 4d.
It is agreed by the commontye[3] of this town that Robert Beverlay,[4] singingman, shall yearly have of the common pece 10s for every quarter from hence forth unto such time as he be priest.
And at this said account John Spencer hath delivered unto the hands of the Church Masters which are now new elect and chosen, 40s in ready money which belonging to the Common Cart.
Memorandum, that Agnes Moore, widow, of her devotion hath given to the honour of God one cross cloth[5] of green sarsenet[6] having on it the Assumption of Our Lady which cloth was bought for 20s, of the costs & charge of the said Agnes Moore & Isabell the wife of William Asseby this year.
New Church Masters for the next year following.
William Kynge.
Robert Dughty.[7]
William Browne, barber.
Robert Proctor.
f. 23v.
Item received the second Sunday after Easter – 5s 8d.
Item for making the indentures of the inell[8] – 2d.

---

1 Tying or packing, or alternatively rehanging. *OED*. Foster, *Cambridge*, p. 484.
2 Page torn at the foot; parts of the line missing.
3 Body of the common people, commonalty, commons. *OED*.
4 In 1548, Robert Beverlay was chaplain of the Trinity guild at the age of forty. He never married and received a pension of £5 13s 4d from 17 December 1544. He was a parish chaplain in the 1550s and possessing lands worth 40s p.a. Foster and Thompson, 'Chantry Certificates', 36, p. 279. Hodgett, *Ex-Religious*, pp. 53, 103. Williamson, 'Religious Guilds', p. 89.
5 A veil covering the Rood figures during Lent. Foster, *Cambridge*, p. 478.
6 Very fine, soft silk material. *OED*.
7 Robert Doughty was churchwarden in 1522/3 and alderman of the Lady guild in 1537 and 1538. Dudding, *Accounts*, p. 217. Goulding, *Corporation Records*, p. 169. He was assessed at £6 13s 4d in the 1524/5 Lay Subsidy. TNA, E179/138/478. Will: TNA, PROB 11/34/36, probate, 30 January 1550/1. Interred 15 July 1550 as *Paterfamilias*. LAO, Goulding Papers, 5/2.
8 Definition unknown.

f. 24r.

[1533–4]

The account of William Kyng, Robert Doughty, Robert Proctor & William Browne, barber, Proctors of the Church of St James of Lowthe, all receipts and expenses on Sunday the Octave of Easter 1533 until the Octave of Easter 1534.
Imprimis, received of the Church Masters in money good & ill – 3s 4d.

Sum – 3s 4d.

Item in sowes of lead.[1]
Item in solder.
Item remaining in the lodge, 1 long piece of timber & one short piece.
Memorandum, that Martyn Mynysterchamber oweth 3s 4d for the burial of John his son in the south porch & for bells ringing for the same John.
William Walker for his wife ringing 4 years.[2]
Imprimis, received the second Sunday after Easter – 5s 8d.
Item the 3rd Sunday – 5s 8d.
Item the 4th Sunday – 3s 6d.
Item the 5th Sunday after – 4s.
Item the 6th Sunday after – 3s 8d.
Item received the Sunday of Pentecost – 5s 1d.
Item received the Sunday of Trinity – 5s 4d.
Item received the 1st Sunday after – 4s 4d.
Item received the 2nd Sunday after – 4s 3d.
Item received the 3rd Sunday after – 4s 8d.
Item received the 4th Sunday after – 3s 5d.
Item received the 5th Sunday after – 4s 10d.
Item received the 6th Sunday after – 2s 10d.
Item received the 7th Sunday after – 3s 11d.
Item received the 8th Sunday after – 4s 2d.
Item received the 9th Sunday after – 4s.
Item received the 10th Sunday after – 4s 3d.
Item received the 11th Sunday after – 4s 8d.
Item received the 12th Sunday after – 3s 4d.
Item received the 13th Sunday after – 3s 4d.
Item received the 14th Sunday after – 3s 11d.
Item received the 15th Sunday after – 3s 5d.
Item received the 16th Sunday after – 3s 6d.
Item received the 17th Sunday – 4s.
Item received the 18th Sunday after – 4s 2d.
Item received the 19th Sunday after – 3s 7d.
Item received the 20th Sunday after – 3s 6d.
Item received the 21st Sunday after – 3s 7d.

[1] No amount stated in this and the following two items.
[2] No amount stated.

Item received the 22nd Sunday after – 3s 3d.
Item received the 23rd Sunday after – 3s 4d.
Item received the 24th Sunday after – 3s 2d.
Item received the first Sunday of Advent – 3s 4d.
Item received the second Sunday of Advent – 3s 1d.
Item received the third Sunday of Advent – 4s 4d.
Item received the fourth Sunday – 3s 6d.
Item received the Sunday after Nativity – 3s 6d.
Item received the Sunday after Circumcision – 3s.
Item received the Sunday after Epiphany – 3s 10d.
Sum – £7 8s 11d.

f. 24v.
Item received the first Sunday after the Octave of Epiphany – 3s.
Item received the 2nd Sunday after – 3s 11d.
Item received the Sunday of *Septuagesima* – 3s 2d.
Item received the Sunday of *Sexagesima* – 3s 8d.
Item received the Sunday of *Quinquagesima* – 3s 1d.
Item received the Sunday of *Quadragesima* – 3s 3d.
Item received the 2nd Sunday of *Quadragesima* – 3s 1d.
Item received the 3rd Sunday of *Quadragesima* – 3s 8d.
Item received the 4th Sunday of *Quadragesima* – 4s.
Item received the Sunday in Passion – 3s 6d.
Item received the Palm Sunday – 3s 6d.
Item received on Good Friday – 4s 1d.
Item received the Sunday after Easter – 4s 6d.
Sum – 46s 5d.
Total of sum collected – £9 15s 4d.
Burials in the churches.

Imprimis, Agnes, wife [of] John Richardson, litster[1] – 6s 8d.
Item Agnes, wife [of] Richard Walker, saddler – 6s 8d.
Item Robert Raynyard – 6s 8d.
Item Alice Talks – 6s 8d.
Sum – 26s 8d.
Witwords to the church.

Imprimis, William Foster to St Mary's church – 12d.
Item Agnes, wife [of] Richard Walker, saddler, to the same – 12d.
Sum – 2s.

f. 25r.
Great bells ringing.

Imprimis, John Williamson – 12d.
Item William Foster – 20d.

---

[1] Litster – a dyer of cloth or someone who makes the edging to a garment. *OED*. Gurnham, *History of Louth*, p. 34. A John Richardson, noted as 'lister', was churchwarden in 1502/3 and 1506/7. Dudding, *Accounts*, pp. 31, 85.

Item Robert Westmold, gentleman – 8d.
Item d John Whyt – 8d.
Item John Gyrdyke – 8d.
Item Robert Wytton, senior – 8d.
Item Richard Ratheby & wife – 8d.
Item Agnes, wife [of] John Richardson, litster – 20d.
Item John Langholme – 8d.
Item Sir John Whyte & Brothers of St Mary's guild – 20d.
Item Agnes, wife [of] Thomas Goshawke – 8d.
Item Elizabeth, wife [of] Robert Johnson, husbandman – 8d.
Item Agnes, wife [of] Richard Walker, saddler – 20d.
Item John Lowthe – 20d.
Item Joanne, daughter [of] Thomas Provost – 8d.
Item Robert, son [of] Henry Sawnderson,[1] shoemaker – 8d.
Item Cecely, wife [of] Robert Richardson – 8d.
Item Thomas Bradlaye, senior – 20d.
John Parnell – 8d.
Thomas Colton, walker – 8d.
Thomas Beverlay – 20d.
Thomas Allerton – 20d.
Stephan Parcens – 8d.[2]
Thomas Gyrdyck & John More – 12d.
Robert Raynyard – 8d.
Item Alice Talks – 20d.
Item John Cade – 8d.
Item Robert Beverlay – 20d.

Sum – 29s 4d.
Total sum received – £12 16s 8d.

f. 25v.

Ministers in the church.

Item Thomas Foster by year – 26s 8d.
Item Robert Beverlay – 20s.
Item the keeper of the clock & chime – 10s.
Item for blowing the organs – 3s 4d.
Item Cloble's wife for washing napery pertaining to the High altar – 2s.
Item the bellman for cleansing the church – 2s 8d.

---

[1] Following the Rising, Nicholas Melton stated that 'it was determined to hang John Beilowe [Bellow] and Mylsent [John Millicent], my Lord Cromwell's servants, who were at Legbourne [priory], [and that] Henry Sanderson [and others] cried to hang them, and the said Sanderson offered wood for a gallows'. *L&P*, XI, 968, p. 390. A Henry Saunderson was buried 15 March 1542/3. LAO, Goulding Papers, 5/2.

[2] 'Gyrdyck' crossed through.

Item Tace for keeping the bells – 4s.
Item Nicholas Upton in fee – 6s 8d.
Item Thomas Provest in fee – 6s 8d.
Item for writing this account – 6s 8d.
Sum – £4 8s 8d.
Expenses about the church.
Imprimis, to my Lord Suffragan for his reward – 6s 5d.
Item for writing the indentures of the wills – 4d.
Item for nails – 1d.
Item to a labourer for his work one day about Aswell[1] – 4d.
Item to 4 men for their labour one day at Aswell – 16d.
Item to William Cawod for making a letter of attorney – 4d.
Item to John Kyrchen[2] for railing at Aswell – 8d.
Item to a labourer there – 4d.
Item to James the glazier for gultyng[3] the cross that be at the new cross cloth ends – 20d.
Item to Thomas Carver for making the copes & the staff – 6d
Item for making 3 pins to the feretor – 2d.
Item for hanging the choir at Corpus Christi day – 8d.
Item for watching the church at the same time – 4d.
Item for carriage away of muck & bringing of stone to the west end of the church – 4d.
Item for mending the lock of the clock house door – 1d.
Item to Thomas Provest for a day's work of himself & one of his servants about the bells – 12d.
Item to William Smythe for wedges to the bells – 2d.
Item for nails – 1d.
Item to Thomas Atkyn for cleansing the aisle windows from spinning webs – 2d.
Item to Tace for raising [the] James bell clapper[4] up & down the steeple – 1d.
Item for nails to be kept in store bought on the fair day[5] – 19d.
Item to Richard Kytchen for a strike of cherkyd coals – 4d.
Sum – 16s 11d.

[1] Aswell or Ashwell Spring, mentioned in documents from 1263 onwards, was the primary source of fresh water in the town and allegedly named after an ancient ash tree. Gurnham, *History of Louth*, p. 20.

[2] A John Keycham was assessed at £6 in the 1524/5 Lay Subsidy. TNA, E179/138/478.

[3] Gilding.

[4] The clapper weighed 121 lbs (51.8kg). Goulding, *Cawod*, p. 7.

[5] Fairs lasting around eight days were held on the third Sunday after Easter, St James's day (25 July) and St Martin's day (11 November). They subsequently came under the auspices of the Corporation. For details, see Goulding, *Markets and Fairs*.

f. 26r.
Item to William Smythe for 4 bars to the chime – 2d.
Item to Henry Deane for a bell-string to the Trinity bell – 2s 2d.
Item for mending the highway to the East Field – 4d.
Item to Robert Spencer for the church business against Master Bradley[1] – 6s 8d.
Item to Nicholas Upton for mending the cross in the Marketstead[2] – 7d.
Item to John Beldy for a horse hide to the bell clappers – 2s.
Item to Thomas Goshalke for warning men of the town to come to the church where agreement was made betwixt the town & Mr Bradlay – 2d.
Item to a smith for a gudgyng [to] a bell – 4d
Item given in a reward to a singingman for the copy of an antyme & his labour in the choir 2 days – 12d.
Item to William Kyng for nails about the bells – 2d.
Item to Thomas Provest for his labour 2 days in the steeple – 12d.
Item to the same Thomas for the silver cross staff – 10d.
Item to old Norman for a bell-string of 12 pounds – 16d.
Item to John Deane for a bell-string of 10 pounds – 13d.
Item to the smith of Spyttell Hyll for his work about mending a bell clapper at St Mary's church – 6d.
Item to Atkyn for sweeping the aisle windows – 1d.
Item to T[homas] Provest for a new wheel to a bell at St Mary's church – 3s 4d.
Item to Tace for cleansing the bell loft at St Mary's church – 3d.
Item to William Worslaye for making 20 nails of silver to the great cross and for [an] ounce weight of silver – 2s 2d.
Item for a quartern[3] of canvas & packthread[4] occupied about the chime – 1½d.
Item for candles about the same chime occupied – 1d.
Item to the clocksmith of Hull for mending the clock & chime paid on St Andrew's day[5] – 5s.
Item to a man for spyttelyng[6] the dirt from the church walls round about the church to his meat and wages – 7d.
Item for carriage away of the same & the purgyng[7] of the leads – 9d.[8]

[1] This is probably Thomas Bradley, merchant of the Staple, who married the widow of Richard Goodrick of Bolingbroke. Their son John (d.1590) was also a staple merchant. Swaby, *History of Louth*, p. 181. Maddison, *Lincolnshire Pedigrees*, 50, p. 169.
[2] For discussion on the cross, see Everson and Stocker, 'Markitte Stede', pp. 330–71.
[3] A quarter or fourth part. *OED*.
[4] A strong cord or twine used for sewing or tying up packs or bundles. *OED*.
[5] November.
[6] Spittling – to dig in or pare with a spittle, a spade. *OED*.
[7] Cleaning.
[8] '8d' crossed through.

Item to William Smythe in the town for mending the same work to the clock & chime immediately broken after the last mending, for his coals & wages and for mending the great lock of the south church door – 4s 1d.
Item to Robert Bayly for iron occupied about the same work & wire, and for nails occupied about the steeple – 2s 8d.
Item to the neterd for seeking the common bull – 2d.
Item to Thomas Provest for one day's work in the steeple – 6d.
Item for a bushel of coals to the clerk watching in the church at Christmas holydays – 6d.
Item for cherkyd coals to the censers – 2d.
Item for scouring the candlesticks against Christmas – 6d.
Item to Nicholas Upton for lime & stone occupied in the steeple & for workmanship – 15d.
Item for a strike of lime – 3d.
Item to Nicholas Upton for hewing stone ready to be occupied to the windows of St James's church – 2s 8d.
Item to Norman for a bell-string & a line to the vale[1] – 18d.
Item to James Glasyer for glass & mending the high windows of the north aisle – 3s 4d.

Sum – 47s 11½d.

f. 26v.
Item to James the gylter[2] for his stuff and labour in gilding St George – 46s 8d.
Item to Thomas Provest for making the scaffold about St George at that time he was gilded for the workman to stand upon – 5s.
Item to Henry Deane for a bell-string to St George bell – 12d.
Item to Thomas Provest for his work one day in the steeple – 6d.
Item for dightyng[3] St George suerde[4] – 5d.
Item to William Smythe for mending the clock[5] to the Rood loft door – 8d.
Item to Thomas Provest for a table that *Sanctus & Agnus*[6] be prycked[7] over the choir – 4d.
Item to John Rede & Robert West for watching four nights in the church – 12d.
Item for cherkyd coals against Easter – 3d.
Item to said John & Robert for watching five nights in the church – 15d.
Item to the bellman's wife for scouring the candlesticks against Easter – 6d.

[1] Veil.
[2] Gilder.
[3] Dighting – to dress, prepare. *OED*.
[4] Sword?
[5] Probably lock.
[6] Both settings for the Mass.
[7] Pricked, copied or marked with musical notation. *OED*. The 'table' was probably a wooden board.

Item to Thomas Provest for the making of the scaffold about St George at the time of his gilding – 5s.[1]
Item to Thomas Provest for one day work in the steeple – 6d.
Sum – £3 4s 9d.[2]
Item paid to William Assheby for a pair beads to St George's head – 4d.
Item paid a year to James the gilder for his labours and reward in gilding St George – 13s 4d.
Item given in reward to Thomas Carver for making the covering of the font with part of his wage – 19s.

   Total to be paid predicted £12 5s 5½d, and so remains 4s 8d
Church Masters.[3]
Walter Fyswyk.
Hugh Beverlay.[4]
John Browne, younger.[5]
Robert Acred, cardmaker.[6]

f. 27r.

Item it is agreed by the parishioners[7] assembled at this account that to the buying of scale ladders, making iron hooks & other things necessary for resing[8] about scathe fires[9] in times of need there shall be taken of Our Lady guild (6s 8d), of the Trinity guild (6s 8½d) of Corpus Christi guild (3s 4d), of St Peter's guild (3s 4d) and of the Plough light (23d).
Overseers of the foresaid works.
Thomas Foster.
Thomas Carver.
Buyers of the ladder kans.[10]
Robert Browne.

---

[1] Line crossed through.

[2] Crossed through.

[3] '24s 8½d' noted at foot of page.

[4] Hugh Beverley, mercer, was churchwarden in 1522/3 and 1534/5. Dudding, *Accounts*, p. 217. Williamson, 'Religious Guilds', p. 89. He was interred 2 January 1544/5. LAO, Goulding Papers, 5/2.

[5] Following the Rising, a John Brown of Louth made a declaration implicating various people. He also stated that 'it was published that the Bishop's Chancellor would take away the jewels of the church', the initial catalyst for the revolt. *L&P*, XI, 854, p. 343, 24 October 1536.

[6] A maker of cards for combing wool. *OED*. Robert Acred, Acrid, Acarhed was interred 31 May 1563. LAO, Goulding Papers, 5/2.

[7] 'Parishioners' is possibly a term used to describe a committee or vestry to oversee the running of the church and perhaps the appointment of the churchwardens.

[8] To attack or assault (the fire)? *OED*. Goulding suggests 'refuge'. Goulding, Papers, 5/3.

[9] A destructive fire or conflagration. *OED*.

[10] Leather cans – buckets? LAO, Goulding, Papers, 5/3.

Robert Baily.
f. 27v. [blank].

f. 28r.

[1534–5]

The account of Walter Fyswyck, Hugo Beverlay, mercer, John Browne, junior, Draper & Robert Acred, cardmaker, Proctors of the Church of St James of Lowthe, all receipts and expenses on Sunday the Octave of Easter 1534 until the Octave of Easter 1535.

Imprimis, received of the Church Masters that were the year before in money – 4s 8d.
Item in sowes of lead lying in St Mary's church – 22cwt 3 quarters.
Item in solder lying in the Church Master's hutch – 2 stone & 13lbs.
Item 2 pieces of timber remaining in the lodge, one long piece.
Memorandum, that Martyn Mynysterchamber oweth 3s 4d, for the burial of John his son in the south porch & for ringing of the Trinity bell to the same.
Item William Walker for his wife's ringing 4 years.[1]

Received with the pece.[2]

First, received the second Sunday after Easter – 4s.
Item received the 3rd Sunday – 8s 5d.
Item received the 4th Sunday – 3s 4d.
Item received the 5th Sunday – 3s 8d.
Item received the Sunday after Ascension – 3s 2d.
Item received the Sunday of Pentecost – 5s 8d.
Item received the Sunday of Trinity – 3s 4d.
Item received the 1st Sunday after – 4s.
Item received the 2nd Sunday after – 3s 4d.
Item received the 3rd Sunday after – 4s 6d.
Item received the 4th Sunday after – 3s 4d.
Item received the 5th Sunday after – 5s.
Item received the 6th Sunday after – 2s 10d.
Item received the 7th Sunday after – 6s 8d.
Item received the 8th Sunday – 3s 7d.
Item received the 9th Sunday – 3s 11d.
Item received the 10th Sunday – 3s 4d.
Item received the 11th Sunday – 5s 7d.
Item received the 12th Sunday – 3s 8d.
Item received the 13th Sunday – 4s 3d.
Item received the 14th Sunday – 3s 5d.

[1] No amount stated.
[2] 'Pece' – piece: money collected piece by piece as in the Sunday collections. Goulding, *Grammar School*, p. 7. Clive Burgess suggests *precium*, price or value. Burgess, *Church Book*, p. xlii.

Item received the 15th Sunday – 4s 5d.
Item received the 16th Sunday – 3s 1d.
Item received the 17th Sunday – 5s.
Item received the 18th Sunday – 3s 4d.
Item received the 19th Sunday – 4s 8d.
Item received the 20th Sunday – 3s.
Item received the 21st Sunday – 3s 6d.
Item received the 22nd Sunday – 3s 7d.
Item received the 23rd Sunday – 4s 4d.[1]
Item received the 25th Sunday – 3s 1d.
Item received the 26th Sunday – 3s 10d.
Item received the first Sunday of Advent – 2s 6d.
Item received the second Sunday of Advent – 4s 9d.
Item received the third Sunday of – 3s 3d.
Item received the fourth Sunday – 4s 2d.
£7 5s 4d.

f. 28v.
Item received the Sunday after Nativity – 3s 7d.
Item received the Sunday after the Circumcision – 4s 5d.
Item received the Sunday after Epiphany – 2s 10d.
Item received the Sunday after Octave Epiphany – 5s 2d.
Item received the Sunday of *Septuagesima* – 3s.
Item received the Sunday of *Sexagesima* – 4s 4d.
Item received the Sunday of *Quinquagesima* – 3s.
Item received the Sunday of *Quadragesima* – 5s 2d.
Item received the second Sunday of *Quadragesima* – 2s 9d.
Item received the third Sunday – 3s 5d.
Item received the fourth Sunday – 3s 5d.
Item received Passion Sunday – 4s 7d.
Item received Palm Sunday – 4s.
Item received Easter Day – 4s 8d.
Item received the Sunday after Easter – 2s 4d.
Sum – 56s 8d.
Burials in the church & witwords.
Imprimis, given by Thomas Spencer to the upholding of the church when Agnes his wife was buried in St Mary's churchyard – 6s 8d.
Item Beatrice, wife [of] George Spyllesby – 6s 8d.
Item William Walker – 6s 8d.
Item Elizabeth, wife [of] Thomas Foster – 6s 8d.
26s 8d.
Witwords to the church.

[1] '24th Sunday' not entered.

First, by Johnson of Fawnthorpe[1] for his wife to the church & the High altar and ringing of the bells, a cow sold by Hugh Beverlay – 8s 3d.
Item received for a pair of small beads of coral – 20d.
Sum – 9s 8d.

f. 29r.
Great bells ringing.

Imprimis, Symon Lyncoln – 8d.
Item John Williamson – 12d.
Item Robert Raynyarde – 8d.
Item Richard, son [of] Walter Fyswyck – 8d.
Item Richard Okeland – 8d.
Item Agnes Spencer, wife [of] T[homas] Spencer – 20d.
Item Robert Westmold, gentleman – 8d.
Item James Marynell – 8d.
Item John Cawod – 20d.
Item Margaret, wife [of] William Dods – 8d.
Item John Gyrdyke – 8d.
Item John White, priest – 8d.
Item William Imttyng – 8d.
Item John Langholme – 8d.
Item John Whyte & Robert White, chaplains – 20d.
Item Katherine, wife [of] Alan Baynton – 8d.
Item Isabell Jacson – 8d.
Item Beatrice, wife of Gregory Spyllesby – 12d.
Item John Lowth – 20d.
Item John Ponell – 8d.
Item Thomas Bradley, senior – 20d.
Item William Walker – 20d.
Item William Walker – 20d.
Item Thomas Mordew – 8d.
Item Thomas Beverlay – 20d.
Item Thomas Allerton – 20d.
Item Thomas Gyrdyke, chaplain, John Beverlay[2] overall – 2s.
Stephan Parcens – 20d.
Item Margaret, wife [of] Allen Holden – 8d.
Item Elizabeth, wife [of] Thomas Foster – 20d.
Item Robert Ranyarde – 8d.

---

[1] Fanthorpe. This settlement is to the north-east of Louth, and although mentioned in the Domesday Book, no longer exists. It was once a grange of Tupholme Abbey (Premonstratensian Canons), which in 1535 was worth £6. Foster and Longley, *Domesday*, p. lv. *VE*, IV, p. 37.

[2] John Beverlay, merchant, was churchwarden in 1506/7. Dudding, *Accounts*, p. 85.

Sum – 31s 8d.
Total sum received – £13 14s 8d.

f. 29v.

Ministers in the church.

Imprimis, Thomas Foster by year – 26s 8d.
Item Arthur Graye[1] – 40s.
Item the keeper of the clock & chime – 10s.
Item for blowing the organs – 3s 4d.
Item Cloble's wife for washing pertaining to the High altar – 2s: 20d.[2]
Item Belman cleansing the church – 2s 8d.
Item Tace for keeping the bells[3] – 4s.
Item Nicholas Upton in fee – 6s 8d.
Item Thomas Provest in fee – 6s 8d.
Item for writing this account – 6s 8d.

Sum – £5 8s 8d.

Expenses about the church.

Imprimis, paid to Lawrence Penygton for a common bull for part of payment left unpaid by the old Church Masters – 6s 8d.
Item to William Smith for mending one of the organ stops – 1d.
Item to John Green for watching by a fourteen night[4] in the church – 20d.
Item to John Green for watching in the church by a fourteen night – 14d.
Item to Robert Smith for mending the iron candlestick – 3d.
Item to William Harryson & Robert Smythe for mending the Trinity bell clapper – 4s 10d.
Item to John Brown for keeping the common bull by the space of 14 nights – 9d.
Item to John Green for watching in the church by the space of fourteen night – 14d.
Item for cleansing the grate at the east end of the church & carrying away thereof – 2d.
Item for watching in the church at Corpus Christi tide – 4d.
Item for a lock to the church yard gate at the west end with a key – 4d.
Item to Henry Deane for a string to the Cope bell (16d) & to Symon Inbroghe for a string (16d) to the same – 2s 8d.
Item to Nicholas Upton for mending the bell flower – 4d.
Item to John Beverlay for lying in the church – 6d.

---

[1] Arthur Grey, Gray, Graye, mercer, was a singingman in St Mary's guild; later granted a pension of 40s dated 17 September 1544. Hodgett, *Ex-Religious*, pp. 53, 104. He is noted in the 1551 Corporation charter as one of the first assistants and was elected warden in 1556. In his will dated 12 December 1556, Grey left the grammar school two cottages worth 4s 8d p.a. TNA, PROB 11/39/28. Interred 15 December 1556. LAO, Goulding Papers, 5/2. Goulding, *Corporation Records*, pp. 4, 19, 124, 178.

[2] 3s 8d. Amount crossed through.

[3] Marginalia – 'Burrett'.

[4] Fortnight?

Item to John White for his bedding to William Richardson[1] lying in the church when there was no clerks – 4d.

21s 3d.

f. 30r.

Item for soldering the holy water vat at the south door – 1d.
Item for removing the pageands[2] – 16d.
Item to R Smythe for a bolt of iron for a curtain to ring upon at St John's altar – 6d.
Item for rings to the same curtain – 1d.
Item to John Tace for a reward – 4d.
Item to Norman for a string to the chime containing 2 stone & [a] half of hemp – 3s 10d.
Item for carrying of a load of wood to St Mary's church for the casting of the lead & the carting of the same – 4d.
Item to Thomas Provest for wainscot to the sollering[3] of the Sir Thomas Kyroke choir[4] & workmanship that of – 12d.
Item to the plumber for his labour shotting & laying lead over the north side of the church – 8s.
Item to William Fawer of 5 loads of lead – 10d.
Item to William Fawer for carrying 6 loads of wood & lead – 12d.
Item for carting[5] 2 loads of wood – 4d.
Item for the plumber's work in laying lead – 4s.
Item to Thomas Provest for sarking board to the north side & workmanship thereof – 3s 4d.
Item for mending the antyme book – 8d.
Item to the said plumber – 12s.
Item to Robert Norman for a string to the chime wheel containing 2 stone of hemp – 3s.
Item to William West for 2 loads of wood – 5s.
Item to 2 men for working 2 days at Stuton[6] Gate & Legburn[7] Gate – 16d.
Item to William Newton for a horse hide to bell collars – 2s.

---

[1] A William Richardson, weaver, left a will: TNA, PROB 11/55/110, probate 28 February 1572/3.

[2] Pageants.

[3] Sollar or flooring, a raised floor. *OED*.

[4] This choir, also known as John Louth's or All Hallows chantry, was situated on the north side of the church. Goulding, *Parish Church*, p. 9 and note. Following the Rising, Nicholas Melton alleged that Sir Thomas Kirk, chantry priest, gave 20s to the rebels. *L&P*, XI, 968, p. 391. Noted as 'Dom Kyrke, cantar' his stipend in 1526 was £8 11s. Salter, *Subsidy*, p. 12. He was interred 16 June 1541. LAO, Goulding Papers, 5/2.

[5] 'Laying' crossed through.

[6] Stewton.

[7] Legbourne.

Item paid to Robert Bayly for thack boards & nails occupied on the north side of the church – 2s 3d.
Item to Hugh Beverlay for nails occupied about the same – 19d.
Item to William Smythe for 2 springs to the chime hammers – 5d.
Item to William Smythe for mending a bell yoke – 7d.
Item to Nicholas Upton for hewing stone – 12d.
Item to Sir Christopher for mending the broken leaves of certain books – 3d.
Item to Thomas Provest for making a trestle & other work about the bells & the stocks[1] – 17d.
Item to Master Vicar[2] of the gift of Johnson of Fawnthorpe to the High altar for his wife in the price of a cow – 20d.[3]
Item to Sir Christopher for dressing certain books in the choir – 8d.
Item to a glazier for mending certain defaults in the church windows to meat & wages – 3s 8d.
Item to Walter Fyswycke for glass & candle – 20d.
Item to the same Walter for solder – 12d.
Item to Ednald for serving the glazier by the space of 5 days – 16d.
Item for a calf skin to William Newton for covering of books – 5d.
Item to Thomas Provest for making on the north side a new stall – 16d.
Item for a strike of lime – 3d.
Item to the smith for making a hammer to be occupied about the chime & for mending of the lock – 2d.
Item to a man for fetching a cow from Fawnthorpe – 1d.
f. 30v.
Item for a load of clay to old Sowthe occupied at the east end of the lodge – 2d.
Item to Hugh Beverlay for nails, wax, rosell, & pyche[4] – 4d.
Item to Robert Smythe for 3 wedges of iron & other things about the bells – 6d.
Item to William Smythe for mending the chime – 5d.
Item to Overay Paynter for mending the pax of the High altar – 12d.
Item for 16 yards of cloth to albs – 8s.
Item to Thomas Provest for trussing of 2 bells & stuff to a bell wheel – 2s 8d.
Item to John Whyte's wife for making 2 albs with their amices[5] & mending old – 18d.
Item to a fellow for seeking the common bull – 1d.

[1] The main upright part; a vertical beam, a stem. *OED*.
[2] Although he is not mentioned by name anywhere in the accounts, this is probably the ill-fated Thomas Kendall; instituted 2 October 1534. Cole, *Chapter Acts*, I, p. 184.
[3] Manicule in margin.
[4] Pitch?
[5] A priest's white linen neckcloth. Friar, *Parish Church*, p. 473.

Item for boards, nails & crooks[1] to the song school house door – 11d.[2]
Item to John Kytchen for the making thereof – 5d.
Item to Nicholas Upton for lime & his labour done at St Mary's church stile & the church – 8d.
Item for a key to the west church stile lock – 2d.
Item to Walter Fyswyck for an ympuall[3] – 18d.
Item for silk occupied about the canopy – 12d.
Item for satin occupied about the same – 10d.
Item to Byllingaye for mending the same – 16d.
Item for watching the church 2 nights when the west window of [the] Trinity choir was open – 6d.
Item to Overay Paynter for taking the glass of the same window down & setting it up again – 2s.
Item to Walter Fyswyck for a wisp of glass – 8d.
Item for 2 strikes of lime to G[eorge] Spyllesby – 6d.
Item for wood to the same window glass – 2½d.
Item for nails and rosell – 1½d.
Item to the masons for their labour [by the space][4] – 10s.
Item to Matthew Belman's wife for scouring the candlesticks – 6d.
Item to Atkyn for sweeping the windows – 1d.
Item for fetching the common bull – 1½d.
Item for an ell[5] & a half of canvas to the covering of the High altar – 8d.
Item to John Lupton for finding the common bull by the space of 20 weeks – 3s 4d.
Item to William Ratheby for meatyng[6] the same bull by the space of 3 weeks – 18d.
Item to Robert Goldsmythe for mending the feretor & a pyx[7] – 12d.
Item to Thomas Provest for a hook of iron for scathe fires weighing 22 lbs – 3s 8d.

Sum – £3 2s 4½d.[8]

Item to Thomas Provest for mending in the church diverse stalls & in the Trinity choir – 8d.

Sum – £6 16s 8½d.

---

[1] A crooked or incurved piece of timber. *OED*.
[2] For the song school, see Introduction.
[3] Ampule.
[4] [Crossed through]. Marginalia – '35s 2d'.
[5] Generally 45 inches (114.3cm). The term 'ell' seems to have been variously taken to represent the distance from the elbow or from the shoulder to the wrist or to the fingertips. *OED*.
[6] Mating or meating is 'feeding' in the sixteenth century according to the *OED*.
[7] The vessel or box in which the consecrated bread of the Eucharist is kept. *OED*.
[8] Crossed through.

Sum £12 5s 4½d, and remaining 29s 3½d, thereof paid for an inventory 10d, and to Thomas Rede for stone leading 12d, and so remains 27s 5½d.
Church Masters.
William Gossehauke.[1]
Robert Bayly.
Matthew Wardell.
Henry Fernstede.
f. 31r.
Memorandum, that William Barbar[2] & Richard Walker received of the gathering of the Plough light which they did bring in this account over and above the charge of a taper made to be borne about the sacrament – 10d.
Memorandum, that at this present account there was delivered to the hands of George Spyllesby 20s, & Robert Browne his surety therefore & to Alexander Mychelson[3] 20s and John Larmowthe[4] his surety therefore which belonged to the Common Cart and they to lead 20 load of stone every one of them to places necessary in this town for this same within this year following.
Memorandum, that William Glene hath given this year a reed to the lighting of the Sepulchre light and other lights in the church containing 5 yards length.
f. 31v. [Blank].

f. 32r.

[1535–6]

The account of William Goshauke, draper, Robert Bayly[5], mercer, Henry Fernysyd, sherman[6] & Matthew Wardale, shoemaker,[7] Proctors of the Church of St James in Lowthe, all receipts and expenses on Sunday the Octave of Easter 1535 until the Octave of Easter Sunday the year following.[8]
Imprimis, received of the Church Masters being the year before in money good & evil – 26s 5½d.
Item of the remainder of the Plough light – 10d.
     Sum – 28s 3½d.

---

[1] A William Gossauke, draper, was churchwarden in 1510/11. Dudding, *Accounts*, p. 125. He was assessed at £26 13s 4½d in the 1524/5 Lay Subsidy. TNA, E179/138/478. He was buried 16 March 1540/1. LAO, Goulding Papers, 5/2.

[2] Following the Rising, Nicholas Melton, shoemaker, said that William Barbor and William Kynge were 'paymasters of the Lowthe men'. *L&P*, XI, 828, p. 322, 21 October 1536.

[3] Mychelson was assessed at 40s in the 1524/5 Lay Subsidy. TNA, E179/138/478.

[4] John Larmouth was assessed at £8 in the 1524/5 Lay Subsidy. TNA, E179/138/478. He was interred 1 December 1539. LAO, Goulding Papers, 5/2.

[5] It was at Robert Bayly's shop that leading citizens of the town met to discuss the situation on the first day of the Rising. Ward, *Rising*, p. 14. He was interred 27 March 1545. LAO, Goulding Papers, 5/2.

[6] Shearman – a shearer of woollen garments. *OED*.

[7] A Mathew Wardall was buried 19 October 1568. LAO, Goulding Papers, 5/2.

[8] Noted as *sequent* – the year following, i.e. 1536.

Item received the 2nd Sunday after Easter – 6s 10d.
Item received the 3rd Sunday after – 5s 4d.
Item received the 4th Sunday after – 4s 2d.
Item received the 5th Sunday after – 4s 1d.
Item received the 6th Sunday after – 5s 3d.
Item received the Sunday of Pentecost – 6s 1d.
Item received on Trinity Sunday – 4s 6d.
Item received the first Sunday after – 4s 6d.
Item received the second Sunday after – 6s 7d.
Item received the 3rd Sunday after – 4s.
Item received the 4th Sunday after – 3s 8d.
Item received the 5th Sunday after – 4s.
Item received the 6th Sunday after – 4s.
Item received the 7th Sunday after – 4s 8d.
Item received the 8th Sunday after – 4s 4d.
Item received the 9th Sunday after – 5s.
Item received the 10th Sunday after – 3s 4d.
Item received the 11th Sunday after – 5s.
Item received the 12th Sunday after – 6s 4d.
Item received the 13th Sunday after – 3s 8d.
Item received the 14th Sunday after – 4s 2d.
Item received the 15th Sunday – 3s 3d.
Item received the 16th Sunday – 3s 10d.
Item received the 17th Sunday – 3s 4d.
Item received the 18th Sunday – 3s 8d.
Item received the 19th Sunday – 3s 7d.
Item received the 20th Sunday – 3s 9d.
Item received the 21st Sunday – 2s 9d.
Item received the 22nd Sunday – 3s 10d.
Item received the 23rd Sunday – 2s 11d.
Item received the 24th Sunday – 3s 9d.
Item received the 25th Sunday – 2s 11d.
Item received the 26th Sunday – 3s 10d.
Item received the first Sunday of Advent – 3s 4d.
Item received the second Sunday of Advent – 3s 10d.
Item received the third Sunday of Advent – 3s 4d.
Item received the fourth Sunday of Advent – 4s.
Item received the Sunday after the Nativity – 3s 4d.
Item received the Sunday after the Crucifixion – 4s 1d.
Item received the Sunday after the Epiphany – 3s.
      Sum – £8 5s 10d.

f. 32v.
Item received the second Sunday after Epiphany – 3s 5d.
Item received the third Sunday – 2s 10d.
Item received the fourth Sunday – 3s 3d.

Item received the 5th Sunday – 2s 5d.
Item received the Sunday of *Septuagesima* – 3s 6d.
Item received the Sunday of *Sexagesima* – 2s 10d.
Item received the Sunday of *Quinquagesima* – 4s 1d.
Item received the first Sunday of *Quadragesima* – 3s.
Item received the second Sunday – 3s 4d.
Item received the third Sunday – 3s 4d.
Item received the fourth Sunday – 3s 8d.
Item received the Passion Sunday – 3s 9d.
Item received on Palm Sunday – 4s 4d.
Item in Easter Day – 3s 6d.
Item received the Octave of Easter – 3s 9d.
     Sum – 51s 9d.
    Sum of total received – £10 17s 7d.
     Burials in the church.
Imprimis, James Bromflett – 6s 8d.[1]
Item Jane, the wife of Thomas Grantham[2] – 6s 8d.
Item Margaret, wife [of] John Norman – 6s 8d.
Item Anne, daughter [of] John Chapman – 3s 4d.
Item Katherine, wife [of] John Branchmore – 6s 8d.
Item Dorothy Beverlay[3] – 6s 8d.
Item William Lawrence – 6s 8d.
Item John Anderson[4] – 6s 8d.
Item Jenet Curtas – 6s 8d.
Item Elizabeth, wife [of] Thomas Richardson – 6s 8d.
     Sum – £3 3s 4d.
    Witwords to the churches.
First, James Bromflett to St Mary's Church – 12d.
Item Jenett Curtas to the same – 6d.
     Sum – 18d.

f. 33r.
     Great bells ringing.
Item Robert Beverlay – 20d.
Item James Bromflett – 20d
Item Simon Lyncoln – 8d.

---

[1] Bromflett was assessed at £34 in the 1524/5 Lay Subsidy. TNA, E179/138/478.

[2] Thomas Grauntham, tailor, was churchwarden in 1521/22. Dudding, *Accounts*, p. 210. He was assessed at £5 in the 1524/5 Lay Subsidy. TNA, E179/138/478.

[3] Dorothy Beverlay was assessed at £13 in the 1524/5 Lay Subsidy. TNA, E179/138/478.

[4] John Anderson was assessed at £13 6s 8d in the 1524/5 Lay Subsidy. TNA, E179/138/478.

Item Alice Talks – 8d.
Item Jane, wife [of] T[homas] Grantham – 8d.
Item John Williamson – 12d.
Item Elizabeth, wife [of] T[homas] Foster – 20d.
Item John Cawod – 20d.
Item James Bromflett – 8d.
Item Robert Westmold, gentleman – 8d.
Item Margaret, wife [of] John Norman – 20d.
Item John Whyte, chaplain – 8d.
Item Robert White, chaplain & other brothers of Our Lady guild – 20d.
Item John Langholme, gentleman – 8d.
Item Katherine, wife [of] William Louthes – 20d.
Item Katherine, wife [of] John Branchemore – 20d.
Item John Cortt – 8d.
Item Jenet, wife of Ranulf Johnson – 20d.
Item Johanne, daughter [of] Christopher Bery – 8d.
Item Jenett Fenn, widow – 8d.
Item Dorothy Beverlay – 20d.
Item John Lowthe – 20d.
Item Jenett Fenn – 8d.
Item William Walker – 8d.
Item William Lawrence – 20d.
Item Thomas Bradley, senior – 20d.
Item John Parnell – 8d.
Item John Anderson – 20d.
Item Jenett Curtas – 20d.
Item William Barton, chaplain – 8d.
Item Thomas Beverlay – 20d.
Item Thomas Allerton & John Taylor – 20d.
Item John Anderson – 20d.
Item Jenet Curtas – 20d.
Item Thomas Parcens, Henry Bootheby – 8d.
Item Jenet, wife [of] Bartholomew Claxton – 8d.
Item Elizabeth Crosseland – 8d.
Item Thomas Guyrdyck, chaplain – 12d.
Item William, son [of] Martin Ministerchambers – 8d.
Item Robert Ranyarde – 8d.
Item Robert Beverlay – 20d.
Item Elizabeth, wife [of] Thomas Richardson – 20d.
Item Symon Lyncoln – 8d.
Item John Cawod, son [of] William Cawod – 20d.
                    Sum – 51s 4d.
            Total sum received – £18 2s ½d.

f. 33v.
Ministers in the church.
Imprimis, Thomas Foster by year – 26s 8d.[1]
Item Arthur Graye – 40s.
Item the keeper of the clock & chime – 10s.
Item for blowing the organs – 3s 4d.
Item Cloble's wife for washing cloths pertaining to the High altar – 2s.
Item Belman for cleansing the church – 2s 8d.
Item Burrett for keeping the bells – 4s.
Item Thomas Provest in fee – 6s 8d.
Item Nicholas Upton in fee – 6s 8d.
Item for writing this account – 6s 8d.
Sum – £5 8s 8d.
Expenses about the church.
Imprimis, paid to William Ratheby for keeping the common bull by the space of 4 weeks – 16d.
Item to Robert Bayly for a wisp of glass – 8d.
Item Overay for glazing the windows – 12d.
Item to Richard Kytchen for cherked coals – 4d.
Item to Thomas Maners for mending copes & vestments – 12d.
Item to the same Thomas again – 13d.
Item to John Browne for cherkyd coals – 4d.
Item to John Kytchen for 5 days work at the lodge – 2s 6d.
Item to Thomas Bowland for 3 days work there – 18d.
Item to Bylyngay for mending a banner – 2d.
Item to William Smythe for a lock & a key to the lodge door – 4d.
Item to Robert Bayly for 6 yards of buckram, cruells[2] & thread occupied about mending the copes – 3s.
Item for a bunch of latts[3] to the lodge – 3d.
Item for nails to the same lodge – 3d.
Item to the smith for making a pair of manacles[4] – 10d.
Item to 2 wrights for a day and a half for their working about the song school seating – 18d.
Item to Matthew Bellman for watching the Sepulchre at Corpus Christi even – 3d.
Item for 6 polls to the work of the song school – 6d.
Item for watching the church on Corpus Christi day – 3d.
Sum – 17s 1d.

[1] Amounts noted in quarters above each entry.
[2] Possibly 'crewls', a thin worsted yarn of two threads, used for tapestry and embroidery. *OED*.
[3] Probably laths, thin strips of wood used for roofing. *OED*.
[4] Handcuffs – possibly for restraining prisoners when transported to Lincoln. *OED*.

f. 34r.
Item for half a thousand thack¹ to the lodge – 4s.
Item for timber to the lodge mending – 4s 4d.
Item to Thomas Provest for his labour 2 days about the bells – 12d.
Item to Thomas Maners for mending vestments – 8d.
Item to the plumber for 6 days work upon the leads of the north aisle – 3s.
Item for the cleansing of Aswell – 6d.
Item to Sir Christopher for mending the Legend Book – 4d.
Item to the plumber for [an]other 6 days' work there – 3s.²
Item to Nicholas Upton for mending the walls of the south church porch & paving the floor – 6d.
Item to the plumber for 5 days work – 2s 6d.
Item for solder – 8d.
Item for lime – 3d.
Item for 3 boards – 18d.
Item for a bell-string to Our Lady bell – 16d.
Item for writing an inventory for things contained in the sacristy³ to the parish priest at his interning – 1d.
Item to Walter Fyswyck for the carriage of the vestments from London⁴ sent by Master Parson⁵ – 10d.
Item for a hook of iron to St Sunday⁶ picture – 1d.
Item to Robert Bayly for nails, thack board, thread & buckram & red saye⁷ & long boards – 2s 8d.
Item to William Smythe for mending the clock chime wheel – 12d.
Item for making a hedge betwixt the Corn [Field] and the East Field – 3s 8d.⁸
Item for felling ryse⁹ to the same – 2d.
Item for slicing the bell-string – 1d.
Item for watching the church on St James's day¹⁰ – 2d.
Item to Henry Deane for a string to the clock plumb – 8d.

1   Thatch.
2   '3d' crossed through.
3   A room where church valuables are secured. Friar, *Parish Church*, p. 397.
4   Via modern roads, the distance to London is around 160 miles (257km).
5   This was probably the prebendary of Louth. Master Henry Williams held the post from 1535/6 until 1554. Le Neve, *Fasti*, Lincoln, 1300–1541, p. 87.
6   Nine Lincolnshire wills from 1520 to 1540 noted gifts to a 'St Sunday light'. Lincoln, St Mary Wigford, Rowston, Belton (Axholme), West Rasen, Algarkirk, Donington in Holland, Mareham on the Hill, Edenham and Lutton. The name allegedly derives from that of St Dominic (1170–1221). Goulding, *Parish Church*, p. 9, note.
7   Say – a red twilled woollen fabric resembling serge. *OED*.
8   Manicule in margin, with the line repeated.
9   Rice ryse, ryce – twigs, small branches or brushwood. *OED*.
10 July.

Item in a reward to my Lord Suffragan when he came to hallow vestments sent by Master Parson – 5s.
Item for girdles & mending of towels¹ – 20d.
Item to Robert Goldsmythe for mending the sensers² – 6d.
Item to Henry Plumer³ for mending the leads over the north side by the space of a day & half – 10d.
Item to the same Henry for a pound & [a] half of solder – 6d.
Item to Thomas Provest for 3 days work in the steeple – 18d.
Item for a surplice⁴ containing 7 yards & the making thereof to the use of the church remaining for strange singingmen when they come to sit in the choir which to the honour of God & the honest of the town – 4s 2d.
Item for a thatcher's labour by the space of 1 day thatching at the lodge – 4d.
Item to a man for serving him that space – 4d.
Item to Nicholas Upton for cleansing the church walls – 4d.
Item to William Johnson for 1,000 thatch to be brought hither at the feast of the Annunciation of Our Lady – 8s.⁵
Item to George Spyllesby in part of payment of 4 marks for the making of the chimney in the lodge – 13s 4d.
Sum – £3 9s 6d.

f. 34v.
Item to a poor man for cleansing the lodge – 2d.
Item to John Scott for 2 great calf skins – 3s 4d.
Item to George Spyllesby a yeoman⁶ for part of payment for his foresaid bargain – 26s 8d.
Item for scouring the candlesticks [be]longing to the High altar – 4d.
Item to the plumber for mending the handbell – 4d.
Item to Robert Acred, William Barbar, William Worslay for their charges in stopping a[n] indictment at Horncastell⁷ 3 years past that Master Bradelay would have taken out the town – 2s 4d.
Item to Thomas Provest for one days working in the steeple before Christmas for one servant & himself – 10d.

---

¹ A cloth, either of linen for use at communion, or of silk or other rich material for covering the altar. *OED*.
² Censers.
³ At the start of the Rising, Henry Plummer was one of the men who defended the church treasures. He was also noted as one of the ringleaders, 'receiving money from diverse priests'. *L&P*, XI, 975, p. 402.
⁴ A loose vestment of white linen. *OED*.
⁵ Manicule in margin. Lady Day, 25 March.
⁶ Yeoman – a man holding a small landed estate; a freeholder under the rank of a gentleman; a commoner or countryman of respectable standing, especially one who cultivates his own land. *OED*.
⁷ Horncastle.

Item to the same Thomas for 2 shafts of wire to the iron ankers made for causalities[1] – 12d.
Item to George Spyllesby for more part of his bargain – 10s.
Item to Richard Curson[2] for making up William the singingman's[3] wage that could not be gathered – 2s 4d.
Item to Thomas Provest for mending the feretor frame – 6d.
Item to Nicholas Upton for hewing stone – 12d.
Item to Robert Smithe for a hook to hang the feretor frame upon – 2d.
Item to William Smythe for mending a lock & a key to the south church door – 5d.
Item to Robert Bayly for stuff taken upon him at diverse times as coals, candles, nails & a lock with the key to the gate at the east end of the church – 14d.
Item to Thomas Foster for writing a square upon the 8 tunes[4] – 16d.
Item to William Browne for 5 strikes of lime occupied about St Mary's church – 15d.
Item to Nicholas Upton & George Armstrong for their labour in mending the buttress there – 5s.
Item to Thomas Provest for making the Paschall foot[5] – 20.[6]
Item to Robert Smyth for making 2 rings thereto – 8d.
Item to John Holderness for keeping the common bull – 4s.
Item to Robert Smith for making an iron ring to the bush for the bell-string to ring in – 15d.
Item to William the singingman – 6s 8d.
Item to Henry Plumer for setting in the iron – 6d.

[1] A casual or incidental charge or payment. *OED*.

[2] Richard Curson was an attorney and a prominent citizen of the town and was assessed at 40s in the 1524/5 Lay Subsidy. TNA, E179/138/478. He served as churchwarden in 1527/8, 1538/9 and 1548/9 and was chamberlain of the Lady guild in 1538 and alderman of the Trinity guild in 1545. Goulding, *Corporation Records*, pp. 169–70. Williamson, 'Religious Guilds', p. 88. During the Rising, Curson composed a letter to the king that reflected the grievances of the rebels during the Rising. *L&P*, XI, 568, p. 225, 6 October 1536: *ibid.*, 828, 2 (iii), p. 323, 23 October 1536. Interred 5 August 1554. LAO, Goulding Papers, 5/2.

[3] Maybe the son of Thomas Foster, also a singingman. Williamson, 'Religious Guilds', p. 89.

[4] Probably the eight tones within Gregorian chant notated within a 'tonary'. The 'square' is a style of notation used at the time. It could also indicate that polyphony was used in the *Magnificat*, performed at Evensong. Williamson, 'Religious Guilds', p. 87.

[5] Although there is no evidence, the 'Easter Foot' was possibly symbolically bathed on Maundy Thursday, replicating Christ washing the feet of his disciples. Alternatively, a base for the Paschall candle.

[6] Not cited as shillings or pence.

Item to Thomas Provest for one day's work in the steeple – 6d.
Item to Overay Paynter for mending the west window at St Mary's church, for stuff & his labour – 16d.
Item to William singingman for pricking a square upon the 8 tunes – 12d.
Item to the bellman for scouring the candlesticks – 4d.
Item for a yard of linen cloth to albs – 6d.
Item to Robert Bayly for lead, nails and coals – 23d.
Item to Nicholas Upton for working in the steeple – 6d.
Item to Thomas Provest in part of payment for a pane of stalling under St George – £4.
Item to Richard Kytchen for cherkyd coals – 4d.
Item for watching the church & choir over Easter Day – 2d.
Item to John Whyte's wife for mending one alb – 2d.
Item to Richard Curson for making up William singingmans wage that could not be gathered – 15d.
f. 35r.
Item to Robert Bayly for stuff taken off him for the pageands[1] against Corpus Christi tide – 3s 8d.
Sum – £8 4s 7d.
Total sum [of] expenses – £17 19s 10d, and remaining – 2s 2½d.[2]
It is agreed by [the] parish that Master John Godeall schoolmaster of grammar shall have yearly toward his living and wages 40s, that is to say 10s of Our Lady guild, 6s 8d, of the pece which he now hath, 13s 4d of St Michael light, 5s of Corpus Christi guild & 5s of St Peter's guild.
William Cawode.[3]
John Davy.
Master John Chapman.
Thomas Holywell.
f. 35v. [Blank].

f. 36r.

[1536–7]

The account of William Cawod, John Davy, fuller, John Chapman, gentleman[4] & Thomas Hallywells, Proctors of the Church of St James of Lowthe, all receipts and expenses on the Octave of Easter Sunday 1536 until the Octave of Easter Sunday the year following.[5]

1   Pageants.
2   Latin.
3   Crossed through.
4   John Chapman was churchwarden in 1536/7, 1547/8 and 1557/8. He was also one of the first six assistants to the Corporation and was elected warden in 1556. Swaby, *History of Louth*, p. 178. Goulding, *Corporation Records*, pp. 4, 19. Buried 26 December 1564. LAO, Goulding Papers, 5/2.
5   1537.

Imprimis, received of the churchwardens being the year before – 13s 6½d.
Memorandum, that William Elsam, butcher,[1] oweth to the church which is payable at the feast of St Michael[2] – 6s.
Imprimis, received the second Sunday after Easter – 5s 8d.
Item received the third Sunday after – 5s 5d.
Item received the 4th Sunday after – 3s 3d.
Item received the 5th Sunday after – 3s 8d.
Item received the 6th Sunday after – 2s 6d.
Item received the Sunday of Pentecost – 4s 6d.
Item received on Trinity Sunday – 5s.
Item received the first Sunday after – 3s 8d.
Item received the 2nd Sunday after – 3s 1d.
Item received the 3rd Sunday after – 3s 4d.
Item received the 4th Sunday after – 3s 9d.
Item received the 5th Sunday after – 4s 3d.
Item received the 6th Sunday after – 3s 3d.
Item received the 7th Sunday after – 3s 11d.
Item received the 8th Sunday after – 4s 1d.
Item received the 9th Sunday after – 3s 7d.
Item received the 10th Sunday after – 3s 6d.
Item received the 11th Sunday after – 2s 8d.
Item received the 12th Sunday after – 4s.
Item received the 13th Sunday after – 3s 2d.
Item received the 14th Sunday after – 3s 1d.
Item received the 15th Sunday after – 3s 4d.
Item received the 16th Sunday after – 2s 10d.[3]
Item received the 17th Sunday after – *nihil propter tumultum populi*.[4]
Item received the 18th Sunday after – 2s 8d.[5]
Item received the 19th Sunday *nihil*.[6]
Item received the 20th Sunday *nihil*.[7]

---

[1] A William Elsam was assessed at £8 in the 1524/5 Lay Subsidy. TNA, E179/138/478.

[2] Michaelmas, 29 September.

[3] Sunday, 1 October 1536. The vicar of Louth, Thomas Kendall, preached an allegedly contentious sermon that was purportedly a catalyst for the Lincolnshire Rising.

[4] Sunday, 8 October. Latin – 'Nothing because of the rising of the people.' This the only direct mention of the revolt in the accounts. A considerable number of parishioners were probably absent, having taken up arms.

[5] Sunday, 15 October. Collection taken. People were by then probably drifting back from Lincoln after the Rising had culminated.

[6] Sunday, 22 October. Latin – nothing. The revolt was largely over, but the lack of a congregation perhaps suggests fear of arrest.

[7] Sunday, 29 October. Latin – nothing. The service was again not performed, probably due to the presence of the king's forces in the town.

Item received the 21st Sunday – 3s.
Item received the 22nd Sunday – 3s.
Item received the 23rd Sunday – 2s 9d.
Item received the 24th Sunday – 3s 6d.
Item received the first Sunday of Advent – 2s 3d.
Item received the second Sunday of Advent – 3s 10d.
Item received the 3rd Sunday of – 3s.
Item received the 4th Sunday – 3s 8d.
Item received the Sunday after Nativity – 3s 2d.
Item received the Sunday after Epiphany – 2s 10d.
Item received the second Sunday after – 2s 8d.
Item received the third Sunday after – 2s 8d.
Item received for the offall[1] of *plasshyng* a hedge in the East Field – 8d.
Sum – £6 4s 9d.

f. 36v.
Ministers in the church.[2]
Item received the Sunday of *Septuagesima* – 3s.
Item received the Sunday of *Sexagesima* – 3s 2d.
Item received the Sunday of *Quinquagesima* – 2s 6d.
Item received the first Sunday of *Quadragesima* – 3s 1d.
Item received the second Sunday – 3s 8d.
Item received the third Sunday – 3s 2d.
Item received the fourth Sunday – 3s.
Item received Sunday in Passion – 2s 11d.
Item received on Palm Sunday – 3s 8d.
Item received Easter Day – 3s 3d.[3]
Item received the week after Easter – 2s 8d.
Sum – 34s.
Sum total collected – £7 18s 9d.
Burials in the church.
Imprimis, William Brown – 6s 8d.
Item Agnes, wife [of] Guy Came[4] – 6s 8d.
Item Jenet, wife [of] Robert Proctor – 6s 8d.
Item Robert Frow – 6s 8d.
Item John Richardson, litster – 6s 8d.
Item William Cawod – 6s 8d.
Sum – 40s.

---

[1] Offal – shavings, chips of wood. *OED*.
[2] Line crossed through.
[3] Marginalia – '31s 4d' crossed through.
[4] Possibly Guy Kyme, a notable participant in the Rising; later executed. Ward, *Rising*, p. 36.

Legacies to the churches.

Imprimis, Thomas Haunsell of North Somercotes – 4d.[1]

f. 37r.

Great bells ringing.

Imprimis, John Williamson, gentleman – 12d.
Item James Bromflett – 20d.
Item Robert Westmold, gentleman – 8d.
Item John Cawod, senior & junior – 20d.
Item Sir John Whyte – 8d.
Item John Gyrdycke – 8d.
Item John Langholme & Anna [his] wife – 8d.
Item brethren and sisters of Our Lady guild – 20d.
Item William Browne – 20d.
Item Agnes, wife [of] Guy Came – 20d.
Item William Hudson – 20d.
Item Agnes, wife [of] William Page, litster – 8d.
Item William Browne – 20d.
Item Agnes, wife [of] Guy Came – 20d.
Item John Lowth – 20d.
Item Robert Norman – 8d.
Item Jenet, wife [of] Robert Proctor – 8d.
Item William Walker – 8d.
Item Thomas Bradlay – 20d.
Item Robert Frow – 8d.
Item John Parnell – 8d.
Item John Anderson – 20d.
Item Thomas Beverlay – 20d.
Item Jenet Curtas – 20d.
Item Robert Frow – 8d.
Item Thomas Allerton – 20d.
Item John Richardson, litster – 20d.
Item William Cawod – 20d.
Item William Cawod – 20d.
Item John Gyrdyke, chaplain – 12d.
Item Thomas Graunt – 8d.[2]
Item Robert Raynard – 8d.[3]

Sum – 39s.
Sum total received – £12 11s 7d.

---

[1] Thomas Hauncell or Auncell of North Somercotes noted in his will of 20 November 1535 a gift of 4d to the 'churche warks' of Louth St James. LAO, LCC, 1535–7, *f.* 101.

[2] Marginalia – '38s 4d'.

[3] Marginalia – '39s'.

f. 37v.
Ministers in the church.
Imprimis, Thomas Foster by year – 26s 8d.
Item Arthur Graye – 40s.
Item the keeper of the clock & chime – 10s.
Item for blowing the organs – 3s 4d.
Item for washing cloths pertaining to the altar – 2s.
Item bellman for cleansing the church – 2s 8d.
Item Burrett for keeping the bells – 4s.
Item Thomas Provest in fee – 6s 8d.
Item Nicholas Upton in fee – 6s 8d.
Item for writing this account – 6s 8d.
Sum – £5 2s.
Expenses about the church.
Imprimis, to William Kyng for a load of rysse occupied for the defence of the East Field – 10d.[1]
Item for felling thereof – 2d.
Item for carriage thereof – 4d.
Item for dyking[2] & hedging – 2s.
Item to John Wylson[3] for hewing the raile[4] – 2d.
Item for mending the rochet belonging to the parish priest for to go in visitation with – 2d.
Item to the bellman for warning the streets to be made clean against Corpus Christi day – 1d.
Item to Thomas Provest for one day's work about the bells – 6d.
Item for watching the church on Corpus Christi day – 2d.
Item to Norman for a bell-string to the Morrow Mass bell – 10d.
Item to Matthew Bellman for the sacrament watching on Corpus Christi even at night – 2d.
Item for mending the church door key – 2d.
Item for carrying thatch to the lodge – 2d.
Item paid to William the singingman for fulfilling his wage at Midsummer which could not be gathered – 8s 10d.
Item for mending the candlestick – 7s 6d.

[1] Marginalia – 'East Field'.
[2] Diking – digging or cleaning a ditch or sewer. *OED*.
[3] In the deposition of John Brown following the Rising, a John Wylson, alias Jok Unsant, carpenter, 'went with an armed company to [Louth] church and took the keys of the treasure house from the churchwardens'. He later rang the common bell; a warning signal. Ward, *Rising*, pp. 14, 36. *L&P*, XI, 854, p. 343, 24 October 1536. A John Wilson is among the names listed as being 'condemned at Lincoln to suffer death the 6th day of March [1537] and not put to execution'. *L&P*, XII (i), 581, p. 268, 6 March 1536/7. A man of that name was interred in October 1538. LAO, Goulding Papers, 5/2.
[4] Probably rail.

Item for wood & coals to the casting of the same – 14d.
Item to Walter Fyswyck for a wisp of glass – 7d.
Item for mending the window in the revestry[1] – 6d.
Item for washing the corporax[2] pertaining to the altar – 4d.
Item to the Suffragan for his reward – 5s.
Item to the plumber for one day's work over the north side of the church & solder – 11d.
Item for wood to the same – 3d.

Sum – 30s 10d.

f. 38r.

Item to Henry Plummer for 5 days work on the north side – 2s 6d.
Item for 2 lbs solder – 7d.
Item to William Fawer for a load of sand – 3d.
Item to John Rede for thatching upon the lodge by the space of 3 days for his server & himself – 2s 6d.[3]
Item for 3 bunches of sewing rope[4] – 3d.
Item to Henry Plummer for 2 days work on the middle ronels[5] – 12d.
Item for 3 pounds of solder – 12d.
Item to John Davy for wood then occupied – 3d.
Item to the plumber for half a day's work – 3d.
Item to the smith for a key – 2d.
Item to William Smythe for mending the handbell – 6d.
Item to John Tayler for carrying the mape[6] from Lowthe Park – 2d.
Item to Overay Paynter for setting up a glass window in the clerk's chamber – 11d.
Item for iron hooks to St Peter's choir & the High choir door – 9d.
Item for nails – 1d.
Item to Norman for a bell-string to the Fore bell – 12d.
Item to William Smythe for a sneck & other iron work about the north churchyard door – 2d.
Item to Nicholas Upton for mending the stile on the north side – 8d.
Item to William Man[7] for his wages at Michaelmas – 20s.

---

[1] A vestry or sacristy. *OED*.

[2] A cloth, usually of linen, upon which the consecrated elements are placed during the celebration of the Mass, and with which the elements, or the remnants of them, are covered after the celebration. *OED*.

[3] Marginalia with manicule – 'bought by William Goshaulk that year'.

[4] Rope used for scaffolding and thatching. *OED*. Dudding, *Accounts*, p. 21, note 2.

[5] Runnel – a gutter. *OED*.

[6] Possibly a map, perhaps illustrating the landholdings of Louth Park Abbey, suppressed 8 September 1536.

[7] William Man was master of the song school, and it was noted in the inquiry following the Rising that he 'sings bass in the choir at Lowthe'. *L&P*, XII (i), 70 (I), p. 33, 12 January 1536/7.

Item to Thomas Provest for his labour & one servant one day in the steeple about the bells – 10d.
Item to William Smythe for mending [an] axle tree[1] [for] the chime – 3s.
Item to Thomas Provest for a table to the pardons[2] – 2d.
Item to Overay Paynter for mending the glass windows by 2 days for his stuff & labour – 16d.
Item for dressing a lock to the steeple – 2d.
Item to the bellman's wife for scouring the candlesticks against Christmas – 4d.
Item to George Spyllesby for 2 freestones – 12d.
Item to T[homas] Matlot for [carrying the present sent][3] doing the town's business – 4d.
Item to George Mason for his labour 2 days & [a] half in laying down the throwghes[4] in the middle alye[5] which were without the church – 17d.
Item to the clerks for to buy coals with again expenses for their reward for watching – 3d.
Item to Burret & his fellow for making[6] the defence of the East Field – 4s.
Item to John Whyte's wife for mending 6 albs – 12d.
Item to William Man for his wages at Christmas – 6s 8d.
Item to [Henry Deane][7] for a bell-string to the second bell made by Symon Newbrowgh[8] – 10d.
Item to Nicholas Upton for finishing the gallery – 8d.
Memorandum that there was gathered of the Plough light money – 8s 10d.[9]
Whereof paid to the Plough men – 2s.
And for 3 torches 6s 8d, & so remaineth – 2d.
Item to Thomas Provest for 2 days work in the steeple – 12d.
Item for lime occupied in the church windows when the great wind was – 4d.
Sum – £3 3s 10d.

f. 38v.
Item to Overay for 2 days work in mending the glass windows – 12d.
Item to Nicholas Upton for his work about the windows by the space of 2 days – 12d.
Item for nails occupied about the leads – 2d.

---

[1] A fixed beam of wood on which wheels revolve. *OED*.
[2] Possibly a list of pardons or indulgences inscribed on a wooden board?
[3] [Crossed through].
[4] Tomb covers previously lying in the churchyard.
[5] Aisle.
[6] 'Plashing' crossed through.
[7] [Crossed through].
[8] Simon Newborough was interred 20 April 1558. LAO, Goulding Papers, 5/2.
[9] Manicule in margin.

Item to Sir Thomas Fowler[1] for to make tapers with for the sacrament, which remained of the gathering of the Plough light the year before – 5s 4d.
Item for lime occupied about the leads – 5d.
Item to the plumbers for their labour on the south side after the great wind – 15s 8d.
Item for wood occupied about casting the lead – 10d.
Item to the glazier then – 2s.
Item for nails then occupied – 19d.
Item to Nicholas Upton for his labour there – 12d.
Item to William Man for his wages – 6s 8d.
Item to Richard Sadler for mending the spouts – 4d.
Item to the bellman's wife for scouring the candlesticks at Easter – 5d.
Item to the smith for 2 keys & other iron work about the new stalls – 8d.
Item for bearing the old stools[2] into the lodge – 2d.
Item to Robert Bayly for nails occupied about the new stalls – 19d.[3]
Item for cherked coals occupied at Easter – 6d.
Item to Thomas Provest for one day's work in the steeple of his man & himself – 6d.
Item for lime – 3d.
Item to the schoolmaster part of his wages granted by the town the last year – 3s 4d.[4]

Sum – 43s 5d.
Total sum – £12 1d.
And so remains clear – 11s 6½d.

Lord Burgh given for water of Monks' Dike as of old times – 2s.[5] Total – 13s 6½d.

f. 39r. [blank].
f. 39v.

IHUS.

Memorandum, that the forty shillings belonging to the Common Cart remaineth within the hands of George Spyllesby & Alexander Michelson as appearth at the end of the second account before this.

Memorandum, that John Smyth, mercer, felled & led away certain trees growing at the Small Wells belonging to the commonte of this town for which he oweth yet.

Sum.[6]

---

[1] Dom Thomas Fowler, Fouler, is noted in 1526 as having a stipend of £5. Salter, *Subsidy*, p. 12. Buried 5 June 1541. LAO, Goulding Papers, 5/2.

[2] Possibly 'stalls' with reference to the lines above and below.

[3] Marginalia – '37s 3d', '11d' crossed through.

[4] Marginalia – '43s 8d'.

[5] *De dno Burgh dat pro aqua de Monks' Dike ut ex antique.* This is probably Sir Thomas Burgh KG, 1st Baron Burgh of Gainsborough (c.1488–1550).

[6] No amount stated.

f. 40r.

IHUS.

[1537–8]

The account of Thomas Argram,[1] William Asseby, mercer, Richard Walker & William Askew, Proctors of the Church of St James of Lowth, all receipts and expenses on the Octave of Easter Sunday 1537 until the Octave of Easter Sunday the year following.[2]

Imprimis, received of the churchwardens the year before as appearith at the end of the [ac]count – 13s 6½d.
Imprimis, received the second Sunday after Easter – 6s 1½d.
Item received the 3rd Sunday – 5s 1½d.
Item received the 4th Sunday – 4s 4d.
Item received the 5th Sunday – 3s.
Item received the 6th Sunday – 3s 8d.
Item received the Sunday of Pentecost – 4s 4d.
Item received in Trinity Day – 5s 10d.
Item received the first Sunday after – 3s 5d.
Item the second Sunday after – 4s.
Item the 3rd Sunday after – 4s.
Item the 4th Sunday after – 4s 4d.
Item the 5th Sunday after – 3s.
Item the 6th Sunday after – 4s.
Item received the 7th Sunday – 5s 2d.
Item received the 8th Sunday – 4s 8d.
Item received the 9th Sunday – 3s 4d.
Item received the 10th Sunday – 3s 5d.
Item received the 11th Sunday after – 4s 4d.
Item received the 12th Sunday after – 4s 2d.
Item received the 13th Sunday after – 2s.
Item received the 14th Sunday after – 2s 8d.
Item received the 15th Sunday after – 3s 8d.
Item received the 16th Sunday after – 4s 10d.
Item received the 17th Sunday after – 3s.
Item received the 18th Sunday after – 3s 6d.
Item received the 19th Sunday after – 3s.
Item received the 20th Sunday after – 2s 9d.
Item received the 21st Sunday after – 3s 6d.
Item received the 22nd Sunday after – 2s 11d.
Item received the 23rd Sunday after – 2s 8d.
Item received the 24th Sunday after – 3s 6d.

---

[1] Argram was assessed at £6 in the 1524/5 Lay Subsidy. TNA, E179/138/478. He was buried 8 July 1541. LAO, Goulding Papers, 5/2.

[2] 1538.

Item received the 25th Sunday after – 23d.
Item received the 26th Sunday after – 3s 1d.
Item received the first Sunday of Advent – 2s 8d.
Item received the 2nd Sunday of Advent – 3s 3d.
Item received the 3rd Sunday of Advent – 2s 4d.
Item received the 4th Sunday of Advent – 2s 9d.
Item received the Sunday after Nativity – 2s 5d.
Item received the Sunday after Circumcision – 3s.
Item received the Sunday after Epiphany – 2s 3d.
      Sum – £7 11d.

f. 40v.
Item received the second Sunday after – 3s.
Item received the third Sunday after – 2s 6d.
Item received the 4th Sunday after – 3s 6d.
Item received the 5th Sunday after – 2s 1d.
Item received the Sunday of *Septuagesima* – 2s 4d.
Item received the Sunday of *Sexagesima* – 2s 6d.
Item received the Sunday of *Quinquagesima* – 3s 4d.
Item received the first Sunday of *Quadragesima* – 2s.
Item received the 2nd Sunday – 2s 5d.[1]
Item received the 3rd Sunday of *Quadragesima* – 2s 9d.
Item received the 4th Sunday of *Quadragesima* – 3s.
Item received Passion Sunday – 2s 5d.
Item received Palm Sunday – 2s 8d.
Item received in Easter Day – 2s 4d.
Item received in Sunday the Octave of Easter – 3s 4d.
      Sum collected – £9 13d.[2]
      Burials in the church.
Imprimis, John Kyrck – 6s 8d.[3]
Item John Bowland – 6s 8d.[4]
Item Margaret, wife [of] William West – 6s 8d.
Item William Grene, priest[5] – 6s 8d.
Item Ales [Alice] Gyles, widow – 6s 8d.
Item Margaret Lawrence, widow[6] – 6s 8d.

---

[1] '4d' crossed through.
[2] £9 1s 1d.
[3] In his will of 16 April 1537, John Kirk or Kyrke of Trusthorpe, husbandman, requested interment in St James's. LAO, LCC, 1535–7, *f.* 211. He left an estate worth £64 18s. LAO, Inventory, Box 6, p. 75.
[4] 'Burial' crossed through.
[5] Dom Willelmus Grene is noted in 1526 as having a stipend of £5 6s 8d. Salter, *Subsidy,* p. 12.
[6] 'Uxor' crossed through.

Sum – 40s.
Witwords to the church.

Alison Edith, a kercher[1] sold by the Church Masters – 7d.
Master Mason of Grymesby[2] – 6s 8d.
Item given by the devotion of a certain priest in Northfolk[3] for to pray for the soul of Symon Lyncoln – 3s 4d.
Item given by Robert Frow [a] legacy to St Mary's church – 6d.
Item received of Hodlyng for a back stall of the old stalls – 16d.

f. 41r.

Great bells ringing.

Imprimis, Robert Beverlay – 20d.
Item Symon Lyncoln – 8d.
Item John Williamson – 12d.
Item John Gybson – 8d.[4]
Item John Kyrck – 20d.
Item Robert Westmold, gentleman – 8d.
Item Sir John Whyte & brethren of the Trinity guild – 8d.
Item John Gyrdyck – 8d.
Item Margaret, wife [of] Bartholomew Claxton, saddler – 8d.
Item Thomas Bowland – 20d.
Item John Langholme, gentleman – 8d.
Item Margaret, wife [of] William West – 20d.
Item the brethren & sisters of Our Lady guild – 20d.
Item William Brown, miller – 20d.
Item Raulf Jonson of Faunthorpe – 20d.
Item Thomas Bowland – 20d.
Item Margaret, wife [of] William West – 20d.
Item Agnes Williamson, widow – 8d.
Item Raulf Johnson – 8d.
Item John Lowth – 20d.
Item Robert, son [of] Richard Watson – 8d.
Item William Walker – 8d.
Item Thomas Bradlay, senior – 20d.
Item John Parnell – 8d.

---

[1] 'kercher' – kerchief, cloth for covering a woman's head.

[2] In her will, Jenet (Joanne) Mason, noted as the widow of Peter Mason, alderman and burgess of Grimsby, donated 6s 8d to St James's church, probably in the name of her husband. LAO, LCC, 1535–7, *f.* 117, 17 September 1535. Peter Mason left a will dated 5 January 1534/5 but does not mention Louth. LAO, LCC, 1535–7, *f.* 5. His estate was valued at £121 15s. LAO, Inventory, Box 5, p. 110.

[3] Norfolk.

[4] John Gybson is noted as working on the spire. Goulding, *Spire*, p. 6.

Item John Anderson – 8d.
Item Thomas Beverlay – 20d.
Item Thomas Allerton – 20d.
Item Jenett Curtas & William Cawod – 20d.
Item Stephan Parkons & Thomas Gyrdyck – 12d.
Item Christopher Heblethwate – 8d.
Item William Grene, priest – 20d.
Item Alice Gyles, widow – 20d.
Item William Grene, priest – 8d.
Item Robert Raynard – 8d.
Item Richard Smyth, fletcher – 8d.
Item Margaret Lawrence, widow – 20d.
Item Robert Beverlay – 20d.
Item Simon[1] Lyncoln – 8d.
Item Alice Gyles, widow – 8d.
Item Richard Watson – 8d.
John Williamson – 12d.

    Sum – 46s 4d.
   Total sum received – £14 13s 4½d.

f. 41v.

    Ministers in the church.

Imprimis, Thomas Foster by year – 26s 8d.
Item Arthur Graye – 40s.
Item William Man – 26s 8d.
Item the keeper of the clock & chime – 10s.
Item for blowing the organs – 3s 4d.
Item for washing cloths pertaining to the High altar – 2s.
Item the bellman for cleansing the church – 2s 8d.
Item Burrett for keeping the bells – 4s.
Item Thomas Provest in fee – 6s 8d.
Item Nicholas Upton in fee – 6s 8d.
Item for writing this account – 6s 8d.
    Sum – £6 15s 4d.
   Expenses about the church.

Imprimis, paid unto Thomas Provest in part of 40s, yet due to him for the pawne[2] of new stalls – 10s.
Item to Arthur Graye for part of his quarter wage behind of the last quarter – 3s 4d.
Item to William Smythe for 2 keys to the choir door – 3d.

---

[1] 'William' crossed through.
[2] Pledge. *OED*.

Item for coals occupied in the Marketsted when my Lord Admiral[1] was here – 2s.[2]
Item to Robert Goldsmyth for mending the cross of silver called Our Lady Cross – 3s 4d.
Item paid unto Thomas Provest in more part of the same – 14s.
Item paid to Thomas Provest the remnant of his duely[3] – 16s.
Item to the Suffragan for his reward & costs being here a day – 7s 6d.
Item for a bushel of lime to George Spyllesby – 6d.
Item to Henry Plumer for his labour 2 days in the high gallery (12d) & his help[er] Nicholas Upton (4d) – 16d.
Item to George Spyllesby for the last payment of 4 marks committed with him for making the chimney in the lodge as appearith in the account of William Goshaulke & Robert Bayly – 3s 4d.[4]
Item for a string to the clock plumb to Norman – 10d.
Item for a bushel of lime to John Larmouth occupied at the Marketstead cross – 6d.[5]
Item to Nicholas Upton for his labour there – 12d.
Item for hedging the East Field – 6d.
Item for nails occupied about mending stools in Our Lady choir – 1d.
Item to Thomas Provest for his labour about the same – 4d.
Item for a basket for Holy Bread[6] – 2½d.[7]

f. 42r.

Item to Henry Plumer (21d) for his labour in fining lead ashes by the space of 3 days & [a] half & George Armstrong (14d) by like space with others – 2s 11d.
Item to James [7d] & Baggott [4d] helpers to bear the lead & their labour about the same – 11d.
Item for nails occupied to a trough – 1½d.
Item to John Haryson for his bellows that time – 16d.
Item for wood spent & burnt about the same lead – 2s.
Item to Lancaster for his house room – 4d.

---

[1] William Fitzwilliam, 1st earl of Southampton (1490–1542) and Lord Admiral of England, 1536–40. *DNB*, https://doi.org/10.1093/ref:odnb/9663 (Accessed 7/8/2018). This entry is probably connected with the occupation of Louth on Friday, 27 October by the king's forces. Gunn, *Brandon*, p. 161 and note 32.
[2] '12d' crossed through.
[3] The extent or degree that is due. *OED*.
[4] Manicule in margin.
[5] Marginalia 'mending the Marketstead Cross'. John Larmouth was buried 1 December 1539. LAO, Goulding Papers, 5/2.
[6] Holy Loaf (*pani sanctificatus*). White bread that was blessed (not consecrated) by the priest following Mass and distributed to the congregation. Addy, *Church and Manor*, pp. 287–9. Cox, *Churchwardens*, p. 58. The basket holding the bread, generally made of wicker, was called a mand or maund. *OED*. Peacock, 'Kirton', p. 20.
[7] Page torn.

Item for leading the same lead to St Mary's church – 2d.
Item to John Holdernes for finding a common bull to the town kye[1] – 4s.
Item William Smythe for mending the chime – 12d.
Item given in reward by the hands of Richard Curson to a servant of the Queens Grace's [one] purse[2] – 20d.
Item to William Smyth for a lock to the song school door – 4d.
Item to Old Norman for 2 bell-strings to the …[3] – 21d.
Item to the glazier mending windows at the west end and about the church by 3 days – 3s.
Item to the glazier again – 3s 2d.
Item to Richard Spencer & John Lowthe for their labour 2 days & [a] half in diking betwixt Lowthe Field and Legburn Gate – 18d.
Item for ale, bread & wine spent in the Marketsted at the general procession for joy of the nativity of Prince Edward[4] – 3s 9d.
Item to Henry Plumer for his labour 2 days about the high gallery of the steeple – 12d.
Item for nails (1d) occupied there & lime (3d) – 4d.
Item to Nicholas Upton for his labour there – 4d.
Item to Fawer for a load [of] clay to the lodge – 2d.
Item for leading a load of earth forth of the churchyard that was about the walls – 1d.
Item to a thatcher for thatching the lodge & his server there meat & wages – 20d.
Item to Henry Plumer for half a day's work about the leads mending – 3d.
Item to Robert Smyth for certain work about Our Lady bell – 10d.
Item to John Rede for making a coffer for young *cores*? – 2d.[5]
Item to Overay Paynter for mending windows at both churches (18d) by 3 days space & glass & solder (4d) – 22d.
Item to Henry Plumer for his helpers for stopping holes in both steeples for stopping out doves by 2 days space – 14d.
Item for an elme[6] of linen cloth (7½d) to an alb sleeves mending and to John Whyte's wife for mending (3d) – 10½d.
Item to Thomas[7] Provest for making a new wheel to the Trinity bell & hanging the same – 8s.
Item to Robert Smyth for iron work to the same – 2d.

[1] Cattle. Manicule in margin.
[2] Queen Jane Seymour, died Wednesday, 24 October 1537. Goulding suggests, *pro urso*, 'for the bear'. Goulding, *Annals*, p. 33.
[3] Line incomplete.
[4] Born Friday, 12 October 1537 at Hampton Court.
[5] Corse – corpse. *OED*. Perhaps children's coffins?
[6] Ell.
[7] 'Robert' crossed through.

Item to Overay Paynter for making badges to the poor folks[1] – 6d.
f. 42v.
Item for revesing[2] girdles (4d) & nails (2d) – 6d.
Item for coals to the clerks against expenses for their reward for watching – 3d.
Item to George Spyllesby for mending the chimney in the clerk's chamber & his stuff – 18d.
Item to Robert Bayly for wire occupied about the chime & a board to the mending of a bere[3] – 6d.
Item for lime to Nicholas Upton occupied about the windows and his labour – 3d.
Item to Robert Smyth for a bolt of iron to the Our Lady bell & other iron work – 4d.
Item to Thomas Provost for his labour at that bell – 4d.
Item to Henry Plumer for stuff & his labour in mending over the Rood loft & the bellman – 12d.
Item to William Smyth for 2 keys to the choir door and a chest to lay these books in – 4d.
Item for writing the letter that was sent by the town to Master Bellow[4] – 4d.
Item to Overay Paynter for glass windows mending about the bellhouse – 12d.
Item for making and writing the supplication sent by the town to the Lord Privy Seal – 20d.[5]
Item to Nicholas Upton for stopping the dove holes in the church – 2d.
Item to the bellman for doing certain reparations necessary in the church – 8d.
Item to Richard Burton[6] for going the town message – 8d.
Item for half [a] hide of white leather to [the] bell collars – 10d.
Item for copying the Duke's letter sent to the town – 4d.[7]
Item to the riders about with the Dukes grace's letter & other expenses about the same business – 4s.[8]
Item to William Goshaulke for thatch occupied about the lodge – 12d.
Item to the same riders for their horses – 2s 6d.

---

[1] Possibly an insignia showing they were residents of the Bedehouse and later to acknowledge the receivers of aid from the poor box. Alternatively, a licence to beg issued under the Vagabonds Act of 1530 (22 Henry VIII c.12).

[2] To clothe, apparel, attire. *OED*. Mending?

[3] Bier – cart used for carrying coffins or shrouded bodies to a grave. *OED*.

[4] This is probably a letter of contrition for Bellow's imprisonment at the commencement of the Rising. For John Bellow, see Introduction.

[5] The Lord Privy Seal was Thomas Cromwell (c.1485–ex.1540).

[6] A Richard Burton was assessed at £20 in the 1524/5 Lay Subsidy. TNA, E179/138/478. Interred 5 November 1541. LAO, Goulding Papers, 5/2.

[7] Charles Brandon, 1st duke of Suffolk (c.1484–1545). *DNB*, https://doi.org/10.1093/ref:odnb/3260. He owned extensive lands in Lincolnshire through his marriage to Katherine Willoughby (1519–80).

[8] '3s' crossed through.

Item to the bellman for mending stools in the church that were faulty – 6d.
Item for cherke coals at Easter – 6d.
Item to William Kyng – 8d.
Item to Thomas Provest for mending the Trinity bell – 6d.
Item for scouring the candlesticks at Easter – 6d.
Item to Richardson for going the town message (4d), to Nicholas Upton (1d), to the smith for wedges to the bell (1d) – 6d.
Item to John Smyth's wife for baking venison & charges bestowed upon the Duke's Grace when he came through the town – 11s.
                    Sum – 32s 4d.
f. 43r.
Total of all allowances and payments £13 18s ½d & remain 15s 4d, over & above 16d found in the purse & so remain 16s 8d, whereof given in reward to George Spyllesby for amendment of his costs & loss about the making of the chimney at the lodge – 13s 4d, and so remains – 3s 4d.
Memorandum, that forty shillings pertaining to the Common Cart is delivered in to the hands of George Spyllesby (20s) & Thomas Provest (20s), their sureties be Robert Brown & William West and they shall lead, dig & carry of their own proper costs and charges this year, at the sight & assignment of the churchwardens 40 loads [of] stone between them and lay it in places necessary.
Churchwardens.
Robert Brown.
Richard Curson.
Thomas Lawrence.
George Sutton.[1]
f. 43v. [Blank]

f. 44r.
                                        [1538–9]
The account of Robert Brown, Richard Curson, Thomas Lawrence & George Sutton, Proctors of the Church of St James in Lowthe, all receipts and expenses on the Octave of Easter Sunday 1538 until the Octave of Easter Sunday following.[2]
Imprimis, received by the delivery of the old churchwardens – 3s 4d.
Imprimis, received the second Sunday after Easter – 3s 11d.
Item received the 3rd Sunday after Easter – 4s 11d.
Item received the 4th Sunday after – 3s.
Item received the 5th Sunday after – 2s 8d.
Item received the 6th Sunday after – 3s 4d.

---

[1] Interred 3 April 1558. LAO, Goulding Papers, 5/2.
[2] 1539.

Item received the Sunday of Pentecost – 2s 4d.
Item received on Trinity Sunday – 3s 9d.
Item received the first Sunday after – 2s 5d.
Item received the second Sunday – 2s 10d.
Item received the third Sunday – 2s.
Item received the 4th Sunday – 3s 2d.
Item received the 5th Sunday – 2s 8d.
Item received the 6th Sunday – 3s 7d.
Item received the 7th Sunday – 2s 8d.
Item received the 8th Sunday – 2s 11d.
Item received the 9th Sunday – 2s 4d.
Item received the 10th Sunday – 3s 5d.
Item received the 11th Sunday – 2s 4d.
Item received the 12th Sunday – 3s.
Item received the 13th Sunday – 2s.
Item received the 14th Sunday – 2s 8d.
Item received the 15th Sunday – 2s.
Item received the 16th Sunday – 3s 3d.
Item received the 17th Sunday – 2s 4d.
Item received the 18th Sunday after – 2s 8d.
Item received the 19th Sunday after – 3s 7d.[1]
Item received the 20th Sunday after – 3s 2d.
Item received the 21st Sunday after – 21d.
Item received the 22nd Sunday after – 3s.
Item received the 23rd Sunday after – 22d.
Item received the first Sunday of Advent – 2s.
Item received the second Sunday of Advent – 2s.
Item received the third Sunday of Advent – 2s 7d.
Item received the fourth Sunday of Advent – 2s.
Item received the Sunday after Christmas Day – 2s 6d.
Item received the Sunday after Circumcision – 20d.
Item received the Sunday after Epiphany – 2s 6d.
Item received the Sunday after the Octave? of Epiphany – 19d.
Item received the second Sunday after – 2s 5d.
f. 44v.
Item the Sunday of *Septuagesima* – 2s 4d.
Item the Sunday of *Sexagesima* – 2s 8d.
Item the Sunday of *Quinquagesima* – 2s.
Item the first Sunday of Lent – 3s.
Item the second Sunday – 2s.

[1] '11d' and '18d' both crossed through.

Item the third Sunday of Lent – 2s 5d.
Item the fourth Sunday of Lent – 2s 9d.
Item the Passion Sunday – 2s 3d.
Item on Palm Sunday – 2s 6d.
Item on Good Friday – 2s 9d.
Item on Low Sunday – 2s.
Item the second Sunday after Easter – 2s 4d.
Sum of Sunday collection – £6 12s 9d.
Burials in the church.

Robert Brampton[1] – 6s 8d.
Item Thomas Argram – 6s 8d.
Item Jenett Buckyngham – 6s 8d.
Item Anna, wife [of] Robert Howlatt – 6s 8d.
Item Elizabeth, wife [of] William Newton – 6s 8d.
Item William Allen,[2] wheelwright – 6s 8d.
Item Anne, daughter [of] Master Marlings – 3s 4d.
Item Isabell, wife [of] William Asby – 6s 8d.
Item Thomas Rychardson – 6s 8d.
Item Alison Carter, widow – 3s 4d.
Item John Spencer[3] – 3s 4d.
Item Ellen, wife [of] Robert Colingwod, south porch – 3s 4d.
Item Henry Fernesyde – 6s 8d.
Sum – £3 13s 4d.
Whitwords or bequests.

Imprimis, Thomas Argram to both churches – 2s.[4]
Item Jenett Buckyngham – 4d.
Item Robert East[5] to St Mary's church and St John's chapel – 4d.
Sum – 2s 8d.

f. 45r.
Great bells ringing.

Imprimis, Robert Brampton – 20d.

---

[1] A Robert Brampton was churchwarden in 1516/17. Dudding, *Accounts*, p. 183. He was assessed at £5 in the 1524/5 Lay Subsidy. TNA, E179/138/478.

[2] This is possibly William Eleyn or Elleyn, who, along with John Browne, John Bellow and John Millicent, was captured by the rebels at Legbourne Priory on Monday, 2 October. Ward, *Rising*, p. 15. *L&P*, XI, 854, p. 343, 24 October 1536.

[3] John Spencer had been steward of the manor court and also churchwarden in 1508/9, 1514/15 and 1524/5. Goulding, *Annals*, p. 33. Spencer was assessed at £15 in the 1524/5 Lay Subsidy. TNA, E179/138/478. Buried 18 February 1538/9. LAO, Goulding Papers, 5/2.

[4] St James's and St Mary's.

[5] East was assessed at 10s in the 1524/5 Lay Subsidy. TNA, E179/138/478.

Item Robert Gybson – 8d.
Item Robert Westmeles – 8d.
Item Robert Brampton – 8d.
Item Richard Watson – 8d.
Item Thomas Argram – 20d.
Item John Gyrdyke – 8d.
Item Jenett Buckyngham – 20d.
Item Thomas Argram – 8d.
Item Robert East – 20d.
Item Isabell, wife [of] Richard Spencer – 8d.
Item Jenett Buckyngham – 8d.
Item John Langholme – 8d.
Item Thomas Bowland – 20d.
Item brethren & sisters of Our Lady guild – 20d.
Item Margaret, wife [of] William West – 12d.
Item John Lowth – 20d.
Item Elizabeth, wife [of] William Newton – 8d.
Item William Allen – 8d.
Item Anne, daughter [of] Master Merlings.[1]
Item Isabell, wife [of] William Asby – 20d.
Item William Walker – 8d.
Item Thomas Bradley – 20d.
Item Isabell, wife [of] William Asby – 20d.
Item Jenet Curtes – 12d.
Item John Parnell – 8d.
Item Marion Cloblay – 8d.
Item John Anderson – 8d.
Item Thomas Beverlay – 20d.
Item Thomas Allerton – 20d.
Item Thomas Rychardson – 20d.
Item Stephan Parcas & Thomas Gyrdyke – 12d.
Item Elizabeth, wife [of] Bartholomew Hanson – 8d.
Item Thomas Rychardson – 20d.
Item Alison Carter.[2]
Item Richard Smythe – 8d.
Item Thomas Bemond & Jenett, [his] wife – 8d.
Item John Spencer – 8d.
Item Ellen, wife [of] Robert Colingwod – 20d.
Item Robert Ranyard – 8d.
Item Robert Beverlay – 20d.
Item Henry Fernesyde – 8d.

[1] Line crossed through, no amount stated.
[2] No amount stated.

Sum – 43s 8d.
Item received by them for old iron candlesticks pertaining to the church – 8s.
Total sum received – £13 3s 9d.

f. 45v.

Ministers in the church.

Thomas Foster this year – 20s.
Arthur Gray – 30s.
The keeper of the clock & chime – 10s.
The blower of the organs – 3s 4d.
The washer of the High altar cloths – 2s.
The bellman cleansing the church – 2s 8d.
Burrett for keeping the bells – 4s.
Thomas Provest in fee – 6s 8d.
Nicholas Upton in fee – 6s 8d.
John Goddalle writing this account – 6s 8d.

Sum – £4 12s.

Expenses.

Imprimis, for fleakes[1] set betwixt the Fallow Field & East Field – 8d.
Item to Richard Curson for writing the sessement[2] to the country[3] – 2s.
Item to John Goodale for writing & attending all Easter week about the town business – 3s 4d.
Item to four men of Grimolby[4] for their labour 3 days in diking the common sewer at Haregarthes – 4s.
Item to Thomas Maners for his work 6 days about mending copes & vestments to meat & wages – 2s 7d.
Item to Thomas Maners for mending the best copes 2 days – 10d.
Item to the plashers of the hedge at Haregarthes – 2s.
Item to Robert Bayly for thread occupied about mending copes – 3d.
Item for freestones bought of George Tyler – 14d.
Item to the dikers of the common sewers – 8s.
Item to Thomas Woolerby for stuff occupied about mending the copes – 7d.
Item to the dikers of the common sewer – 8s 8d.

Sum – 34s 1d.

f. 46r.

Item to the hands of William Asseby – 6s 8d.
Item to Robert Bayly for certain stuff occupied about mending copes – 12d.
Item to Symon Newbrugh for a bell-string – 12d.
Item for peres[5] sent to the Dukes Grace – 8d.

---

[1] Flakes – a wattled hurdle. *OED*.
[2] Assessment, probably for tax purposes.
[3] The local area or region. *OED*.
[4] Grimoldby.
[5] Pears?

Item to Drakes for mending the way at Legburne Gate – 3d.
Item given to the gatherers at Sawthrop[1] church – 2s.
Item to William Allain for boards to the lead shafts – 4d.
Item to 2 men for their labour 2 days in shifting the lead shafts & doing other necessaries about the same – 16d.
Item to Gylbert Fyssher for nails about the same & other necessaries to the church – 5d.
Item to Thomas Provest for his stuff & labour in making a lectern for the bibles – 2s.
Item to Norman to a chime rope – 4s 3d.
Item for 2 skins to book coverings – 6d.
Item to William Newton for a calf skin to a book covering – 8d.
Item for chains & irons made for Kydd – 2s.
Item to Thomas Provest & his 2 servants for their work in the steeple at All Hallows tide[2] – 16d.
Item to Walter Fyswyck for nails – 1d.
Item to William Smyth for 2 locks at St Mary's church new door and their keys – 6d.
Item to William Fawer for 2 loads stone laid in the church yard – 4d.
Item to Walter Fyswyck for 9 yards linen cloth to a surplice to the parish priest – 4s 6d.[3]
Item to John Whyte's wife for making it – 16d.
Item to the bellman for going about the town[4] – 2d.
Item for wood (20d) to the trundle[5] & the making (2s 8d) – 4s 4d.
Item to William Haryson for iron work to the same – 7d.
Item to Thomas Provest for making a new stall in the church & boards to a book covering – 10d.
Item to John Holdernes for finding a common bull to the town for the whole year – 5s.
Item for the register book of burials & weddings – 6d.[6]
Item to Bartholomew Claxton for leather to the books clasps – 10d.

[1] Sausthorpe. This was possibly a brief regarding a collection for an unknown purpose. A brief is a document issued by official or legal authority or a royal letter or mandate; a writ or summons. *OED*. This system was abolished in 1828. Goulding, Papers, 5/3. For discussion on royal briefs, see Goulding, *Briefs*, n.p.
[2] 1 November.
[3] Manicule in margin.
[4] Probably acting as the town or common crier.
[5] Trendle, Trindle, Trundle – a suspended hoop or wheel on which tapers were fixed, forming a chandelier, used in churches before the Reformation. A trindle can also be a roll of taper wax cut to size for lights surrounding a shrine. Alternatively, a small wheel sometimes attached to gates to bear the weight. *OED*.
[6] This is the first mention of a Parish Register specified in the Royal Injunctions of 1538. Williams, *Historical Documents*, p. 813.

Item to William Smyth for mending iron work about the clock & chime – 10d.
Item to John Spencer for his labour in dressing certain books belonging to the choir – 13s 4d.
Item to Hugh Cardmaker for helping the priest to say Mass at St Mary's church in the plague times – 4d.[1]
Sum – 57s 11d.[2]

f. 46v.
Item for a skin to a book covering – 7d.
Item to Owtred Wilson for wood occupied about the lead shafts – 10d.
Item to Nicholas Upton for making a door at St Mary's church chancel – 5s 10d.
Item for a quire of paper to Walter Fyswick – 2d.
Item for a strike of coals to the clerks at Christmas – 3d.
Item to a glazier for his stuff & labour about 2 panes of a window in Trinity choir – 12d.
Item to Thomas Provest for one day's work of him & his servant in the steeple – 10d.
Item to the bellman & clerks for their office about the burial of 3 poor folks – 12d.
Item to the labourers for bearing away the image of St George after it was taken down – 3d.[3]
Item to Thomas Provest for his labour in taking down the image and his servants – 6s 8d.
Item to Robert Bayly for red skins occupied about dressing the books – 18d.
Item to a glazier for mending a window in the Trinity choir – 4d.
Item for lime (3d) & mending a window in the gallery – 6d.
Item for 2 bars of iron & lead nails – 2d.
Item to the hands of William Ashby and Robert Dowghty for my Lady Fytzwilliam[4] – 9s.
Item to labourers for bearing away the horse pertaining to St George image – 12d.
Item to Symon Newbrugh for a bell-string to St George bell – 16d.
Item to Thomas Maners for mending the vestments & copes – 11d.

---

[1] This entry suggests that St Mary's was still a consecrated church. The generic term 'plague' was used to indicate any significant outbreak of sickness. Louth was 'visited' in 1516–17, 1518–19/20, 1521, 1538–9, 1540–1, 1543–4, 1587, 1625–7 and 1631. Goulding, *Parish Church*, p. 9 note. In 1562, Leverton churchwardens paid 20d for 'the books ... for praying and fasting in the time of the plague'. Thompson, *Boston*, p. 568.

[2] '37s' crossed through.

[3] This was the first action noted in Louth following the Royal Injunctions concerning 'the taking down of feigned images'. Williams, *Historical Documents*, V, p. 812.

[4] This is possibly either Margaret Wygersley, wife of John Fitzwilliam of Mablethorpe (d.1547), or Mary Skipwith, spouse of John's son George Fitzwilliam (d.1559). Maddison, *Lincolnshire Pedigrees*, 50, pp. 357–8.

Item to John Whyte's wife for mending certain altar cloths – 12d.
Item to Norman for a string to the clock – 10d.
Item to John Whyte for cherked coals against Easter (4d) & for noting (4d) the names of weddings, burials & christenings – 8d.
Item to Richard Curson for registering the same – 8d.
Item to Thomas Provest for his work in the steeple certain days & about other necessaries – 12d.
Item for ribbon to mending the vestments – 2d.
Item for a line to the basin hanged up in the High choir – 8d.
Item to Robert Bayly for 2 yards buckram & other stuff taken of him about mending the vestments & copes – 15d.
Item to the bellman for scouring the great candlesticks against Easter – 6d.
Sum – 38s 11d.

f. 47r.
Item to John Goodale for one quarter of his wages ended at the Annunciation of Our Lady – 13s 4d.
Item to Robert Goldsmyth for mending a vial[1] of silver – 4d.
Item for the clerks & the bellman doing about the burial of 3 poor folks – 8d.
Item to a tinkler[2] for mending the basin hanging in the High choir – 14d.
Sum – 15s 6d.
Sum of all allowances this year £11 18s 5d, and remain 25s 5d in money good & ill whereof paid to the hands of Thomas Lawrence which he paid to the labourers at the common sewer 8d, & sold to Arthur Graye certain broken silver for the which he paid in good money 2s 8d, and so this there remaineth clear 23s 4d in good money.[3]
Memorandum, that the money pertaining to the Common Cart by the assignment of the parishioners shall remain for the year following in the hands of George Spyllesby & Thomas Provest, and they shall lead therefore forty load[s] of stone ready digged & carried at their own expense, costs & charge and lay them where the churchwardens shall appoint them.
Churchwardens.
Thomas Spencer.
Alexander Mychelson.
Thomas Grene.[4]
Thomas Kechen.
f. 47v. [Blank].

---

[1] Phial – a small bottle or container, in this case probably for holy oil or unguent. *OED.*

[2] Itinerant metal worker. *OED.*

[3] Marginalia – 'in loss 17d'.

[4] In 1548, Thomas Grene received a pension of 26s 8d from the possessions of the St Mary guild. Foster, 'Certificate', p. 287. A Thomas Grene was interred 24 January 1543/4. LAO, Goulding Papers, 5/2.

f. 48r.

[1539–40]

The account of Thomas Spencer, draper, Alexander Mychelson, taylor, Thomas Grene, taylor, & Thomas Kechen, husbandman, Proctors of the Church of St James of Lowthe, all receipts and expenses on Sunday the Octave of Easter 1539 until the Octave of Easter the year following.[1]

Imprimis, received in good money by the delivery of the old churchwardens – 23s 4d.
Item received the 3rd Sunday after Easter – 3s 4d.
Item received the 4th Sunday after – 3s 8d.
Item received the 5th Sunday after – 2s 5d.
Item received the 6th Sunday after – 2s 6d.
Item received the Sunday of Pentecost – 3s 4d.
Item received the Trinity Sunday – 3s 8d.
Item received the first Sunday – 23d.
Item received the second Sunday after – 3s 8d.
Item received the 3rd Sunday after – 2s 4d.
Item received the 4th Sunday after – 2s 1d.
Item received the 5th Sunday after – 2s 1d.
Item received the 6th Sunday after – 3s 1d.
Item received the 7th Sunday after – 2s 4d.
Item received the 8th Sunday after – 2s 11d.
Item received the 9th Sunday after – 23d.
Item received the 10th Sunday after – 19d.
Item received the 11th Sunday after – 2s.
Item received the 12th Sunday after – 2s 11d.
Item received the 13th Sunday after – 2s 4d.
Item received the 14th Sunday after – 16d.
Item received the 15th Sunday after – 2s.
Item received the 16th Sunday after – 2s 1d.
Item received the 17th Sunday after – 3s.
Item received the 18th Sunday after – 3s 7d.
Item received the 19th Sunday after – 22d.
Item received the 20th Sunday after – 2s.
Item received the 21st Sunday after – 2s 1d.
Item received the 22nd Sunday after – 2s 8d.
Item received the 23rd Sunday after – 2s 1d.
Item received the 24th Sunday after – 2s 6d.
Item received the 25th Sunday after – 15d.
Item received the first Sunday of Advent – 2s 7d.
Item received the second Sunday of Advent – 2s 4d.
Item received the third Sunday of Advent – 2s 3d.

[1] 1540.

Item received the fourth Sunday of Advent – 20d.
Item received the Sunday after Christmas Day – 2s 7d.
Item received the Sunday after Circumcision – 2s.
Item received the first Sunday after the Octaves – 20d.
Item received the Sunday of *Septuagesima* – 2s 1d.
Item received the Sunday of *Sexagesima* – 2s 6d.
Item received the Sunday of *Quinquagesima* – 3s.
f. 48v.
Item received the first Sunday of *Quadragesima* – 2s 3d.
Item received the second Sunday – 2s 9d.
Item received the third Sunday – 23d.
Item received the fourth Sunday – 2s 9d.
Item received on Passion Sunday – 2s 1d.
Item received on Palm Sunday – 2s 7d.
Item received on Good Friday – 18d.
Item received the first Sunday after Easter – 3s 10d.
    Sum of collections – £6 6d.
      Burials.
Dorothea, wife [of] Richard Beverlay – 6s 8d.
Robert Rowte – 6s 8d.
John Larmowth – 6s 8d.
      Sum 20s.
      Legacies.
Imprimis, Thomas Hill to St John's chapel – 4d.
f. 49r.
    Great bells ringed.
Imprimis, Symon Lyncoln – 8d.
Item John Williamson – 12d.
Item Henry Fernesyde – 8d.
Item Thomas Hill – 20d.
Item Robert Westmelles – 8d.
Item Thomas Argram[1] – 8d.
Item Sir John Whyte & brethren & sisters of the Trinity guild – 8d.
Item John Gyrdyke & others – 8d.
Item Thomas Hill – 8d.
Item Jenett Buckyngham – 8d.
Item Richard Walker – 20d.
Item Thomas Bowland – 8d.
Item Dorothea, wife [of] Richard Beverlay – 20d.
Item John, son [of] Robert Wallays – 8d.

---

[1] 'Hyll' crossed through. Thomas Argram was interred 8 July 1541. LAO, Goulding Papers, 5/2.

Item Robert Rowte – 20d.
Item John Lowth – 20d.
Item William Allen – 8d.
Item John Larmowth – 12d.
Item John Archard – 8d.
Item Thomas Bradlay – 20d.
Item Marion Cloblay – 8d.
Item John Parnell – 8d.
Item William Walker – 8d.
Item Jenet Curtes – 12d.
Item Thomas Beverlay – 20d.
Item Thomas Allerton – 20d.
Item Robert Johnson, smith – 20d.
Item Stephen Parcens & Thomas Gyrdyke – 12d.
Item John Spencer – 8d.
Item Jenett, wife [of] Nicholas Upton – 8d.
Sum total – £9 14s 6d.

f. 49v.
Ministers in the church.

John Goodale in fee – 53s 4d.
The keeper of the clock & chime – 10s.
The blower of the organs – 3s 4d.
The washer of the High altar cloths – 2s.
The bellman cleansing the church – 2s 8d.
Burrett keeping the bells – 4s.
Nicholas Upton in fee – 6s 8d.
Thomas Provest in fee – 6s 8d.
Sum – £4 8s 8d.
Expenses about the church.

First, to John Goodale for writing the will of Master T[homas] Taylor[1] sent to Master Jennay – 16d.

Item to Thomas Provest & his servant for their labour one day in the steeple – 10d.

Item to the clerks and the bellman for their office doing about burial of poor folks – 8d.

Item for storing a ladder – 2d.

Item for 2 locks & the keys to the churchyard gates whereof Master Vicar hath taken charge – 4d.[2]

Item to William Smythe mending the great lock of the church door – 4d.

---

[1] Thomas Tayllyer was assessed at £20 in the 1524/5 Lay Subsidy. TNA, E179/138/478. For Taylor, see Introduction.

[2] Manicule in the margin.

Item to John Mylner for stuff & workmanship about mending the gate & stile at St Mary's churchyard – 8d.
Item to John Holderness for finding a common bull to the town for the whole year – 4s.
Item to Symon Newbrughe for a bell-string – 16d.
Item to Symon Newbrughe for a rope to the chime – 2s 6d.
Item given in reward to a poor gentleman that preached here with the assent of Master Vicar and the parishioners – 2s.
Item paid for hedging the East Field for sowing the corn – 16d.
Item to Wathe for casting the vat at the south church door – 11d.
Item to William Haryson for hasps & staples to the churchyard gates – 3d.
f. 50r.
Item in part of a reward to certain *videlicet fabule actoribus*[1] of my Lord of Suffolk's servants being in the town – 23d.
Item to a smith for an iron stenicheon[2] to a window – 2d.
Item to a smith for mending a lock at the south church door – 6d.
Item to Wathe for mending windows about the church for his stuff & labour – 20d.
Item to Thomas Provest for a chest standing at the north side of the High choir door for keeping the register book in & other necessaries – 10s.
Item to the same for his labour about the bells at All Hallows and other necessaries – 20d.
Item to Thomas Spencer for 2 wainscots occupied about necessaries in the church – 2s.
Item to William Kyng that he paid to my Lord of Suffolk's secretary for writing the letter of commandment sent from his grace to the town for ordering the obstacle – 2s.
Item paid for 1 yards & [a] half [of] cloth, 8d to the Sunday alb sleeves & for making the same 2d – 10d.
Item to William Rowthe for mending the lock of the steeple door – 6d.
Item to Robert Burnschale for sawing timber occupied about the grate at the north stile – 2s 2d.
Item for a strike [of] coals to the clerks against expenses – 3d.
Item for wire & nails occupied about [the] chimes – 11d.
Item to 2 labourers for their labour about the grate at the north stile – 3d.
Item to Thomas Provest for making the same, 12d & for making 2 gallery doors in the steeple, 12d – 2s.
Item to a smith for bolts of iron & door bands there – 6d.
Item to William Haryson for ironwork to Our Lady bell – 7d.
Item to Thomas Provest for his labour in hanging the same bell – 4d.

[1] 'That is to say acting agents.'
[2] Stanchion – upright bar, stay, prop. *OED*.

Item to Robert Lawson[1] for an ounce of silver to the foot of the frankincense ship[2] & his labour in making the same – 6s.
Item to William Haryson for shotting iron bars about the glass windows – 2d.
Item to William Smythe for mending the axle tree to the chime wheel – 3s 4d.
Item to George Tyler for glass to the windows – 8d.
Item to Wathe for mending the windows & leads – 2s 10d.
Item to William Haryson for making iron bars – 2d.
Item to Wathe for stuff & workmanship about mending windows in the Trinity choir – 18d.
Item to James Anderson[3] for mending 2 great candlesticks in Our Lady choir & one in the High choir – 3s.
Item for a strike of lime – 3d.
Item to John Rede for stuff & his labour about mending the lodge – 6d.
Item given in reward to a singingman being here certain days – 2s.
f. 50v.
Item for a new bible of the largest volume – 22s.[4]
Item to Robert Bayly for iron occupied about the clock & chime & for nails – 2s 2d.
Item for coals to the church against Easter – 3d.
Item for cherked coals against Easter – 6d.
Item for mending certain stalls in the church to the hands of Thomas Provest – 16d.
Item to John Rede for scouring the candlesticks – 6d.
Item to Richard Curson for the making of a pair [of] indentures of bargain betwixt Master Bellowe and Richard Beverlay[5] for two copes buying to the use of the church, half part – 16d.
Sum – £4 13s 5d.
Total sum allocated £9 2s 1d, and so remaining clearly 12s 6d, to which they be charged with 4s 5d, received by them of the clear expenses of the Plough light this year, and so remaining clear 16s 11d, in money good & ill.

---

[1] A Robert Louson, Lawson, goldsmith, was churchwarden in 1518/19. Dudding, *Accounts*, p. 195. Buried 15 June 1542. LAO, Goulding Papers, 5/2.

[2] Gum or resin used to make incense, in this case within a container designed like a ship. *OED*.

[3] A James Anderson, described as a tinker (an itinerant metal worker, *OED*), was interred 13 October 1562. LAO, Goulding Papers, 5/2.

[4] In September 1538, Thomas Cromwell issued an injunction that churches were to provide, 'one boke of the hole [*sic*] bible of the largest volume in English'. Merriman, *Letters*, II, p. 152.

[5] This is possibly the Richard Beverlay noted in the deposition of William Moreland following the Rising, having 'lent unto him an elmen [elm] bow and eight shafts'. *L&P*, XII (i), 380, p. 177, 9 February 1536/7. In 1513–14, Beverley was dean of the Lady guild. Williamson, 'Religious Guilds', p. 89. Interred 31 July 1546. LAO, Goulding Papers, 5/2.

Churchwardens.
Robert Fyssher.
William West.
Gylbert Fyssher.
William Colyngwod.
f. 51r. [Blank].
f. 51v.
Memorandum, that the forty shillings pertaining to the Common Cart remaineth for the year following by the assent of the parishioners in the hands of Thomas Provest carpenter & John Tenand, husbandman, which have promised to the said parishioners for the use of the said money to lay in such places as the churchwardens shall appoint them, either of them thirty loads of stone ready digged & carried of their own expense costs & charges within the year, and for the repayment of the said money, William West is surety for Thomas Provest, and William Kyng & Walter Fyssewyck be sureties for John Tenand.

f. 52r.

[1540–1]

The account of Robert Fyssher, William West, Gilbert Fyssher, mercer & William Colingwod, weaver, Proctors of the Church of St James of Lowthe, all receipts and expenses on Sunday the Octave of Easter 1540 until the Octave of Easter the year following.[1]
Imprimis, received of the old churchwardens in money good & evil – 16s 6d.
Item received the 2nd Sunday after Easter – 4s 9d.
Item received the 3rd Sunday after – 3s 7d.
Item received the 4th Sunday after – 3s 3d.
Item received the 5th Sunday after – 2s 8d.
Item received the Sunday after Ascension – 3s 10d.
Item received the Sunday of Pentecost – 4s.
Item received the Trinity Sunday – 3s 6d.
Item received the first Sunday within Octaves – 2s 8d.
Item received the first Sunday after – 3s 8d.
Item received the second Sunday after – 2s 9d.
Item received the third Sunday after – 3s 10d.
Item received the fourth Sunday after – 2s 6d.
Item received the 5th Sunday after – 3s 9d.
Item received the 6th Sunday after – 3s 7d.[2]
Item received the 7th Sunday after – 3s 8d.
Item received the 8th Sunday after – 2s 2d.
Item received the 9th Sunday after – 3s 4d.
Item received the 10th Sunday after – 2s.

---

[1] 1541.
[2] '11d' crossed through.

Item received the 11th Sunday after – 3s 7d.
Item received the 12th Sunday after – 2s 2d.
Item received the 13th Sunday after – 3s 3d.
Item received the 14th Sunday after – 2s.
Item received the 15th Sunday after – 3s.
Item received the 16th Sunday after – 2s 7d.
Item received the 17th Sunday after – 3s 8d.
Item received the 18th Sunday after – 2s 9d.
Item received the 19th Sunday after – 2s 9d.
Item received the 20th Sunday after – 22d.
Item received the 21st Sunday after – 4s 6d.
Item received the 22nd Sunday after – 20d.
Item received the 23rd Sunday after – 2s 8d.
Item received the 24th Sunday after – 2s 5d.
Item received the 25th Sunday after – 2s 8d.
Item received the first Sunday of Advent – 22d.
Item received the second Sunday of Advent – 2s 6d.
Item received the third Sunday of Advent – 2s.
Item received the fourth Sunday of Advent – 3s.
Item received the Sunday after the Nativity – 2s 8d.
Item received the Sunday after the Circumcision – 3s 4d.
Item received the Sunday after […][1] – 2s 7d.
Item received the first Sunday after the 20th day – 3s.
Item received the second Sunday – 2s 8d.
Item received the third Sunday – 2s 6d.
Item received the 4th Sunday – 2s.
f. 52v.
Sunday in *Septuagesima* – 2s 3d.[2]
Sunday in *Sexagesima* – 20d.
Item in *Quinquagesima* – 2s 10d.
Item first Sunday of *Quadragesima* – 2s 8d.
Item second Sunday of *Quadragesima* – 3s.
Item third Sunday of *Quadragesima* – 3s.
Item fourth Sunday of *Quadragesima* – 3s.
Item Passion Sunday – 2s 10d.
Item received Palm Sunday – 2s 11d.
Item received Easter Sunday – 17d.
Item received the Sunday after Easter[3] – 3s 2d.
                     Sum – £7 17s 10d.

---

[1] Illegible.
[2] This and the next ten lines are written in Latin shorthand.
[3] Written as 'in albis'. Easter Week was known as *ebdomada alba* (white week) or *in albis* (in white) from the white robes worn by those baptised at Easter. Regan, *Advent to Pentecost*, p. 242.

Burials in the church.

Sir Peter Langholme, priest,[1] in the south porch of the church – 3s 4d.
Item William Newton – 6s 8d.
Item William Asseby – 6s 8d.
Item d William Nothawk – 6s 8d.
Item Thomas Halywells – 6s 8d.
Item Joanne Foster, widow – 6s 8d.
Item Alice, wife [of] John Spalding – 6s 8d.
Item Robert Wentforth.[2]
Item Robert Forman, priest – 6s 8d.
Item Isabel, wife [of] Robert Brown – 6s 8d.
Item Robert Page – 6s 8d.
Item William Goshauke – 6s 8d.

Legacies.

Imprimis, William Asseby – 3s 4d.
Item Robert Davy – 4d.

Sum – £3 13s 8d.

Item received of Robert Spencer for money spared in buying the new bible which he received the year before – 6s 8d.

f. 53r.

Great bells.

Imprimis, Henry Fenesyde – 8d.
Item Robert Raynyard – 8d.
Item Thomas Grantham[3] – 20d.
Item Robert Beverlay – 20d.
Item Symon Lyncoln – 8d.
Item Sir Peter Langholme – 20d.
Item John Williamson – 12d.
Item Robert Westmeles – 8d.
Item Sir Peter Langholme – 20d.
Item Jane Heron, widow – 8d.
Item Sir John Whyte – 8d.
Item John Gyrdyke with others – 8d.
Item Richard Walker – 20d.
Item William Newton – 8d.

---

[1] Dom Petrus Langholme, the brother of John Langholme of Conisholme, is noted in 1526 as having a stipend of £5 6s 8d. Salter, *Subsidy*, p. 12. Maddison, *Lincolnshire Pedigrees*, 51, p. 580. Buried in Louth 19 April 1540. LAO, Goulding Papers, 5/2.

[2] Line crossed through, no amount stated.

[3] In William Moreland's deposition following the Rising, he was brought to the shop of Thomas Grantham, tailor, where he was compelled to read the contents of a book of reckonings given to him for safe keeping by John Frankish, the bishop's registrar. *L&P*, XII (i), 380, p. 174, 9 February 1536/7. Interred 26 March 1540. LAO, Goulding Papers, 5/2.

Item John Langholme – 8d.
Item Sir John Whyte & brethren of Our Lady guild – 8d.
Item William Asseby – 20d.
Item Christopher Bery – 8d.
Item Sir William Nothawke – 20d.
Item Thomas Halywells – 20d.
Item John Lowthe, merchant – 20d.
Item Joanne Foster, widow – 20d.
Item John Davy – 20d.
Item Alice, wife [of] John Spalding – 20d.
Item John Davy – 8d.
Item Thomas Bradlay – 20d.
Item William Cawod – 12d.
Item Robert Wentforth.[1]
Item Thomas Beverlay – 20d.
Item Thomas Allerton – 20d.
Item Robert for Brown's wife[2] – 20d.
Item Master Richard Wether – 20d.
Item Robert Page – 8d.
Item Janet, wife [of] Robert Akerhed – 12d.[3]
Item John Gyrdyk with others – 12d.
Item Robert Beverlay – 20d.
Item William Goshauke – 20d.
Item Symon Lyncoln – 8d.
Item William Foster – 8d.
      Sum – 45s 8d.
      Total – £15 9d.

f. 53v.
      Ministers in the church.
John Goddalle – 40s.
The keeper of the clock & chime – 10s.
The blower of the organs – 3s 4d.
The washer of the High altar clothes – 2s.
The bellman for cleansing the church – 2s 8d.
The keeper of the bells – 4s.
Thomas Provest in fee – 6s 8d.
Nicholas Upton in fee – 6s 8d.
For writing this account – 10d.[4]
      Sum – £3 16s 2d.

---

[1] No amount stated.
[2] Isabel Brown, interred 25 February 1540/1. LAO, Goulding Papers, 5/2.
[3] Recorded as Joanna Acred. Buried 10 March 1540/1. LAO, Goulding Papers, 5/2.
[4] For a quarter.

Expenses.

Imprimis, for a key to the steeple door – 1d.
Item for a key to the clerk's chamber door – 3d.
Item paid to the hands of William Asserby & Robert Dowghty that they paid for redeeming the cross that was in pledge – 2s 4d.[1]
Item to a smith for mending a lock – 1d.
Item for thread, wax and nails & other necessaries – 4d.
Item to Wathe for his work 2 days about mending the leads to meat & wages – 12d.
Item for 2 bell-strings – 2s 2d.
Item to John Holdernes for finding the town a common bull – 4s.
Item for making a dam that cattle may have water to drink – 4d.
Item to the smith for ironwork about the chime mending – 4d.
Item to Thomas Provest for one day's work for him & his servant in the steeple – 10d.
Item to John Rede for dressing St Mary's churchyard gate & other necessaries about the church & for nails – 8d.
Item to the vestment maker for making the High altar cloth to meat drink & wages – 6s 8d.

f. 54r.

Item to John Wathe[2] for his labour & stuff about mending all the faults about the church windows – 20s.
Item to Robert Fysher for 3 strikes [of] lime – 9d.
Item for mending the way at Legburn Gate & tornyng[3] the water – 6d.
Item to Gybson for carrying a tree to the same – 2d.
Item to William Haryson for making iron bars to the glass windows – 12d.
Item to Thomas Provest for a day's work of himself & his servant in the steeple & mending a chest in Our Lady choir – 12d.
Item for mending a latten[4] cross (4d) & nails (2d) – 6d.
Item for a strike [of] lime (3d) & for a men labouring (3d) about dressing the walls & windows of the church – 6d.
Item to a man for burnishing certain images in the church – 7d.
Item to Simon Mikelbarow for dressing the little images of the Rood loft – 2s 8d.[5]
Item to Richard Syll for wires making & other work about the clock – 4d.
Item to Thomas Maners for mending the coverlet [be]longing to the High altar – 7d.
Item to the cardmaker for a lantern – 14d.

---

[1] This was perhaps a loan repaid to the guilds for financing the construction of the spire, using the cross as collateral; example in Dudding, *Accounts*, p. 58.
[2] John Wathe was interred 12 May 1558. LAO, Goulding Papers, 5/2.
[3] Possibly turning. *OED*.
[4] Latten – yellow metal resembling brass. *OED*.
[5] '20d' crossed through.

Item to the clerks for their service doing of about the sick folks – 4d.
Item to Thomas Provest for his labour about the bells at Christmas – 6d.
Item for an elne[1] of velvet & 14 yards & [a] half of Towres[2] ribbon, yellow thread & searing candle – 21s.
Item for 9 yards [of] cloth & the colouring of the same for the lining of the High altar cloth – 6s 7d.[3]
Item in a reward to the vestment maker for making the High altar cloth – 2s.
Item paid 2 men for bringing of a dead corse[4] to town that was found dead in Hayrgarthers in the great snow – 4d.
Item in a reward to a man in Costragate[5] visited with plague to provide for himself in the country – 2s.[6]
Item to a smith for mending the chime – 14d.
Item the clerks for a strike [of] coals – 3d.
Item to Mykylbarow for scouring glass windows – 5d.
Item to Mykylbarow for scouring [the] north side [of the] church – 12d.
Item John White for going with constables[7] for his writing – 2d.
Item to a singingman in a reward – 20d.
               Sum – £4 6s 3d.

f. 54v.
Item to Thomas Provest for 2 days work about the bells – 16d.
Item to John Wath for mending glass windows in this church & St Mary's church – 2s 4d.
Item to William Rowth for mending the chime wires and other things – 3s 4d.
Item for 8lb [of] wax – 3s 8d.
Item for the chrismatory[8] mending – 6d.
Item for nails – 1d.
Item for a provand lyem[9] – 1½d.
Item to John Red for scouring candlesticks – 6d.
               Sum – 11s 10½d.
Item for cherk coals of Easter even – 6d.
Item to Robert Tods for [...] for certain leads lying in his house – 8d.
               Sum – 14d.

---

[1] Ell.
[2] Names of a product made at or associated with Tours in France, such as Tours taffeta. *OED*.
[3] A cross in the margin and a new hand.
[4] Corpse.
[5] Cisterngate. A house owned or rented by the church on Sasten Gate, Saxtengate or Saxongate was deemed remote enough from the town to be used for isolation purposes in time of plague. Green, *Streets of Louth*, p. 60.
[6] Perhaps given money to leave town so as not to spread disease.
[7] This is the first entry that mentions the constables as town officials.
[8] A vessel containing chrism or consecrated oils. *OED*.
[9] Meaning unknown.

Sum total £8 15s 5½d, and so remains clear £6 5s 3½d, and also is remains of the clear gatherings of the Plough light 2s 8d, all which money lyeth and remain in a coffer in Our Lady hutch, which coffer the key is of remains with the new churchwardens. Item paid of the same money to John Smyth for our house in Sastan Gate 12d, and to John Red 20d, and so remains clear £6 5s 3½d.
New churchwardens.
John Holdernes.
Thomas Wollerby.
Thomas Wardell.
William Taylyor.

f. 55r.

[1541–2]

The account of John Holdernes, Thomas Wollerby, Thomas Wardyll & William Taylyor, Proctors of the Church of St James of Louth, all receipts and expenses on Sunday the Octave of Easter 1541 until the Octave of Easter the year following.[1]
Imprimis, received the 2nd Sunday after Easter – 4s 4d.[2]
Item in 3rd Sunday – 3s 5d.
Item in 4th Sunday – 19d.
Item 5th Sunday – 2s 8d.
Item Sunday [after] Ascension – 2s 3d.
Item Sunday [of] Pentecost – 3s 9d.
Item Trinity Sunday – 3s 5d.
Item first Sunday after Trinity – 3s 3d.
Item 2nd Sunday – 3s 1d.
Item 3rd Sunday – 2s 6d.
Item 4th Sunday – 2s 4d.
Item 5th Sunday – 3s 3d.
Item 6th Sunday – 2s 11d.
Item 7th Sunday – 3s 1d.
Item 8th Sunday – 2s 2½d.
Item 9th Sunday – 2s 8½d.
Item 10th Sunday – 2s 9d.
Item 11th Sunday – 2s 6d.
Item 12th Sunday – 23d.
Item 13th Sunday – 2s 1d.
Item 14th Sunday – 2s 1½d.
Item 15th Sunday – 2s 6d.
Item 16th Sunday – 2s 6d.
Item 17th Sunday – 22d.

[1] 1542.
[2] The following items written in Latin shorthand.

Item 18th Sunday – 2s 4d.
Item 19th Sunday – 2s 2d.
Item 20th Sunday – 2s 6d.
Item 21st Sunday – 2s 4d.
Item 22nd Sunday – 2s 4d.
Item 23rd Sunday – 2s 3d.
Item 1st Sunday [of] Advent – 18d.
Item 2nd Sunday [of] Advent – 22d.
Item 3rd Sunday [of] Advent – 2s 4d.
Item 4th Sunday [of] Advent – 2s 6d.
Item Nativity Sunday.[1]
Item Sunday [of] Circumcision – 2s 8d.
Item Sunday after Epiphany – 22d.
Item 1st Sunday after Epiphany – 2s 7d.
Item 2nd Sunday – 16d.
Item 3rd Sunday – 2s 1d.
f. 55v.
Item Sunday [of] *Septuagesima* – 2s 6d.
Item Sunday [of] *Sexagesima* – 2s 7d.
Item Sunday [of] *Quinquagesima* – 17d.
Item first Sunday [of] *Quadragesima* – 2s 1d.
Item second Sunday – 22d.
Item third Sunday – 2s 5d.
Item fourth Sunday – 21d.
Item in Passion – 2s 5d.
Item Palm Sunday – 2s 6d.
Item Easter Day – 2s 8d.
Item Sunday after Easter[2] – 2s 2d.
      Sum – 24s 4d.
Received for a bible – 9s 8d.
     Burials.
Robert Brown – 6s 8d.
William Harry – 6s 8d.
Sir Thomas Fouler – 6s 8d.
Sir Thomas Kyrke – 6s 8d.
Richard Forby – 6s 8d.
Thomas Argram – 6s 8d.
Henry Rowson – 3s 4d.
John Cartar – 3s 4d.
Elizabeth Bessby, *monialis*[3] – 6s 8d.

---

[1] No amount stated.
[2] 'In albis'.
[3] Nun. This is probably Elizabeth Biesby Bursbye, Besby, Prioress of Stainfield

Elizabeth, wife [of] Robert Fyshar – 6s 8d.[1]
Margaret, wife [of] Matthew Wardall – 6s 8d.[2]
Wife [of] Robert Colynwod – 6s 8d.[3]
Richard Spencer – 6s 8d.
John Norman – 6s 8d.
Robert Holett.[4]
Gylbert Fyshar – 6s 8d.
Robert Wentforth – 6s 8d.

Sum – £5.
Legacy
William Henryson, smith – 8d.
Sir John Hudson – 12d.[5]

f. 56r.

Great bells.

John William – 12d.
Wife [of] John Goodayll – 8d.[6]
Robert Brown – 20d.
John Wryght – 8d.
William Harryson – 20d.
Robert Westmells – 8d.
Robert Brown for his month's day.[7]
James Bromflet – 12d
Sir Thomas Fouler – 8d.
Sir John White – 8d.
Wife [of] William Colynwod – 8d.[8]
Sir Thomas Fouler – 8d.
Sir Thomas Kyrke – 20d.
Richard Forby.[9]
John Gyrdyke – 8d.
Thomas Argram – 8d.
Henry Rowson – 8d.

Priory (Benedictine nuns) at the time of its suppression, post-7 August 1536. She was granted a pension of £18. Buried 13 September 1541. Smith, *Heads*, III, pp. 692–3. *L&P*, XIII (i), 1520 (52), p. 577. LAO, Goulding Papers, 5/2.

[1] Interred 7 October 1541. LAO, Goulding Papers, 5/2.
[2] Buried 16 October 1541. LAO, Goulding Papers, 5/2.
[3] Agnes Collynwod, interred 21 October 1541. LAO, Goulding Papers, 5/2.
[4] No amount stated. Burial fee paid the following year.
[5] Page torn.
[6] Joanna Goddall, buried 23 April 1541. LAO, Goulding Papers, 5/2.
[7] No amount stated. Known as the 'months mind', the bells were rung during a Requiem Mass, performed thirty days after the funeral.
[8] Margaret Collynwod, interred 5 June 1541. LAO, Goulding Papers, 5/2.
[9] No amount stated.

Thomas Red – 8d.
John Cartar – 20d.
John Langholme – 8d.
Sir John White – 12d.
Wife [of] Thomas Mychell – 8d.[1]
Elizabeth Besby, *monialis* – 20d.
Elizabeth, wife [of] Robert Fyshar – 20d.
Elizabeth Besby, *monialis* – 20d.
Sir William Nottoke – 8d.
Wife [of] Matthew Wardall – 20d.[2]
Wife [of] Robert Colynwod – 20d.[3]
Robert Rount – 8d.
Richard Spencer – 20d.
John Louth, merchant – 20d.
John Norman – 20d.
Robert Holoyt.[4]
Gylbert Fyshar – 20d.
Item John Davy – 8d.
John Nelson – 8d.
Myles Wilson.[5]
Gilbert Fyshar – 20d.
William Walker.[6]
Thomas Bradlay – 20d.
John Parnell – 8d.
William Cawod – 8d.
Thomas Beverlay – 20d.
Thomas Allerton – 20d.
Perkons & Gyrdyke – 12d.
Robert Beverlay – 20d.[7]
f. 56v.

Ministers in the church.

Imprimis, John Whet[8] – 6s 8d.
The keeper of the clock & chime – 10s.
The blower of the organs – 3s 4d.
The washer of the High altar cloths – 2s.

[1] Elizabeth Michell, buried 9 September 1541. LAO, Goulding Papers, 5/2.
[2] Margaret Wardall, interred 16 October 1541. LAO, Goulding Papers, 5/2.
[3] Agnes Collynwod, buried 21 October 1541. LAO, Goulding Papers, 5/2.
[4] No amount stated.
[5] No amount stated. Interred 5 December 1541. LAO, Goulding Papers, 5/2.
[6] No amount stated.
[7] Foot of the page damaged.
[8] Probably 'White'.

Thomas Provest in fee – 6s 8d.
The bellman for cleansing the church – 2s 8d.
The keeper of the bells – 4s.
Nicholas Upton in fee – 6s 8d.
For writing this account – 3s 4d.
Sum – 46s.[1]
Expenses.
Imprimis, paid to William Fawer[2] for digging & leading 6 load of stone to Legburn Gate – 23d.
Item for mending the latyn[3] cross – 8d.
Item for finding the common bull to John Holdernes – 4s.
Item to Thomas Provest for a bell wheel mending – 6d.
Item for nails and wood for the sawer – 2d.
Item for rent in Sastangait of certain cottages – 5s.
Item for pricking a book of 8 tomes[4] – 4d.
Item to William Rowth mending the clock watch – 12d.
Item to Simon Mykylbarow for cleansing windows – 3d.
Item paid to a bereward[5] – 20d.
Item to glazier for mending glass windows – 12d.
Item white lead for a bell clapper collar in St Mary's church – 2d.
Item Thomas Provest and his servant for one day's work about the bells – 10d.
Item Nicholas Upton for cleansing the grates at [the] church stile – 1d.
Item for girdles to vestments at the High altar – 4d.
Item for 2 bell-strings to Trinity bell and Cope bell – 2s 6d.
Item for collars to the clock – 3d.
Item for 2 crooks for a door in the steeple – 2d.
Item Thomas Provest and his servant for a day's work in the steeple – 10d.
f. 57r.
Item for mending silver censers – 8d.
Item for a stall mending in the church – 6d.
Item to W[illiam] Fawer for 9 loads of stone carrying to Legburn Gate and his labour – 3s 4d.
Item to W[illiam] Fawer for 3 stone there – 12d.
Item John Wathe for mending glass windows – 13d.
Item to W[illiam] Rowth for making iron bars for glass windows – 6d.
Item strike of lime – 3d.
Item T[homas] Provest for mending a bell wheel – 12d.

---

[1] '4d' crossed through.
[2] Interred 18 April 1547. LAO, Goulding Papers, 5/2.
[3] Latten.
[4] Eight tunes.
[5] Bear keeper. *OED*. The animal was possibly part of an entertainment group.

Item to Nicholas Upton for laying down leads of the church that was blown up with wind – 2d.
Item for mending of the organs – 16s 8d.
Item for string to the veil – 2d.
Item for charcoals for ovens – 6d.
Item for scouring the great candlesticks – 6d.
Item paper – 1d.
                    Sum – 52s 1d.[1]
Item paid for a horse hide – 2s 8d.
Item for mending clock and chime workmanship and iron – 10s.
Sum of all payments this year is £5 10s 1d, so remaineth clear this year £8 7s, which is laid in Our Lady hutch in a bible coffer with the money gathered the year before the new churchwardens having the key of the said coffer.
New churchwardens.
Richard Hynd.
Robert Hartburn.
Barkyl.[2]
f. 57v.
Received of the gathering for the Plough light this year 5s 5d, which the new churchwardens hath received.
[Memorandum that the 40s that was given for finding the Common Cart remaineth now with the new churchwardens that is made this year].[3]
Memorandum, that the money pertaining the Common Cart remains in the hands of William Reed and John Skupholme,[4] husbandman, which hath promised to lead either of them 30 loads stone to certain places within the town where need is assigned by the church masters, Thomas Spenythorn & Thomas Ketchyn bound for[5] John Skupholme, Thomas Wollerby and John Tenant bound for William Red.
Robert Kyrkby is new chosen the parish clerk this year and Master Jeffray Baly, vicar,[6] William Worslay, Robert Odlyn[7] and William Kay[8] hath promised

---

[1] '48s 10d' crossed through.
[2] Foot of page damaged, but possibly Bartholomew Claxton.
[3] [Crossed through].
[4] John Skupholm, son of John, was interred 13 October 1560. LAO, Goulding Papers, 5/2.
[5] 'Bound for' – acting as sureties.
[6] Geoffrey Baily, vicar 1537–49. Goulding, *Vicars*, p. 11.
[7] Robert Odlyng, Odlen, Odling is mentioned on 105 occasions in the accounts. Buried in 1578. Accounts III, *f.* 99v. Odlyng's two wives, Margaret and Mary, and five children, in order, William, Joanna, Joanna, Margaret and William, all predeceased him. LAO, Goulding Papers, 5/2.
[8] Interred 26 February 1551/2. LAO, Goulding Papers, 5/2.

the church masters to be bound for the said Robert Kyrkby as well for his duty doing as for his truth.

f. 58r.

Memorandum, that the fourth shillings pertaining the Common Cart remaining in the hands of Thomas Provest and John Tenant and them to lead as much stone as they did the year afore and his sureties as appears in the said year.

f. 58v.

> [There remains this year all things discharged – £9 9s 6½d.
> Total sum – £13 3s 9½d.
> Total sum allocated – £4 4s 4d].[1]

f. 59r.

[1542–3]

The account of Richard Hynd, Robert Hartburn, Bartholomew Claxton & William Draux, Proctors of the Church of St James of Louth, all receipts and expenses on Sunday the Octave of Easter 1542 until the Octave of Easter the year following.[2]

Imprimis, received the 2nd Sunday after [the] feast [of] Easter – 3s 1d.[3]
Item 3rd Sunday – 2s 7d.
Item 4th Sunday – 3s 3½d.
Item 5th Sunday – 2s 8d.
Item received the Sunday after Ascension – 2s 7½d.
Item Pentecost – 4s.
Item Trinity Sunday – 2s 4d.
Item received the first Sunday after Trinity – 2s 6d.
Item second Sunday – 3s.
Item third Sunday – 2s 9d.
Item fourth Sunday – 2s 9d.
Item fifth Sunday – 2s 8d.
Item sixth Sunday – 2s 6d.
Item 7th Sunday – 2s 7d.
Item 8th Sunday – 2s 11d.
Item 9th Sunday – 2s 11d.
Item 10th Sunday – 2s 4d.
Item 11th Sunday – 22d.
Item 12th Sunday – 2s 4d.
Item 13th Sunday – 2s 8d.
Item 14th Sunday – 2s 8d.
Item 15th Sunday – 2s 1d.

---

[1] [All lines crossed through].
[2] 1543.
[3] The following entries in Latin shorthand.

Item 16th Sunday – 2s 8d.
Item 17th Sunday – 2s 2d.
Item 18th Sunday – 2s 9d.
Item 19th Sunday – 22d.
Item 20th Sunday – 2s 8d.
Item 21st Sunday – 18d.
Item 22nd Sunday – 2s 3d.
Item 23rd Sunday – 2s 8d.
Item 24th Sunday – 2s.
Item 25th Sunday – 23d.
Item received the first Sunday of Advent – 2s 8d.
Item second Sunday – 2s 2d.
Item third Sunday – 2s 4d.
Item fourth Sunday – 2s 1d.
                    Sum – £4 10s 9d.

f. 59v.
Item received the Sunday after Nativity – 2s 11d.
Item received the first Sunday after Epiphany – 22d.
Item received the Sunday after the Octave of Epiphany – 2s 10d.
Item Sunday [of] *Septuagesima* – 2s 6d.
Item Sunday [of] *Sexagesima* – 2s 6d.
Item Sunday [of] *Quinquagesima* – 2s.
Item first Sunday [of] *Quadragesima* – 2s 9d.
Item Second Sunday [of] *Quadragesima* – 2s 4d.
Item third Sunday [of] *Quadragesima* – 2s 4d.
Item fourth Sunday [of] *Quadragesima* – 2s 4d.
Sunday in Passion – 2s 3d.
Palm Sunday – 2s.
Item Easter Day – 3s 1d.
Item Sunday in Easter – 22d.[1]
                    Sum – 33s 6d.
                    Burials.
Robert Lawson – 6s 8d.
Master Kyme's child – 3s 4d.[2]
John Croxton – 6s 8d.
Joanna, wife [of] Robert Hartburn – 6s 8d.
Master Bradlay's child – 5s.[3]

---

[1] Noted as *albis*.
[2] Charles Kyme, son of Thomas, gentleman, interred 21 June 1542. LAO, Goulding Papers, 5/2.
[3] Maria Bradley, daughter of John, buried 1 November 1542. LAO, Goulding Papers, 5/2.

Master Sampall's child – 5s.¹
Master Robynson – 6s 8d.
Robert Holot – 6s 8d.
Wife [of] Robert Lawson – 6s 8d.²
Roger Bowman – 6s 8d.
Thomas Spenythorne – 6s 8d.
Sir Thomas Lyncoln³ – 6s 8d.
Received for wood of the hedge in Hayrgarthes.
First, 3 loads 3s, 6 loads 6s, 8 loads 8s 3d.
One load, 12d of Robert Akershed for wood of the said hedge – 6s 4d.
Item of William Glen in a reward towards making the new stalls – 12d.
Item Robert Baly for the same – 5s.
               Sum – £5 3s 11d.

f. 60r.

               Great bells.
Kathryn Constable – 12d.
Symon Lyncoln – 8d.
Robert Brown for Symon Thews child – 8d.
John Williamson – 12d.
Robert Westmols – 8d.
Richard Walkar – 12d.
Trinity guild – 20d.
John Gyrdyke – 8d.
Robert Lawson – 20d.
Master Kyme's child.⁴
Master Langholm – 8d.
For Our Lady guild – 20d.
Joanna, wife [of] Robert Hartburn – 20d.
Thomas Penyngton.⁵
Master Sampall's child.⁶

---

¹ This is probably Jacob or James, son of Thomas Sempull (St Poll), interred 14 September 1542. LAO, Goulding Papers, 5/2.
² Joanna Lawson, buried 27 January 1542/3. LAO, Goulding Papers, 5/2.
³ In 1526, Dom Thomas Lincoln, chaplain, is noted as having a stipend of £5 13s 4d. Salter, *Subsidy*, p. 12. In his deposition following the Rising, William Moreland stated that on Tuesday, 3 October, Sir Thomas Lincoln and other priests were 'elected' by the rebels to ride to Caister; no doubt to raise support. *L&P*, XII (i), 380, p. 175, 9 February 1536/7. Interred 29 March 1543. LAO, Goulding Papers, 5/2.
⁴ Line crossed through, no amount stated.
⁵ No amount stated.
⁶ No amount stated. This is probably Thomassina, daughter of George St Paule or Pole, interred 24 August 1542. LAO, Goulding Papers, 5/2.

Elizabeth Besby – 8d.[1]
Robert Hudson – 8d.[2]
Master Robynson – 20d.
Richard Spencer – 8d.
William Walker for last year – 8d.
John Louth – 20d.
John Nelson – 8d.[3]
William Walker – 8d.
Thomas Bradlay – 20d.
Robert Brown – 20d.
Wife [of] Robert Lawson – 20d.[4]
T[homas] Beverlay – 20d.
T[homas] Allerton – 20d.
Parkons & Thomas Gyrdyck – 12d.
Wife [of] Roger Bowman – 20d.[5]
Thomas Spenythorne – 20d.
John Croxton – 20d.
Sir Thomas Lyncoln – 20d.
Robert Wentforth – 20d.
Thomas Dynys – 20d.
Sum – 39s 8d.

f. 60v.
Expenses to ministers in the church.

Imprimis, keeper of the clock & chimes – 10s.
Item the blower of the organs – 3s 4d.
Item the washer of the High altar cloths – 2s.
Item Thomas Provest in fee – 6s 8d.
Item the bellman for cleansing the church – 2s 8d.
Item the keeper of the bells – 4s.
Item Nicholas Upton in fee – 6s 8d.
Item for writing this account – 4s.
Sum – 38s 8d.
Expenses of the church.

Paid for one quarter six penny nails (9d), one quarter five penny nails (7d), one quarter four penny nails (5d) – 21d.
Mending the holy water vat – 1d.
Item paid for a lock unto the gate in the churchyard – 4d.

---

[1] Former nun.
[2] Hudson was assessed at 40s in the 1524/5 Lay Subsidy. TNA, E179/138/478.
[3] '2s 3d' crossed through.
[4] Joanna Lawson, interred 27 January 1542/3.
[5] Joanna Bowman, buried 26 February 1542/3. LAO, Goulding Papers, 5/2.

For a band for the same gate – 1d.
For a purse to put in the church money in – 1d.
For lime to the church walls – 12d.
To 2 labourers about the same – 4d.
Nicholas Upton for working – 8d.
Item to Robert Hotoft for working about the church walls – 6d.
For leading 2 loads of stone for St Mary's church – 4d.
To Fyshar for a 5 ounces lime – 6d.
Item another labourer about the church walls – 7d.
Item Nicholas Upton 4 days about the church walls – 16d.
Item for lime – 3d.
Item to a labourer – 4d.
Item Nicholas Upton for the church walls – 10d.
Item to John Reed for watching at Corpus Christi day – 2d.
Item to the Sawer for mending stalls in the church – 2d.
Item for a lock mending – 2d.
Sum – 9s 7d.

f. 61r.
Paid to Symon Roper for making the chime rope weighing 2½ stone – 3s 2d.[1]
Item to workmen for cleansing the sewer beside Hayrgarthes – 10s 5d.[2]
Item St Peter priest for part of his wages – 5s.
Item for paper delivered to the parish priest to make a book to write the names of weddings and of christenings – 1d.
Item in a reward to the Bishop's Suffragan – 6s 8d.[3]
Item the justice's clerk for writing a bill for mending the common ways – 8d.
Item to Jenkyn Holdernes for the common bull – 4s.
Item for mending the parish priest's surplice – 2d.
Item for mending the glass window – 12d.
Item to a vestment maker – 20d.
Item for nails – 1d.
Master Vicar for a sytacon[4] – 6d.
Item to John Wath for mending the west widow in St John's chapel – 12d.[5]
Item for nails – 5d.
Item for nails – 7½d.[6]
Item to John Wath and his servant for 6 days about the church and St Mary's church of the leads – 4s 3d.

[1] Manicule in margin.
[2] Also written in margin.
[3] Manicule in margin.
[4] Citation.
[5] This chapel in the Market Place was therefore still functioning.
[6] Manicule in right margin.

Item the same about the leads a glass windows 5 days – 3s 6d.
Item the same for 7lb of solder – 2s 4d.
Item the same for glass, lead and solder – 12d.
Item paid for a strike [of] lime – 3d.
Item half [a] horse hide for bell clappers – 12d.
Item nails – 1d.
Item John Wathe for mending the leads over the porch by 2 days work – 10d.
Item his servant 2 days – 6d.
Item 2lbs solder – 8d.
Item the clerks for 2lbs candle[s] for searching the church – 2d.
Item to William Lathes and his servant by two days for mending St Mary's church garth gate – 18d.
Item for wood for the same gate – 12d.
Item for a vertavell for the same gate – 1½d.
Sum – 57s 8d.

f. 61v.
To Thomas Maners for mending diverse vestments by four days meat and wages every day 6d, sum 2s.
Half dozen girdles – 3d.
The Bayn[1] for the same – 2d.
To the clerks for helping him – 2d.
For a strenkyll[2] – 1d.
To George Armstrong for a day [and a] half about the holy water vat – 6d.
5 ounces lime – 6d.
For fetching a stone to the church – 1d.
For carrying a load [of] stone from Louth Parke – 8d.[3]
For leading the same – 3d.
For 4 iron clasps to the holy water vat – 3d.
One strike lime – 3d.
George Armstrong 2 days – 8d.
To Nicholas Upton for his work – 2s 4d.
Paid to T[homas] Provest and Robert Odlyn for a payce[4] for the High altar and for certain stalls in the church making in part of the payment – 40s 4d.[5]
Item to T[homas] Provest – 6s 8d.
Item to Robert Odlyn – 13s 4d.

[1] Possibly a derivation of 'bone' – in this context, a set of bobbins or pins (typically made of bone or ivory) on to which the individual threads are wound. *OED*.
[2] Manicule in margin. Strinkle – a holy water sprinkler: an aspergillum. *OED*.
[3] For many years following its suppression, stone was brought from the abbey site and reused. For Louth Park, see Introduction.
[4] Probably a pax.
[5] Manicule in margin.

Item to T[homas] Provest – 26s 8d.
Item to Robert Odlyn – 6s 8d.[1]
Item to T[homas] Proveste – 8s 12d.
To Thomas Provest for a day's work amongst the bells – 6d.
The same for mending a stall and 2 letters[2] – 8d.
For mending [...][3] of a canopy – 1d.
For a horse hide for bell collars – 8d.
For mending a silver fyalle[4] – 16d.
For making iron for glass windows – 3d.
Item for a key for steeple door – 2d.
Item for mending windows – 12d.
Item for writing the names of dead persons, weddings and christenings – 12d.
For plashyng[5] the hedge at Hayrgarthes, every rod 1½d, paid first in hand another time sum [of] the whole payment for plashyng the hedge – 20s 6d.[6]
f. 62r.
To Robert Baly [for] 2lbs great wire to the chime – 10d.
A silk yellow for vestments – 2d.
Item 3½lbs [of] coloured glass – 2d.
Item 2 bell-strings weighing 20cwt – 22d.
Item for making 4 great serges[7] found by the Plough light – 12d.
Item for cleansing the new stalls and mending of a well in the churchyard – 3d.
Item for the holy water vat – 6d.
Item for chercolls[8] for [the] parish oven – 6d.
Item for bearing away old wood out of the church – 2d.
Item to Mytchell for paving in the church – 4d.
Item for scouring [the] great candlesticks – 6d.
Item for lime – 3d.
Item for measuring Hargarthes hedge of Robert Acarhed's part – 2d.
Item for mending the pace[9] in St Mary's church and a stall in the High choir – 12d.
Item for a board to the holy water vat – 2d.
Item in a reward to Robert Odlyng for making new stalls – 5s.
Item in a reward to Thomas Provest – 20d.
Sum – 14s 6d.

[1] 12d added.
[2] Perhaps an engraving.
[3] Possibly an omitted word.
[4] Vial.
[5] Plashing – the interweaving or plaiting of a hedge. *OED*.
[6] Manicule in margin; '4s', '5s 6d', '10s 4d' all crossed through.
[7] Searge, serge, cierge – large candles. *OED*.
[8] Charcoals.
[9] Pax.

Total sum allocated, £12 18s 5d, and remains 9s 5d, and 4s 5d by them received the last year of the Plough light whereof paid for wax, 16d, and this is wanting that not be found 13d, and is remaining 11s.[1]
New churchwardens, William Glover, Robert Colynwod, John Spalding[2] & John Spenlof.

f. 62v.
Memorandum, this is gathered of the Plough light which is delivered to the new churchwardens – 5s 4d.
John Tenant hath promised to lead 10 loads[3] [of] stone which he hath unled afor the feast of the Nativity of St John [the] Baptist.[4]
[And Thomas Provest 10 loads for the said feast.[5]
Item William Reed 20 loads for the said feast.
Item John Skupholm 20 loads for the said feast].
Memorandum, that the money pertaining to the Common Cart remaining in the hands of Thomas Anderson [and Richard Gybson][6] which hath promised to load either of them 20 loads [of] stone to certain places within the town where need requireth, assigned by the churchwardens Richard Hynd[7] and Bartholomew Claxton[8] sureties for Thomas Anderson and Robert Acarhed and Waryng Bery for Richard Gybson.

f. 63r.

[1543–4]

The account of Robert Spencer,[9] Robert Colynwod, John Spenlof & John Spaldyng, Proctors of the Church of St James of Louth, all receipts and expenses on Sunday the Octave of Easter 1543 until the Octave of Easter the year following.
Item the arrearages[10] of last year and the Plough light the same year – 16s 4d.
Imprimis, the second Sunday after Easter – 3s 2d.[11]
Item received the third Sunday after – 2s 9½d.

---

1 '5d' crossed through.
2 Yeoman. Will: TNA, PROB 11/54/51, probate, 7 February 1571/2.
3 '14' crossed through.
4 June.
5 [This and the next two lines partially crossed through].
6 [Crossed through]. Gybson, noted as *Paterfamilias*, was interred 8 April 1552. LAO, Goulding Papers, 5/2.
7 Buried 16 September 1546. LAO, Goulding Papers, 5/2.
8 Described as a saddler. Will: TNA, PROB 11/33/147, probate, 27 March 1550. Interred 17 August 1549. LAO, Goulding Papers, 5/2.
9 'William Glene' crossed through. He was buried 29 June 1543. LAO, Goulding Papers, 5/2.
10 Arrears of a payment that is due. *OED*.
11 The following entries are in Latin shorthand.

Item 4th Sunday – 3s 1d.
Item 5th Sunday – 2s 9½d.
Item Sunday after Ascension – 2s 5d.
Item Sunday in Pentecost – 4s 8d.
Item Trinity Sunday – 3s 4d.
Item first Sunday after Trinity – 3s.
Item second Sunday – 2s 10d.
Item third Sunday – 3s 11d.
Item fourth Sunday – 2s 7d.
Item fifth Sunday – 3s 4d.
Item sixth Sunday – 2s 10d.
Item seventh Sunday – 3s 1d.
Item eighth Sunday – 2s 6d.
Item ninth Sunday – 2s 1d.
Item tenth Sunday – 3s 11d.
Item eleventh Sunday – 2s 9d.
Item twelfth Sunday – 3s 4d.
Item thirteenth Sunday – 2s 5d.
Item fourteenth Sunday.[1]
Item fifteenth Sunday – 2s 4d.
Item sixteenth Sunday – 2s 1d.
Item seventeenth Sunday – 2s.
Item eighteenth Sunday – 22d.
Item nineteenth Sunday – 2s 1d.
Item twentieth Sunday – 2s 5d.
Item twenty first Sunday – 3s.
Item twenty second Sunday – 2s 8d.[2]
Item twenty third Sunday – 17d.
Item twenty fourth Sunday – 2s.
Item twenty fifth Sunday – 2s.
Item twenty sixth Sunday – 23d.
Item twenty seventh Sunday – 18d.
Item first Sunday of Advent – 2s 3d.
Item second Sunday of Advent – 2s 7d.
      Sum – £4 12s 10d.

f. 63v.
Item third Sunday of Advent – 2s 4d.
Item fourth Sunday of Advent – 3s 2d.
Item Sunday after Nativity – 2s 3d.
Item Sunday after Circumcision – 3s 1d.

[1] No amount stated.
[2] Manicule in margin pointing up.

Item Sunday after Epiphany – 23d.
Item Sunday after Octave of Epiphany – 2s 2d.
Item second Sunday after – 2s 4d.
Item 3rd Sunday – 2s 5d.
Item Sunday [of] *Septuagesima* – 2s 3d.
Item Sunday [of] *Sexagesima* – 3s.
Item Sunday [of] *Quinquagesima* – 23d.
Item first Sunday [of] *Quadragesima* – 2s 3d.
Item second Sunday [of] *Quadragesima* – 23d.
Item third Sunday [of] *Quadragesima* – 2s.
Item fourth Sunday [of] *Quadragesima* – 21d.
Item Passion Sunday – 21d.
Item Palm Sunday – 2s 8d.
Item Easter Day – 3s.
Item Sunday after Easter[1] – 2s 3d.

Sum – 44s 5d.

Received for Maiden chapel of T[homas] Spencer – 31s 8d.[2]
Thomas Anderson for a thrughe – 3s paid & quit.

Burials.

Wife [of] John Merlyngs – 6s 8d.[3]
Anne, wife [of] Thomas Holdernes – 6s 8d.
William Glean – 6s 8d.
John Merlyngs – 6s 8d.[4]
Robert Fyscher – 6s 8d.[5]
Margaret Parych – 3s 4d,
Wife [of] William Goshauke – 6s 8d.[6]
William Bard[7] – 6s 8d.
The bequest of Robert Fyscher – 6s 8d.
The bequest of Sir William Aylby – 6s 8d.[8]

Sum – 56s 8d.

There was gathered this year by the churchwardens of charity by the King's commandment to aid the Emperor against the Turk – 53s 4d.[9]

---

[1] *In albi*.
[2] The Maiden chapel was in St Mary's church.
[3] Katherine Marlyns was interred 30 April 1543. LAO, Goulding Papers, 5/2.
[4] Amount crossed through.
[5] Fyscher left a will: TNA, PROB 11/31/42, probate, 5 February 1545/6.
[6] Isabel Goshawcke, buried 17 February 1543/4. LAO, Goulding Papers, 5/2.
[7] Probably the servant of Sir William Ayscough, mentioned in accounts of the Rising. Ward, *Rising*, p. 16. Interred, 6 March 1543/4. LAO, Goulding Papers, 5/2.
[8] '£3 3s 4d' crossed through.
[9] Probably the campaign against Turkish pirates in North Africa. Periodically,

f. 64r.

Bells.¹

Thomas Spenythorn – 20d.
Robert Beverlay – 20d.
Symon Lyncoln – 8d.
Sir Thomas Lyncoln – 8d.
John Williamson – 20d.
Wife [of] John Marlyngs.²
John Whit, priest – 20d.
Robert Westmells – 8d.
John Gyrdyke and Lamp light³ – 8d.
Anne, wife [of] Thomas Holdernes – 20d.
William Glean – 20d.
Robert Lanson – 20d.
William Glean – 20d.
John Langholm – 8d.
John Whit, priest and brethren of Our Lady guild – 20d.
Robert Hudson – 8d.
William Walker – 8d.
Agnes Gybson – 8d.
John Marlyngs.⁴
John Louthe – 20d.
Robert Fyscher – 20d.
Wife [of] John Bell.⁵
Alice Rykard – 8d.

---

money was raised through royal briefs throughout England to pay for the release of Christian captives, notably in Tunis and Algiers. In 1543, Emperor Charles V (1519–56) made an alliance with Henry VIII in opposition to Francis I of France (1515–47), who was covertly supporting the Turks. Goulding, *Briefs*, n.p. A similar brief in Louth in 1670 raised £4 12s 7d, collected from 190 parishioners. Brears, *Lincolnshire*, p. 66. In 1568, the Leverton churchwardens paid 16d for a 'Boke of prayers agaynst the Turkis'. Thompson, *Boston*, p. 568.

1   'Burials' crossed through.
2   No amount stated.
3   The Fraternity of the Lamp Light is mentioned in the will of Thomas Sudbury, vicar of Louth (1461–1502). A large silver cross donated by Sudbury, weighing 237 ounces, was to be used at the burial of members. Another donation was to the 'Sudbury Hutch', a chest that today (2023) stands in the south-eastern chapel of the parish church. On the facing side are carved the portraits of Henry VII and his wife Elizabeth of York. Sudbury died in 1504 and left considerable sums to the church. Dudding, *Accounts*, pp. 61, 75, 94. Goulding, *Vicars*, pp. 8–9.
4   No amount stated.
5   No amount stated. Agnes Bell was buried 2 December 1543. LAO, Goulding Papers, 5/2.

Robert Fyscher – 20d.
T[homas] Bradlay – 20d.
T[homas] Beverlay – 20d.
T[homas] Allerton – 20d.
John Whit.[1]
Gyrdyke – 12d.
Wife [of] William Goshauke – 20d.
T[homas] Burnshall – 8d.
Sir W[illiam] Aylby – 8d.
W[illiam] Bard – 20d.
A stranger – 8d.
Alexander Dought[y] – 8d.
Sir Thomas Lyncoln – 20d.
Thomas Spenythorn – 20d.
Robert Beverlay – 20d.
William Bayard – 20d.
                    Sum.[2]

f. 64v.
                  Standing fees.
First to the keeper of clock and chime – 10s.
Item the blower of the organs – 3s 4d.
Item the washer of the High altar cloths – 2s.
Item T[homas] Provest for his fee – 6s 8d.
Item bellman for cleansing the church – 2s 8d.
Item the keeper of the bells – 4s.
Item Nicholas Upton for his fee – 6s 8d.
Item for writing this account – 4s.
                Sum – 38s 8d.
Received for Maiden chapel of Thomas Spencer – 31s 8d.[3]
             Expenses and reparations.
Imprimis, paid for iron work to the chime – 10d.
Item a plumber one day on the leads – 6d.[4]
Item his servant one day – 4d.
Item 2 pounds solder – 8d.
For making a beare[5] – 3d.
Item for cleansing the common sewer at Hayrgayrs – 4d.
Item mending a silver cross, a vial and St John of the Feretor – 2s 10d.

---

[1] No amount stated.
[2] Page damaged.
[3] Line crossed through.
[4] Manicule in margin with bracket indicating this and the following two lines.
[5] Bier?

Item for making 2 pair [of] butts[1] – 2s.
Item to John Holdernes for the common bull – 4s.
Item for 3 strikes lime for the church wall – 9d.
Item a labourer about the same – 4d.
Item to Nicholas Upton for mending the church wall – 3s.
Item a strike of lime – 3d.
Item to the bellman for watching of Corpus Christi night – 2d.
Item R[obert] Spencer, R[obert] Baly that is paid to Mr Beloo for his house in Saxtongate when the plague[2] – 3s 4d.
Sum – 19s 7d.

f. 65r.
Item paid for rope to the clock plumb of 16 fathoms[3] – 7d.
Item paid for hedging betwixt the East Field and the Corn Field – 2s.[4]
Item for ryese to the same – 17d.
Item for the great chime ropes – 3s 2d.
Item to Bishop's Suffragan in a reward – 5s.
Item for a new cross staff – 5d.
Item for mending the latten cross – 4d.
Item a brush for the church – 1d.
Item mending the church wall by 2 days to a workman – 8d.[5]
Item a labourer – 4d.
Item lime 3 strikes – 9d.
Item in a reward the King's bearward[6] – 20d.
Item for mending a stall in the church – 1d.
Item for cleansing the common sewer at Hayrgathes – 4d.
Item for carrying a priest prisoner to Lyncoln – 3s 6½d.[7]
Item paid to the clerk of [the] market – 10s.
Item to William Rowth for mending the chimes – 8d.[8]
Item paid for the charges of the fire breaking at Saltfleethaven and the watch – 6d.
Item for the mending of a bell wheel and nails – 3d.

---

[1] For the archery butts, see Introduction.
[2] Probably rented for isolation purposes during epidemics.
[3] A fathom equals approximately 6 feet (1.82m); therefore the rope was about 96 feet (29m). *OED.*
[4] Manicule with bracket indicating this and the line below.
[5] This and the next two lines are bracketed in the margin.
[6] Keeper of the bears. *OED.*
[7] The churchwardens appear to have had the right of jail delivery. See Introduction. The circumstances of the priest's alleged nefarious activities are unknown.
[8] Manicule in margin.

Item for half [a] stone iron and mending a bell clapper of St Mary's church – 20d.[1]
Item to Lawson for scouring the common sewer in Hayr Gayrthes – 4d.
To the clerks 2lbs [of] candles for searching the church – 3d.
Item to John Wathe for taking down lead of Mades chapel[2] – 14d.
Item T[homas] Provest for a day's work about the bells and his servant – 10d.
For nails – 3d.
Thomas Provest and his servant 2 days – 20d.
Item boards and nails to the bell wheels – 15d.
To Nicholas Upton for carrying a spout to the same for buying presses for glass windows – 8s 4d.
To Lowson for scouring the sewer in Hayrgayrthes – 4d.
To Nicholas Upton for working in the church – 4d.
f. 65v.[3]
To the clerks for searching church 3lbs candles – 3d.
Item for a ladder – 8d.
Item to Nicholas Upton about the church window – 3d.
Item for a bell-string for James bell weighing a stone and [a] half – 2s 8d.
For a legend book – 9s 7d.
To Mychell for his business – 1d.
Thomas Provest and his man a day's work in steeple – 10d.
To Maltby, smith, for iron work – 7d.
To Robert Odlyng for making new stalls in the church – 26s 8d.[4]
Item to Nicholas Upton for his business – 1d.
Item making new clappers – 6d.
Item a strike of chare coals for parish oven – 6d.
Item T[homas] Provest for making new stalls in the church – 32s 8d.
Item to Robert Odlyng for making doors to the stalls in St Peter's choir and mending diverse other stalls in the church – 3s.
Item paid for a dinner to Master Hennegde[5] and his servants – 8s.
Item for mending the great latten candlestick – 2s 4d.
Item a door for a closet in St Peter's choir – 12d.
     Sum – £4 9s 8d.
Item for flooring 2 stalls – 8d.
Item [paid for costs] and charges of Master Woloby[6] [and his servant when he assigned men for the King – 10s].[7]

1 Manicule in margin.
2 Maiden chapel. Manicule in margin.
3 [A small piece of paper with Latin text is attached to this page].
4 Manicule in margin.
5 Heneage.
6 Probably Willoughby.
7 [Items crossed through].

Item for mending the silver cross – 2s 4d.
Item for scouring candlesticks – 6d.
Item for watching the High altar of Easter Day – 1d.
Item parchment – 4d.
Sum – 3s 11d.
Total sum £9 12s 11½d, and that remaining in ill money £4 12s 6d, which is delivered to the new churchwardens whereof paid to a skinner for mending diverse books in the High choir, 8s 4d.
f. 66r.
Memorandum, delivered to the churchwardens this year of the clear proceeds of the Plough light, 5s 5d.
The 40s of the Common Cart.
Item delivered to Thomas Anderson 20s, for which he hath promised to load 20 loads [of] stone this year, Robert Baly and John Brown is his sureties.
Item delivered to Richard Gybson the elder 20s, for which he hath promised to load 20 loads [of] stone this year, Robert Colynwod and John Fyscher is his sureties.
20th day of April *Anno* H8 35.[1]
Item 4 score load [of] stone is unload at this day as appears in the last year's account.

f. 66v.

[1544–5]

The account of William Kyng, Robert Dughtie, William Brown & William Camron, Proctors of the Church of St James of Louth, all receipts and expenses on Sunday the Octave of Easter 1544 until the Octave of Easter following.[2]
Item the accountants be charged with the arrearages of the last year, £4 9s 7d.
Item with the receipts as follows, first.[3]
Item 2nd Sunday after Easter – 3s 8d.
Item third Sunday – 3s 7d.
Item fourth Sunday – 3s 5d.
Item fifth Sunday – 3s.
Item Sunday after Ascension – 2s 7d.
Item Sunday of Pentecost – 3s 8d.
Item Trinity Sunday – 3s 3d.
Item first Sunday after Trinity – 2s 7d.
Item second Sunday – 2s 1d.
Item third Sunday – 3s 1d.
Item fourth Sunday – 3s 9d.
Item fifth Sunday – 3s 6d.
Item sixth Sunday – 3s 1d.

---

[1] 1543/4.
[2] 1545.
[3] The following entries in Latin shorthand.

Item seventh Sunday – 2s 6d.
Item eighth Sunday – 3s 1d.
Item ninth Sunday – 21d.
Item tenth Sunday – 3s 6d.
Item eleventh Sunday – 22d.
Item twelfth Sunday – 3s 3d.
Item thirteenth Sunday – 2s 3d.
Item fourteenth Sunday – 2s 8d.
Item fifteenth Sunday – 2s 5d.
Item sixteenth Sunday – 2s 7d.
Item seventeenth Sunday – 4s 1d.
Item eighteenth Sunday – 3s.
Item nineteenth Sunday – 20d.
Item twentieth Sunday – 2s 11d.
Item twenty first Sunday – 2s 7d.
Item twenty second Sunday – 2s 7d.
Item twenty third Sunday – 2s.
Item twenty fourth Sunday – 2s 7d.
Item first Sunday of Advent – 2s 8d.
Item second Sunday of Advent – 2s 3d.
f. 67r.
Item third Sunday of Advent – 2s 4½d.
Item 4th Sunday – 22d.
Item Sunday after Nativity – 2s 3d.
Item Sunday after Circumcision – 10d.
Item Sunday after Epiphany – 2s 10d.
Item Sunday after the Octave of Epiphany – 3s 1d.
Item second Sunday – 2s.
The Sunday of *Septuagesima* – 2s 9d.
The Sunday of *Sexagesima* – 2s 7d.
The Sunday of *Quinquagesima* – 2s 2d.
The 1st Sunday of *Quadragesima* – 2s 1d.
The second Sunday – 2s 5d.
The third Sunday – 2s 6d.
The fourth Sunday – 23d.
Passion Sunday – 3s 2d.
Palm Sunday – 2s 5d.
Easter Sunday – 9d.
The Sunday after Easter[1] – 2s.
f. 67v.

        Burials.

William Weest – 6s 8d.

---

[1] *In albis.*

Wife [of] John Okland – 6s 8d.¹
Master Barton's child – 6s 2d.²
John Hoperton – paid & quit.
Stevyn Stoker – 3s 4d.
Hugh Beverlay – 6s 8d.
Wife [of] Richard Capper – 6s 8d.
Robert Baly – 6s 8d.
f. 68r.

Bells.

John Williamson, senior – 12d.³
Symon Lyncoln – 8d.
Robert Westmels – 12d.
John Whet, priest for Trinity guild – 20d.
John Gyrdyke – 8d.
William Glean – 20d.
William West – 20d.⁴
Wife [of] John Okland.⁵
William West – 20d.
John Langholm – 8d.
John Whet, chaplain – 20d.
Master Barton's child.⁶
John Hopton.⁷
Wife [of] John Overay – 8d.⁸
Stevyn Stoker – 20d.
Robert Fyssher – 20d.
John Lowth – 20d.
Stewyn Stoker – 8d.
Thomas Beverlay – 20d.

---

¹ Margaret Okland (Oakland), interred 16 July 1544. LAO, Goulding Papers, 5/2.

² This child could be Humphry Berton or Barton, son of John, gentleman. Interred 24 July 1544. LAO, Goulding Papers, 5/2.

³ '22d' crossed through.

⁴ West left a will, TNA, PROB 11/31/43, probate 5 February 1545/6. Interred 28 February 1545/6. LAO, Goulding Papers, 5/2.

⁵ Crossed through, no amount stated.

⁶ No amount stated.

⁷ No amount stated.

⁸ Margaret Overa, interred 20 October 1544. LAO, Goulding Papers, 5/2. Following the Rising, her husband, John Overay, a woolpacker, declared that 'the priests were the occasion of this business'. 'The parsons of Helloff [Belleau] offered them 40s and the parsons of Somarcokes [Somercotes] and Welton and dean of Mukton [Muckton] aided and encouraged them.' 'Guy Cayme [Kyme] went from Lincoln to York and John Bell from Lowthe to Hull, and the two met at York: before that there was no stir in the North.' *L&P*, XI, 972, p. 397, 3 November 1536.

Thomas Allerton – 20d.
Hugh Beverlay – 20d.
William Bayrd – 20d.
Wife [of] Richard Capper – 20d.
Ralph John.[1]
Robert Baly – 20d.
William Walker – 8d.
Wife [of] John Okland – 20d.
Robert Beverlay – 20d.
      Total sum received – £14 14s 3d.

f. 68v.
      Fees
Keeper of the clock and chime – 10s.
Blower of organs – 3s 4d.
The washer of High altar cloths – 2s.
Thomas Provest for his fee – 6s 8d.
Belman for cleansing the church – 2s 8d.
Keeper of bells – 4s.
Nicholas Upton for his fee – 6s 8d.
For writing this account – 4s.
      Sum – 39s 4d.
      Allowances and expenses.
Item paid for mending a highway of this Halyngton[2] – 6s.
Item for 5 ounces lime – 6d.
Item nails for a bell wheel – 1d.
Item for mending the chime to a smith – 1d.
Item John Holdernes for common bull – 4s.
Item Lawson for scouring the sewer in Hayrgayrthes – 4d.
Item for writing an antephener[3] and nottyng[4] the same – 4s.
Item for hedging the East Field – 6s 6d.
Item for mending the high[way] toward Stewton Lane – 16d.
Item for mending new velvet copes – 7d.
Item binding an antyfymer – 3s 4d.
Item writing and noting the same – 13s 4d.
Item to Nicholas Mason for making at Gelyan Bowar[5] a new cross – 3s.

 [1] No amount stated.
 [2] Hallington.
 [3] Antiphoner or antiphonary – a book containing a set of antiphons, music sung by one choir in response to another. *OED*.
 [4] Noting – to write or compose – musical notation. *OED*.
 [5] Julian Bower, situated today within the London Road Cemetery. Although possibly prehistoric in origin, in the Saxon period the site was used a meeting place for the Louthesk Wapentake; 'aesk' meaning ash tree. Gurnham, *Early Louth*, pp. 8–9.

Item a skin of parchment – 3d.
Item a key – 2d.
Item for a bell-string to Our Lady bell weighing 11lbs – 21d.
Item the Bishop's Suffragan – 5s.[1]

f. 69r.

Item for nails to bell wheels – 4d.
Item for 3 books for the procession[2] – 12d.
Item for a bell-string to Coo bell weighing 15lbs – 2s 2d.
Item for writing the book of burying and christenings – 8d.
Item for scouring a sewer in Hayrgars – 4d.
Item another book for the procession – 3d.
Item for hanging and mending the Coo bell and Second bell wheels – 5s.
Item for wine for Master Sampall[3] [and] Mr Skypwith – 12d
Item for making iron bars in a glass window – 4d.
Item for writing and binding 3 books; antiphoner, a verse book and a little grail – 13s 4d.
Item for carrying a load dug out of the churchyard – 1d.
Paid for mending the chime – 3d.
For 2 sheep skins for books – 6d.
For washing cloths of St John's altar – 6d.
John Wathe for his workmanship about the church – 20d.
For a bush to the bell – 1d.
Paid to Maltby, smith, for his work about the chime – 16d.
Item for 2lbs [of] candles for searching [the] church – 2½d.
Item for nails – 1d.
Item to Thomas Carver for mending chime wheels – 6d.

On Wednesday, 4 October 1536, the mound became a rallying point during the Rising. Nicholas Melton stated that 'a muster was held on the hill by the cross called Julian Bowre and captains chosen', notably John Chapman, Guy Kyme, Henry Fernstede and Thomas Foster. *L&P*, XI, 828 (i), p. 321, 21 October 1536: *ibid.*, 968, p. 390. Ward, *Rising*, p. 23.

[1] Text at the foot of the page crossed through and illegible.
[2] A processioner – a liturgical volume used for processions. *OED*.
[3] Probably George St Poll (c.1499–1558) of Louth Park, North Carlton and Snarford, where the family tombs still lie in the parish church. Maddison, *Lincolnshire Pedigrees*, 52, pp. 844–5. In 1548, he is noted as having an income of 13s 4d from the possessions of the dissolved St Mary's guild in Louth. Foster, 'Certificate', p. 287. St Poll was MP for Lincoln and Lincolnshire on numerous occasions between 1542 and 1558. Bindoff, *House of Commons*, III, pp. 260–1. Following the Rising, Mathew Mackerall, abbot of Barlings, stated that a Thomas Kirton of Scothern revealed that 'Mr Sampoull, a man of fourscore [80], had been taken from his bed to be sworn, and to send his son and heir with them.' Mackerall also related that men were sent to enlist six monks to join the rebels and that a 'Mr Sampcotes was their captain'. *L&P*, XI, 805, pp. 311–12, 20 October 1536.

Item Nicholas Upton for his work about [the] church – 12d.
Item paying for a breakfast to Master E[…][1] – 3s 4d.
Item for a stole[2] of cloth of gold – 2s.
Item a piece of willow for bushes – 2d.
Item T[homas] Carver and his servant [for] a day in the steeple – 10d.
Item to the same for wood and nails – 3d.
Item the same for him and his servant one day – 10d.
For scouring a sewer in Hayrgayrthes – 4d.
For string and thatching the lodge – 10d.
For a lock to a door in the steeple – 4d.
Paid to Maltby, smith, for forlocks[3] and cotylls[4] to Our Lady bell – 20d.
To Thomas Provest and his servant 2 days in church and steeple – 20d.
For mending the solaryng[5] in St Peter and Our Lady choir – 2s.

f. 69v.
For 2lbs candles for searching [the] church – 2d.
Paid to the constables for hiring horses for the King when lead was carried from Louth Parke in *sekyng* wains – 6s 4d.[6]
Item to T[homas] Carver for mending [the] bell frame in [the] steeple – 2s 1d.
For timber occupied in the steeple to William Brown – 3s 2d.
Item making 6 bell collars – 12d.
To Nicholas Upton – 4d.
A strike of lime – 3d.
2 bars of iron for a glass windows – 4d.
Mending a surplice – 1d.
For mending the High altar cloth – 5d.
For scouring the common sewers in Haregarthes – 4d.
Item to John Wathe for mending glass windows and about the leads and for glass and solder – 2s 8d.
Item Nicholas Upton for pergettyng[7] the glass windows with lime – 4d.[8]
To John Wathe for glass solder and workmanship about the glass windows in the church – 2s 8d.

---

[1] Name illegible.

[2] An ecclesiastical vestment consisting of a narrow strip of silk or linen, worn over the shoulders and hanging down to the knee or lower. *OED*.

[3] Forelock – an iron wedge thrust through a hole in the end of a bolt to keep it in place. *OED*.

[4] Cotterells – a pin, key, wedge or bolt that fits into a hole and fastens something in its place. *OED*.

[5] Sollaring – flooring. *OED*. Goulding suggests ceiling. Goulding, Papers, 5/3.

[6] '2s 4d' crossed through. This was probably lead from the roofs of the abbey, melted down for the king's use. The bells and lead from the monastery were valued at the questionable figure of £598 13s. Swaby, *History of Louth*, p. 112.

[7] Pargeting – 'The vessels of Glasse are pargetted and fenced' (1576). *OED*.

[8] '4d' written twice.

For making 6 keys and mending 3 locks to the choir doors – 13d.
For new making the silver piece – 20d.
Item to Thomas Carver for making a new stall by the font and a new door by the clerk's chamber – 22s.
Item for charcoals of Easter even – 6d.
Item paid towards the building of the new house of T[homas] Taylor's gift – 26s 8d.[1]
For scouring [the] great candlesticks – 6d.
For keeping the High altar after Easter morn – 2d.
To Nicholas Upton for his work about church and a strike [of] lime – 2s 3d.
There is loss in ill silver that was sold at London, the sum of 9s 6d.
f. 70r.
Total sum £10 9s 9d, and that remaining clear £3 15s, whereof paid to Nicholas Upton for making Legburn new 3s,[2] and that remains £3 13s, whereof paid for making of 4 great serges 9d, paid to the Common Cart 10s, for is remaining £3 2s 7d, which is delivered to the new churchwardens.
                    The Common Cart – 40s.
Item delivered to Thomas Anderson 20s, for which he promised to lead 20 loads [of] stone, John Brown and William Brown his sureties.
[10s of the other 20s pertaining the price and Richard Gybson oweth the other 10s.][3]
Item delivered to John Cogull[4] 20s, for which he hath promised to load 20 loads [of] stone, William Cameron[5] and George Spylsby sureties for the one half and Richard Wodhall for the other half.
10s of the foresaid 40s is taken out of the price and Richard Gybson oweth 10s, Robert Colynwod hath promised to sue for the same.
The Plough money as a purse by a bill was accounted by Thomas Wollerby.

[1545–6]

New churchwardens.
Walter Fyswyke.
William Brown, barber.
William Whet.[6]
Gylbert Blanncherd.[7]

---

    [1] See also note 821, p. 150.
    [2] Presumably a repair of Legbourne Gate.
    [3] [Crossed through].
    [4] Possibly John Coggle, described as *Paterfamilias*. Interred 28 February 1548/9. LAO, Goulding Papers, 5/2.
    [5] Buried 7 September 1546. LAO, Goulding Papers, 5/2.
    [6] Recorded in 1561 as a yeoman. Burton, *Old Lincolnshire*, p. 118.
    [7] Gilbert or Gylbert Blanchard, mercer and yeoman, left a will in which he

f. 70v.

It is agreed that the new Church Masters shall buy 2 bulls and deliver them to Robert Akerhed which hath promised to oversee them and to keep the one of them sufficiently all winter to May Day next of his cost having for his meat the winter season 16d of the church, and the other bull he shall kill against Christmas to his own use after paying for him as the Church Masters paid when they bought him first, provided the Church Masters shall assign whether the bull shall be killed.

[Item that Gylbart Blanchand doth owe to the church 20 stone [of] lead & 6lbs by that he borrowed].[1]

Item that John Wathe owes to the church 49 stone leads which he owes for.

f. 71r.

Bells.

Symon Lyncoln – 8d.
William Dughte child – 8d.[2]
Wife [of] T[homas] Wollerby – 20d.[3]
John Williamson – 12d.
Robert Baly – 20d.
Robert Westmels – 8d.
John Whett and brethren and sisters of Our Lady guild – 20d.
John Gyrdyke, Lamp light – 8d.
William West – 20d.
Wife [of] William Kyng – 20d.[4]
Thomas Northe – 20d.[5]
Master Langholm – 8d.
John Whet, priest – 20d.
Wife [of] John Nelson – 8d.[6]
Thomas Northe – 8d.
Wife [of] Thomas Mychell – 20d.[7]

---

bequeathed 20s to the grammar school. TNA, PROB 11/70/189, probate, 5 April 1587. Goulding, *Corporation Records*, pp. 4, 19, 125. He was churchwarden in 1545/6, 1553/4, 1563/4, 1573/4 and 1582/3. Blanchard was one of the first 'six assistants' of the Corporation in 1551 and was elected warden in 1558, 1567, 1574, 1580 and 1585. For the Blanchard family, see Swaby, *History of Louth*, pp. 178–9.

[1] [Crossed through].
[2] John Dowghte, buried 13 April 1545. LAO, Goulding Papers, 5/2.
[3] The parish register records a Joanna Willerbe, wife of Thomas, interred 23 April 1545. LAO, Goulding Papers, 5/2.
[4] Isabel Kyng, interred 18 July 1545. LAO, Goulding Papers, 5/2.
[5] Will: TNA, PROB 11/31/57, probate, 12 February 1545/6. Buried 4 August 1545. LAO, Goulding Papers, 5/2.
[6] Margery Nelson was buried 12 August 1545.
[7] Marginalia – '20d'. Isabel Mychell was interred 14 October 1545.

Wife [of] Bartram – 8d.[1]
Nicholas Upton – 8d.
Wife [of] John Fyshe – 20d.[2]
John Lowthe – 20d.
Robert Fysher – 20d.
Item Thomas Foster – 20d.
For Master Brodlay – 20d.
Item Thomas Berly – 20d.
Thomas Foster – 20d.
For Hugh Barly – 8d.
William Barbor – 8d.
Thomas Allerton – 20d.
For Mistress Spencer – 8d.
Item for Lawrence Penynton – 20d.
Item Robert Bordle – 20d.
Item for Robert Barley obit – 20d.
Servant of Lyncoln[3] – 8d.
Margytt Necolson – 8d.
Sir Richard of Mabbyllthorpe[4] – 8d.
Master Wylliamson, senior – 12d.
    Sum of the bells – 43s 8d.
The 4th October.
Delivered to Gylbert Blancherd of ill money to exchange at London 23s, and a knope of silver to the value of 8d by estimation.[5]
f. 71v.
Paid to the keeper of the clock and chime – 10s.
To the blower of the organs – 3s 4d.
For washing the High altar cloths – 2s.
Thomas Carver for his fee – 6s 8d.
The belman for cleansing the church – 2s 8d.
The keeper of the bells – 4s.
Nicholas Upton for his fee – 6s 8d.
For keeping the sewer in Hayrgarythes – 1s 4d.
For writing & making this account – 4s.
    Sum – 40s 8d.
Paid for a red bull – 12s 7d.
    Sum – 12s 7d.

---

 [1] Alice Galion? Wife of Bartram, interred 20 November 1545. LAO, Goulding Papers, 5/2.
 [2] Joanna Fisshe and her daughter, also Joanna, were both buried 25 November 1545. LAO, Goulding Papers, 5/2.
 [3] Possibly the bishop's servant.
 [4] Mablethorpe.
 [5] Remainder of page damaged and illegible.

Allowances.

Paid to the bellman for nails – 1d.
To labourers for diking Monks' Dyke – 16d.
Paid for 3 strikes lime to the cross – 9d.
To Nicholas Upton for mending a cross of the north side of the church – 8d.
For paper – 1d.
T[homas] Carver for mending [the] Trinity bell – 12d.
To John Holdernes for [the] common bull the year past – 4s.
To William Whet for mending hayr [...].[1]
Robert Hartburn for dighting a hod[2] that the priest uses about the sacrament – 3d.
John Reed for watching the sacrament of Corpus Christi day – 2d.
For mending the hedge in Hayrgayrthes – 2d.
For writing a book of the names of christenings and buryings – 8d.
For making and sewing the hodd -2d.
For hedging East Field thorns[3] – 12d.
Labourers 2 days – 8d.[4]
For leading[5] *thorns* – 7d.[6]

f. 72r.

To Nicholas Upton for cleansing church walls – 12d.
For a strike of lime – 3d.
A load [of] sand – 2d.
For washing albs – 8d.
Paid for building the New Inn – 40s.
To Thomas Carver for a plank to a gutter in Hayrgars hedge – 20d.
Item for scouring the same gutter – 3d.
For mending the chime – 6d.
Paid for white lead for mending a bell collar – 8d.
Paid in expenses for riding to the Justices of Sewers[7] – 17d.
Paid for writing the copies of a verdict of the sewers – 8d.
Paid for 2 bell-strings weighing 25lbs – 3s 4d.
To Maltby, smith, for new work to a bell – 8d.
For mending a bell clapper for St Mary's church – 6s 8d.
Item for trussing 2 bells in the steeple to Thomas Carver himself and his servant 2 days and nails – 2s 1d.

---

[1] No amount stated. Hayr can mean grey haired, old or venerable. *OED*.
[2] Possibly the hood of his amice, or a tabernacle for the pyx. *OED*.
[3] '12d' written twice. The use of thorns, often noted in the accounts, was probably a security measure to protect both crops and animals. A cheap form of defence and enclosure.
[4] '8d' written twice.
[5] Leading, to carry or convey. *OED*.
[6] Page damaged and illegible.
[7] Commissioners of the Sewers, overseeing the repair of dikes and ditches in order to prevent flooding, especially important in the marshlands to the east of Louth.

To the constables for the charges of a prisoner to Lyncoln – 4s 3d.
Paid for 2lb candle to search the church to the clerks – 4d.
Paid to Robert Odlyn for mending the pump – 2d.
To John Wathe for mending a glass widow and solder to the same – 12d.
Item paid to John ...*dy for a ren...d* – 12d.
Item to John Red for going about the town – 1d.
Item [.........] *feswork* for thread for mending of albs – 1d.
Item to [......................................] of the clock & chime – 2s 6d.
Item to [......................................] – 10d.
Item to [...] Kyrkby [...] cloth – [...]
Item to Maltby, smith, for the bells – 3d.[1]
[Item to Wade's wife – 4d].[2]

        Sum – 63s 2d.

f. 72v.

Item paid to Robert Spencer for the new house – £3.
Item to the belman for the mending of the gate of St Mary's churchyard – 6d.
Item to Wady's wife – 4d.
Item paid to Thomas Provest – 18d.
Item to John Red for mending chest and bere – 2d.
Item to M[aster] Dothty[3] for a quarter's rent for school house – 12d.
Item to Auncell Gese for mending of the chime rope – 6d.
Item to the belman – 2d.
Item Thomas Karver mending of the bells – 6d.
Paid to the belman for going about the town – 1d.
Paid to the fosserd[4] scouring the common sewer – 4d.
Paid to Gelbert Blancherd that he laid forth at John Smyth for wine for M[aster] Skypwith and M[aster] Kyme [when they] sat there for [the] subsidy & musters[5] – 12d.
Item paid to the Suffragan – 3s 4d.
Item paid to Wayde's wife – 4d.
Item to Thomas Carverer & his servant – 10d.
Item for a chain for a stryngkyll – 2½d.
Item to Master Dowthy for a quarter's rent – 12d.
Item for mending of bell collars – 4d.
Item for a cord to Auncell Gese – 2d.
Item to Maltby, smith – 20d.

---

 [1] Following line crossed through and illegible.
 [2] [Crossed through].
 [3] Doughty. A Robert Doughty was vicar from 1558/9 to 1600.
 [4] Fossor – person who digs ditches. *OED*.
 [5] Muster – to assemble soldiers to be counted, inspected as to condition and equipment, exercised, displayed, enlisted into service or sent into battle. *OED*.

Item to Thomas Carver for working in the steeple and about the church with 2 servants – 4s 8d.
Item to John Red – 4d.
Whereof the said Thomas Carveres has allowed for Thomas Sanderson – 4s.
Item to Walter Feswyke for thread – 1d.
Thomas Carever for a spar & nails – 4d.
Item for the mending of the churchyard of St Mary's – 9d.
Item to Mesterchamers for the same for a spar – 2d.
Paid to Robert Acryd for making of the East Field hedge at May Day – 3s 4d.
Paid to Walter Fyswycke for *cockyney* strings & thread – 5d.
Paid to Hoparton's wife for 3 new bell-strings which are occupied.[1]
Left in ill silver that was sold by Gylbart Blanchard & William Whyt – 4s.
Paid to Johanna Hoparton for the overplus[2] of the 3 bell-strings that we had for her husband's burial – 8d.[3]
Paid for a breakfast? for Sir William Skypwith[4] & Master Sampall – 5s.
Paid for charcoals – 4d.
For scouring 3 great candlesticks – 6d.
2 bell collars – 4d.
For all that the corviser[5] had – 3d.

Sum – £4 15s 1½d.
Sum total of all payments – £11 5s 2½d.

Item allowed to the said churchwardens for decays lost by negligence of writing – 3s 6½d.

f. 73r.

Sum of the money that remains of this reckoning £3 13s 2d, whereof paid to William White for keeping of the common bull – 3s.
Item paid to Thomas Spencer for one pump set in the Market Place 13s, and so remaineth clear which was delivered to the hands of the new churchwardens underwritten, 56s 10d.

Churchwardens.

Robert Acred.
Mathew Wardell.
William Baliffe.
William Doughtie.

---

[1] Entry crossed through.
[2] That left over, a surplus. *OED*.
[3] John Hoperton was interred 13 September 1544. LAO, Goulding Papers, 5/2.
[4] Sir William Skipwith (c.1487–1547) of South Ormsby JP MP, was the head of a prosperous Lincolnshire gentry family. During the Rising, he was taken prisoner at Louth and signed letters expounding the rebels' grievances to the king. With the duke of Suffolk's army advancing to put down the rebellion, Skipwith managed to evade his captors and submitted. Following its suppression, he leased the house and site of Markby Priory. He died intestate. Bindoff, *House of Commons*, III, pp. 325–6.
[5] Shoemaker or leather worker. *OED*.

For the Common Cart.

Memorandum, delivered in the sight of all the parishioners to John Cogill, 20s for which he hath promised to lead 20 loads of stone by the appointment of the churchwardens, William Cameron & George Spillesby being sureties for their half and Richard Nodhall[1] for the other half.

Item delivered to Thomas Anderson [an]other 20s, for which he hath promised 20 loads [of] stones. John Brown and William Brown being sureties.

Two bulls.

Memorandum, it is agreed that the new churchwardens shall buy one bull for serving the township and to be at their order for the most profit of the town [and] 2 bulls *videlicet* remaining & another to be bought *ut supra*.[2]

Lead delivered by weight to the new churchwardens.

This year was Nicholas Parnell chosen to be one of the parish clerks and Master Vicar, Master Kyng, Robert Walle his sureties that he shall do his service & for his Tenth.[3]

Memorandum, it is agreed that Nicholas Parnell shall have the office of keeping of the church book[4] & to have for the same 4s by year over and besides 16s assigned likewise to him for his diligent service in the choir yearly to be paid by the churchwardens.

f. 73v.

Item paid to Robert Spencer for the New Inn – £3.[5]

Item to Wade's wife – 4d.[6]

Item paid to the bellman for the mending of [...............] – 6d.[7]

Imprimis, the first Sunday gathered – 3s 7d.[8]

Item the second Sunday gathering – 2s 8d.

Item the third Sunday gathering – 2s.

Item the 4th Sunday – 22d.

Item the 5th Sunday gathered – 18d.

Item the 6th Sunday gathered – 2s 8d.

Item the 7th Sunday gathered – 2s 2d.

Item the 8th Sunday – 2s.

Item the 9th Sunday – 20d.

Item the 10th Sunday – 14d.

Item the 11th Sunday – 20d.

---

1 Interred 25 June 1546. LAO, Goulding Papers, 5/2.

2 As above.

3 Tithe. *OED*.

4 Probably the churchwardens' accounts or a book containing receipts of tithes, of which Parnell was later the scribe. Page 189, *f. 79v.*

5 Line crossed through.

6 Indistinct.

7 Line crossed through.

8 The lists of collections and burials usually follow the preamble to the new financial year.

Item the 12th Sunday – 2s 5d.
Item the 13th Sunday – 14d.
Item the 14th Sunday – 22d.
Item the 15th Sunday – 2s 1d.
Item the 16th Sunday – 18d.
Item the 17th Sunday – 13d.
Item the 18th Sunday – 21d.
Item the 19th Sunday – 19d.[1]

f. 74r.

The obits & burials.

For Robert Westmelles – 8d.
Item for John Browne, goldsmith – 8s 4d.
Item for Sir John Wyte.[2]
Item for Annes Whale – 8d.
Item for Jenet Hyde – 4s 4d.
Item for Master Martin Maysterchamers – 3s 4d.
Item for John Girdake – 8d.
Item for Woddnyll – 8d.
Item for Annes Bryan – 12d.
Item for Aylles Tonke -8d.
Item for Jenet Spedle – 8s 4d.
Item for Robert Collingwood – 8s 4d.
Item for Ayllys Gray – 8s 4d.
Item for John Tenant – 8d.
Item for Sir Robert Butllar – 8s 4d.
Item for Jenett Kyng – 8s 4d.
Item for Master John Langham – 8d.
Item for Sir John Wyte – 20d.
Item for Thomas Spencer – 8d.

f. 74v.

[1546–7]

The account of William Baylle, Robert Acred, William Doughtie & Mathew Wardyll, Proctors of the Church of St James of Louth, all receipts and expenses on Sunday the Octave of Easter 1546 until the Octave of Easter following.[3]
Imprimis, received the second Sunday after Easter – 3s 7d.
Item received the 3rd Sunday – 2s 9d.
Item received the 4th Sunday – 2s.
Item received the 5th Sunday – 22d.
Item received the 6th Sunday – 18d.

---

[1] '19th' written as 'xviiij'. The collections for 1545/6 finish here.
[2] Amount illegible.
[3] 1547.

Item received the 7th Sunday – 2s 8d.
Item received the 8th Sunday – 2s 2d.
Item received the 9th Sunday – 2s.
Item received the 10th Sunday – 20d.
Item received the 11th Sunday – 14d.
Item received the 12th Sunday – 20d.
Item received the 13th Sunday – 2s 5d.
Item received the 14th Sunday – 14d.
Item received the 15th Sunday – 22d.
Item received the 16th Sunday – 2s 1d.
Item received the 17th Sunday – 18d.
Item received the 18th Sunday – 13d.
Item received the 19th Sunday – 21d.
Item received the 20th Sunday – 20d.
Item received the 21st Sunday – 21d.
Item received the 22nd Sunday – 14d.
Item received the 23rd Sunday – 2s 4d.
Item received the 24th Sunday – 2s 10d.
Item received the 25th Sunday – 3s.
Item received the 26th Sunday – 3s.
Item received the 27th Sunday – 2s 8d.
Item received the 28th Sunday – 2s 10d.
Item received the 29th Sunday – 2s 7d.
Item received the 30th Sunday – 2s 10d.
Item received the 31st Sunday – 2s 1d.
Item received the 32nd Sunday – 2s 4d.
Item received the 33rd Sunday – 2s.
Item received the 34th Sunday – 2s.
Item received the 35th Sunday – 22d.
Item received the 36th Sunday – 22d.
Item received the 37th Sunday – 18d.
Item received the 38th Sunday – 22d.
Item received the 39th Sunday – 2s.
Item received the 40th Sunday – 2s.
Item received the 41st Sunday – 22d.
Item received the 42nd Sunday – 22d.
Item received the 43rd Sunday – 19d.
Item received the 44th Sunday – 13d.
Item received the 45th Sunday – 16d.
f. 75r.
Item received the 46th Sunday – 19d.
Item received the 47th Sunday – 18d.
Item received the 48th Sunday – 19d.
Item received the 49th Sunday – 2s 4d.

Item received the 50th on Good Friday – 20d.
Item received the 51st Low Sunday – 17d.
Sum – £4 18s 2d.
Great bells ringing.

John Browne, goldsmith – 20d.
Robert Westmells – 8d.
Sir John White, priest – 20d.
Annes, wife [of] Robert Whale – 8d.
Jenet, wife [of] Richard Hynd – 20d.
Martin Mynsterchabars – 20d.
Perkings and Girdyke – 8d.
Richard Wodall – 8d.
Annes, wife [of] Robert *Than* – 8d.
Alys Kooke, *monialis*[1] – 8d.
Jenet, wife [of] John Spencer – 20d.
Robert Collyngwood – 20d.
Alys Gray, wife [of] Arthur Gray – 20d.
Jenet, wife [of] John Tenant – 8d.
Sir Robert Butlar, priest – 8d.
Jenet, wife [of] William Kyng the younger – 20d.
Master John Langton – 8d.
Sir John Wyte, priest – 20d.
Thomas Spencer, younger – 8d.
Richard Beverlay – 20d.
William Kameron – 20d.
Olyver Bowland, major[2] – 20d.
Richard Hynde – 20d.
The founders of the chantry – 20d.
William Kameron – 20d.
Thomas Foster – 20d.
Thomas Moore – 20d.
Thomas Bradelay – 20d.
Thomas Beverlay – 20d.
Thomas Allerton – 20d.
Isabell Fyswike – 20d.
Thomas Moore, priest[3] – 8d.

---

[1] Nun. An Alice Coke was noted at the Gilbertine priory of North (Nun) Ormsby; suppressed in September 1538. Similar to the other nuns, she was probably given a pension of £2. *L&P*, XIV (i), 1355, 91b, p. 600, 12 December 1538.

[2] Senior.

[3] Dom Thomas More is noted in 1526 as having a stipend of £5 6s 8d. Salter, *Subsidy*, p. 12. Following the Rising, Nicholas Melton stated that Sir Thomas Moore

Robert Baylle – 20d.[1]
Robert Beverlay – 20d.

f. 75v.

Burials.

John Brown, goldsmith – 6s 8d.
Jenet Hynde, wife [of] Richard Hinde – 6s 8d.
Martin Mysterchambars – 6s 8d.
Jenet Spendle, wife [of] John Spedle – 5s 8d.
Robert Collingwood – 6s 8d.
Alice, wife [of] Arthur Gray – 6s 8d.
Robert Buttler, priest – 6s 8d.
Jenet, wife [of] William King – 6s 8d.
William Kameron – 6s 8d.
Elyn Bouland, *puella*[2] – 6s 8d.
Richard Beverlay – 6s 8d.
Richard Hynd – 6s 8d.
Thomas Moore, priest – 6s 8d.

Sum – £4 6s 8d.

Bequests.

Richard Hynde to St Mary's church – 4d.
Richard Beverlay to both churches – 7s 8d.[3]
And to St John's chapel – 12d.[4]
Item to the common bull sold by the wardens – 18s.

Sum – 27s.

Sum of the whole charge of the receipts – £15 14s 4d.
Received from Our Lady's guild – £4 8s 8d.
Received for a bull – [18s].[5]

Sum – £5 6s 8d.

f. 76r.

Expenses of the church.

The keeper of the clock & chime – 10s.
The blower of the organs – 3s 4d.
The bellman for his fee by year – 13s 4d.

---

gave 5s to the rebels. *L&P*, XI, 968, p. 391. Buried 31 December 1546. LAO, Goulding Papers, 5/2.

[1] Will: TNA, PROB 11/31/44, probate 5 February 1545/6. Buried 27 March 1545. LAO, Goulding Papers, 5/2.

[2] Girl. Ellen was the daughter of Thomas Bowland. She was however charged the full price for burial (children were usually interred for 3s 4d, suggesting she had reached her majority); 14 July 1546. LAO, Goulding Papers, 5/2.

[3] These are the last recorded donations to St Mary's church.

[4] This is the final reference to St John's chapel.

[5] Crossed through.

Thomas Provest in fee by year – 6s 8d.
Nicholas Parnell in fee by year – 20s.
Master Doughtie by year for the school house – 4s.
Sum – 57s 4d.
Imprimis, paid for sealing of a quittance[1] before the Commissary – 2d.
Item paid for a winding rope to the chime – 2s 8d.
Item to Thomas Provest for a wheel to Trinity bell that he took by great[2] – 13s 4d.
Item Richard Smith for nails & iron and his work about the bells – 16d.
Item for watching the feretor upon Corpus Christi day within the church – 3d.
Item paid for wine to Sir William Skypwith when he was here for the town's business – 2s 8d.
Item the bellman going about the town – 1d.
Item given in alms to poor people – 2s 4d.[3]
Item John Wath for work about the high gallery that he took by great of the churchwardens – 33s 4d.
Item to William Fawer for 3 loads [of] sand & 2 loads [of] clay to that work – 13d.
Item a bushel of lime to the same work – 7d
Item John Bello[4] for serving of Welton town folks when they were visited with plague to keep them out of the town & to buy victuals & for his pains – 18d.
Item John Rede for a bell collar and mending a string – 3d.
Item given in alms to poor people – 4s.
Item to George Dowthgty[5] for writing a copy of Master Talor's will[6] – 20d.
Item for 3 pounds of wire for the chime – 15d.
Item to Thomas Provest & his man for 2 days work in the steeple about the bells – 20d.
Item to Mistress Bale for nails to the same work – 5d.
Item given in alms to poor people – 2s 8d.
Sum – £3 11s 3d.

[1] The action of freeing from a debt, obligation or obligatory payment. *OED*.

[2] At a fixed price for completion of the whole task or for each piece. *OED*.

[3] This is the first record in the accounts of giving to the poor, something that became a regular occurrence in subsequent years. With the dissolution of the guilds, monasteries and chantries, some form of charitable provision had to be created to sustain the destitute. Collections placed in 'poor boxes' became the means by which parishioners could perform acts of benevolence.

[4] A John Bello, glover, was interred 9 October 1546. LAO, Goulding Papers, 5/2.

[5] George Doughtie was auditor of both the Trinity and St Mary guilds, receiving an annuity in 1548 of 3s 4d and 6s 8d respectively. Foster, 'Certificate', p. 287.

[6] This was probably in connection with the dissolution of the chantries, although Thomas Taylor's bequest was never fulfilled. For Taylor, see Introduction.

f. 76v.

Expenses of the church.

Item paid for a dinner when Master Goodryke[1] and Master Bellow was here to view the lands of the guilds – 6s 4d.[2]

Item Thomas Provest for a bush to St George bell & a door mending at the broach foot, 2 days for his man & himself – 20d.

Item for wood to a throssauld[3] & a [*da* …] to the same door & to the bushes & nails – 12d.

Item for mending of a great winding wheel – 10d.

Item to Symon Newbrouth for 3 bell-strings one to the Cobe bell and one to Our Lady's bell and another to St George bell – 3s 11d.

Item lost in evil silver changing – 20d.

Item given in alms to poor people – 3s 4d.

Item paid for a bell clapper making – 7s.

Item for coals & bread & drink to the same – 2s 3d.

Item paid for iron to the same – 4s 4d.

Item to John Rede for helping of the smith & a collar to the same bell – 3d.

Item given in alms to poor people – 2s 9d.

Item to John Wathe for thatching of the north porch & solder occupied to the same – 4s 8d.

Item given in alms to poor people – 2s 4d.

Item to Thomas Provest for one day's work and his man about the clock house – 10d.

Item to Master Vicar[4] for a *plake* to the same – 8d.

Item given in alms to poor people – 23d.

Item for vestments & copes mending – 2s 8d.

Item given in alms to poor people – 2s 3d.

Item paid for a piece of a torch to Sir William Dycham[5] for searching of the church – 6d.

Item for mending of the churchyard walls – 23d.

Item for one bushel of lime to the same – 7d.

---

[1] For Goodrich, see Introduction.

[2] Probably with a view to suppression.

[3] Threshold – timber that lies below the bottom of a door; the sill of a doorway. *OED*.

[4] Probably Geoffrey Baily (Baylie).

[5] Sir William Dychaund, Dychande, Dichande was the chantry priest of the John Louth chantry, part of the Holy Trinity chantry, having a net value of £11 16s 11d. He is noted in 1547 as being fifty-two and 'by no means fit to serve the cure'. Dychaund, who never married, was granted a pension of 10 marks (£6 13s 4d). He was also rector of Raithby by Louth until 1567/8 and was buried in 1574. Goulding, *Corporation Records*, p. 174. Foster and Thompson, 'Chantry Certificates', 36, p. 278. Hodgett, *Ex-Religious*, pp. 21, 49. Swaby, *History of Louth*, p. 138. Accounts III, *f.* 81r.

Item to John Wathe for the chowting[1] of lead & water flashes in the lower gallery – 2s.
Item given in alms to poor people – 12d.
Item paid for 4 quarters of lime – 6s 8d.
Item paid for a latten cross mending, a great candlestick foot & a little one pertaining to the High altar – 16d.
Item to poor people given in alms – 22d.
Item paid for wood to mending of Aswell – 12d.
Item for 2 pound candles for searching the church – 4d.
Item for a strike of coals to the clerks of Christmas even – 4d.
Item given in alms to poor people – 6d.
Item paid to Thomas Provest for one day's work & his man about the bells – 10d.
      Sum – £3 9s 11d.

f. 77r.

[1547–8]

The account of Thomas Meres, gentleman,[2] John Chapman, gentleman, George Spyllesbe & Thomas Pellson,[3] Proctors of the Church of St James of Louth, all receipts and expenses on Sunday the Octave of Easter 1547 until the year following.[4]
    The receipts of the Sunday gathering.[5]
Imprimis, the second Sunday after Easter – 3s 6d.
Item the third Sunday – 2s 11d.
Item the fourth Sunday – 2s 4d.
Item the fifth Sunday – 2s 3d.
Item Sunday after Ascension [of Our] Lord – 2s.
Item Sunday [of] Pentecost – 3s 7d.
Item Trinity Sunday – 2s 1d.
Item first Sunday after Trinity – 2s 2d.
Item second Sunday – 2s 7d.
Item third Sunday – 2s 5d.
Item fourth Sunday – 2s 2d.
Item fifth Sunday – 2s 8d.
Item sixth Sunday – 2s.
Item seventh Sunday – 2s 4d.
Item eighth Sunday – 2s 4d.
Item ninth Sunday – 3s 2d.
Item tenth Sunday – 2s 9d.

---

[1] Possibly 'clouting' – to mend with a clout or patch. *OED*.
[2] Interred 26 January 1557/8. LAO, Goulding Papers, 5/2.
[3] Buried 14 February 1567/8. LAO, Goulding Papers, 5/2.
[4] 1548.
[5] Entries written in Latin shorthand.

Item eleventh Sunday – 22d.
Item twelfth Sunday – 2s.
Item thirteenth Sunday – 22d.
Item fourteenth Sunday – 2s 4d.
Item fifteenth Sunday – 2s 3d.
Item sixteenth Sunday – 2s.
Item seventeenth Sunday – 22d.
Item eighteenth Sunday – 2s.
Item nineteenth Sunday – 23d.[1]
Item the twenty first Sunday – 21d.
Item the twenty second Sunday – 2s.
Item the twenty third Sunday – 21d.
Item the Sunday before Advent – 16d.

f. 77v.

Item first Sunday of Advent – 20d.
Item second Sunday of Advent – 22d.
Item third Sunday of Advent – 17d.
Item the fourth Sunday of Advent – 18d.
Item the Sunday after Nativity of Our Lord – 12d.
Item received of the common box – 2s 2d.
Item Sunday *Septuagesima* – 18d.
Item Sunday *Sexagesima* – 12d.
Item Sunday *Quinquagesima* – 20d.
Item first Sunday *Quadragesima* – 18d.[2]
Item received of the common box – 14d.
Item second Sunday *Quadragesima* – 20d.
Item 3rd Sunday *Quadragesima* – 10d
Item received from the common box – 14d.
Item the 4th Sunday *Quadragesima* – 18d.
Item Passion Sunday – 11d.
Item received of the box – 6d.
Item Palm Sunday – 18d.
Item Good Friday – 4d.
Item received of the box – 16d.
Received for a hedge in the East Field – 2s.
Received of Thomas Spencer of the 40s that he had dd[3] to London for the town's business – 2s 8d.
Received of Thomas Wollarbe & Robert Acred for the Plough light – 6d.
Paid to William Dowghty & Robert Akerhed, churchwardens in part of

---

[1] 20th Sunday after Trinity appears to be missing.
[2] Noted as 'xl': possibly fortieth day.
[3] *Dimidium* – half.

payment of £19 borrowed of them £4 8s 8d, which sum they have paid to John Chapman & Thomas Meres, gentlemen, £4 8s 8d.

Burials.

Item William Fawer in the church porch – 40d.
Item Jenet Gray,[1] daughter of Arthur Gray for her burial – 6s 8d.
Robert the son of John Spalding – 5s 4d.
Peter the son of Richard Robynson – 6s 8d.
George Spellysbe.[2]
William Kyng.[3]
Elizabeth Boswell.[4]
[Following four lines illegible]
Received of Master Dowghte & Gylbard Blancherd which was delivered to Thomas Spencer when he went to London for the towns business – 40s.

f. 78r.

Expenses of the church.

Item to John Wathe for mending of a window in the clerk's chamber – 4d.
Item to a Wright to meat & wages a day about the song school house – 6d.
Item for wood to a throssewold[5] & the door frame to the same work and nails – 4d.
Item for a load of clay & walling to the same – 6d.
Item a lock and key to the same school door – 2d.
Item given in alms to poor people – 22d.
Item paid to Arnalld for the mending of the second silver cross with broken silver – 3s.
Item paid for dinner when Sir William Skypwith was here on the town's business – 8s 2d.
Item for mending a chrismatory[6] – 10d.
Item given in alms to poor folk – 22d.
Item paid to John Shellton for the church lofe[7] – 10d.
Item for mending of the walls of the church & about the churchyard – 5s 6d.
Item for stone & carriage to the same – 2s.
Item John Wathe for mending of glass windows in St Mary's church – 3s 4d.
Item given to poor folks – 23d.
Item to Mistress Baylle for a bull keeping.[8]

---

[1] Jenet Grey is noted as 'Joanna' in the Parish Register when buried on 30 July 1547. However, there is another 'Joanna Grey, daughter of Arthur' noted as having been interred on 11 June 1552. Arthur's wife Alice was buried 23 July 1546, so she is possibly the daughter of a second marriage. LAO, Goulding Papers, 5/2.

[2] No amount stated.

[3] No amount stated.

[4] Wife of Edward Boswell. No amount stated.

[5] Threshold.

[6] The vessel containing the chrism or consecrated oil. *OED*.

[7] Probably the Holy Loaf.

[8] No amount stated. Page cut at this point.

f. 78v.

Memorandum, that the receipt of this year gathered and received by the churchwardens aforesaid amounts to £15 14s 4d, with their arrearages as it appears by the particulars aforesaid in this account and the same total of the charges and payments paid by the same churchwardens the same year is £12 8s 9d, and so remains clearly all things discharged £3 5s 7d, which is delivered to John Chapman, gentleman, George Spyllesby, Thomas Mers gentleman[1] & Thomas Pelson,[2] deanys[3] elect for the year following.

Item the £4 8s 8d pertaining to Our Lady's guild mentioned in this book at the last account is delivered at this account to the rulers of the common hutch in the revestry unto a convenient time.[4]

f. 79r.

Great bells.

John Williamson – 20d.
Robert Westmelles – 8d.
John Browne, goldsmith – 20d.
William Fawer – 8d.
Sir John Wyte – 20d.
John Gyrdike – 8d.
Master Martin Mysterchamber – 8d.
Richard *Bran* – 20d.
John Langhom, gentleman – 8d.
Sir John Wyte, priest, with the brethren & sisters of Our Lady's guild – 20d.
Robert Spawlling, son of John Spallyng – 8d.[5]
John Watts – 8d.
Isabell, the wife of Thomas Abot – 8d.
Peter, the son of Richard Robinson – 8d.
Thomas Bradlay – 20d.
Thomas Beverlay – 20d.
Thomas Allerton – 20d.
George Spillesby.[6]
William Kyng, junior.[7]
Elizabeth Boswell, junior.[8]

f. 79v.

---

[1] Buried 26 January 1557/8. LAO, Goulding Papers, 5/2.

[2] Thomas Pelson, yeoman, was churchwarden in 1557/8 and 1565/6. Will: TNA, PROB 11/50/218, probate, 5 July 1568. Interred 14 February 1567/8. LAO, Goulding Papers, 5/2.

[3] Possibly deans.

[4] Page cut at this point.

[5] Line crossed through.

[6] No amount stated.

[7] No amount stated.

[8] No amount stated.

Fees.

Robert Kyrkebe for keeping the clock & chime – 10s.
The blower of the organs – 3s 4d.
The washer of the cloths pertaining [to] the choir – 2s.
Thomas Provest for his fee – 6s 8d.
John Reed for keeping the bells – 4s.
John Reed for cleansing the church – 2s 8d.
John Reed for his fee – 6s 8d.
Robert Doughte for the school house – 3s.
Nicholas Parnell for his fee – 16s.
Nicholas Parnell for writing this account – 4s.

48s 4d.

Allowances and expenses.

Imprimis, for paper for this book – 1d.
Item paid for a dinner when Sir Thomas Heneage[1] was here at a sessions – 4s 4d.
Item paid to Richard Smith for 2 keys mending pertaining to the church door & the revestry and for 2 new keys to chests in the High choir – 6d.
Item to Thomas Provest mending of the same chest – 2d.
Given in alms to poor people – 4d.
Item paid to Thomas Provest for 2 days work & 2 of his men about the bells – 2s 4d.
Item given in alms to poor people – 4d.
Item to John Browne, pinder,[2] for driving the field[3] – 4d.
Item for nails occupied in the church – 2d.
Item John Rede for watching of the feretory at Corpus Christi tide – 3d.
Item in alms – 2d.
Item paid to Margaret Smythe at one […].[4]

f. 80r.

Paid to T[homas] […], clerk & to Thomas […] – 2s 4d.
Item to John Browne, pinder, for driving of the field – 2d.
Item to George Nettlewode for letting forth water out of Monks' Dyke to serve the field – 4d.
Item paid for a pot of ale when Wydern[5] bayne was here – 7d.

---

   [1]   Thomas Heneage of Hainton (c.1480–1553), Gentleman of the Privy Chamber and brother of George Heneage (1482–1549), dean of Lincoln. He was also the bishop's steward for the manor of Louth on a retainer of £3 6s 8d. Both he and his wife Katherine Skipwith (d.1575) are buried in Hainton church. *DNB*, https://doi.org/10.1093/ref:odnb/12920 (Accessed 11/4/2018). Swaby, *History of Louth*, p. 104.
   [2]   A man in charge of impounding stray animals within the pinfold. *OED*.
   [3]   To make (a furrow) by ploughing. *OED*.
   [4]   Foot of the page damaged and illegible.
   [5]   John Swaby suggests 'Withern'. The Domesday Book records *Widerne*. Swaby, *History of Louth*, p. 166, note 2. Foster and Longley, *Domesday*, 13/4, p. 73.

Item paid to Wyderne play[ers] – 6s 8d.
Item paid to William Kyng for 3 load of ryse for hedging in the East Field – 3s.
Item to John Browne, pinder, for hedging of the same field – 22d.
Item to Richard Smythe for a piece of iron to a glazed window – 1d.
Item paid to John Holdernes for one bull to serve the township for their kine[1] – 17s.
Item paid to Thomas Wollarbe for the Plough light – 4s.
Item paid to John Rede for going about the town – 1d.
Item given in alms – 2d.
Item paid to John Chowman given for leading of the ryse that the East Field was hedged with – 12d.
Item to Thomas Provest for mending of the stalling on Our Lady's choir – 6d.
Paid for a load of ryse leading to William Brown to the hedging of the East Field – 6d.
Item paid to Sir Robert Clarke for mending of a book pertaining to the choir – 20d.
Item paid for a book making to George Dowghty of the christening & burying – 16d.
Item to John Reade for a strinkill – 1d.
Item for a glass – 1d.
Item in alms – 4d.
Item paid for to the workmen in the new dyke – 30s.
Item in nails occupied about the steeple – 2d.
Item paid in alms – 4d.
Item paid for 2 challdar[2] of lime – 13s 4d.
Item paid to Thomas Tyllar & his servant for a fortnights work to meat & wages – 8s.
Item for a sawers work to meat & wages.[3]

f. 80v.

Item to George Doughte for a pair of indentures & an obligation made betwixt the churchwardens & they that had up the plate of the churches – 20d.
Paid to Thomas Corvesar's wife – 2d.
Item paid to Thomas Tylar for work that he took by great of the wardens – 10s.
Item given in alms – 8d.
Item to John Rede for making clean the choir that was wyted[4] with lime & for making of waxed candles – 6d.

---

[1] Cattle.
[2] Chalder – 12 quarters or 30–40 bushels of dry measure. *OED*.
[3] Amount illegible, as is the line below.
[4] Whited, whitewashing, possibly covering wall paintings. There is no previous record of 'whiting the walls'; therefore the church was probably covered in painted murals.

Item paid to Thomas Tyllar in erlles[1] of a bargain that he took by great of the churchwardens for wyting of the church – 3s 4d.
Item given in alms – 1d.
Item given in alms – 18d.
Item paid to a clocksmith for mending of the clock – 8s 4d.
Item paid to the new dyke making – 13s 4d.
Item paid to the same – 10s.
Item paid for a challder of lime – 6s 8d.
Item paid to Thomas Tylar the later end of his bargain that he took of the churchwardens for wytyng of the church – 7s.
Item paid to the clerks for a strike [of] coals for Christmas even – 4d.
Item given in alms – 4d.
Item paid to John Rede for dressing the windows in the steeple – 6d
Given in alms – 9d.
Paid to John Wathe for mending [a] glass window – 8d.
Paid to George Dowghty for the book of christenings – 4d.
Item given in alms – 8d.
Item paid for a bancket[2] when Sir William Wyllebe[3] was here in the town – 7s.
Item given in alms – 2d.
Item given in alms – 8d.
Item paid to Walter Fyswyke for casting down a dyke in the East Field – 8d.
Item paid to Saltmarsh & to Wayd for scouring of a common sewer betwixt Stewton & us – 3s 4d.
Item given in alms – 8d.
Item paid to the constables for their horse hire & their bill making when they did write to Master Bolles[4] of [the] town's business – *12d.*
Item given in alms – 12d.
Item paid to George Doughte for making of an obligation – 4d.
Item paid for a bell clapper setting in belonging to the High altar – 1d.
Item paid for diking in the East Field – 12d.
Item given in alms – 6d.

[1] Possibly 'arles' – 'to give earnest-money'. *OED*.
[2] Banquet, breakfast?
[3] Probably Sir William Willoughby, 1st Baron Willoughby of Parham in Suffolk (c.1515–70), who was MP for the county in 1545. Despite Stanley Bindoff's suggestion that 'he had an unblemished record during the rebellion of 1536', within the deposition of Matthew Makerall, abbot of Barlings (ex.1537), was mentioned a 'Mr Willoughbybye' as the 'grand captain of the whole host', with Thomas Mawre, a monk of Kirkstead, also revealing him as 'William Willoughbye'. *L&P*, XI, 805, p. 312, 20 October 1536: *ibid.*, 828 (vii), pp. 324–5, 3 November 1536. Bindoff, *House of Commons*, III, pp. 630–1. James, 'Obedience and Dissent', pp. 45, 76.
[4] This is the first reference to the Bolles family; later residents of Thorpe Hall. Swaby, *History of Louth*, pp. 183–90.

f. 81r.

Item delivered dd[1] to Thomas Spencer when he went to London of the towns business – 40s.

Item paid to John Wathe for mending of a glass window in St Thomas choir – 3s 4d.

Item paid to Saltmarsh & Wade for diking betwixt Stewton and this town – 5d.

Item given in alms – 7d.

Item paid to Saltmarsh & Wade for diking betwixt Steuton and this town – 3s 4d.

Item given in alms – 3d.

Item paid to the constables – 8d.

Item given in alms – 12d.

Item given in alms – 16d.

Item paid to Master Curson for making of writings & bills – 5s.

Item paid when the book was casted[2] and for drink – 2d.

Item paid for candles to Thomas Holland that was spent in the church – 3s 2d.

Item paid for making the book of Our Lady's guild & Trinity & the [...] of the Bishop – 6s.

Item given in alms – 14d.

Item paid to Bonnar for making of Master Erbe[3] & *closted* to his stuff & workmanship – 10s.

Item paid to Robert Odlyng & J[ohn] Rede for 3 days labouring taking down of the Rood, Mary & John – 9s 4d.[4]

Item paid to St George priests – 2s 8d.

All things counted & allowed in the end of the [a]ccount of Mr John Chapman, Thomas Meres, gentlemen, Thomas Pelson, William Askew, there remained 22s 5d, which is delivered to the hands of Richard Cursin, Thomas Holande, John Swyne[5] & John Fysshe.[6]

f. 81v.

[1548–9]

Churchwardens elected for this year, Richard Curson, Thomas Holland, John Swyne and John Fysshe.

---

[1] Half.

[2] To count or reckon. *OED*.

[3] Irby? The Irbys were an influential family from the Holland district. Maddison, *Lincolnshire Pedigrees*, 51 (1903), pp. 541–3.

[4] The figures of Christ on the cross (the Rood), St Mary and St John the Evangelist stood on the Rood loft. That it took two men three days to accomplish the task suggests the figures were of considerable size and weight.

[5] Buried 13 February 1557/8. LAO, Goulding Papers, 5/2.

[6] Recorded in 1561 as a yeoman. Burton, *Old Lincolnshire*, p. 118.

Anno Domini 1548.

Imprimis, received of the churchwardens the year before as apperyth at the end of the account – 22s 5d.

The Common Bull.

Memorandum, that there is one bull to serve the town.

The Common Cart – 40s.

Item delivered to Thomas Anderson – 20s, for which he hath promised to lead 20 load stone and to lay them where the churchwardens shall appoint him, William Browne his surety, the other 20s hath John Cogill after manner and form afor rehearsed, John Chapman, gentleman & Walter Fyswyke his sureties.

f. 82r.

Item received the 2nd Sunday after Easter – 12d.
Item received the 3rd Sunday after – 15d.
Item received the 4th Sunday after – 13d.
Item received the 5th Sunday after – 8d.
Item received the Sunday after the Ascension – 12d.
Item received the Wyte Sunday[1] – 2s 5d.
Item received Trinity Sunday – 21d.
Item received the first Sunday after Trinity – 16d.
Item received the 2nd Sunday after Trinity – 16d.
Item received the 3rd Sunday after Trinity – 16d.
Item received the 4th Sunday – 21d.
Item received the 5th Sunday – 16d.
Item received the 6th Sunday – 11d.
Item received the 7th Sunday – 20d.
Item received the 8th Sunday – 12d.
Item received the 9th Sunday – 21d.
Item received the 10th Sunday – 14d.
Item received the 11th Sunday – 18d.
Item received the 12th Sunday – 15d.
Item received the 13th Sunday – 17d.
Item received the 14th Sunday – 12d.
Item received the 15th Sunday – 20d.
Item received the 16th Sunday – 5d.
Item received the 17th Sunday – 13d.
Item received the 18th Sunday – 20d.
Item received the 18th – 13d.[2]
Item received the 19th Sunday – 20d.[3]
Item received the 20th Sunday – 22d.

---

[1] Whit Sunday – Whitsun.
[2] '18th' is written twice but with different amounts.
[3] This noted as the 'ix' Sunday.

Item received the 21st Sunday – 21d.
Item received the 22nd Sunday – 16d.
Item received the 23rd Sunday – 10d.
Item received the 24th Sunday – 16d.
Item received the 25th Sunday – 21d.
Item received the first Sunday in Advent – 21d.
Item received the 2nd Sunday in Advent – 11d.
Item received the 3rd Sunday in Advent – 13d.
Item received the 4th Sunday of Advent – 21d.
Item received the Sunday after the Nativity.[1]
Item received the Sunday after the Twelfth Day.[2]
Item received the first Sunday after Epiphany – 2s 2d.
Item received the second Sunday after – 14d.
Item received the Sunday after – 13d.
Item received the 3rd Sunday – 13d.
Item received the 4th Sunday – 9d.
Item received the Sunday in *Septuagesima* – 17d.
Item received the Sunday in *Sexagesima* – 17d.[3]
f. 82v.
William Rychardson, the keeper of the clock & chime – 10s.
Mawborne the blower of the organs – 3s 4d.
Jenet Kyrbe, the washer of the cloths pertaining to the altar – 2s.
John Reade, the keeper of the bells – 4s.
John Reade, the cleansing of the church within & out – 2s 8d.
John Reade, the fee for throwes laying down – 6s 8d.
Nicholas Parnell, the writer of this account – 4s.
Nicholas Parnell for helping to maintain the service – 16s.
Paid to Robert Horling – 6s 8d.

The Common Box.

Item *imprimis*, received of the Poor Man's box the first, second and 3rd week after Easter – 2s.
Item received of the box the 5th Sunday – 4d.
Item received of the box – 1d.
Item received of the box – 6d.
Item received of the box – 2d.
Item received of the box – 8d.
Item received of the box – 2d.
Item received of the box – 3d.
Item received of the box – 3d.
Item received of the box – 3d.

---

[1] Amount illegible.
[2] Amount illegible.
[3] The list of collections concludes here.

Item received of the box – 3d.
Item received of the box – 4d.
Item received of the box – 4d.
Item received of the box – 4d.
Item received of the box – 3d.
Item received of the box – 2d.
f. 83r.

Charges.

First, paid for a book called the *Paraphrases*[1] – 11s.
Item paid to Master Curson for making of a book of all the goods pertaining to the church – 5s.[2]
Item paid to George Doughte for writing the inventory of the said goods – 4d.
Item paid for 4 loads of ryse for hedging in the East Field – 4s.
Item paid to workmen for the same doing – 16d.
Item paid for paper – 1d.
Item given in alms – 4d.
Item given in alms – 10d.
Item paid for leading 4 loads of ryse for hedging the East Field – 2s 8d.
Item paid for the constables for a horse hired to David Bradlay to the Justice – 10d.
Item given in alms – 1d.
Item paid to Master Curson for writings making for a bill copying of the inventory of the goods of the church – 2s 8d.
Item given in alms – 7d.
Item paid for one load of thorns to the East Field hedging – 13d.
Item paid to Richard Smythe for mending of the clock – 4d.
Item given in alms – 2d.
Item paid to John Browne, pinder, for hedging of the East Field – 12d.
Item given in alms – 8d.
Item given in alms – 4d.
Item given in alms – 4d.
Item given in alms – 2d.
Item given in alms – 3d.
Item paid to Robert Odling for mending the chime wheel – 16d.
Item given in alms – 3d.
Item paid to a painter for putting out images of two cloths pertaining to the altar – 6d.

---

[1] *Paraphrases upon the Epistles*. This volume by Desiderius Erasmus (1466–1536) featured paraphrases of the Gospels. In the 1547 Injunctions, Edward VI ordered it to be 'set up in some convenient place in the church where their parishioners may most commodiously resort to the same'. Frere and Kennedy, *Articles*, p. 179.

[2] In 1549, there was a requirement that an inventory of church goods including bells and plate should be provided. This once again raised fears that the government wished to confiscate the wealth of the parish churches, rumours of which had become the catalyst for the Rising in 1536. Duffy, *Altars*, p. 456 and note 17.

Item given in alms – 4d.
Item given in alms – 3d.
Item paid to John Reade for 4 days work in helping of the painter to make his scaffolds – 16d.

f. 83v.
Item given in alms – 2d.
Item given in alms – 3d.
Item given in alms – 3d.
Item given in alms – 4d.
Item given in alms – 5d.
Item given in alms – 2d.
Item paid to John Browne, pinder, for making of a drain to let in water to serve the towns cattle – 4d.
Item paid to John Reade for serving the sick folks – 5s.
Item given in alms – 4d.
Item paid for a pound of wire to the clock – 6d.
Item given in alms – 6d.
Item paid to John Wathe part of his covenant for glazing of the church – 12s.
Item given in alms – 3d.
Item given in alms – 4d.
Item given in alms – 4d.
Item given in alms – 3d.
Item paid to Master Bradlay for half a year rent for the school house – 2s.
Item given in alms – 12d.
Item paid for paper for christenings & buryings – 1d.
Item paid to Symon Newbrough for 2 bell-strings – 3s 4d.
Item paid to George Doughte for his forekeeping a book of the names of all the christenings and buryings – 12d.
Item paid for a poor womans burial – 4d.
Item given in alms – 4d.
Item paid to Richard Smithe for iron bars to a glass window – 6d.
Item given in alms – 4d.
Item given in alms – 7d.
Item paid to Saltmarsh for diking in St Mary's churchyard – 6d.
Item given in alms – 2d.
Item given in alms – 10d.
Item paid for the mending of a stall – 2d.
Item paid to Thomas Holand for candle occupied in the church 6 pounds – 12d.
Item paid to Richard Smythe for iron bars to a glass window & a key to the church door – 16d.
Item paid to Spalding for exchange of money – 12?[1]

---

[1] Not stated whether shillings or pence.

f. 84r.
[All things discharged of this account remaining in debts and money ill to the new churchwardens – £4 5s 4d].[1]
16th day [of] April, the 7th year of the reign of Edward VI.
The account of Robert Spencer of such money as the said Robert received as well for the 3 bells in St Mary's church as for certain other things received by him as hereafter followeth.[2]
First, received by him for the said 3 bells – £26 11s 8d.
Item received of Anne Balif, widow, for Our Lady's crown – £4.[3]
Item received of Richard Curson for ones bequest to Aswell Lane – 10s.
Item received of Thomas Pelson for the bequest of Richard Clarke[4] – 10s.
    Sum received – £31 11s 8d.
Paid for the paving of Aswell Lane – £13 18s 2d.[5]
Item for the diking, setting and hedging of Haregarthes – £16 9s 3d.
    Total sum – £30 7s 5d.
And so remaining in debts upon the said Robert Spencer, 24s 9d.[6]
For which said sum [the said][7] Robert Spencer the son of the said Robert Spencer hath promised to deliver his bill obligations to the hands of the new churchwardens to be paid in the feast of St Michael the Archangel next coming and further Arthur Grey hath undertaken to pay the said sum at the said feast if he said Robert Spencer do make default in the payment thereof.[8]

f. 84v.
                  [1549–50]
The account of George Sutton, William Colynwood, Thomas Palmer and William Evans, Churchwardens of the Parish Church of St James in Lowthe in the County of Lyncoln of all their receipts and payments & expenses from the Sunday on the Octaves of Easter in the year of Our Lord God 1549 unto the same Sunday in the year of Our Lord God 1550 that is to say for one whole year.[9]
First, received of the churchwardens being the last year in money – 40s.
Item received on the second Sunday after Easter – £2.

---

 1 [Line crossed through].
 2 The sale of St Mary's bells following its cessation as a place of worship.
 3 A crown on an image of the Virgin as Queen of Heaven. Williamson, 'Religious Guilds', p. 87.
 4 Clarke was assessed at £6 13s 4d in the 1524/5 Lay Subsidy. TNA, E179/138/478. A Richard Clarke senior was buried 25 September 1549. LAO, Goulding Papers, 5/2.
 5 Paid for partly by the sale of St Mary's bells. LAO, Goulding Papers, 5/3.
 6 Line crossed through.
 7 [Crossed through].
 8 The remainder of the page damaged.
 9 This is the first instance of the preamble to the accounts being written in English.

Item received the 3rd Sunday after Easter – 2s 2d.
Item on the 4th Sunday after Easter – 2s 2d.
Item on the 5th Sunday after Easter – 21d.
Item on the Sunday after the Ascension Day – 2s.
Item received on Whitsunday – 2s 2d.
Item received on Trinity Sunday – 13d.
Item on the first Sunday after Trinity – 8d.
Item on the second Sunday after Trinity – 12d.
Item on the third Sunday after Trinity – 15d.
Item on the 4th Sunday after Trinity – 16d.
Item on the 5th Sunday after Trinity – 22d.
Item on the 6th Sunday after Trinity – 14d.
Item on the 7th Sunday after Trinity – 18½d.
Item on the 8th Sunday after – 2s.
Item on the 9th Sunday after Trinity – 21d.
Item on the 10th Sunday after Trinity – 12d.
Item on the 11th Sunday after Trinity – 17½d.
Item on the 12th Sunday after Trinity – 10d.
Item on the 13th Sunday after Trinity – 6d.
Item on the 14th Sunday after Trinity – 15d.
Item on the 15th Sunday after Trinity – 15d.
Item on the 16th Sunday after Trinity – 11d.
Item on the 17th Sunday after Trinity – 7d.
Item on the 18th Sunday after Trinity – 3d.
Item on the 19th Sunday after Trinity – 15d.
Item on the 20th Sunday after Trinity – 15d.
Item on the 21st Sunday after Trinity – 12d
Item on the 22nd Sunday after Trinity – 10d.
Item on the 23rd Sunday – 21d.
f. 85r.

Receipts.

Item on the 24th Sunday after Trinity – 9d.
Item on the 25th Sunday after Trinity – 13½d.
Item on the 26th Sunday – 11d.
Item received on the 27th Sunday after Trinity – 17½d.
Item received the Sunday next after Christmas – 12d.
Item received the Sunday before Twelfth Day – 11d.
Item received the Sunday after Twelfth Day – 12d.
Item received the second Sunday after Twelfth Day – 22d.
Item received on the third Sunday after 12th Day – 18d.
Item received on the 4th Sunday after Twelfth Day – 22d.
Item on the 5th Sunday after 12th Day – 6d.
Item received on the Sunday before Passion – 13d.

Item on the first Sunday in Lent – 8d.
Item on the second Sunday in Lent – 18d.
Item on the 3rd Sunday in Lent – 8d.
Item on the 4th Sunday in Lent – 22d.
Item on the 5th Sunday in Lent – 17d.
Item received on Palm Sunday – 2s 2d.
Item received on Easter Day – 8d.
Item received on the first Sunday after Easter – 17d.
Sum – £3 2s 3½d.
Burials in the church.
Item received for the burial of Jenet Rychardson – 6s 8d.
Item received for the burial of Richard Clerk – 6s 8d.
Sum – 13s 4d.
Receipts to the use of the Poor Man's box.
Item received to the use of the Poor Man's box given by Jenet Rychardson – 12d.
Item received at another time to the same use – 10d.
Item received at another time to the same use – 4d.
Item received another time – 1d.
Item received to the use aforesaid at another time – 2d.
Item at another time – 8d.
Item at another time – 13d.
Item received to the use of the Poor Man's box – 9s 4d.
Sum – 13s 6d.
Item received of John Browne for certain old boards – 20d.
Total.

f. 85v.
Item received of John Cogle's debts – 20s.[1]
Item owing by George Worsley – 25s 4d.
Sir Robert Beverlay & William Nosley sureties.
Item owing by William Kyng – £3.
Whereas received on Candlemas last – 20s.[2]
Item received for an old hedge in the East Field – 2s.
Item received for an old hedge in the North Field – 12d.
Item received for old boards of Robert Cardemaker – 12d.
Item received for certain things belonging to the church by us sold – 42s.[3]
Item received for certain old clothes – 9s 6d.

---

[1] A wife and child, cited only as 'Cogle', received charity off the parish for some period of time (see below).
[2] Line crossed through.
[3] Line crossed through.

Item received of Gilbert Blancherd and William Whyte for the overplus of 2 chalices as apperith by their bills – £10 11s 9d.[1]
Item for certain things belonging to the church sold by us – 50s 4d.
Sum – £19 11d.[2]
Sum of all the receipts – £25 11s 8½d.
Memorandum, that the 40s pertaining to the Common Cart by the assignment of the parishioners did remain this present year in the hands of Thomas Anderson and Robert Westerby[3] and they did lead forty loads [of] stone therefore ready digged & carried & laid them where the churchwardens did appoint them.
f. 86r.
Payments and allowances.
First, paid to William Rychardson for keeping the clock & chime – 13s 4d.
Total.
Item paid to John Reade for keeping the bells and leads & the church – 13s 4d.
Total.
Item to Mawborne for blowing of the organs – 10d.
Total.
Item to Nicholas Parnell for helping to maintain the service – 4s.
Total.
Item paid for the writing of this account – 4s.
Total.
Item for writing the book of christenings, weddings and burials – 2s 8d.
Total.
Other expenses about the church and money given in alms.
First, paid for 9 books called psalters to serve the choir – 10s 8d.[4]
Item paid to Bracebryge for mending the dikes & hedges of St Mary's churchyard – 8d.
Item paid for a book of the new service – 3s 8d.[5]
Item paid for paper for the choir – 3d.
Item to Gilbert Blanchard for a load of thorns – 12d.
Item to John Mylner for hedging of the same thorns – 6d.
f. 86v.
Payments & allowances.
Item for a bell-string – 9d.
Item to John Harryson for mending a wheel – 4d.
Item given in alms – 1d.
Item paid to William Browne for leading one load of thorns & loading of them – 10d.

---

[1] '£4 11s 8d' crossed through.
[2] '£18 12s 7d' crossed through.
[3] Robert Westerbe was buried 2 May 1554. LAO, Goulding Papers, 5/2.
[4] Volumes of psalms, later incorporated within the new Book of Common Prayer.
[5] Book of Common Prayer.

Item for washing towels pertaining to the altar – 1d.
Item given in alms – 4d.
Item given at another time in alms – 12d.
Item paid to John Wathe for mending the leads of St Mary's church – 8d.
Item for nails to the said work – 3d.
Item paid to Symon Newbrugh for a chime string of 2½ stone of hemp with the workmanship – 5s 2d.
Item given in alms – 2d.
Item paid for an axle tree of the chime wheel – 12d.
Item given in alms – 2½d.
Item for writing and making perfect of the books of christenings, weddings & burials – 12d.
Item to the Commissioners servant for certifying his master of the perfect making of the said books – 8d.[1]
Item paid to the dean's servant for a suspension[2] – 12d.
Item for making the bill of enclosures to the Justices – 4d.[3]
Item paid to George Sutton for enclosing the churchyard & for wood and workmanship for the same – 7s 4d.
Item paid to Bate for carrying one load of thorns – 8d.
Item paid to 2 men for hedging in the East Field – 2s 4d.
Item for a book of the service done in the church – 4s 8d.
Item paid to Walter Anderson for carrying of 2 loads of thorns – 18d.
Item given in alms – 2d.
Item paid for a load of thorns for hedging in the East Field – 3s.
Item given in alms – 3d.
Item for scouring candlesticks that stands in the high ally[4] – 1d.
Item for watching the East Field before it was hedged – 4d.
Item given in alms – 1d.
Item paid to Robert Odlyng for his quarter's wages for keeping the bells – 20d.
Item given in alms – 4d.

Sum – 36s 3½d.

f. 87r.

Payments and allowances.

Item paid to John Harryson for mending the clock & chimes – 2s.

---

[1] Probably the bishop's commissioners on an inspection of St James's.

[2] 'Deprived of the Communion of the Sacraments' (1581). *OED*.

[3] Enclosure in Louth during this period appears to have been of a temporary nature, most fields up to the edges of the town being in common. From spring to August, meadows were fenced and protected by thorns to safeguard crops and animals. There appears to have been little attempt to build permanent walling. A letter from the Queen's Council dated 1584 concerning the formation a commission of inquiry into enclosure and its final outcomes is recorded in Goulding, *Corporation Records*, pp. 92–5. For enclosure, see Robinson, *Book of Louth*, pp. 79–86.

[4] Aisle.

Item paid for selling a piece of wood over the grate by the church stile – 3d.
Item paid to William Rychardson for his pains in helping John Harryson for helping & mending the clock & chimes – 4d.
Item given in alms – 4d.
Item for washing of cloths – 2d.
Item given in alms – 2d.
Item for nails & washing a surplice – 2d.
Item given in alms – 2d.
Item for a pound of candles – 2d.
Item for washing of cloths – 2d.
Item given in alms – 1d
Item more in alms – 6d.
Item more – 2d.
Item in alms to the 2 bedehouses[1] – 12d.
Item paid for a book of *Homilies* and the *Injunctions* – 2s.[2]
Item given in alms – 12d.
Item more given – 2d.
Item paid to Richard Hanson's wife for mending of Mr Wilson's surplice – 4d.
Item given in alms – 6d.
Item for a mat – 2d.
Item given in alms – 8d.
Item paid to Robert Odlyng for his quarter's wages – 20d.
Item for paper – 1d.
Item in alms – 4d.
Item to Mr Chapman for diking the common dike – 18s 4d.
Item for making a new trundell at the west end of the church – 10s.
Item given in alms – 8d.
Item to John Reade the pulpit steps & the steps where he reads the chapters[3] and the stile against Easter – 6d.
Item given in alms – 8d.
Item to Walter Anderson for laying one load stone at John Browne's door – 2d.
Item to Saltmarsh for diking the common dike between Haregarth & Stewton closing – 6s 8d.[4]
Item given in alms – 6d.
Item at another time – 18d.
Item at another time – 6d.
Item more in alms – 4d.

Sum – 52s 5d.

[1] Houses for the poor, previously administered by the two guilds. See Introduction.
[2] For the changes in spiritual texts, see Introduction.
[3] This suggests at least a 'two-decker' pulpit.
[4] Manicule in margin with the sentence repeated.

f. 87v.
Payments and allowances.

Item paid for burying of Margaret Thomson – 6d.
Item given in alms – 13d.
Item paid for 2 bulls going with the common herd 2 years to Jenkyn Holderness – 10s.
Item given in alms – 6d.
Item paid to John Syver for a ryddell[1] – 4d.
Item given in alms – 8d.
Item to John Wathe for the glazing of windows – 20s.
Item given in alms – 14d.
Item for making mortar for the glass windows – 2d.
Item paid to Mr Eresby for 2 books – 4s.[2]
Item to John Fyssh for a lether[3] – 8d.
Item given in alms – 5d.
Item paid for washing of a surplice and certain table napkins – 4d.
Item paid for paper – 1d.
Item paid to John Wathe for mending the glass windows – 20s.
Sum – 59s 11d.

Item paid for 2 bell collars – 4d.
Item paid to Robert Odlyng for his half year's wages – 3s 4d.
Item paid for spelles[4] for the glass windows – 20d.
Item paid for mending a *brike*[5] between Lowthe and Stewton – 12d.
Item paid to Gylbert Blanchard for 2 loads of thorns – 2s.
Item given in alms – 4s 6d.
Item to John Wathe for mending the leads about St Mary's church – 8d.
Item more in alms – 2d.
Sum – 13s 8d.

Item paid to Mr Chapman for hedging & making the common dike – 4s.
Item paid to Mr Vicar for a book of the *Homilies* – 14d.
Item paid for setting forth 2 pikemen being soldiers for the harnesses[6] & other furnishers as apperath by certain bills – £6 13s 5d.
Sum – £6 18s 7d.

---

[1] Riddel – a curtain at one end of an altar. *OED.*

[2] Lawrence Eresbe, Eresby, was interred 9 January 1561/2. LAO, Goulding Papers, 5/2. Will: TNA, PROB 11/45/47, probate, 13 February 1562. For Lawrence Eresby, see Introduction.

[3] Ladder.

[4] A bar, rail or rung. *OED.*

[5] Possibly 'bridge'.

[6] Body armour of a man-at-arms or foot-soldier; military equipment or accoutrement. *OED.*

Item paid for digging the common pit[1] at Burton Bridge[2] – 5s 10d.
Sum.[3]

f. 88r.
Total sum of all their payments and allowances – £18 19½d.
And remains £7 10s 1d whereof owing by William Kyng – 40s.
Item by William Worsley & Sir Robert Beverley as apperith by their bill – 25s 4d.
Whereof received of Sir Robert Beverlay – 12s 7d.
And so remaineth in money – £4 4s 4d.[4]
Which moneys delivered unto the hands of John Holdernes, Thomas Wardall, Thomas Blanchard and John Palmer, churchwardens for the year next coming.
Item delivered to the said churchwardens in money gathered for the Plough light – 7s.
Item delivered to the said churchwardens to those of the Poor Man's box, 9s of the Lamp light money.
Memorandum, that the 40s for the Common Cart doth remain for this year next following in the hands of Thomas Anderson and Robert Westerby & they to lead 40 loads of stone and to lay the same where they shall be appointed by the churchwardens.

f. 88v.

[1550–51]

The account of [John Holdernes, William Taillor],[5] Thomas Wardell, Thomas Blanchard[6] & John Palmer, Churchwardens of the Parish Church of St James in Lowthe in the County of Lincoln of all the receipts & payments & expenses from the Sunday in the Octave of Easter in the year of Our Lord God 1550 unto the said Sunday in the year of Our Lord 1551, that is to say for one whole year.
First, received of the money of the churchwardens the last year as appearith by their account – £4 4s 4d.
Item more received of the money gathered for the Plough light – 7s.
Item received to the use of the Poor Man's box of the Lamp light money – 9s.
Sum – £5 4d.
Item received the second Sunday after Easter – 3s 5d.
Item received the 3rd Sunday after Easter – 2s 6d.
Item received the 4th Sunday after Easter – 2s 2d.

---

[1] Probably a saw pit.
[2] The whereabouts of Burton Bridge is so far unknown.
[3] No amount stated.
[4] '9d' crossed through.
[5] [Crossed through]. Holderness was interred 23 April 1550. LAO, Goulding Papers, 5/2. Will: TNA, PROB 11/33/228, probate 21 May 1550.
[6] Thomas Blanchard, yeoman, was elected Corporation warden in 1564, 1571 and 1577, and churchwarden in 1559/60 and 1569/70. Goulding, *Corporation Records*, p. 19. Burton, *Old Lincolnshire*, p. 118.

Item received to the use of the Poor Man's box – 1d.
Item received the 5th Sunday after Easter – 18d.
Item received on the Sunday after the Ascension Day – 4s.
Item received on Whitsun Sunday – 2s 10d.
Item received on Trinity Sunday – 2s 6d.
Item received on the first Sunday after Trinity – 2s 4d.
Item received on the second Sunday after Trinity – 22d.
Item received on the 3rd Sunday after Trinity – 23d.
Item received on the 4th Sunday after Trinity – 2s 7d.
Item received for brass – 21s.
Item received more for brass – 7s 6d.
Item received for iron – 12d.
Item received for a bell clapper – 16d.
Item more received for old iron – 12d.
Item received on the 5th Sunday after Trinity – 2s 9d.
Item received on the 6th Sunday after Trinity – 23d.
Item received the 7th Sunday after Trinity – 9½d.
Item received the 8th Sunday after Trinity – 2s 4d.
Item received the 9th Sunday after Trinity – 2s 4d.
Item received the 10th Sunday after Trinity – 20d.
Item received the 11th Sunday after Trinity – 20d.
Item received the 12th Sunday after Trinity – 9d.
Item received the 13th Sunday after Trinity – 13d.
Item received the 14th Sunday after Trinity – 22d.
£3 16s 8d.[1]

f. 89r.
Item received on the 15th Sunday after Trinity – 13d.
Item received on the 16th Sunday after Trinity – 13d.
Item received on the 17th Sunday after Trinity – 15d.
Item received on the 18th Sunday after Trinity – 18d.
Item received on the 19th Sunday after Trinity – 7d.
Item received on the 20th Sunday after Trinity – 21d.
Item received on the 21st Sunday after Trinity – 16d.
Item received on the 22nd Sunday after Trinity – 2s 4d.
Item received on the 23rd Sunday after Trinity – 22d.
Item received on the 24th Sunday after Trinity – 2s.
Item received on the 25th Sunday after Trinity – 2s 2d.
Item received on the first Sunday in Advent – 23d.
Item received for a stone vat[2] – 12d.
Item received on the second day in Advent – 21d.
Item received on the 3rd Sunday in Advent – 19d.

[1] Total recorded for the first time in 'Arabic' numerals. The total, minus the entries unconnected with the collections, is £3 5s 8½d.
[2] Noted as 'ffate'.

Item received for lokkers under the altars – 3s.[1]
Item received for 2 strikes of lime – 4d.
Item received on the 4th Sunday in Advent – 16d.
Item received on the first Sunday after Christmas – 20d.
Item received on the second Sunday after Christmas – 21d.
Item received on the 3rd Sunday after Christmas – 20d.
      33s 3d.[2]
     Burials in the church.
Item received for the burial of Robert Dowghty – 6s 8d.
Item received more for the bells – 20d.
Item received for the burial of Isabell, the wife of Robert Spencer – 6s 8d.
Item received for the burial of John Holdernes – 6s 8d.
Item more for the bells – 20d.
Item received for the burial of John Thorneley's wife – 6s 8d.[3]
Item received for the burial of Thomas Spenlow – 8s 4d.
Item received for the burial of Margaret Smythe, wife of John Smythe – 6s 8d.
Item received for tile – *6d*.[4]
Item received for the burial of Thomas Spencer – 20s.[5]
      £3 5s 8d.
    Received of Gilbert Blanchard.[6]

f. 89v.
    Receipts to the use of the Poor Man's box.
Item received at one time – 6d.
Item received at another time – 4d.
Item received at another time – 4d.
Item received at another time – 5d.
Item received at another time – 4d.
Item received at another time – 8d.
Item received at another time – 6d.
Item received at another time – 12d.
Item received at another time – 4d.
Item received at another time – 1d.
Item received at another time – 4d.
Item received at another time – 4d.
Item received for a top of a […] – 3s 4d.

---

[1] These were possibly containers holding relics associated with the initial dedication of the altar.

[2] The listing is incomplete. The subtotal without the added entries is 21s 4d, making a total of £4 11s ½d.

[3] Isabel Thornley, buried 1 May 1550. LAO, Goulding Papers, 5/2.

[4] Page torn.

[5] Page torn.

[6] No amount stated.

Item received to the use of the Poor Man's box – 12d.
Item received at another time – 4d.
Sum – 10s 1d.[1]
Item received on the 4th Sunday after Christmas – 21d.
Item received on the 5th Sunday after Christmas – 16d.
Item received on the 6th Sunday after Christmas – 2s.
Item received on the 7th Sunday after Christmas – 2s 4d.
Item received on the first Sunday in Lent – 16d.
Item received on the second Sunday in Lent – 22d.
Item received on the 3rd Sunday in Lent – 13d.
Item received on the 4th Sunday in Lent – 19d.
Item received on the 5th Sunday in Lent – 20d.
Item received on Palm Sunday – 2s 2d.
Item received on Good Friday – 18d.
Item received for lead taken out of the Rood loft – 12s.
Item received for wax of Arthur Gray & Thomas Blancherd – 32s 4d.
Item received of John Wayth & William Rede for the bell frame at St Mary's church – 6s.
Item received of John Wayth for a locker – 3s.
Item received the long pays that was before the High altar – 8s.
£3 19s 11d.
Item received for 6 boulders[2] that was [in] St Mary's church – 3s.
Item received on the first Sunday after Easter – 2s 7d.
Item received to the use of the Poor Man's box – 2s 2d.
Item received for an old pew in the bellhouse – 5s.[3]
Sum – 12s 9d.

f. 90r.
£11 4s 9d.
£18 18s 9d.

f. 90v.
Item given in alms – 15d.
Item paid for a common bull going with the town kye – 20s 8d.
Item given in alms – 14d.
Item paid for hedging in the East Field – 2s.
Item given in alms – 8d.

---

[1] '9s 11d' crossed through.

[2] Possibly glacial deposits of dolerite bluestones; an example can be seen outside the Louth Museum. Benton, *Early Days*, p. 46.

[3] One of only three instances of the term 'pew', as against stool or stall, used in relation to the main body of the church. There is no record of charges for the renting of pews. Rates at St Laurence's in Ludlow varied from 20d to 6s 8d, being largely dependent on the position of the seat and the status of its occupant. Wright, *Churchwardens' Accounts*.

Item paid to John Wathe for the rest of his wages in mending of the windows of the church – 13s 4d.
Item given in alms – 8d.
Item more given in alms – 4d.
Item paid to bellman for batting the dogs out of the church[1] – 2d.
Item more to him for mending the stalls – 4d.
Item paid for making a lectern above the pulpit – 2s.
Item given in alms – 18d.
Item given in alms – 21d.
Item paid to John Wathe for mending of the leads – 2s.
Item given in alms – 4d.
Item paid to Rauf Page for mending a stool at the organs – 1d.
Item given in alms – 16d.
Item to John Reade for mending the stools in the church – 3d.
Item given in alms – 1d.
Item more in alms – 8d.
Item given in alms – 12d.
Item paid for making a pyk.[2] – 12d.
Item given in alms – 2d.
Item given in alms – 6d.
Item more in alms – 5d.
Item more in alms – 4d.
Item for making of pits in the quarry[3] for the Boon day[4] – 4s.
Item given in alms – 13d.
Item more in alms – 2d.
Item more in alms – 6d.
Item more in alms – 11d.
Item given in alms – 10d.

[1] The position of dog whipper, assigned to remove stray animals, was common to many parish churches. A note in the accounts for 1588/9 states that the whipper also received 4s for 'setting good order amongst children and unruly persons' and in 1609/10 was awaking 'them that sleep in the church'. Accounts III, *ff.* 135v, 192r. Goulding, *Customs*, p. 11.

[2] Pick or pyx?

[3] These pits, as against the saw pits, were probably for digging out stone. The quarry was where the present livestock market is now situated (2023), off London Road. It was also the location of the butts used for archery practice and where tennis and other 'unlawful' games took place. Green, *Origins*, p. 119.

[4] A practice whereby tenants of the lord of the manor were required to work one 'Boon-Day' for him every week in harvest time. *OED*. Later, the term was used to describe the annual maintenance of local roads and bridges, especially following the 1555 Highways Act. The word is recorded as Bound, Bune, Boune and Boundais but is transcribed as 'Boon'. Brears, *Lincolnshire*, pp. 90–1.

Item given in alms – 14d.
Item for a surplice for Master Vicar – 9s 4d.
Item given in alms – 6d.
Item given in alms – 14d.
Item given in alms – 7d.
Item paid for the mending of a lock – 2d.
Item given in alms – 2d.
Item given in alms – 12d.
Item paid for a key making to the church door – 4d.
£3 15s 11d.

f. 91r.
Item for a trough mending – 4d.
Item given in alms – 12d.
Item paid for a candle – 2d.
Item given in alms – 8d.
Item given in alms – 8d.
Item paid to John Reade for thatching of the lodge – 20d.
Item paid for a bunch of sewing rope – 1½d.
Item given in alms – 6d.
Item more in alms – 7d
Item more in alms – 2d.
Item spent for taking down the altars – 8d.[1]
Item paid for mending of the chimes – 4d.
Item in alms – 3d.
Item in alms – 9d.
Item paid to John Joyner for making the church gate – 8d.
Item paid to John Wake, the smith, for iron gear to the church gate – 8d.
Item paid for making of a key – 16d.
Item given in alms – 6d.
Item more in alms – 6d.
Item paid to Robert Odlyng for his wages – 20d.
Item for mending of a wheel & other work – 4d.
Item paid for 2 sawters[2] for the church – 4s.
Item given in alms – 8d.
Item paid for walling of St Mary's church windows – 4d.[3]
Item paid for paper – 1d.
Item paid to John Wathe for mending the church windows – 6s 8d.
Item given in alms – 4d.
Item given in alms – 10d.

[1] Altars were removed and replaced by a communion table.
[2] Psalters.
[3] By this period, St Mary's was closed. A short time later, it became premises for the refounded grammar school.

Item for a quarter [of] thatch for the lodge – 2s 3d.
Item given in alms – 3d.
Item to Robert Odlyng for setting up the bell in the Marketstead – 20d.[1]
Item given in alms – 8d.
Item for laying of stones & cleansing the choir of the church – 3s 10d.
Item to John Reade for working in the church – 3s.
Item given in alms – 8d.
Item paid for a barrow – 4d.
Item paid for the table that is set in the High choir – 11s.[2]
Item paid for a pound of candles – 2d.
Item for whyting the church walls – 4d.
       51s. ½d.

f. 91v.
Item to John Reade for his wages – 13s 4d.
Item to William Rychardson for keeping the clock & chime – 13s 4d.
Item for making & writing of this account – 4s.
Item for writing the book of christenings, weddings & buryings – 2s 8d.
Item paid for nails – 1d.
Item paid John Reade for working in the church – 18d.
Item paid to Jeames Story for working in the church – 10d.
Item paid to Thomas Wardall for his men & other men's wages for working in the church – 3s 4d.
Item given in alms – 8d.
Item given in alms – 4d.
Item paid to John Hill for making the stalls in the church – 3s 4d.
Item paid to William Evans for carrying the prisoner to Lincoln – 6s 5d.
Item given in alms – 10d.
Item given in alms – 3d.
Item given in alms – 6d.
Item paid to Odlyng for his wages – 10d.
Item given in alms – 6d.
Item given in alms – 2d.
Item given in alms – 8d.
Item more in alms – 2d.
Item more in alms – 10d.
Item paid to a workman for helping to take down the bells in St Mary's church & working there – 6d.[3]
Item in alms – 4d.

---

[1] Page damaged. The bell was probably used to signify the commencement of the market. Goulding, *Markets and Fairs*, n.p. Was it one of those removed from St Mary's (see below)?
[2] A communion table, replacing the altars.
[3] Further evidence that St Mary's had been abandoned as a place of worship.

Item given in alms – 8d.
Item given in alms – 11d.
Item more in alms – 2d.
Paid to Arthur Gray that he paid to John Smythe's wife when my Lord Welloby[1] was in the town to the sum of – 10s.
Paid for taking down of 3 bells at St Mary's church to John Wathe & William Red to meat & wages & [leading][2] – 2s.
To Arthur Gray […] & there remain still sum – 69s 5d.

f. 92r.
Paid for a pew making in the high aisle – 13s 8d.
Paid John Wathe for mending the windows – 6s 8d.
Item paid for dressing of Langholme choir – 10d.
Item in alms – 6d.
Paid for a surplice washing – 1d.
Paid to Odlyng for his wages -10d.
Item given in alms – 7d.

Sum – 23s 2d.

Total sum of all the payments and allowances of this accounted – £10 19s 6½d.
And so remaineth due & to be paid by the said churchwardens – £7 19s 11d.
Which said sum of £7 19s 11d the said churchwardens hath delivered & paid to Robert Spencer, John Spenlow,[3] Thomas Holdernes[4] & William Somerscales[5] the churchwardens the year now next ensuing.
Item received of Sir Robert Beverlay for his part of George Worslers[6] bill – 12s 8d.
Item more received of William Browne for the Plough light – 6s 6d.
Item more received for Willowes[7] field – 12d.
Item there is due to be paid £5 whereof received £5 by Robert Acrede for brass metal, £5 12s, he hath promised to pay at this side [of] Midsummer […] 4 days after which was paid to the hands of the churchwardens.[8]
Item there is owing by William Kyng – 40s.

---

1   Willoughby. Possibly Richard Bertie (1517–82), second husband of Katherine Willoughby (d.1580) and MP for Lincolnshire in 1563. *DNB*, https://doi.org/10.1093/ref:odnb/2276; http://www.historyofparliamentonline.org/volume/1558-1603/member/bertie-richard-1517-82.
2   [Crossed through].
3   A John Spenlay was buried 24 March 1556/7. LAO, Goulding Papers, 5/2.
4   Holderness was recorded in 1561 as a yeoman. Burton, *Old Lincolnshire*, p. 118. Will: TNA, PROB 11/55/111, probate 28 February 1573. His daughter Emma (25 April 1547) and wife Catherine (9 October 1564) both predeceased him. LAO, Goulding Papers, 5/2.
5   William Somerskaills was interred 12 December 1565. LAO, Goulding Papers, 5/2.
6   Worseley?
7   Possibly George Willows, churchwarden 1557/8.
8   Part of page is damaged.

Item there is owing more by William Worseley for the debt of George Worseley his son – 12s 8d.
Item the said new churchwardens hath received of Gilbert Blancherd for his debt of Corpus Christi guild – 13s 4d.
£10 19s 6½d.
Restored – £7 19s 1½d.

f. 92v.
Item received more by the said churchwardens of Gilbert Blancherde twenty stone & 8lbs of lead. 20 stone & eight pounds of lead.[1]
Item there remaining in the custody of John Wathe for which he must answer to the said churchwardens of lead forty and nine stone. 49 stone of lead.[2]
Memorandum, that 40s for the Common Cart is committed and delivered this year to Thomas Anderson & Robert Westabye and they to lead for the repairs of the highways 80 loads, that is to say for the last year 40 loads & for this year coming [an]other 40 loads, and to lay the same in such places as they shall be assigned by the said churchwardens – 40s.[3]
William Browne, Richard Woolsby, smith, sureties for Thomas Anderson.
William Taylor, Walter Brown, sureties for Robert Westabye.
Item delivered to the hands of the new churchwardens for St George's sword sold to William Worseldy – 3s 4d.
Memorandum, that Mr Vicar of Lowthe,[4] Thomas Palmer, William Farrand, William White & William Raythbye doth promise from henceforth to pay yearly to churchwardens of Lowthe for the time being for the sum of 14d, as it doth appear here under written for easement of such common grounds as they have in their several tenures, that is to say.
Mr Vicar – 4d.
William White – 4d.
Thomas Palmer – 2d.
William Raythbye – 2d.
William Farrand – 2d.
This is granted to the Poor Man's box.[5]

f. 93r.
The copy of the bill indentured betwixt Mr Goodryk & Arthur Gray, William Whyte & others made to them upon the receipt of the town's plate.

---

[1] Written twice.

[2] Written twice.

[3] This entry is noteworthy in that local highway maintenance was being administered by the churchwardens prior to the Highways Act of 1555.

[4] This is possibly John Louthe, purportedly vicar of St James's in 1549. He is however recorded in a list of incumbents at Chew Magna in Somerset from 1562 until his resignation in 1566. In 1565, he was appointed archdeacon of Nottingham, a position he held until his death in 1590. Nevertheless, there is no reference to his Louth or Chew Magna incumbencies in Louthe, 'Reminiscences', pp. 7–59.

[5] Remainder of page damaged.

Contents of the plate.[1]
First of gilt 543 ounces.
Item parcel gilt[2] 162 ounces.
Total Sum – 705 ounces.
Richard Goodrick, L[awrence] Eresbie.
The copy of Mr Goodryk letter the same time.
[After most hearty commendations this shall be to advertise you that I have received into my custody at the request of they of your neighbours certain parcels of plate appearing by one bill indented made betwixt them and me which shall be ready for you at all times when you shall demand the same, and as touching your guild & chantry lands this bringer can presently declare unto you the state of the same whom I have caused the longer to tarry that you might be fully advertised[3] therein. And this I wish you heartily well to fare from [......][4] Christmas Day which bill indented of the said plate was delivered to the aforesaid friends hands of the said Mr Goodryck upon the full payment of the money due for the said plate by the whole agreement of the parishioners of Lowthe].[5]
To his loving friends & neighbours then inhabitants of the township of Lowthe these be given.
Memorandum, that Gylbert Blanchard has [...] to Thomas Bradley – [...].[6]
Robert Spencer, William Topclyffe £33 14s 1d, & certain bills belonging to that account remains in [the] keeping of the churchwardens.
Item the bill that [...] in duty of the plate.[7]

f. 93v.

[1551–2]

The account of Robert Spencer, John Spenlow, Thomas Holdernes and William Somerscales, Churchwardens of the Parish Church of St James in Lowthe in the County of Lincoln of all their receipts, payments & expenses from the Sunday in the Octave of Easter in the year of Our Lord 1551 unto the same Sunday in the year of Our Lord God 1552 that is to say one whole year.
First, received in money of the churchwardens the last year as appearith in the foot of the accounts in certain parcels.
Item received on the second Sunday after Easter – 4s 1½d.
Item received on the 3rd Sunday after Easter – 2s.

---

[1] This is the total amount of surviving church plate removed following changes to the liturgical layout. It sold for £95. Swaby, *History of Louth*, p. 139. Any interest was given to the poor. Goulding, Papers, 5/3.
[2] Silverware partly gilded, notably on the inner surface. *OED*.
[3] Goulding suggests 'adcertain' – ascertain? Goulding, *Grammar School*, p. 6.
[4] Page damaged.
[5] [Paragraph crossed through].
[6] Illegible.
[7] Page damaged.

Item received on the 4th Sunday after Easter – 2s 8d.
Item received on the 5th Sunday after Easter – 3s 2d.
Item received on the 6th Sunday after Easter – 23d.
Item received on Wytson Sunday – 3s 7d.
Item received on Trinity Sunday – 18d.
Item received on the first Sunday after Trinity – 2s 6½d.
Item received on the second Sunday after Trinity – 2s 3½d.
Item received on the third Sunday after Trinity – 3s 8d.
Item received on the 4th Sunday after Trinity – 21d.
Item received on the 5th Sunday after Trinity – 2s 8d.
Item received on the 6th Sunday after Trinity – 2s 8d.
Item received on the 7th Sunday after Trinity – 2s 6d.
Item received on the 8th Sunday after Trinity – 2s 8d.
Item received on the 9th Sunday after Trinity – 2s 8d.
Item received the 10th Sunday after Trinity – 3s 2d.
Item received on the 11th Sunday after Trinity – 3s.
Item received on the 12th Sunday after Trinity – 2s 1d.
Item received on the 13th Sunday after Trinity – 12d.
Item received on the 14th Sunday after Trinity – 20d.
Item received on the 15th Sunday after Trinity – 16d.
f. 94r. [Blank].
f. 94v.
Item that William Brown & Richard Nycollason, smith,[1] owes for 4 stone of iron – 6s 8d.
Item there is hung at William Howenys a great hook of iron that is for pulling down houses when there is a scathe fire.
Item that there [is] belonging to the church a gaff loke[2] of iron & 3 picks of iron.
Item that there is in the hutch that is in the keeping of the churchwardens a great chalice & pyxes with covering of silver.
That there is at St Mary's church certain lead in [w]*eshes*
Item that John Smetthe owes of account of the land of Our Lady's guild – £3 6s 8d.
Item that there 4 great serges of wax & banner cloth & other gear that belonged to St George's horse bridles & other belongings.
f. 95r.
The account of Robert Spencer, John Spenlowe, William Somerscales and Thomas Holdernes, Churchwardens of the Parish Church of St James in Lowth in the County of Lyncoln of all their receipts, payments & expenses from the

---

[1] Interred 25 February 1555/6. LAO, Goulding Papers, 5/2.
[2] Gablock or Gavelock – an iron crowbar or lever. *OED*.

Sunday in the Octave of Easter *Anno Domini* 1551 unto the same Sunday *Anno Domini* 1552 that is to say one whole year.[1]
First, received in money of the churchwardens being the last year – £7 19s 11d.
Item more received of Sir Robert Beverlay for his part of George Worsley's bill – 12s 8d.
Item more received of William Browne for the Plough light – 6s 6d.
Item more received for Wyllowes Field – 12d.
Item received of William Kyng – 40s.
Item received of Gylbert Blanchard for the debt of Corpus Christi guild – 13s 4d.
Item received of William Worsley for St George's sword – 3s 4d.
Item received of Robert Akand in part of payment of £5 12s for brass metal – £5.
Item received for a bull to Gilbert Blanchard, William Whyte, William Browne, John Spencer, William Somerscales & Robert Akryd – 33s 4d.
Item received for the plasshing of one hedge sold to William Browne & Robert Acrad – 16s.
Item received of Thomas Blanchard for 2 stone & 4 pounds of lead – 2s 3d.
£19 8s 4d.
Receipts on the Sundays.[2]

f. 95v.
Item received on the 16th Sunday after Trinity – 11d.
Item received on the 17th Sunday after Trinity – 20d.
Item received on the 18th Sunday after Trinity – 19d.
Item received on the 19th Sunday after Trinity – 2s 3d.
Item received on the 20th Sunday after Trinity – 2s 2d.
Item received on the 21st Sunday after Trinity – 17d.
Item received on the 22nd Sunday after Trinity – 16d.
Item received on the 23rd Sunday – 21d.
Item received on the 24th Sunday – 13d.
Item received on the 25th Sunday – 22½d.
Item received on the 26th Sunday – 17½d.
Item received on the 27th Sunday which was the first Sunday in Advent – 18½d.
Item received on the second Sunday in advent – 2s.
Item received on the 3rd Sunday in Advent – 17d.
Item received on the 4th Sunday in Advent – 15½d.
Item received on the Sunday after St Stephen's day[3] – 2s.
Item received on the first Sunday after the Epiphany – 2s 8d.

   [1]   This is a repeat of the preamble on page 213, *f.* 93v.
   [2]   The collection entries that precede these are exact copies of those on page 213, *f.* 93v. This list therefore commences on the sixteenth Sunday after Trinity, following on from that previously recorded.
   [3]   December.

Item received on the second Sunday after – 2s 1½d.
Item received on the 3rd Sunday after – 22d.
Item received on the 4th Sunday after – 22d.
Item received on the 5th Sunday after – 2s 6d.
Item received on the Sunday called *Septuagesima* – 21½d.
Item received on the Sunday called *Sexagesima* – 14½d.
Item received on *Quinquagesima* Sunday – 20d.
Item received on the first Sunday in Lent – 21d.
Item received on the second Sunday in Lent – 2s.
Item received on the 3rd Sunday in Lent – 2s 4d.
Item received on the 4th Sunday in Lent – 2s.
Item received on the 5th Sunday in Lent – 19d.
Item received on Palm Sunday – 2s 1d.
Item received on Good Friday – 21d.
Item received on the first Sunday after Easter – 19d.
£5 9s 2d.[1]

f. 96r.

Burials in the church.

First, received for the burial of Agnes, the wife of John Swyne – 6s 8d.
Item received for the burial of Cuthbert Story's wife – 6s 8d.[2]
And for the bells – 20d.
Item received for the burial of Agnes Beverlay – 6s 8d.
Item received for the burial of John Richarson – 6s 8d.[3]
And for the bells – 20d.
Item received for the burial of George Spylesby – 6s 8d.
Item received for the burial of Jenet Richarson – 6s 8d.
And for the bells – 20d.
Item received for the burial of Thomas Goshawke – 6s 8d.
And for the bells – 20d.
Item received for the burial of William Colynwood's wife – 6s 8d.[4]
And for the bells – 20d.
Item received for the burial of Richard Gybson, taylor – 6s 8d.
And for the bells – 20d.
Item received for the burial of Thomas *Gren* the elder – 6s 8d.
£3 16s 8d.

Receipts to the use of the Poor Man's box.

Item received at one time – 15d.
Item at another time – 15d.
Item at another time – 3d.

---

[1] This total figure includes the collections on page 213, *f.* 93v.
[2] Emott Story, interred 5 September 1551. LAO, Goulding Papers, 5/2.
[3] John Richardson left a will: TNA, PROB 11/34/496, probate 4 December 1551.
[4] Joanna Collynwod, buried 23 March 1551/2. LAO, Goulding Papers, 5/2.

Item at another time – 10d.
Item at another time – 2d.
Item at another time – *16d*.[1]
Item at another time – 22d.
Item at another time – 23½d.
Item at another time – 12d.
Item at another time – 4d.
Item at another time – 12d.
11s 8d.
Total Sum – £29 7s 8d.

f. 96v.
Payments & allowances.

First, paid for writing this account – 4s.
Item paid for writing of the book of christenings, weddings & buryings – 2s 8d.
Sum – 6s 8d.

Item paid to Robert Kyrkby for keeping the clock and chime, the leads and bells – 13s 4d.
Sum – 20s.

Other payments and allowances done by the said churchwardens.
First, given in alms – 20d.
Item for washing of cloths – 6d.
Item more given in alms – 9d.
Item paid to Leonard Russhby & his fellow for 6 days working about 2 gates & the making of them, the one beyond Master Chapman's mill & the other at Monks' Dyke – 6s 8d.
Item paid to 2 labourers for 3 days working about the said gates – 15d.
Item paid for carriage of one of the said gates – 4d.
Item given in alms – 12d.
Item paid to the smith for iron to the 2 gates & workmanship thereof – 2s 4d.
Item paid for the carriage of the gate to the Monks' Dyke Head – 2d.
Item paid to John Wright for dressing of stalls in Master Langholme choir – 8d.
Item given in alms – 8d.
Item paid for wood stoops,[2] rails with spurs[3] to the said gates – 11s 6d.
Item paid to Thomas Lathes & his man for working about the well in the Market Place – 2s 8d.
Item for wood & planks to the same – 4s.
Item paid to Maltby, smith, for working about the said well – 16d.
Item for nails – 3d.
35s 5d.

[1] Page cut.
[2] Stoop – a post, pillar. *OED*.
[3] A short strut or stay set diagonally to support an upright timber. *OED*.

f. 97r.

Payments & allowances.

Item paid to Jakson for a shew[1] of leather that covered the staff[2] in the well – 4d.
Item paid to a labourer for drawing out of the water of the well – 7d.
Item paid to Willy for going to Fotherby for the Subsidy Book[3] – 2d.
Item paid for the keeping of the common bull – 6s 8d.
Item paid to William Bayly – 13s 4d.
Item paid for the mending of the chimes – 4d.
Item paid for the mending of the gate – 4d.
Item given in alms – 9d.
Item paid for a roop[4] to the plumber – 7s.
Item paid for a lock to the churchyard[5] gate – 4d.
Item given in alms – 8d.
Item more in alms – 4d.
Item paid to Topclyp for blowing the organs – 8d.
Item paid for mending of stalls in the north aisle – 6d.
Item given in alms – 4d.
Item paid for nails – 2d.
Item paid for mending of Stewton Lane – 4d.
Item in alms – 4½d.
Item paid to Robert Spencer for mending the highway at East Mill bridge – 2s 8d.
Item paid for mending the wheel of the chimes – 4d.
Item given in alms – 6d.
Item more in alms – 8d.
Item more in alms – 6½d.
Item paid for a bull for the town – 26s.
Item given in alms – 6d.
Item paid for making of a new fled[6] for the clock – 3d.
Item paid for a lock for the organs – 4d.
Item paid for mats & bassocks[7] for the choir – 2s 9d.
Item given in alms – 6d.
Item paid to John Spaldwyn for carrying the mad women out of the town – 20d.
Item given in alms.[8]

---

[1] Shew – to fasten, attach or join pieces of leather. *OED*.
[2] Possibly part of the gear mechanism for winding up the bucket. *OED*.
[3] A book recording the names of those liable to pay a subsidy or tax. *OED*.
[4] Rope.
[5] Noted as 'Kyrkarth'.
[6] Possibly 'flee' or flay' – 'To clarify oil': 'I flaye oyle with water, whan it boyleth', 1530. *OED*.
[7] Hassocks. *OED*.
[8] Page cut through.

Item more in alms.[1]
Item paid for a pound of candles – 4d.
Item paid to John Read for going with the bell – 1d.
Item given in alms – 8d.
Item paid to Robert Odlyng for making a bell wheel – 2s.
Item paid for nails & stays – 2d.
Item in alms – 4d.
Item paid to Robert Odlyng for a plank & a rail for the stalls – 16d.
Item more to him for 3 days work in mending the stalls to meat & wages – 3s 4d.
Item paid for nails – 8d.
Item paid to John Reade for going with the bell – 1d.

f. 97v.

Payments & allowances.

Item paid in alms – 11½d.
Item more in alms – 6d.
Item more in alms – 1d.
Item paid for cleansing the common sewer at Haregares of seven score & 10 rods – 13s 4d.
Item paid in alms – 6d.
Item paid to John Wathe for mending the leads in this church & St Mary's church – 2s 4d.
Item paid in alms – 6d.
Item paid for plashyng the common hedge by Aleyn Holdernes close contain[ing] 56 rods – 9s 4d.
Item paid in alms – 6d.
Item paid for nails – 4d.
Item paid in alms – 7d.
Item paid to Robert Odlyng for mending a bell wheel & for nails – 6d.
Item given to William Wythell in alms – 12d.[2]
Item paid to Robert Odlyng for 2 days work about the bell wheels & for boards & nails to the same – 2s 8d.
Item given in alms – 6d.
Item paid for a rope of 2 stone for the greatest bell – 6s 8d.
Item given in alms – 20d.
Item paid for making of iron bars for the glass windows – 16d.
Item given in alms – 6d.
Item given to Arthur Capper in alms – 8d.
Item paid to John Wathe for mending of the glass windows[3] – 13s 4d.
Item given in alms – 8d.

---

[1] Page cut through.
[2] This is the first occasion that a recipient of alms is named.
[3] 'Leads' crossed through.

Item paid for stopping the holes in the church where doves come in – 8d.
Item paid in alms – 2d.
Item paid for lime – 2s.
Item paid for the nursing of a poor child – 20d.
Item paid to John Wathe for mending the glass windows – 10s.
Item paid to Maltby, smith, for mending of iron work about the north door of the church – 8d.
Item paid to John Wathe for mending glass windows & solder – 6s 8d.
Item paid for making an iron bar & a key to the lock of the organs – 6d.
Item paid for making 3 picks and a gavelok of the church's iron – 4s.
Item paid for 4 nails for 4 picks – 4d.
Item paid for sharpening the said picks for Aswell Lane – 8d.

£4 5s 2½d.

f. 98r.

Payments & allowances.

Item paid for mending of iron bars for glass windows – 6d.
Item paid for making 8 new iron bars – 20d.
Item paid for a band, a crook & a clasp of iron for one of the gallery doors – 6d.
Item paid for iron bars – 20d.
Item paid for filling the rails with thorns at the Monks' Dyke Head – 4d.
Item paid to John Wathe for mending of the glass windows – 10s.
Item given in alms – 4d.
For burying of a poor child – 1d.
Item given in alms – 2d.
Item paid for paper – 2d.
Item given in alms – 6d.
Item paid to William Browne for keeping of the bull – 6s 8d.
Item that whereas there was at the day of the King's First Proclamation[1] in money in the box £3 3s 2d, as it before went whereof we ask allowance for the loss in the same money by virtue of the said Proclamation, 15s 9½d.
Item that whereas there was in the box of the church money at the Second Proclamation as money went before that day £3 10s 9d, whereof we ask allowance for loss in the same money, 23s 7d.
Item paid to John Reade for dressing of the church & helping of the bells – 13s 4d.
Item given in alms – 3d.

£3 19s 6½d.

Total sum of all payments and allowances, £14 16s ?d.[2]
And so remaineth due to be paid by the said churchwardens – £14 16s 5d. Which said sum of £14 16s 5d, the said churchwardens hath delivered & paid to [William Kyng and Edward Boswell],[3] William Browne, John Spaldwyn,

---

[1] A formal order issued by a monarch or other legal authority and made public. *OED*.
[2] Line cut through.
[3] [Crossed through]. Edward Boswell was buried 12 April 1563. LAO, Goulding Papers, 5/2.

William Kyng and Edward Boswell churchwardens chosen & appointed for the year now following.
Item owing to the said churchwardens by Robert Kyrkby – 3s 4d.
f. 98v.
Memorandum, that the 40s for the Common Cart is committed & delivered this year to Thomas Anderson & Walter a Wood,[1] and they to lead for the repairing the highways 20 loads & to lay the same in such places as they shall be assigned & appointed by the churchwardens.
William Whyte, Stephen Buk,[2] sureties for Thomas Anderson.
William Kyng, Thomas Blancherd, sureties for Walter a Wood.
Memorandum, that William Worsley doth owe unto the said churchwardens for George Worsley's debt – 12s 8d.
Item that there is remaining in the hands of John Wathe 12 stone 4 pounds of lead for which he must answer to the churchwardens.
Item owing by Robert Cardemaker[3] to the churchwardens for the rest of certain brass – 12s.[4]
Item paid unto the hands of the new churchwardens for the Plough light – 6s 1½d.[5]
Item that there is in the custody of Master St Pole, 15 stone & 10 pounds of lead for which he must answer to the churchwardens of Lowthe.

f. 99r.

[1552–3]

The account of William Browne, John Spaldwyn, William Kyng & Edward Boswell Churchwardens of the Parish Church of St James in Lowthe in the County of Lyncoln of all their receipts, payments and expenses from the Sunday in the Octaves of Easter in the year of Our Lord God 1552 unto the same Sunday then next following, that is to say for one whole year.
Receipts.
Item received in money of the churchwardens being the last year as appearith in the foot of their account – £14 16s 5d.
Item received more by them for the Plough light mentioned in the foot of the last account – 6s 1½d.
Sum – £15 2s 6½d.

---

[1] Possibly a kinsman of John a Wood of Tetney who was related to the monk William Moreland, connected with the Rising. Swaby, *History of Louth*, p. 114.

[2] Stephen Buck was recorded in 1561 as a yeoman. Burton, *Old Lincolnshire*, p. 118. A Stephen Buck, cited as son of Stephen, was interred 8 May 1564. LAO, Goulding Papers, 5/2.

[3] Robert Cardmaker was alleged to have been one of the 'petty captains' during the Rising. *L&P*, XI, 972, p. 398, 3 November 1536.

[4] Noted next to total: 'days given to the said Robert Acred unto Midsummer next'.

[5] Marginalia – text in Latin: *neratur in anno sequenti ut patet in sequenti folio.* It is owed in the next year as set out on the following folio.

Receipts on the Sundays with the pece.
Item received on the second Sunday after Easter – 4s 4d.
Item received on the 3rd Sunday after Easter – 5s 2d.
Item received on the 4th Sunday after Easter – 2s 10½d.
Item received on the 5th Sunday after Easter – 3s 6½d.
Item received on the 6th Sunday after Easter – 2s 3½d.
Item received on Whit Sunday – 3s 1d.
Item received on Trinity Sunday – 18½d.
Item received on the first Sunday after Trinity – 3s 8d.
Item received on the second Sunday after Trinity – 2s 3d.
Item received on the 3rd Sunday after Trinity – 3s 3d.
Item received on the 4th Sunday after Trinity – 2s 9d.
Item received on the 5th Sunday after Trinity – 2s 10d.
Item received on the 6th Sunday after Trinity – 2s 5½d.
Item received on the 7th Sunday after Trinity – 2s.
Item received on the 8th Sunday after Trinity – 23d.
Item received on the 9th Sunday after Trinity – 3s 1d.
Item received on the 10th Sunday after Trinity – 2s 1d.
Item received on the 11th Sunday after Trinity – 3s 1½d.
Item received the 12th Sunday after Trinity – 2s 1d.
Item received the 13th Sunday after Trinity – 2s 6d.
Item received the 14th Sunday after Trinity – 2s ½d.
Item received the 15th Sunday after Trinity – 2s 1d.
    Sum – 59s 11½d.

f. 99v.

Anno Domini 1552.
Item received the 16th Sunday after Trinity – 2s.
Item received the 17th Sunday after Trinity – 2s 4d.
Item received on the 18th day after Trinity – 15d.
Item received on the 19th day after Trinity – 2s 6d.
Item received on the 20th day after Trinity – 2s 5d.
Item received on the 21st day after Trinity – 2s 6d.
Item received on the 22nd day after Trinity – 2s 6½d.
Item received on the 23rd day after Trinity – 2s 1d.
Item received on the first Sunday in Advent – 22d.[1]
Item received on the second Sunday in Advent – 2s 2d.
Item received on the third Sunday in Advent – 19d.
Item received on the fourth Sunday in Advent – 21d.
Item received on Christmas Day – 2s 7d.
Item received on New Year's Day – 2s 7d.
Item received on the Sunday after Twelfth Day – 2s 2d.
Item received on the second Sunday after Twelfth Day – 2s 7½d.

---

[1] Marginalia – '£5 18s 10d'.

Item received on the third Sunday after – 19½d.
Item received on the fourth Sunday after called *Septuagesima* – 2s ½d.
Item received on the Sunday named *Sexagesima* – 2s 1d.
Item received on the Sunday called *Quinquagesima* – 2s 2½d.
Item received on the first Sunday in Lent – 20d.
Item received on the second Sunday in Lent – 22½d.
Item received on the 3rd Sunday in Lent – 19½d.
Item received on Midlent[1] Sunday – 3s 2d.
Item received on Passion Sunday – 2s 3d.
Item received on Palm Sunday – 2s 10½d.
Item received on Good Friday – 19d.
Item received of Lord's Sunday – 2s 5½d.
      Sum – £3 4d.

f. 100r.
      Receipts of burials in the church.
Item received for the burial of Cuthbert Story – 6s 8d.[2]
Item received for the bells – 8d.
Item received for the burial of Sir John Goshawke[3] – 6s 8d.
Item received for the burial of Arthur Grey's wife – 6s 8d.[4]
Item received for the bells – 20d.
Item received of the executors of William Geldall for the bells – 6d.
Item received for the burial of Agnes Palmer – 6s 8d.
Item received for the bells – 20d.
Item received for the burial of Thomas Candeler – 6s 8d.
Item received the bells – 20d.
Item received for the burial of Katheryn Dowghty – 6s 8d.
Item received for Robert West – 4d.

---

 [1] Mid-Lent Sunday is the middle or fourth Sunday in Lent, also called Mothering Sunday or Refreshment Sunday. *OED*.
 [2] Interred 20 April 1552. LAO, Goulding Papers, 5/2. Cuthbert Story, weaver, left two wills. One is dated 20 December 1546 but with a probate date of 20 May 1553, LAO, LCC, 1543–56, *f.* 82. The second, probably a codicil, was dated 30 December 1552. LAO, LCC, 1551–2, *f.* 114. His estate was valued at £5 14s 7d. LAO, Inventories, Box 20, p. 92, 20 April 1552. Rowson, *Inventories*, n.p.
 [3] John Goshauke was prior and chaplain to St Mary's guild with a salary of £5 13s 4d. Hodgett, *Ex-Religious*, pp. 53, 57. In 1526, he received a stipend of 36s 8d and was noted in 1547 as being forty-four years old. Salter, *Subsidy*, p. 12. Foster and Thompson, 'Chantry Certificates', 36, p. 280. He was buried 16 May 1552. LAO, Goulding Papers, 5/2. In his will, dated 5 May 1552, Goshauke gave his soul to God, Mary and the saints, a conservative preamble, and also donated to the poor man's box. LAO, LCC, 1551–2, *f.* 71. He left an estate valued at £6 6s 10d. LAO, Inventories, Box 20, p. 231, 17 May 1552.
 [4] This is possibly Arthur Grey's second wife, not recorded in the Parish Register. See page 187, note 1.

Item received for the burial of Jenet Wentforth – 6s 8d.
Sum – 53s 2d.
Receipts for the use of the Poor Man's box.
Item received at one time – 4d.
Item received at another time – 1d.
Item received at another time – 1d.
Item received at another time – 7d.
Item received at another time by the gift of Thomas Holland – 2s.[1]
Sum – 3s 1d.
f. 100v.
Other receipts.
Item received of John Smythe and George Somerscales for the frame and organs in the Lady's choir – 18s.
Item received of William Kyng of a board that was over the Sepulchre – 3s 4d.
Item received of Arthur Grey for a stone[2] – 6d.
Item received of William Whyte for a cofer[3] – 4s.
Item received of Thomas Palmer for 2 foot stools and a lettern[4] – 6d.
Item received of William Browne for a chest – 8d.
Item received more of William Whyte for wooden candlesticks – 3s 4d.
Item received for stone – 14d.
Item received of Thomas Denys for his part of Langholme's choir – 10s.
Item received of William Dowghty for stone – 12d.[5]
Item received for a chest in Our Lady's choir – 2s.
Item received toward the reparations of the church by Walter Fyswike – 3s 4d.
Sum – 47s 10d.
Item received more for a bull – 13s 4d.
Item received of Richard Smyth for iron – 11s 10d.
Item received more of the Plough light gathered this present year with the sum of 14d for the rent of certain common grounds in diverse places of the town – 5s 8d
Total sum received – £27 17s 9d.
Item received more of Thomas Pelson for his part of Langholme's choir – 10s.
Item received of him for one cloth that did hang in the High choir – 5s.
Item received T[homas] Taylor for a chest with banner cloths – 12s.
Total sum – £29 4s 9d.
f. 101r.
Payments and allowances.
First, paid to Robert Odlyng for his wages for the last year – 3s 4d.

---

[1] Will: TNA, PROB 11/35/303, probate, 12 September 1552. Interred 9 August 1552; recorded as *Paterfamilias*. LAO, Goulding Papers, 5/2.
[2] Probably a gravestone.
[3] Coffer – strong box or chest. *OED*.
[4] Lectern.
[5] Marginalia – '£4 7s 10d'.

Item paid to William Somerscales towards his loss that he had in the money that he borrowed of the church money – 3s 4d.
Item given in alms – 1d.
Item given in alms – ½d.
Item given in alms – 3d.
Item given in alms – 4½d.
Item paid to Richard Smyth for making a key to – 4d.
Item given in alms – 2d.
Item more in alms – 2d.
Item more in alms – 2d.
Item more in alms – 3d.
Item paid for serving of Fotherby folks[1] – 2s 4d.
Item more in alms – 1d.
Item paid more for serving Fotherby folks – 12d.
Item paid to Saltmarsh for serving of Fotherby folks – 2s.
Item given in alms – 1d.
Item paid to Saltmarsh's wife – 2s.
Item paid to Robert Odlyng for mending of a wheel – 4d.
Item given in alms – 2d.
Item paid for paper – 1d.
Item paid to William Kyng for the expenses at Reyson[2] when they were with the Leftenants[3] and writing of the inventory of the church goods – 11s 8d.
Item paid to Saltmarsh's wife – 2s.
Item paid to John Spaldwyn & Edward Boswell for their expenses at Reyson – 16d.
Item paid to Richard Smyth for a pick & mending of the clock – 9d.
Item paid to Saltmarsh's wife – 2s.
Item paid to Saltmarsh's wife – 12d.
Item more paid to Saltmarsh's wife – 12d.
Item paid to Richard Smyth for a bolt to the clock – 4d.
Item paid to Richard Curson for money that he paid to the players – 4s.[4]
Item paid to John Richardson for mending of the Haregarth – 6d.
Item paid to Geldall's wife for mending of a boys' leg – 2s 8d.
Item paid to John Reade for making of 3 bell collars – 4d.
     Sum – 44s 2d.

f. 101v.

---

[1] There appears to have been an outbreak of disease in Fotherby, with provision paid from Louth's parish funds.

[2] 'Rasen'; probably East (Market) Rasen.

[3] The original spelling and expression of the present-day lieutenant. See *OED* for gradual changes in idiom.

[4] Magnus Williamson suggests these were the Corpus Christi players. Williamson, 'Religious Guilds', p. 88. This is the last record of players in the accounts, although they continued to be noted in the Corporation records. Goulding, *Corporation Records*, p. 55.

Item paid to Saltmarsh's wife – 2s.
Item paid for wine for my Lord's Council – 18d.
Item paid for watching of the Haregares one night to 2 men – 8d.
Item paid to Gilbert Blanchard for mending of the Haregares – 20d.
Item paid for a pound of candles – 3d.
Item paid to Aleyn Reade for keeping the Haregares – 2s.
Item paid to Robert Kyrkby for destroying the sterlings[1] – 6d.
Item paid for the making of a book at the visitation – 4d.
Item paid to John Spaldyng for riding to Master Heneage & for keeping of Grene seven nights in hold – 8d.
Item given in alms – 2d.
Item paid for dressing of a lantern – 6d.
Item paid to a poor man for keeping the Haregares – 12d.
Item paid for a pound of candle and bread – 3½d.
Item paid for wine – 1½d.
Item paid for bread – 1d.
Item paid for paper – 1d.
Item paid for bread – 1d.
Item paid for wine – 1d.
Item paid for a shovel – 1d.
Item paid to Gilbert Blanchard for thorns – 12d.
Item paid to William Kyng for a book – 5s.
Item paid to Robert Odlyng for a bell wheel and nails – 5s 2d.
Item paid for a staple – 2d.
Item paid for dightyng of a grate – 1d.
Item paid for wine – 6d.
Item paid for bread – 1d.
Item paid for mending a bell-string – 4d.
Item paid for a pair of pynsons[2] for turning a wire to the chimes – 6d.
Item paid for a quire of paper – 3d.
Item paid for taking down the Trinity bell & setting & hanging her up – 14d.
Item paid to Robert Odlyng & his man for work about the Trinity bell – 5s 8d.
Item paid for dressing the windows in the bell frame – 12d.

Sum – 33s.

f. 102r.
Item paid for writing of this account – 4s.
Item paid for making the books of christenings, weddings & buryings – 2s 8d.
Item paid to John Reade for dressing of the church & helping the bells – 13s 4d.
Item paid to Robert Odlyng for his wages – 3s 4d.

---

[1] Starlings. The parish was required to keep birds under control to protect crops within 'An Act to dystroye Choughes, Crowes and Roks', 24 Henry VIII, Chapter X, 1532/3. *Statutes* III, pp. 425–6.

[2] Pincers?

Item paid to Robert Kyrkby for keeping the clock & chime – 13s 4d.
Item paid to Richard Smyth for dressing the ironwork about the said bells – 2s.
Item paid to Robert Kyrkby for carrying a sick child to Minting – 2s.
Item paid to the clerk for wire to the chimes – 6d.
Item for nails – 1½d.
Item paid for wine & bread – 8d.
Item paid for mending of a bell collar – 3d.
Item paid to Robert Adlyngton for mending a stall – 4d.
Item paid to Richard Smyth for 2 jemers[1] – 4d.
Item paid for wine – 16d.
Item paid for the common skep[2] – 12d.
Item paid for mending of the Coo bell – 8d.
Item paid to William East[3] for blowing of the organs – 10d.
Item paid for 2 staples & a hook to Robert Cottam for the common skep – 3d.
Item paid to Thomas Watson for hedging in the Haregares – 11d.[4]
Item paid to John Rychardson for felling of ryse in Lowthe Wood to the same hedging – 12d.[5]
Item paid for 4 trees for the well in the Market Place – 5s 4d.
Item paid for ten boards to the same – 4s 2d.
Item paid for nails & stubbs[6] to the same – 6d.
Item paid for the door bands & crooks – 10d.
Item paid to 2 man for 3 days to meat, drink & wages – 4s.
Item paid for making of a stool for the scholars in Our Lady's choir & mending of the panel in St Peter's choir – 2s.
Item paid for keeping of the common bull – 6s 8d.
                    Sum – £3 11s 8½d.

f. 102v.
Item paid for melting of the lead – 12d.
Item paid for nails, boards & workmanship in Our Lady's choir – 12d.
Item paid to Saltmarsh's wife for serving of Fotherby folks when they were sick – 2s.

---

[1] Gimmer, gemmer – hinge. *OED*.
[2] A container of varying sizes usually of wickerwork: perhaps a beehive. *OED*.
[3] William East is recorded numerous times in the accounts undertaking work varying from 'keeping the bells and chimes', washing altar cloths, blowing the organs and later as a dog whipper. Although appearing to be a general factotum, he was nevertheless a member of the Lady guild, obtaining a pension of £1. He was married and worked as a weaver but is also noted as 'celebrating', for which he is paid £4. Hodgett, *Ex-Religious*, p. 103. Magnus Williamson suggests he was a chaplain of the Lady guild, therefore possibly ordained. Williamson, 'Religious Guilds', p. 91, note 70.
[4] Marginalia with manicule – '£6 5s 4½d'.
[5] Page torn.
[6] Stob – a short, thick nail. *OED*.

Item paid for scouring of Aswell – 12d.
Item paid to Master Crathorne for the levy – 7s 11d.
Item paid for making of the butts – 3s.
Item paid for leading of 12 loads of sods – 2s.
Item paid for lime to St Mary church & for bearing it in – 20d.
Item paid for a bull for the town – 18s.
Item paid for fetching[1] of the foot bridge and staking it down at the East Mill – 6d.
Item paid for leading 2 loads of ryce to Haregares – 12d.
Item paid to 2 men for meat, drink & wages – 9d.
Item paid to Richard Smyth for mending the clock & chimes and a key for the church door – 2s.

Sum – 41s 11d.

For mending of the common sewer in Padholle Bridge.[2]
Paid to the hands of Thomas Acrad for leading stone to the said work – 2s 2d.
Item for sand leading – 9d.
Item to the labourers for wages – 15d.

Sum – 4s 2d.

Paid for 18 quarts of malveson[3] at 5d the quart spent at Easter – 7s 6d.[4]
Item for bread the same time – 14d.
Item for 2 loads of thorns – 2s 8d.
Item for scouring of Aswell to 4 men – 2s.
Item owing by Master Chapman – 10s.[5]
Item by John Browne & William Worsley – 6s 8d.[6]
Item to Thomas Michell for a[n] iron *temme* to the common skeppe – 2s.
Item for mending of the North choir – 16d.
Item to Gilbert Blancherde for his charges at Lincoln before the Commissioners – 2s 8d.

Sum – 23s 6d.
Total Sum paid – £10 14s 3½d.

f. 103r.

Sum total received as particularly appearith above by this account declared the next Sunday after Easter 1553, £29 4s 9d, whereof by the churchwardens as also particularly appearith by the said account, £10 14s 3½d. And so remaineth in debt upon the said churchwardens £18 10s 5½d, whereof for money disbursed

---

[1] To make good, recoup, restore. *OED*.
[2] Padehole (toad-hollow) is an earlier name for Northgate. Green, *Origins*, p. 114.
[3] Malvasia (Malmsey) wine from a variety of white grape widely produced in Spain and Italy. *OED*.
[4] Marginalia with manicule – 'scouring of Aswell Lane'.
[5] Line crossed through.
[6] Line crossed through.

to Mr Lyndesey in reward, 6s 8d. And yet remaineth £18 3s 9½d is paid to the hands of the new churchwardens, which made that the sum of 40s for the Common Cart is committed & delivered this present year to Walter Woode and John Skupholme and they to lead for the repairing of the highways 20 loads of stone to be laid in such places where the new churchwardens shall appoint.
Sureties for W[alter] Woode.
William Kyng.
Thomas Blancherd.
Sureties for John Skupholme.
William Doughtie.
John Brandon.

Arrearages yet owing.

First by W[illiam] Worsley owing for the debt of his son for which he hath promised to deliver his bill [of] obligation with one surety to be paid at March next to the new churchwardens 12s 8d, whereof paid to the churchwardens 5s, and the rest provided by the whole parish.
Item by Robert Acred for the rest of the brass metal to be paid a[t] this side Midsummer next 12s, whereof paid to the churchwardens 8s and the rest provided by the whole parish.
f. 103 v.
The contents of the lead owing by these persons following.
First by Mr Sayntpolle[1] 15 stone 10lbs.
Item by John Wathe 12 stone 4lbs.
Memorandum, it is agreed by the whole parish that the rest of the lead remaining in the charge of the churchwardens shall be weighed and the contents thereof to be entered in this book immediately.
f. 104r.

[1553–4]

Churchwardens appointed to office *Anno Domini* 1553, Gilbert Blancherd, John Brown, John Brandon & Stephen Bucke.
Memorandum, there is remaining in the charge of the churchwardens this present year £18 3s 9½d, besides one bull of the age of 3 years and 13s received of Robert Acred and William Worsley of the old arrearages.

Receipts.

Item received on the second Sunday after Easter – 4s 4d.
Item received on the 3rd Sunday after – 3s 7½d.
Item received on the 4th Sunday after – 4s 2½d.
Item received on the fifth Sunday – 4s 3½d.
Item received on the sixth Sunday – 2s 11d.
Item received on Whit Sunday – 2s 10d.

---

[1] St Poll.

Item received on Trinity Sunday – 2s 1½d.
Item received on the first Sunday after – 2s ½d.
Item received on the second Sunday after – 2s 1½d.
Item received on the third Sunday after – 2s 1d.
Item received on the 4th Sunday after – 2s 8½d.
Item received on the 5th Sunday after – 2s 9½d.
Item received on the 6th Sunday after – 22d.
Item received on the 7th Sunday after – 22d.
Item received on the 8th Sunday[1] after – 2s 2¾d.
Item received on the 8th Sunday after – 2s 2d.
Item received on the 9th Sunday after – 2s 2½d.
Item received on the 10th Sunday after – 2s.
Item received on the 11th Sunday after – 2s 2d.
Item received on the 12th Sunday after – 2s.
Item received on the 13th Sunday after – 22½d.
Item received on the 14th Sunday after – 12½d.
Item received on the 15th Sunday after – 17¼d.
Item received on the 16th Sunday after – 21¼d.
Item received on the 17th Sunday after – 23½d.
Item received on the 18th Sunday after – 22d.
Item received on the 19th Sunday after – 13d.
Item received on the 20th Sunday after – 14¼d.
Item received on the 21st Sunday after – 16½d.
Item received on the 22nd Sunday after – 2s 4¾d.[2]
f. 104v.
Item received on the 23rd Sunday[3] after – 18¼d.
Item received on the 23rd Sunday after – 2s 1d.
Item received on the 24th Sunday after – 2s 8¼d.
Item received on the 25th Sunday after – 2s 3d.
Item received on the 26th Sunday after – 2s 10d.
Item received on the 27th Sunday after – 2s 4d.
Item received on the 28th Sunday after – 3s 3½d.
Item received on the first Sunday after Christmas – 3s 10d.
Item received on the second Sunday after – 3s 1d.
Item received on the third Sunday after Christmas – 3s 7¼d.
Item received on the 4th Sunday after – 3s 8d.
Item received on the 5th Sunday after – 3s 7¼d.
Item received on the 6th Sunday after – 2s 8½d.
Item received on the first Sunday in Lent – 3s 5¼d.
Item received on the second Sunday in Lent – 2s 6d.
Item received on the 3rd Sunday in Lent – 3s 1½d.

---

[1] '8th Sunday' noted twice.
[2] Marginalia – '£2 8s 4½d'.
[3] '23rd Sunday' noted twice.

Item received on Mid-Lent Sunday – 2s 8d.
Item received on Passion Sunday – 3s 9d.
Item received on Palm Sunday – 2s 8d.
Item received of Good Friday – 3s 2½d.
Item received on the first Sunday after Easter – 21¼d.[1]
        Sum total of Sunday receipts – £6 8s 9½d.

f. 105r.
        Receipts for the burials and for the bells.
Item received for the Trinity bell for Bowgham – 8d.
Item received of Arthur Gray for the bells for his mother – 8d.[2]
Item received for certain linen fold[s] and awbes[3] – 54s 6d.
Item received for the burial of Luca Crosse, widow – 6s 8d.
Item received of John Browne for a bull – 14s.
Item received of John Makerell[4] for the one half of the brig[5] that was at the end of William Graunt's house – 2s.[6]
Item received of Robert Chapman[7] for the bells – 20d.
Item received for the Trinity bell for Roger Mawvyn's wife – 8d.[8]
Item received for the Trinity bell for William Farrand – 8d.
Item received for the overplus of all the ornaments of the church which was sold at Whitsuntide last past – £3 5s 4d.
Item received of Arthur Gray for Robert Spencer's money due to the church – 24s 3d.[9]
Item received for 2 serges that was upon the heirs of Agnes Aleyn – 8d.
Item received for the burial of Agnes Aleyn – 6s 8d.[10]
Item received for the Trinity bell – 8d.
Received of Steven Boucke for the Plough light – 5s 4d.[11]
        Total Sum – £9 4s 5d.
Total sum of all the receipts received the said year by the said churchwardens declared in this account – £34 10s.

f. 105v.
        Payments.
Item paid to William East for his first quarter's wages for keeping of the clock & chime – 5s.

---

1   Marginalia – '£3 5d'.
2   Possibly Joanna Grey, interred 30 July 1547. LAO, Goulding Papers, 5/2.
3   'Aubs' or Albs.
4   Was this John Mackerell a relation of Mathew Mackerell, the former abbot of Barlings executed in 1537 for his part in the Rising?
5   Bridge?
6   Graunt was buried 8 November 1557. LAO, Goulding Papers, 5/2.
7   A Robert Chapman left a will: TNA, PROB 11/55/59, probate 6 February 1572/3.
8   Elizabeth, interred 9 March 1553/4. LAO, Goulding Papers, 5/2.
9   Marginalia – '£3 11s 1d'.
10 Agnes Allen was buried 30 March 1554. LAO, Goulding Papers, 5/2.
11 Marginalia – '13s 4d'.

Item paid for burde lime[1] – 1d.
Item paid to William Brown for his expenses and charges in the suit against William White commenced in the county – 3s 4d.
Item paid for a common bull – 15s 1d.
Item paid to John Rychardson for mending of the Haregares for 3 days – 15d.
Item paid for one ley[2] in Haregares by the space of 2 years [ended at Michaelmas][3] [th]at the gate standith on – 16d.
Item paid to [Sellby and][4] Ferryby and his fellow for double diking and hedging of the common hedge betwixt Elkington Field and Lowth Field to the number [of] 30 rods at 3d a rod – 7s 6d.
Item paid on Whit Sunday for wine – 15d.
Item paid for bread on Whit Sunday – 3d.
Item paid to Odlyng for a wheel to St George's bell – 10s.
Item paid to him for mending of the Second bell wheel and of other bells – 3s 4d.
Item paid for nails and iron work – 5d.
Item paid to a labourer for helping about the bells – 2d.
Item paid for pynding[5] the bull at Cokryngton[6] – 1d.
Item paid for bread and wine on Trinity Sunday – 10½d.
Item paid for a plumb rope to Cater – 12d.
Item paid to a wright for mending of the Haregarth gate – 2d.
Item paid to William East for blowing of the organs and whipping the dogs – 10d.
Item paid for writing this account and the book of christenings for one quarter – 20d.
Item paid to William East for his second quarter wages for keeping the clock and chime – 5s.
Item paid for 2 nails to 2 picks and for laying one of them and for a new shaft to it – 5d.
Item paid for half a load of ryce for wynding[7] of the bank at Graunt's house – 10d.[8]

f. 106r.

Item paid for drink to the workmen of the said ryce – 3d.
Item paid for 9 song books – 3s.
Item paid to Robert Westerby for 2 weeks for keeping of the Haregares – 12d.

---

[1] Possibly 'bird lime', a glutinous substance spread upon twigs, by which birds may be caught and held fast. *OED.*
[2] Lea. ley, leye, lay – land that has been uncultivated, pasture, grassland. *OED.*
[3] [Crossed through].
[4] [Crossed through].
[5] Pinding.
[6] North or South Cockerington.
[7] Widening?
[8] Marginalia – '59s 10½d'.

Item paid to John Anderson[1] for one quarter wages for keeping of the leads – 2s.
Item paid to Robert Westerby for 2 weeks in keeping of the Haregares – 12d.
Item paid to Richard Curson for a bill for the presentment of the quesi[2] at the Dean's Court – 12d.
Item paid to Sir Robert Beverlay for 2 boards and 2 trestles and a bassok and one stock lock[3] with 2 keys belonging to William Man's schoolhouse – 12d.[4]
Item paid on the 23rd day of July for bread and wine – 13½d.[5]
Item paid for wine spent on the day of the Proclamation of Queen Mary – 10s.[6]
Item paid for ale at Cursons at the making of the said Bill of Presentment – 4d.
Item paid to Robert Westerby the 6th day of August for 2 weeks for keeping the Haregares – 12d.
Item paid for a load of ryce for hedging of Lyncoln Close – 16d.[7]
Item paid to George Sympson for the carriage thereof – 10d.
Item paid to John Richardson for hedging the same – 7d.
Item paid Symon Kellum[8] and John Byllyngey for 4 days for mending the highway at the East Mills and the bridge to meat & wages – 2s.
Item paid to George Kyme for certain labourer's wages that *wrought at the forte*[9] – 28s 3d.
Item paid for bread & wine on the 20th day of August – 8d.
Item paid on the said day for keeping the Haregares – 12d.
Item paid on the 3rd day of September for keeping of the Haregares – 12d.
Item paid for bread & wine on the 17th day of September – 7½d.
Item paid on the said day for the keeping of the Haregares – 12d.
Item paid to John Wath for glazing of the windows – 2s 4d.
Item paid to Westerby by the first day of October – 12d.
Item paid to William East for his third quarter for the keeping of the clock and chimes – 5s.[10]

f. 106v.

Item paid to the said William East for the whipping of dogs and blowing the organs – 10d.
Item paid to John Anderson for his second quarter for keeping the leads – 2s.

---

[1] Interred 3 December 1559. LAO, Goulding Papers, 5/2.
[2] Possibly 'sought for; asked or enquired about': questioned or petitioned at the court. *OED*.
[3] A lock enclosed in a wooden case, usually fitted on an outer door. *OED*.
[4] Probably the song school.
[5] Probably concerning celebrations for the accession of Queen Mary.
[6] Mary was proclaimed in London on 19 July 1553. *DNB*, https://doi.org/10.1093/ref:odnb/18245 (Accessed 30/8/2023).
[7] Manicule in margin.
[8] Buried 23 November 1557. LAO, Goulding Papers, 5/2.
[9] Meaning unknown.
[10] Marginalia – '£3 7s 4d'.

Item paid for the second quarter for writing the account and the book of christenings – 20d.
Item paid to Westerby on the 15th Day of October for keeping of the Haregares – 12d.
Item paid to Richard Smyth for a pick – 8d.
Item paid to Thomas Leche for 4 staples and 2 espes[1] for the church gates – 10d.
Item paid to William Jakson for mending of the church stiles and for wood – 8d.
Item paid to Sympson for 2 loads of sand and leading of a load of stone to the church stile – 12d.
Item paid to Wady for 3 days & a half in mending of the church walls – 2s 4d.
Item paid to Robert Sympson for 3 days about the same for serving the said Wady to meat & wages and cleansing the grate – 16d.
Item paid for [bread][2] and wine – 8½d.
Item paid to William East for bread – 3d.
Item paid to William East for driving out of the doves – 6d.
Item paid to Martyn Chapman[3] for cleansing of Aswell – 8d.
Item paid to Herre Mawborn[4] and Rauf Robson[5] for dressing of Aswell – 2s.[6]
Item paid to John Enderby[7] for mending the common hedge on the south side of Haregares – 12d.
Item paid to Thomas Smyth for a lock to the churchyard gate – 6d.
Item paid to Symon Roper for 2 bell-strings – 3s.
Item paid to Robert Sympson for dressing up of lime in St Mary's church – 2d.
Item paid to Thomas Michell for going to Kennyngton[8] on a message for the town – 4d.
Item paid to 3 men for cleansing and scouring of the Small Wells.[9]
Item paid to the constable for keeping of Bastard in the hall – 4d.
Item paid to the poor people of the money taken of the linen ware – 9s 8d.
Item paid on the 10th day of December for bread and wine – 7d.
Item paid for half a pound of wire for the chime – 5d.[10]

[1] Hasps.
[2] [Crossed through].
[3] Chapman was interred 14 April 1569. LAO, Goulding Papers, 5/2.
[4] Henry Mawborn, buried 11 February 1564/5. LAO, Goulding Papers, 5/2.
[5] Ranulf Robson's bastard daughter Margaret was interred 4 July 1567. LAO, Goulding Papers, 5/2.
[6] 'Dressing' can relate to either cleansing or repairing, so was this a refurbishment of the town's water source or a form of well-dressing still practised today, notably in Derbyshire? Well-dressing is cited in the *OED* as late as 1819. At one time, the spring supplying Aswell may have been venerated as a holy well. Bayley, *Notitiæ Ludæ*, pp. 210–12. See also Caitlin Green at https://www.caitlingreen.org/2015/04/of-sacred-springs-commerce-and-crime.html (Accessed 20/6/2019).
[7] Buried 24 August 1566. LAO, Goulding Papers, 5/2.
[8] Keddington.
[9] No amount stated.
[10] Marginalia – '32s 5½d'.

f. 107r.
Item for nails to the chimes – ½d.
Item paid to Auncell Jeff for a string to the Trinity bell – 3s 4d.
Item paid for a yard of cloth to an amice – 11d.
Item paid for tukkyng strings[1] and tabbes[2] – 1d.
Item paid for latten sawter[3] – 6d.
Item paid for a collar to the Trinity bell – 4d.
Item paid for dressing of the Small Wells to Saltmarsh, Ferryby & Penny – 2s.
Item paid to William East for blowing the organs & whipping the dogs for the 4th quarter – 10d.
Item paid to the same William his 4th quarter for keeping the clock & chime – 5s.
Item paid for the third quarter wages for writing the account – 20d.
Item paid to John Anderson[4] for his third quarter wages for dressing the leads – 3s 4d.
Item paid for leather to a collar to the Lady bell – 2d.
Item paid to Robert Odlyng for mending of the ceiling on the north side of St Peter's choir – 20d.
Item paid more to him for dressing the bushes of the Trinity bell and a cross shaft – 8d.
Item paid to Robert Odlyng for his half year's wages – 20d.
Item paid to Richard Smith for mending of the chime – 2d.
Item paid to Thomas Mysterchambers for a manual[5] and a dirige book[6] – 4s 6d.
Item paid for a mass book – 5s.[7]
Item paid to William King for a holy water bucitt[8] & a pair of censers – 4s.
Item paid for 2 candlesticks of 6lb for the altar – 2s 8d.
Item paid for a cross of copper – 6s 8d.
Item paid for a suit of vestments of blue and red velvet – £3 13s 4d.
Item paid for a cross cloth – 2s.
Item paid for a vestment of black russels[9] with a red cross – 5s 4d.
Item paid for dressing of the censers and candlesticks and 5 chemes[10] to the censers – 18d.[11]

   1 Possibly strings of a 'tucking girdle' worn with the alb. *OED.*
   2 Tab – a short strap attached at one end to one side of a coat, jacket, vest, etc. *OED.*
   3 Latin psalter.
   4 'Reade' crossed through.
   5 A book containing the instructions in the administration of the sacraments. *OED.*
   6 A volume comprising the offices for the dead. *OED.*
   7 The purchase of a Mass book, manual and dirige book along with the procurement of liturgical fixtures is the first evidence of doctrinal changes following the accession of Queen Mary.
   8 Bucket.
   9 A strong twilled woollen cloth formerly used for clothing and footwear. *OED.*
   10 Chains.
   11 Marginalia – '£2 7s 4½d'.

f. 107v.

Item paid to the relief of sick people in Saltfleethaven on the second week of January – 2s.[1]

Item paid for a sacring bell – 4d.

Item paid to John Bellingay for digging 6 loads of stone for the altar – 14d.

Item paid to the relief of the people of Saltfleethaven for the 3 weeks, 3rd week of January – 2s.

Item paid to William Reade for serving the poor people in Saltfleethaven – 6d.

Item paid to the relief of Saltfleethaven people for the 3rd week in January – 2s.

Item paid to William Reade for the second week for serving people in Saltfleethaven – 6d.

Item paid for 2 loads of stone to the altar – 5d.

Item paid to John Smith for leading 8 loads of stone and 22 of sand for the altar – 9s 8d.

Item paid to Henry Squyrall for 6 days to meat & wages in making the altar – 4s.

Item paid to Thomas Freman for 6 days in making of the altar – 2s 6d.

Item paid to William Dyxson[2] for 4 days work about the said altar – 2s 2d.

Item paid for a manual – 3d.

Item paid for mending of a surplice for the curate – 4d.

Item paid to Robert East for helping and working about the altar – 2d.

Item paid to William Reade for the 3rd week for serving the people in Saltfleethaven – 6d.

Item paid for the 4th week for the relief of the said people – 2s.

Item paid for the relief of Saltfleethaven people for the 5th week – 2s.

Item paid to William Reade for the 5th week in serving the said people – 6d.

Item paid to Thomas Palmer for a piece of a cowcher[3] – 6s 8d.

Item paid to Edward Argram for a whole cowcher for the same half year – 16s.

Item paid for bread and ale at the raising of the altar stone – 5d.[4]

Item paid to William Dyxson for 2 days work about the altar – 13d.

Item paid to Henry Squyrall for two days and a half about the said altar – 20d.

Item paid to Thomas Freman for 2 days and a half in serving the workmen – 13d.

Item paid for strings to 2 awbes[5] – 4d.

Item paid for 52 brick tiles to the altar & holy water vat – 15d.

Item paid to Richard Curson for 4 obligations for the church money – 3s 4d.

---

[1] Probably an outbreak of disease in Saltfleethaven, to which the churchwardens allotted funds doubtless to prevent the inhabitants from travelling to Louth for relief and spreading the disease.

[2] William Dyxson, Dixson, tiler, was interred 5 February 1569/70. LAO, Goulding Papers, 5/2.

[3] Coucher – a large breviary (a book containing the divine office); a cartulary or register. *OED*.

[4] The re-introduction of stone altars was evidently a cause for much celebration.

[5] Albs.

f. 108r.
Item paid for frankincense – 1d.
Item paid for soap for washing of the surplice – 2d.
Item paid to the relief of Saltfleethaven people -2s.
Item paid for serving of them – 6d.
Item paid to the relief of Holme and his wife – 12d.[1]
Item paid to the relief of Syll's wife – 6d.[2]
Item paid to the relief of Martyn Smith – 6d.[3]
Item paid to William Whyte for a grail and 2 pieces of a cowcher – 13s 4d.
Item paid William East for the washing of a surplice – 1d
Item paid to Robert Odlyng for making a pax before the altar – 22s.
Item paid to Gilbert Blannchard for nails and boards to the same pax – 8s 3d.
Item paid to William Read for serving the people in Saltfleethaven – 6d.
Paid for 7 yards hare cloth[4] to the High altar at 7d a yard – 4s 1d.
Paid Robert Odlyng for the making of the rail of the back side of the altar & a foot to the cross – 2s 6d.
Item paid to the relief of Saltfleethaven people – 2s.
Item paid to William Reade for serving of them – 6d.
Item paid to John Wathe for beating of 8 stone of lead to 2 holy water vats & melting thereof – 2s.
Item paid to the said John for glazing and stopping of windows on the south side of the church – 16d.
Item paid to the relief of Saltfleethaven and for serving of them – 2s 6d.
Item for 2 holy water strynkells – 2d.
Item for 4 yards of canvas to the altar – 3s.
Item for writing of a bill that was sent to the Commissioners from Mr Heneage – 4d.
Item for sewing of the altar cloth and the hare cloths – 4d.
Item paid to Edward Argram for an altar cloth – 2s 6d.
Item paid to George Somerscales for a grail book – 4s.
Item paid to the relief of Saltfleethaven people and serving of them – 2s 6d.
Item paid to John Reed for serving of the people of Saltfleethaven – 6d.
Sum – 73s 2d.
f. 108v.
Item paid for wine that was carried to Master John Skypwith[5] – 10d.
Item given to his clerk – 12d.
Item paid to Robert Kyrkby for wax making – 2s 4d.

---

[1] Line crossed through.
[2] Line crossed through.
[3] Line crossed through.
[4] Possibly rough cloth for the shirts worn by penitents or ascetics. *OED.*
[5] This is possibly John Skipwith (d.1585) of Walmesgate, son of Sir William Skipwith (d.1547) and his second wife Alice Dymoke. He was born in Louth in 1527. Maddison, *Lincolnshire Pedigrees*, 52, pp. 889, 895.

Item paid to Jordan – 6d.
Item paid to William Whyte for 12 pounds of wax – 12s.
Item for 4 pounds of wax paid to William Kyng – 3s 4d.
Item paid to George Somerscales for 4 pounds of wax – 3s 10d.
Item paid for a pound and a half of wax – 6d.
Item paid to John Wathe for a Sepulchre – 2s.[1]
Item paid for butter for dryving[2] of the wax – 2d.
Item paid for a cord to hang the cloth of the sacrament – 1d.
Item paid to Arthur Grey for money laid out by the said Arthur whereas he went to Lincoln concerning the enclosures – 11s 8d.
Item paid to Thomas Palmer for 3 painted cloths to the Sepulchre – 10s.
Item paid for whipping of the dogs and blowing of the organs – 10d.[3]
Item paid for a lock to the Sepulchre – 1½d.
Item paid to Robert Odlyng for his last half year's wages – 20d.
Item paid to the writer of the account for his last quarter's wages – 20d.
Item paid to Robert Odlyng for a frame for [the] lenten light – 2s.
Item paid to him for an arme [4]over the altar for the sacrament – 8d.
Item paid to him for 2 pairs of clasps – 20d.
Item paid for mending of the hearse[5] about the Sepulchre – 8d.
Item paid to John Anderson for his 4th quarter wages for the dressing of the leads & bells – 2s.
Item paid to Thomas Mysterchambers for an altar cloth to be above the altar – 5s.[6]
Item paid to Gilbert Blanchard for a canopy of red silk embroidered with gold and the fringe – 5s.
Item for a skene[7] of red silk – 2d.
Item for a yard of stripe worsted for the altar cloth – 16d.
Item for a yard of buckram for lining the same – 6d.
Item to Jervis Denys for making of the canopy – 8d.
f. 109r.
Item for 4 yards of black spannys[8] silk and a black silk knop for the sacrament – 8d.
Item for a plumb of lead to the same – 2d.

[1] Perhaps the start of the process of reinstating an Easter Sepulchre; probably removed in Edward VI's reign.
[2] Driving – possibly for removing wax from altar cloths?
[3] '6d' crossed through.
[4] *Armoire* (French) – cupboard.
[5] An elaborate framework originally intended to carry a large number of lighted tapers and other decorations over the bier or coffin while placed in the church at the funerals of distinguished persons. *OED*.
[6] Marginalia – '£3 4s 6½d'.
[7] Skin. *OED*.
[8] Possibly Spanish black lace.

Item paid for the setting out of the sowldgors[1] over and beside the money gathered in the town for them – £6 18s 4d.[2]
Paid to Thomas Lecheman[3] for 2 irons for the staying of the back of the altar – 4d
Item paid to the gatherers for the poor on Good Friday – 3s 4d.
Item paid for watching of the Sepulchre – 4d.
Paid to Steven Boucke for wood to the hallowed fire[4] of *Pash Albi*[5] – 4d.[6]
Total sum of the several payments laid forth by the said churchwardens, £32 9d.
Total sum received as particularly appearith above by this account declared by Gilbert Blancherd, John Brown & others the churchwardens the next Sunday after Easter *Anno* 1554 £34 10s, whereof paid by the said churchwardens as appearith particularly by their account above declared £32 9d, and yet remaineth upon the said churchwardens by the said account 49s 3d, to be delivered to the hands of the new churchwardens for the year following.
Memorandum, the sum of 40s for the Common Cart is committed and delivered this present year to Walter Woode and John Skupholme & they to lead for the repairing of the highways 20 loads of stone to be laid in such places where the new churchwardens shall appoint. William Kyng & Robert Odlyng have undertaken & become sureties for W[alter] Wood & William Deughte & Thomas Richardson sureties for John Skupholme.

f. 109v.

[1554–5]

Churchwardens appointed to office *Anno Domini* 1554, William Whyte, William Balif, Thomas Richardson[7] & Thomas Leche.
Received of the old churchwardens as appearith in the foot of the last account, 49s 3d.
Item more received of them on the money in the Rood loft[8] with one obligation

---

1   Soldiers. Perhaps raised by Mary to secure the throne from Lady Jane Grey.
2   Marginalia – '£2 6s 10d'.
3   Lechman's wife Margaret and his daughter Joanna were buried on the same day, 17 January 1557/8. LAO, Goulding Papers, 5/2.
4   Wood for a fire lit and blessed, *Benedictio ignis*, on Easter Eve (Saturday) signifying Christ's victory over darkness following his decent into Hell. (*Gospel of Nicodemus*, Chapters 15–18). Parishioners took the flame into their houses as a form of blessing. Wright, *Churchwardens' Accounts*, pp. 1–2, note 3.
5   White Easter.
6   Marginalia – '4s 4d'.
7   Recorded in 1561 as a yeoman. Burton, *Old Lincolnshire*, p. 118.
8   A chest containing church documents and valuables placed on the Rood loft for safekeeping.

of 34s 4d of Mr Topclyff, wherewith John Bradeley,[1] Robert Spencer & Richard Topclyff[2] was charged £6 5s 3d.

Receipts with the pece.

Item received on the second Sunday after Easter – 4s 4½d.
Item received on the third Sunday after – 3s 10½d.
Item received on the 4th Sunday after – 2s 10d.
Item received on the 5th Sunday after – 2s 3d.
Item received on the 6th Sunday after – 2s 1d.
Item received on Whit Sunday – 2s 10½d.
Item received on Trinity Sunday – 2s 11½d.
Item received on the first Sunday after – 22d.
Item on the second Sunday after – 2s 3d.
Item received on the 3rd Sunday after – 23½d.
Item received on the 4th Sunday after – 2s 9d.
Item received on the 5th Sunday after – 3s 2d.
Item received on the 6th Sunday after – 2s 4d.
Item received on the 7th Sunday after – 19d.
Item received on the 8th Sunday after – 20d.
Item received on the 9th Sunday after – 22½d.
Item received on the 10th Sunday after – 2s 9d.[3]

Sum – 43s 6d.

f. 110r.

Receipts of burials and other things.

Item for the burial of Edward Same[4] – 6s 8d.
Item for the Trinity bell ringing – 8d.
Item received for the burial of Richard Curson – 6s 8d.
Item for the bells.[5]
Item for the burial of Nicholas Thorndik's wife – 6s 8d.
Item for the bells – 20d.
Item for the Trinity bell for Agnes Cyll – 8d.
Item for the burial of Edward Boswell's wife – 6s 8d.[6]
Item for the bells – 20d.

---

[1] In 1551, John Bradley, merchant of the Staple, was one of the first of the six assistants to the Corporation and elected warden in 1565 and 1575. Goulding, *Corporation Records*, pp. 4, 19. He married Francis Fairfax of Swarby (d.1608, aged eighty-four), who has a plaque dedicated to her on the south wall of St James's. Bradley was buried in Louth 6 December 1590. Maddison, *Lincolnshire Pedigrees*, 50, p. 169. Will: TNA, PROB 11/77/22, probate, 9 January 1591. For details of Bradley's extensive property in Louth, see Swaby, *History of Louth*, p. 181; Goulding, *Louth Houses*, n.p.

[2] Interred 13 February 1558/9. LAO, Goulding Papers, 5/2.

[3] The list of collections finishes here.

[4] Edward Same of Aby interred 2 June 1554. LAO, Goulding Papers, 5/2.

[5] No amount stated.

[6] Margaret, buried 10 October 1554. LAO, Goulding Papers, 5/2.

Item for the burial of Nicholas Thorndik's child – 20d.[1]
Item received for the James bell at the burial of Anne Marshall – 12d.
Item received for the wood that was sold belonging to the plague house[2] – 2s 6d.
Item received for the burial of John Hilton, clerk[3] – 6s 8d.
Item for the bells – 12d.
Item for the burial of George Ramforth – 6s 8d.
Item received for the bells at the burial of Peter Farrand's wife – 12d.
Sum – 51s 10d.

f. 110v.
Payments.
Item paid to William East for keeping of the clock and chime – 20s.
Item paid to him for the blowing of the organs – 3s 4d.
Item paid to the writer of this account – 6s 8d.
Item paid to John Anderson for keeping of the leads – 13s 4d.
Item paid to Thomas Odlyng for his wages – 3s 4d.
Item paid to Martin Chapman for scouring of Aswell for half a year – 12d.
Item paid to John Anderson for recompense for this last year's wages as it was agreed by the parish – 16d.
Item paid to Rauf Jakson for 2 books – 2s.
Item paid to Sir John Whetley[4] for a preffion[5] in parchment – 3s.
Item paid for a quire of paper – 3d.
Item paid to William Evans for certain books – 3s 4d.
Item paid to Edward Boswell for a book – 2s.[6]
Item paid to the pavyer[7] for paving on the Corne Hill, 3 days [and a] half at 9d a day – 2s 7½d.[8]

---

[1] William, interred 2 October 1554. LAO, Goulding Papers, 5/2.

[2] Probably the building on Cisterngate used for isolation purposes. Green, *Streets of Louth*, p. 60.

[3] John Hilton, Hylton or Hiltonne was previously an Augustinian canon of Thornton Abbey. Following its suppression, he was awarded a pension of £6. *L&P*, XV, 1032 (140), p. 548, 2 February 1539/40. He received dispensation to hold a benefice, 27 January 1539/40. Chambers, *Faculty Office*, p. 207. Hilton became a vicar in Louth on a stipend of £7 6s 8d and was buried 19 January 1554/5. Hodgett, *Ex-Religious*, p. 103. LAO, Goulding Papers, 5/2.

[4] John Wheatley, Weikeley, aged sixty, was a former chaplain to the St Mary guild with a pension of £5 13s 4d. He was unmarried and was noted in 1526 as having a stipend of £6. Hodgett, *Ex-Religious*, pp. 102–3. Salter, *Subsidy*, p. 12. Interred as John Wheatle on 3 April 1558. LAO, Goulding Papers, 5/2. He left a will dated 26 March 1557, in which Sir William Dychand was appointed his supervisor and his books were donated to John Goodall the schoolmaster. LAO, LCC, 1558 (ii), *f.* 99.

[5] Possibly 'profession' – taking a vow.

[6] '20d' crossed through.

[7] Pavior – a person who lays paving slabs. *OED*.

[8] Marginalia – 'The Corn Hill paved by the churchwardens.'

Item paid to John Wath for mending and making the glass windows in the church – 6s 8d.
Item paid to John Wath for 7 pounds [and a] half of solder – 2s 8d.
Item paid to him and his man for 5 days work – 4s.
Item paid to Robert Odlyng for mending the Fore bell and St George bell – 16d.
Item paid to Richard Smyth the 20th day of May for iron work to the windows & the clock – 4d.
Item paid to Symon Roper for a bell-string to the Coo bell – 3s.
Item paid to John Reade for 2 troughs laying – 8d.
Item to Symon Roper for a bell-string – 3s 2d.
Item paid to Symon Kellum for digging of stone – 12d.
Sum – £4 5s ½d.

f. 111r.
Item paid to William Browne for leading of sand and stone to the Market Hill – 2s.[1]
Item paid to Robert Odlyng for 2 bushes and nails – 4d.
Item paid to Symon Kellum for digging of stone on the bowne day[2] – 18d.
Item paid to Robert Odlyng for the wages of 2 men for mending the bells – 20d.
Item paid to Richard Smyth for mending the irons to the bells – 8d.
Item paid to Thomas Leche, smith, for mending of the grate & the church gates – 4d.
Item paid for helping to hang the James[3] – 2d.
Item paid to Robert Odlyng for 2 boards for the holy water vat – 8d.
Item paid to him for mending the Trinity bell – 20d.
Item paid to Robert Odlyng in part of payment for the wheel for the James bell – 8s.
Item paid to Awncell Jeff for a string to the James bell – 6s 4d.
Item paid to John Anderson[4] for covering the grave of Mr Curson – 4d.
Item paid to Robert Odlyng for the rest of the James wheel – 5s 4d.
Item paid to Symon Newbrugs for mending the chime string – 16d.
Item paid to John Richarson for felling of 2 loads of ryce – 6d.
Item paid Thomas Watson for 3 days for hedging the Haregares – 15d.
Item paid to Symon Kellum and John Bellingey for digging of 9 loads of stone, 2½d the load – 22d.
Item paid for felling 2 loads of rice – 6d.
Item paid to Dyxson for 6 days work about the altars – 4s 6d.
Item paid to George Lowes[5] for 6 days about the same work – 3s.
Item paid for 6 loads of sand to Sympson – 2s.

[1] '4d' crossed through.
[2] Boon day.
[3] James bell.
[4] 'Reade' crossed through.
[5] Buried 27 May 1564. LAO, Goulding Papers, 5/2.

Item paid to Thomas Watson for 2 days [and a] half working in the Haregares – 12d.
Item paid for laying down the thrugh of Nicholas Thorndik's wife – 4d.
Item paid to Thomas Watson for 2 days work on the Haregares – 10d.
Item paid to John Richarson for felling of ryce to the Haregares – 6d.
Item paid to Thomas Watson for one day in hedging of Haregares – 5d.
Sum – 47s.

f. 111v.

Payments.

Item paid to Robert Odlyng for mending of St George bell, the James bush and the Fore bell – 3s 4d.
Item paid to William Kyng for 6 loads of thorns to the Haregares – 3s.
Item to William Browne for carrying 2 loads [of] rice to the Haregares – 12d.
Item to John Anderson for covering the thrugh of Margaret Boswell – 4d.[1]
Item to John Anderson for covering the thrugh of Arthur Grey's mother – 4d.
Item to Peper in part of payment of the making of the Rood – 6s 8d.[2]
Item to Robert Minghell for irons to the Trinity bell – 12d.
Item to Robert Odlyng for mending of the Trinity bell, Our Lady's bell and the Fore bell – 3s.
Item for a horse skin – 8d.
Item paid to Peper for the rest of the money for making of the Rood – 3s 4d.
Item for washing the altar cloth – 1d.
Item paid to Robert Babsor [for] painting of the Rood – 7s.
Item to Robert Odlyng for mending of the bells – 12d.
Item to John Anderson for covering the thrugh of John Hilton, clerk – 4d.
Item paid to 3 men for dressing the bridge at East Mills – 3s.
Item paid to John North for a horse skin – 3s.
Item paid to Sir John Wheatley for candles – 4d.
Item paid to Robert East for mending the chimes – 2d.
Item paid to Richard Smith for mending the chime and bells – 22d.
Item to Symon Roper for 2 altar cloths of 6 yards – 3s.
Item to Richard Nicolson for mending a lock – 2d.
Item to Robert Akred for mending a lantern – 14d.
Item paid for washing a surplice – 2d.
Item for covering the trough of George Ramforth – 4d.
Item for making 2 obligations – 8d.
Item paid to William Peper for one day's work about the Rood to meat and wages – 9d.
Item for washing an alb and an amice and washing thereof – 3d.

---

[1] Interred 10 October 1554. She was possibly the second wife of Edward Boswell; his first, Elizabeth, was buried 1 March 1547/8. LAO, Goulding Papers, 5/2.

[2] William Peper; '10s' crossed through. Probably replacements for the Rood figures removed during the previous administration.

Item for 400 of stowring[1] nails that John Wath had about the leads – 8d.
Item for wood for the melting of lead – 4d.
Item for mending the picks 2 times – 10d.
Item for 2 corporax cloths – 2s.
Item to William Dixson and Rauf Robson for whiting the church walls – 6s.
Sum – 55s 10d.

f. 112r.
Item more to Dixson for certain other works – 18d.
Item to Agnes Scott in charity – 2d.
Item to William Hewet[2] for 2 planks for the Rood – 4s.
Item to Robert Odling for a stock for the cross foot – 2d.
Item to Martin Chapman for scouring Aswell – 12d.
Item for the digging of stone to the common work – 3s.
Item to the Clerk of the Market for the town skep – 3s 4d.
Item paid for the Sepulchre – 6s 8d.
Item paid for nails – 1d.
Item for 2 yards of linen cloth for 2 towels for the altar – 2s 1d.
Item for making of them – 2d.
Item for a bull – 16s 6d.
Item for a cross case – 6d.
Item for a new rope to the chimes to Symon Newbrugh – 12s.
Item for scouring of 2 Alman Ryvetts[3], 3 sallets[4], 3 pairs of splints[5] & 3 gorgits[6] – 9s 4d.[7]
Item for 8 yards & [a] half of canvas for 2 altar cloths – 5s 8d.
Item for 14 pounds [and a] half of wax for the Sepulchre light at 16d a pound – 18s.

---

[1] Stour – stout, massive, bulky. *OED*.

[2] William Hewit, Hewicke, Hewick, shoemaker, left a will: TNA, PROB 11/54/150, probate, 21 April 1572. Buried 31 January 1571/2. LAO, Goulding Papers, 5/2.

[3] Almain Rivet – a type of flexible light armour, originating in Germany, featuring overlapping plates sliding on rivets. *OED*. In his deposition, William Moreland noted that after he fled to Yorkshire following the Rising, he sought to serve Sir Robert Constable of Holderness, who gave him 'a pair of Almain Rivets'. *L&P*, XII (i), 380, p. 178, 9 February 1536/7. In 1598, the Wigtoft churchwardens recorded: 'Item one Allmend fully furnished, 2 corselets, 2 bows, 2 calivers, 2 girdles, 6 swords and 6 daggers.' Nichols, *Illustrations*, pp. 245–6.

[4] A light globular headpiece, either with or without a visor and without a crest. *OED*.

[5] Plates or strips of overlapping metal on medieval armour. *OED*.

[6] Gorget – section of armour protecting the throat. *OED*. Illustration at https://collections.royalarmouries.org/object/rac-object-24417.html (Accessed 16/4/2020).

[7] Presumably the parish kept armaments in readiness for local disturbances, or even armed insurrection during the early years of Queen Mary's reign. Equipment was later procured during the Northern Rebellion of 1569.

Item to Robert Kirkby for making 26 pounds of wax at 1½d the pound – 3s 3d.
Item for 4 yards [and] a quarter [and] a half [a] quarter of canvas for a cloth to the High altar – 3s 3d.
Item for 2 yards [and] a quarter of green chamblet[1] for the new altar cloth – 6s 9d.
Item for the altar cloth of silk & emiges[2] [of] gold – 13s 4d.
Item for 4 yards of linen for the High altar cloth – 4s 8d.
Item for making thereof – 1d.
Item for 7 yards of linen for 2 side altar cloths – 5s 10d.
Item for making them – 2d.
Item for 14 yards canvas for the vale[3] in the choir – 16s.
Item for sewing the same together and hanging them with curtain rings and ynkill[4] for the rings – 16d.
Item for 9 yards [and] 3 quarters of canvas for a vale[5] for the Rood – 6s 6d.
Item for sewing the same – 4d.
Item for a piece of wood for the cloth to hang on – 4d.
Item to Thomas Lathes for mending the gate at the West Mills for wood & workmanship – 20d.
Item for nails and a vertiwell to the said gate – 5d.
Item for Peper for one day about the Rood for meat and wages – 9d.
Item for a piece of wood to the Rood – 10d.
Item for 3 spakes for pyn wood – 2d.[6]
Item to Robert Kirkby for a ladder of 12 stowers[7] for standing in the Rood loft – 12d.
Item for ½ yard [of] Rone[8] buckram green for lining a piece of the altar cloth – 6d.
Item for 7 yards [of] canvas for covering the 2 side altars – 4s 8d.
Item for 1 yard [and] 3 quarters of linen cloth and a quarter half of blue russells[9] for the same – 2s.
Sum – £7 18s.

[1] Camlet – a name originally referring to costly eastern fabrics; later applied to various imitations. *OED*.
[2] Possibly images or edging of gold?
[3] 'Walle' crossed through. This was possibly a covering for the wall, similar to a tapestry, on which were painted images, perhaps replacing wall paintings previously removed.
[4] Inkle – linen tape. *OED*.
[5] Veil.
[6] Spakes and pyn – possibly a wooden peg, nail or spike. Alternatively, a bolt or latch on a door or gate. *OED*.
[7] Rung of a ladder. *OED*.
[8] Rone or Rome – meaning unknown in this context.
[9] Russel – a strong twilled woollen cloth. *OED*.

f. 112v.

Item to John Wath for part payment of his work in glazing – 6s 8d.
Item to John Earl for working of a pew in the church that Thomas Palmer's wife settith in, for 9 days meat and wages – 7s.
Item to him for stocks[1] for serges to stand about the Sepulchre – 4d.
Item to Bab for painting 2 altar cloths cont[aining] in length and breadth 10 yards – 3s 4d.
Item and for more for painting the vales in the choir and for the Rood cont[aining] 34 yards – 6s 8d.
Item to Luke Painter for painting the cloth before the High altar – 4s.
Item for packthread for sewing on the altar cloth and nails – 1½d.
Item for an altar cloth to St Peter's altar – 3s 4d.
Item to William Dowghty for 3 vestments & a cope – 33s 4d.
Item more for a canopy, a corporax case, a Sepulchre, a Sacre bell & 2 cruets – 10s.
Item for a pyx, a cross foot of latten and scouring the cross foot – 4s 1d.
Item to James Mainfeld for mending a cope, purchasing a new altar cloth and lining the same, buying 2 amices and lining them – 20d.
Item for 9 yards of white yncle – 1½d.
Item paid to William King for the table over the Sepulchre – 3s 4d.
Item paid by William White, John Baily,[2] William Fyswik for the soldiers at London, *Anno Domini* 1553 – 12s 1d.[3]
Item for mending and hedging the common sewer in the North Field to 3 men one day – 16½d.
Item to 2 men for 2 days about the said work – 22d.[4]
Item to Thomas Richarson for his lee in the Haregares that the gate standith on – 8d.[5]
Item to Odling and his man for one day's work about the bells to meat and wages – 12d.
Item more paid to John Wath for glazing – 6s 8d.
Item to John Earl for making a stool for 3 days to meat and wages – 2s.
Item paid for mending the chrismatory – 10d.
Item to John Anderson for dressing the church stiles – 2d.
      Sum – £5 10s 7½d.
Total sum of the whole payments paid by the churchwardens – £22 16s 6d.
Sum of the whole receipts appearing in this year's accounts – £16 19s 10¼d.
And so the churchwardens be in surplusage – £5 16s 8d.

 [1] The main upright, a vertical beam or stem. *OED*.
 [2] Recorded in 1561 as a yeoman. Burton, *Old Lincolnshire*, p. 118.
 [3] Possibly relating to the rebellion of Sir Thomas Wyatt and the subsequent execution of Lady Jane Grey.
 [4] '11d' crossed through.
 [5] '20d' crossed through.

f. 113r.
[Memorandum, the said churchwardens chargeth themselves to have received of diverse things sold within the said church of £102 12d].[1]
Sum of the surplusage due to the said churchwardens as appearith on the other leaf next before £5 16s 8d, whereof the said churchwardens do charge themselves to have received of the Plough gatherings of the said year 6s 8d. Item they do charge themselves for the arrearage due upon the reckonings to the poor declared in the latter end of this book, 28s 5½d. And yet remaining in surplusage, £4 18½d.
Item the said churchwardens chargeth themselves with the sum of one hundred [and] two pounds twelve pence remaining in their hands by the appointment of the whole parish £102 12d, whereof paid as appearith by 15 obligations delivered over unto the new churchwardens £95 6s 8d. And there remaineth of this reckoning remaining upon the old churchwardens 14s 4d.
Memorandum, the sum of forty shillings for the Common Cart is of new committed to Walter Woode and John Skupholme upon like conditions and sureties as in the year next before they were charged and the said sureties to be charged not only for the payment of the said money but also for the carriage of the stone in default of the said Walter Wood & John Skupholme, *videlicet* 35 loads that is 20 loads for the year coming & 11 loads for the last year yet being sold the last year.
Memorandum, where the old churchwardens doth owe upon the said reckoning of £102 12d, the sum of £6 14s 4d, the same churchwardens doth ask allowance of the surplusage likewise above declared and that surplusage allowed to them yet there remaineth in debt upon the said churchwardens of the said reckoning, 52s 9½d.
Item more due by them received by them of the money assigned for the relief of them, £9 10s 8d, yet remaining in debt upon the said old churchwardens £12 3s 5d, over and before 17s.
f. 113v.
[Memorandum, the old churchwardens. Memorandum, there is owing yet of old debt for two horses by William Whyte & William Fishewyke][2] 50s. Whereof 4d there is owing by Robert Spencer for one horse delivered by William Whyte, 30s 10d, by William Whyte in his manner *videlicet* for 1 writ of latitat[3] with the serving of the same 7s, and in ready money to the new churchwardens in *Anno* 1555 27s, and so contented & paid and acquitted by the whole parish.

[1]   [Crossed through].
[2]   [Lines crossed through].
[3]   A writ summoning a defendant assumed to be in hiding to answer in the Court of King's or Queen's Bench. *OED*.

f. 114r.

[1555–6]

Churchwardens appointed to office *Anno Domini* 1555, William Doughtie, Robert Acred, Robert Chapman and Edward Argram. *Anno Domini* 1555.

Receipts with the pece.[1]

Item on the second Sunday after Easter – 2s 8d.[2]

Memorandum, the old churchwardens hath delivered over to the new churchwardens 15 obligations of diverse persons amounting in the whole to the sum of £95 6s 8d.

Item they have likewise delivered to the said new churchwardens in ready money for the debt remaining upon the account declared in the first side of the leaf next before, £13 5½d.

One common bull.

Item they have likewise delivered over to the new churchwardens to the use of the township one bull at 16s 6d.

Item William Fyshwyke & William Whyte hath paid to the hands of the said new churchwardens for the price of one horse, 20s.

In witness of the same the persons underwritten being present at the declaration of the said account have subscribed their names the 24th day of April *Anno Domini* 1555.[3]

L[awrence] Eresbye.

John Makrell['s] mark[4], by me Gylbert Blanchard

William Kyng.

Robert Acred['s][5] mark, [by me] Arthur Grey.

William Dowghty.

Robert Chapman, by me Edward Argram, by me Thomas Blanchard.

Robert Marshall['s] mark,[6] by me John Baily,

by me Thomas Mytchell.

William Atkin['s] mark.[7]

f. 114v.

Receipts with the pece.

Item on the second Sunday after Easter – 2s 8d.

Item on the 3rd Sunday after – 3s 2d.[8]

Item on the 4th Sunday after – 2s 2½d.

Item on the 5th Sunday after – 4s 9d.

---

[1] Line crossed through.
[2] Line crossed through.
[3] The following names appear to be signatures; those who were probably illiterate made their marks and were witnessed by others.
[4] A circle.
[5] A square with a small rectangle attached to the right.
[6] A circle with a line through.
[7] A square.
[8] '8d' crossed through.

Item on the 6th Sunday after – 5s 1½d.
Item on Whitsunday – 8s 1d.¹
Item on Trinity Sunday – 6s.
Item on the first Sunday after – 5s 1½d.
Item on the second Sunday after – 4s.²
Item on the 3rd Sunday after – 2s 2d.
Item on the 4th Sunday after – 2s.
Item on the 5th Sunday after – 22d.
Item on the 6th Sunday after – 17d.
Item on the 7th Sunday after – 16d.
Item on the 8th Sunday after – 2s 1d.
Item on the 9th Sunday after – 2s 5d.
Item on the 10th Sunday after – 21d.
Item on the 11th Sunday after – 22d.
Item on the 12th Sunday after – 2s 2½d.
Item received on the 13th Sunday after – 18d.
Item on the 14th Sunday after – 22d.
Item on the 15th Sunday after – 2s.
Item on the 16th Sunday after – 18½d.
Item on the 17th Sunday after – 20d.
Item on the 18th Sunday after – 2s.
Item on the 19th Sunday after – 2s.
Item on the 20th Sunday after – 19d.
Item on the 21st Sunday after – 2s.
Item on the 22nd Sunday after – 19d.
Item on the 23rd Sunday after – 2s.
Item on the 24th Sunday after – 16d.
Item on the first Sunday in Advent – 19d.
Item on the second Sunday in Advent – 20d.
Item on the 3rd Sunday in Advent – 2s.
f. 115r.
Item on the 4th Sunday in Advent – 20d.
Item on the first Sunday after Christmas – 21d.
Item on the 2nd Sunday after Christmas – 22d.
Item on the 3rd Sunday after Christmas – 2s 3d.
Item on the 4th Sunday after Christmas – 19d.
Item on the 5th Sunday after Christmas – 2s.
Item on the 6th Sunday after Christmas – 20d.
Item on the 7th Sunday after Christmas – 2s 1½d.
Item on the 8th Sunday after – 20d.
Item on the first Sunday in Lent – 19d.

[1] '7s' crossed through.
[2] '½d' crossed through.

Item on the second Sunday in Lent – 19d.
Item on the 3rd Sunday in Lent – 2s.
Item on Mydlent Sunday – 16d.
Item on the 5th Sunday in Lent – 2s 4d.
Item on Palm Sunday – 2s 7d.
Item on Good Friday – 23d.
Item on Low Sunday – 13d.
Sum – £5 17s 5d.
Receipts of burials.
Item for the burial of Richard Wryght – 6s 8d.
Item for the bells – 20d.
Item of the executors of Richard Nicolson for the bells – 12d.
Item of [the executors][1] [of] John Bawdwin[2] for the bells – 12d.
Sum – 10s 4d.
Sum received besides the money due by especialties[3] – £20 8s 2½d.
Sum of the payments – £19 8s.
Remains – 20s 2½d.

f. 115v.
Payments.
Item paid to William East for his wages for the clock & chime – 20s.
Item paid to Anderson for his wages – 13s 4d.[4]
Item to the writer of this account – 6s 8d.
Item for blowing the organs – 3s 4d.
Item to Odling for his wages for carpenters office about the bells – 3s 4d.
Sum – 46s 8d.
Item paid to John Earl for banner staves – 2s 8d.
Item for washing the scripture in the Rood loft – 4d.[5]
Item for banner cloths – 10s.
Item for writing 3 copies of the orders taken at Easter court – 12d.
Item for watching the Sepulchre to William East – 12d.[6]
Item to Shadworth for a day's work about church yard – 8d.
Item to Roger Ymos[7] for 3 days [and a] half work about St Mary's churchyard – 14d.
Item to William Peper for a banner staff – 18d.

---

[1] [Crossed through].
[2] John Bawdewyn was assessed at 40s in the 1524/5 Lay Subsidy. TNA, E179/138/478.
[3] A contract by deed. *OED*.
[4] Marginalia – 'for the bells & leads'.
[5] Was the text being cleaned or removed?
[6] Marginalia – 'not for the bellman'.
[7] Possibly Roger Hymas, buried 25 February 1557/8. LAO, Goulding Papers, 5/2.

Item paid to Leonard Russhby and his 2 men for working about the pale[1] of St Mary's churchyard for 14 days [and a] half to meat and wages – 11s 8d.
Item paid to 2 sawyers for sawing of boards for 4 days to meat and wages – 6s 8d.
Item to Robert Akred for timber wood, that is to say 9 pieces – 3s 4d.
Item to William Dowghty for 5 trees and 2 posts – 16s 8d.
Item to William Evans for meat for the bull – 5s.
Item for carrying 2 prisoners to Lincoln – 12s.[2]
Item to Mr Chapman for scouring the common dike, hedging and thorning the hedge betwixt Elkyngton & Lowthe – 9s 6d.
Item to Robert Cottam for a hesp, 2 staples, a hoop [and] a pick to St Mary's church gate – 6d.
Item for washing the vicar's surplice – 2d
Item to George Wright for a day's work about St Mary's churchyard – 8d.
Item paid to John Tyler for leading of stone to Legburn Lane – 12d.
Item to Robert Akred for a piece of wood – 2d.
Item to Symon Kellum for digging of stone – 3d.
Item to Thomas Crosier[3] for a day's work in mending the highway – 4d.
Item paid for wire to the *Jymes*[4] – 3s 6d.
Item to Herry Mawborne,[5] George Harrison and William Graunt for making a pair of butts in the quarry – 2s 2d.
Item to Robert Minghell for a pick – 6d.
Item to Reade for bringing up the East Mill bridge – 2d.
Item for nails to St Mary's churchyard – 3s 6d.
Item for a bell clapper slowting[6] – 6s 8d.
      Sum – £5 2s 1d.[7]

f. 116r.
Item for mowing of Merbanks – 2s.
Item to Bab[8] for painting of banner staves – 12d.
Item for a lock to the churchyard – 12d.
Item paid for paper – ½d.
Item to the bellman for burying a wench that died in the street – 1d.

---

 1 To enclose with pales or a fence. *OED*.
 2 '11s' crossed through.
 3 Crosier's three sons, Thomas, Richard and Robert, all predeceased him. LAO, Goulding Papers, 5/2.
 4 Possibly the James bell, or alternatively another form of jemers or gemmers – hinges.
 5 Buried 11 February 1564/5. LAO, Goulding Papers, 5/2.
 6 Possibly 'slotting' – secured by shooting a bolt. *OED*.
 7 '£7 7s 1d', crossed through.
 8 Possibly William Babbe, whose daughter Ellen was interred 8 July 1568. LAO, Goulding Papers, 5/2.

Item to John Wathe for glazing the church windows – 6s 8d.
Item to Auncell Jeff for a bell rope – 3s.
Item to Symon Kellum in part payment for digging of a pit – 3s.
Item to Robert Odling for a bell wheel – 13s 4d.
Item to George Kyme for helping up with the said wheel – 2d.
Item for great nails to the bell – 6d.
Item for small nails to the leads – 6d.
Item to John Wathe for 2 days to him and his man about the leads – 2s.
Item for a pound of candles – 2d.
Item to Symon Kellum in part of payment for digging of a pit – 12d.
Item to Robert Odling 3 days to him and his man about the bells – 4s.
Item to him for nails – 2d.
Item for gear to the mending of the bells – 11d.
Item to Roger Halle[1] for 2 days about the bells – 12d.
Item to Arthur Hill for helping about the bells – 4d.
Item to John Anderson for 2 days about the bells – 12d.
Item to Robert Minghell for a cudgion,[2] 2 crames[3] & 2 clasps for the bells – 20d.
Item to Thomas Lechman for mending of the clock – 21d.
Item for great nails to the clock – 6d.
Item to Symon Kellum in part payment for digging a pit – 8d.
Item for keeping of Aswell – 12d.
Item paid to William King for a piece of willow for the James – 6d.
Item to William Peper for mending a stall – 2d.
Item for washing of the vicar's surplice – 2d.
Item to Jeff for shotting[4] a bell-string – 12d.
Item to John Anderson for covering [the] grave of Richard Wright – 3d.
Item to Wake for a book – 12d.
Sum – 50s 7½d.

f. 116v.

Payments to the poor.

Item on the second Sunday after Easter to Cotts, Father Wood, Arthur Capper & Adam Dixon[5] – 16d.
Item to Burle, John May, Holme – 3d.
Item to Walker's wife, Arthur Mylner and Lede's wife – 6d.
Item to Todd's wife – 1d.

---

[1] Buried 30 June 1559. His son John was baptised and buried on 26 October 1548. LAO, Goulding Papers, 5/2.

[2] Gudgeon.

[3] To fasten or mend with cramps or hold-fasts. *OED*.

[4] In this case, shotting is a term for splicing a rope. *OED*.

[5] Adam Dixon was interred 10 April 1559. LAO, Goulding Papers, 5/2. Although receiving charity, he was not one of the seventeen parishioners noted in the registers as being a pauper.

Item to Margaret Bery, Blind Emma, Thomas Humble, Allyn Whyte, Story's wife – 10d.
Item to Mother Eldon, Alice Thomlynson, Margaret Lenny, Agnes Davyson – 8d.
Item to Martyn Smith, Margaret Wright the senior, Mother Dawton, Beatrix Elwold, Mother Lowth, Elizabeth Becham, Jenet Crumdall, Lele's wife, Turner's wife – 20d.
Item to Arthur Capper, Father Wood & Adam Dixon and Cotes – 16d.
Item to John May and Holme – 4d.
Item to Robson's wife – 6d.
Item to Agnes Scott – 6d.
Item to Todd's wife – 4d.
Item to Roger *Jimos*[1] – 2d
Item to Humble – 2d.
Item to Father Grene & Wilson – 6d.
Item to a poor man in alms – 2d.
Item to Temple in alms – 8d.
Item to Agnes Scott – 6d.
Item to Mother Robson & William Clerk – 12d.
Item to Father Wood – 4d.
Item to Adam Dyxson – 2d.
Item to Arthur Capper and Cotts – 8d.
Item to Robson's wife – 6d.
Item to Mother Louth – 2d.
Item to Father Holme – 2d.
Item to Agnes Reynold, Todds & her sister – 12d.
Item to Father Grene and Temple – 8d.
Item to Crofts and Fets household – 4d.
Item to Robert Wady's household – 2d.
Item to Wady's wife and her 3 children – 2d.
Item to clerk Furrier departed – 6d.
Item Crosier *Jimos*, Mother Robynson – 6d.
Item to Bartholomew Hanson – 4d.
Item to Mother Thomlynson – 2d
Item to Randall's daughter – 2d.
Item to Isabell Coryar – 3d.
Item to Father Wood – 4d.
Item to Arthur Capper – 4d.
Item to Adam Dixson and Cotts – 4d.
Item to Robson's wife – 4d.
Item to Mother Lowthe & Holme – 4d.
Item to Agnes Reynold – 4d.
Item to Todds and her sister – 6d.

---

[1] Surname uncertain.

Item to Father Grene, James Barton, Crofts, Fets household, Robert Wady's household, Wady's wife and her children and Crosier – 13d.

Sum – 22s 3d.

f. 117r.

Item to *Jimos*, Mother Robinson, Bartill[1] Hanson, Mother Thomlynson, Isabell Coryar, Agnes Diconson and Randall's daughter – 14d.

Item to Turner's wife – 4d.

Item to Jenet Story – 2d.

Item to Anthony Collnwood – 1d.

Item to Father Wood, Adam Dixson, Arthur Capper, Father Cotts, Robson's wife – 23d.

Item to Mother Lowth, Holme, Agnes Reynold, Todds & her sister & Grene – 20d.

Item to James Burton, Crofts, Fets household, Robert Waday, Wady's wife & Crosier – 12d.

Item to *Jimos*, Bartill Hanson, Mother Tomlynson, Isabell Coryar, Randall's daughter and Turner's wife – 17d.

Item more given to other poor people – 20d.

Item given on Trinity Sunday to the poor people above named – 8s 8d.

Item to Cogle's boy – 2d.

Item on the first Sunday after Trinity to the poor above named – 5s 3d.

Item on the second Sunday after to the poor – 3s 4d.

Item on the 3rd Sunday after to William Smithson in his sickness – 8d.

Item to Arthur Capper & to Walker's wife – 2d.

Item to Mother Robson – 2d.

Item to Todd's wife & her sister – 2d.

Item to Thomas Grene – 2d.

Item to Margaret Huggard – 2d.

Item to Margaret Scott – 3d.

Item the 4th Sunday after Trinity to Mother Hobson – 2d.

Item to Mother Hobson – 6d.

Item to Arthur Capper – 2d.

Item to Father Holme – 1d.

Item to Father Wood – 1d.

Item to Father Grene – 2d.

Item to Agnes Reynold – 2d.

Item to Mother Robson – 6d.

Item to Richard Bylton – 2d.

Item to Agnes Renold – 2d.

Item to Father Wood, Arthur Capper, Burle, Adam Dixson, Thomas Grene, Dawton's wife, Newton's daughter, John May – 12d.

Item on the 6th Sunday after to Mother Robson – 6d.

Item to Anne Scott – 2d.

---

[1] Bartholomew.

Item on the 7th Sunday to Agnes Renold – 2d.
Item to Mother Robson – 6d.
Item to Arthur Capper, Thomas Grene, Father Wood & Thomas Holme, Beatrix Elwold & John May – 6d.[1]

f. 117v.
Item to Dawton's wife & Jenet Glenton – 2d.
Item to Adam Dixson – 1d.
Item to Arthur Capper, Father Holme, Father Burle & John May – 8d.
Item to Father Grene, Agnes Renold & Dawton's wife – 4d.
Item to Mother Robson – 6d.
Item to Father Wood, Arthur Capper, Adam Dixson, Burle and John May – 8d.
Item to Father Grene – 1d.
Item to Father Wood, Arthur Capper, Adam Dixson, Burle, John May & Father Grene – 12d.
Item to Father Holme & Dawton's wife and Mother Lowthe – 6d.
Item to Agnes Renold – 2d.
Item to Todd's wife – 1d.
Item to Arthur Capper, Adam Dixson, Thomas Grene, Dawton, John May and Richard Wood – 12d.
Item to Father Holme – 1d.
Item to Arthur Capper, Adam Dixson, John May and Father Wood & Holme – 10d.
Item to Elizabeth Dawton, Agnes Scott and Todd's wife and Thomas Agred – 6d.
Item to Mother Lowth and Agnes Beche – 2d.
Item to Arthur Capper, Adam Dixson, Richard Wood, John May, Elizabeth Dawton, Thomas Gene, Father Holme, Cogle's wife – 13d.
Item to Father Burle – 6d.
Item to Agnes Scott – 2d.
Item to Agnes Halle – 1d.
Item to Arthur Capper, Father Wood, Adam Dixson and John May – 4d.
Item to Father Holme, Thomas Grene, Burle – 8d.
Item to Elizabeth Dawton, Jenet Story, Todd's wife's sister – 6d.
Item to Agnes Halle – 1d.
Item to Mother Lowth – 1d.
Item to Alison Dawtney – 1d.
Item to Arthur Capper, Father Wood, Adam Dixson and John May – 4d.
Item to Thomas Grene, Father Holme, Elizabeth Dawton – 3d.
Sum – 11s.

f. 118r.
Item to Agnes Scott – 2d.
Item to Jenet Story – 1d.

---

[1] Marginalia – 'Sum 33s 7d'.

Item to Cicele Lowth – 1d.
Item to Isabell Newton – 2d.
Item to Arthur Capper, Adam Dixson, John May, Thomas Grene – 4d.
Item to Holme, Elizabeth Dawton – 2d.
Item to Agnes Scott, Jenet Story, Mother Lowth and Isabell Newton – 4d.
Item to Father Wood – 1d.
Item to Alice Becham – 1d.
Item to Ellyn Whyte – 1d.
Item to Isabell Story – 1d.
Item to Arthur Capper, Adam Dixson and Father Wood – 4d.
Item to John May, Dawton's wife, Jenet Story and Elizabeth Whyte – 4d.
Item to Thomas Grene, Father Holme, Agnes Halle and Agnes Scott – 6d.
Item to Alice Beche and Mother Lowth – 2d.
Item to Agnes Parris & Car's wife, Isabell Corriar, Isabell Newton, Lokwood's wife – 6d.
Item to Arthur Capper, Adam Dixson, Father Holme & John May – 8d.
Item to Father Cotts, Mother Lowth, Dawton's wife, Father Wilson – 8d.
Item to Story's wife, White's wife, Bechman's wife and Halle's wife – 8d.
Item to Isabell Newton, Cogle's wife, Mother Edon, Isabell Corryar – 4d.
Item to Thomas Grene and Agnes Reynold – 4d.
Item to Arthur Capper, Adam Dixson, Father Holme and John May – 8d.
Item to Father Cotts – 2d.
Item to Dawton's wife, Story's wife, White's wife, Halle's wife, Isabell Newton – 5d.
Item to Cogle's wife, Mother Edon – 2d.
Item to Thomas Grene, Mother Lowth – 3d.
Item to Agnes Reynold, Isabell Coryar – 2d.
Item to Bechum's wife – 1d.
Item to Arthur Capper, Adam Dixson, Father Holme and John May – 4d.
Item to Father Cotts, Dawton's wife, Story's wife, White's wife, Halle's wife & Isabell Newton, Cogle's wife & Mother Edon – 8d.
Item to Thomas Grene & Mother Lowth – 2d.
Item to Agnes Renold, Isabell Corur – 2d.
Item to Father Wilson & Becham's wife – 2d.
f. 118v.
Item to Arthur Capper & Adam Dixson – 4d.
Item to Father Grene & John May – 3d.
Item to Dawton's wife – 2d.
Item to Father Holme & Cotts – 2d.
Item to Ellyn White – 1d.
Item to Jenet Story – 1d.
Item to Jenet Walker – 1d.
Item to Cogle's wife & Margaret Bery – 2d.

Item to Mother Lowth & Alice Dawbney and Agnes[1] Davison – 3d.
Item to Mother Edon & Isabel Story – 2d.
Item to Croft's wife and Agnes Scott – 4d.
Item to Lokwood – 1d.
Item to Anthony Milner's wife – 1d.
Item to Todd's wife – 1d.
Item to Arthur Capper & Adam Dixson – 4d.
Item to Father Grene and John May – 3d.
Item to Dawton's wife, Father Holme & Cotts – 4d.[2]
Item to Ellin White, Jenet Story & Jenet Walker – 3d.
Item to Cogle's wife, Margaret Bery – 2d.
Item to Mother Lowth, Alice Dawbney, Agnes Davison, Mother Edon & Isabell Story – 5d.
Item to Croft's wife & Agnes Scott – 4d.
Item to Todd's wife – 2d.
Item to Halle's wife – 1d.
Item to Arthur Capper, Adam Dixson – 4d.
Item to Thomas Whyte – 4d.
Item to Margaret Burton – 2d.
Item to Father Grene and John May – 4d.
Item to Dawton's wife, Father Holme & Cotts – 6d.
Item to Margaret Bery – 1d.
Item to Jenet Walker – 1d.
Item to Ellyn White & Jenet Story – 2d.
Item to Jenet Ledis & Edon's wife – 2d.
Item to Mother Lowth & Agnes Halle – 2d.
Item to Alice Bechum & Agnes Davison – 2d.
Item to Cogle's wife & Alice Thomlinson – 2d.
Item to Todd's wife – 2d.
Item to Croft's wife – 2d.
Item to Thomas – 2d.
Item to Isabell Corryar – 1d.
Item to Arthur Capper, Adam Dixson – 4d.
Item to Father Grene, John May – 4d.
Item to Father Holme and Cotts – 4d.
Item to Father Wood & Dawton's wife – 3d.
      Sum – 9s 3d.

f. 119r.
Item to Cogle's wife and Wilson – 2d.

---

[1] 'Jenet' crossed through.
[2] '2d' crossed through.

Item to Ellyn[1] White & Jenet Story – 2d.
Item to Ledis's wife & Walker's wife – 2d.
Item to Margaret Bery & Croft's wife – 2d.
Item to Car's wife, Alice Thomlinson, Mother Lowth & Alice Bechum – 4d.
Item to Agnes Davison, Margaret Wright – 2d.
Item to Todd's sister, Halle's wife, Edon – 3d.
Item to Philip Forman – 1d.
Item to Arthur Capper, Adam Dixson, Father Grene and John May – 8d.
Item to Father Holme, Cotts, Father Wood & Dawton's wife – 8d.
Item Beatrix Elwold – 1d.
Item to Cogle's wife, Wilson, Ellyn White & Jenet Story – 4d.
Item to Ledis's wife, Walker's wife, Croft's wife – 4d.
Item to Mother Lowth and Alice Bechum – 3d.
Item to Agnes Davison, Todd's sister, Halle's wife – 4d.
Item to Isabell Corier, Thomas White's wife and to a boy of Lokwood – 4d.
Item to Halle's wife – 2d.
Item to Dawton's wife – 4d.
Item to Arthur Capper, Adam Dixson, Father Wood, Father Holme, John May, Father Grene & Father Cotes and Thomas Crosier – 2s.
Item to Mother Lowth, Walker's wife, Jenet Story, Alice Bechum – 4d.
Item to Mother Edon, Margaret Bery, Ledis's wife, Alice Wady – 4d.
Item to Margaret Sands, Agnes Davison, Cogle's wife, Halle's wife – 4d.
Item to Agnes Scot – 2d.
Item to Burton's daughter & Croft's wife and Isabell Corrier & Todd's sister and Todd's wife – 10d.
Item to Thomas Crosier in his sickness – 10d.
Item to Arthur Capper (2d), Adam Dixson (2d), Father Wood (2d), Father Holme (1d), John May (1d), Father Grene (2d) and Father Cotes (1d) – 11d.
Item to Ellyn White (1d), Beatrix Elwold (1d), Margaret Bery (1d), Mother Edon (1d), Jenet Story (1d), Alice Wady (1d), Margaret Burton (1d) – 7d.
Item to Mother Lowth (1d), Alice Bechum (1d) – 2d.
Item to Agnes Thomplinson, Jenet Walker – 2d.
Item to Agnes Scott (2d), Margaret Dawton (2d) – 4d.
Item to Jenet Thissilton and Margaret Wright – 2d.
Item to Jenet Crofts & Jenet Halle – 2d.
      Sum – 12s 4d.

f. 119v.
Item to Agnes Davison & Jenet Newton – 2d.
Item to Isabell Coryer and Seamer's wife – 2d.
Item to Arthur Capper & Adam Dixson, John May and Father Wood – 8d.
Item to Father Holme – 2d.
Item to Bylting – 4d.

---

[1] 'Agnes' crossed through.

Item to Beatrix Elwold and Isabell Newton – 2d.
Item to Father Grene – 2d.
Item to Ellyn Whyte, Mother Edon, Margaret Bery, Jenet Walker, Ledis's wife, Margaret Wright, Halle's wife, Cogle's wife – 16d.
Item to Mother Lowth, Alice Bechum, Father Cotts – 4d.
Item to Alice Wady, Margaret Burton, Alice Thomplinson, Agnes Davison, Father Wilson, Croft's wife, Mother Story, Burket's wife, Jenet Glenton & Isabell Corier – 10d.
Item to Agnes Scott – 2d.
Item to Wady's wife – 1d.
Item to Arthur Capper, Adam Dixson, Father Wood – 6d.
Item to John May, Father Holme – 4d.
Item to Beatrix Elwold, Margaret Hutter, Cogle's wife, Todd's wife – 5d.
Item to Margaret Wright, Alice Wady – 2d.
Item to Jenet Story, Ellyn White – 2d.
Item to Richard Bylton – 2d.
Item to Father Cotts & Grene – 4d.
Item to Margaret Bery, Halle's wife – 2d.
Item to Agnes Scott, Agnes Davison – 4d.
Item to Mother Lowth, Edon – 2d.
Item to Jenet Walker – 1d.
Item to Croft's wife – 2d.
Item to Robert Wady – 1d.
Item to Arthur Capper, Adam Dixson, Father Wood, John May & Father Holme – 10d.
Item to Father Cotts, Father Grene – 4d.
Item to Thomas Bose – 4d.
Item to Ellyn White, Mother Edon, Alice Bechum and Mother Lowth – 4d.
Item to Bylting – 2d.
Item to Margaret Bery, Jenet Walker, Alice Thomlinson, Ledis's wife – 4d.
Item to Halle's wife, Mother Story, Alice Wady, Agnes Davison, Croft's wife, Robert Wady – 6d.
Item to Agnes Scott – 2d.
Item to Cogle's wife, Father Wilson, Todd's sister, Isabell Story – 4d.
Item to Martin Smithson – 1d.

Sum – 11s 1d.

f. 120r.
Payments.

Item paid to Dixson for 4 days work about the church walls – 2s 8d.
Item to Anderson for 4 days work about the same walls – 2s.
Item to Thomas Smith for mending the chimes – 2s 8d.
Item paid for a book to the church – 6d.
Item paid to Sir Christopher for an altar cloth – 2s 5d.
Item paid to Robert Mychell for staples and hasps to the church gates – 8d.

Item paid for 2 locks – 4d.
Item to Edward Argram for a yard of russells for mending of a vestments – 18d.
Item paid to a tailor for mending a cope – 4d.
Item to Robert Mychell for a budgill[1] to the Second bell – 6d.
Item to Robert Cottam for iron gear about the Sepulchre – 2s 6d.
Item to Robert Odlyng and his 2 men for 2 days work about the bells and the Sepulchre – 4s.
Item paid for a plank and nails in Our Lady's choir – 11d.
Item to John Anderson for burying a boy that came from Tattershall – 2d.
Item given to Anthony Mylner for keeping the same boy – 5d.
Item to William East for bearing a cross – 2d.
Item to Richard Smith's man for rings for the curtain afore the altar – 2d.
Item to Geff for 2 cords afore the Rood – 4d.
Item to Robert Odling for making the Little bell wheel and half a day's work among the bells – 3s.
Item to Richard Smith's man for reed and nails to the said bell – 2d.
Item to Robert Kerkby for making of wax for the Sepulchre – 3s.
Item to Auncell Jeff for a bell rope for the Second bell and a long cord of 20 fathoms[2] – 3s.
Item to John Erle for a cross and staff – 10d.
Item for painting of an altar cloth and the Lenten cross to Luke Brown – 3s 8d.
Item for washing of altar cloths – 8d.
Item paid for mending the chime – 4d.
Item for writing the book of the poor men's names – 4d.[3]
Item for watching the Sepulchre to William East – 12d.

Sum – 38s 3d.

f. 120v.
Item to Robert Odling of bushes – 8d.
Item to Sir John Whetley for candle spent in winter – 4d.
Item for scouring of Aswell – 12d.
Item to Robert Chapman for wood to the fire on Easter even – 2d.[4]
Item for leading timber to St Mary's church – 4d.
Item for scouring the grate – 1d.
Item to Edward Argram for 4 pounds[5] of wax – 5s 4d.
Item to him for 3 yards [and a] half of canvas for an altar cloth – 20d.
Item for paper – 3d.
Item for nails to the chimes – 1d.

Sum – 9s 11d.

[1] Meaning unknown.
[2] Approximately 120 feet (36.57m).
[3] It appears that the names of the poor were registered in a separate volume from the accounts.
[4] Probably for the 'Easter Fire'. See p. 228, note 1091.
[5] '10' crossed through.

f. 121r.
Item to Arthur Capper, Father Dixson, Father Wood, Father Cotts, John May and Father Grene – 12d.
Item to Byltyng and Alice Briggs – 4d.
Item to Father Holme – 2d.
Item to Beatrix Elwold, Walker's wife, Story's wife, White's wife, Ledis's wife, Alice Wady – 6d.
Item to Mother Edon, Margaret Bery – 2d.
Item to Todd's wife & her sister – 2d.
Item to Mother Lowth & Mother Bechum – 2d.
Item to Agnes Scott – 2d.
Item to Davison's wife, Alice Tomlinson, Margaret Wright, Halle's wife, Margery Deane, Jenet Glentam, Croft's wife, Wady's wife, Isabell Corryar, Martin Smyth's boy – 20d.
Item to Thomas Bose – 2d.
Item to Arthur Capper, Father Dixson, Father Wood, Father Cotts, John May & Grene – 12d.
Item to Father More, Alice Briggs – 8d.
Item to Agnes Reynold, Martin Smith's boy – 4d.
Item to Story's wife – 2d.
Item to Todd's wife & her sister – 4d.
Item to Bylting and Croft's wife – 4d.
Item to Isabell Story, Cogle's wife, Mother Lowthe – 6d.
Item to Agnes Davison, Agnes Halle and Mother Edon & Dawton's wife – 8d.
Item to Arthur Capper (2d), Father Dixson (2d), Father Wood (4d), Father Cotts (2d), John May (1d) & Grene (2d) – 13d.
Item to Halle's wife – 2d.
Item to Jenet Story, Ellyn White – 2d.
Item to Father Holme, Jenet Walker, Cogle's wife, Alice Thomlinson, Martin Smith & Mother Edon – 6d.
Item to Agnes Davison – 1d.
Item to Margaret Todd & her sister – 2d.
Item to Father Wilson, Wady's wife – 2d.
Item to Beatrix Elwold, Jenet Glentam – 2d.
Item to Mother Louth, Alice Bechum – 2d.
Item to Anne Scott – 2d.
Item to Bose – 2d.
Item to Jenet Crofts – 2d.
Item to Richard Bylting – 1d.
Item to Jenet Wady – 1d
Item to Anthony Collingwood's wife – 1d.
Item to Isabell Story – 1d.
                              Sum – 12s.

f. 121v.
Item to Arthur Capper, Father Wood, Father Grene, Adam Dixson, Father Cotts & May – 12d.
Item to Anthony Collingwood – 2d.
Item to Bose – 2d.
Item to Father Holme, Father Wilson, Bilting – 3d.
Item to Agnes Scott – 2d.
Item to Story's wife, Walker's wife, White's wife, Halle's wife – 6d.
Item to Mother Lowth, Alice Bechum, Mother Davion, Beatrix Elwold & Ledis's wife – 6d.
Item to Todd's wife & her sister – 2d.
Item to Alice Tomlinson, Alice Wady, Mother Edon, Jenet Blanton, Croft's wife & Margaret Wright, Robert Wady's wife – 7d.
Item to Isabell Corriar – 1d.
Item to Arthur Capper, Father Wood, Father Dixson, Father Grene, Father May & Cotts – 10d.
Item to Jenet Story, Jenet Walker, Ellyn White and Agnes Halle – 4d.
Item to Holme, Beatrix Elwood, Jenet Glentam and Wilson – 4d.
Item to Isabell Newton, Wady's wife, Alice Tomlinson, Jenet Ledis, Margaret Bery, Bilting, Margery Deane (2d), Jenet Wady, Agnes Scott (2d) – 11d.
Item to Alice Bechum and Mother Lowth – 2d.
Item to Margaret Capper & Agnes Davison – 2d.
Item to Martyn Wilson, Mother Edon – 2d.
Item to Bose – 2d.
Item to Croft's wife – 2d.
Item to Isabell Story – 1d.
Item to Father Wyndell[1], Father Cotts, Adam Dixson, Arthur Capper, Father Grene, Father Wood and John May – 8d.
Item to Anthony Mylner, Father Holme – 6d.
Item to Jenet Walker, Story's wife, Halle's wife, White's wife, Mother Edon and Margaret Wright – 6d.
Item to Ledis's wife, Margaret Bery, Margery Deane, Cogle's wife, Alice Wady & Croft's wife – 6d.
Item to Agnes Reynold, Thomas Bose, Bylting – 6d.
Item to Mother Lowth, Alice Bechum & Agnes Davison, Alice Tomlinson, Wady's wife & Isabell Coryar – 6d.
Sum – 10s 1d.
f. 122r.
Item to Todd's wife & her sister & Martyn Wylson – 3d.
Item to Arthur Capper, Father Wood, Adam Dixson, Father Cotts, Father Grene, Father May – 11d.

---

[1] Crossed through.

Item to John Dean's wife, Ellyn White, Old Edon, Jenet Walker, Agnes Halle, Agnes Davison, Thomas Holme, Margaret Bery – 8d.
Item to Jenet Story, Beatrix Elwold, Jenet Glenton & Alice Tomlinson, Richard Bylton, Jenet Ledis, Thomas Bose, Mother Lowth, Todd's wife – 9d.
Item to Agnes Scott – 2d.
Item to Wady's wife, Burret's wife, Croft's wife, James Barton, Smithson's wife – 5d.
Item to the other Wady wife – 1d.
Item to Nicholas Williamson – 1d.
Item to Arthur Capper, Father Wood, Adam Dixson, Father Cotes, Father Grene – 10d.
Item to Father Holme, John May – 4d.
Item to Todd's wife & her sister – 4d.
Item to Anthony Mylner – 4d.
Item to Jenet Walker, Agnes Halle, Agnes Davison, Jenet Story, Beatrix Elwold – 5d.
Item to Mother Lowth, Richard Bylton – 2d.
Item to Croft's wife – 1d.
Item to Margaret Wright, Bechum's wife, Burret's wife, Cogle's wife, Ledis's wife, Bery's wife, Robert Wady's wife, White's wife, Mother Edon, Alice Tomlinson, Agnes Renold – 12d.
Item to James Barton – ½d.
Item to Isabell Corriar – ½d.
Item to Mother Edon – ½d.
Item to Alice Wady – ½d.
Item to Glenton's wife – ½d.
Item to Arthur Capper, Father Grene, Adam Dixson, Father Cotts and Father Wood – 10d.
Item to Todd's wife, Wady's wife – 2d.
Item to John May & Jenet Story – 2d.
Item to Father Wilson & Anthony Collingwood – 2d.
Item to Father Holme & Ellyn White – 2d.
Item to Maryon Stoker and Blind Anne – 2d.
Item to Margaret Bery & Ledis's wife – 2d.
Sum – 8s 10½d.

f. 122v.

Memorandum, to the churchwardens doth charge themselves to have received by the pece this present year and for burials [over and besides][1] with the money received by them of the old churchwardens & of William Whyte & William Fyshwyke besides the money due by especialties, £20 8s 2½d. Whereof paid by them in diverse parcels as appearith by the particulars of their account above declared £19 8s, and so owing upon the old churchwardens over and

---

[1] Crossed through.

besides the money due by specialities amounting to the sum of £95 6s 8d upon this account, 20s 2½d.
Item there remaineth more of the said churchwardens for money received of William Whyte for the price of a horse that Robert Spencer had above declared, 23s.
Item more for the Plough light, 4s 9½d.
£8 7s 7d, besides £4 13s 4d.
Sum – £13 11d.

f. 123r.

[1556–7]

Churchwardens appointed to office *Anno Domini* 1556, Mr Thomas Mores, Mathew Wardall, Symon Thew & Richard Robertson.[1]
Memorandum, the old churchwardens hath delivered unto the hands of the new churchwardens to the use of the said church to be employed to the inhabitants of the same town upon interest upon good assurance and especiality[2] to be made to the said new churchwardens £100 whereof £4 13s 4d in ready money is delivered to the new churchwardens to be put to likewise as the rest of the hundred pounds.
Item the said old churchwardens have likewise delivered to the hands of the said new churchwardens in ready money with 4s 9½d for the Plough light & 23s for one horse which Robert Spencer had paid by the hands of William Whyte to the use of the church, £7 4s 8d, whereof paid by the new churchwardens to Thomas Blancherde for the charges of a prisoner to Lyncoln – 5s 9d.
Item to Thomas Holdernes for finding of the common bull – 10s.
Item to William Kyng for the taking away of the ceiling above the Sepulchre – 8d.
Item to Thomas Richardson for one ley that the gate standith on in Haregarthis – 8d.[3]
Memorandum, also that the forty shillings charged for the Common Cart is now delivered to the hands of the new churchwardens to remain in their hands to the use of the church for the space of seven years *videlicet* during the time of the statute for the amendment of the highways, 40s.[4]
One common bull – 42s 3d.
Memorandum, that one common bull late in the keeping of Thomas Holdernes is delivered over unto the charge of the new churchwardens.

[1] Richard Robinson, weaver, left a will: TNA, PROB 11/55/335, probate 11 August 1573.
[2] Speciality; particularly; in detail. *OED*.
[3] Marginalia – '17s 10d'.
[4] This is the first direct reference to the 'Act for Mending the Highways' of 1555, which states: 'This Acte to contynewe for seven yeeres next after the begynnyng of thys Parlyament …', 2 & 3 Philip & Mary, Chapter VIII, *Statutes* IV (i), pp. 284–5.

f. 123v.
The election of the Surveyors of the Highways *pro Anno Domini* 1556 to Gilbert Blancherd & John Brown.
      The days appointed for the amendment of the highways.
1 The Tuesday next after Lowth Fair.[1]
2 The Friday in Cross Week.[2]
3 The Tuesday before Corpus Christi day.
4 The Tuesday after St Barnabas day.[3]
      The receipts with the pece of the parishioners.[4]
Item received of them at Midsummer – 44s ½d.
Item received at Michaelmas – 39s 3d.
Item more received of this quarter – 20½d.
Item received for the Plough light – 4s 8d.
Item received on Christmas quarter – 24s 3d.
Item more received on this quarter – 6s.
Item more on this quarter – 15d.
Item received on Gilbert Blanchard of the money that [is] left for mending the highways – 2s 3d.
Item received at Easter quarter – 23s 4d.
      Receipts of burials and for the bells.
Item received for the bells at the burying of Robert Wright – 20d.
Item received for the burial of William Worsley's wife – 6s 8d.[5]
Item for the bells – 20d.
Item for the burial of Thomas Palmer's wife – 6s 8d.
Item for the bells – 20d.
Item received for the burial of Sir Roger Bonus[6] – 6s 8d.
For the bells – 20d.
Item that he gave to the Poor Man's box – 10s.
Item for the burial of Arthur Grey – 6s 8d.[7]
Item for the bells – 20d.

---

  [1] The third Sunday after Easter for eight days. Goulding, *Markets and Fairs*, n.p.
  [2] Rogation week.
  [3] June.
  [4] The Sunday collections are now recorded quarterly with the exception of 1564/5.
  [5] Agnes Worsley, buried 16 August 1556. LAO, Goulding Papers, 5/2.
  [6] Roger Bonus, Bawnus alias Ascue, was a former chaplain to the Trinity guild receiving a pension of 113s 4d. Foster, 'Certificate', p. 287. Hodgett, *Ex-Religious*, pp. 53, 104. He was appointed schoolmaster in 1541 at the age of thirty-five on a stipend of £5 13s 4d and from 1551 was usher (*subpedagogi*) to the grammar school under John Goodall. Gurnham, *Free School*, pp. 13–14. Buried under the name Askew on 2 November 1556. LAO, Goulding Papers, 5/2.
  [7] Interred 15 December 1556. LAO, Goulding Papers, 5/2.

Item for the burial of William Worsley – 6s 8d.[1]
Item for the bells – 20d.
Item received for a bull – 42s.[2]
Item for the burial of John Spenlow – 6s 8d.[3]
Item for the bells – 20d.
f. 124r.
Item more received with the pece at Easter quarter – 2s 5d.
Item more received at Easter quarter with the pece – 2s 4d.
Item more received with the pece on Black Monday[4] – 5s.
Item more received on Low Sunday – 7d.
f. 124v.

Payments.

First, paid to Bartill Hanson in part payment of his wages for the execution of the office of bedler[5] – 3s 4d.
Item to Thomas Mysterchambers for clapboard[6] spent the last year – 18d.
Item paid to Henry Mawbarne and Robert Sympson for 2 days work either of them about graving[7] of sods and making the common butts after the rate of 16d a day to meat & wages – 2s 8d.
Item paid to John Smith, husbandman & Robert Sympson for leading 10 loads of sods to the said butts – 2s 8d.
Item to James Anderson for mending a pyx on the High altar – 6d.
Item paid for bowstrings bought at the muster – 1d.
Item paid for 3 quarters of thatch for thatching of the school in the churchyard[8] – 12s.
Item for bread and drink to the bringing thereof – 4d.
Item to John Anderson & [an]other 2 labourers for 8 days work in walling the said schoolhouse at 5d a day to meat & wages – 3s 4d.

---

[1] Buried 30 November 1556. LAO, Goulding Papers, 5/2.

[2] Line crossed through.

[3] Interred 24 March 1556/7. LAO, Goulding Papers, 5/2.

[4] Fordun's *Scotichronicon* (c.1449) relates that the army of the Black Prince sustained terrible losses from a storm on Easter Monday 1357. A similar incident occurred on 14 April 1360 when large numbers of Edward III's army died of the cold before Paris (both *OED*). Also Wright, *Churchwardens' Accounts*, p. 91, note 2.

[5] Bedle, bedler or beadle – 'an official appointed by the parish to keep order in the church, punish petty offenders, and act as a general servitor or messenger of the parish; a parish constable'. *OED*. Bartholomew (Bartill) Hanson also appears in the accounts as a regular receiver of alms. Possibly the office of beadle was given to him as a form of gainful employment. Hanson's wife Elizabeth predeceased him in 1538/9, and he was interred 29 December 1557. LAO, Goulding Papers, 5/2.

[6] A smaller size of split oak, imported from north Germany and used by coopers for making barrel-staves; in later times also for wainscoting. *OED*.

[7] To dig out, excavate. *OED*.

[8] Probably the song or petty school.

Item to John Smith for leading 6 loads [of] clay & one load of stone for the said house – 19d.
Item for 3 small spars[1] & plaister[2] stakes to the said house – 8d.
Item for nails – 2d.
Item to a wright for putting in the spars – 4d.
Item for 2 thraves of straw to the said house – 4d.
Item paid to a thatcher for 3 days [and a] half in thatching of the same house – 2s 4d.
Item paid for sewing rope – 4d.
Item paid to the Queen's Majesty's servants whereas they played in the church – 12s.[3]
Item for mending the church pyx – 2d.
Item to Bartill Hanson in part of his wages for the execution of the office of the bedler for his second quarter – 3s 4d.
Item to John Smith for leading 2 loads of sand – 8d.
Item paid for 24 yards of linen to surplices – 18s.
Item for a key to the schoolhouse and mending a pick – 3d.
             Sum [of] payments – £3 6s 7d.

f. 125r.
Item paid to William East for wages[4] for keeping the clock & chime – 20s.
Item more to him for blowing the organs and whipping the dogs – 3s 4d.
Item to John Anderson for his wages for keeping the leads & […][5] the church – 13s 4d.
Item to the writer of this account – 6s 8d.
Item paid to Odlyng for his wages for looking to the bells – 3s 4d.
Item to a boy for carrying sand to the church – 1d.
Item for a skin of parchment – 4d.
Item for another skin of parchment for making of the book of the names of the inhabitants of the town – 4d.[6]
Item for writing of the said book – 12d.
Item to Robert Odlyng for mending and taking up of the Trinity bell and Our Lady's bell – 2s 1d.
Item to William Johnson for laying of a gudgyon of the Trinity bell – 8d.
Item to William Brown for a bush to the Second bell – 4d.
Item to 6 men for raising of Our Lady's bell and St George bell – 8d.
Item paid to Thomas Lorryman, mason and his servant for mending and working about the steeple and church in part of payment for his wages – 12s 4d.

[1] Rafters. *OED*.
[2] Plaster. *OED*.
[3] These were possibly members of the Chapel Royal. Consequently, the choir of St James's would appear to have been held in some esteem.
[4] 'His first quarter' crossed through.
[5] Illegible.
[6] Possibly for taxation purposes.

Item to John Anderson for 5 days in serving the mason and other works about the church – 2s 1d.

Item paid to Leonard Russhby for making a cradle[1] and putting in pins in the broach of the steeple[2] and mending a lether[3] – 2s 3d.

Item to East for nails to the church – ½d.

Item for a clasp of iron to the cradle and nails – 9d.

Item to Richard Robinson for a board to the cradle – 3d.

Item to Thomas Lorryman, mason at another time for mending and working about the steeple & church – 20s.

Item to John Anderson for serving the mason for 5 days [and a] half – 2s 3d.

Item for bolts of iron and chains of iron and [...][4] – 16d.

Sum of payment – £4 14s 10d.

f. 125v.

Item paid to Thomas Smith for making of a pulley of iron and other work about the clock – 2s.

Item paid to the mason & his 3 men for one weeks work about the church – 23s.

Item for tile – 2d.

Item to John Anderson for serving the mason for one week – 2s 6d.

Item for bolts and chains – 12d.

Item for 2 bolts breaking and a kytt[5] garthing that was broken – 3d.

Item paid to the masons for working about the church *fest* by great – 4s.

Item paid for painting the images – 12s.

Item to Peper for making the three images – 22s.

Item to Elizabeth Robynson for dighting the Small Wells – 2d.

Item paid to Thomas Smith for irons to the images – 4d.

Item paid to Robert Akred for the image of James – 2s 4d.

Item paid to Mr Bradeley for 2 quarters of lime – 7s.

Item paid to Mrs Mysterchambers[6] for making 4 surplices & a rachett[7] – 4s.

Item allowed to the scrivener[8] for thread to his surplice – 1d.

Item paid to Thomas Lecheman, smith, for making 3 keys to a chest – 9d.

Item to him for making an iron to the chime wheel – 7d.

Item paid to Bartholomew Hanson for his third[9] quarter wages for his execution of his office of the bedle – 3s 4d.

---

[1] Any framework of bars, cords, rods, etc. united by lateral ties; a grating, or hurdle-like structure. *OED*.

[2] The spire.

[3] Ladder.

[4] Illegible.

[5] Kit – a circular wooden vessel, made of hooped staves. *OED*.

[6] This is the first example of a spouse recorded as 'Mrs'; Elizabeth Mysterchambers, widow, was buried 9 February 1569/70. LAO, Goulding Papers, 5/2.

[7] Rochet.

[8] A scribe, copyist or a clerk, a person authorised to draw up or certify contracts, deeds and other legal documents. *OED*.

[9] 'Second' crossed through.

Item to John Anderson for covering the grave of William Worsley's wife[1] – 4d.
Item to him for dressing the churchyard – 6d.
Item to William East for knylling[2] the bell in Harvest for gathering of the pescods[3] – 4d.
Item to Robert Odlyng for mending the wheels of the Trinity bell & St George's bell – 2s 4d.
Item to Jeff for a string for St George's bell – 3s 4d.
Item for washing of an aub[4], an altar cloth and a surplice – 4d.
Item to East for a strinkle – 1d.

Sum – £4 12s 9d.

f. 126r.
Item to John Smith for leading 4 pieces of wood from Burton Bridge – 3d.
Item for covering the grave of Thomas Palmer's wife – 4d.
Item paid for 2 boards to John Baily for the wheels – 3d.
Item for nails – 1d.
Item for tar – 2d.
Item to Thomas Smithe for making of iron gears to the bells – 6d.
Item for a strinkle – 1d.
Item for washing of Mr Vicar's surplice – 2d.
Item paid to certain labourers for taking up the James & the Trinity[5] – 2s.
Item to Thomas Leche, smith for a gowchion[6] making and other iron work to the James – 3s.
Item to Odlyng for his 2 men for 2 days[7] for working about the bells – 3s 4d.
Item paid to William Evans for carrying the earth in Aswell[8] – 2s 4d.
Item to Odlyng for 3 boards and nails about the bells – 8d.
Item to Leonard Russhby for nailing up a gate and *footing a form*[9] – 2d.
Item to Martyne Chapman for dighting of Aswell – 12d.
Item to Gervys Dyinys's wife for her relief being sick and poor for one week being at the feast of the Conception of Our Lady[10] – 12d.
Item to her for one other week – 6d.
Item to Leonard Russhby for working about the chambers & mending the stalls in the space of 4 days – 3s.[11]
Item to him for nails – 2d.

---

1   Agnes, interred 16 August 1556. LAO, Goulding Papers, 5/2.
2   Knolling – tolling. *OED*.
3   Peasecods – pod or legume of the pea plant, a peapod. *OED*.
4   Alb.
5   Bells.
6   Gudgeon.
7   'And a half' crossed through.
8   'He laid out for paving of' crossed through.
9   Meaning unknown.
10 December.
11 '8d' crossed through.

Item to *uxor*[1] Dynnys for one week – 12d.
Item to Robinson for a piece of wood to the barrel of the chamber – 12d.
Item to him for a plank – 8d.
Item for a pound of candles to work by in the chime house – 3½d.
Item for washing of 4 surplices, one alb and a towel – 4d.
Item to Thomas Leache, smith for making of iron work to the clock & the chambers – 2s 8d.

Sum – 24s 10¾d.

f. 126v.
Item to John Anderson for laying down the graves of Arthur Grey and for Sir Roger Bonus – 8d.
Item paid for a cope of tawny silk[2] – 6s 10d
Item to 2 men for helping the clerk about the chime wheel – 2d.
Item to John Anderson for laying down William Worsley's grave – 4d.
Item to him for mending the church styles – 4d.
Item to 3 men for helping about the chime – 6d.
Item for 4 pounds of wax – 4s 8d.
Item for a form – 12d.
Item to William Whyte for a child that was set forth of the town – 4d.
Item paid to Denny's wife in alms – 12d.
Item to William Reade in alms – 6d.
Item paid to Erle for a bear chest – 10d.
Item to Odlyng for mending the door of St Peter's choir – 18d.
Item to him for doing work about the leads[3] – 12d.
Item paid to Thomas Leche for mending the chime and making a gudchon to the Second bell – 2s.
Item for nails – 2d.
Item to Henry Verley nailes – 4d.
Item to the bellman for hanning[4] away muck from the church door – 5d.
Item to the organ player in reward by the advice of the town – 6s 8d.
Item to Bartill Hanson for his wages for the quarter for his office of the bedler – 3s 4d.
Item paid for two keys to the High choir door and mending the locks – 8d.
Item to Edward Cotts for driving out pigeons in the church – 4d.
Item for mending a jak[5] of the church harness – 4d.
Item to Edward Cotts more for driving out of pigeons in the church – 4d.

[1] Wife.
[2] A composite colour, consisting of brown with a preponderance of yellow or orange. *OED*.
[3] 'Steeple' crossed through.
[4] A variant of 'have'. *OED*. Sweeping or clearing?
[5] A short, padded, quilted jacket or tunic usually made of layers of leather or canvas stuffed with linen and wool, often worn as a protective garment. *OED*.

Item to William Jakson for mending stools in the church – 14d.
Item for 4 spars for the said stools – 16d.
Item for mules¹ for the said stools – 3d.
Item for 2 boards for the said stools – 8d.
Item to John Wheteley for candles – 6d.
f. 127r.
Item given in alms to a poor man – 1d.
Item to Thomas Smith for mending of the clock – 4d.
Item for dressing the lock and key to the steeple door – 4d.
Item paid to Bartill in augmentation of his wages – 20d.
Item paid for a bull to Mr Whittington² – 46s 8d.
Item to William Browne in part of payment for keeping the bull – 6s 8d.³
Item paid to the bellman for covering the grave of John Spenlow – 4d.
Item paid⁴ of the increase money to Richard Wright⁵ & Thomas Lathes to the use of the poor folks – 20s.
Item paid to John Wathe for mending the glass windows *fest* by great – 13s 4d.
Item to Martyne Chapman for dressing of Aswell – 12d.
Item for 2 lbs [and a] half of wax for making of the Sepulchre – 3s.
Item for wick to the same – 5d.
Item for a corde that was occupied for the Rood cloth – 1d.
Item to Richard Mawborne for digging of 10 loads of sods to the making of a pair of butts after 1½d a load – 15d.
Item to George Sympson for leading 10 loads [of] sods to the said butts – 2s 6d.
Item paid on Palm Sunday to Richard Wright & Thomas Lathes of the increase money to the use of the poor – 10s.
Item paid to the said George Sympson for leading 18 loads of sods to the said butts – 4s 4d.
Item to Richard Mawborne for digging the said 18 loads [of] sods – 2s 2d.
Item to the said Richard Mawborne & Thomas Wake for 3 days to meat & wages for making the said butts – 3s 4d.
Item for washing the surplice of the vicar – 2d.
Item for washing the altar cloths & 3 surplices, a rachet⁶ & towels – 6d.

---

¹ Perhaps some form of soft material to stop the stools scraping on the stone floor?

² Possibly Alexander Whittington, gentleman; churchwarden 1571/2. Will: TNA, PROB 11/54/209, probate 14 May 1572.

³ '2s' crossed through.

⁴ 'Delivered' crossed through.

⁵ Richard Wright was founder of Wright's Coal and Butter Charity, following his death in 1575. Will: TNA, PROB 11/58/282, probate, 12 July 1576. Goulding, *Corporation Records*, pp. 178, 182. For details of the various payments by the charity, see Goulding, Papers, 5/9.

⁶ Rochet.

Item for wood to the fire – 2d.
Item paid for 2 candlesticks that stand on the High altar to Mrs Nailer – 6d.
Sum – £6 4s 4d.[1]

f. 127v.
Item paid to William East for keeping of the Sepulchre & setting it up – 12d.
Item to Edward Cotts for keeping doves out of the church – 4d.
Item paid to Odling for the mending of the Trinity bell & the nails – 10d.
Sum – 2s 2d.
Sum of the allowances & payments as appearith before in this book – £23 9½d.
Item allowed to them further for Hugh Todd's charge for conveying him out of the town & for mending the church hedge in Haregarthes – 7s 3d.
Item for the interest of £3 which there laid out for necessary charges of the church which £3 pounds was not lent upon interest – 6s.
Item allowed to them for the gown of Bartholomew Hanson – 14s.[2]
Item to Thomas Dynnys for conveying a woman to Lincoln.[3]
Sum total allocated £24 8s ½d, and remaining £108 16½d, whereof they have delivered in specialities £95 6s 8d, *et debent* £12 14s 8½d, over and besides with a bull price 46s 8d.

f. 128r.

[1557–8]

Item John Chapman, gentleman, Thomas Pelson, John North & George Willows are chosen churchwardens for the year following by the assent of the whole parish.
Item they have chosen Surveyors of the Highways for this year Robert Acred & John Spalding.
And the Boon days to be kept the same day that they were before the last year.
The Tuesday next after the 3rd Sunday after Easter.
The Friday in Cross Week.
The Tuesday before Corpus Christi day.
The Tuesday after St Barnabas day.
f. 128v.
Money lent.
First, lent to George Moore[4] upon the pawn of his copy after the value of 8d […][5] – 6s 8d.
Lent John Browne upon a speciality to be paid at Candlemas next – 6s 8d.
Lent to the same John Browne & John Northe to be paid at the same day upon a speciality – 13s 4d.

---

[1] '£5 19s 8d', crossed through.
[2] Possibly his uniform as beadle.
[3] Line crossed through.
[4] Buried 4 January 1564/5. LAO, Goulding Papers, 5/2.
[5] Illegible.

Paid to Bartyll Hanson for his first quarter's wages.[1]
Lent to Robert Westerbe upon a speciality to be paid [at the] Octave of Candlemas next coming – 6s 8d.
Lent William Wytt, Thomas Rychardson, Robert Chapman, John Swyne & Thomas Lane upon a speciality to be paid at Candlemas next for Symon Newbrowgh – 20s.
Lent to Robert Odlyng & to Roger Mawuyn upon a speciality to be paid at Candlemas next – 10s.

f. 129r.

The payments for this year following.

First, paid to Thomas Dynnys, constable, for the charge of carrying a prisoner to Lincoln – 2s.
Item to 3 poor men for dressing of Small Wells the space of one day after 3d apiece – 9d.
Paid to Thomas Lechman for [the] mending of a wheel to the clock – 4d.
Paid to Herey Tottery to meat & wages for 3 days for making the common gate – 3d.
Paid more to 2 wright[s] that was his servant[s] for 3 days to meat & wages – 5s.
Paid more to William Keys for one day to meat & wages – 4d.
Paid more [to] John Mylner for one day to meat & wages – 4d.
Paid more to one blacksmith for half a day to meat & wages – 2d.
Paid more to Thomas Letche, smith for ironwork to the same gate – 20d.
Paid more to Thomas Pelson for wood that made the common gate, the bars, the stoops & the rails – 13s 4d.
Paid for a bell – 33s 11d.
Paid more to Edward Argram for to relieving of the poor folks – 6s 4d.
Item paid to William East for Midsummer quarter – 5s 10d.
Item for mending of the pike that belongith to the church – 6d.
Paid to Bartholomew Hanson for his quarters wages that Symond Thew should have paid him – 5s.
Paid Thomas Smythe for setting a wheel post – 6d.
Paid to John Colman for Midsummer quarter – 3s 4d.
Paid to Robert Odlyng for mending the leads – 12d.
Paid to the same Robert for Midsummer quarter – 10d.
For mending Our Lady's bells – 4d.
Paid to Bartholomew Hanson for Midsummer quarter – *5s.*
Paid that was taking to the setting forth thereof the men that served my Lord Clynton[2] – 46s 8d.
Paid to John Gray[3] for mending of the gate – 4d.

---

[1] Line crossed through.
[2] For Clinton, see Introduction.
[3] Recorded in 1561 as a yeoman. Burton, *Old Lincolnshire*, p. 118.

Paid more to John Gray for remaining [......] & cott... [...] of the rails.¹
Sum – £6 17s.

f. 129v.
Paid to John Bolyngbrowk for the carriage of 2 poor folks – 12d.
Paid to John Belmore for laying down the stones whereas Argram was buried – 4d.
For nails into the steeple – 1d.
Paid more to the relieving of the poor folks – 5s 4d.
Paid to William East for Michaelmas quarter – 5s 10d.
Paid to Symond Nebrowghe for a rope that went to the clock – 18d.
Paid to John Belmore for Michaelmas quarter for his wages – 3s 4d.
Paid to Bartelle Hanson for Michaelmas quarter – 5s.
Paid to Father Wood in relief – 4d.
Paid to Mother *Eff....e*² in relief – 4d.
Paid for a bolt [for] mending the clock – 2d.
Paid to Thomas Wenstable – 1d.
Paid that I sent to London for books to the church – 20s.³
Paid more to Merecock for a *rent* book – 2s.
Paid more to John North that he laid out of this *parthe* – 18d.
Paid more in relief to Ferebe – 6d.
Paid more in relief to Symon Holland – 6d.
Paid more to one Mylborne in relief – 6d.
Paid more for nails to the steeple doors & about the bells – 2d.
Paid for bringing the common bull from Wethecall⁴ – 1d.
Paid more to James Barton in relief – 4d.
Item paid to Edward Cotts – 20d.
Item paid to Bartyllamew Hanson – 20d.
Item paid to J[ohn] Anderson for the Christmas quarter – 3s 4d.
Item paid to Martyn Chapman for Aswell – 12d.
Item for covering the grave of Edward Maddysloe – 4d.⁵
Item for covering the grave of William Jackeson – 4d.
Paid to Mylborne in alms – 6d.
Paid to James Barton in alms – 6d.
Paid to Robert Westerbe in alms – 8d.
Paid more to Thomas Piper for a table [for] Our [Lady's] altar – 20s.⁶
Paid to William East for the Christmas quarter – 5s 10d.⁷
Sum – £4 4s 9d.

---

1. Page damaged, some text illegible.
2. Illegible.
3. '15s' crossed through.
4. Withcall.
5. Edward Maddison, interred 15 November 1557. LAO, Goulding Papers, 5/2.
6. Part of the line missing.
7. Remainder of the page damaged.

f. 130r.
For washing the altar cloths & other necessaries belonging to the church – 16d.
Paid for minding the bridges at the opening of the town to chapman[1] – 16d.
Paid to Sympson for keeping away at the time he was keeping in his house – 12d.
For nails to the church – 3d.
Paid more to James Bartone in alms – 6d.
Paid more to Robert Odlyng for Michaelmas & Christmas quarters – 20d.
Paid more to the said Robert for mending the bells & the choir doors & 2 doors in the steeple – 6s 8d.
Paid to Thomas Lecheman for work about the James bell – 2d.
Paid to Myles Clarke for meat & wages – 10d.
For wood for the minding of Aswell – 12d.
Paid to Cots Wylly[2] for his relief – 8d.
Paid for a stryngyll – 2d.
Paid to Mrs Weyttley for [a] candle – 8d.
Paid to Edward Cots more in money – 20d.
Paid more to Anseyll Jefe for a bell-string – 2s 4d.
Paid to John Belman for covering Robert Marshall's wife's grave – 4d.[3]
Paid more to William East for Easter quarter – 5s 10d.
Paid to Ansselle Jeffe for a rope to the clock – 16d.
Paid to the charges of my Lord Welebe[4] at that time that he was in the town – 10s 2d.
Paid to Thomas Tempell for marking the Sepulchre light – 2s 6d.
Paid to the furniture of the fyerbeckeyn[5] – 6d.
Paid for nails at 2 times – 4d.
Paid for the repairing of Hargarthe – 3s 8d.
Paid to Thomas Blanchard for a piece of wood – 7d.
Paid to Robert Cotame for 2 locks – 20d.
Paid to John Belman for Easter quarter – 3s 4d.
Paid for cloths washing – 16d.
Paid to Robert Odlyng for Easter quarter – 10d.
Paid to the same Robert for mending of the bells – 6d.
Paid to William Pelson[6] for 5 quarters wax – 5s 3d.
Paid for covering Robert Bowland's grave – 4d.

---

[1] People engaged in buying and selling; market people. *OED*.
[2] 'Scottish' written above. Scotland at this period was a 'foreign' country, and its inhabitants therefore seen as 'aliens'.
[3] Elizabeth Marshall, buried 24 December 1559. LAO, Goulding Papers, 5/2.
[4] Willoughby.
[5] Fire beacon.
[6] William Pelson, mercer, left a will. TNA, PROB 11/43/557, probate 26 October 1560.

Paid for covering Mr Weytlay's grave – 4d.
To John North for 2 *kydes* of Good Friday – 2d.
Sum – 59s 3d.
Total of the whole payments – £14 12d.

f. 130v.
Gatherings in the church quarterly as after followeth for this year following.
Item gathered the first quarter – 29s 2d.
Item gathered at Michaelmas quarter – 32s.
Item gathered the first Sunday in the new year being the third quarter – 12s 10d.
Item gathered more of the same quarter – 16s.
Item gathered at Easter – 30s 2d.
Sum – £6 2d.

f. 131r.
Memorandum. the said old churchwardens hath likewise declared their account for the said sum of £95 6s 8d before mentioned.

First they charge themselves with the increment that they have received for the loan of the said sum for one whole year £9 13s 4d, whereof they ask allowance for money by them disbursed at several times to diverse aged & impotent persons living of alms as appearith by a book of parcels 51s, and so remaineth of the said increment, £6 12s 4d, over & besides the said sum of £95 6s 8d in the whole £101 19s, which the said old churchwardens hath delivered to the hands of the new churchwardens, *videlicet* in especialties £95 6s 8d,[1] and in ready money £6 12s 4d, and so is therefore discharged.

The new churchwardens are to be charged for money received by them of the surveyors of the common ways *videlicet* with the sum of 4s 6d.

Men's names appointed to survey the bells.
William White.
William Evans.
Richard Robynson.
Thomas Blanchard.
John Spalding, Mathew Wardall, with the churchwardens.

f. 131v.
The account of William Ormesby.
Received of William Rychmonde for a bull – 21s.[2]
Received by the hands of William Whyte and William Browne of that gathered on Plough Monday – 7s.
Received of William Red for a cross of wood that fell down – 6d.
Remaining in the purse in ready money – £4 12s 4d.

f. 132r. [Blank].

---

[1] '£16 13s 4d' crossed through.
[2] This and the next three lines crossed through.

f. 132v.

[1558–9]

The account of William Ormesby, William Richimond, William Evans & John Fissh, Churchwardens of the Parish Church of St James in Lowth in the County of Lincoln as well of all their receipts as of their payments from the first Sunday after Easter in the year of Our Lord God 1558 unto the same day in the year of Our Lord 1559, that is to say for one whole year.

Receipts

First, they charge themselves of money received by them of Thomas Pelson as appearith in the foot of the last account – £7 16s 2½d.

Item more received of the said Thomas Pelson of the mercement[1] of their obligations – £6 12d 4d.[2]

Item more received of the surveyors of the common works – 4s 6d.

Item more received of the parishioners in money of them gathered quarterly for one whole year as appearith by the quarter book[3] – £4 19s 6½d.

Item received of William Browne & William Richmond for the Plough money – 7s 4d.

Item received of William Richmond for a bull – 21s.

Item of Thomas Booth for another – 30s.

Item received for the skin of a bull which died at Robert Akrid's – 5s 8d.

Item received of John Spalding for Agnes Young – 16d.

Item received for a cross of wood – 6d.

Sum – £16 6s 1d.[4]
Receipts of burials & for the bells.

First received of John Swyne – 7s 4d.

Item received for George Sutton – 6s 8d.[5]

Item received for William Dowghtie's child – 3s 4d.

Item received for Mr Meares – 8s.

Item received for George Somerscales – 7s 8d.

Item received for John Wathe – 20d.

Item received for Thomas Sampson – 2s.

Item received for Anne Bayly[6] – 7s 4d.

Item received for Thomas Lamb – 12d.

Item received for William Dyngley – 8s.

---

1 Amercement – the imposition of a penalty or fine. *OED*.
2 Line crossed through.
3 A volume containing quarterly accounts. *OED*.
4 '£22 6s 9½d' crossed through.
5 '7s 4d' crossed through.
6 Anne Bayly was one of only two women from Louth during this period who deposited their will with the Prerogative Court of Canterbury. TNA, PROB 11/41/122, probate, 12 October 1558. Interred 17 June 1558. LAO, Goulding Papers, 5/2.

Item received for William Collinwood – 7s 4d.
Item received for Symond Thew[1] – 7s 8d.
f. 133r.
Item more received for Alice Gilbert – 8s.
Item more received for John Browne – 8s.
Item more received for William Farrand – 2s.
Item more received for Godfrey Thomas – 7s 8d.
Item more for the burial of Thomas Blanchard's wife – 8s.
Item for James Archbolde – 8s.
Item for Robert Jakson – 20d.
Item for Thomas Grene – 8s.
Item for Mr Topcliff – 8s.
Item for Mother Wardall – 8d.
Item for Mr Eresbie's maid – 4s.
Item of Mr Grey for Thomas Rankyn – 12d.
Item of John Willoby – 8d.
Item for Roger Theker's wife – 8d.
Item for James Manfeld's mother – 6s 8d.
Item of Bonus's wife – 20d.
Sum – £7 2s 8d.
Sum of all the receipts for this year – £23 8s 9d.
Memorandum, that the burial of Mrs Meares as yet is unpaid and also for Jakson's wife & his maid.
f. 133v.
Payments paid by the foresaid churchwardens as hereafter following.
First, paid to Roger Halle for keeping the field when Reade was sick – 20d.
Item paid to John North for the winter meat of one of the bulls – 4s.
Item paid to Martyn Chapman for dressing of Aswell – 12d.
Item paid to William East for keeping the Sepulchre – 12d.
Item paid to Thomas Pelson by the parish commandment for work at Grymesby[2] – 10s.
Item paid to Mr Chapman for winter meat of one bull – 4s.
Item paid to Gilbert Blanchard for the carriage of a letter of my Lord Willabie's[3] to the Mayor of Lincoln – 16d.
Item paid to the constables for making 2 pairs of butts in the quarry – 3s 4d.
Item paid for paper – 2d.
Item paid for 4 gallons of ale when the bells were hanged up – 8d.
Item paid to a poor man for driving of the bull to Spilesby[4] when he was sold – 6d.
Item paid for one bull – 21s 10d.

---

[1] Symon Thew was churchwarden 1556/7. Buried 23 September 1558. LAO, Goulding Papers, 5/2.

[2] Grimsby.

[3] Willoughby. The mayor of Lincoln from 1557 to 1558 was Thomas Grantham MP.

[4] Spilsby, 16 miles (26km) from Louth.

Item paid to Anthony Fen for mending the church leads – 12s.
Item to Thomas Mysterchambers for clapboard to the same – 12d.
Item paid for nails to the same – 4d.
Item paid to Sir William Dichon for 2 ymalls[1] – 22d.
Item paid to William Kyng for a standing lectern in the choir – 2s 6d.
Item paid for a lock for the bell chamber door & another to the clock house door – 16d.
Item paid to Thomas Lechman for the chimes – 10d.
Item more paid to him for 5 keys & mending of 5 locks in the High choir – 16d.
Item paid to William Reade for keeping the field – 3s 4d.
Item paid for the burial of John Watson in Walkergate – 6d.
Item paid for a lock & key for William Man – 4d.
Item paid for 2 holy water strinkells – 3d.
Item to Awncell Jeff for a bell-string – 20d.
                    Sum – £3 16s 9d.

f. 134r.
Item paid for digging of a pit in the field by the commandment of William White & William Browne – 2s.
Item paid to Mr Corkar for money by him laid out for the antiphoner – 5s 2½d.
Item paid for making of the same book – 3s 4d.
Item paid to Mr Gooddall for certain parchment leaves to the same book – 2s.
Item paid to William East for washing the surplices – 6d.
Item paid to William Jakson for 3 days for repairing & mending the churchyard stile & the gates to meat & wages – 2s.
Item paid to William Russhby for 2 days to meat & wages for the same work – 16d.
Item paid to John Fissh for wood to the same – 3s.
Item paid to William Ormesby for one piece of wood for rails to the same – 8d.
Item paid to Thomas Lechman for 2 keys for the staple[2] doors – 8d.
Item more to him for 4 staples for the bells – 4d.
Item more paid to him for ironwork for the chimes – 4d.
Item paid to John Anderson for digging of holes – 2d.
Item paid to Thomas Bonnar[3] for mending his wife's stool – 2d.
Item paid to Robert Odlyng for mending of 3 coffins[4] – 3s.
Item paid to Thomas Boothe for a bull – 26s 8d.
Item for melting the Sepulchre wax – 6d.
Item for 12 pounds of iron & making of the same for 2 chains for the hooks – 4s 6d.
Item paid to William Kyng for poles for the hooks – 18d.

[1] Hymnals – a hymn-book. *OED*.
[2] Steeple?
[3] Buried 3 September 1559. Francis, his daughter, was interred 4 December 1559. LAO, Goulding Papers, 5/2.
[4] These were probably the 'town coffins' used to convey the deceased, wrapped in a shroud for burial and then reused.

Item they ask allowance for bull that died – 21s 10d.
Item paid to Robert Akrid for meat to the same & slaying of the same – 2s 3d.
Item to Odlyng for making the poles to the hooks – 18d.
Item paid to Auncell Jeff for 2 ropes for the said poles & hooks – 6s 8d.
Item to Bryan Luter for mending all the windows in the church – 26s 8d.
Sum – £5 16s 9½d.

f. 134v.
Payments laid out for the charges of the bells.
Item paid to William Jakson & Robert Wynter for a tree for 3 bell yokes – 6s.
Item paid to Robert Odlyng for making for making a new yoke & for ironwork to the Trinity bell – 20s.
Item more to him for making 3 new yokes & one new wheel & for ironwork to the said bells – £3 10s.
Item given to him in recompense for his pains by the parish mynds[1] – 20s.
Item more paid to the said Robert for Our Lady's bell & mending 2 wheels – 4s 4d.
Item paid to Thomas Smith for the ironwork of the same bell & for a lock – 2s 4d.
Item paid to Richard Robynson for 2 pieces of willow to the bell wheels – 16d.
Sum – £6 4s.
Item more paid to William East for one year's wages for the clock & chime – 23s 4d.
Item to John Anderson for his year's wages for keeping the leads & dressing the church – 13s 4d.
Item to George Dowghty for his wages for writing the book of christenings, weddings & burials – 4s.
Item to Robert Odlyng for his year's wages for looking to the bells – 3s 4d.
Item paid to Father Coles for half a year's wages – 6s 8d.
Item paid to Martyn Chapman – 12d.
Item paid to William Pelson for 14 pounds of wax to the Sepulchre light – 10s 6d.
Item to Robert Kirkby for making of 24 pounds [of] wax at 2d a pound – 4s.
Sum – £3 6s 2d.
Sum total of payment aforesaid – £19 3s 8½d.

f. 135r.

[1559–60]

Memorandum, to the old churchwardens *videlicet* William Ormesby, William Richmond, William Evans & John Fissh have declared their account before the whole parish the first Sunday next after Easter *Anno Domini* 1559 for one whole year ending at the said feast and there remaineth in debt upon the said churchwardens upon the determination of the account, £4 6½d.

---

[1] Mentions, records. *OED*.

Which said sum of £4 5s ½d,[1] was delivered to the hands of the new churchwardens, that is to say Thomas Wardall, Thomas Blanchard, William Hewytt & Robert Kighley, churchwardens appointed for the year following.

Item the said new churchwardens are to be charged with money received of the sureties of the common wains[2] *videlicet* Richard Robynson & John Palmer – 2s 8d.

Memorandum that the said new churchwardens are to be charged with one common bull, and also for the burial of Mrs Meares as yet unpaid.

Item received by the new churchwardens of the old churchwardens a chalice with a patent[3] & 6 skins of parchment & a broken bell clapper.

f. 135v.

Memorandum, that the said churchwardens have likewise declared their account for the said sum of £101 19s, before mentioned which said sum of £101 19s the said old churchwardens have delivered unto the hands of the new churchwardens *videlicet* especialties [of] £90 & for the increment of the obligations £9 4s 6d[4] for the whole sum of one whole year, whereof they ask allowances for money by them dispensed at diverse and several times to diverse impotent & aged persons as appearith by a book of parcels thereof made.

And so remaining upon the said amercement 35s 10d, over & besides the said sum of £90,[5] and more they have delivered in ready money to the new churchwardens with 40s which Thomas Pelson paid to the behoff[6] of the town, £11 19s in the whole £103 14s 10d, and so is thereof discharged.

f. 136r.

Memorandum, that the old churchwarden *videlicet* Thomas Blansherd, Thomas Wardale, Robert Kyghby, William Huyt have declared their account before the whole parish the first Sunday next after Easter *Anno Domini* 1560 for one whole year ending at the said feast, and they remaineth in debt upon the said churchwardens upon the determination of their account for the foot of this account for the last year as on the overleaf plainly appearith, being the sum of £103 14s 10d, besides 2 bulls that remaineth for the use of the town over & besides the sum before mentioned. Also the said churchwardens are to be charged for their collection this year which commith to the sum of £12 9s 8d.

Total Sum – £116 4s 6d.

Whereof the said churchwardens appearith allowance for this year for such charges about the church & for the distribution to the poor as in this book particularly as expressed being the sum of £19 12s 2d, also the said churchwardens appearith allowance of 40s, which they were charged withal in

---

[1] '5s' added and '6d' crossed through.
[2] Common Cart, common account.
[3] Paten – a plate or shallow dish on which the Host is laid during the Eucharist and that also served as a cover for the chalice. *OED*.
[4] '£13 17s 6d' crossed through.
[5] '£91 15s 10d' crossed through.
[6] 'Behoof' – use, benefit, advantage. *OED*.

Thomas Pelson's account. Sum of all the said charges to be allowed to the said churchwardens £21 12s 2d, & so remaineth in the hands of the said churchwardens for this full account over & besides their said allowance in ill money the sum of four score fourteen pounds 12s 4d,[1] over & besides the said 2 bulls before mentioned. Which said sum of money & 2 bulls is to be delivered to the new churchwardens, that is to say, John Palmer, William Somerscales, William Fyswyk & Gearrott Arundall,[2] churchwardens appointed for the year following.

Memorandum, that the said new churchwardens have to received those burial[s] hereafter mentioned that is to say:

Item for Myster Forster's burial & for the bells – 8s 4d.[3]

For Thomas Dynnes's wife's burial & bells – 6s 8d.[4]

To receive of Thomas Holdernes for the Great bell ringing for his brother – 12d.

Item that the rents for the Plough for the year past is to be reckoned for.[5]

f. 136v.

Received by the new churchwardens of the old churchwardens a chalice with a paten, 6 skins of parchment & 2 iron picks made of broken bell clappers.

Memorandum, the 13th April *Anno Domini* 1561, it is agreed by the whole township to discharge the said churchwardens of the sum of £88 14s 8d, wherewith they are charged in the next page before in this account, whereof there is lost by the fall of money[6] £9 6s 6d, and so the clear of that money is £79 8s 2d, which is in Thomas Blanchard's hands to be delivered to the warden[7] and assistants of the school by the ascent of the most of the parish whose names are written[8] in the first beginnings of the book of churchings[9] and burials [of the which said sum].[10]

---

[1] £94 12s 4d.

[2] Jarrat Allendale.

[3] That is, 6s 8d for burial within the church and 20d (1s 8d) for the bells.

[4] Joanna Dynnes, Dennys, interred 10 March 1559/60. LAO, Goulding Papers, 5/2.

[5] No amount stated.

[6] Inflation was problematic during most of the Tudor period, and this statement indicates some of its consequences.

[7] The warden for 1561 was William Brown, yeoman. Goulding, *Corporation Records*, p. 19, note 2. He was also churchwarden in 1533/4, 1544/5 and 1552/3. Brown died in office and was buried 16 February 1560/1. LAO, Goulding Papers, 5/2.

[8] This was the beginning of the process by which the town purchased the manor of Louth from the Crown in 1564. Goulding, *Corporation Records*, pp. 77–80. The £79 8s 2d was the church's contribution to the final cost of £233. For the signatories, see Goulding, *Corporation Records*, pp. 77–80. LAO, Louth, St James, PAR, 1/1, p. 1.

[9] Parish Register. Churching – the public appearance of a woman at church to take communion and give thanks for the safe delivery of her child. The ceremony is in reference to the Purification of the Virgin Mary and typically took place on the fortieth day following the birth. *OED*.

[10] [Crossed through].

Received of Thomas Blansherd of the sum above named for diking & setting in the North Field between Kennyngton & Louth Field the sum of £14 15s 3d. *Anno Domini* 1561.
Received of the said Thomas Blansherd, more of the said sum by the hands [of] Gilbert Blancherd, Steven Buck,[1] John Gray & Richard Gyrsby, churchwardens for the repayment of the church & over the church works the sum of £7. *Anno Domini* 1563. [............].[2]
By me Gilbert Blanchard.
By me John Grey.
By me Steven Bowck.
f. 137r.
Videlicet new book.[3]
ff. 137v. to *142r.* [Blank].
f. 142v.
These persons be appointed to council with the new churchwardens for the continuance of the money letten out by obligation for the relief of the poor.
Master Dyon.[4]
Master Bradley.
L[awrence] Eresbye.
Arthur Grey.
William Whyte.
Gilbert Blancharde.
William Brown.
William Kyng.
William Evans.
John Makrell.
Mr Chapman.
William Dughtye.[5]
Thomas Pelson.
John Brown.
Received of Walter Anderson – 3s 4d.
Memorandum, that Richard Gibson and Walter Browne and John Skupholme of Lowth have borrowed of the churchwardens 6s 8d at this 6th May 1555 to be repaid again with 14 days warning.

---

1   Steven Bucke, draper, left a will: TNA, PROB 11/76/355, probate, 26 November 1590.
2   Illegible.
3   Written later in pencil with a manicule.
4   John Dyon of North Somercotes and Tathwell, left a will, LAO, LCC, 1583 (ii), *f.* 18. His estate came to £19 13s 4d. LAO, Inventories, Box 68, p. 113, 15 April 1583. In 1552, an indenture was drawn up between Dyon and the Louth prebendary, Henry Williams, for the lease of 'all that his prebende or parsonage of Louthe ... at a rent of £24'. Cole, *Chapter Acts*, III, p. 77.
5   Crossed through.

And that George More[1] hath borrowed of the said churchwardens the said day and year 3s 4d to be paid at Whit Sunday next; Robert Akred surety.

And that William East hath of the church money 6s 8d, to be repaid at Midsummer next; Thomas Wardall surety.

And that Leonard Russhby hath borrowed of the church 6s 8d, to be repaid at the said day.

[The] 3rd day of November [in the year of] the reign [of] Philip and Mary, King and Queen 5th and 6th.[2]

Lowth. Repaid the day and year above said of the constables of Lowthe for the King & Queen's majesty's tax, and unto the said Sovereign Lord & Lady Philip & Mary the sum of £12 13s 2½d, by John Nocton & John Barbar, deputies for Mr Upton, collector, by me Hammond Upton.

f. 143r.

Imprimis, received of Thomas Grene for his [mother in law's burial – 3s 4d].[3]
And for the bells ringing – 20d.[4]
Item received of Master Dyon for the reparations of the church – 12d.[5]
Item given to Bartyllimeue Hanson for his wages – 3s 4d.[6]
And paid to Thomas Anderson[7] for covering of Worsely's wife's grave – 4d.
Item for dressing of the churchyard – 3d.
Item given William East for nollyng of the Pesecode bell – 4d.
Item given to Robert [Odlyng] for mending of 2 bell wheels, the Trinity & St George – 2s 4d.
Item given to the said Robert Odlyng for his half[8] year's wages – 20d.

f. 143v.[9]

Payments paid by William Whyte, William Bayly, Thomas Richardson and Thomas Leche, churchwardens of Lowth for this year, that is to say the year of Our Lord 1554 out of the sum £8 8s 10d,[10] to them delivered by the other

---

[1] More was interred 4 January 1564/5. LAO, Goulding Papers, 5/2.

[2] Latin. King Philip II of Spain (d.1598) married Queen Mary on 25 July 1554 (St James's Day) in Winchester Cathedral; hence the differing regnal years. Mary died 17 November 1558 (St Hugh's Day).

[3] [Crossed through].

[4] Line crossed through.

[5] Line crossed through.

[6] Line crossed through. Hanson was interred 29 December 1557. LAO, Goulding Papers, 5/2.

[7] 'Rede' crossed through.

[8] 'Quarter' crossed through.

[9] This page is out of sequence with the rest of the accounts. No mention is made of payments to the poor during the years 1554 to 1555, although the names of the churchwardens correspond. Therefore, these items may have been left out of the original account. Page 239. Accounts II, *f.* 109v. Alternatively, the pages were possibly placed incorrectly when the volume was bound.

[10] '£14 14s 1d' crossed through.

churchwardens before them [as appearith in the beginning of the account].[1]
And so remains 28s 5½d in debt upon the churchwardens.
Item paid to Margaret Todds and Isabel her sister on the 8th day of April – 6d.
Item to Hobson's wife – 2d.
Item to Alice Huttoft – 2d.
Item to Edward Cotts – 2d.
Item to Anthony Collynwood – 4d.
Item on the 15th day of April to Alice Huttoft – 2d.
Item to Margaret Todds & her sister – 6d.
Item to Hobson's wife – 2d.
Item to Edward Cotts – 2d.
Item to Anthony Colynwood – 4d.
Item to Arthur Capper and Adam Dyxson – 4d.
Item to Holme – 2d.
Item paid on the 22nd April to Alice Huttoft – 4d.
Item to Anthony Collynwood – 2d.
Item to Arthur Capper – 4d.
Item to Thomas Holme – 2d.
Item to Adam Dyxson – 2d.
Item to Hobson's wife – 4d.
Item to Margaret Todds and her sister – 6d.
Item to Barthelmew Hanson – 4d.[2]
Item to Jenett Kirkby – 2d.
Item to Jenett Ledys – 2d.
Item to Edward Cotts – 2d.
Item to Arthur Capper on the 30th day of April – 2d.
Item to Alice Huttoft – 4d.
Item to Holme – 1d.
Item to Hobson's wife – 2d.
Item to Mother Lowth and Alice Bycham – 4d.[3]
Item to Margaret Todds – 4d.
Item to Bartill Hanson – 1d.
Item Jenet Kyrkby – 1d.
Item to Anthony Colywood – 1d.
Item to Father Wood – 2d.
f. 144r.
Item paid on the 6th day of May to Arthur Capper – 2d.
Item paid on the 12th May to Arthur Capper – 2d.
Item to Mother Robson – 2d.

---

[1] [Crossed through]. Marginalia – '£8 8s 10d whereof paid in alms to the poor as appearith by this account'.
[2] This entry seems at odds, as Hanson was interred 29 December 1557.
[3] '2d' crossed through.

Item to Margaret Wright – 2d.
Item to Margaret Todds & her sister – 4d.
Item Mother Lowth – 2d.
Item to Alice Becham – 2d.
Item to Holme – 2d.
Item to Arthur Capper and Cogle's wife on the 20th day of May – 4d.
Item to Holme's wife – 1d.
Item to Alice Robson – 2d.
Item to Margaret Todds – 2d.
Item to Lowth's wife – 2d.
Item to Margaret Wright – 1d.
Item to Arthur Capper and Cogle's wife on the 26th May – 4d.
Item to Holm's wife – 1d.
Item to Alice Robson – 2d.
Item to Margaret Todds – 2d.
Item to Lowth's wife – 2d.
Item to Margaret Wright – 2d.
Item to John May – 1d.
Item on the 3rd day of June to Arthur Capper – 2d.
Item to Mother Lowth – 2d.
Item to Margaret Todds – 2d.
Item to Cogle's wife – 1d.
Item to Beatrix Wright – 2d.
Item on the 10th June to Robert Eastgate – 4d.
Item to Mother Lowth – 2d.
Item to Mother Hobson – 2d.
Item to Mother Cogle – 2d.
Item to Holme – 1d.
Item to Arthur Capper – 2d.
Item to Margaret Todds – 2d.
Item on the 22nd day of June to Robert Eastgate – 4d.
Item to Mother Cogle – 1d.
Item to Alice Robson – 1d.
Item to Arthur Capper – 2d.
Item to Holme – 1d.
Item to Margaret Todds – 2d.
Item to Arthur Capper and Mother Robson – 4d.
Item to Holme – 2d.
Item to Eastgate – 2d.
Item to Dawton's wife, Mother Lowth, John May & Becham – 4d.[1]

---

[1] Foot of page damaged, text illegible.

f. 144v.
Item to Jenet Kyrkby – 2d.
Item to Mother Lowth on the first day of July – 4d.
Item to Arthur Capper – 2d.
Item to Alice Robson – 2d.
Item to Robert Eastgate – 1d.
Item to Todd's wife – 2d.
Item on the 8th of July to Todd's wife and her sister – 4d.
Item to Jenett Kyrkby – 2d.
Item to Arthur Capper – 2d.
Item to Alice Robson – 2d.
Item to Holme – 1d.
Item to Mother Lowth – 4d.
Item to Mother Wyndell – 4d.
Item to Eastgate – 1d.
Item to Mother Cogle – 2d.
Item to Mother Lowth on the 15th of July – 4d.
Item to Arthur Capper – 2d.
Item to Mother Cogle – 2d.
Item to Alice Robson – 2d.
Item to Todd's wife – 2d.
Item to Jenet Kyrkby – 1d.
Item on the 22nd July to Mother Lowth – 4d.
Item to Arthur Capper – 2d.
Item to Mother Cogle – 2d.
Item to Alice Robson – 2d.
Item to Todd's wife – 4d.
Item to Jenett Kyrkby – 2d.
Item on the 29th day of July to Walter Pyper being sick – 6d.
Item to Arthur Capper – 2d.
Item to Alice Robson & Margaret Todds – 4d.
Item to Mother Cogle – 2d.
Item to Jenett Kirkby – 2d.
Item to Holme – 1d.
Item to John May & Mother Louth – 2d.
Item on the 6th day of August to Walter Pyper – 6d.
Item on the 13th of August to Alice Robson – 4d.
Item to Walter Pyper – 6d.
Item to Todd's wife – 2d.
Item to Mother Cogle – 2d.
Item to Alice Robson – 4d.
Item to Walter Pyper – 6d.
Item to Todd's wife – 4d.

f. 145r.
Item to Mother Cogle – 2d.
Item to Mother Lowth – 2d.
Item to Arthur Capper – 2d.
Item to Jenet Kyrkby and Alan – 2d.
Item on the 26th day of August to Arthur Capper and Cogle's wife – 4d.
Item to Jenett Kyrkby – 1d.
Item to Todd's wife – 2d.
Item to Holme – 1d.
Item to Father May – 1d.
Item to [Mother][1] Alice Robson – 2d.
Item on the 2nd day of September to Arthur Capper and Cogle's wife – 4d.
Item to Jenett Kyrkby – 1d.
Item to Todd's wife – 2d.
Item to Holme and Father May – 2d.
Item to Alice Robson – 2d.
Item to Roger Hynes – 1d.
Item to Mother Edon – 1d.
Item to Father Wood – 2d.
Item on the 9th day of September to Arthur Capper – 2d.
Item to Todd's wife and to Father Wood – 4d.
Item to Father Wyndell & Mother Lowth – 4d.
Item to Mother Edon and Roger J[…][2] – 2d.
Item to Jenett Kyrkby and Holme – 2d.
Item to John May & Cogle's wife – 2d.
Item to James Wady – 1d.
Item to Mother Robson – 2d.
Item on the 16th September to Arthur Capper and John May – 4d.
Item to Father Wyndell – 2d.
Item to Mother Cogle – 2d.
Item to Holme – 1d.
Item to James Wady – 1d.
Item to Mother Dalton – 1d.
Item to Jenet Kyrkby and Mother Robson – 4d.
Item to Father Wood – 2d.
Item to Mother Edon – 2d.
Item to Todd's wife & her sister – 2d.
Item to Mother Lowth – 4d.
Item to Roger J[…][3] Martyn Smith – 3d.

[1] [Crossed through].
[2] Surname indecipherable.
[3] Surname indecipherable.

Item on the 23rd September to Arthur Capper and Wyndell – 4d.
Item to Jenet Kyrkby & Mother Robson.[1]
Item to Mother Lowth.[2]

f. 145v.
Item on the last of September to Dyxson's wife – 4d.
Item to Burrett's wife – 4d.
Item to Mother Robson – 2d.
Item to Mother Lowth – 4d.
Item to Arthur Capper – 2d.
Item to Mother Edon – 1d.
Item to Jenett Kyrkby – 1d.
Item to Todd's wife – 2d.
Item to John May & Dawton's wife – 2d.
Item on the 2nd October to Arthur Capper – 2d.
Item to Dixson's wife – 4d.
Item to Father Wood – 2d.
Item to Mother Edon and Mother Robson – 4d.
Item to Mother Cogle – 4d.
Item to Todd's wife – 2d.
Item to Jenett Kyrkby – 1d.
Item to Mother Louth – 2d.
Item to Burrett's wife – 1d.
Item on the 14th of October to Windell – 2d.
Item to Mother Robson – 2d.
Item to Mother Lowth – 2d.
Item to Todd's wife and her sister – 4d.
Item to Jenet Sorby – 2d.
Item to Jenet Kirkby – 1d.
Item to Agnes Scott – 1d.
Item to Dawton's wife & Mother Edon – 2d.
Item to Arthur Capper & Holme – 2d.
Item to John May – 1d.
Item to Jenett Holdernes – 1d.
Item to Father Wood – 2d.
Item on the 21st of October to Jenet Kirkby and Alice Robson – 2d.
Item to Burrett's wife – ½d.
Item to Mother Cogle – 4d.
Item to Mother Seresby – 1d.
Item to Todd's wife – 1d.
Item to Mother Louth – 2d.

[1] Page damaged.
[2] Page damaged.

Item the 28th of October to Todd's wife – 2d.
Item to Mother Robson – 2d.
Item to Jenet Kyrkby – 1d.
Item to John May – 1d.
Item to Arthur Capper – 2d.
Item on the 4th of November to Mother Lowth – 2d.
Item to Alice Robson – 2d.
Item to Jenet Kirkby & Mother Edon – 2d.
Item to Arthur Capper – 2d.
Item to Burrett's wife & Jenet Story – 2d.
Item to Todd's wife – 2d.[1]

---

[1] Page damaged.

The Louth St James Churchwardens' Accounts: 1560–70[1]

f. 1r.

[1560–1]

1560.

The account of John Palmer, William Somerskaills, William Fysswick and Jarrat Alendaill,[2] Churchwardens of the Parish Church of St James in Lowthe in the County of Lyncoln of all their receipts, payments and expenses from the Sunday in the Octaves of Easter in *Anno* 1560 to the same Sunday in *Anno* 1561 that is to say for one whole year.

First, received of the old churchwardens being the last year in ready money the sum of five pounds thirteen shillings and four pence – £5 13s 4d.

Item received more one chalice with a paten, six skins of parchment[3] and 3 iron picks which was made of the broken bell clapper.

Item received more by the hands of Thomas Blanchard in money – 2s 8d.

Item more in evil money – 20d.

Item received for old planks and other broken wood that belonged to Steueton Bridge[4] – 3s.

Item received for the collection gathered by the churchwardens due for three quarters of this year – £3 14s 10½d.

Received of John Palmer for 12 rods of thorns – 5s.

Item received of Thomas Smyth, butcher for 12 rods of thorns – 5s.

f. 1v.

Item received of John North for 20 rods of thorns – 8s 4d.

Item received of William Somerskells for 15 rods of thorns – 6s 3d.

---

[1] LAO, Louth St James, PAR/7/3. The pages commence from *folio* 1.

[2] Jarrat Allandale, tanner, left a will dated 26 January 1586/7, donating 40s, along with cloth and coal to the poor via the Sudbury Hutch. TNA, PROB 11/82/9, probate, 5 February 1593/4. Goulding, *Corporation Records*, p. 147. Gurnham, *History of Louth*, p. 72.

[3] In 1563, a Bill was presented to Parliament stating that 'all former church books of 24 yeeres continuance' should be written 'into great deacent books of parchment'. A clause from the 1597 Convocation affirmed that 'the registers were for the future to be kept on parchment and parchment copies were to be made of those old registers which were on paper'. Cox, *Parish Registers*, pp. 5–6. There was apparently no requirement for churchwardens' accounts to be similarly treated.

[4] Stewton.

Received of the churchwardens for the collection of the last quarter of this year – 22s 9½d.
Item received for one bull sold by the churchwardens – 26s 8d.
Sum – £13 8s 7d.
f. 2r.
This be the payments and allowances unto the ministers of the church due to them as standing fees and paid yearly as hereafter it doth appear.
First, paid to the writer of this account and for keeping of the book of christenings, weddings and burials.[1]
Item paid to the blower of the organs.
Item paid for keeping the bells, the leads and for dressing of the church.
Item paid to the keeper of the clock and chimes and ringing of the Day bell.[2]
Item paid to Robert Odlyng for his fee.
f. 2v. [Blank].
f. 3r.
1560.
The receipts for burials and for ringing of the bells and also to the Poor Men's box as hereafter appearith.
First received for the burial of Robert Wynter's wife for the Great bell – 12d.[3]
Item received of Richard Wayrd, carver, for his legacy bequeathed to the poor folks in Lowthe and to be distributed by the churchwardens above said four pounds – £4.
Item received for the burial of Mr John Toplis and for the bells – 7s 6d.
Item received of Thomas Dynnys for the burial of his wife & his mother – 16s 4d.
Item received for the burial of Johanna, the wife of William Taller & for the bells – 7s 4d.
Item received for the burial of Mrs Foster[4] and for the bells – 7s 8d.[5]
Item received for the burial of Peter Worledge – 7s 8d.
Item received for the burial of William Skelton and for the bells – 6s 7½d.
Received for the burial of Alice Cowper – 6s 8d.
Received for the burial…[6]
Sum – £7 9½d.
Total sum received [and] paid – £20 9s 4½d.

---

[1] No amounts are stated for this and the next four entries.
[2] This was rung as a summons to worship and as the curfew bell at the end of the day. Goulding, *Customs*, p. 2. Dudding, *Accounts*, pp. 13–14.
[3] Emott Wynter was interred 10 November 1560. LAO, Goulding Papers, 5/2.
[4] Possibly Emott Foster, buried 27 November 1559. LAO, Goulding Papers, 5/2.
[5] This calculates as 6s 8d for burial inside the church and 12d for ringing the James bell. If the Trinity bell was rung, the cost would be 7s 4d.
[6] Sentence incomplete.

f. 3v.
Arrearages yet owing for the burials as appearith in the last account.
First, for the burial of Mrs Foster & for the bells – 8s 4d.[1]
Item for the burial of Thomas Dynes's wife and for the bells – 7s 8d.
Item for the ringing of the Great bell for John Holdernes – 12d.
Item the rent of Plough is to be accounted for the year 1559.
f. 4r. [Blank].
f. 4v. [Blank].
f. 5r.

Anno Domini 1560.

Payments and allowances of other expenses as well about the church in money given in alms to the poor folk as is hereafter subscribed.
Item given in alms to the poor folks of the second Sunday after Easter which was the 28th day of April – 2s 5d.
Item paid to Thomas Lechman, the smith for the making of 3 bars of iron for the glass windows and for the shotting of one great fire hook – 2s.
Item paid for half hundredth[2] [of] nails to the glass windows – 3d.
Item paid to Richard Wright for this paper book – 2s 4d.
Item paid to the bedle for his quarter's wages due at May Day, five shillings – 5s.
Item given in alms the 3rd Sunday after Easter to the poor folks – 3s 4d.
Item given in alms to the poor folks the 4th Sunday after Easter – 4s 3d.
Item given in alms to the poor folks the 19th day of May – 5s.
Item paid to the mason for workmanship about the glass windows – 8s 6d.
Item paid to Enderbe for mending of a hedge betwixt Hagthorpe Field and Louyth Field – 2s 6d.
f. 5v.

1560.

Item paid to William Jacson for hanging of a gate at Monks' Dyke Head – 16d.
Item paid for a hook to the same – 4d.
Item paid to Auncell Jef for a bell-string and for 6 trayses[3] – 2s 8d.
Item paid to the poor folk the 25th day of May – 4s 4d.
Item paid to Robert Salman for looking to them that lay the dung at Gosbell[4] End to corrupt it – 6d.
Item paid to the poor folks on the 2nd day of June – 5s.
Item paid to Bryan Jacson in part of payment for mending of the glass windows – 20s.
Item paid to John Fyssche for one tree to the repair of Lowith Bridge – 8s 6d.
Item paid to Richard Gregbey for sawing the said tree – 3s.

[1] This and the next three entries are noted as 'discharged' and crossed through.
[2] Fifty nails or alternatively half a hundredweight = 56 lb.
[3] Traces – the end-piece of a bell-rope. *OED*.
[4] Probably Gospelgate. Green, *Streets of Louth*, p. 95.

Item paid to John Skepholme for carriage of the said tree to the bridge – 6d.
Item paid to Leonard Rushbe, the wright, for his work 2 days and a half – 22d.
Item paid to Ralf Robson for ramming[1] about the said bridge – 8d.
f. 6r.

1560.

Item paid to John Palmer for 3 pieces of timber for sleepers to the said bridge – 6s 8d.
Item paid to Brian Jacson for glazing of the library[2] and sweeping and dressing of it – 5s 6d.
Item paid to him for 3 provands[3] of lime to the work – 7d.
Item paid Robert Salmon for given attendance to them that corrupt Gospell End with dung – 2d.
Item paid to William East for his quarter's wages for keeping clock and chimes – 5s 10d.
Item paid to the bellman for his fee – 3s 4d.
Item paid to William East for making of the church brocke[4] – 4d.
Item paid to Leonard Rushbe for making of the gates in the churchyard and for one piece of wood to the same – 12d.
Item paid to John Palmer for carrying of planks and sleepers to Steuton Bridge and for bringing of the old wood to the town – 20d.
f. 6v.

1560.

Item paid to Bryan Jacson for mending of the glass windows – 13s 4d.
Item paid to Thomas Leche, smith, for one bolt and 2 staples to the church gates – 7d.
Item paid for one gallon [of] wine which was sent to my Lord Wyllowbe[5] the 18th day of July – 20d.
Item for washing Mr Vicar's surplice at Lammas[6] – 2d.
Item paid to Richard Riggs for scouring of 2 Almayn Rivyts and 3 pair of splints and one sallet – 6s.
Item paid to the bedle for his quarter's wages due at Lammas – 5s.

---

[1] Ramming – compressing the ground. *OED*.
[2] This room was built over the south porch in the fifteenth century. Gurnham, *Early Louth*, p. 124. In 1504/5, the accounts note: 'Item, for makyn the stewed [study] in the south Kyrke porch', and 'divers books to it'. Dudding, *Accounts*, p. 72. Swaby, *History of Louth*, p. 52. The chamber later acted as a meeting room for the Corporation. It was removed during refurbishments in 1868–9. Goulding, *Parish Church*, p. 8.
[3] Meaning unknown.
[4] Meaning unknown.
[5] Willoughby.
[6] Lammas Day, 1 August. The accounts record the feasts of Lammas and Martinmas, both recognised as Quarter Days in Scotland and Northern England. *OED*.

Item paid to Leonard Rushbe for mending of stalls and for nails to the said work in Our Lady's choir – 7d.
Item paid to the writer of this account and for writing of the books of christenings & burials for his quarter's wages due at Lammas – 20d.
Item paid to Leonard Rushbe for mending of the turdle of the church gate at the west end of the church – 12d.

f. 7r.

1560.

Item paid to Thomas Lechman for mending of the clock – 8d.
Item paid to William East for his quarter's wages due at Michaelmas – 5s 10d.
Item paid to Robert Odlyng for his quarter's wages – 20d.
Item paid to the bellman for his quarter's wages – 3s 4d.
Item paid for the burial of Thomas Parke – 3d.
Item paid to Auncell Jeffe for the slicing of the plumb rope – 6d.
Item paid to William Rede & Ralff Robson for scouring the well in the Market Place – 2s.
Item paid to Herre Mylls for carrying away of the mud from the well – 2d.
Item paid to the vicar for a book of admonition concerning marriages[1] – 4d.
Item paid to Mr Sidens for a book named the *Paraphrases* – 10s.
Item paid for a little book of the articles made by the Bishop of Canterbury[2] – 2¼d.

f. 7v.

1560.

Item paid to Gilbert Blanchard for boards & nails which was bestowed of the well in the Marketstead – 2s 11d.
Item paid to William Jacson for working about the said well – 7½d.
Item paid to the bedle for his quarter's wages at Martinmas[3] – 5s.
Item paid to the writer of this account and for writing of the book of christenings and burials due at Martinmas – 20d.
Item paid to William East the 24th day of November for his quarter's wages due to him at Christmas next coming – 5s 10d.
Item paid to Thomas Leche, smith for 2 bands to the well in the Market Place – 4½d.
Item paid for washing of 2 surplices to the vicar – 3d.

---

[1] Probably a volume listing prohibitions concerning family affinities within marriage.

[2] Matthew Parker, archbishop of Canterbury (1559–75). These Articles were probably the outcome of a synod at Lambeth in 1561; the resultant work being 'A declaration of certain principal articles of religion for the unity of doctrine to be taught'. *DNB*, https://doi.org/10.1093/ref:odnb/21327 (Accessed 17/3/2018).

[3] The feast of St Martin, 11 November, when there was also a fair in Louth.

Item paid for the washing of Mr Man's[1] surplice for one year ended at Michaelmas last past] – 4½d.

f. 8r.

1560.

Item paid to the bellman for his quarter's wages due at Michaelmas – 3s 4d.
Item paid to Robert Odlyng for his wages due at Christmas – 10d.
Item paid to the bellman for covering of Thomas Dynnys's mother and wife's graves – 8d.
Item paid to Mr Pormort[2] for the charges of the common bull being cawyghtyd[3] with him 9 weeks – 3s ½d.
Item paid to bellman for covering of Mr Toplif & William Taller's wife's grave – 8d.[4]
Item paid to the bedle for his quarter's wages due at Candlemas – 5s.
Item paid to 2 plumbers servants to my Lord Clynton for working of the leads certain days – 38s 6d.
Item paid for board and nails to Gilbert Blancherd which was bestowed of the said leads – 6s.
Item paid to Robert Saltmarsh and Symson for plasshynge of the common hedge at Haregarth – 32s 6d.
Item paid to the bellman quarter wages at the Annunciation of Our Lady – 3s 4d.
Item paid for the covering of Mrs Foster, Peter Worghlege, William Skelton, William Brown and Alice Cowper's graves – 20d.

f. 8v.

Item paid to Martyn Chapman for his year's fee for the keeping of Aswell – 2s.
Item paid to Robert Odlyng for his quarter's wages due at Our Lady Day – 10d.
Item paid to him for his work about the bells at Easter – 3s 4½d.
Item paid to Robert Kyrckbe for his quarter's wages due at Our Lady Day – 5s 10d.
Item paid to Thomas Leche for iron and for his labour in working of 36 pounds – 10s.
Item paid for washing of the vicar's surplice & other clothes – 4½d.
Item paid to Leonard Rischbe for the hanging of one gate at the east end of the town – 3d.
Item paid for the burial of Jenet Thymolbe – 4d.
Item paid to John Palmer for keeping the common bull – 3s 4d.
Item paid for carriage of the gate from Monks' Dyke to the East Field – 6d.

---

[1] William Man.

[2] This is possibly Christopher Pormort (d.1584), second son of George Pormort of Keddington (d.1541). He was churchwarden 1569/70 and mayor of Grimsby in 1578 and was buried there. Will: LAO, LCC, 1585(i), *f.* 176. Maddison, *Lincolnshire Pedigrees*, 52, pp. 789–90.

[3] Quartered?

[4] Joanna Tailler was buried 12 May 1560. LAO, Goulding Papers, 5/2.

Item paid to the writer of this account for his quarter's wages due at Candlemas – 20d.
Item paid to William Somerskells for 7 boards to the plumber's mould & for making of the plumber's pane[1] – 3s.

f. 9r.

1560.

Item lost in the churchwardens hands at the fall of money – 20s 7d.
Sum of all the payments £16 14s, and remaineth £3 15s 4½d, whereof paid to the Queen's Majesty for amercement[2] set over the town of Louthe by the Justices of Assizes for that they gave not evidence against William West the sum of 6s 8d, and yet there remains £3 13s 8½d. To the which they charge themselves with the rents gathered of the Plough light, 3s 10½d. And so the sums put together amount to £3 12s 7d, which sum of £3 12s 7d they have delivered to Thomas Holdernes, John Spalding, the old churchwardens, and John Baylye and John Rygald the new churchwardens for the year next following.
The said new churchwardens are to be charged the next year with one bull and 5s to be taken of the parishioners for half of the new *Paraphrases*, and 6s 8d for the burial and bells for Elizabeth Skelton, buried the 28th February the year of Our Lord 1560[3] & is the money coming of 72 rods of plasshing of the common hedging in Haregarthes.

f. 9v.

Six skins of parchment, one chalice with a paten and 3 iron picks, one iron gavelock and one silver piece.

[1561–2]

Surveyors for the Highways.

Robert Kyngley and John Fysshe, the 13th April in *Anno Domini* 1561, made their account before the whole parish and delivered to the Poor Man's box 12d, above all charges & the said parish have chosen Surveyors for the year following, Leonard Russebye and Robert Chapman, tanner.

f. 10r.

The payments and allowances with other expenses as here followeth the present year, *Anno* 1561.
Item paid to Roger Stut[4] for one bible – 12s.
Item paid to Robert Kyrkbe & to the bellman for the burial of Jenet Thymelbe – 6d.[5]

---

[1] A rectangular piece of wood fitting into a larger wooden framework. *OED*.

[2] The imposition of a penalty or fine. *OED*.

[3] This date tallies with the Parish Registers. A Stephen Skelton, presumably a relative, was interred on 2 March 1560/1. LAO, Goulding Papers, 5/2.

[4] A Roger Stut (Stutte) was commemorated with a plaque on the north wall of the church stating that he 'dyed Maii 1st 1604'. Holles, *Church Notes*, p. 94. He was warden in 1586, 1593 and 1599. Goulding, *Corporation Records*, pp. 19–20.

[5] Joanna Thymelbe was buried 27 March 1561. LAO, Goulding Papers, 5/2.

Item paid to John Soyrbe[1] for keeping of the sewer at Gospell End – 4d.
Item paid for nails bestowed of the bells – 12d.
Item paid to the bedle for his quarter's wages due at May Day – 5s.
Item paid for one bull – 30s.
Item paid to the writer of this account and for the writings of christenings & burials due at May Day – 3s 4d.
Item paid for the making of the butts – 3s 1½d.
Item paid to Jeffray Wilson for one bell-string to the James and another to the Fore bell – 8s 3d.
Item paid to Mr Pormort for keeping of the common bull which was due to him at the last account – 3s 4d.
Item paid to Ralf Robson for his quarter's wages at Midsummer – 3s 4d.
Item paid for the writing of the quarter collection book – 4d.
Item paid to the vicar for the table and the frame containing the commandments & other sentences of scripture – 2s 5d.[2]

f. 10v.

Anno 1561.

Item paid for a new calendar[3] set forth by my Lord of Canterbury – 8d.
Item paid to Robert Kyrckbe for his quarter's wages due at Midsummer – 5s 10d.
Item paid to Robert Odlyng for his quarter's wages due at Midsummer – 10d.
Item paid for the covering of Elizabeth Skelton's grave – 4d.
Item paid to Robert Kyrkbe for painting of the letters with the hands of the clock – 16d.[4]
Item paid to the bedle for his quarter's wages due at Lammas – 5s.
Item paid to the writer of this account and for the writing of christenings, burials & weddings due for his quarters wages at Lammas – 3s 4d.
Item paid to Johnson, smith, for mending of the tache[5] to the chimes – 4d.
Item paid to Robert Cotton for mending of the chimes and for work about the church gates – 20d.
Item paid to the bedle for his quarter's wages due at Martinmas – 5s.
Item paid to Robert Kyrkbe for his quarter's wages due at Michaelmas – 5s 10d.

30s 2d.

---

[1] A John Soirbe was interred 13 April 1564. LAO, Goulding Papers, 5/2.

[2] A board on which was written the Ten Commandments, the Lord's Prayer and other observances sanctioned under Queen Elizabeth.

[3] Listed in the Book of Common Prayer: 'A Table and Kalender, expressing the ordre of the Psalmes and Lessons'. *OED*.

[4] Evidence that the church clock face displayed hands, not always the case in this period.

[5] Fastening two parts; a clasp, buckle, hook and eye. *OED*.

f. 11r.

Anno 1561.

Item paid for the washing of the vicar's surplice and other clothes at Michaelmas – 4d.

Item paid to Ralf Robson for his quarter's wages at Michaelmas – 3s 4d.

Item paid for the covering of William Draycks's grave – 4d.

Item paid to Herre Skurall & his server for mending of the churchyard walls – 2s 7d.

Item paid to Robert Odlynge for his quarter's wages due at Michaelmas – 10d.

Item paid to him for one plank to the church grate – 12d.

Item to him for one piece of wood bestowed about the chime hammer – 2d.

Item more to him and William Jacson for one day's work about the bells – 2s.

Item paid to Robert Cottam[1] for ironwork about the bells – 8d.

Item paid to the writer of this account and writings of burials, christenings & weddings due at Martinmas – 3s 4d.

Item paid to Martyn Chapman for his half year's wages in keeping of Haswell[2] – 12d.

Item paid to Robert Mylner for a horn – 15d.

Item paid to the plumber for his work about the church and for wood & nails – 4s 6d.

Item paid to Robert Kirckbe for his quarter's wages due at Christmas – 5s 10d.

27s 2d.

f. 11v.

Anno 1561.

Item paid to Ralf Robson for his quarter's wages at Christmas – 3s 4d.

Item paid for one bushel of lime to the mending of the church walls – 10d.

Item paid to the wrights for taking down the Rood loft – 5s 4d.[3]

Item paid to the bedle for his quarter's wages due at Candlemas – 5s.

Item paid to Leonard Hanson for keeping of the bull this winter – 13s 4d.

Item paid to the writer of this account and writing of burials, weddings & christenings due at Candlemas – 3s 4d.

Item paid to Robert Cotton for ironwork about the bells – 5s.

Item paid for packthread occupied about the chimes – 4d.

---

[1] The two sons of Robert Cottam, William and Thomas, predeceased him. LAO, Goulding Papers, 5/2.

[2] Aswell.

[3] The *OED* describes a Rood loft as 'a loft or gallery, often panelled and ornately decorated, running along the top of a Rood screen in a church'. Therefore, this is probably only the loft itself and not the entire screen. The figures on the Rood must therefore have been removed previously, although there is no mention of this in the text. A loft is last recorded in the accounts of 1628 when 3s was paid to 'Massingale for mending over the Rood loft.' LAO, Louth St James, 7/5 (i), *f.* 34.

Item paid to Robert Kyrkbe for his quarter's wages due at Lady Day – 5s 10d
Item paid to Ralf Robson for his quarter's wages due at the same day – 3s 4d.
Item paid to Robert Odlyng for his half year's wages due at Our Lady's Day, the Annunciation – 20d.
f. 12r.

Anno 1561.

Item paid to Robert Odlyng for dressing of the Trinity bell – 3s.
Item paid to Ralf Robson for one day's work about the said bell – 8d.
Item to him for covering of Edward Pystor's grave – 4d.[1]
Item paid to Robert Kyrckbe for washing of the vicar's surplice and other clothes – 4d.
The 29th day of May in the seventh year of the reign of our Sovereign Lady Queen Elizabeth.[2]
There remained in the hands of Thomas Blanchard the 13th day of April *Anno Domini* 1561 of the church money as appearith in our old church book the sum of £79 8s 2d, whereof the said Thomas paid for the diking of a dike between Kedyngton and Lowthe as appearith in the same old books the sum of £14 15s 3d.
Item paid by the said Thomas Blanchard to Gilbert Blanchard and Richard Grison, churchwardens 1563, £7.
Item paid to Mr Smith of Boston for his council and drawing a book for the corporation[3] and fee farm,[4] £7 13s 4d.
Sum of the payments £28 8s 7d, and so remaineth £50 19s 7d, whereof,

f. 12v.

NB. Although entered in the churchwardens' accounts, the following records relate to the Corporation and grammar school. They are dated separately and therefore out of sequence with the churchwardens' financial records. This continues to *f.* 14v inclusive.

In the hands of Roger Waite £8, and paid by Mr Warden to the churchwardens for their surplusage in their account this year 69s 9d. Paid by him more to

---

[1] Edmund Pistor, buried 10 February 1561/2. LAO, Goulding Papers, 5/2.
[2] 1564.
[3] This is the first direct reference in the churchwardens' accounts to the Louth Corporation, which, along with the grammar school, was established in a charter of Edward VI, 21 September 1551. They were governed by a warden and six assistants, who, in 1564, purchased the manor of Louth from the queen, the churchwardens providing nearly £80. Pages 282–3. Accounts II, *f.* 136v. Goulding, *Corporation Records*, pp. 1–7; list of wardens, pp. 19–23. Goulding, *St Mary's*, p. 10, note.
[4] A fixed annual rent payable to the monarch by chartered boroughs or to a lord on the creation of a tenancy. Bristow, *Glossary*, pp. 68–9.

the new churchwardens in ready money towards the repair of the church 24s 6d, and so remaineth £38 5s 4d besides the said £8 in Roger Wath's hands.
Item paid more by Mr Bradley, the warden, to the hands of Mathew Wardall for the use of the church – £3.
Memorandum that all the money above named mentioned to be in the hands of Thomas Blanchard is now returned into the hands of Mr Warden and the assistants. Item paid by Mr Gilbert Blanchard, the warden, to the churchwardens the 7th day of July *Anno* 1566 of the sum above named in part of payment thereof the sum of £3.
Item paid more by the said warden to Thomas Pelson over of the churchwardens as appearith in the receipt of this account which was bestowed in charges about the dressing of Aswell, 40s.
Item paid more by the aforesaid Mr Warden to the said Thomas Pelson the 6th day of April *Anno* 1567 as appearith in the same account of receipt the sum of 20s.

f. 13r.

Item paid to John North and his fellow churchwardens by the hands of Mr John Purvey,[1] the warden of the school, as appearith in the receipt of their account *Anno Domini* 1567 the sum of £4, whereof was paid by the hands of Gilbert Blanchard, 40s.
Item paid more to John North and his fellows the 17th of April by the hands of Mr Bradle for Mr Purvey the warden as appearith in their account, £3.
Item paid more to Mr Ormsbe[2] and his fellow churchwardens by the 27th day of November *Anno* 1568, by Mr White,[3] the warden of the school, as appearith in the receipt of their account, 20s.[4]
Item paid more by the said Mr White to the use of the church at the account of Low Sunday and so remaineth owing by the warden and assistants in money twenty pounds five shillings and four pence besides eight pounds remaining in Roger Wait's hands, which sum of £8 William White & William Kyng[5] of Lowth hath promised for them both & their executors to pay yearly of Low

---

[1] John Purvey MP (c.1525–83), was elected warden 1568, 1573, 1582. Goulding, *Corporation Records*, p. 19. He married secondly Margaret (Magdalene) Eresby, widow of Lawrence Eresby, at Louth on 19 December 1562. Bindoff, *House of Commons*, III, p. 163. Margaret's will: TNA, PROB 11/76/302, probate, 11 November 1590.

[2] William Ormsby, died without issue. Buried 27 July 1584. Maddison, *Lincolnshire Pedigrees*, 51, p. 739. Accounts III, *f.* 119r.

[3] William White, Whyte, was warden in 1560, 1569, 1576 and 1581. Goulding, *Corporation Records*, p. 19 and note 5. Will: TNA, PROB 11/67/378, probate, 24 October 1584.

[4] '40s' crossed through.

[5] William Kyng was elected warden in 1572 and 1578. Goulding, *Corporation Records*, p. 19.

Sunday 20s to the said sum of £8 to be paid. In witness whereof they have set to their hands in the presence of the whole parish the 17th April 1569 by me William White, by me William Kyng.[1]

Item paid more by the hands of Mr White the 4th day of June *Anno* 1569 as appearith in the receipts of the account of Mr Pormort and Thomas Blanchard churchwardens, the sum of 20s.

Item paid more by Mr Kyng, the warden, the 7th October 1571, as appearith in the receipts of the accounts of Mr Whittyngton and Jarrat Alendall, churchwardens – 40s.

f. 13v.

Item paid more by the said warden the 4th day of November following as appearith in the receipts of [the] accounts of the said Mr Whittyngton & his fellow churchwardens, 40s.

Item paid by Mr Bradley, deputy for Mr Purvey, the warden as appearith in the account of William Kyng & his fellow churchwardens made in *Anno Domini* 1573, 40s.

Item paid by Mr Blanchard, the warden, the 26th day of December *Anno* 1573 as appearith in the writings of his account being churchwardens with Robert Marshall and others, 40s.

Item paid by Mr White, the warden, the last day of June *Anno Domini* 1575 as appearith in the receipts of his account being churchwarden with Thomas Richardson and other – £3.

Item paid to William Ormsbe, gentleman, the 13th day of May *Anno* 1576 as appearith in the receipts of his account, being churchwardens with John Northe, William Graunt and John Blanchard,[2] £8. This was paid by Mr White to them being wardens of the school.

And so remains 5s 4d, which the warden & six assistants have paid to William Ormsby, John Northe, William Grawnte and John Blanchard, churchwardens, *Anno Domini* 1576, together with £6 13s 4d which the said warden & assistants have given at the same to the said churchwardens towards the repair of the church & have also promised to pay £20 more towards the repairs of the church in four years more next coming. That is to say every year £5 in consideration of £14 15s 3d, which was paid out of the sum which remained for diking between Kenyngton & Louthe & £6 13s 4d of the said sum given to Mr Smythe for drawing a book for the corporation.[3]

f. 14r.

The sum within written being £20 is promised by us in manner & form before written to be paid by me Thomas Blanchard, warden.

---

[1] Marginalia – '£20 5s 4d'.

[2] John Blanchard, yeoman, died in 1574. He gifted 40s to the poor in his will dated 20 December 1574: TNA, PROB 11/57/30, probate, 23 January 1574/5.

[3] Marginalia – signatures: 'Received by us by Mr William Ormesby, John Northe, his mark, William Graunt, his mark and John Blanchard.'

[Signatures].
John Purevy.
John Bradley.[1]
Gilbert Blanchard.
William Whyte.
William Kynge.
      Promised on expense of us.
[Signatures].
Thomas Broxholme.[2]
Robert Dowghte, clerk.[3]
John Blanchard.
John Fishe.
Robert Chapman.
Richard Brown & diverse others.
Received in part payment of the £20 above promised by the said warden and assistants, the 26th day of November 1576 of Thomas Blanchard, warden the sum of we say received three pounds by us William Ormesby, John Northe, William Graunt and John Blanchard, churchwardens for the said year, £3.
      By me John Blanchard.

f. 14v.
Received in part of payment of Roger Wate's debt as appearith in *Anno* 1570, 20s.
Received in part payment of Roger Wait's debt as appearith in the account of William Kyng and Nicholas Coventre in *Anno* 1573, 20s. Received more in *Anno* 1573 [an]other 20s as appearith in the account of Mr Blanchard and Robert Marshall with others.
Received more as appearith in the account of Steven Bucke and Richard Grysbe[4] *Anno* 1574 [an]other 20s.

---

[1] Recorded in 1561 as a gentleman. Burton, *Old Lincolnshire*, p. 118.

[2] Thomas Broxholme, counsellor at law, died 1590/1. Maddison, *Lincolnshire Pedigrees*, 50, p. 193.

[3] Robert Doughty was the first married vicar of Louth (1558/9–1600). At the time of his death, he also held the title of warden, the only clergyman 'elected' to the Corporation. As vicar, his income was £12 p.a., and he is described in 1576 as aged forty, 'skilled in Latin and well versed in sacred learning'. Doughty was also rector of Grainsby and the south moiety of Grimoldby; both relinquished in 1577. Will: TNA, PROB 11/97/95, probate, 10 February 1601. Goulding *Vicars*, pp. 11–12. Swaby, *History of Louth*, pp. 141–2. Foster, *Episcopal Records*, p. 184.

[4] Richard Grysbe, Greesbye, Greesby or Gresbye, yeoman. Will: TNA, PROB 11/63/50, probate 31 January 1581. He possibly married Anne Walles, mentioned in his will, a former nun of Sixhills Priory (Gilbertine nuns and canons), suppressed 29 September 1538. In 1548, she was still receiving a pension of £2, first granted 4 February 1538/9. *L&P*, XIV (i), 1355 (181), p. 602, 2 February 1539/40. In 1554, Anne was living in Market Rasen but probably moved to Louth upon her marriage. The last

Received more as doth appear in the account of William Whyte and Thomas Richardson, *Anno* 1575 – 20s.

Conclusion of the Corporation Accounts.

f. 15r.

Anno 1561.

The receipts for burials and to the Poor Man's box & also all others due for this present year as is following.
First received for the burial of William Draycks – 6s 8d.
Item received for the burial of Walter Stoker's wife – 3s 4d.[1]
Item received for one bull that was sold – 33s 4d.
Item received of John Thew[2] for the case of the organs – 13s 4d.
Item received for the burial of Mr Ersbe[3] – 8s 4d.
Item received that was given by Mr Ersbe to the reparations of the church – £5.
Item received for the burial of William Balley[4] – 8s 4d.
Received of Richard Spencer for a pair of bellows – 2s.
Received for the burial of Thomas Skynner – 8d.
Received for the burial of Elizabeth Hudson – 8d.
Received for the burial of Brian Jacson – 8d.
Received for the burial of Edmund Pystor – 8d.
Received for the burial of Elizabeth Skelton – 6s 8d.
Received for the vailcloyth[5] sold to William Somerskells – 6s.
Received more of the churchwardens for the collections gathered in the whole year [which there was 6d for the Plough][6] – £5 10d.
Received more of the old churchwardens [in ready money with the money belonging to the Plough light upon the end][7] of their account – £3 12s 7d.

f. 15v.

Anno 1562.

Received more for 72 rods of plasshinge in Haregarthes and 3d the load – 18s.
Sum of all the receipts above written is £19 9s 5d, whereof paid as appearith

---

prior of Sixhills, James Wallis, was possibly a relative, although Anne is not mentioned in his will of 21 April 1539. LAO, LCC, 1538–40, *f.* 194. Hodgett, *Ex-Religious*, pp. 39, 110, 147. Knowles and Hadcock, *Religious Houses*, p. 196.

[1] Joanna Stoker, buried 31 August 1561. LAO, Goulding Papers, 5/2.
[2] John Thew was bailiff of the Corporation and drew up the account for 1554/5. *VCH Lincs*, p. 463.
[3] Lawrence Eresbie.
[4] William Baille, Balley. Bayliff was churchwarden in 1546/7 and 1554/5, and an assistant of the Corporation, being elected warden in 1559. Goulding, *Corporation Records*, pp. 4, 19. Interred 21 October 1561. LAO, Goulding Papers, 5/2.
[5] Veil cloth.
[6] [Crossed through].
[7] [Crossed through].

in 3 leases before written £10 23½d. And yet remaineth in their hands £10 7s 5½d, whereof they desire to be allowed for their loss sustained at the fall of money, 11s. And yet there remaineth £9 16s 5½d, which sum of £9 16s 5½d they have paid by the hands of the churchwardens hereafter appointed, that is to say William King, Edward Boswell, Nicholas Coventre and Robert Marshall for the year following over and besides one bull, one chalice and a paten, 3 iron picks, one iron gavelock and one silver piece and 6 skins of parchment[1] sold to Mylys Graye[2] and other ornaments which contained in an inventory delivered [to] the said new churchwardens. Made that the said new churchwardens shall receive of Robert Odlyng for certain old timber that was of the Rood loft, 13s 4d to be paid the 4th Sunday next after Easter 1562, the said [sentence continued to *f.* 16r.].

f. 16r.

Anno 1562.

[from *f.* 15v.] new churchwardens must be charged with 107 pounds of tin and other in layer metal 15 pounds, in wax 15lbs, 12 copes and vestments and two awbes,[3] 2 banner chests in St Peter's choir, 2 chests & one ark in the church, 3 pieces of wood, 3 banner staves and ladders.

Memorandum, that Mr Vicar of Lowthe, Thomas Palmer, William Farrand, William White and William Raithbe doth promise from henceforth to pay yearly to the churchwardens of Lowthe for time being for ever the sum of 14d, as it doth appear here underwritten for easement of such grounds as they have in their several tenures, that is to say:

Master Vicar – 4d.
William White – 4d.
Thomas Palmer for Thomas Northe – 2d.
William Raithbe – 2d.
William Farrand for Donnay [Dounay] Ground[4] – 2d.
                                    14d.

All this is granted to be given to the Poor Man's box.

Memorandum, to be paid by the manor of Lowth Parke yearly for easement of waters from Aswell, due to be paid on Plough Day – 2s.

---

1   Marginalia – 'pieces of the skins 2s, to be paid [to] the new churchwardens'.
2   Myles Gray, gentleman, was elected warden in 1562, 1563 and 1570, and churchwarden in 1564/5. Goulding, *Corporation Records*, p. 19. In delivering the town's petition to the queen regarding the purchase of the Louth manor, Gray allegedly bribed his way into Windsor Park and personally presented the application to the monarch. Swaby, *History of Louth*, p. 159. Will: TNA, PROB 11/64/51, probate 1 February 1581/2.
3   Albs.
4   The only place with a similar name today is 'Donna Nook', now on the east coast 2½ miles (4km) north of North Somercotes (TF 422 998). The *OED* suggests for 'donary' – a gift or donation.

f. 16v.

[1562–3]

Anno Domini 1562.

The account of new churchwardens for the present year of all the receipts from the Sunday in the Octaves of Easter in *Anno* 1562 unto the same Sunday *Anno* 1563, that is to say for one whole year.

First, received that was delivered to the hands of the said churchwardens as appearith in the foot of the last account the sum of £9 16s 5½d.
Item received more for six skins of parchment – 2s.
Received for the burial of George Cottam and for the bells – 8s.
Received for the bells by the gift of Richard Sawayghe – 3s.
Received of the plumber for one year's rent of the house in the churchyard – 6s 8d.
Received for the burial of Jenet Nut & for the bells – 7s 8d.
Received of Robert Marshall for hay in Elmyers[1] – 4s.
Received of William Rede for hay in Elmyers – 2s 8d.
Received for half years rent of the plumber's house due at Lammas – 3s 4d.
Received for a bull sold by the churchwardens price – 33s 4d.

f. 17r.

Anno 1562.

Received of James Mansyll for a dead heagle[2] in Elmyers – 5s.
Received for the burial of Leonard Rushbe's wife and for the bells – 7s 4d.[3]
Received for old wood which was sold to Edward Boswell & Nicholas Coventre – 2s 4d.
Received for the burial of Gylyan Walker[4] and for the bells – 7s 8d.
Received for the burial of Isabell Wait and for the bells – 7s 8d.
Received for five score and four pounds of tynne[5] at 6d a pound – 52s.
Received for the burial of Robert Forrest, William Coocke, Thomas Moore and Agnes Nycholson – 3s 4d.
Received that was gathered in the church for the whole year – £5 10d.
Received more for 10lbs of tynne that was sold at 6d the pound – 5s.
Received for the burials of Jenet Flower, Allan Rede, Jenet Freman, Richard Marshall and William Lamb – 3s 4d.
Received more that was gathered in the church by the churchwardens – 3s 5d.

Sum of the whole receipts this year – £23 5s ½d.

---

[1] Two private carriageways are cited in the 1805 Enclosure Award as 'Great and Little Elmire Roads', possibly a derivation of 'Elmyers'. LAO, Louth St James, PAR/17/1. The roads ran left from Stewton Road, now Stewton Lane. Swaby, *History of Louth*, p. 264.

[2] Eagle?

[3] Dorothy Ruschbe was buried 31 October 1562. LAO, Goulding Papers, 5/2.

[4] Julie Walker, widow, was buried 6 March 1562/3. LAO, Goulding Papers, 5/2.

[5] Tin.

f. 17v.
Anno 1562.¹

f. 18r.
Anno 1562.

The payments and allowances with other expenses as here followeth for this present *Anno* 1562.

Item paid to John Serbe for keeping of the sewer at Gosbelle End² – 4d.
Item paid for covering of George Cottam's grave – 4d
Item paid to William Rede for keeping the town kye from Low Sunday to May Day – 4s.
Item paid to Herre Mauborn and James Storre for hedging of the common ground in Elmyers to meat and wages for 4 days at 8d the day – 5s 4d.
Item paid for one cow at Borwell fair³ which the netthord hath – 28s 4d.
Item paid to the writer of this account for his quarter's wages due at May Day – 3s 4d.
Item paid to the plumber for 7 days and a half working [in] the church at 12d the day to meat and wages – 7s 6d.
Item to his servant for 2 days – 2s 1d.
Item for casting and laying of 20 stone [of] lead – 3s 4d.
Item for 8lbs of solder – 5s 4d.
Item paid to the swineherd – 10s.
Item paid for making of the butts – 3s 4d.
Item paid for a ladder – 12d.
Item paid for helping the plumber to Ralf Robson for 7 days – 3s 6d.

£3 17s 9d.

f. 18v.
Anno Domini 1562.

Item for leading of sods to the butts – 2s 8d.
Item paid for 2 locks for the doors going to the leads – 10d.
Item paid to Robert Marshall for stowps⁴ & other wood for the gate at Monks' Dike – 4s.
Item paid to William White for willows to the same gate – 2s.
Item paid for making & setting the said gate – 4s 8d.
Item paid for leading of the stowps & for drink to the waynes⁵ that lead thorns – 6d.
Item paid for a vertevelle, one pick and one howppe⁶ to the gate – 18d.

---

¹ Remainder of the page is blank.
² Gospel End.
³ Burwell, Tuesdays and Thursdays. A charter was granted 5 October 1240 to Ralph de Haya, uncle to Nicholaa de la Haye (d.1230), constable of Lincoln Castle and sheriff of Lincolnshire. *CClR*, 1237–42, p. 228.
⁴ Stoops, posts. *OED*.
⁵ Wainers – a driver of a wain, a wagoner. *OED*.
⁶ Hoop?

Item paid to Mrs Ersbe[1] for 200 of resse[2] for enclosing of Elmyers – 8s 4d.
Item paid to Thomas Grey for 3 mats to the choir – 12d.
Item paid to Ralf Robson for his quarter's wages due at Midsummer – 3s 4d.
Item paid to Robert Kyrkbe for his quarter's wages due at Midsummer – 5s 10d.
Item to William Kyng for wood that the plumber had which was spent in casting of lead – 14d.

35s 10d.

f. 19r.

Anno Domini 1562.

Item paid to Andrew the glazier for mending of the windows about the church – 23s 4d.
Item for mending the vicar's surplice – 4d.
Item paid to the bedle for his quarter's wages due at May Day – 5s.
Item paid to Thomas Leichman for a lock & a bolt to the organs – 12d.
Item paid to Leonard Rushbe that was spent of the Bune Day[3] – 11d.
Item paid to Thomas Gonnell for his wages blowing the organs from Whitsun Day to Midsummer – 4d.
Item paid to Thomas Cowper of Theddylthorpe for a bull – 20s 5d.
Item paid for covering of Jenet Nute's grave – 4d.
Item paid to John Fyswick and Nicholas Thorndicke which was sessed[4] to be paid by the town of Lowthe for draining of the water at Myhell Harphan – 10s.[5]
Item paid to Burton for the town of Lowthe for his fee in keeping the Book of the Sewers – 5s.
Item paid to Gylbert Blanchird for one strike of lime spent about the church – 4d.
Item paid to Gylbert Blanchird in part payment of a pair of shoois[6] that Coggell had – 4d.

£3 7s 4d.

f. 19v.

Anno Domini 1562.

Item paid to one Knyght, a preacher for his sermon given of the benevolence by the township – 6s 8d.[7]

---

[1] Possibly Magdalen Eresby (née Cheke), the widow of Lawrence Eresby (d.1562) and sister-in-law of William Cecil, Lord Burghley. Alford, *Kingship*, p. 145.

[2] Rice.

[3] Boon day.

[4] Assessed.

[5] Harpham is a village between Driffield and Bridlington (TA 092 617). It contained a holy well dedicated to St John of Beverley (d.721), who was allegedly born in the village. Farmer, *Saints*, p. 259. Mykell means Great. *OED*.

[6] Shoes?

[7] Possibly an itinerant preacher authorised to spread the new doctrines.

Item paid to Herre Skurralle[1] for mending of the Crosse and Cawood graves – 16d.
Item paid to the bedle for his quarter's wages due at Lammas – 5s.
Item paid to Nicholas Toye for mowing of the common clois[2] at Elmyers – 3s 4d.
Item paid for making of a gate at St Mary's church with wood for the same – 20d.
Item paid more for mowing in Elmyers – 16d.
Item paid for making of the said hay – 6s.
Item to Robert Marshall for leading of 3 loads from Elmyers – 2s.
Item paid to the writer of this account for his quarter's wages due at Lammas – 3s 4d.
Item paid to Ralf Robson for serving the plumber 7 days – 3s 6d.
Item paid to the plumber for 7 days to meat & wages – 7s.
Item paid more to the plumber for 6 days and a half – 6s 6d.
Item to Ralf Robson for serving him 6 days – 3s.
50s 8d.

f. 20r.

Anno Domini 1562.
Item paid for 9lbs of solder that was occupied about the leads – 6s 4d.
Item paid to Gylbert Blancherd for 400 of six penny nails – 2s.
Item paid for a pound of rosell for the plumber – 2d.
Item paid for 2 strikes of lime – 12d.
Item paid to Robert Kyrckbe for his quarter's wages due at Michaelmas – 5s 10d.
Item paid to Ralf Robson for his quarter's wages due at Michaelmas – 3s 4d.
Item paid to Thomas Gunnel for his wages – 10d.
Item paid for washing of the vicar's surplice – 4d.
Item paid to William Rede for hedging and diking the common hedge – 6d.
Item paid for the covering of Leonard Rushbe's wife's grave – 4d.
Item paid for mending of the stalls in the church by Leonard Rushbe for 3 days – 2s 4d.
Item paid for a plank and nails to the same stalls – 12d.
Item paid for mending of the chimes and for a labourer about the same – 7s 10d.
Item paid for mending of the organs – 12d.
32s 10d.

f. 20v.
Item paid for wood that the plumber spent about [the] leads in making of his fire – 12d.
Item paid to John Parghe, the roper, for two bell-strings – 7s 6d.
Item paid to the bedle for his quarter's wages due at Martinmas – 5s.

---

[1] Henry Skurrall's wife Agnes (5 May 1569), his son John (27 July 1552) and daughter Dorothy (22 January 1558/9) all predeceased him. LAO, Goulding Papers, 5/2.
[2] Close?

Item paid to the writer of this account for his quarter's wages due at Martinmas – 3s 4d.
Item paid for washing of the church cloths at Christmas – 4d.
Item paid for mending of surplices – 4d.
Item paid for paper – 4d.
Item paid for mending of the church picks – 12d.
Item paid to Robert Kyrckbe for his quarter's wages due at Christmas – 5s 10d.
Item paid to Thomas Gunnell for his wages – 10d.
Item paid for one great tree for planks to Aswell – 10s.
Item paid for one tree for making of trestles – 20d.
Item paid for our double spar spent at Aswell – 16d.
Item paid for sawing of the great tree in planks to Gregbe – 3s 4d.
Item to two wrights for their work at Aswell to meat & wages for 3 days – 6s.
Item paid for carriage of the wood to Aswell – 12d.
Item paid to Ralf Robson for his quarter's wages due at Christmas – 3s 4d.
52s 2d.

f. 21r.
Item paid to Robert Cotton for a bolt of iron to Aswell – 6d.
Item paid for dd[1] a lb. of iron ware to the clock – 4d.
Item for one axe hammer to the clock – 14d.
Item paid to Cater for a rope to the said clock – 12d.
Item paid to Thomas Lechman for working about the clock by the space of 14 days – 14s 4d.
Item to William Richardson for his pains about the same – 2s.
Item paid to the bedle for his quarter's wages due at Candlemas – 5s.
Item paid to the writer of this account for his quarter's wages due at Candlemas – 3s 4d.
Item paid to Herre Skurrall and his son for their labour in the church for one day to meat and wages – 2s.
Item to his son for 1 day and a half to meat and wages – 18d.[2]
Item paid to Ralf Robson for 3 days to meat & wages serving them – 18d.
Item paid to Ralf Robson for covering of Gyleane Walker's grave – 4d.
Item paid to Robert Marshall for carrying of trough stones from St Mary's church to this church porch – 16d.[3]
34s 4d.

f. 21v.
Item paid to Mr Bradley for one quarter of lime – 4s.
Item paid to him for 2 hundred of 4 penny nails and a 100 of 6 penny nails – 14d.

---

[1] Half.
[2] '2s' crossed through.
[3] Possibly transferring tomb covers from the now redundant St Mary's to be used in south porch interments.

Item paid for marking all the altar cloths and mending of two surplices – 6d.
Item paid to Kirkbe for washing of the church cloths – 4d.
Item paid to Ralf Robson for his quarter's wages due at Our Lady Day – 3s 4d.
Item paid to Thomas Gunnell for his wages due at the same day – 10d.
Item paid to Ralf Robson for covering of Isabell Wait's grave – 4d.[1]
Item paid to William Richardson for his quarter's wages due at Our Lady Day for keeping the clock and chimes – 7s 6d.
Item paid to Robert Cottame for ironwork to the clock – 4d.
Item to Robert Odlynge for his whole year's wages – 3s 4d.
Item paid to him for working in the steeple and Our Lady's choir – 2s.
Item paid for nails that William Richardson had to the chimes and clock – 4d.

24s.

f. 22r.

Sum of all the payments £18 14s 11d, and yet remaineth in their hands £4 10s 1½d, to the which said churchwardens are charged with 13s 4d received of Robert Odling for the Rood loft, and so remaineth £5 3s 5½d, whereof allowed for the hedge in Haregarthes yet unreceived 20s. And yet there remaineth £3 5s 5½d, which sum the said churchwardens have paid to Gilbert Blanchard, Stephen Buck, John Gray, younger and [Leonard Russhebye][2] & Richard Girsbye, the new churchwardens, over and besides one bull, one chalice and a paten, 2 iron picks, one iron gavelock and one silver piece. Also the said new churchwardens must be charged with 2s received of John Bayllye by the hands of Thomas Baylly.[3] Also they must receive of the old churchwardens 15 pounds[4] of lay[er] metal, 15 pounds of wax, 12 copes and vestments, two albs, 2 bound chests[5] in St Peter's choir, 2 chests and an ark in the church, 3 banner staves and 3 ladders. Also they must receive of certain men for plasshinge in Haregarthes 18s [sold by John],[6] which is to be answered by John Palmer and his fellows which sold the same. Also the said new churchwardens must be charged with 6s which hath been received by the Plough over and above all charges.[7] Also they must be charged with 14d, received and *sparid*[8] by the surveyors of the Boon days. Also the said churchwardens are to be charged with one cow remaining with William Rede the netehurd.[9]

---

[1] Marginalia – the names of John Skelton, William Shepley, Richard Skelton written in a different hand. These are repeated at the foot of the page. Isabel Waite, wife of Roger, buried 16 March 1562/3. LAO, Goulding Papers, 5/2.
[2] [Crossed through].
[3] Recorded in 1561 as a yeoman. Burton, *Old Lincolnshire*, p. 118.
[4] '40' crossed through.
[5] Chests with iron bands for reinforcement.
[6] [Crossed through].
[7] Marginalia – 'received the first day £4 12s 7½d'.
[8] Meaning unknown.
[9] Neatherd, a cowherd. OED.

f. 22v.

Memorandum, their parishioners have chosen John Worth and George Anderson, surveyors for the highways for the year next following, who with the assent of the parishioners have appointed those Boon days hereafter following, that is to say the first to be on Thursday next before the Fair, the second on Friday next after Holy Thursday, the third on Tuesday next after Trinity Sunday, the fourth on Thursday next before Midsummer Day.

[1563–4]

The account of the new churchwardens for this present year of all the receipts from the Sunday in the Octaves of Easter *Anno* 1563 unto the same Sunday in *Anno* 1564, that is to say for one whole year.

First, received that was delivered to the hands of the said churchwardens as appearith in the foot of the last account, the sum of £4 12s 7½d.[1]

Received of William Richmond[2] for his burial 6s 8d & for the bells – 12d.

Received for the hide of the common bull that was bought at Borwell,[3] which died in the field the 17th May – 7s.

Received that was given by Robert Acryd for a legacy to the Poor Man's box – 3s 4d.

Received by the churchwardens which was collected for the quarter to the maintaining of the church due at Midsummer, 25s 11½d.

f. 23r.

Received by the churchwardens which was collected for the quarter for the maintenance of the church due at Michaelmas – 32s 5d.

Received of Thomas Blancherd the 13th day of January of such money as he hath in his hands to the use of the said church works the sum of £7.

Received by the churchwardens which was collected for the quarter to the maintaining of the church due at Christmas, 24s 7d.

Received of John Regall and Robert Odlyng & William White for thorns as appearith in the foot of this account, 13s 6d.

Received for the Plough of the collectors at Plough Day, 3s 8d.

Received of the churchwardens that was collected for the quarter at Our Lady Day, 28s.

Received of Robert Saltmarsh for a rotten willow wrote under Barnard Borne's[4] Close – 4d.

      Total sum – £18 19s 1d.

---

[1] Also written in the margin.
[2] Will: TNA, PROB 11/46/300, probate 9 July 1563. Interred 28 April 1563. LAO, Goulding Papers, 5/2.
[3] Burwell.
[4] Bernard Born.

Received for the burials & the bells in another place is written for such as died this year sum – 51s 8d.
Total sum of all receipts & gatherings this year is £21 10s 9d.
Whereof paid in charges as followeth, £16 14s 11½d, and so remains in the hands of the churchwardens, £4 15s 9½d.
f. 23v. [Blank].
f. 24r.
The receipts for the burials and for the bells as hereafter followeth, the year *Anno* 1563.
First, received at the burial of William Gregbe for the Trinity bell – 8d.
Received of Edward Boswell for the Great bell – 12.+*[1]
Received of John Hanson for the Great bell – 12d.
Received of Robert Whalley for the Great bell – 12d.+*
Received of Thomas Carter for the Trinity bell – 8d.+*
Received of John Bryngkle for the Trinity bell – 8d.+*
Received of Hugh Bowell for the Trinity bell – 8d.
Received for the burial of Robert Acred – 6s 8d,+* and for the Great bell – 12d.+*
Received of Symon Leaper for the Trinity bell – 8d.+*
Received of William Swetyng for the Trinity bell – 8d.+*
Received of Alice Snarforth for the Trinity bell – 8d.*
Received of Margere Salmone of the Trinity bell – 8d.+*
Received of Elizabeth Thomasson – 8d.*
Received of Allice Crosland for the Trinity bell – 8d.*
Received of Robert Patchit for the James – 12d.*
Received of Thomas Watson for the Trinity bell – 8d.+*
Received of Robert Anderson for the Trinity bell – 8d.+*
Received of Isabell Wright for the Trinity bell – 8d.
Received of Bettris Gregbe for the Trinity bell – 8d.+*
Received of Robert Wright for the Trinity bell – 8d.
Received of John Grey, harper, for the Trinity bell – 8d.+*
Received of Jenet Richardson for the Trinity bell – 8d.+*
Received of Annes Grene for the Trinity bell – 8d.
Received of Cateryn Brafurth for the Great bell – 8d.*[2]
Received of Walter Brown for the Great bell – 12d.+*
Received of John Brafurth for his wife's burial in the church porch – 3s 4d.+*
Received of Jenet Lyons for the Trinity bell – 8d.+*
Received of Isabell Raithbe for the James[3] bell – 12d.+*

---

[1] + These names are recorded with a cross in the left margin possibly signifying being in arrears, and those noted as 'received'* are in the right margin.
[2] '12d' crossed through.
[3] 'Trinity' crossed through.

Received of Robert Sall for the Great bell – 12d.+*[1]

f. 24v.

Received of Isabell Brownrick – 8d.*

Received of Catern, the wife of Mr Allote – 12d,* and for her burial – 6s 8d.*

Received for Master Robert Allote for burial in the church – 6s 8d.*

Received for the greatest bell for the same Mr Allote – 12d.*

Received of Edward Nycolls for the Great bell – 12d.*

Received of Bettris Lamb for the Great bell – 12d.*

Received of Thomas Mychell for the Great bell – 12d.

Received of Agnes, the wife of Mathew Wardall for her burial, 6s 8d, and for the bells, 12d.

Sum of the receipts that is received for the burials and the bells which is received – 51s 8d.

Item that there is remaining for the bell that is owing which is unpaid – 6s 4d.

Item that this *Plough* owes for the year rent of the church house this year past 1564 – 6s 8d.[2]

f. 25r.

Anno 1563.

The payments and allowances with other expenses as hereafter followeth for this present *Anno* 1563.

First, paid to John Soirbe for keeping of the sewer at Gospell End – 4d.

Item paid to the bedle for his quarter's wages due at May Day – 5s.

Item paid to the writer of this account and for writing of christenings, weddings and burials – 3s 4d.

Item for one bull bought of Borwell Fair day price – 28s 4d.

Item paid for one cow bought at Lowth Fair day delivered to the swineherd – 26s.

Item paid to Walter Anderson for leading of 19 loads of sods to the great butts – 6s.

Item paid to Auncell Glentham & Thomas Whit for working 2 days about the said butts to meat & wages – 2s 8d.

Item paid to Herre Mawborn & James Storre for labouring & diking 6 days about the said butts to meat & wages – 8s.

Item paid for drink spent at making of the said butts – 4d.

Item paid to Robert Saltmarsh & John Hodgsone for scouring of 140 rods of the north side in the new dike betwix Keddyngton Field and Lowth at a 1d the rod, sum – 11s 8d.

Item paid the same Robert & John for 41 rods scouring more where the wall stood in the same dike at 1½d the rod which was at May Day – 5s 1½d.[3]

---

[1] 'Trinity' crossed through.
[2] This is probably the clergy house situated on Westgate.
[3] Marginalia – '£4 16s 9½d'.

f. 25v.

Anno 1563.

Item paid to Robert Odlyng and his man for 3 days work apiece of them about the dressing of the Fore bell and the Second bell & the Little bell and for stays to St George bell and the Trinity bell at 20d the day to meat & wages – 5s.

Item paid to the said Robert for 2 boards of 7 foot a piece to the mending of the Second bell wheel – 10d.

Item paid to him for 7 stays of wood to the bells – 3d.

Item given to William Richardson for his pains taking about the bells – 4d.

Item paid for a 100 lath nails[1] and 16 penny nails – 4d.

Item paid to Thomas Lechman, the smith for a new clapper of iron to the Second bell and mending the ironwork and for 20 stubbs to the said bell – 20d.

Item to William Richardson for the covering of Robert Acrid and William Richmond's graves – 8d.

Item paid to William Richardson for his quarter's wages for keeping the clock & chimes due at Midsummer – 7s 6d.

Item paid more to him for keeping the bells and the leads due at this day – 3s 4d.

Item paid to Thomas Gonnell for his quarter's wages due at this day – 10d.[2]

f. 26r.

Anno 1563.

Item paid to Robert Kyrkbe for washing the church cloths due at Midsummer – 4d.

Item paid for mending Mr Mychell's surplice and one other surplice – 2d.

Item paid for 2 stone of hemp for a bell-string to the James – 6s.

Item paid to two men for keeping the butts of St James Day in the quarry – 6d.

Item paid for one bull bought of Lammas Day at Ludfurth,[3] price – 26s 9d.

Item paid to Robert Kyrckbe for washing of the church cloths due at Michaelmas – 4d.

Item paid to Thomas Gunnell for his quarter's wages at Michaelmas – 10d.

Item paid to William Richardson for his quarter's wages for keeping the clock & chimes, the bells and leads due at Michaelmas[4] – 10s 10d.

Item paid to the writer of this account and for writing of Christenings, weddings & burials due at Lammas[5] for his quarter's wages – 3s 4d.

Item paid to Thomas Smith for dressing of the chime wheel[6] new in the clock house – 2s 8d.

Item paid to Richard Kirckbe for making of a new table cloth that was given to the communion table this year – 2d.[7]

---

1. Nails for fixing laths upon battens. *OED*.
2. Marginalia – '20s 9d'.
3. Ludford.
4. 'Midsummer' crossed through.
5. 'May Day' crossed through.
6. 'James' crossed through.
7. Marginalia – '51s 11d'.

f. 26v.

Anno 1563.

Item paid to Thomas Pelson for 3 loads of thorns to the hedge betwix Kedyngton and Lowth Field – 6s.

Item paid for one load of hay to William Reade the netterd for his cow – 5s 4d.

Item paid to Mr Ormsbe for 2 gallons [of] wine given to Justices of the Sewers when they sat at Mr Ormsbie's – 2s 8d.

Item paid for a load of hay to the swineherd for his cow – 6s.

Item paid for 2 stone & 2 lbs of hemp to the chime strings – 6s 5d.

Item paid to Jeffrey Wilson for making it – 17d.

Item paid to John Fishwick [and] Garboray[1] for the leavy[2] to Theddlethorpe Corner for 95 acres [of] land in the South Field of Lowith at ½[d] the acre – 3s 11½d.

Item paid for 2 loads of thorn fellings bought of Thomas Pelson and best wood of the hedge betwix Kedyngton & Lowith – 12d.

Item paid to Oliver Watterhous for a day & a half in scouring of Aswell – 10d.

Item paid for 5 stone of hemp to 2 strings to the James[3] and the plumb strings and to the ekynge[4] of the chime string – 12s 6d.

Item paid to Jeffrey's wife for making the same strings – 2s 8d.

Item paid for 2 loads of rysse in Lowith Wood to the hedge betwix Kedyington and Lowith Field – 5s.

Item paid for felling of the said rysse – 12d

Item paid to Auncell Parker and others for carriage of the same 6 loads at 16d – 8s.[5]

Item paid to Herre Mawborne and others for 700 of setts[6] to the said dike – 2s 4d.[7]

£3 5s 1½d.

f. 27r.

Anno 1563

Item paid to Saltmarsh for himself there at the diking & hedging for 10 days and a half at 8d per day to meat & wages – 7s.

Item paid to John Hodgshone for the like work there for 9 days & a half at 8d the day to meat & wages – 6s 4d.

---

[1] In 1566, a John Garbora was recorded as repairing Theddlethorpe Corner. Page 337. Accounts III, *f.* 48v.

[2] Levy – assessment, tax. *OED*.

[3] James bell.

[4] Increase, add to, lengthen. *OED*.

[5] '18d' crossed through.

[6] Possibly 'set sods' – turf used in building up a bank of a ditch. *OED*.

[7] Marginalia – '£3 5s 1½d'.

Item paid for the exchange of a red white-backed cow and a calf bought at Ketsbe[1] Fair which the swineherd had – 2s 6d.
Item paid for the bulls meat[2] at Turrington[3] which strayed thither – 6d.
Item paid to Thomas Grene for fetching him there – 10d.
Item paid Andrew the glazier for work he did last year in William Kyng's time which was owing over [the] year to him – 2s 8d.
Item paid for laying of a bridge over the common dike betwix Steueton Close and Haregarths and for staking and winding[4] of the bank and filling it up at the end of the bridge – 4d.
Item paid to George Kent[5] for carrying of Herre Coggle as prisoner to Lyncoln, the 15th December *Anno predicto*[6] – 5s 6d.
Item paid to the said Kent for the jailer when he received the said prisoner – 12d.
Item paid more to the jailer for straw and irons – 4d.
Item paid Hushe for carrying the pied[7] bull to Cowpers the 22nd of December – 4d.
Item paid for 200 setts more & to Saltmarsh for one day setting them and scouring the dike – 18d.[8]
Item paid for great nails that Robert Odlyng had for mending the stools in the church – 2d.[9]

f. 27v.

Item paid to Thomas the bedle for his quarter's wages due at Lammas – 5s.
Item paid to William Richardson for his quarter's wages for keeping the clock & chimes, the bells and the leads due at Christmas – 10s 10d.
Item paid to Thomas Gunnell for his quarter's wages due at that day – 10d.
Item paid to Robert Kirckbe for the washing of the church cloths due at this day – 4d.
Item paid to the writer of this account & for writing of the christenings, weddings and burials due at Martinmas before – 3s 4d.
Item paid for covering of Mr Allot's grave – 4d.
Item paid to Robert Odlyng for 3 quarters of his wages ended at Christmas – 2s 6d.
Item paid more to him for mending the Trinity wheel and for stays to the same – 8d.

---

[1] Ketsby.
[2] Provide (an animal) with fodder or feed. *OED*.
[3] East or West Torrington, 12½ miles (20km) from Louth.
[4] Widening?
[5] George Kent's two daughters and a son all died within two months of each other. Ellen, 12 June 1561, George, 22 August and Frances, 23 August. LAO, Goulding Papers, 5/2.
[6] 'Year aforesaid' i.e. 1563. The Cogle family were regular receivers of alms.
[7] Marked, dappled, speckled. *OED*.
[8] Marginalia – 'the same dike'.
[9] Marginalia – '29s'.

Item paid to him for mending of 2 seats in the church whereof the one is before Mrs Grey's stool and the other behind St George's choir – 8d.

Item paid to William Whit for one whole years rent for the house that the swineherd dwelleth in – 3s 6d.[1]

f. 28r.

Item paid to William Richardson for his quarter's wages for keeping the clock & chimes, the bells and the leads due at Our Lady Day[2] – 10s 10d.

Item paid to the bellman for covering of Mr Allat[3] & Agnes Wordall's graves – 8d.

Item paid to Thomas Gonnell for his quarter's wages due at this day – 10d.

Item paid for washing the church cloths – 4d.

Item paid to Robert Odlyng for his quarter's wages due at Our Lady Day – 10d.

Item to him for work about the bells – 12d.

Item paid to John Sorbe for the latter half year for keeping the sewer at Gospell – 4d.

Item paid Mawborne for mending the hedge betwix Mr Simcott's close & Gilbert Blancherd's close in Haregarthes – 4d.

Item for nails that Thomas Smithe had for fitting one lock of St Peter's & Our Lady's choir doors – ½d.

Item paid to the same Thomas for 2 keys to the same choir doors – 8d.

Item paid for an iron staple to the west gate in the churchyard – 2d.

Item paid William Jacksone for mending the trundell there – 14d.

Item paid Thomas Smyth for a spring of iron to one of the hammers that leadeth it to strike of the bell – 4d.

£17 17s 5½d.

f. 28v.

Item paid for sack and sugar[4] when William Whit, William King and we went to speak with Mr Tyrwhit[5] & Mr Captain Copledike[6] for order of the town's harness – 10d.

Item paid Thomas Pellson for 2 bulls keeping in his pasture a fortnight apiece of them after Martinmas – 16d.

---

[1] Marginalia – '28s'.

[2] 'Christmas' crossed through.

[3] Robert Allotte, gentleman, was interred 15 January 1563/4, a month after his wife Catherine (17 December 1563). LAO, Goulding Papers, 5/2. Will: TNA, PROB 11/47/85, probate, 4 March 1564.

[4] Sack – a generic name for a class of white wines formerly imported from Spain and the Canaries. *OED*. The sugar was added as a sweetener.

[5] This is possibly Marmaduke Tyrwhitt of Scotter (c.1533–1600), MP for Grimsby in 1558, who in 1564 was noted as being commissioner of the sewers for Lincolnshire. Bindoff, *House of Commons*, III, p. 500 and note.

[6] Probably John Copledike (c.1527–85), sheriff of Lincolnshire in 1567. He was the son of Sir John Copledike (d.1557), MP for the county in November 1554. Bindoff, *House of Commons*, I, p. 694. Maddison, *Lincolnshire Pedigrees*, 50, p. 268.

Item paid for a load of rice to the mending of the hedge from the gate in Our Lady's Close to alongest against the *[E]lmyers* and for stakes – 2s.
Item paid Robert Marshall for leading of the same load – 18d.
Item paid for a crust[1] of a plank to a bridge over the same dike betwixt Kenington Field and us – 6d.
Item paid Saltmarsh & John Hodeson for hedging of the same & for scouring of the dike either of them 2 days apiece at 8d the day to meat and wages being four days the both – 2s 8d.
Item paid to Gilbert Blancherd for keeping of the common bull this winter – 10s.
Item paid Robert Odling in recompense of the timber of the Rood loft which he bought over dear, by the ascent of all the parish at the last [a]count day – 3s 4d.
Item paid the writer of this account & for christenings, weddings and burials for his quarter due at the Annunciation of Our Lady – 3s 4d.
f. 29r.
Paid Robert Saltmarsh for mending certain gaps betwixt Elkington and us – 4d.
Total sum of the charges £16 14s 11½d.[2]
And so remain over and above all charges allowed in the hands of our churchwardens, £4 15s 9½d. Also there remaineth to the use of the church 2 bulls & 2 kyen, which kyen as in the hands of the swineherd & neteherd.
Item that Thomas Plumber oweth for one year's rent of the church house – 6s 8d.
Item owing for the bell as appearith in the book for certain causes[3] – 6s 4d.[4]
Item that Mr Bradley or Walter Browne's wife do owe for a plank – 8d.
Memorandum, that it was agreed that Robert Odlen shall have yearly for his lea of ground that the common hedge standith upon in the North Field – 6d. And the said Robert is paid for the same for all years by past before this day 1564, the 8th day of April.
Memorandum, that the old churchwardens have delivered the sum of £4 15s 9½d above named into the hands of the new churchwardens whose names do consequently follow.

[1564–5]

William Whyte and Thomas Richardson, Myles Gray & George Anderson are elect & chosen to be churchwardens new for this year following, *Anno Domini* 1564.
The Surveyors for the Highways this year following as Nicholas Coventry & Robert Marshall.
f. 29v. [Blank].
Anno 1564.[5]

---

1. A plank cut from the outside of a tree-trunk. *OED*.
2. Marginalia – '17s'.
3. Cause Book – a book in which legal causes are entered. *OED*.
4. '8d' crossed through.
5. Remainder of the page is blank.

f. 30r.

Receipts on Sundays by the churchwardens *Anno* 1564.
First, received the 2nd Sunday after Easter – 23d.
Item received the 3rd Sunday – 2s 10d.
Item received the 4th Sunday – 3s 5½d.
Received the 5th Sunday – 9d.
Received the 6th Sunday – 2s 4d.
Received on Whit Sunday – 2s 8d.
Received on Trinity Sunday – 3s.
Received the 4th day of June – 2s 8d.
Received the 11th day of June – 18d.
Item there was no collection by Thomas Richardson and George Anderson the 18th day of June.[1]
Received the 25th day of June – 6s 5¼d.[2]
Received the 2nd day of July – 3s 8d.
Received the 9th day of July – 3s 7d.
Received the 16th day of July – 2s 8d.
Received the 23rd of July – nothing.[3]
Received the 30th day of July – 2s.
Received the 6th day of August – 3s 4d.
Received the 13th day of August – 2s 4d.
Received the 20th day of August – 2s 9d.
Received the 27th day of August – 15¾d.
Received the 3rd day of September – 2s 2½d.
Received the 10th day of September -2s 3d.
Received the 17th day of September – 21½d.
Received the 24th of September – 2s 3d.
Received the first day of October – 3s 8d.
Received the 10th day of October[4] – 12d.

f. 30v.

Received the 15th day of October – 2s 10d.
Received the 22nd October – 14d.
Received the 29th day of October – 16½d.
Received the 5th day of November – 2s 1d.
Received the 12th day of November – 23d.
Received the 19th day of November – 18d.
Received the 26th day of November – 3s 3½d.
Received the 3rd day of December – 2s 4d.

---

[1] Richardson and Anderson were churchwardens for the year. Did they personally take the collection in church during the service, or were they just nominally in charge?
[2] Increased amount, possibly added on from the previous Sunday.
[3] This is the first time since the Rising that nothing had been collected.
[4] This should be Sunday the 8th of October; the tenth was a Tuesday.

Received the 10th day of December – 2s 9d.
Received the 17th day of December – 2s 8d.
Received the 24th day of December – 4s 2d.
Received the 31st day of December – 2s 8d.
Received the 7th January – 2s 9½d.
Received the 14th January – 19d.
Received the 21st January – 3s 8½d.
Received the 28th day of January – 23d.
Received the 4th day of February – 21d.
Received the 11th day of February – 21d.
Received the 18th of February – 3s ¼d.[1]
Received the 25th day of February – 18d.
Received the 4th day of March – 2s 2½d.
Received the 11th day of March – 2s 1d.
Received the 18th day of March – 23¾d.
Received the 25th of March – 2s 7d.
Received the first day of April – 2s 10d.
Received the 8th day of April – 2s.
Received the 15th day of April – 3s 1d.
Received the 22nd day of April – 12d.
Received the 29th day of April – 4s.[2]

f. 31r.

Receipts for the burials and for the bells as here followeth, *Anno* 1564.
Received for the burial of Peter Welborn for the Trinity bell – 8d.*[3]
Received for the burial of Isabell, the wife of John Northe and for the bells – 7s 4d.*
Received for the burial of Richard Swelynge – 12d.*
Received that was gathered by the Common Plough – 13d.
Received of Catern Holdernes for the Great bell – 12d.*
Received of Eustache Booth for the Great bell.[4]
Received of Allane Banton for the Great bell – 12d.*
Received for the burial of George Lowes – 8d.*
Received for the burial of Mr Chapman and for the bells – 7s 8d.*
Received for the burial of John Macrith and for the bells – 7s 8d.*
Received of Robert Kirckbe for the burial of Robert Patchit's wife which was owing for last year – 12d.*[5]

Sum – 29s 5d.

f. 31v. [Blank].

---

1. '2d' crossed through.
2. Marginalia – '£3 8s 5½d'.
3. Those marked * noted as 'Discharged'.
4. No amount stated.
5. Joanna Pattrick, buried 9 August 1564. LAO, Goulding Papers, 5/2.

f. 32r. [Blank].

f. 32v.

The receipts of all things due to the church of Lowith for this present year besides the bells and burials and the collections with the pece as hereafter followeth.

Received for a cow that was the swineherd's – 15s.

Received of Thomas Butcher for the ridlyng bull[1] – 20s 6d.

Received of Thomas Richardson for to exchange at London for single pennies – 6s 8d.

Received for the burial of Eustace Bowthe and for the bells – 7s 8d.

Sum – 49s 10d.

Sum of all receipts this year was £4 15s 9½d of old money delivered to the churchwardens and of new money collected this year £10 10s 1d, in all £15 5s 10½d.

ff. 33r to *34v.* [Blank].

f. 35r.

Anno 1564.

The payments and allowances with other expenses as hereafter followeth for the present year *Anno* 1564.

First to John Berche for diking and hedging the common hedge in Haregarthe – 8d.

Item paid to Smithson the swineherd at the entering of his service – 1d.

Item paid more to his wife for him in recompense of a cow which he had from May Day to the 28th of the same month and then required to deliver the said cow to the hands of the churchwardens and was content to have in money 10s, which was paid him by the said churchwardens, where upon Gilbert Blancherd & Richard Girsbe is sureties that if he do not serve the whole year that they shall repay so much of the said 10s as is not served for by the said Robert Smythson.

Item paid by William White *Anno* 1564, the 14th day of June to [the] plumber's servant to my Lord Clynton in recompense of 10s which was due to him and other of his fellows for work done by them of the church leads *Anno* 1560,[2] this sum – 5s.

Item paid to Robert Kyrckbe for washing the church cloths at Midsummer – 4d.

16s 1d.

f. 35v.

Item paid to Thomas Gonnell for his quarter's wages at Midsummer – 10d.

Item paid to William Richardson for his quarter's wages due at Midsummer for keeping the clock with the chimes, the bells and the leads – 10s 10d.

Item to the writing of this account & for the writing of christenings, weddings and burials due at May Day – 3s 4d.

---

[1] Possibly a castrated bull. *OED.*

[2] Page 296. Accounts III, *f.* 8r.

Item paid to Andrew Fene for dressing of all the low windows of both sides in the church, he finding all charges except lime and sand – 13s 4d.
Item paid to Auncell Parker for one load of sand – 4d.
Item paid to William Richardson for bearing of sand to the glazier – 2d.
Item paid to him for covering Isabel North's grave – 4d.
Item paid to William Richardson of working with the plumber about the church – 12d.
Item paid to the plumbers for removing ashes in the lead house – 2d.
Item paid for wire to the clock and chimes – 12s.
Item paid to Andrew Fene & another plumber for working of the leads – 11s 2d.
Item paid for the leading 4 loads of stone for the mending of the church walls – 12d.

54s 6d.

f. 36r.
Item paid to Gilbert Blancherd for ten bushels of lime for mending the walls about the churchyard and for lime bestowed about windows by the glazier – 10s.
Item paid to Nicholas Toye for stakes to the hedging of the north side of the new bridge at the east end of the town – 6d.
Item paid to the writer of this account for writing of christenings, weddings and burials due at Lammas – 3s 4d.
Item paid Isabell Wylingam for dressing of Aswell – 8d.
Item paid to Thomas Gonnell for his quarter's wages due at Michaelmas – 10d.
Item paid for the mending of the church lantern – 10d.
Item paid to Robert Kirckbe for washing the church cloths at Michaelmas – 4d.
Item paid to William Richardson for his quarter's wages at Michaelmas for keeping the clock with the chimes, the bells and the leads – 10s 10d.
Item paid for the charges of Mr Smith's man to Lyncoln castle – 6s 8d.
Item paid to Thomas Grey for one nat[1] in the high ally – 4d.
Item paid for candles occupied about the chimes in the steeple – 8d.

35s.

f. 36v.
Item to Herre Mawborne for making the fleick[2] to cover the well in the Market Place – 4d.
Item paid to Ralf Flower for carrying a prisoner to Lyncoln – 3s 4d.
Item paid to Thomas Gonnell for his quarter's wages at Christmas – 10d.
Item paid to Robert for washing the church cloths at Christmas – 4d.
Item paid to Robert Odlyng & his servant for working about the bells and the clock 9 days – 6s.
Item paid to William Richardson for his quarter's wages at Christmas for keeping the clock with the chimes, the bells and the leads – 10s 10d.

---

[1] A mat used in church, presumably to kneel upon. *OED*.
[2] Possibly a flitch, planks fastened side by side to form a compound beam. *OED*. Edward Peacock suggests 'fleak', a hurdle. Peacock, 'Sutterton', p. 61.

Item paid to William Richardson for mending of stones in the church walls – 4d.
Item paid to William Jacson for one piece [of] wood to the barrel for the chimes – 3s.
Item paid to Thomas Gonnell for his quarter's wages at Our Lady Day – 10d.
Item paid to Martyn Chapman for dressing of Aswell – 6d.
Item paid to Jenet Richmond for one piece of wood for the barrel to the chimes – 2s 4d.
Item paid to the writer of this account and writings of christenings, weddings & burials due for Michaelmas and Candlemas quarters – 6s 8d.

35s 4d.

f. 37r.

Item paid to William Richardson for his quarter's wages at Our Lady Day & for keeping the clock & chimes, the bells and leads – 10s 10d.
Item for the covering of Mr Chapman, Eustace Booth[1] and John Macrythe's graves – 10d.
Item paid to Arthur Bentley by Thomas Richardson in part of payment for mending the chimes – 8s.
Item paid to William Whyte for exchange of pence at London and had them not – 6s 8d.
Item paid to Arthur Bentley in part of payment for mending the chimes, paid by George Anderson – 6s 8d.
Item paid more by George Anderson to the said Arthur for mending the said chimes – 12s.
Item paid more by George Anderson to the said Arthur for mending the said chimes – 46s 8d.
The parcels paid by William White as here follow.
First paid for the carriage of one cow to the Fair to be sold – 4d.
Item paid to my Lord's men the 22nd July 1564 – 5s.[2]
Item paid to Dixson, tiler, for 5 days and a half about the church walls the 5th August – 3s 8d.
Item paid to him that served him the same time for 5 days work – 2s 6d.
Item paid to Ralf Flower for the carriage of a prisoner to Lyncoln the 19th day of August – 3s 4d.
Item paid for a service book – 4s.

£5 5s 10d.

f. 37v.

Item paid for a 100 of lead nails – 4d.
Item paid for white wax – 2d.
Item paid for 10lbs 6 ounces of puder[3] – 6s 1d.

---

[1] Eustace Booth, son of Eustace, gentleman, buried 2 March 1564/5. LAO, Goulding Papers, 5/2.

[2] Marginalia – 'this is not in charge'.

[3] Either powder or pewter. *OED*.

Item paid for a 100 of nails – 6d.
Item more for nails – 2d.
Item paid for great nails – 4d.
Item paid to the plumber in money the 18th day of August – 12d.
Item more for a 100 of great nails – 15d.
Item paid for one load of hay for William Rede – 6s.
Item paid more for nails – 4d.
Item paid for 8 yards and [a] quarter of linen cloth for a surplice to the Vicar at 16d the yard – 11s.
Item for thread to the same surplice – 2d.
Item paid to Mrs Misterchambers for making of the same – 22d.
Item paid to Arthur Bentley the maker of the chimes in part of payment of his wages – 20s.
Item paid to Ralf Flower for his charges at Lyncoln and in reward for the harness – 4s 2d.[1]
Item paid for iron and workmanship of the bolts about the church gates – 18d.
Item paid for 2 double padlocks about the same gates – 16d.
Item paid for laying down a plank at Stueton Bridge – 4d.
Item paid for a lock to the font – 4d.[2]
Item to Diconson for mending the church gates – 4d.
Item paid to John Grey, Wright & Diconson for working 16 days about the chimes – 10s 8d.
Item paid to Thomas Lechman, smith for work about the bells, the 12th of March – 4s.
Item paid to him for working about the clock – 6d.
£3 13s 10d.

f. 38r.
Item paid more for an axle tree about the chimes – 6d.
Item paid more for working about the clock – 8d.
Item paid to him [Thomas Lechman] for iron for the font – 6d.
Item paid to him for a lock and a key to the bell house door – 10d.
Item paid for keeping of the bulls from Martinmas to May Day – 20d.
Item paid for a homily book delivered to Mr Vicar – 4s 6d.
Item paid to Robert Odlyng for his whole year's wages – 3s 4d.[3]
Item paid to Robert Kirckbe for washing the church cloths due at Our Lady Day – 4d.
Item to Robert Odlyng for one lea in the North Field that the common hedge standith upon – 6d.
Sum of all payments £17 11s 9d, & so the said churchwardens are in surplusage

[1] Flower would have worn a form of armour (harness) when transporting prisoners.
[2] Fonts were covered and locked to preclude theft of the consecrated baptismal water for nefarious purposes.
[3] Marginalia – '31s 2d'.

45s 10¾d. Paid more to Gilbert Blanchard as appearith by his bill for one bull 21s, a yard of harden cloth[1] 6d, for nails 1d, for a yard of canvas 6d & for 15lbs & [a] half of iron, 22d. Which bill in all cometh to the sum of 23s 11d, and the surplusage is £3 9s 9d, which the warden of the town and school is contented to pay of such money as is in his hands and is also contented further to deliver to the new churchwardens this year 24s 6d, and for the whole sum which the said warden hath paid the said church is £4 14s 3d.

f. 38v.

[1565–6]

Anno Domini 1565.

Memorandum, that the parish hath elected for the year following, Robert Chapman, Tanner and Mathew Wardall, the old churchwardens and Robert Holland and Roger Stut, the new churchwardens.

The said churchwardens are charged with two bulls & one cow in the keeping of William Rede & with 24s 6d paid to them by the hands of John Bradley, warden.

Item Thomas Plommer oweth for two years rent to the house in the church yard at 6s 8d by year to be received by the said churchwardens.

Item there is owing for bells 4s, *videlicet* Margaret Grymsbie 8d, Henry Mawburne 8d, Isabel Penny 8d, Jenet Michelson 12d & Agnes Parker 12d.

For highways.

The names of the Surveyors for Highways for this year 1565; William Sandeson, gentleman, Thomas Wake, Robert Holland & Anthony Wilson.

The first Boon day, the 8th of May; the second, the 15th of May; the third, the 22nd of May; the 4th, the first of June; the 5th, the 7th of June; the 6th, the 30th of June.

Memorandum, that the said surveyor have made their account the 21st of October 1565 for the year last past according to the statute & there remains in their hands over & besides all their charges & payments to be delivered to the new surveyors the sum of 8s besides the amercements of certain men which have not laboured in the Boon days.

f. 39r.

The 29th day of May in the seventh year of the reign of Our Sovereign Lady Queen Elizabeth.

There remained in the hands of Thomas Blanchard the 13th day of April *Anno Domini* 1561 of the church money as appearith in our old church book the sum of £79 8s 2d. Whereof the same Thomas hath paid for the diking of a dike betwixt Kedington and Lowth as appearith in the same old book the sum of £14 15s 3d.

Item paid by the said Thomas Blanchard to Gilbert Blanchard and Richard Girsbe, churchwardens 1563, £7.

---

[1] A coarse fabric made of flax or hemp. *OED*.

Item paid to Mr Smith at Boston for his counsel and drawing a book for the corporation & fee farm, £6 13s 4d.
Sum of the Payments – £28 8s 7d.
And so remaineth £50 19s 7d. Whereof in the hands of Roger Wathe £8, and paid by Mr Warden to the said churchwardens for their surplusage in their account this year 69s 9d. Paid by him more to the new churchwardens in ready money towards the repair of the church 24s 6d. And so remaineth £38 5s 4d, besides the said £8 in R[oger] Wat's hands.

Paid more by Mr Bradle the warden to the hands of Mathew Wardall for the use of the church, £3.[1]

Memorandum, that all the money above named to be in the hands of Thomas Blanchard is now returned into the hands of the warden & assistants paid by Gilbert Blanchard, warden, to the churchwardens 7th July 1566 of the sum above named in part payment thereof the sum of £3.

Received more of Mr Gilbert Blanchard, warden, in part of this sum by the hands of the churchwardens *Anno Domini* 1566, the sum of 40s.

Received more of the said warden by the said churchwardens the 6th day of April 1567 the sum of 20s more.

f. 39v.

Anno Domini 1565.
Receipts for burials and for the bells as here followeth.

Received of Agnes Parker for the Great bell – 12d.
Received of Walter Cowper for his burial and for the bells – 7s 8d.
Received of Thomas Wynskall for the Great bell – 12d.
Received of William Somerskells for the bell – 12d.
Received of John Croslande for the bell -12d.
Received of Thomas Croslande – 8d.
Received of Herre Mawborn – 8d.
Received of William Hawe – 12d.
Received of Jenet Mychelson for her burial and for the bells – 7s 8d.
Received of Richard Shepperd – 12d.
Received of Elizabeth Robynson.[2]
Robert Cowper – 8d.
Received of John Wilkynson – 8d.
Received of Thomas Inglyshe – 8d.
Received of Robert Robynson – 12d.
Received for the burial of Thomas Inglyshe – 6s 8d.
32s 4d.

---

[1] The text is in different hands spread unevenly across the page, perhaps indicating later additions concerning the Corporation. This also illustrates the close cooperation between the two entities, church and local authority.

[2] No amount stated.

f. 40r.

Anno Domini 1565.

Receipts on Sundays by the churchwarden.

Received the 6th day of May for the first collection – 3s 7d.
Received the 13th day of May – 2s 2½d.
Received the 20th day of May – 3s 1½d.
Received the 27th day of May – 2s 1¾d.
Received the 3rd day of June – 2s 3¼d.
Received the 10th day of June – 2s 11½d.
Received the 17th day of June – 3s 10d.
Received the 24th day of June – 3s 5½d.
        23s 7d.
Received which was collected by the quarter of the year from Midsummer to Michaelmas the sum of 35s 9d.
Received at Christmas which was collected by the quarter the sum of 26s 1d.
Received at Our Lady Day collected by the quarter – 34s 5d.
Received by the constables of certain highways payable of the Plough Day – 12d.
        £4 17s 3d.

Sum of the collections for the whole year is £6 10d.

f. 40v. [Blank].

f. 41r.

Anno Domini 1565.

The receipts of all things due to the church of Lowthe for this present year besides the bells and burials and the collection with the pece as hereafter followeth.

Received first of Mr Bradley, the warden, as appearith before written to the use of the church in the foot of the last account, £3.
Received for 2 bulls that was sold, price 56s.
Received more as appearith in the foot of the last account the sum of 24s 6d.
        £7 6d.
Sum total of the whole charge wherewith the churchwardens as charged with this year, £14 13s 8d.

f. 41v.

The payments and allowances with other expenses for this present year as hereafter followeth.

First, paid to a brick layer[1] for his work about the north side of the church wall – 5s.
Item for a bushel of lime to the same work – 12d.
Item paid for leading 8 loads of stone and sand to the same work – 2s 8d.

---

[1] This is the first entry in the accounts that uses the term 'brick layer', as against 'tiler' or 'brick tiler'.

Item paid to Thomas Holdernes for stone that was digged the last year to the highways & not allowed in the last account – 20d.
Item paid to William Richardson for his labour about the chimes the last year when Arthur Bentley made them – 2s 6d.
Item for the writing of this account and the writing of weddings, burials & christenings due at this May Day for his quarter's wages – 2s 4d.
Item paid to Ralf Flower for bringing harness from Lyncoln – 12d.
Item paid to Smithson the swineherd in recompense of one cow for one whole year – 10s.
Item paid the hands of Gylbert Blanchard which he paid to John Fishwicke for landlaw[1] of 80 acres[2] to Theddlethorpe Corner at a penny the acre as appearith by a quittance[3] for the same – 7s 11d.
Item paid for making of the butts in the quarry – 5s 6d.
Item paid to Richard Gyrsbe for leading of 13 loads [of] sods to the same butts – 3s.
Item paid to Thomas Gonnell for his quarter's wages due at Midsummer – 10d.
44s 5d.

f. 42r.
Item paid to Robert Kirckbe for washing the church cloths at Midsummer – 4d.
Item paid to William Richardson for his quarter's wages due at Midsummer for keeping the clock and chimes, the bells and the leads – 10s 10d.
Item paid to Anthony Wylson, one of the constables, to make up the whole sum of the tax money – 20d.
Item paid to William Rede, the netherd for one load of hay – 5s 4d.
Item paid for one key to the little house in the churchyard – 4d.
Item paid for one cruyck[4] to the gate at the new bridge – 4d.
Item paid for rosell to the glazier – 1d.
Item paid for 3lb of solder to the glass windows – 21d.
Item paid to the glazier for 2 days work and a half – 20d.
Item paid to the writer of this account for writing christenings, weddings and burials due at Lammas – 3s 4d.
Item paid to Herre Skenrall for 4 days in mending Bishop Bridge[5] – 4s.

---

[1] Law of a land or country; the 'law of the land' originated in the use of the land for grazing. *OED*.
[2] The text is unclear as to the actual amount.
[3] The action of freeing from a debt or obligation. *OED*.
[4] Cruck?
[5] Bishop's Bridge was associated with the Hall Mill, noted in the *compotus* of the manor court in 1565. In 1545, William King, the bailiff, and Richard Curson, both described as 'yomen', leased a water mill called the Hall Mills from the bishop. Benton, *Early Days*, p. 52. Cole, *Chapter Acts*, II, p. 106. Goulding, *Corporation Records*, p. 64, note 1. Lincs to the Past, MLI91837.

Item paid for 4 strikes of lime – 2s.
Item for leading a load of stone to the said work – 4d.
Item paid to Gilbert Blanchard for wine given to the Justices of the Sewer for viewing of a strait[1] towards Stueton Bridge – 2s.
34s.

f. 42v.
Item paid to Thomas Gonnell for his quarter's wages at Michaelmas – 10d.
Item paid to William Richardson for his quarter's wages at Michaelmas for keeping the clock and chimes, the bells and the lead – 10s 10d.
Item given in reward to a glazier that did come to see work about the church – 20d.[2]
Item paid to Herre Totte for making scaffolds in the steeple and for helping the glazier to stay[3] his ladders – 3s 4d.
Item paid to the bellman for covering Walter Cowper's grave – 4d.
Item paid to Andrew Fene for 18 days work about the church windows – 15s 2d.
Item paid to William Cooke for 19 days work about the same windows – 16s.
Item paid to William Richardson for serving them 19 days – 3s 4d.
Item paid to Wyndkell's wife for solder to the same work – 2s 4d.
Item paid to Mr Bradley for 4 sheifs[4] of glass – 10s.
Item paid to the writer of this account due at Martinmas for writing of christenings, weddings and burials – 3s 4d.
Item for a year's rent of Thomas Grey, the swineherd which he charged this town withal – 8s.
£7 15s 2d.

f. 43r.
Item paid for one bull bought at Martinmas Fair – 26s 9d.
Item paid for 2 labourers of Kedyngton for diking of the common hedge betwix Lowth & Keddyngton for 9 hundred rods – 16s.
Item paid to Thomas Lecheman for making a new pulley to the clock with other work – 2s 4d.
Item paid to Gilbert Blanchard for 3 strikes lime […][5] in July to William Richardson […][6] 3 strikes of lime – 18d.
Item paid to Thomas Gonnell for his quarter's wages at Christmas – 10d.

---

[1] Street. Alternatively, a way, passage or channel so narrow as to make transit difficult. *OED*.
[2] There appears to have been a considerable amount of work on the windows over a lengthy period. Was this possibly a process of replacing stained glass with plain?
[3] Hold.
[4] Sheaf or sheiffes – plates of glass. *OED*.
[5] Illegible.
[6] Indecipherable.

Item paid to William Richardson for his quarter's wages due at Christmas for keeping the clock and chimes, the bells and the leads – 10s 10d.
Item paid for covering Jenet Mychelson's grave – 4d.
Item paid for one rope to the plumber – 22d.
Item paid to William Rushebe & Thomas Diconson for 5 days [and a] half working of the house in the churchyard – 5s.
Item paid for 2 pane pieces to the house – 4s.
Item paid for 15 spars and 2 wyvers[1] – 6s 4d.
Item for plaster stacks and nails – 3s 7d.
Item paid to a glazier for one day's work about the church – 8d.
Item paid to Jeff for one bell-string – 18d.
$$£4\ 18d.$$

f. 43v.
Item paid to William Richardson for helping the wrights about the church house – 8d.
Item paid to Robert Odlyng for his half year that was due at Martinmas – 20d.
Item to him for one day's work about the bells and for one board and nails to the said work – 16d.
Item paid to the writer of this account due at Candlemas for writing of christenings, weddings & burials – 3s 4d.
Item paid to William Rushbe and Thomas Diconson for 2 days [and a] half work about the church gates and the trundell – 3s 4d.
Item for wood to the same work – 3s 10d.
Item paid for ironwork to the same – 14d.
Item paid to William Richardson for his quarter's wages due at Our Lady Day for keeping the clock and chimes, the bells and the leads – 10s 10d.
Item paid to Thomas Gonnell for his wages due at that day – 10d.
Item paid to Robert Odlyng for his half year's wages due at Our Lady Day – 20d.
Item paid to the vicar for one piece of wood that remains in the steeple for mending the glass windows – 20d.
Item paid to William Kyng for one piece of wood remaining in the steeple – 2s 2d.[2]
Item to him boards that was occupied in the church – 8d.
$$33s\ 2d.$$

f. 44r.
Item paid for mending of St Peter's choir door – 2d.
Item paid for paper – 1d.
Item paid for 4 yards [of] linen cloth for one surplice to the clerk – 4s 6d.
Item for 2 psalters to the church – 3s.

---

[1] Wiver – a long beam of wood in the roof of a house. *OED.*
[2] '20d' crossed through.

Item paid to John Erlle [Earl] for mending stools in the church and for sleepers[1] and nails to the same – 14d.
Item paid to William Richardson for covering of the graves of Mr Lawrence Ersbe[2] and Thomas Inglishe[3] – 8d.
Item paid to Robert Holland for keeping the common bull 2 weeks – 10d.
Item for laths and nails to Roger Stute spent about the house in the churchyard – 2s 8d.
Item paid to William White for keeping of the common bull from Martinmas to May Day – 10s 4d.
23s 5d.
Sum total of all payments this year £14 11s 8d, & so remains in the churchwardens hands of their receipts this year over & besides those payments to be delivered to the new churchwardens, 2s.
Remaining also in the hands of the old churchwardens to be delivered unto the new churchwardens, one bull & one cow in the hands of William Reade, whereof paid to Robert Odlen for the rent of one lea in the North Field that the common hedge standith upon next Kennyngton town 6d, & so remains in money in the old churchwardens hands, 18d.

f. 44v.

[1566–7]

1566

The surveyors of the common works appointed this year for the highways are Thomas Pelson, William Hewet, Robert Salmon & John Scopholm the which surveyors have received of the old surveyors the sum of 8s 4d.
Also they are charged with the collection certain marsyments[4] of certain persons which have not laboured according to the statute in the Boon days
And these be the Boon days for this year following
1 The first Boon day is the 9th day of May.
2 The second is the 20th day of May.
3 The third is the Friday after the Ascension Day.[5]
4 The fourth if the Thursday in Whitsun Week
5 The fifth is the 17th day of June.
6 The sixth is the 21st day of June.
The said surveyors above named have made their account the 6th day of April

---

[1] A horizontal beam, plank. *OED.*
[2] This entry is puzzling as Lawrence Eresbe was interred 9 January 1561/2. LAO, Goulding Papers, 5/2.
[3] Thomas Inglishe (Inglisch) was buried 13 March 1565/6. LAO, Goulding Papers, 5/2.
[4] Amercement.
[5] May.

1567 for the year then ended & they have delivered of the remainder of their collections 6s in money before three new picks that they have made & also 2 old picks & a gavelock that was made before, which 6s in money 5 picks and a gavelock are delivered into the hands of the new surveyors for the year following whose names be hereafter written, that is to say Thomas Blancherd, Steaven Spaldyng, Roger Stut & John Sowthe.

f. 45r.

1566.

Memorandum, that Richard Robenson & Thomas Pelson are the old churchwardens for this year following & Thomas Smyth, butcher, & William Holland for the new churchwardens.

The said churchwardens are charged with one bull & with one cow in the hands of William Reade & also with 18d in money, which they have received of the old churchwardens for the last year past 1565, besides 2 iron picks & a gavelock and the said 18d was paid to Isabell Wyllyngam for her fee for dressing of Aswell for 3 quarters of the year ended at May Day next written, the 21st day of April.

These be the receipts collected by the churchwardens quarterly as hereafter doth appear that is to say at Midsummer for the first quarter the sum of – 29s 9d.

Item, collected by the churchwardens at Michaelmas for the second quarter – 26s 4d.

Item, collected by the churchwardens at Christmas for the 3rd quarter – 25s 10d.

Item, collected by the churchwardens at Our Lady Day for the last quarter – 24s.

£5 5s 11d.

f. 45v.

Anno Domini 1566.

Receipts for the burials and for the bells as is following.[1]

Received of John Somerskells for the Great bell – 12d.
Received of Jenet Crosland – 12d.
Received of Richard Walker – 8d
Received of Elizabeth Erlle – 8d.
Received of William, the son of William Balley for his burial and for the bells – 7s 8d.
Received of George, the son of William Symcot, gentleman for his burial and for the bells – 7s 8d.
Received of Elizabeth, the wife of William Rowce for the bells – 8d.
Received of Thomas, the son of Thomas Crosland.[2]

---

[1] Those marked * have 'allo^r' for *allocatur* written in the margin: translated 'it is allocated'.

[2] No amount stated.

Received of Allis Crosland, widow – 8d.
Received of Margaret Watson.[1]
Received of Anthony Ranold – 8d.*
Received of John Grey, wright – 12d.
Received of William Beysbe – 8d.
Received of John Holme – 12d.
Received of Phillip Forman – 8d.[2]
Received of Annes Burret – 8d.*
Received of William Galside.[3]
Received of Thomas Tomson.[4]
Received of Annes Joy – 12d.*[5]
Received of Richard Askew – 8d.*
Received of Jenet Catterall.*[6]
Received of Richard Spaldynge – 12d.*
Received of John Skopholm – 12d.*
Received of Christopher Chapman – 12d.*
Received of Elizabeth Leve – 12d.*
Memorandum, owing by Thomas Pattyson for one year's rent of the work house[7] in the churchyard endith at May Day *Anno* 1567 – 5s.

f. 46r.

The receipts of all things due to the church this present year, besides the bells and burials and the collection which the piece as hereafter followeth.
Received first for the hide of a bull which was given to the poor folks – 8s.
Received of Mr Gilbert Blancherd, warden, the 7th of July 1566 in part of payment of a more sum which the said warden & assistants as charged in a former account to pay unto the churchwardens the sum of £3.
Received for the branches and flowers[8] that was of the coppice which was sold to John Morley the goldsmith of Lyncoln – 40s.
Received of Thomas Blancherd for one little hand bell – 6d.[9]
Received of William Kyng for one pair of censors – 12d.

[1] No amount stated. Marginalia – '22s 8d'.
[2] '12d' crossed through.
[3] No amount stated. Marginalia – '22s 8d'.
[4] No amount stated.
[5] Agnes Joye, interred 17 January 1566/7. LAO, Goulding Papers, 5/2.
[6] No amount stated.
[7] Possibly the plumber's house?
[8] Possibly to be turned into ornamental work. *OED*.
[9] The following entries indicate that church fittings previously used in Catholic ceremonies were being sold in order to adhere to new liturgical regulations. This process probably commenced in the early years of Elizabeth's reign, and these entries were being compiled and eventually deposited at the cathedral. At Saxilby in 1566, Alexander Pereson was paid 20d to travel to Lincoln with the 'Inventory of Superstitious Ornaments'. Gibbons, 'Saxilby', p. 387. See Introduction.

Received of William White for one crosseit[1] and one holy water vat – 3s.
Received of John South for 2 candlesticks – 3s 4d.
Received of Robert Holland for 2 small candlesticks – 20d.
Received of Thomas Blancherd for 2 sides of wood that belonged to the Sepulchre light – 3s 4d.
Received of William Holland for one passyon cloth[2] – 2s 8d.
Received of Thomas Blanchard for one cloth that did hang before the Rood – 3s 6d.
Received of William Kyng for one painted altar cloth – 16d.
Received of Thomas Smythe, butcher, for one painted altar cloth – 10d.
Received of Gilbert Blancherd in money to the charges bestowed about Aswell – 40s.
Sum of the receipts £14 18s 5d.[3]
Received more of Mr Gilbert Blancherd, warden, by the said churchwardens the 6th day of April 1567 as appearith in another account before witnesses the sum of 20s.[4]
Total Sum – £15 18s 5d.
f. 46v. [Blank].
f. 47r.
Anno Domini 1566.
These be the payments and allowances unto the ministers of the church due unto them as standing fees and paid yearly as hereafter it doth appear.
First paid to the writer of this account and for writing of christenings, weddings and burials due at May Day to be paid quarterly the sum of 3s 4d – 13s 4d.
Item paid to William Richardson for his fee due at Midsummer for keeping the clock with the chimes, the bells and the leads to be paid quarterly, 10s 10d, [total] 43s 4d.
Item paid to Robert Odlyng for his fee due at Midsummer to be paid quarterly 10d, [total] – 3s 4d.
Item paid to Thomas Gonnell for blowing of the organs due at Midsummer – 3s 4d.
Item paid to Robert Chapman for washing church cloths due at Midsummer – 16d.
Item paid to Isabell Willyngam for keeping and dressing of Aswell due at May Day – 2s.
Total Sum – £3 6s 8d.
Item more to Robert Kirckbe for his services in the choir due at Midsummer to be paid quarterly, 3s 4d, [total] – 13s 4d.
£3 14s 8d.

---

[1] Either a cruet or a crosselette, a small cross. *OED*.
[2] A cloth that covered the Rood during Lent.
[3] Marginalia – '£8 9s 2d'.
[4] Marginalia – '£8 1s 2d'.

f. 47v.

Anno Domini 1566.

The payments and allowances with other expenses for the present year as hereafter followeth.

First paid for making of a gate at Monks' Dike wrought by Thomas Bradley – 16d.

Item paid for a hook and a bolt of iron for the same – 6d

Item paid for wood to the same gate – 3s.

Item paid to Thomas Ingram of Carlton[1] for a thousand of thatch to the house in the churchyard – 11s.

Item paid to George Chapman, thatcher for 3 days work on the church house in thatching and walling the same at 8d per day to meat & wages – 2s.

Item paid to his wife & his daughter for their work about the said house at 3d apiece to meat & wages – 18d.

Item paid for shaking the thatch by the said George – 2d.

Item paid to Richard Robynson for one spar to the same house – 8d.

Item paid more to George Chapman for thatching of the said church house for 2 days to meat and wages for himself, his wife and his daughter serving him – 2s 8d.

Item paid for sewing rope to the same work – 8d.

Item paid for 2 loads of clay to the said house – 7d.

Item paid for 6 thraves of straw to the same – 18d.

Item paid at the visitation of the chancellor's clerk for our bills – 6d.

Item paid to Smythson, the swineherd, in recompense of a cow for one year – 10s.

36s 1d.

f. 48r.

Anno 1566.

Item paid to a plumber for viewing of the decayed places of the church leads – 12d.

Item paid to Herre Day of Skidbrouke[2] for the copy of a streyt[3] wherein the new bridge was in pain of amercement – 8d.

Item paid to the pariter's[4] fees when we were at Lyncoln at the visitation – 12d

Item paid to Mr Tailer for his fees there – 20d.

Item paid for ourselves and our horse's charges there – 8d.

Item paid for mending a door in Our Lady's choir – 4d.

Item paid for mending the *wr...th*[5] of the clock – 4d.

Item paid to William Rede, the netterd, for one load of hay – 6s.

Item paid for mending the bridge at Stueton Lane and against Bargars[6] – 8d.

---

1 Either Great or Little Carlton.
2 Skidbrooke.
3 Possibly strait or street.
4 Apparitor – an officer of an ecclesiastical court. *OED*.
5 Indecipherable.
6 Possibly a misspelling of Haregarth, a part of the south field of Louth.

Item paid for one strike of lime and one load of sand for mending of decayed places about the leads – 11d.
Item paid to a bell founder that did see the ryven bell[1] – 8d.
Item paid in charges for 2 times riding to the Commissioners at Alforthe[2] – 18d.
Item paid to the bellman for covering of the graves of William Baille & George Symcot – 8d.

16s 1d.

f. 48v.
Item paid to Robert Odlyng for his work about the bells, the 3rd day of October – 10d.
Item for boards & nails to the same work – 8d.
Item paid to Auncell Jeff for a bell rope to the Second bell – 18d.
Item paid to William Dixon, tiler for 3 days labour about Aswell at 10d the day to meat and wages – 2s 6d.
Item paid to Ralf Robson for 2 days to meat and wages – 14d.
Item paid to William Bell for leading a load of stone & clay – 16d.
Item paid to Walter Smyth for mending of the fethers[3] and wedges about the Trinity bell – 18d.[4]
107r
Item paid for nails bestowed upon the decayed doors in the steeple – 1d.
Item paid to John Garbora for the repair of Theddlethorpe Corner – 7s 11d.
Item paid to John Craggs for the digging of 10 loads of stone at Lowth Park which was bestowed at Haswell[5] – 3s 4d.
Item paid to Robert Odling for his work about the Trinity [bell] – 16d.
Item paid for a bull to Thomas Butcher – 30s.
Item paid for our bull pinding and slaughtering at Kedington – 12d.
Item paid for a lock to the chest in the bell house – 6d.
Item paid to Heri Skorell and his son for 3 days work about the church porches & other decayed places at 10d the day – 2s 6d.[6]

f. 49r.
Anno 1566.
Item paid to Gilbert Blancherd for 3 strikes of lime to the said work – 15d.
Item paid Richard Stowte for mending of the steeple door lock & for the staple to the same – 5d.
Item for tile stones to the south porch – 4d.

---

    1   Riven – torn, rent, split, cracked. *OED*.
    2   Alford.
    3   Fetters – chains, fasten, shackle. *OED*.
    4   Marginalia – 'November'.
    5   Aswell. Louth Park Abbey was apparently still being used as a stone quarry, thirty years after closure.
    6   Marginalia – '58s 8d'; '56s 2d' crossed through.

Item paid to Brian Parish for his work about Aswell – 3s.
Item paid for a piece of wood to Robert Sheperd that was occupied about the spout – 16d.
Item paid to Leonard for sawing the said piece of wood and for laying it at the said spout – 10d.
Item paid to the constables for carrying Saltmarsh[1] to Lyncoln castle – 5s.
Item paid for the carrying of Ferrebe to the same castle – 3s 6d.
Item paid for making of a surplice to the clerk – 8d.
Item paid for 4 yards and a quarter of linen cloth for a surplice to William Mychell and for the making of it – 3s 10d.
Item paid to Robert Odlyng for the rent of one ley in the North Field that the common hedge standith upon toward Keddyngton town side – 6d.
Item paid to Gilbert Blanchard for one chalder and 3 bushels of lime bestowed upon Aswell – 15s 10d.
Item for 500 of brick tile to the same work – 6s 8d.
Item paid for carriage of 6 loads of stones from St Mary's church to Aswell – 2s.[2]

42s 5d.

f. 49v.
Item paid for 3 loads of sand to the same work – 12d.
Item for 5 loads of chalk stones from the quarry to Aswell – 15d.
Item more in lime to Aswell, one bushel – 10d.
[Item for one strike of lime spent about the church – 5d].[3]
Item paid to William Dixon for making the pit in the quarry and for digging of stone – 20d.
Item paid to Robert Robynson for working about the same pit 2 days – 16d.
Item paid to Craggs for felling of 20 loads[4] of stone at Lowth Park – 7s 4d.
Item to Bell for leading one load of sand – 7d.
Item paid to Herre Skurrall and his son for 3 days work at 10d the day – 5s.
Item paid to Herre Surrall's boy for 3 days work – 18d.
Item paid to Dixson, tiler, for 4 days work there – 3s 4d.
Item paid to George Lobley for 2 days work – 14d.
Item paid to Bryan Parysh for one day's work – 7d.
Item paid more to Dixson for one day – 10d.
Item paid to Herre Skurrell and his son and William Dixson for 5 days work at 10d the day about the same work – 12s 6d.

---

[1] This is presumably the same Robert Saltmarsh mentioned elsewhere in the accounts. In 1553–4, Saltmarsh, along with Ferrebe (line below), was paid 2s for 'dressing of the Small Wells'. Page 235. Accounts II, *f.* 107r.

[2] St Mary's church was possibly in the process of demolition, although apparently the former chancel was retained as a chapel after the grammar school vacated the premises in c.1558. Goulding, *St Mary's*, p. 10.

[3] [Crossed through]. Marginalia – 'this is not in charge'.

[4] '2 loads' crossed through.

Item paid to Herre Skurrell's boy for 5 days at 6d the day – 2s 6d.
Item paid to Herre Skurrell and his son and to Dixson in Easter week for 3 days – 7s 6d.
Item paid to Herre Skurrell's servant for 3 days work – 18d.
Item paid to Oliver Watterhouse for 3 days – 2s.

f. 50r.

Item to Oliver Watterhouse for scouring of Aswell Head – 4d.
Item paid for 6 loads of stone to Thomas Pelson from the quarry to Aswell – 18d.
Item paid to Thomas Lechman for mending certain locks and other work due to be paid the last year – 2s 6d.
Item paid to Thomas Hutchynson for carrying of Robert Swetyng[1] and Dugles[2] to Lyncoln castle – 9s 4d.
Item for charges about bringing home the bull that died in the field and for dressing[3] which was given to the poor – 14d.[4]
Item paid to William Graunt for keeping of the common bull for this year *Anno* 1566 – 15s.

Total Sum – 24s 10d.

Sum total £15 5s 2d of all the payments this year & so remains [in] the old churchwardens hands of their receipts over & besides those receipts 13s 3d, & also one bull & also one cow in the hands of William Read.

52s 5d.

f. 50v

[1567–8]

1567

The new surveyors appointed for this year, 1567, be these, Thomas Blancherd, Steaven Spaldyng, Roger Stutt & John Sowth, & they have received of the old surveyors 6s in money, 5 picks & a gavelock which they are now charged with as it appearith in the foot of the old surveyor's account before written.
Boon days.
The first to be the 16th of April.
2 The second to be the 24th of April.
3 The third to be the 22nd of May.
4 The fourth to be the 27th May.
5 The fifth to be the third day of June.
6 The sixth to be the 12th of June.

---

[1] Swetyng later escaped or was released, and a 'hue and cry' was raised. Page 361. Accounts III, *f.* 66v.
[2] Douglas?
[3] In this case to divide into pieces; to cut up. *OED*.
[4] Marginalia – '13s 8d' and '14s 10d', both crossed through.

A copy of a letter from Sir William Skipwith[1] unto Herre Edward the contents whereof appearith following.

'There hath been with me certain of the township of Lowth for their carriages[2] and as they do allege their carriage be weak and their hay spent wherefore you cannot have of them so many carriages as you would but they be content to let you have 4 carriages which be well for this time, wherefore I pray you be contented and molest them no further for this time and think it no duty but contented at the Justices request for this time to help as they may binding no custom and so I end. From Ormsbe[3] the first of May *Anno* 1567'.

Your friend, William Skipwith.

f. 51r.

1567.

Memorandum, that John North, George Willos are old churchwardens, James Marshall & Robert West for the new churchwardens for the same year.

Memorandum, that the same churchwardens are charged with one bull & one cow in the hands of William Read & 13s 3d in money, which they have received of the old churchwardens.

Also they are charged with the collection of 10s 8d, due for the bells ringing for certain causes apparent in the [a]count for bells & burials.

Also they are charged with 20s in money taken of Thomas Blancherd for certain velvet vestments which were sold to him with consent of the parish.

Also they are charged with a great chalice of silver & gilt & a cover for the same chalice with certain other things appertaining to the choir apparent by an inventory indented whereof one part remaineth with the clerk & the other part with the churchwardens.

Also they are charged with 20d in money which they have received of John Wygon for one year's rent of a piece of gresground[4] with willows at the east side in Lincoln Close, which year ended the 24th day of March last past.

Also they are charged with certain money to be gathered for the Plough going out of certain men's grounds, sum 14d.

Also they are charged with money promised for Monks' Dike by Mr Guavero,[5] 2s.

Also they are charged with a new brewing lead[6] in the hands of William

---

[1] Sir William Skipwith of South Ormsby JP, MP (1510–86), was sheriff of Lincolnshire in 1552–3 and 1563–4. Bindoff, *House of Commons*, III, p. 326.

[2] Probably an actual carriage or wagon, as against 'an action performed by someone'. *OED*.

[3] South Ormsby.

[4] Grass ground?

[5] Possibly Francis Velez de Guevara from Segura in Spain. He was buried at Stenigot 12 February 1592/3. Goulding, *Customs*, p. 10. Maddison, *Lincolnshire Pedigrees*, 51, p. 433.

[6] A vessel for brewing. *OED*.

White served for 2 year's rent of the house in the churchyard, [ap]praised in the Lord's court to 10s.
f. 51v.

Anno 1567.

The account of the new churchwardens for this present year of all the receipts from the Sunday in the Octaves in Easter, *Anno Domini* 1567 unto the same Sunday *Anno* 1568, that is to say for one whole year as it doth appear hereafter. Received of the said churchwardens quarterly in the church with the piece is as appearith following, that is to say at Midsummer for the first quarter the sum of 24s.

Item received of the said churchwardens for the 2nd quarter at Michaelmas the sum of 20s 4d.

Received more for the 3rd quarter which was collected at Christmas, the sum of 23s 4d.

Item collected by the said churchwardens for the last quarter [that] endith at Our Lady Day the sum of 26s 8½d.

The receipts for burials and for the bells as hereafter it doth appear by their names following.[1]

Received of Jenet Warde for the Trinity bell – 8d.*

Received of Jenet Dynnys – 8d.

Received of Auncell Jeff – 8d.

Received of John Helwode of Theddlethorpe[2] sent for his burial and for the bells – 7s 8d.*

Received of Catern Moore[3] for her burial and for the bells – 7s 8d.*

Received of Bettris Robynson for her burial and for the bells – 7s 6d.*

Received of Isabell Girsbe for her burial and for the bells – 7s 8d.*

Received of Richard, son [of] Askew – 8d.*[4]

f. 52r.

Anno 1567.

Received of Mylles Clarke – 8d.*

Item of John Bawdwyn – 7s 8d.*

Item of William Hay – 2s.*[5]

---

1 Those marked * have '*allor*' for *allocatur* written in the margin: translated 'it is allocated'.

2 John Helwod or Elwod was buried 20 April 1567. LAO, Goulding Papers, 5/2. Will: LAO, LCC, 1567, *f.* 199.

3 Catherine Moore, wife of John, a clerk, was buried 19 May 1567. Goulding Papers, 5/2. The Clergy Marriage Act 1548, titled an 'Acte to take awaye all posityve Lawes againste Marriage of Priestes', allowed former priests to marry. Statutes IV (i), p. 67. Queen Elizabeth was opposed to wedded clergy, despite her own archbishop, Matthew Parker, being married.

4 Line crossed through. Richard Askew was the son of William Askew, interred 25 January 1566/7. LAO, Goulding Papers, 5/2.

5 '12d' crossed through.

Item of Anne Pennyngton – 2s.
Item of William Sowth – 8d.*
Item of Thomas Pelson – 7s 8d.*
Received of John Tailler, batchelor – 8d.*
Received of William Coppuldicke, gentleman[1] – 7s 8d.
Received of Annas, the wife of Herre Milis – 8d.*
Received of Margaret Helwod [for her burial][2] – 7s 8d.*
Rafe Goslynge – 8d.
John Freman – 8d.
Elizabeth Askew[3] – 8d.
f. 52v.
The receipts of all things due to the church this present year besides the bells and burials and the collection with the piece as hereafter appearith.
Received of Thomas Blanchard in part of payment for certain vestments sold by the churchwardens, 1566 – 10s.[4]
Received of Mr Purvey the warden in part of payment of a more sum as appearith before written in the 12th leaf of this book the sum of £4, whereof was paid by the hands of Gilbert Blanchard, 40s.[5]
Received of Thomas Blanchard in part of payment for vestments and coips[6] sold by him being churchwarden – 10s.[7]
Received for 2 bulls sold by the churchwardens – 34s.
Received for ashes that was sold to strangers – 8s.
Received of Mr Purvey, warden, by the hands of Mr Bradley the 17th day of April – £3.
Sum total of all receipts for this present year £20 6s 10½d, whereof they have paid in charges as hereafter followeth £17 9d, & so remains in their hands to be delivered to the new churchwardens £3 6s 1½d in money & debts & other things besides one common bull & one cow in the hands of Robert Forman. Of the which remainder is owing for the bells & burials 16s 8d, & so remains in money 49s 5½d, besides the said bull & cow whereof they ask allowance for 2s paid to Isabell Willyngam for dressing of Aswell & 6d paid to Robert Odlen for the rent of a lea whereupon the common hedge standith & so remains in their charge to be accounted upon, besides the said 16s 8d due for bells & burials, the sum of 46s 11½d with one bull & a cow.

---

[1] William Copledike was the third son of Sir John Copledike MP of Harrington (d.1557) and Elizabeth Littlebury of Stainby (d.1552). Maddison, *Lincolnshire Pedigrees*, 50, p. 268. Interred 16 February 1567/8. LAO, Goulding Papers, 5/2.

[2] [Crossed through].

[3] Elizabeth Askew was buried 14 April 1568. LAO, Goulding Papers, 5/2.

[4] Line crossed through. Marginalia – 'this is not in charge'.

[5] Page 301. Accounts III, f. 13r.

[6] Copes or coifs: the latter a close-fitting cap covering the top, back and sides of the head? *OED*.

[7] Line crossed through. Marginalia – 'this is not in charge'.

Also they ask allowance for a brewing lead in the hands of William Whyte, 10s.
Also they ask allowance 4s 4d, for certain burials that cannot be gotten, that is to say for Agnes Watson 8d, William Gatesyde 8d, Thomas Thomson 8d, Jenet Catherall 12d, Jenet Dynnes 8d, of Thomas Crosland 8d.
f. 53r.
These be the payments and allowances unto the ministers of the church due to them as standing fees and paid yearly as hereafter it doth appear.
First, paid to the writer of this account and for writing of christenings, weddings and burials to be paid at 4 several times in the year – 13s 4d.
Item paid to the bellman for his yearly wages for keeping the clock and chimes, the bells and the lead and the Day bell – 43s 4d.
Item paid to Robert Odlyng for his year's fee – 3s 4d.
Item paid to Thomas Gonnell for blowing of the organs the whole year – 3s 4d.
Item paid to Robert Chapman by the year for washing of church cloths – 16d.
Item paid to Robert Kirckbe for his year's wages for singing and maintaining divine service in the choir – 13s 4d.
Sum – £3 18s.
f. 53v.
The payments and allowances with other expenses for this present year as is hereafter following.
Item paid to Herre Edward for the out end of Saltfleethaven – 8s.
Item paid for making of a gate in the west end of the town for the safe keeping of the corn field – 10d.
Item paid to Robert Chapman for willows to the same gate – 18d.
Item paid to George Willis for a piece of wood to the head of the said gate – 4d.
Item paid for a vestevell and a crook to the said gate – 10d.
Item paid to George Buck for hedging the lane for safeguard of the corn – 2d.
Item paid to the plumber for his work 4 days of the church at 10d the day – 3s 4d.
Item paid to his boy for 4 days work in serving his master about the church – 12d.
Item paid to Gilbert Blanchard for 4 boards bestowed of the leads – 8d.
Item paid to Mr Bradley for 100 of nails spent of the leads – 8d.
Item paid to John North for one thick plank to raise the leads – 16d.
Item paid to Mrs Mysterchambers for solder bestowed upon the leads – 2s.
Item paid for covering the grave of Bettris Robynson – 4d.[1]
20s 11d.
f. 54r.
Anno 1567.
Item paid for a string to the Little bell – 11d.
Item paid to Robert Odlynge for mending the James bell – 10d.
Item paid to William Richardson for serving of the plumber about the leads – 12d.

---

[1] Beatrix Robynson, wife of Richard, was interred 25 May 1567. LAO, Goulding Papers, 5/2.

Item paid to him for covering John Helwod's grave – 4d.
Item paid for making of the butts – 3s.
Item paid to Herre Skurrall and William Dixon for making of the stone bridge in the South Field – 12s 4d.
Item paid for a bull bought by the churchwardens – 22s.
Item paid for the charges in buying the said bull and for ryenge[1] of him being straid[2] – 8d.
Item paid to Smythson, the swineherd for his quarters wages due at Lammas – 2s 6d.
Item paid for leading of 6 loads of stone from Lowth Park to Hargarths Corner to the new bridge – 4s 4d.
Item paid for 4 loads of chalk leading from the quarry to the said bridge – 12d.
Item paid for 7 bushels of lime to the same bridge – 5s 10d.
Item paid for a fille[3] that William Richardson had – 4d.
Item paid for bearing a gate from Monks' Dike Head to the East Bridge – 2d.
Item paid for a vertevell to the same gate – 3d.
Item paid to James Mansill for a pound and a half of puder[4] – 9½d.
Item paid to the plumber the 3rd day of September for 2 days work of the church at 17d the day – 2s 10d.
Item paid to William Richardson for serving the plumber 2 days – 6d.

59s 7½d.

f. 54v.
Item paid for a pound of solder to Mrs Mysterchambers – 7½d.
Item paid to Robert Chapman's wife for 1½ lbs of solder – 9d.
Item paid to Gilbert Blanchard for one strike of lime – 5d.
Item paid to the bellman for covering the graves of Catern Moore and Isabell Grisbe – 8d.
Item paid to the nethord for one load of hay – 6s.
Item paid to George Chapman and his fellows for scouring and diking the common hedge betwix Lowth and Keddyngton – 13s 4d.
Item paid to Mr Bradley for 3 bars to the new gate by the West Mill – 12d.
Item paid to Robert Smithson, the swineherd, at Martinmas in part payment of his wages – 5s.
Item paid for one bull bought this year – 24s 4d.
Item paid to George Chapman the 7th day of December for diking and scouring the common hedge betwix Lowth and Keddyngton – 10s.
Item paid to Bernard Born for leading of 9 loads of yew to the said hedge – 12s.

[1] Ringing?
[2] Strayed?
[3] Meaning unknown.
[4] Powder, pewter, both in *OED*.

Item paid for a Register Book of paper for christenings, weddings and burials with 4d for carriage of it from London – 5s 4d.
Item paid to Bernard Born for leading riesse to the common hedge betwix Lowth and Kedyngton – 5s 4d.
Item paid to George Chapman and his fellows for hedging there – 5s 4d.
Item paid more to Bernard Born for leading the last part of 17 loads of riesse – 5s 4d.
£4 15s 5½d.

f. 55r.
Item paid to Robert Kirckbe for a net to catch crows – 6s 8d.[1]
Item paid for a paper book[2] for the clerk for the christenings, weddings and burials to be written therein – 5d.
Item paid to George Chapman and his fellows at the ending of their work of the common hedge betwix Lowth and Keddyngton – 20d.
Item paid to Saltmers[3] for diking of five rods of the common piece of ground at Haregars – 20d.
Item paid to Thomas Lechman for ironwork to the clock and chimes – 4s 4d.
Item paid for covering of John Bawdwyn's grave – 4d.
Item paid to Robert Odlyng for making a bush to one of the bells – 4d.
Item paid for covering of Thomas Pelson's grave – 4d.
Item paid to Thomas Lechman for making of a new key to the south church door and for 8 nails to set on the lock of the said door – 18d.
Item paid for covering Mrs Helwod's grave – 4d.
Item paid for carrying a plank to the West Mill Bridge – 4d.
Item paid to James Mansill for keeping the common bull this winter – 20s.
Item paid for 4 mats for people to kneel on in the High choir – 14d.
Item paid to Mr Goddall for 4 prick song books to the choir – 5s.
Item paid to the swineherd for the last part of his wages this year – 2s 6d.
46s 7d.

f. 55v.
Item paid to William Kyng for 4 C one quarter[4] of wood at 9s 4d the hundred – 39s 8d.
Item paid to William Rushbe [for] mending of [the] gate at West Mill – 6d.
Item paid to Isabell Willyngam – 2s.
Sum total of the receipts.[5]

---

[1] The illumination of vermin was stipulated in the 1566 'Act for the Preservation of Grain', 8 Elizabeth, Chapter XV (ii). *Statutes* IV (i), p. 498.

[2] This should be of parchment, not paper. Page 292, note 1. Accounts III, *f.* 2r.

[3] Probably Saltmarsh, who appears to have been released from his incarceration in Lincoln Castle. Page 337. Accounts III, *f.* 49r.

[4] Four hundreds and one quarter of a hundred.

[5] Line crossed through.

Item Robert Odlyng for the rent of one lea towards Keddyngton Field, such to be paid yearly – 6d.

[1568–9]

Anno Domini 1568.

Thomas Anderson,[1] Christopher Pormorte, William Grawnte & James Mansell are appointed surveyors of the highways for this present year following & they have received of the old surveyors five picks & gavelock which they are charged with & seven shillings in money & also one new pick made this last year.

Boon days.

1 The first to be upon the 14th day of May.
2 The second to be on the 21st day of May.
3 The third Boon day, the last day of May.
4 The fourth upon the 11th day of June.
5 The fifth day upon the 21st of June.
6 The sixth Boon day the 25th of June.

f. 56r.

Anno Domini 1568.

William Ormesby, John Fyshe, old churchwardens, Steaven Spaldyng & Thomas Jackson[2] are elected for new churchwardens for this present year following.

Memorandum that the said churchwardens are charged with 32s 11d in money which they have received of the old churchwardens.

Also they are charged with a brewing lead in the hands of William Whyte & also they are charged with a cow and a bull and also they are charged with the collection of 11s 8d due the last year ended for bells and burials yet ungathered *videlicet* William Copuldick, gentleman 7s 8d, Ann Penyngton 2s, Rafe Goslyng, J[ohn] Freman, Elizabeth Aske 2s.

Also they are charged with a great chalice of silver & gilt & a cover for the same with certain other things belonging to the choir apparent by an inventory indented whereof one part remaineth with the clerk & the other part with the churchwardens.

Also they are charged with certain money to be gathered for the Plough going out of certain men's grounds [as appearith in the 16th leaf of this book][3] – 14d.

Also they are charged to receive of Olyver Kennythorpe for rent for piece of common ground lying within his close due at the feast of the Annunciation

---

[1] 'Richard Gresby' crossed through. A Richard Grescroft, son of John, was buried 7 July 1567. LAO, Goulding Papers, 5/2.

[2] A Thomas Jackson, shoemaker, left a will: TNA, PROB 11/72/116, probate, 3 February 1588.

[3] [Crossed through].

of Our Lady last past,[1] 20d, & for the year's rent of the same piece this year following, 20d.

Also they are charged with certain wax & rosell & 2s 8d in money which they have received of Richard Robynson.

[Also they are charged with two shillings to be received of Mr Gravers for the manor of Lowth Park for easement of water from Aswell due to be paid every Plough Day – 2s].[2]

Sum in money – 50s 1d.

f. 56v.

Anno Domini 1568.

The receipts with the price in the church to be paid quarterly as it does appear following *videlicet*.

Received at the first quarter at Midsummer the sum of.[3]

Received at Michaelmas.

Received at Christmas.

Received at Our Lady Day.

Total – £4 6s 11d.

The receipts for bells and burials is here subscribed.

Received for the burial of Em[ott] the wife of John Goddall[4] and for the bells – 7s 8d.

Received of William Penyngton for his wife's burial – 12d.[5]

Received for John Freman for the Trinity bell – 8d.

Received for the burial of Judithe, the wife of Richard White and for the bells – 7s 8d.

Received for [the] Trinity bell for Hwe Smith[6] – 8d.

Received for the burial of Mathew Wardall – 7s 8d.

Received for the burial of Elizabeth Askwe – 8d.

Received for the burial of John Marshall – 8d.

Received for the burial of George Gedney – 7s 8d.

Received for the burial of Ellyn Hodgson – 8d.

Received for the burial of Ralf Flower – 7s 8d.[7]

[1] March.
[2] [Crossed through].
[3] [Separate totals not recorded].
[4] Presumably John Goodall the schoolmaster. Emott Goodall was interred 5 May 1568. LAO, Goulding Papers, 5/2.
[5] Ann Penyngton, buried 28 October 1567. LAO, Goulding Papers, 5/2
[6] Hugh.
[7] Flower is frequently recorded transporting prisoners to Lincoln. He was buried 7 March 1568/9. LAO, Goulding Papers, 5/2. His son Leonard was interred the following day. Both his other sons, Richard (buried 21 June 1545) and Thomas (8 February 1552/3), along with his wife Joanna (10 October 1562), predeceased him. LAO, Goulding Papers, 5/2.

Received for the burial of Elizabeth Kyng – 7s 8d.
Received for the burial of John Cooke[1] – 8d.
                    Sum – 50s.
Of Mr Simcote for his daughter[2] – 7s 8d.
f. 57r.
                Anno Domini 1568.
                [Remainder Blank].
f. 57v.
                Anno Domini 1568.
The receipts of all things due to the church this present year besides bells and burials and the collections with the piece as hereafter appearith.
Received of Oliver Kenythorpe for one year's rent due before the 24th day of March 1567 – 20d.
Received for a cow sold by the said churchwardens – 16s 6d.
Received for one bull sold by them, price – 29s.
Received of Mr White, the warden, the 27th November to the repair of the church – 20s.
Received for a coat that was Ralf Stubbs's servant which hanged himself – 4s.
Received of Mr White for one bull that was sold to him – 20s.
Received the 17th day of April of Mr White, the warden, to the repair of the church – 20s.
                Sum £5 9s 6d.
Total sum of all receipts received by the churchwardens in money this year – £15 5s 2d.
f. 58r.
The payments and allowances unto the ministers of the church with other yearly payments as follows.
First, to be paid to the writer of this account for his year's wages and for the writing of christenings, weddings and burials the sum of – 13s 4d.
Item to the bellman by the year for keeping the clock and chimes, the bells and the leads and also the Day bell – 43s 4d.
Item to Robert Odlyng for [a] year's fee – 3s 4d.[3]
Item to Thomas Gonnell for blowing of the organs by the year – 3s 4d.
Item to Robert Kirckbe for maintaining divine service for his year's wages – 13s 4d.
Item to Robert Chapman in the year for washing the church cloths – 2s.
Item to Robert Odlyng yearly for the rent of a ley whereupon the common hedge standith betwix Lowth and Keddyngton – 6d.[4]

---

[1] Will: TNA, PROB 11/51/269, probate 29 June 1569.
[2] Susan Symcote, interred 2 April 1569. William Symcote is recorded as a gentleman. LAO, Goulding Papers, 5/2.
[3] Marginalia – 'Discharged'.
[4] Marginalia – 'Discharged'.

Item to Isabell Willyngam for keeping and dressing Aswell yearly, whereof paid for 3 quarters 18d, and more, 6d – 2s.
£4 14d.

f. 58v.

Anno Domini 1568.

Item paid to Richard Wright for making of a collection book for the churchwardens – 4d.
Item paid to Olyver Kenythorpe for one bull – 24s.
Item paid for covering Mrs Goodall's grave – 4d.
Item paid to John North for a sheep skin bestowed about the organs and glue to the same – 6d.
Item paid to Richard Story the glazier the 20th day of September for mending of the leads about the church – 20s.
Item paid for the making of two surplices that was old altar cloths and for washing of the same – 6d.
Item paid for covering of Suzan White's grave – 4d.
Item paid to Leonard Rushbe and Thomas Bradley for their work 2 days upon the vestry at 10d per day either of them – 4s 2d.
Item paid for timber bought of Mrs Thew to the same work – 2s 8d.
Item paid for nails to the said work – 12d.
Item paid to Patchet for mending windows in the steeple with certain boards – 8d.
Item paid for one strike of lime bestowed upon the glass windows – 5d.
Item paid to Richard Story the glazier for mending all the windows in the church – 40s.
Item paid to the Crowner[1] Mr Baird, for Ralf Stubb's servant that hanged himself – 13s 4d.
Item paid for 2 bell-strings to the roper weighing 3 stone 5lbs [and a] dd[2] the price – 10s 4d.
Item paid to Robert Wynter, the wright for 3 days work at Aswell to meat & wages at 10d the day – 2s 6d.
Item to Thomas Bradley for the like work to meat and wages for 2 days [and a] half at 10d per day – 2s 1d.
£6 3s 2d.

f. 59r.

Item paid to Isabell Willyngam for 3 long spars for trestles to bear the planks – 2s.
Item paid to John Fishe for 3 spars for rails to the same work – 18d.
Item paid to Stevyn Spaldynge for hanging of a gate at the Corn Field side – 12d.
Item paid to John Fishe for a post to the gate at the west end of the church – 6d.
Item paid to Thomas Bradley for his day's wages for dressing and mending the said gate – 8d.

[1] Coroner.
[2] Half.

Item paid for covering of Mathew Wardall's grave to the bellman – 4d.
Item paid for one bull bought of Mr White the 8th day of December – 21s 9d.
Item paid to Richard Riggs for dressing of the town's harness & for mending certain faults about the same – 5s.
Item paid to William Dixson, tiler, and his boy for 3 days work to meat & wages in making up the decayed places of the church wall – 3s 4d.
Item paid to Widow Pelson for 3 bushels of lime to the same work – 3s.
Item paid for one book called Mr Beacon's *Postells*[1] – 4s 8d.
Item paid for the dressing of Gilian Bower[2] – 12d.
Item paid to Thomas Wynter for nails to the windows – 8d.
Item paid to John Waite for 6 ropes at 2d the piece to tie the bell-strings – 12d.
Item paid for covering of George Gedney, Ralf Flower, Isabell Kyng and William Coppuldike – 16d.
Item paid for a new key to the prasse[3] in St Peter's choir – 4d.
Item for mending the clock – 4d.
Item paid to Mr White for the meat of the bull and for exchange of a bull – 20s.
Item paid more to Robert Pelson for his lea – 6d.
£3 8s 11d.

f. 59v.

Total sum of the payments this present year £13 13s 4d, & so remains in the hands of the old churchwardens to be set over to the new churchwardens in money, 31s 11d.
Whereof they desire allowances as followeth, that is to say for the burial of the wife of Hugh Goslyng[4] – 8d.
Item for the burial of William Copeldyke – 6s 8d.
Item for the burial of Sewson,[5] daughter of Mr Symcots – 7s 8d.
Which sums conferred together do amount to 16s, & so remains in their hands 15s 11d, which sum of 20s 11d must be delivered to the new churchwardens.

[1569–70]

Surveyors for the highways this year.
Richard Gyrsbe.
John Righton.
Thomas Salmon.
Robert Odlyng.

[1] A Postil is a sermon on the Epistles and Gospels, in this case written by the reformist theologian Thomas Becon (1512–67). *DNB*, https://doi.org/10.1093/ref:odnb/1918 (Accessed 14/5/2018).
[2] Julian Bower.
[3] Press?
[4] Rose Goslynge was buried 15 February 1567/8. LAO, Goulding Papers, 5/2.
[5] Susan.

Which have received of the old surveyors 5 picks, one iron gavelock and in money the sum of 7s 4d.
Boon days.
1 The 22nd of April.
2 The 29th of April.
3 The 6th of May.
4 The 13th of May.
5 The 7th of June.
6 The 14th of June.
f.60r.

Anno Domini 1569.

Thomas Blanchard, Robert Kyngley, Christopher Pomorte & John Sowthe, churchwardens elected & chosen for this present year to whom was delivered as appearith before written by the old churchwardens the sum of 15s 11d. Also they are charged with the collection for the burial of Rafe Goslyng 8d, and for the burial of William Copuldick, gentleman, 7s 8d.
A note of all things to be enquired of by the whole parish of Lowth at the account upon Law Sunday every year as is following.
1 First to take account of the churchwardens.
2 Item to see certain implements in the clerk's charge contained in a bill indented.
3 Item to enquire of all things belonging to the communion table whether there be one communion cup [of] parcel gilt weighing 15 ounces wanting the half quarter. Also one white communion cup of silver in weight 10 ounces and 3 quarters.
4 Item to enquire of all other things pertaining to the church.
5 Item whether they be 2 bibles, a greater and a less.
6 Item 2 books named *Erasmus's Paraphrases* of one volume.
7 Item one book called *Beacon's Postells* of a small volume.
8 Item to see the clerk's book of christenings, weddings and burials and to confer it with the register that no name be left unwritten upon pain to forfeit, and to pay to the Poor Man's box for every default omitted by the said clerk, 12d. Also to take the like forfeiture of the keeper of the register book for every name omitted by his negligence.
Item the surveyors of the highways are answerable yearly for one iron gavelock and 5 picks.
f. 60v.

Anno Domini 1569.

The receipts this year with the pece in the church to be paid quarterly as it doth appear following *videlicet*.
Received at Midsummer, the first quarter the sum of – 27s 4d.
Received at Michaelmas – 32s 8d.
Received at Christ's Nativity – 27s 9d.
Received at Our Lady Day in Lent – 30s 9d.

£5 18s 11d.

Receipts for bells and burials as is here subscribed.

Received for the burial of John Hopkyn – 8d.
Received for the burial of Widow Rantforth – 8d.
Received for William Rushbe's wife's burial – 8d.[1]
Received for the burial of Richard Archer – 8d.
Received for the burial of Jenet Somerskaills – 7s 8d.
Received for Richard Harpam's wife's burial – 8d.[2]
Received for the burial of Robert Sympson – 8d.
Received for the burial of Willor's daughter – 8d.[3]
Received for the burial of Suzan Kyng – 7s 8d.
Received for the burial of Annas, wife of Herre Skurrall – 8d.
Received for the burial of the son of John Johns – 8d.[4]
Received for the burial of Elizabeth, wife of Richard Raithbe – 8d.
Received for the burial of Roger, the son of John Dikes – 8d.
Received for the burial of Jenet, wife of Thomas Jacson – 7s 8d.
Received for the burial of John Brathat – 8d.
Received for the burial of Herre, the son of Thomas Rushurth – 8d.
Received for the burial of Robert Lowson.[5]
Received for the burial of Joan, the wife of William Evans.[6]
Received for the burial of Cecill, the wife of John East – 8d.
Received for the burial of Joan Bower, widow – 7s 8d.
Received for the burial of Jenet Grene, widow.[7]
Received for the burial of Elizabeth Mysterchambers – 7s 8d.[8]
Received for the burial of Herre Read – 8d.
Received for the burial of Eleanor, wife of William Evannes – 8d.
Received for the burial of Suzan, daughter of William Symcot, gentleman – 7s 8d.

£9 11s 2d.[9]

f. 61r.

Anno Domini 1569.

Receipts of all things due to the church this present year besides bells and burials, the collections which the piece as hereafter appearith.

[1] Ann Ruschbe, interred 10 May 1569. LAO, Goulding Papers, 5/2.
[2] Elizabeth Harpam, buried 7 May 1569. LAO, Goulding Papers, 5/2.
[3] Possibly Joanna, daughter of Thomas Wilson, interred 8 October 1569. LAO, Goulding Papers, 5/2.
[4] John Johns, son of John, *Medici Physicus*. Buried 21 June 1569. LAO, Goulding Papers, 5/2.
[5] No amount stated.
[6] '8d' crossed through. The name 'Everington' is written above 'Evans'.
[7] No amount stated.
[8] Buried 9 February 1569/70. LAO, Goulding Papers, 5/2.
[9] '£9 17s 10d' crossed through.

Received of the old churchwardens, Mr Ormsbe and his fellows, for arrearages that was collected after their account, 5s 10d.
Received of Mr White, the warden, to the repair of the church the 4th of June *Anno* 1569 – 20s.
Received for one bull sold by Thomas Blanchard to Jarrat and John Sowth price – 30s.
Received for 2 chalices and one paten gilt weighing 42 ounces and half a quarter, sold by Roger Stute at London for 5s 4d the ounce – £11 4s 8d.
Received of James Story for rent of two leis[1] that the common hedge standith of toward Keddyngton – 10d.
    Sum of all receipts – £23 12s 6d.[2]

f. 61v.

Anno Domini 1569.

The payments and allowances unto the ministers of the church with other yearly payments and expenses as here followeth *videlicet*.
First, to be paid to the writer of this account for his years wages and for keeping the register book of christenings, weddings and burials *videlicet* – 13s 4d, whereof paid at May Day – 3s 4d, at Lammas – 3s 4d, at Martinmas – 3s 4d, more at Christmas for half a quarter […] – 3s. 4d.
Item to William Richardson for keeping of the clock and chimes & for ringing the Day bell – 30s, whereof paid at Midsummer – 7s 6d, Michaelmas – 7s 6d, more 7s 6d, 7s 6d.
Item to Ralf Robson, the bellman for dressing the church, the leads and for keeping the bells – 13s 4d, whereof paid at Midsummer – 3s 4d, & more 3s 4d, more 3s 4d and 3s 4d.
Item to Robert Kirckbe for maintaining of divine services the choir – 13s 4d, whereof paid at Midsummer – 3s 4d, more 3s 4d, more 3s 4d and 3s 4d.
Item to Thomas Gommell for blowing of the organs -3s 4d, whereof paid at Midsummer 10d, more 10d, more 10d and 10d.
Item to Robert Chapman for washing the church cloths – 2s 8d, whereof paid at Midsummer – 8d,[3] more 8d, more 8d and 8d.
Item to Robert Odlyng for his fee about the steeple in mending of the bells – 3s 4d, whereof paid at Midsummer – 10d, Michaelmas, 10d and more, 20d.
Item to Isabell Willyngam for keeping and dressing of Aswell – 2s.[4]
Item to Robert Odlyng for the rent of a lea which upon the common hedge standith between Lowth & Keddyngton – 6d.[5]
    £4 3s 6d.

[1] Lea.
[2] '19s 2d' crossed through. Marginalia – '£14 16d'.
[3] 6d crossed through.
[4] Marginalia – 'discharged'.
[5] Marginalia – 'discharged'.

f. 62r.

Anno 1569.

Item paid to Robert Wynter and Rigald for hanging a gate at the [...]¹ new bridge with wood bestowed upon the same – 18d.

Item paid to Mr Christopher Pormort for one gun – 16s.²

Item paid to 3 men for wearing the town's harness 3 days before their captains to meat and wages – 6s.

Item paid for mending a coat of plate & for poynts and lasyng the same – 4d.³

Item paid for mending William Holland's gun, staff and matches – 4d.⁴

Item paid to 4 labourers for 4 days work in making of the butts to meat & wages and for leading of sods and also for leading of 2 loads of rise to the same – 13s 6d.

Item paid to William White for gun powder and for lase and for flockes⁵ to the sallets – 2s 1d.

Item paid to 3 labourers one day to meat and wages for digging and finishing the butts – 18d.

Item paid for a vertival and a crook and for wood to make 3 short bars to the gate at Robert Chapman's mills with workmanship to the same – 13d.

Item paid to the swineherd for his quarter's wages at Midsummer – 20d.

Item paid to the making of Saltfleethaven fire beacons – 6s 8d.⁶

Item paid to Robert Odlyng for 3 workmen 2 days about the bells to meat & wages – 3s 4d.

Item paid to Thomas Lechman for making 2 keys and other work and also for ironwork bestowed upon the Great James – 3s 8d.

Item paid 3 men for carrying the town's harness to Borwell⁷ to meat & wages – 2s 6d.

£3 2d.

f. 62v.

Anno Domini 1569.

Item paid for a girdle⁸ bestowed upon one of the soldiers – 2d.

Item paid to Mr Christopher Pormort for wood that was bestowed upon the turnpike⁹ in Westgate – 20d.

---

1   Indecipherable.
2   This is the first of a number of entries regarding the purchase of weapons and armour relating to the Northern Rebellion of November 1569. See Introduction.
3   Here the parish is paying for mending plates of armour and purchasing lacing to connect the different parts.
4   Probably relating to a matchlock musket.
5   Flock – a material consisting of the coarse tufts and refuse of wool or cotton, *OED*, doubtless used for padding to the sallets, a type of helmet.
6   Beacons were possibly lit to warn of enemy ships approaching the coast.
7   Burwell.
8   A belt worn round the waist as a means of carrying a weapon. *OED*.
9   A spiked barrier fixed in or across a road or passage, as a defence against sudden attack; in this case across Westgate. *OED*.

Item paid to the glazier for almost 5 lb of solder – 2s 10d.
Item paid to Robert Wynter, the wright, for one piece of wood and plaster stakes to the repair of the church house and for mending the bridge against Lowth Wood – 18d.
Item paid to him and his servant to meat and wages about the same work for one day and a piece of a day – 20d.
Item paid more to him for one other piece of wood – 6d.
Item paid for a horse to carry the town's harness to Borwell – 4d.
Item paid to William Dixson, tiler, and his son for one day's work to meat & wages about the leads – 14d.
Item paid to Jacson and William Rushbe for one day's work and a half to meat and wages for making the turnpike in the churchyard – 2s.
Item paid for covering of the graves of Joan Somerskells, Suzan Kyng and Jenet Jacson – 12d.
Item paid to the bellman for 3 days work upon the leads – 8d.
Item paid for a stock lock and a key to the church house – 6d.
Item paid for one rope of 24 fathoms to the plumber and for one great rope to the chimes of 60 and 3 fathoms price – 9s.[1]
Item paid for laying down of certain webs of lead blown up with the wind – 3s.
Item paid to the clock smith of Horncastell for mending the clock and making a new wheel of iron – 12s.

38s.

f. 63r.
Item paid to Thomas Lechman for 3 locks and 3 keys to the doors that opens to the leads upon the church – 15d.
Item paid for dressing of the town gun – 20d.
Item paid to him [Lechman] for one day's work for himself and his servant about the steeple – 6d.
Item paid to Arthur Hill for keeping the gate at the new bridge – 4d.
Item paid to Ralf Robson for serving the plumber one day and a half about the church at the laying down of the leads – 6d.
Item paid for a cord to the clock & chimes – 7d.
Item paid to Gilbert Blanchard for 18 lbs of *Dainysh*[2] iron bestowed about the bells – 3s 2d.
Item paid for wood about the town butts – 4s 2d.
Item paid for one bushel & 2 pecks[3] of lime – 12d.
Item for one half yard of harden cloth and for nails to the clock – 4d.
Item paid for nails spent in repairing of the lodge – 10d.

---

[1] feet (115m).
[2] Danish?
[3] A quarter of a bushel. Bristow, *Glossary*, p. 258.

Item paid for a corslet¹ and a coat of plate with other furniture received at Grymsbe – 8s 4d.²
Item paid to John Blanchard for the receipt of them at the ship and delivering them to be kept at Mr Cook's – 12d.
Item paid to William Rede for his quarter's wages at Midsummer – 20d.
Item paid to Gilbert Blanchard for one quarter of gun powder – 4d.
Item paid for a common bull to the town – 24s.
Item paid for one communion cup parcel gilt in white 15 ounces, wanting the half quarter at 6s the ounce – £4 9s 3d.
Item paid for one white communion cup of silver weighing 10 ounces and 3 quarters at 5s 8d the ounce – 58s 10d.

£9 18s 2d.

f. 63v.

Anno Domini 1569.

Item paid to William Dickson, tiler and his son for 5 days work in making a decayed piece of the north end of the church wall to meat and wages – 3s 9d.
Item paid to the bellman for covering of the graves of Joan Everyngam, Joan Bower and Elizabeth Mysterchambers – 12d.
Item paid to Walter Stoker³ for white leather for a collar to [the] James bell (16d), and to John Clark for white leather (4d), and to John Jacson for the like (1d) – 21d.
Item paid to Richard Riggs for dressing of a corslet 2 times and also for scouring other harnesses besides – 4s 4d.
Item paid to Gilbert Blanchard for 5 strikes of lime bestowed about the church walls – 2s 1d.
Item paid to him for a quarter of a quarter of a pound of gun powder the 30th November – 4d.
Item paid to him for carriage of 2 harnesses from Grymsbe to Lowth – 12d.
Item paid to Robert Odlynge for staves and nails and for workmanship to the Trinity bell – 12d.
Item paid for boards and nails to the Trinity wheel – 14d.
Item for workmanship to the same – 8d.

17s 1d.

Sum of the payments £19 16s 11d, & so remains to be delivered to the new churchwardens £3 15s 7d, whereof paid to Mr Whittyngton for keeping of the town bull the winter last past 13s 4d, & so remains £3 2s 3d.
The said old churchwardens have also received more 14d gathered by the Plough which they must pay to the new churchwardens.

---

¹ A piece of armour covering most of the body. *OED*.
² Undoubtedly part of the defence against the northern rebels, the armour being brought in by sea rather than by road during winter.
³ Walter Stoker, glover. Will: TNA, PROB 11/61/6, probate 7 April 1578.

f. 64r.

[1570–1]

Anno Domini 1570.

William Hewet & John Pallmer are elected & chosen for the old churchwardens & Rychard Ryggs & Richard Holdernes for the new churchwardens for this present year now finished now following to whom was delivered by the old churchwardens £3 3s 5d. Also they are charged the collection for the burials of William Everingham's wife, 7s 8d, & for burial of William Copeldyke 7s 8d, & for the burial of Jenyt Grene 8d, & for the burial of Robert Lowson 8d. Also they are charged with one bull of *coler brandit myrkit*.[1]

Thomas Rychardson, Thomas Hutchenson, John Dyke & Thomas Wynter are chosen for the Surveyors of the Highways for this present year following and they are answerable for one iron gavelock and 5 picks and in money.[2]

Boon days.

1 The first to be the 7th day of April.
2 The 13th of April.
3 The 20th of April.
4 The 27th of April.
5 The 23rd of May.
6 The first of June.

f. 64v.

The receipts with the piece in the church to be paid quarterly as doth appear following *videlicet*.

Received at Midsummer – 30s 7d.
Received at Michaelmas – 25s 10d.
Received at Christmas – 24s 8d.
Received at Our Lady Day – 29s 7d.

     Sum – £5 10s 8d.[3]

Received more the quarter that was delivered – 18d.

    Receipts for bells and burials as followeth.

Received for the burial of Ann Taller – 12d.
Received for the burial of Alls Bornskell – 7s 8d.
Received for the burial of Jane Faddon – 8d.
Received for the burial of William Copuldicke – 7s 8d.
Received for the burial of the wife of William Everyngam – 7s 8d.[4]
Received for the burial of Jenet Grene – 8d
Received for the burial of Robert Lowson – 8d.
Received for the burial John, son of J[ohn] North – 12d.

---

[1] Meaning unknown, other than the animal's colour.
[2] No amount stated.
[3] Marginalia – '£5 12s 2d'.
[4] Joanna Everyngam, interred 16 September 1569. LAO, Goulding Papers, 5/2.

Received for the burial of Ann Hutchynson – 7s 8d.[1]
Received for the burial of Jenet Knowth – 8d.
Received for the burial of John Barret, piper – 12d.
Received for the burial of John Mackerell – 7s 8d.[2]
Received for the burial of Isabell Tomson – 12d.
Received for the burial of Robert Chapman – 7s 8d.
Received for the burial of Thomas Wardall[3] – 7s 8d.
Received for the burial of Cuthbert Wille – 7s 8d.
Received for the burial Ceall, wife of Thomas Wright – 12d.[4]
Received for the burial of Anthony Fletcher – 12d.
Received for the burial of Margaret Holtbe – 12d.
Received of Christopher Langham, esquire – 7s 8d.[5]
Received of John Jacson, glover – 12d.
Received of Herre Mylls – 12d.
Received of Thomas Wells – 8d.
Received of Auncell Glentham – 8d.
Received of Catern Lyon – 8d.
Received of Margaret Wardall – 7s 8d.
Received of Agnes Dolman – 12d.
Received of William Watson – 8d.
Received of John Martyndall – 8d.
Received the wife of James Mansill – 7s 8d.[6]
Isabell Taller, widow – 12d.
Received for the burial of Thomas Carter in the church porch – 3s 4d.
                    Sum £5 4s 8d.

f. 65r.

Anno Domini 1570.

The receipts of all things due to the church this present year besides burials and the collection which the piece as here after it doth appear.

[1] Buried 24 June 1570. LAO, Goulding Papers, 5/2.

[2] Possibly John Mackerell, shearman of Binbrook, interred 9 August 1570. LAO, Goulding Papers, 5/2. Will: LAO, LCC, 1570, p. 26.

[3] Thomas Wardall, tanner, left a will. TNA, PROB 11/54/441, probate, 25 October 1572. Buried 28 September 1570. LAO, Goulding Papers, 5/2.

[4] Cecelia Wright, interred 28 October 1570. LAO, Goulding Papers, 5/2.

[5] This is probably the second son of John Langholm of Conisholme (d.1527) and Maud Gilliot, interred 4 January 1570/1. LAO, Goulding Papers, 5/2. Maddison, *Lincolnshire Pedigrees*, 51, p. 580.

[6] Joanna Mansell, buried 10 April 1571. Five of James (Jacob) Mansill's children predeceased him. Three sons, Thomas (9 September 1544), John (28 July 1554) and Richard (12 May 1559), and two daughters, Susanna (1 April 1567) and Margaret (23 October 1570). LAO, Goulding Papers, 5/2.

Received of certain men for three sheep goyngs[1] in the quarry before May Day – 14d.
Received of John Palmer for one piece of a broken bell clapper – 11d.
Received of Mr Vicar for 3 boards taken down in St Peter's choir – 15d.
Received more of him for the one half of Mr Jewel's book[2] 5s 6d, so that the said book is now his own and the churchwardens bearing no part thereof – 5s 6d.
Received of James Mansell and Richard Riggs for 2 tabernacles[3] taken down in St Peter's choir – 2s.[4]
Received of John Rechard, alias Regall, for one piece of wood – 6d.
Received for certain willow rails upon the commons – 6s 8d.
Received of Robert Odlyng for wood about the Rood loft – 6s 8d.
Received of Thomas Hutchynson for a piece that was before the High altar – 4s.
Received of William White for one lead[5] taken for rent of the house in the churchyard – 10s.
Received more of him for the debt of Roger Waite – 20s.
Received for the common plough – 14d
Received of Cuthbert Lanckester, John Melton and William Mychell for 20 rods of the common hedge at 4¾d the rod – 7s 11d.
Received of James Mansell for 10 rods at 5d the rod – 4s 2d.
Received of Saltmars[6] for 4 rods – 2s.
Received of Robert Odlyng for 19 rods at 5d the rod – 7s 11d.

£4 22d.[7]

Sum total of rents with £3 3s 5d remaining of last year £18 2s 1d, and so remaineth to be accounted upon 51s 3½d, whereof their allowances for burials 22s 4d, and so remains 29s 10½d, paid more to them 4d.

f. 65v.

The payments and allowances to the ministers of the church with other yearly payments and expenses as hereafter followeth.

---

1 Possibly sheep 'gangs', the three days preceding Ascension Day (Holy Thursday), during which religious processions took place; a Rogation Day. *OED*. Goulding, *Markets and Fairs*, n.p. The quarry area was also used as a livestock market, as it still is today.

2 John Jewel, bishop of Salisbury (1560–71). His work, *Apologia pro Ecclesia Anglicana* (1561), was an official defence of the newly established church. He was also author of a book of homilies, part of which was 'An Homily Against Disobedience and Willful Rebellion' (1571), a treatise relating to the ill-fated Northern Rebellion of 1569. *DNB*, https://doi.org/10.1093/ref:odnb/14810 (Accessed 15/5/2018).

3 An ornamented receptacle for the pyx containing the consecrated host. *OED*.

4 These are the last examples of church valuables, reinstated during Mary's reign, to be sold; twelve years after Elizabeth's accession. Gurnham, *History of Louth*, pp. 73–4.

5 Brewing lead.

6 Saltmarsh.

7 £4 1s 10d.

First, paid to the writer of this account for his year's wages and for keeping the register book of christenings, weddings and burials – 13s 4d.
Item paid to William Richardson for keeping the clock & chimes & ringing the Day bell – 26s 8d.
Item paid to Ralf Robson, the bellman for keeping of the bells and dressing of the church and leads – 13s 4d.
Item paid to Robert Kyrckbe for maintaining of divine service in the choir – 13s 4d.
Item paid to Thomas Gonnell for blowing of the organs at service time – 3s 4d.
Item paid to Robert Odlyng for his fee about the steeple in mending the bells – 3s 4d.
Item paid to Robert Chapman for washing of the church cloths – 2s 8d.
Item paid to Isabell Willyngam for keeping and dressing of Aswell – 2s.
Item paid to Robert Odlyng for the yearly rent of lea whereupon the common hedge standith between Lowth and Kedyngton – 6d.

£3 18s 6d.

f. 66r.

Anno Domini 1570.

Item paid to the netherd for 9 days of April for amercement of his wages – 5s.
Item paid to the swineherd for the like – 5s.
Item paid for one new staple and for mending of a lock thereto the plumb house – 4d.
Item paid to John North for half of one end of white leather to the James collar – 14d.
Item paid for bringing a plank to the West Mill Bridge that was carried away with the violence of the water – 4d.
Item paid for covering of Alls Burnskell's grave – 4d.
Item paid for the one half of Mr Juells book – 5s 6d.
Item paid to William Coocke, glazier for mending of all the glass windows about the church and for the repair of the leads this year ending at Easter next – 40s.
Item paid for one bell-string – 2s.
Item paid for one horn to the swineherd – 8d.
Item paid to Thomas Myddelton for serving the glazier – 6d.
Item paid to John Erlle for making of 20 bars to stay the glass windows – 10d.
Item paid to him for mending the stools in the church – 6d.
Item paid to the bellman for serving of the plumber upon the boards, 3 days – 12d.
Item paid for covering of Ann Hutchynson's grave – 4d.
Item paid for covering of Thomas Wardall, Robert Chapman and John Mackerall's graves – 12d.
Item paid for charcoal for drying the organs – 2d.

Sum £3 4s 7d.

f. 66v.

Item paid for mending the clock and for a huppe[1] and a staple to the church gate and for a bolt to the Great James – 8d.

Item paid to Arthur Hill and Richard Emet for making hue and cry[2] after Robert Swetyng[3] from Lowth to Barton and Caster,[4] for their labour and expenses, 4s 4d, and for the hire of 2 horses to Thomas Hutchynson & George Lobley – 2s 8d.

Item paid to Robert Odlyng and John Earlle for 3 days work upon the Rood loft to meat and wages, that is to John Earlle 2s 4d and to Robert Odlyng 2s, sum – 4s 3d.[5]

Item paid for nails to the said work – 7d.

Item paid for one rope to the great plumbs and chimes – 6s.

Item paid for one string to the Second bell – 2s 2d.

Item paid to the keepers of the Sudberies Hutch[6] for 5 lbs of solder – 2s 1d.

Item paid to Ralf Robson for 2 lbs of solder – 10d.

Item paid to Mr Dowghty the vicar, for 10 boards bestowed for painting of the Rood loft – 4s 8d.[7]

Item paid for 30 cotterells and 8 wedges to the bells – 2s 4d.

Item paid to the smith for the laying of ten stirrups[8] and making of 2 anckers,[9] one of 5lbs and the other of 9lbs – 20d.

Item paid for one key to the clock house door and for work about the clock – 8d.

32s 11d.

f. 67r.

Item paid to Fawdyngworth, the mason, for making of 4 moynylls[10] to 2 glass windows, the one on in St Peter's choir and the other in the north side of the High ally – 20s.

Item paid to 3 labourers at Bishop Briggs one day and a half, to meat and wages for wood bestowed there – 2s 3d.

Item paid for making of iron bars to the glass windows before mentioned, which iron was gotten in taking down of the Rood loft – 20d.

---

1 Hoop?
2 A proclamation for the capture of a criminal. *OED.*
3 Swetyng had previously been sent to Lincoln Castle but appears to have escaped or was a fugitive. Page 339. Accounts III, *f.* 50r. He must however have been recaptured, as Thomas Lech was later paid for giving evidence against him at Lincoln. Page 362. Accounts III, *f.* 67v.
4 Caister.
5 Part of the Rood loft appears to be still standing.
6 Sudbury's Hutch.
7 Possibly for painting scriptural texts on a board attached to the Rood screen.
8 An appendage to a bell. *OED.*
9 Anchors.
10 Mullions?

Item paid for covering of Cuthbert Wille's grave – 4d.
Item paid for the charges of a bull that strayed to Skamelsbe[1] and for keeping him 15 days – 12d.
Item paid to Robert Odlyng for taking up St George bell and the 2 bells for 4 days work of 2 wrights at 6d the day – 4s.
Item paid to him for the mending of the James wheel and for nails and stays to the same – 16d.
Item paid to William Coocke in recompense of charges for making and mending of glass windows after the great storm – 20s.[2]
Item paid to William Kyng for 3 *provambs*[3] of lime spent about the glass windows – 7½d.
Item paid to labourers for bearing in of stones that was of the 2 crosses and for digging and labouring in the churchyard – 3s 6d.
Item paid for carrying a plank to the West Mill that was born away with the flood – 4d.
Item for mending the Trinity bell-string with new hemp by work [of] the roper – 12d.
Item for scouring and mending of the common hedge towards Keddyngton – 12d.
f. 67v.
Item paid to Thomas Leich, smith, for giving evidence at Lyncoln against Robert Swetyng – 3s 4d.
Item paid for covering of Mr Langham and Widow Wardall's graves – 8d.
Item paid to William Jacson for storing of 2 ladders and for making a new fid[4] on one of them – 8d.
Item paid to Saltmarsh and Hogdson for plasshynge and diking of 53½ of rods of the common hedge towards Legborn Lane – 13s 4d.
Item paid to Gilbert Blanchard for nails and one strike of lime – 6d.
Item paid to John Earll for setting scaffold to the Rood for painting of it and for taking down of it with nails bestowed about the same – 14d.
Item paid to William White for one bull – 20s.
Item paid to Mr Vicar for solder for mending of the leads – 15d.
Item for paper and nails – 2d.
Item paid to William Hewet and Olyver Kenethorpe for keeping the two common bulls – 20s.
Item paid to Luke Smith for painting scripture on the Rood loft[5] – 11s.

[1] Scamblesby, 7 miles from Louth.
[2] Raphael Holinshed (c.1525–80?) noted in his *Chronicle* of 1577 that 'this year [1570], the fifth of October, chanced a terrible wind and rain both by sea and land … [and at] Mumbie chappell, the whole town was lost [and] … the church was wholly overthrown except the steeple',
[3] Meaning unknown.
[4] A wooden or metal bar or pin. *OED*.
[5] A board containing scriptural texts, replacing the figures of Christ, Mary and John above the screen.

Item paid to Richard Riggs for dressing and keeping in order the town's harness for this year – 20d.
Item paid to Robert Odlyng for taking up the Fore bell and making a wheel to the Lady bell – 20d.
Item paid to Richard White for 2 psalm books – 2s 10d.
Item paid to John Wadsley for bars to the glass windows – 6d.
£3 18s 9d.
Sum – £15 11s 9½d.

APPENDIX 1

LOUTH ST JAMES CHURCHWARDENS: 1500–70

Date	Name/Occupation	References
1499–1500	John Chapman, Merchant John Hoberthorn, Gentleman Symon Lyncoln, Merchant Thomas Bradelay, Mercer	LAO, Goulding Papers 5/3.
1500–1	Robert Ynglych, Barker Thomas Alderton, *alias* Cardmaker William Keyll, Tailor Thomas Fox, Shoemaker	Dudding, *Accounts*, p. 1.
1501–2	Thomas Tayleyor, Draper Robert Beverlay, Mercer Thomas Argram, Draper William Joneson, Weaver	Dudding, *Accounts*, p. 15.
1502–3	Robert Gyrdyke, Mercer Thomas Messanger, Goldsmith John Rychardson, Lister John Rycroft, Draper	Dudding, *Accounts*, p. 31.
1503–4	William Fitzwilliam, Gentleman Symond Lyndsay, Merchant Richard Beverlay, Mercer Thomas Bradlay, Merchant	Dudding, *Accounts*, p. 47.
1504–5	John Chapman, Mercator[1] Simond Lincoln, Mercator Thomas Alderton Richard Raythby, Butcher	Dudding, *Accounts*, p. 59.
1505–6	Thomas Tayleyor, Draper William Inglich, Butcher Edward Hewbaunke John Gonnyle, Draper	Dudding, *Accounts*, p.74.
1506–7	William Butelar, Merchant John Beverlay, Merchant John Richardson, Lister John Thomson, Sadler	Dudding, *Accounts*, p. 85.

[1] Mercator – Latin, merchant.

Date	Name/Occupation	References
1507–8	Robert Gyrdyke, Mercer James Bromflett, Weaver John Kechyn, Fletcher John Okeland, Tailor	Dudding, *Accounts*, p. 94.
1508–9	John Spencer, Clerk Richard Burton, Butcher William Gray, Corvesar[2] William Joneson, Corvesar	Dudding, *Accounts*, p. 106.
1509–10	Thomas Tayleyor, Draper Richard Beverlay, Mercer Richard Raythby, Butcher John Gonylde, Draper	Dudding, *Accounts*, p. 115.
1510–11	William Gossauke, Draper Alexander Rychardson, Corviser John Norman, Roper Richard Clarke, Capper	Dudding, *Accounts*, p. 125.
1511–12	Robert Beverlay, Mercer Thomas Alderton, Yeoman Robert Stefnson, Yeoman Robert Route, Mercer	Dudding, *Accounts*, p. 133.
1512–13	Robert Smyth, Butcher William Goldsmith Gilbert Erchebold, Weaver William Pyght, Corviser	Dudding, *Accounts*, p. 141.
1513–14	Thomas Bolar, Wright William Helsame, Butcher Thomas Maundfild Robert Spencer, Draper	Dudding, *Accounts*, p. 158.
1514–15	Thomas Bradelay, Merchant Thomas Tayleyor, Draper Richard Beverlay, Mercer John Spencer, 'Steward of Court, Lord Lincoln'[3]	Dudding, *Accounts*, p. 165.
1515–16	John Kechyn, Fletcher William Walker Richard Bouher William Broune, Mylner[4]	Dudding, *Accounts*, p. 174.

[2] Corvesar, Cordwainer – shoemaker. *OED*.
[3] Steward of the Manor Court of the bishop of Lincoln.
[4] 'Mylner' – miller. *OED*.

Date	Name/Occupation	References
1516–17	Thomas Argram, Draper John Alford Robert Brampton, Corviser John Foster, Smith, def[5] John Thomas, Fuller[6]	Dudding, *Accounts*, p. 183.
1517–18	Robert Moor, Corviser Thomas Provest, Carffare[7] William West William Bernard, Butcher	Dudding, *Accounts*, p. 188.
1518–19	William Proketure, Weaver John Pernell, Husbandman Robert Louson, Goldsmith William Neuton, Glover	Dudding, *Accounts*, p. 195.
1519–20	Gilbard Clarke, Carpenter Robert Pagge, Butcher Richard Hynde, Mylner Christopher Smilay, Capper	Dudding, *Accounts*, p. 200.
1520–1	Robert Peyrpoynt, Gentleman Thomas Beverlay, Mercer John Layrmond, Glover Robert Fysher, Tanner	Dudding, *Accounts*, p. 205.
1521–2	William Cawod Thomas Rychardson, Glover Thomas Grauntham, Tailor Robert Corneford, Tailor	Dudding, *Accounts*, p. 210.
1522–3	William Kyng Robert Doughty Walter Fyswike, Mercer Hugh Beverlay, Mercer	Dudding, *Accounts*, p. 217.
1523–4	William Gunby, Gentleman Robert Treigolde, Gentleman John Curtas, Yeoman Robert Baly, Mercer	Dudding, *Accounts*, p. 222.
1524–5[8]	John More John Spencer Richard Beverley William Gosshauke	Goulding, Papers, 5/3

[5] 'def' – defunct. Goulding Papers, 5/3.
[6] Cleaner of cloth. *OED*.
[7] 'Carffare' – carver, carpenter. Goulding Papers, 5/3.
[8] Few accounts surviving. Gosshauke – alderman of the Trinity guild.

Date	Name/Occupation	References
1525–6[9]	[...], Thomson, Sadler [...], Shoemaker [...], Brampton John? Davy	Goulding, Papers, 5/3.
1526–7[10]		
1527–8	Robert Browne, Draper Richard Curson Alex[ander]..., Tailor[11] Thomas Spencer, Draper	Page 1. Accounts II, f. 1r.
1528–9	Thomas Richardson, Glover William West Robert Fyssher, Tanner Thomas Wollerby, Mercer?	Page 12. Accounts II, f. 5r.
1529–30	Thomas Hyll, Weaver John Holdernes, Butcher Richard Hynde, Mylner Richard Spencer	Page 20 Accounts II, f. 9r.
1530–1	William Browne, Miller William Lawrence Robert Hartburn, Walker William Glene, Mercer	Page 29. Accounts II, f. 13r.
1531–2	Thomas Bowland Robert Lawson Robert Collingwod Robert Richardson	Page 37. Accounts II, f. 16r.
1532–3	Robert Spencer William Newton Thomas Spenethorne George Spillesby	Page 47. Accounts II, f. 20r.
1533–4	William Kyng Robert Doughty Robert Proctor William Browne, Barber	Page 56. Accounts II, f. 24r.

---

[9] Document damaged.
[10] No accounts surviving.
[11] Surname missing. Goulding suggests Alexander Tayleor. Goulding, Papers, 5/3. His name could be Alexander Mychelson, churchwarden and tailor, 1539/40. Accounts II, p. 101.

Date	Name/Occupation	References
1534–5	Walter Fyswyck Hugo Berverlay, Mercer John Browne, Junior, Draper Robert Acred, Cardmaker	Page 63. Accounts II, *f.* 28r.
1535–6	William Goshauke, Draper, Robert Bayly, Mercer, Henry Fernysyd, Sherman Matthew Wardale, Shoemaker,	Page 71. Accounts II, *f.* 32r.
1536–7	William Cawod John Davy, Fuller John Chapman, Gentleman Thomas Hallywells	Page 79. Accounts II, *f.* 36r.
1537–8	Thomas Argram, Draper William Asseby, Mercer Richard Walker William Askew	Page 86. Accounts II, *f.* 40r.
1538–9	Robert Browne Richard Curson Thomas Lawrence George Sutton	Page 94. Accounts II, *f.* 44r.
1539–40	Thomas Spencer, Draper Alexander Mychelson, Taylor Thomas Grene, Taylor Thomas Kechen, Husbandman	Page 101. Accounts II, *f.* 48r.
1540–1	Robert Fyssher William West Gilbert Fyssher, Mercer William Colingwod, Weaver	Page 107. Accounts II, *f.* 52r.
1541–2	John Holdernes Thomas Wollerby Thomas Wardayll William Taylyor	Page 113. Accounts II, *f.* 55r.
1542–3	Richard Hynd Robert Hartburn Bartholomew Claxton William Draux	Page 119. Accounts II, *f.* 59r.
1543–4[12]	Robert Spencer Robert Colynwod John Spenlof John Spaldyng	Page 127. Accounts II, *f.* 63r.

---

[12] William Glene (d.1543) crossed through.

Date	Name/Occupation	References
1544–5	William Kyng Robert Dughtie William Brown William Camron	Page 134. Accounts II, *f.* 66v.
1545–6	Walter Fyswyke William Brown, Barber William White Gylbert Blanncherd	Page 140. Accounts II, *f.* 70r.
1546–7	William Baylle Robert Acred William Doughtie Mathew Wardyll	Page 147. Accounts II, *f.* 74v.
1547–8	Thomas Meres, Gentleman John Chapman, Gentleman George Spyllesbe Thomas Pellson	Page 153. Accounts II, *f.* 77r.
1548–9	Richard Curson Thomas Holland John Swyne John Fysshe	Page 161. Accounts II, *f.* 81v.
1549–50	George Sutton William Colynwood Thomas Palmer William Evans	Page 166. Accounts II, *f.* 84v.
1550–1[13]	Thomas Wardell Thomas Blanchard John Palmer	Page 173. Accounts II, *f.* 88v.
1551–2	Robert Spencer John Spenlow Thomas Holdernes William Somerscales	Page 182. Accounts II, *f.* 93v.
1552–3	William Browne John Spaldwyn William Kyng Edward Boswell	Page 190. Accounts II, *f.* 99r.
1553–4	Gilbert Blancherd John Brown John Brandon Stephen Bucke	Page 198. Accounts II, *f.* 104r.

---

[13] The names of John Holdernes (d. 1550) and William Taillor are both crossed through, therefore only three churchwardens appear to have been elected.

Date	Name/Occupation	References
1554–5	William Whyte William Balif Thomas Richardson Thomas Leche	Page 208. Accounts II, *f.* 109v.
1555–6	William Doughtie Robert Acred Robert Chapman Edward Argram	Page 216. Accounts II, *f.* 114r.
1556–7	Thomas Meres Mathew Wardall Symon Thew Richard Robertson	Page 232. Accounts II, *f.* 123r.
1557–8	John Chapman, Gentleman Thomas Pelson John North George Willows	Page 240. Accounts II, *f.* 128r.
1558–9	William Ormesby William Richmond William Evans John Fissh	Page 245. Accounts II, *f.* 132v.
1559–60	Thomas Wardall Thomas Blanchard William Hewytt Robert Kighley	Page 249. Accounts II, *f.* 135r.
1560–1	John Palmer William Somerskaills William Fysswick Jarrat Alendaill	Page 259. Accounts III, *f.* 1r.
1561–2[14]	Thomas Holdernes John Spalding John Baylye John Rygald	Page 265. Accounts III, *f.* 9v.
1562–3	William King Edward Boswell Nicholas Coventre Robert Marshall	Page 273. Accounts III, *f.* 16v.

---

[14] Holdernes and Spalding are recorded as the old churchwardens, Baylye and Rygald as the new on page 264.

Date	Name/Occupation	References
1563–4[15]	Gilbert Blanchard Stephen Buck John Gray, Younger Richard Girsbye	Page 279. Accounts III, f. 22v.
1564–5	William Whyte Thomas Richardson Myles Gray George Anderson	Page 287. Accounts III, f. 29r.
1565–6[16]	Robert Chapman, Tanner Mathew Wardall Robert Holland Roger Stut	Page 294. Accounts III, f. 38v.
1566–7[17]	Richard Robenson Thomas Pelson Thomas Smyth, Butcher William Holland	Page 300. Accounts III, f. 44v.
1567–8[18]	John North George Willos James Marshall Robert West	Page 307. Accounts III, f. 50v.
1568–9[19]	William Ormesby John Fyshe Steaven Spaldyng Thomas Jackson	Page 314. Accounts III, f. 55v.
1569–70	Thomas Blanchard Robert Kyngley Christopher Pomorte John Sowthe	Page 319. Accounts III, f. 59v.
1570–1[20]	William Hewet John Pallmer Richard Ryggs Richard Holdernes	Page 325. Accounts III, f. 64r.

[15] Leonard Russhebye crossed through.

[16] Chapman and Wardall are recorded as the old churchwardens, Holland and Stutt as the new.

[17] Robenson and Pelson are recorded as the old churchwardens, Smyth and Holland as the new.

[18] North and Willes are recorded as the old churchwardens, Marshall and West as the new.

[19] Ormesby and Fyshe are recorded as the old churchwardens, Spaldyng and Jackson as the new on page 314.

[20] Hewet and Pallmer are recorded as the old churchwardens, Ryggs and Holdernes as the new.

APPENDIX 2

SUNDAY COLLECTIONS BY YEAR: 1500/1–70/1

Date	£	s	d	Decimal	Date	£	s	d	Decimal
1500/1	7	6	8	£7.33	**1536/7**	7	18	9	£7.94
1501/2	11	5	8	£11.28	**1537/8**	9	13	0	£9.65
1502/3	14	18	11	£14.95	**1538/9**	6	12	9	£6.64
1503/4	12	10	4	£12.52	**1539/40**	6	0	6	£6.03
1504/5	10	13	9	£10.69	**1540/1**	7	17	10	£7.89
1505/6	10	13	1	£10.65	**1541/2**	6	0	7½	£6.03
1506/7	11	2‖	2	£11.11	**1542/3**	6	4	3	£6.21
1507/8	10	2	10	£10.14	**1543/4**	6	17	3	£6.86
1508/9	9	12	10	£9.64	**1544/5**	6	11	1½	£6.01
1509/10	9	2	2	£9.11	**1545/6***	1	16	4	£1.82
1510/11	11	16	4	£11.82	**1546/7**	4	18	2	£4.91
1511/12	12	12	4	£12.57	**1547/8**	4	12	9	£4.64
1512/13	10	3	2	£10.16	**1548/9***	3	7	11	£3.40
1513/14	9	9	5	£9.47	**1549/50**	3	2	2½	£3.11
1514/15	12	10	0	£12.50	**1550/1**	4	9	11	£4.50
1515/16	11	16	0	£11.80	**1551/2**	5	14	1½	£5.70
1516/17	7	9	0	£7.45	**1552/3**	6	0	3½	£5.01
1517/18	9	5	3	£9.26	**1553/4**	6	8	9½	£5.44
1518/19	8	13	1	£8.65	**1554/5***	2	3	6½	£2.18
1519/20	7	0	11	£7.05	**1555/6**	5	17	5	£5.87
1520/1	9	5	1	£9.25	**1556/7+**	7	0	5	£7.02
1521/2	7	12	8	£7.63	**1557/8+**	6	0	2	£6.01
1522/3	8	8	7	£8.43	**1558/9+**	4	19	6	£4.98
1523/4	9	10	0	£9.50	**1559/60+**	12	9	8	£12.48‖
1524/5	Unknown				**1560/1+**	4	17	8	£4.88
1525/6	Unknown				**1561/2+**	5	0	10	£5.04
1526/7	Unknown				**1562/3**	5	4	3	£5.21
1527/8	9	1	7	£9.08	**1563/4+**	5	10	6½	£5.53
1528/9	8	17	0	£8.85	**1564/5**	6	11	2	£6.56

SUNDAY COLLECTIONS BY YEAR: 1500/1–70/1

Date	£	s	d	Decimal	Date	£	s	d	Decimal
1529/30	8	5	7	£8.28	**1565/6+**	6	10	0	£6.50
1530/1	9	6	2	£9.31	**1566/7+**	5	5	11	£5.30
1531/2	10	7	4	£10.37	**1567/8+**	4	14	4½	£4.72
1532/3	8	1	5	£8.07	**1568/9+**	4	6	11	£4.35
1533/4	9	15	4	£9.77	**1569/70+**	5	18	11	£5.95
1534/5	10	0	0	£10.00	**1570/71+**	5	12	2	£5.61
1535/6	10	17	7	£10.88					

* Incomplete or missing.
+ Entered quarterly.
‖ Probably an inaccurate calculation.

INDEX OF PERSONS AND PLACES

County names are added only for places outside of Lincolnshire. The editor is grateful to Mr Simon Neal for completing the indexes for this volume.

—, Alan, 288
Alexander, 33, 39, 367
  Anthony, 86
  Sir Christopher, 79, 86, 102, 109, 259
  Leonard, 69, 338
  Richard, 174
  Abot, Isabel, wife of Thomas, 188
Aby, 240n
Acred (Acarhed, Acrad, Acrede, Acrid,
    Acryd, Agred, Akand, Akerhed,
    Akershed, Akred, Akrid),
  Janet, wife of Robert, 143
  Joanna, 143n
  Robert, 96, 96n, 97, 110, 154, 158–59,
    173, 177, 179, 186, 211, 215, 221n,
    229, 243, 248, 251, 268, 272,
    280, 284, 312–13, 315, 368–70
  Thomas, 228, 255
  Adlyngton, Robert, 227
Africa, North, 161n
Agred, Akand, Akerhed, Akershed, Akred,
    Akrid *see* Acred
Alderton,
  Thomas, 37, 365
  Thomas, *alias* Thomas Cardmaker,
    37n, 364
Alendaill, Alendall *see* Allendale
Aleyn *see* Allen
  Alford (Alforthe), John, 337, 366
Algarkirk, 109n
Algiers, Algeria, 162n
Allat *see* Allot
Allen (Aleyn, Allain, Eleyn, Elleyn),
  Agnes, 231, 231n
  William, 129, 129n, 130, 132, 137
Allendale (Alendaill, Alendall, Allandale,
    Arundall), Jarrat, 282, 282n, 291,
    291n, 302, 370
Allerton, Thomas, 48, 56, 73, 84, 92, 99,
    107, 115, 123, 130, 137, 143, 149, 155,
    163, 169, 174, 181, 188

Allot (Allat, Allote, Allotte),
  Mr, 31718
  Catherine, wife of Robert, 314, 318n
  Robert, 314, 318n
Anderson,
  …, 250, 259
  George, 312, 319–20, 324, 371
  James, 139, 139n, 266
  John, 7, 106, 106n, 107, 115, 123, 130,
    233, 235, 238, 241–43, 246, 252,
    260, 266–70, 274, 279–80
  Robert, 313
  Thomas, 159, 161, 166, 172, 178, 193,
    200, 204, 212, 221, 284, 346
  Walter, 201–202, 283, 314
Androse, John, 53
Archard, John, 137
Archebold (Archebolde, Erchebold),
  Gilbert, 84, 365
  James, 278
Archer, Richard, 352
Argram,
  …, 274
  Edward, 236–37, 248, 260, 273, 370
  Thomas, 120, 129–30, 136, 136n,
    147–48, 364, 366, 368
  Armstrong (Armestrong), George, 77,
    77n, 111, 124, 157
  Arnalld, …, 187
Arundall *see* Allendale
Ascue *see* Askew
Ashby (Asby, Asheby, Asseby, Asserby,
    Assheby),
  Isabel, wife of William, 89, 129–30
  William, 59, 59n, 96, 120, 131, 133,
    142–44, 368
  Asheball, Gilbert, 73
Asheby *see* Ashby
Askew (Ascue, Aske, Askwe, Ayscough),
  Elizabeth, 342, 342n, 346–47
  Richard, 334

INDEX OF PERSONS AND PLACES

Richard, son of William, 341, 341n
Roger, *alias* Roger Bonus, 265n
William, 120, 192, 368
Sir William, 161n
Asseby, Asserby, Assheby *see* Ashby
Aswardby, 25
Atkins (Atkin, Atkyn),
 ..., 89, 94, 103
 Thomas, 85, 93
 William, 248
Auncell *see* Haunsell
Aylby, William, 161, 163
Ayscough *see* Askew

Babbe (Bab),
 ..., 246, 251
 Ellen, daughter of William, 251n
 William, 251n
Babsor, Robert, 24, 243
Bailey (Baille, Baily, Balif, Baliffe,
  Balley, Baly, Bayle, Baylie, Bayliff,
  Baylle, Baylly, Bayllye, Bayly,
  Baylye), 40
 family of, 11
 Mistress, 187
 Anne, widow, 197, 277, 277n
 Geoffrey, vicar of Louth St James, 3n,
  151, 151n, 184n
 John, 246, 248, 269, 297, 311, 370
 Katherine, daughter of Robert, 64–65
 Robert, 36, 36n, 38–39, 43, 43n, 44,
  53, 60–61, 66, 70, 72, 74, 74n,
  75–79, 85, 88, 95, 97, 102, 104,
  104n, 108–109, 111–12, 119, 124,
  126, 131, 133–34, 139, 154, 158,
  164, 166, 168–69, 173, 182, 366,
  368
 Thomas, 311
 William, 177, 179, 218, 239, 284, 304,
  304n, 337, 369–70
 William, son of William, 333
Bain, River, 6
Baird (Bayrd),
 Mr, 349
 William, 169
Baker, William, 83, 83n
Bale, Mistress, 183
Balif, Baliffe, Balley, Baly *see* Bailey
Banton, Alan, 321
Barbor (Barbar),
 - John, 284
 - William, 104, 104n, 110, 174
 Bard, William, 161, 163

Bardney, abbey, abbot of, *see* Barton,
  Peter de
Barley (Barly, Berly),
 - Hugh, 174
 - Robert, 174
 - Thomas, 174
 Barlings, abbey, abbot of, *see*
  Mackerall, Matthew
Barly *see* Barley
Barnard *see* Bernard
 Barret, John, 358
 Barton, 361
Barton (Bartone, Berton),
 - Humphrey, son of John, 168, 168n
 - James, 254, 263, 274–75
 Peter de, abbot of Bardney, 8
 William, 107
 William, vicar, 52n
 Barwick, ..., wife of, 48
 Bastard, ..., 234
 Bate, ..., 201
Bawdwin (Bawdewyn, Bawdwyn), John,
  250, 250n, 341, 345
 Bawesforth, Richard, 53
Bawnus *see* Bonus
 Bayard, William, 163
Bayle, Baylie, Bayliff, Baylle, Baylly,
  Bayllye, Bayly, Baylye *see* Bailey
 Baynton, Katherine, wife of Alan, 99
 Bayo, Walter, 35
Beacon *see* Becon
 Becham (Bechman, Bechum, Bycham),
  256, 263
 Mother, 261
 Alice, 256–59, 261–62, 285–86
 Elizabeth, 253
Beche,
 Agnes, 255
 Alice, 256
Bechman, Bechum *see* Becham
Becon (Beacon),
 Mr, 350
 Thomas, 350n
Beilowe *see* Bellow
 Belbow, John, 66
 Beldy, John, 94
 Bell, 338
 Agnes, wife of John, 162, 162n
 John, 168n
 William, 337
Belleau (Helloff), parsons of, 168n
 Bellingay (Bellingey, Byllingaye,
  Byllyngey, Bylyngay), 103, 108
 John, 233, 236, 242

Bellman (Belman), 49–50, 66, 78, 85, 100, 169
- John, 275
- Matthew, 42–43, 58, 60, 62, 68, 74, 87, 103, 108, 116
Bellow (Beilowe, Bello, Bellowe, Beloo), Mr, 139, 164, 184
  John, 21, 21n, 23, 33n, 92n, 126, 126n, 129n, 183, 183n
Belman see Bellman
Belmore, John, 274
Beloo see Bellow
Belton [in Axholme], 109n
Bemond,
  Janet, wife of Thomas, 130
  Thomas, 130
Bentley, Arthur, 324–25, 329
Berche, John, 322
Berly see Barley
  Bernard (Barnard), William, 72, 72n, 74, 84, 366
Bertie, Richard, 211n
Berton see Barton
Berverlay see Beverley
Bery,
  ..., 263
  Christopher, 143
  Joanne, daughter of Christopher, 107
  Margaret, 253, 256–59, 261–63
  Waryng, 159
Bessby (Besby, Biesby, Bursbye),
  Elizabeth, 149, 155
  Elizabeth, prioress of Stainfield, 147
Betton (Beton, Betyn, Bylton), William, 12, 80, 80n
Beverley (Berverlay, Beverlay),
  family of, 29
  Agnes, 216
  Dorothy, 106, 106n, 107
  Dorothy, wife of Richard, 136
  Hugh, 96–97, 99, 102, 168–69, 366, 368
  Janet, 36, 38
  Janet, widow, 37, 44, 48
  John, 99, 99n, 100, 364
  Richard, 9, 62, 72n, 139, 139n, 181–82, 364–66
  Robert, 37, 37n, 51–52, 55–56, 58, 60–61, 64n, 65–66, 80, 83–84, 89, 89n, 92, 106–107, 122–23, 130, 142–43, 162–63, 169, 182, 364–65
  Sir Robert, 199, 204, 211, 215, 233
  Thomas, 37, 37n, 56, 92, 99, 107, 115, 123, 130, 137, 143, 149, 155, 163, 168, 181, 188, 366
  Thomas, junior, 48
  Thomas, senior, 73, 84
  Thomas, son of Richard, 72–73
Beverley, St John of, 308n
Beysbe, William, 334
Biesby see Bessby
Bilsby, 25
Bilting (Bylting, Bylton, Byltyng),
  ..., 258–59, 261–62
  Richard, 254, 259, 261, 263
Binbrook, 358n
Blanchard (Blanchand, Blancherd, Blancherde, Blanchird, Blannchard, Blanncherd, Blansherd),
  family of, 11, 29
  Gilbert, 11, 14, 172, 172n, 173, 173n, 174, 176–77, 187, 200, 203, 206, 212–13, 215, 226, 228–29, 237–39, 248, 265, 278, 283, 295–96, 300–301, 303, 308–309, 311, 318–19, 322–23, 326–27, 329–30, 334–35, 337–38, 342–44, 355–56, 362, 369, 371
  Thomas, 204, 204n, 207, 215, 221, 229, 248, 264, 275–76, 278, 281–83, 291, 300–303, 312, 326–27, 333–35, 339–40, 342, 351, 353, 369–71
Blanton, Janet, 262
Blind,
  Anne, 263
  Emma, 253
Bocher see Butcher
Boland, Thomas, 78
Bolar, Thomas, 365
Bold, Thomas, 19
Bolingbroke, 94n
Bolles,
  family, 191n
  Mr, 191
Bolyngbrowk, John, 274
Bonnar,
  ..., 192
  Frances, daughter of Thomas, 279n
  Thomas, 279
Bonus (Bawnus),
  ..., 278
  Roger, 270
  Roger, alias Roger Askew, 265
Booth (Boothe, Bowthe),
  Eustace, 321–22, 324
  Eustace, son of Eustace, 324n

Thomas, 277, 279
Bootheby, Henry, 107
Bordle, Robert, 174
Borne (Born), Bernard, 312, 344–45
Bornsale *see* Burnshall
Bornskell *see* Burnskell
Borwell *see* Burwell
Bose,
  ..., 261–62
  Thomas, 259, 261–63
  Boston, ..., 51
Boston, 2, 7n, 24, 300, 327
  church, 8
  clergy of, 3n
  taxation at, 2n
Boswell,
  Edward, 220, 220n, 221, 225, 241, 305–306, 313, 369–70
  Elizabeth, junior, 188
  Elizabeth, wife of Edward, 187, 187n, 243n
  Margaret, wife of Edward, 240, 240n, 243
Boucke *see* Buck
  Bouher, Richard, 365
Bouland *see* Bowland
Bowck *see* Buck
  Bowell, Hugh, 313
Bower,
  Joan, 356; as widow, 352
  Julian, 350
Bowland (Bouland),
  Ellen, 182; as daughter of Thomas, 182n
  John, 121
  Oliver, 181
  Robert, 275
  Thomas, 69, 69n, 70, 108, 122, 130, 136, 367
Bowman,
  Joanna, wife of Roger, 155, 155n
  Roger, 154
Bowthe *see* Booth
  Bracebryge, ..., 200
  Brackenborough (Brakenbrugh), 53
Bradley (Bradelay, Bradlay, Bradlaye, Bradle, Brodlay),
  family of, 11, 29
  Mr, 86, 88, 94, 110, 174, 196, 268, 283, 301–302, 310, 319, 327–28, 330, 342–44
  David, 195
  John, 21, 21n, 64n, 240, 303, 326; as

merchant of the staple of Calais, 240n
  Maria, daughter of John, 153
  Thomas, 67, 37, 56, 65, 115, 130, 137, 143, 149, 155, 163, 181, 188, 213, 336, 349, 364–65
  Thomas, merchant of the staple of Calais, 40n, 65n, 94n
  Thomas, senior, 48, 73, 84, 92, 99, 107, 122
Brafurth,
  John, 313
  Katherine, 313
Brakenbrugh *see* Brackenborough
Brampton,
  ..., 367
  Robert, 129, 129n, 130, 366
Bran, Richard, 188
Branchmore (Branchemore), Katherine, wife of John, 106–107
Brandon,
  Charles, duke of Suffolk, 126n
  John, 229, 369
Brathat, John, 352
Bridlington, East Yorkshire, 308n
Briggs,
  Alice, 261
  Bishop, 361
Brodlay *see* Bradley
Bromflett (Bromflet), James, 106–107, 115, 148, 365
Broune *see* Brown
  Browghton, William, 56, 78
Brown (Broune, Browne),
  Elizabeth, wife of Robert, 64–65
  Isabel, 143, 143n; as wife of Robert, 142
  Joanne, 65; as wife of William, 64, 69, 74
  John, 14, 96, 100, 108, 116n, 129n, 166, 172, 178–79, 181–82, 188–90, 195–96, 199, 202, 228–29, 231, 239, 265, 272, 278, 283, 369
  John, junior, 96–97, 368
  John, son of Robert, 33n
  Luke, 260
  Matthew, 52
  Richard, 303
  Robert, 33, 33n, 39, 71, 76n, 77, 96, 104, 127, 147–48, 154–55, 367–68
  Walter, 212, 283, 313, 319
  William, 62, 62n, 70, 88–90, 111, 114–15, 122, 166, 171–72, 178,

190, 193, 200, 211–12, 214–15,
220–21, 224, 232, 242–43, 267,
271, 276–77, 279, 282n, 283,
296, 365, 367, 369
Brownrick, Isabel, 314
Broxholme, Thomas, 303, 303n
Bryan, Annes, 179
Bryd, Robert, 24
Bryngkle, John, 313
Buck (Boucke, Bowck, Bucke, Buk),
George, 343
Stephen, 221, 221n, 229, 231, 239, 283,
283n, 303, 311, 369, 371
Stephen, son of Stephen, 221n
Buckyngham, Janet, 129–30, 136
Bude, John, fee of, 4n
Buk see Buck
Bulle, William, 18n
Burgh, Thomas, Baron Burgh of
Gainsborough, 119, 119n
Burket, ..., 259
Burle,
..., 252, 254–55
Father, 255
Burnshall (Bornsale, Burnschale),
Robert, 51, 138
Thomas, 163
Burnskell (Bornskell), Alice, 357, 360
Burnstall, John, 42
Burrett (Burret),
..., 108, 116, 118, 123, 131, 137, 263,
289–90
Annes, 334
John, 86
Bursbye see Bessby
Burton,
..., 258, 308
James, 254
Margaret, 257–59
Richard, 126, 126n, 365
Burwell (Borwell), 26, 312, 354–55
fair, 307, 314
Butcher (Bocher),
Bernard, 68
Thomas, 322
Thomas, 337
Butlar (Butelar, Butllar, Buttler),
Robert, 182
Sir Robert, 179, 181
William, 364
Bycham see Becham
Byllingaye, Byllyngey, Bylyngay see
Bellingay

Bylting see Bilting
Bylton see Betton, Bilting
Byltyng see Bilting
Byrd, William, choirmaster and composer,
25n

Cade, John, 92
Caistor (Caster), 27, 33n, 70n, 154n,
361
Calais, Staple of, merchants of, 6n, 29n,
37n, 40n, 65n
Cambridge, Cambridgeshire, 80n
Came see Kyme
Cameron (Camron), William, 166, 172,
178, 181–82, 369
Camolks, John, 65
Camron see Cameron
Canaries, wine from, 318n
Candeler, Thomas, 223
Canterbury, archdiocese, archbishop of,
25, 295, 298
Capper,
..., wife of Richard, 168–69
Arthur, 219, 252–59, 261–63, 285–90
Margaret, 262
Richard, 40
Car, ..., 256, 258
Cardmaker (Cardemaker),
Hugh, 133
Robert, 66, 74n, 199, 221, 221n
Thomas, *alias* Thomas Alderton, 37n,
364
Carever see Carver
Carffare (Carfare),
Agnes, daughter of Thomas, 36
Thomas, 39, 39n, 41–42, 44
Carlton, Great or Little, (Carlton), 336
Carlton, North, 170n
Carter (Cartar),
Alison, 130; as widow, 129
John, 147, 149
Richard, 84
Thomas, 313, 358
Carver (Carever, Carverer, Karver,
Kerver), Thomas, 51, 93, 96,
170–72, 174–77
Caster, see Caistor
Cater, ..., 310
Catterall (Catherall), Janet, 334, 343
Cawood (Cawod, Cawode, Caywod),
..., 309
John, 22n, 30, 44, 44n, 49–50, 55, 59,
65, 73, 84, 99, 107

INDEX OF PERSONS AND PLACES

John, junior, 115
John, senior, 115
John, son of William, 107
William, 70, 93, 112, 114–15, 123, 143, 149, 366, 368
William, son of John, 59, 59n
Cayme *see* Kyme
Cecil (Cecill),
Alice, 48
William, Lord Burghley, 308n
Sir William, 9n, 21
Chapman,
family of, 11, 29
Mr, 43, 59, 202–203, 217, 228, 251, 283, 321, 324
Anne, daughter of John, 106
Christopher, 334
Elizabeth, wife of John, 72, 72n, 73
George, 336, 344–45
John, 11, 37, 37n, 48, 56, 65, 73, 84, 112, 112n, 170n, 185, 187–88, 192–93, 272, 264, 368–70
John, merchant of the staple of Calais, 37n
Martin, 234, 234n, 241, 244, 269, 271, 274, 278, 280, 296, 299, 324
Robert, 231, 231n, 248, 260, 273, 297, 303, 326, 335, 343–44, 348, 353–54, 358, 360, 370–71
Charles V, Holy Roman emperor, 162n
Chew Magna, Somerset, 212n
Chowman, John, 190
Clacksby, Claksby *see* Claxby
Clarke (Clarck, Clark, Clerck, Clercke, Clerk),
Gilbert, 36, 36n, 366
James, 72, 72n, 73
John, 356
Miles, 275, 341
Richard, 197, 199, 365
Richard, senior, 197n
Sir Robert, 190
William, 253
Claxby (Clacksby, Claksby),
..., 41, 50
Richard, 60
Claxton,
Bartholomew, 132, 151n, 152, 159, 368
Janet, wife of Bartholomew, 107
Margaret, wife of Bartholomew, 122
Clerck, Clercke, Clerk *see* Clarke
Clinton (Clynton), Lord, 273, 296, 322
Cloble (Cloblay),

..., wife of, 66, 74, 85, 92, 100, 108
Marion, 130, 137
Clynton *see* Clinton
Cocke, John, 56
Cockerington, North or South, (Cokyngton), 232
Coggle (Coggell, Cogill, Cogle, Cogull),
..., 254–59, 261–63, 286, 288, 308
family, 317n
Mother, 28689
Harry, 317
John, 172, 172n, 178, 193, 199
Coke *see* Cooke
Coles, Father, 280
Collingwood (Colingwod, Collingwode, Collinwood, Collnwood, Collyngwood, Collyngwoode, Collynwod, Collynwood, Colyngwod, Colynwod, Colynwode, Colynwood, Colywood),
Agnes, wife of Robert, 148, 148n, 149, 149n
Anthony, 254, 261–63, 285
Ellen, wife of Robert, 129–30
Henry, 67
Joanna, wife of William, 216, 216n
Margaret, wife of William, 148, 148n
Robert, 69, 69n, 70, 159, 166, 172, 179, 181–82, 367–68
William, 140, 197, 278, 368–69
Colman, John, 273
Colton, Thomas, 92
Colyngwod, Colynwod, Colynwode, Colynwood, Colywood *see* Collingwood
Coningsby (Conysby), 6, 39
Conisholme, 36n, 142n, 358n
church, 36n
Constable,
Katherine, 154
Sir Robert, 244n
Conysby *see* Coningsby
Cooke (Coke, Coocke, Cook, Kooke),
Mr, 356
Alice, 181, 181n
John, 56, 56n, 58, 348
William, 306, 330, 360, 362
Cooper (Couper, Cowper),
Alice, 292, 296
John, 48
Richard, 60
Robert, 327

Thomas, 308
Walter, 327, 330
Copledike (Copeldyke, Coppuldicke,
    Coppuldike, Copuldick,
    Copuldicke),
  John, 318; as sheriff of Lincolnshire,
    318n
  Sir John, 318n, 342n
  William, 342, 342n, 346, 350–51, 357
Corier see Corriar
  Corkar, Mr, 279
  Corneford, Robert, 366
  Corriar (Corier, Corryar, Corur,
    Coryar), Isabel, 253–54, 256–59,
    261–63
Cortt,
  John, 107
  Richard, 76
Corur see Corriar
Corveser (Corvesar),
  Byrt, 46, 54
  Thomas, 190
Coryar see Corriar
Cotame see Cotton
  Cotes, Cots see Cotes
Cotton (Cotame, Cottam, Cottame),
  George, 306–307
  Robert, 227, 251, 260, 275, 298–99,
    310–11
  Thomas, son of Robert, 299
  William, son of Robert, 299
Cotts (Cotes, Cots),
  ..., 252–53, 257–58
  Father, 254, 256, 258–59, 261–63
  Edward, 270, 272, 274–75, 285
Couper see Cooper
  Coventry (Coventre), Nicholas, 303,
    305–306, 319, 370
Coventry, Warwickshire, Charterhouse, 3n
Cowper see Cooper
Craggs,
  ..., 338
  John, 337
Cranmer, Thomas, archbishop of
    Canterbury, 19n
Crathorne, Mr, 228
Croft (Crofts),
  ..., 253–54, 257–59, 261–63
  Janet, 258, 261
Cromwell, Thomas, Lord Privy Seal, 15,
    17, 21n, 33n, 92n, 126n, 139n
Crosier,
  ..., 253–54
  Richard, son of Thomas, 251n

Robert, son of Thomas, 251n
Thomas, 251, 251n, 258
Thomas, son of Thomas, 251n
Crosland, Croslande see Crosseland
Crosse, Luca, widow, 231
Crosseland (Crosland, Croslande),
  Alice, 313; as widow, 334
  Elizabeth, 107
  Janet, 333
  John, 327
  Thomas, 327, 343
  Thomas, son of Thomas, 333
Croxton,
  John, 153, 155
  Thomas, 14
Crumdall, Janet, 253
Curson (Cursin),
  Mr, 195
  Richard, 33, 42, 76n, 111, 111n, 112, 125,
    127, 131, 134, 139, 192, 197, 225,
    233, 236, 240, 329n, 367–69
  Robert, 45, 53
  Janet, 106–107, 115, 123, 130, 137
  John, 9, 36, 36n, 3738, 48, 56, 366
Cutas, Joan, widow, 53
Cyll see Syll

Daddy, Sir Richard, 47n
Dalton, Mother, 288
Davison (Davion, Davyson),
  ..., 261
  Mother, 262
  Agnes, 253, 257–59, 261–63
Davy,
  John, 112, 117, 143, 149, 367–68
  Robert, 142
Davyson see Davison
  Dawbney, Alice, 257
  Dawtney, Alison, 255
Dawton,
  ..., 254–58, 261, 286, 289
  Mother, 253
  Elizabeth, 255–56
  Margaret, 258
Day, Harry, 336
Dayl, Henry, 13n
Dean (Deane, Deyn),
  Harry, 39, 42
  Henry, 50, 50n, 58, 60–61, 74, 86,
    94–95, 100, 109, 118
  John, 94, 263
  Margery, 261, 262
Deeping, Market, 7n, 14, 26
  churchwardens' accounts, 1n, 4

Denny, ..., 270
Dennys (Denys, Dyinys, Dynes, Dynnes, Dynnys, Dynys),
    Gervase (Jervis), 238, 269
    Janet, 341, 343
    Joanna, wife of Thomas, 282, 282n
    Thomas, 155, 224, 272–73, 292–93, 296
Deughte see Doughty
Deyn see Dean
Dichande (Dichon, Dycham, Dychand, Dychande, Dychaund), Sir William, 184, 184n, 241n, 279
    Dickson see Dixon
Diconson,
    ..., 325
    Agnes, 254
    Thomas, 331
Dike (Dikes, Dyke),
    John, 357
    Roger, son of John, 352
    Thomas, 19
Dixon (Dickson, Dixson, Dyxson),
    ..., 242, 289, 324, 338–39
    Father, 261
    Adam, 252, 252n, 253–59, 262–63, 285
    Robert, 68
    William, 24, 236, 236n, 244, 337–38, 344, 350, 355–56
Dods, Margaret, wife of William, 99
Dogdyke, 6
Dolman, Agnes, 358
Donington in Holland, 109n
Dorchester (Dorchester on Thames), Oxon, see, 10
Doughty (Deughte, Dothty, Doughte, Doughtie, Dowthgty, Dowghte, Dowghty, Dowghtye, Dowthy, Dughtie, Dughte, Dughty, Dughtye),
    Mr, 176, 183, 187, 361
    Alexander, 33n, 163
    George, 183, 183n, 190–91, 195–96, 280
    John, 173n
    Katherine, 223
    Robert, 89, 89n, 90, 133, 144, 166, 189, 206, 303, 366–67
    Robert, vicar of Louth St James, 176n, 303n
    Thomas, 55, 57
    William, 173, 177, 179, 186, 224, 229, 239, 246, 248, 251, 277, 283, 369–70

Drakes (Draux, Draycks),
    ..., 132
    William, 152, 299, 304, 368
Driffield, East Yorkshire, 308n
    Dudding, Reginald, rector of Saleby, 1
Duffield, William, 80n
Dughtie, Dughte, Dughty, Dughtye see Doughty
Dugles, ..., 339
Dycham, Dychand, Dychande, Dychaund see Dichande
Dyinys, Dynes, Dynnes, Dynnys, Dynys see Dennys
Dyke see Dike
Dymoke, Alice, 237n
Dynes see Dennys
    Dyngley, William, 277
Dynnes, Dynnys, Dynys see Dennys
Dyon,
    Mr, 283–84
    John, 283n
Dyxson see Dixon

Earl (Earll, Earlle, Erle, Erlle),
    ..., 270
    Elizabeth, 333
    John, 246, 250, 260, 332, 360–62
East,
    ..., 268
    Cecily, wife of John, 352
    Robert, 129, 129n, 130, 236, 243
    William, 227, 227n, 231–35, 237, 241, 250, 260, 267, 269, 272–75, 278–80, 284, 294–95
Eastgate, Robert, 286–87
Edenham, 109n
    Edith, Alison, 122
Ednall (Ednald),
    ..., 102
    Thomas, 67, 67n
Edon,
    ..., 257–58
    Mother, 256–59, 261–63, 288–90
    Old, 263
Edward, Harry, 340, 343
Edward VI, king of England,
    accession of, 5
    birth of, 5, 125
    injunctions by, 195n
Egleston (Egiliston), Thomas, vicar of Louth St James, 3, 36, 36n, 37, 65n
Eldon, Mother, 253
Eleyn see Allen

Elizabeth of York, wife of Henry VII, 162n
Elkington (Elkyngton), 251, 319
Elleyn *see* Allen
Elsam, William, 113, 113n
Elwold (Elwald, Elwod, Elwood, Helwod, Helwode),
    Mrs, 345
    Beatrice, 253, 255, 258–59, 261–63
    Christopher, 53, 58
    John, 341, 341n, 344
    Margaret, 342
Ely, 80
    Ely, diocese, bishop of, see Goodrich, Thomas
Emet, Richard, 27, 361
Enderby (Enderbe),
    ..., 293
    John, 234
Erasmus, Desiderius, 195n
Erbe *see* Irby
Erchebold *see* Archebold
Eresby (Eresbe, Eresbie, Eresbye, Ersbe),
    Mr, 203, 278
    Mrs, 308
    Lawrence, 9n, 21, 21n, 203, 213, 248, 283, 304, 304n, 332, 332n
    Magdalen, widow of Lawrence, 308n
    Margaret, widow of Lawrence, 301n
Erle, Erlle *see* Earl
Ermine Street, 5
    Ersbe *see* Eresby
Evans (Evannes),
    Eleanor, wife of William, 352
    Joan, wife of William, 352
    William, 197, 210, 241, 251, 269, 276–77, 280, 283, 369–70
Everingham (Everyngam),
    Joan, 356
    Joanna, 357
    William, 357

Faddon, Jane, 357
Fairfax, Francis, 240n
Fanthorpe (Faunthorpe, Fawnthorpe), 99, 99n, 102, 122
Farrand (Farrant),
    Peter, 241
    William, 52, 52n, 75, 212, 231, 278, 305
Faunthorpe *see* Fanthorpe
    Fawdyngworth, ..., 361
Fawer,
    ..., 86–87, 125
    William, 52, 52n, 75–76, 101, 117, 132, 150, 183, 187–88
Fawnthorpe *see* Fanthorpe
Feltwell, Norfolk, rector of, 80n
Fen, Fene *see* Fenn
Fenesyde *see* Fernesyde
Fenn (Fen, Fene),
    Andrew, 323, 330
    Anthony, 279
    Janet, 107
Ferebe *see* Ferryby
Fernesyde (Fenesyde, Fernstede, Fernysyd), Henry, 104, 129–30, 136, 142, 170n, 368
Ferryby (Ferebe, Ferrebe), ..., 232, 235, 274, 338
Feswyke *see* Fishwick
Fets, ..., 253–54
Fiennes, Edward, Baron Clinton and Saye, earl of Lincoln, 10, 10n
Fishe (Fisshe, Fyshe, Fyssche, Fyssh, Fysshe),
    ..., wife of John, 174
    Joanna, 174, 174n
    Joanna, daughter of Joanna, 174n
    John, 192, 203, 277, 279–80, 293, 297, 303, 346, 349, 369–71
Fisher (Fissher, Fyscher, Fyshar, Fysher, Fyssher),
    ..., 156
    Elizabeth, wife of Robert, 148–49
    Gilbert, 132, 140, 148–49, 368
    James, son of Robert, 56–57
    John, 166
    Robert, 45, 45n, 74n, 140, 144, 161, 161n, 162–63, 168, 174, 366–68
Fishwick (Feswyke, Fishewyke, Fishwicke, Fisshwyck, Fiswick, Fyshwicke, Fyshwycke, Fyssewyck, Fysswick, Fyswick, Fyswik, Fyswike, Fyswyck, Fyswycke, Fyswyk, Fyswyke),
    Isabel, 181
    John, 308, 316, 329
    Richard, son of Walter, 99
    Thomas, son of Walter, 73
    Walter, 59, 59n, 75, 88, 96–97, 102–103, 109, 117, 132–33, 140, 172, 177, 191, 193, 224, 366, 368–69
    William, 246–48, 263, 282, 291, 370
Fisshe *see* Fishe
Fissher *see* Fisher
Fisshwyck, Fiswick *see* Fishwick
Fitzwilliam (Fytzwylliam),

INDEX OF PERSONS AND PLACES 383

    Lady, 133
    Mr, 76
    George, son of John, 77n, 133n
    John, 77n, 133n
    William, 364
    William, earl of Southampton, 17, 124n
    Flanders, [Belgium], 12
Fletcher,
    Anthony, 358
    Richard, 76
Flodden Field, battle of, 8n
Flower,
    Janet, 306
    Joanna, wife of Ralph, 347n
    Leonard, son of Ralph, 347n
    Ralph, 27, 323–25, 329, 347, 347n, 350
    Richard, son of Ralph, 347n
    Thomas, son of Ralph, 347n
    Forby, Richard, 147–48
Forman,
    Ellen, wife of John, 83–84
    John, 83n
    Philip, 258, 334
    Robert, 66, 86, 142, 342
    Fornas, William, 72
Forrest, Robert, 306
Foster (Forster),
    Mr, 58, 282
    Mrs, 292–93, 296
    Elizabeth, daughter of Thomas, 83–84
    Elizabeth, wife of Thomas, 98–99, 107
    Emott, 292n
    Joanne, 143; as widow, 142
    John, 366
    Thomas, 16n, 40, 40n, 44, 49, 49n,
        50–51, 56–57, 66, 68n, 74, 84,
        92, 96, 100, 108, 111, 111n, 116,
        123, 131, 170n, 174, 181
    William, 39, 39n, 44, 49–50, 56–57,
        66, 74–75, 77, 83–84, 91, 143
    William, son of Thomas, 40n, 57
Fotherby, 23, 225, 225n, 227
Fotherby, …, 218
Fowler (Fouler),
    James, 11n
    Thomas, 119, 119n, 147–48
    Fox, Thomas, 364
Francis I, king of France, 162n
Frankish, John, 16, 16n, 86n, 142n
Frauncheman, …, 33n
Freman,
    Janet, 306
    John, 342, 346–47
    Thomas, 236

Frith, John, 16, 16n
Frow (Fro),
    Robert, 84n, 114–15, 122
    William, son of Robert, 84
Furrier, …, 253
Fyscher, Fyshar see Fisher
Fyshe see Fishe
Fysher see Fisher
Fyshwicke, Fyshwycke see Fishwick
Fyssche, Fyssh, Fysshe see Fishe
Fyssewyck see Fishwick
Fyssher see Fisher
Fysswick, Fyswick, Fyswik, Fyswike,
    Fyswyck, Fyswycke, Fyswyk,
    Fyswyke see Fishwick
Fytzwylliam see Fitzwilliam

Galion, Alice, wife of Bartram, 174, 174n
Galside, William, 334
Garbora (Garboray), John, 316, 316n, 337
    Garrot, …, 36–37
Gatesyde, William, 343
Gaunce, William, 9, 83, 83n
Gedney, George, 347, 350
Geff see Jeff
Geldall,
    …, wife of, 225
    William, 223
Germany, 266
    armour from, 244n
Gese, Auncell, 176
Gibson (Gybson),
    …, 144
    Agnes, 162
    John, 122, 122n
    Richard, 159, 166, 172, 216, 283
    Robert, 130
Gilbert, Alice, 278
Gilder (Gylter), James, 95–96
Gilliot, Maud, 358n
Girdyke (Girdake, Guyrdyck, Gyrdike,
    Gyrdyck, Gyrdycke, Gyrdyk,
    Gyrdyke),
    …, 149, 163, 181
    family of, 29
    John, 8, 36, 36n, 3738, 48, 55, 65,
        84, 92, 99, 115, 122, 130, 136,
        142–43, 148, 162, 168, 173, 179,
        188
    Robert, 364–65
    Thomas, 48, 74, 84, 92, 99, 107, 123,
        130, 137, 155
Girsbye (Girsbe, Gyrsbe, Gyrsby),
    Isabel, 341

Richard, 283, 311, 322, 326, 329, 350, 371
Glazier (Glasyer),
  Andrew, 308, 317
  James, 67, 88, 93, 95
  Glean (Glen, Glene), William, 62, 69, 104, 154, 159, 161–62, 168, 367
Glentham (Glentam, Glenton),
  ..., 263
  Auncell, 314, 358
  Janet, 255, 259, 261–63
Glover, William, 159
Goddall, Goddalle, Godeall see Goodall
Goderick, Goderke, Goderwyck see Goodrick
Goldsmith (Goldsmyth, Goldsmythe),
  Robert, 43, 43n, 66, 85, 103, 110, 124, 134
  William, 86, 86n, 365
Gommell see Gunnell
Gonbye see Gunby
Gonnell, Gonnyle, Gonylde see Gunnell
Goodall (Goddall, Goddalle, Godeall, Goodale, Goodayll, Gooddale, Gooddall),
  Mr, 25, 279, 345
  Mrs, 349
  Emott, wife of John, 347, 347n
  Joanna, wife of John, 148, 148n
  John, 2022, 22n, 30, 50, 57, 66, 74, 112, 131, 134, 137, 143, 241n, 265n, 347n
Goodrick (Goderick, Goderke, Goderwyck, Gooderick, Goodrich, Goodryck, Goodryk, Goodryke),
  Mr, 19, 184, 212
  Richard, 21, 21n, 52, 68, 73, 94n, 213
  Robert, 42
  Thomas, bishop of Ely, 21n
Goshawke (Goshalke, Gosehauke, Goshauke, Goshaulke, Goshawcke, Gossauke, Gossehauke, Gosshauke),
  ..., wife of William, 163
  Agnes, wife of Thomas, 92
  Isabel, wife of William, 161, 161n
  John, 223n
  Sir John, 223
  Thomas, 94, 216
  William, 104, 104n, 124, 126, 142–43, 365–66, 366n, 368
Goslyng (Goslynge),
  Hugh, 350
  Ralph, 342, 346, 351

Rose, 350n
Gossauke, Gossehauke, Gosshauke see Goshawke
Grainsby, rector of, 303n
Grantham (Grauntham),
  chantries in, 21n
  church, 8
  clergy of, 3n
  taxation at, 2n
Grantham (Grauntham),
  Jane, wife of Thomas, 106–107
  Thomas, 106n, 142, 142n, 278n, 366
Graunt (Grawnte),
  ..., 232
  Thomas, 115
  William, 231, 231n, 251, 302–303, 339, 346
Grauntham see Grantham
Gravers, Mr, 347
Gray (Graye, Grey),
  ..., wife of Arthur, 223
  family of, 11
  Mr, 278
  Mrs, 318
  Alice, 179
  Alice, wife of Arthur, 181–82, 187n
  Arthur, 16, 19, 100, 100n, 108, 116, 123, 131, 134, 197, 207, 211–12, 223n, 224, 231, 238, 243, 248, 265, 270, 283
  Lady Jane, 239n, 246
  Janet, daughter of Arthur, 187, 187n
  Joanna, 231n
  Joanna, daughter of Arthur, 187n
  John, 273–74, 283, 313, 325, 334
  John, the younger, 311, 371
  Miles, 305, 305n, 319, 371
  Thomas, 308, 323, 330
  William, 68, 68n, 76, 87, 365
Green (Gren, Grene),
  ..., 226
  Father, 253–55, 257–59, 261–63
  Annes, 313
  Janet, 352, 357
  John, 100
  Richard, 346n
  Thomas, 134, 134n, 135, 254–56, 278, 284, 317, 368
  Thomas, the elder, 216
  William, 121, 121n, 123
Greesby, Greesbye see Gresbye
Gregbe (Gregbey),
  ..., 310
  Beatrice, 313

INDEX OF PERSONS AND PLACES

Richard, 293
William, 313
Gremysby *see* Grimsby
Gren, Grene *see* Green
Gresbye (Greesby, Greesbye, Grisbe, Grysbe),
Isabel, 344
Richard, 303, 303n
Grescroft, Richard, son of John, 346n
Grey *see* Gray
Grimoldby (Grimolby), 131
rector of, 303n
Grimsby (Gremysby, Grymesby, Grymsbe), 2, 7n, 26, 122, 278, 356
aldermen of, 122n
church, 8
friars of, 65n
mayor of, 21n, 296n
MPs for, 76n, 318n
players of, 39
taxation at, 2n
Grisbe *see* Gresbye
Grison, Richard, 300
Grymesby, Grymsbe *see* Grimsby
Grymsbie, Margaret, 326
Grysbe *see* Gresbye
Guevara (Guavero), Francis Velez de, 340, 340n
Gunby (Gonbye),
Mr, 78
Janet, 58
William, 78n, 366
Gunnell (Gommell, Gonnell, Gonnyle, Gonylde, Gunnel),
John, 364–65
Thomas, 308–11, 315, 317–18, 322–24, 329–30, 335, 343, 348, 353, 360
Guyrdyck *see* Girdyke
Gybson *see* Gibson
Gyles, Alice, 121, 123
Gylter *see* Gilder
Gyrdike, Gyrdyck, Gyrdycke, Gyrdyk, Gyrdyke *see* Girdyke
Gyrsbe, Gyrsby *see* Girsbye

Hainton, 189n
church, 189n
Halle,
..., 256–59, 261–62
Agnes, 255–57, 261–63
Janet, 258
John, son of Roger, 252n
Roger, 252, 278
Hallington (Halyngton), 169

Hallywell, Hallywells *see* Holywell
Halton (Haulton),
John, 72, 72n, 73, 84
Thomas, 65
Halyngton *see* Hallington
Halywells *see* Holywell
Hampton Court, Middlesex, 125n
Hanson,
..., wife of Richard, 202
Bartholomew, 253–54, 266–68, 270, 272–74, 284, 284n, 285
Elizabeth, wife of Bartholomew, 130, 266
John, 313
Leonard, 299
Hareson, Robert, 39–42, 44
Hareyson *see* Harrison
Harpam,
Elizabeth, 352n
Richard, 352
Harpham (Harphan), East Yorkshire, 308, 308n
Harrington, 342n
Harrison (Hareyson, Harryson, Haryson),
..., 50–52, 59–60, 66
George, 251
John, 59, 68, 74, 74n, 77, 124, 200–202
John, senior, 79, 84
Robert, 49–50
William, 67–68, 77, 132, 138–39, 144, 148
Harry, William, 147
Harryson *see* Harrison
Hartburn,
Joanna, wife of Robert, 153–54
Robert, 62, 151–52, 175, 367–68
Haryson *see* Harrison
Haulton *see* Halton
Haunsell (Auncell), Thomas, 115, 115n
Hawe, William, 327
Hay, William, 341
Haya, Ralph de, uncle of Nicholas, 307n
Heblethwaite, Christopher, 123
Helloff *see* Belleau
Helsame, William, 365
Helwod, Helwode *see* Elwold
Heneage (Hennedge),
Mr, 165, 226
George, dean of Lincoln, 189n
John, 76n
Thomas, 189n
Sir Thomas, 189
Henry VII, king of England, 162n
Henry VIII, king of England, 162n

dirge of, 6
Heron, Jane, widow, 142
    Hewbauncke, Edward, 364
    Hewet (Hewick, Hewicke, Hewit, Hewytt, Huyt), William, 244, 244n, 281, 332, 357, 362, 370–71
Heydour (Heydour near Ancaster), quarry, 6
Hildyard,
    Elizabeth, daughter of Sir Peter, 72n
    Sir Peter, 72n
Hill (Hyll),
    Alice, 56
    Arthur, 27, 252, 355, 361
    John, 210
    Thomas, 53, 61–62, 136, 367
    Thomas, senior, 53n
Hilton (Hiltonne, Hylton), John, 241, 241n, 243
Hinde (Hynd, Hynde),
    Janet, wife of Richard, 181–82
    Richard, 53, 53n, 151–52, 159, 181–82, 366–68
Hoberthorn see Hobthorn
Hobson,
    …, 285
    Mother, 254, 286
Hobthorn (Hoberthorn),
    Jane, 35, 36, 36n, 37
    John, 364
Hodgson (Hodeson, Hodgsone, Hogdson),
    …, 362
    Ellen, 347
    John, 314, 316, 319
    Hodlyng, …, 122
Hogdson see Hodgson
Holand, Holande see Holland
Holbeach, Henry, bishop of Lincoln, 10
Holbeach All Saints, 67n
    Holden, Margaret, wife of Alan, 99
Holderness (Holdernes, Holdernesse, Holdrenes, Holdrenesse),
    Aleyn, 219
    Anne, wife of Thomas, 16162
    Catern, 321
    Catherine, wife of Thomas, 211n
    Emma, daughter of Thomas, 211n
    Janet, 289
    Jenkin, 156, 203
    John, 53, 61–62, 111, 125, 132, 138, 144, 146, 150, 164, 169, 175, 190, 204, 204n, 206, 293, 367–68, 369n
    Richard, 357, 371
    Thomas, 64–65, 211, 211n, 213–14, 264, 282, 297, 329, 369–70

Holderness, East Yorkshire, 244n
Holett see Holot
Holland (Holand, Holande),
    Mr, 39n
    Robert, 326, 332, 335, 371
    Simon, 274
    Thomas, 192, 196, 224, 369
    William, 26, 333, 335, 354, 371
Hollinshed, Raphael, 362n
Hollis, Gervase, 6n
Holme (Holm),
    …, 237, 252–56, 262, 286–89
    Father, 253–59, 261–63
    Ellen, 48
    John, 334
    Thomas, 255, 263, 285
Holot (Holett, Holoyt), Robert, 148–49, 154
Holtbe, Margaret, 358
Holywell (Hallywell, Hallywells, Halywells), Thomas, 112, 142–43, 368
Hony, Thomas, 18
Hoperton (Hoparton),
    …, 177
    Johanna, 177
    John, 168, 177n
Hopkyn, John, 352
Hopton, John, 168
Horling, Robert, 194
    Horncastle (Horncastell), 6, 110, 355
    Hotoft, Robert, 156
    Howeny (Howenys), William, 28, 214
Howlatt, Anna, wife of Robert, 129
Howsam, William, 72
Hudson,
    Elizabeth, 304
    Robert, 17, 155, 155n, 162
    William, 65, 115
Huggard, Margaret, 254
Hull, 168n
    clocksmith of, 94
Humble,
    …, 253
    Thomas, 253
    Hushe, …, 317
Hutchynson (Hutchenson),
    Anne, 358, 360
    Thomas, 27, 339, 357, 359, 361
Hutter, Margaret, 259
    Huttoft, Alice, 285
Huyt see Hewet
Hyde, Janet, 179
Hyll see Hill

Hylton *see* Hilton
Hymas (Ymos), Roger, 250, 250n
Hynd, Hynde *see* Hinde
Hynes, Roger, 288

Imttyng, William, 99
Inbroghe, Simon, 100
Inglish (Inglich, Inglisch, Inglishe,
    Inglisshe, Inglys, Inglyshe,
    Inglysshe, Ynglych),
  Agnes, widow, 45, 53
  Matthew, citizen and ironmonger of
    London, 47n
  Matthew, son of William, 47–48
  Robert, 364
  Thomas, 327, 332, 332n
  William, 364
Ingoldmells (Ingomels), 2, 2n
Ingram, Thomas, 336
Irby (Erbe),
  family, 192n
  Mr, 192
Ireland, William, 55, 55n

Jackson (Jackeson, Jacksone, Jacson,
    Jakson),
  ..., 60, 61, 218, 355
  Brian, 293–94, 304
  Isabel, 99
  Janet, 355
  Janet, wife of Thomas, 352
  John, 356, 358
  Ralph, 241
  Robert, 278
  Thomas, 12, 346, 346n, 371
  William, 234, 271, 274, 279–80, 293,
    295, 299, 318, 324, 362
Jeff (Geff, Jefe, Jeffe),
  ..., 269, 331
  Auncell, 235, 242, 252, 260, 275,
    279–80, 293, 295, 337, 341
Jenkenson, John, 84
Jennay, Mr, 137
Jewel (Juell),
  John, 359n
  John, bishop of Salisbury, 359–60
Jimos, Roger, 253
John, Ralph, 169
Johns,
  John, 352
  John, son of John, 352n
Johnson (Joneson, Jonson),
  ..., 76, 78, 99, 102, 298
  Elizabeth, wife of Robert, 92

Janet, wife of Ranulf, 107
Ralph, 122
Robert, 41, 64, 68, 68n, 69, 78, 137
William, 75n, 110, 267, 364–65
Jordan, ..., 238
Joy (Joye),
  Agnes, 334n
  Annes, 334
Joyner, John, 209
Juell *see* Jewel

Kameron *see* Cameron
Karver *see* Carver
  Kay, William, 151
Kechyn (Kechen, Ketchyn, Kychen,
    Kytchen),
  John, 103, 108, 365
  Richard, 87, 89, 93, 108, 112
  Thomas, 134–35, 151, 368
Keddington (Keddyngton, Kedington,
    Kedyngton, Kennington,
    Kennyngton, Kenyngton), 234, 283,
    296n, 300, 302, 316, 326, 330, 332,
    337–38, 344–45, 348, 353, 360, 362
Kelby, quarry, 6
Kellum, Simon, 233, 242, 251–52
Kendall, Thomas, 3, 22n, 102v; as vicar of
    Louth St James, 3n, 15, 47n, 113n
Kenethorpe (Kenythorpe), Oliver, 348–49,
    362
Kennington, Kennyngton *see* Keddington
Kent,
  Ellen, daughter of George, 317n
  Frances, daughter of George, 317n
  George, 317, 317n
  George, son of George, 317n
Kenyngton *see* Keddington
Kenythorpe *see* Kenethorpe
Kerkby *see* Kirkby
Kerver *see* Carver
Ketchyn *see* Kechyn
  Ketsby (Ketsbe), fair, 317
Keycham (Kyrchen), John, 93, 93n
  Keyll, William, 364
  Keys, William, 73
Kighley, Robert, 281, 370
King (Kinge, Kyng, Kynge),
  Mr, 178
  Elizabeth, 348
  Isabel, 350
  Isabel, wife of William, 173, 173n
  Janet, 179
  Janet, wife of William, 181–82
  Robert, abbot of Thame, 80n

Susan, 352, 355
William, 9n, 23, 70, 70n, 79, 86, 89–90, 94, 104n, 116, 127, 138, 140, 166, 187, 190, 199, 204, 211, 215, 220–21, 224–26, 229, 235, 238–39, 243, 246, 248, 252, 264, 279, 283, 301, 301n, 302–303, 305, 308, 317–18, 329n, 331, 334–35, 345, 362, 366–67, 369–70
William, junior, 188
Kirk (Kyrck, Kyrke, Kyroke),
John, 121, 121n, 122
Thomas, 147–48
Sir Thomas, 37n, 101, 101n
Kirkby (Kerkby, Kirckbe, Kirkbe, Kyrbe, Kyrckbe, Kyrkbe, Kyrkby, Kyrkebe),
..., 176, 311
Janet, 194, 285, 287–90
Robert, 151–52, 189, 217, 221, 226–27, 237, 245, 260, 280, 296–300, 308–310, 315, 317, 321–23, 325, 329, 335, 343, 345, 348, 353, 360
Thomas, 56
Kirkstead, monk of, 191n
Kirton, Thomas, 170n
Kirton in Lindsey, 7n, 14
churchwardens' accounts, 1n, 5
Knowth, Janet, 358
Knyght, ..., 20, 308
Kooke see Cooke
Kychen see Kechyn
Kydd, ..., 132
Kyghby, Robert, 281
Kyme (Came, Cayme),
Mr, 176
Agnes, wife of Guy, 114–15
Charles, son of Thomas, 153
George, 233, 252
Guy, 74n, 114n, 168n, 170n
Kyme Eau, 6
Kyng, Kynge see King
Kyngley, Robert, 297, 351, 371
Kyrbe see Kirkby
Kyrchen see Keycham
Kyrck see Kirk
Kyrckbe, Kyrkbe, Kyrkby see Kirkby
Kyrke see Kirk
Kyrkebe see Kirkby
Kyroke see Kirk
Kytchen see Kechyn

Lamb,
Beatrice, 314
Thomas, 277
William, 306
Lambeth, Surrey, synod, 295
Lancaster (Lanckester),
..., 124
Cuthbert, 359
Lane, Thomas, 273
Langholme (Langham, Langholm, Langhom),
..., 211, 224
Mr, 61–62, 173, 217, 362
Anne, wife of John, 36n, 115
Christopher, 358
John, 36, 36n, 48, 65, 73, 84, 92, 99, 107, 115, 122, 130, 143, 149, 162, 168, 179, 188, 358n
John, son of John, 36n
Peter, 142
Peter, brother of John, 142n
Langton, John, 181
Lanson, Robert, 162
Larmouth (Larmowth, Larmowthe),
John, 104, 104n, 124, 124n, 136–37
Lathes,
Thomas, 217, 245, 271
William, 78, 157
Lawrence,
Margaret, widow, 121, 123
Thomas, 127, 134, 368
William, 62, 67, 69, 106–107, 367
Lawson (Louson, Lowson),
..., 165, 169
Joanna, wife of Robert, 154, 154n, 155, 155n
Robert, 69–70, 139, 139n, 153, 352, 357, 366–67
Laycock, John, 21n
Layrmond, John, 366
Leache (Lech, Leche, Leich, Letche),
Thomas, 28, 234, 239, 242, 269–70, 273, 284, 294–96, 361n, 362, 370
Leaper, Simon, 313
Lech, Leche see Leache
Lechman (Lecheman, Leichman),
Joanna, daughter of Thomas, 239n
Margaret, wife of Thomas, 239n
Thomas, 28, 239, 252, 268, 273, 275, 279, 293, 295, 308, 310, 315, 325, 330, 339, 345, 354–55
Ledis (Lede, Ledys),
..., 252, 258–59, 261–63

Janet, 257, 262–63, 285
Legbourne, priory, 21n, 33n, 92n, 129n
Leich *see* Leache
Leichman *see* Lechman
Lele, ..., 253
Lenny, Margaret, 253
Letche *see* Leache
Leve, Elizabeth, 334
Leverton, churchwardens' accounts, 1n, 5, 19, 24, 27, 39n, 133n, 162n
Lincoln, archdeaconry, 80n
    Lincoln, deanery, dean of, 2, 25n; *see also* Heneage, George
Lincoln (Lincolln, Lincolne, Lyncoln), diocese,
    ..., bishop of, 365n
    Alexander, bishop of, 13n
Lincoln (Lincolln, Lincolne, Lyncoln), 2, 10, 17, 24, 25n, 28–29, 109n, 116n, 168n, 228, 238, 272, 325, 334n, 362
    castle, 27, 307n, 323, 338–39, 345n, 361n
    cathedral,
    dean and chapter of, 2
    organist and choirmaster at, 25n
    treasurer of, 88n; *see also* Luda, Thomas de
    friars of, 65n
    mayor of, 278; *see also* Grantham, Thomas
    MPs for, 170n
    offences tried at, 10
    people of, 19, 174, 334
    prisoners at, 27, 176, 251, 264, 273, 317, 323–24, 347n, 361n
Lincoln (Lincolln, Lincolne, Lyncoln), family of, 29
    Simon, 6, 6n, 7, 38, 55–56, 65, 80, 83–84, 99, 106–107, 122–23, 136, 142–43, 154, 162, 168, 173, 364
    Thomas, 154, 154n, 155, 162–63
    William, 83n
Lincolnshire, county,
    MPs for, 211n, 318n
    Rising, 3, 15–17, 21n, 33n, 40n, 43n, 80n, 92n, 101n, 104n, 113n, 114n, 170n, 177n, 195n, 244n
    sheriff of, 307n, 340n; *see also* Copledike, John
Lindesay (Lyndesey, Lyndsay),
    Mr, 229
    Simon, 7, 364
Litherland (Lytherland),
    Mr, 88

Henry, 88n
Littlebury, Elizabeth, 342n
Lobley (Loblay),
    George, 338, 361
    Robert, 42
Lokwood, ..., 256–58
London, 24–25, 29, 109n, 172, 174, 186–87, 192, 233n, 274, 322, 324, 353
    Christ's Hospital in, 20n
    coal from, 53
    people of, 47
    soldiers at, 246
Longland, John, bishop of Lincoln, 69n
Lorryman, Thomas, 267–68
Louson *see* Lawson
Louth (Louthe, Lowth, Lowthe),
    bailiff of, 70n
    chapel of St John, 6n, 8–9, 38, 83n, 129, 136, 156, 182
    chapel of St Mary, 8
    charity, 22–23
    churches,
    St James, 13, 15
    Angel Chapel in, 75n
    John Louth chantry in, 37n
    organs in, 42n
    St Mary's, 6n, 89, 38, 45, 55, 64, 68, 75–77, 79, 83, 88, 94, 98, 101, 103, 106, 122, 125, 129, 132–33, 133n, 138, 144, 156–58, 165, 175–77, 182, 187, 196–97, 201, 203, 207, 209–11, 214, 219, 228, 234, 250–51, 260, 309–10, 338, 338n
    Maiden Chapel (Mades Chapel) in, 40, 161, 163, 165
    churchwardens of, 212
    corporation, 10, 21n
    description of, 2
    fair, 29, 265, 295, 314
    guilds, 13
    Corpus Christi, 12, 22, 112, 212, 215, 225n
    Holy Trinity, 11–12, 21, 22n, 29, 36, 43n, 73, 84, 89n, 111n, 122, 136, 168, 183n, 192, 366n
    St George, 61n
    St Mary (Lady guild), 7n, 11, 11n, 12, 21–22, 22n, 29, 33n, 36n, 37, 41n, 45n, 48, 48n, 53, 64n, 65, 72n, 73, 78n, 92, 100n, 107, 111n, 112, 115, 122, 130, 134n, 143, 154,

162, 170n, 173, 182, 183n, 188, 192, 214, 223n, 227n, 241n
St Peter, 12, 22, 112
Trinity, 8, 265n
King Edward VI grammar school, 9, 20–21, 21n
manor, 10, 36n, 189n, 300n, 305n
markets, 29
merchants of, 29
parsonage, 283n
poor of, 3n
prebend, 283n
prebendary of, 109n, 283n
streets and places in,
Agarth, 14n
Ashwell Head (Aswell Head), 339
Ashwell Lane (Aswell Lane), 197, 220, 228n
Ashwell Spring (Ashwell, Aswell, Haswell), 10, 93, 93n, 109, 185, 228, 234, 241, 252, 260, 269, 271, 275, 278, 296, 301, 305, 310, 316, 323–24, 333, 335, 337–39, 342, 347, 349, 360
Aygarth House, 14n
Bishop's Bridge (Bishop Bridge), 329, 329n
Breakneck Lane, 41n
Bridge Street, 52n, 77n
Burton Bridge, 204, 269
Chequergate, 21n
Cisterngate, 23, 145, 145n, 241n
Corn Hill (Corne Hill), 16, 241, 241n
Cornmarket, 16
Dounay Ground, 305
East Bridge, 344
East Field, 124, 169, 191, 195, 199, 201, 207, 296
East Mills, 228, 233, 243
East Mills Bridge, 218, 251
Elkington Field, 232
Elmyers *see* Great and Little Elmore Roads
Gelyan Bowar *see* Julian Bower
Gospelgate (Gosbell End, Gosbelle End, Gospell End), 12, 293–94, 298, 307
Great and Little Elmore Roads (Elmyers), 306, 306n, 307–309
Gulpyn Lane, 43n
Hagthorpe Field, 293
Haswell *see* Ashwell Spring
Hall Mill (Hall Mills), 329n
Haregarth (Haregares, Haregars, Haregarthes, Haregarthis, Haregarths, Hargarthe, Hargarthes, Hayrgars, Hayrgarthes, Hayrgayrs, Hayrgayrthes), 13, 13n, 58, 131, 154, 156, 158, 163, 165, 169–71, 174–75, 197, 202, 219, 225–28, 232–34, 243, 246, 264, 272, 275, 296, 304, 311, 317–18, 322, 336, 345
Haregarth Gate (Haregarth Gate), 232
Haregarth Corner (Hargarths Corner), 344
Julian Bower (Gelyan Bowar), 169, 169n, 170n
Keddington Field (Keddyngton Field), 314, 319, 346
Legbourne Gate (Legburn Gate, Legburne Gate), 101, 125, 132, 144, 150, 172
Legbourne Lane (Legborn Lane, Legburn Lane), 251, 362
Legbourne Road, 14n
Lincoln Close (Lyncoln Close), 233, 340
London Road, 64n, 208n
London Road Cemetery, 169n
Louth Bridge (Lowith Bridge), 293
Louth Field (Louyth Field, Lowth Field, Lowthe Field), 125, 232, 283, 293, 316
Louth Wood (Lowith Wood, Lowth Wood, Lowthe Wood), 227, 316, 355
Maiden Row, 12
Market Place (Marketstead), 8, 12, 17, 29, 59, 83n, 94, 124–25, 156n, 177, 210, 217, 227, 295, 323
Merbanks, 251
North Field, 199, 246, 283, 319, 325, 332
Northgate, 228n
Padehole, 228n
Padehole Bridge (Padholle Bridge), 228
Saracen's Head, 16, 86n
Saxongate (Sastan Gate, Sastangait, Sasten Gate, Saxtengate), 145n, 146, 150, 164
Schoolhouse Lane, 9, 22, 43n
Sheep Market, 12
Small Wells, 77, 77n, 119, 234–35, 268, 273, 338n
South Field, 13n, 58n, 316, 344

South Street, 64n
Southfield Farm, 14n
Spital Hill (Spyttell Hyll), 64, 94
Stewton Bridge (Steueton Bridge,
    Steuton Bridge, Stueton Bridge),
    291, 294, 325, 330
Stewton Close (Steueton Close), 317
Stewton Gate (Stuton Gate), 13, 87, 101
Stewton Lane (Stewton Road, Stueton
    Lane), 13n, 169, 218, 306n, 336
Theddlethorpe Corner, 316, 316n, 329,
    337
Upgate, 12
Walkergate, 279
West Mills, 245, 345, 362
West Mills Bridge, 345, 360
Westgate, 12, 41, 41n, 314n, 354
Willows Field (Willowes, Wyllowes
    Field), 215
vicarage, 3
vicars of, 305; *see also* Doughty,
    Robert
Louth (Louthe, Louthes, Lowth, Lowthe),
    …, 286
    Mother, 253–59, 261–63, 285–87,
        289–90
    Mr, 48
    Cicely, 256
    John, 37, 37n, 56, 65, 73, 84, 92, 99,
        107, 115, 122, 125, 130, 137, 143,
        149, 155, 162, 168, 174
    John, vicar of Louth St James, 212n
    Katherine, wife of William, 107
Louth Park (Louth Parke, Lowth Park,
    Lowth Parke), 76, 170n, 171,
    337–38, 344
    abbey, 13, 13n, 15n, 59n, 76n, 117n, 157,
        157n, 337
    manor, 305, 347
    wood, 70n
Louthes *see* Louth; Louthesk
Louthesk (Louthes), wapentake, 169n
Lowes, George, 242, 321
Lowson *see* Lawson
Lowth *see* Louth
Lowth Park, Lowth Parke *see* Louth Park
Lowthe *see* Louth
Lud, River, 2, 77n
Luda, Thomas de, treasurer of Lincoln, 8
Ludford (Ludfurth), 315
Ludlow, Shropshire, 11, 18
    church of St Lawrence, 4
    churchwardens' accounts, 4, 6, 11n, 19,
        24, 207n

guild of palmers, 13, 29
Lupton, John, 103
Luter, Brian, 280
Lutton, 109n
Lyncoln *see* Lincoln
Lyndesey, Lyndsay *see* Lindesay
    Lynn, Kings, (Bishops Lynn, Lyn),
        Norfolk, 2n, 80
Lyons (Lyon, Lyones),
    …, 19
    Catherine, 358
    Janet, 313
Lytherland *see* Litherland

Mablethorpe (Mabbylthorpe), 76, 77n,
    133n, 174
Mackerall (Mackerell, Makerall, Makerell,
    Makrell),
    John, 231, 231n, 248, 283, 358, 358n,
        360
    Matthew, abbot of Barlings, 80n, 170n,
        191n, 231n
Macrith (Macrithe, Macrythe, Makerith),
    John, 69n, 321, 324
Maddison (Maddysloe),
    Edward, 274
    Sir Edward, 33n
Mainfeld *see* Manfeld
Makerall, Makerell, Makrell *see*
    Mackerall
Malerbe, William, fee of, 4n
Maltby,
    …, 1, 50–52, 58, 60–61, 165, 170–71,
        175–76, 217, 220
    Isabel, wife of John, 50n
    John, 50n
Man,
    Mr, 296
    William, 22n, 117, 117n, 118–19, 123,
        233, 279, 296n
Maners (Manars), Thomas, 44, 52, 67,
    108–109, 131, 133, 144, 157
Manfeld (Mainfeld), James, 246, 278
Mansell (Mansill, Mansyll),
    James, 25, 306, 344–46, 358–59
    Joanna, 358n
    John, son of James, 358n
    Margaret, daughter of James, 358n
    Richard, son of James, 358n
    Susanna, daughter of James, 358n
    Thomas, son of James, 358n
Mareham on the Hill, 109n
Markby, priory, 177n

Marlings (Marlyngs, Marlyns, Merlings, Merlyngs),
    Anne, daughter of Mr, 129–30
    John, 161–62
    Katherine, wife of John, 161, 161n, 162
Marshall,
    Anne, 241
    Elizabeth, wife of Robert, 275, 275n
    James, 340, 371
    John, 347
    Richard, 306
    Robert, 248, 302–303, 305–307, 309–310, 319, 370
    Martyndall, John, 358
Mary, queen of England,
    accession of, 23, 233n
    marriage of, 6n
    proclamation of, 6, 233, 233n
    Maryn, Nicholas, 45, 53
Marynell, James, 99
Mason,
    Mr, 122
    George, 61, 76, 118
    Janet or Joanne, widow of Peter, 122n
    Nicholas, 40, 169
    Peter, 122n
Massingale, ..., 299
Matlot, Thomas, 118
Mauborn, Harry, 307
    Maundfild, Thomas, 365
Mawborne (Mawbarne, Mawborn, Mawburne),
    ..., 194, 200, 318
    Harry, 251, 314, 316, 323, 327
    Henry, 234, 234n, 266, 326
    Richard, 27, 271
Mawre, Thomas, 191n
Mawvyn (Mawuyn),
    Elizabeth, wife of Roger, 231, 231n
    Roger, 273
May,
    Father, 288
    John, 55, 252–59, 261–63, 286–90
Maysterchambers (Mestchamber, Mestechamber, Mesterchamber, Mesterchamers, Ministerchambers, Misterchambers, Mynsterchabars, Mynysterchamber, Mysterchambars, Mysterchamber, Mysterchambers),
    ..., 177
    Mrs, 325, 343–44
    Elizabeth, 352, 356; as widow, 268
    George, son of Martin, 65
    Joanne, daughter of Martin, 83
    John, son of Martin, 72, 74, 84, 90, 97
    Martin, 90, 97, 179, 181–82, 188
    Mary, daughter of Martin, 65
    Thomas, 23, 235, 238, 266, 279
    William, son of Martin, 107
Meares (Meres, Mers),
    Mr, 277
    Mrs, 278, 281
    Thomas, 185, 187–88, 192, 369–70
Mekilbaro, Robert, 38–39
Melton,
    John, 359
    Nicholas, 16, 16n, 40n, 92n, 104n, 170n, 181n
    Richard, 64–65
    William, 101n
Merecock, ..., 274
Meres see Meares
Merlings, Merlyngs see Marlings
Mers see Meares
Messenger, Thomas, 364
Mestchamber, Mestechamber, Mesterchamber, Mesterchamers see Maysterchambers
Michell (Mychell, Mytchell),
    ..., 158, 165
    Mr, 315
    Elizabeth, wife of Thomas, 149, 149n
    Isabel, wife of Thomas, 173, 173n
    Robert, 259–60
    Thomas, 228, 234, 248, 314
    William, 338, 359
Michelson (Mychelson),
    Alexander, 33n, 104, 104n, 119, 134–35, 367n, 368
    Janet, 326–27, 331
Mikelbarow (Mykelbarowgh, Mykylbarow),
    ..., 62, 145
    Simon, 144, 150
Milis see Mylls
Millicent (Mylsent), John, 33n, 92n, 129n
Milner (Mylner),
    ..., wife of Anthony, 257
    Anthony, 260, 262–63
    Arthur, 252
    John, 138, 200, 273
    Robert, 299
Minghell, Robert, 243, 251–52
Ministerchambers see Maysterchambers
Minting, 227
Misterchambers see Maysterchambers
Molter, Patrick, 72–73
Mondy see Munday

INDEX OF PERSONS AND PLACES

Moore (Moor, More),
  Father, 261
  Agnes, widow, 89
  Catherine, 341, 344
  Catherine, wife of John, 341n
  George, 272, 284
  John, 7n, 38, 38n, 64–65, 70–71, 73, 84, 92, 366
  Margery, 55, 57
  Robert, 366
  Thomas, 181, 181n, 182, 306
  William, 68
Mordew, Thomas, 99
More *see* Moore
Moreland, William, 15n, 16n, 76n, 81n, 139n, 142n, 154n, 221n, 244n
Mores, Thomas, 264
Morley, John, 334
  Mossam, Thomas, 67
Muckton (Mukton), dean of, 168n
Mumby (Mumbie), chapel, 362n
Munday (Mondy),
  Isabel, wife of Roland, 64–65
  Roland, 72–73, 84
Mychell *see* Michell
Mychelson *see* Michelson
Myddelton, Thomas, 360
Mykelbarowgh, Mykylbarow *see* Mikelbarow
Mylborne, ..., 274
  Myller, John, 61
Mylls (Milis),
  Annas, wife of Harry, 342
  Harry, 295, 358
Mylner *see* Milner
Mylsent *see* Millicent
Mynsterchabars, Mynysterchamber, Mysterchambars, Mysterchamber, Mysterchambers *see* Maysterchambers
Mytchell *see* Michell

Nailer, Mrs, 272
Nebrowghe *see* Newborough
  Necolson *see* Nicholson
Nelson,
  John, 149, 155
  Margery, wife of John, 173, 173n
Nettlewode, George, 189
  Neuton *see* Newton
Newark, Nottinghamshire, 88n
Newborough (Nebrowghe, Newbrough, Newbrouth, Newbrowgh, Newbrugh, Newbrughe, Newbrugs),
  Simon, 118, 118n, 131, 133, 138, 184, 196, 201, 242, 244, 273–74
Newton (Neuton),
  ..., 87, 254
  Elizabeth, wife of William, 129–30
  Isabel, 256, 259, 262
  Janet, 258
  William, 81, 81n, 101–102, 132, 142, 366–67
Nicholson (Necolson, Nicolson, Nycholson, Nycollason),
  Agnes, 306
  Margaret, 174
  Richard, 214, 243, 250
  Nocton, John, 284
  Nodhall, Richard, 178
Norfolk (Northfolk), county, 122
Norman,
  ..., 58, 61, 76, 94–95, 101, 116–17, 124–25, 132, 134
  Eleanor (Ellen), wife of John, 36–37
  John, 36n, 51, 148–49, 365
  Margaret, wife of John, 106–107
  Robert, 59, 59n, 67, 77–78, 101, 115
North (Northe),
  Isabel, 323
  Isabel, wife of John, 321
  John, 41, 43, 243, 272, 274, 276, 278, 291, 301–303, 340, 343, 349, 360, 371
  John, son of John, 357
  Thomas, 173, 305
Northfolk *see* Norfolk
Norwich, diocese, 80
Nosley, William, 199
Nothawk (Nothawke, Nottoke), William, 142–43, 149
Nottingham, archdeaconry, archdeacon of, 212n
Nottoke *see* Nothawk
Nut (Nute), Janet, 306, 308
Nycholson, Nycollason *see* Nicholson
Nycolls, Edward, 314

Oakland (Okeland, Okland),
  ..., wife of John, 169
  John, 37, 64, 64n, 65, 73, 365
  Margaret, wife of John, 168, 168n
  Richard, 99
Odling (Odlen, Odlin, Odlyn, Odlyng, Odlynge),
  ..., 211, 232, 246, 250, 267, 270, 272, 280
  Joanne, daughter of Robert, 151n

Margaret, daughter of Robert, 151n
Margaret, wife of Robert, 151n
Mary, wife of Robert, 151n
Robert, 18, 151, 151n, 157–58, 165, 176, 192, 195, 201–203, 209–210, 219, 224–26, 235, 237–39, 242–44, 252, 260, 267, 269, 273, 275, 279–80, 284, 292, 295–96, 298–300, 305, 311–12, 315, 317–19, 323, 325, 331–32, 335, 337–38, 342–43, 345–46, 348, 350, 353–54, 356, 359–63
Thomas, 241
William, son of Robert, 151n
Okeland, Okland *see* Oakland
Ormesby (Ormsbe, Ormsbie, Ormsby), Mr, 316, 353
William, 276–77, 279–80, 301, 301n, 302–303, 346, 370–71
Ormsby, North, (Nun Ormsby), priory, 181n
Ormsby, South, (Ormsbe), 177n, 340, 340n
Otel (Otle), Edward, 47–48
Otter, Robert, 73, 73n
Overay (Overa),
..., 108
John, 1680n
Margaret, wife of John, 168, 168n
Oxford, Oxfordshire, 3

Page (Pagge),
Agnes, wife of William, 115
Isabel, 65
Margaret, 55–56
Margaret, *alias* Margaret Bailey, 57
Ralph, 60, 208
Robert, 142–43, 366
Thomas, 33n
William, 69, 69n
Painter (Paynter),
James, 66
Luke, 246
Overay, 102–103, 112, 117–18, 125–26
Palmer (Pallmer, Pallmore),
..., wife of Thomas, 246
Agnes, 223
John, 204, 281–82, 291, 294, 296, 311, 357, 359, 369–71
Thomas, 56, 197, 212, 224, 236, 238, 265, 269, 305, 369
Parcins (Parcas, Parcens, Parkons, Perkings, Perkons),
..., 149, 155, 181
John, 56, 65
Richard, 73

Stephen, 56, 65, 84, 92, 99, 123, 130, 137
Thomas, 107
Parghe, John, 309
Parham, Suffolk, 191n
Paris, 266
Parish (Parysh), Brian, 338
Parke, Thomas, 295
Parker,
Agnes, 326–27
Auncell, 316, 323
Matthew, archbishop of Canterbury, 25n, 26, 295
Parkhous, Thomas, 37
Parkons *see* Parcins
Parnell (Paronell, Parronell, Pernall, Pernell),
John, 47–48, 65, 73, 73n, 84, 92, 107, 115, 122, 130, 137, 149, 366
Nicholas, 22n, 30, 178, 183, 189, 194, 200
Parr,
Katherine, queen of England, 17n
Sir William, 17, 17n
Parret, Hyan, 68
Parris, Agnes, 256
Parronell *see* Parnell
Parson, Mr, 109
Parych. Margaret, 16
Parysh *see* Parish
Pattrick (Patchet, Patchit),
..., 349
Joanna, wife of Robert, 321, 321n
Robert, 313
Pattyson, Thomas, 334
Paynter *see* Painter
Pelson (Pellson),
Widow, 350
Robert, 350
Thomas, 185, 188, 188n, 192, 197, 224, 272–73, 277–78, 281–83, 301, 316, 318, 332–33, 339, 342, 345, 369, 371
William, 24, 275, 275n, 280
Penny,
..., 235
Isabel, 326
Pennyngton (Penygton, Penyngton, Penynton),
Anne, 342, 346, 347n
Lawrence, 100, 174
Thomas, 154
William, 347
Pepper (Peper),
..., 24, 245, 268

INDEX OF PERSONS AND PLACES

Henry, son of William, 68n
Joanna, daughter of William, 68n
Joanna, wife of William, 68n
Thomas, son of William, 68n
William, 68, 243, 243n, 250, 252
Pereson, Alexander, 334n
Perkings, Perkons *see* Parcins
Pernall, Pernell *see* Parnell
Peyrpoynt, Robert, 366
Piper (Pyper),
 Thomas, 274
 Walter, 287
Pistor (Pystor),
 Edmund, 300n, 304
 Edward, 300
Plummer (Plomare, Plommer, Plumber, Plumer, Plummar),
 Henry, 110–11, 117, 124–26
 Matthew, 39
 Thomas, 319, 326
 William, 67–68
Pomorte *see* Pormort
Ponell, John, 99
Pormort (Pomorte, Pormorte),
 Mr, 296, 298, 302
 Christopher, 346, 351, 354, 371
 Christopher, son of George, 296n
Preston, Thomas, 67
Proctor (Procter, Proketure),
 Isabel, wife of Robert, 33n
 Janet, wife of Robert, 114–15
 Robert, 76, 76n, 89–90, 367
 William, 73, 73n, 84, 366
Provost (Provest, Proveste),
 Joanne, daughter of Thomas, 92
 Joanne, widow, 41n
 Thomas, 4, 28, 41, 41n, 42, 44, 49–52, 56–61, 66, 68, 74–75, 77–79, 85–89, 93–96, 100–103, 108–112, 116, 118–19, 123–27, 131–34, 137–40, 143–45, 150, 152, 155, 157–59, 163, 165, 169, 171, 176, 183–85, 189–90, 366
Pullay,
 George, 65
 Gregory, 64
 Marion, wife of William, 33n
Purvey (Purevy),
 Mr, 302, 342
 John, 301, 301n, 303
Puyll, John, 56
Pyght, William, 365
Pynder, John, 68
Pyper *see* Piper
Pystor *see* Pistor

Raithbe (Rathby, Ratheby, Raythby),
 Elizabeth, wife of Richard, 352
 Isabel, 82, 84, 313
 Isabel, senior, 83
 Richard, 37, 37n, 48, 56, 73, 92, 364–65
 William, 49, 49n, 52, 52n, 59, 103, 108, 212, 305
Raithby cum Maltby (Ratheby, Raythby),
 parson of, 56
 rector of, 184n
Ramforth, George, 241, 243
Randall, …, 253–54
Rankyn, Thomas, 278
Ranold, Anthony, 334
Rantforth, Widow, 352
Ranyard, Ranyarde *see* Raynard
Rasen, Market, (East Rasen, Reyson), 225, 303n
Rasen, West, 109n
Rathby *see* Raithbe
Ratheby *see* Raithbe; Raithby cum Maltby
Raynard (Ranyard, Ranyarde, Raynyard, Raynyarde), Robert, 91–92, 99, 107, 115, 123, 130, 142
Raynforthe, George, 67
Raynyard, Raynyarde *see* Raynard
Raythby *see* Raithbe; Raithby cum Maltby
Reade (Read, Red, Rede, Reed),
 …, 251, 278
 Alan, 226, 306
 Harry, 352
 John, 18, 67, 86, 95, 117, 125, 139, 144–46, 156, 175–77, 183–84, 189–92, 194, 196, 200, 202, 208–10, 219–20, 225–26, 237, 242
 Thomas, 104, 149
 William, 151, 159, 207, 211, 236–37, 270, 276, 279, 295, 306–307, 309, 311, 316, 325–26, 329, 332–33, 336, 339–40, 356
Rechard, John, *alias* John Regall, 359
Red, Rede, Reed *see* Reade
Regall *see* Rigald
Renold *see* Reynold
Revesby, abbey, abbot of, 43
Reynold (Renold), Agnes, 253–56, 261–63
Reyson *see* Rasen, Market
Richardson (Richarson, Richerson, Rychardson),
 …, 127
 Agnes, wife of John, 91–92
 Alexander, 365
 Cicely, wife of Robert, 92

Elizabeth, wife of Thomas, 106–107
Gerard, 48
Janet, 199, 216, 313
John, 91n, 114–15, 216, 216n, 225, 227, 232–33, 242–43, 364
Robert, 69–70, 367
Thomas, 45, 45n, 129–30, 239, 246, 264, 273, 284, 302, 304, 319–20, 322, 324, 357, 366–67, 370–71
William, 101, 101v, 194, 200, 202, 210, 310–11, 315, 317–18, 322–24, 329–32, 335, 343–44, 353, 360
Richmond (Richimond, Rychmonde),
Janet, 324
William, 276–77, 280, 312, 315, 370
Rigald (Regall, Rygald),
..., 354
John, 297, 312, 370
John, *alias* John Rechard, 359
Riggs (Ryggs), Richard, 25, 294, 350, 356–57, 359, 363, 371
Righton, John, 350
Rischbe *see* Rushbe
Robenson *see* Robinson
Robertson, Richard, 264, 370
Robinson (Robenson, Robynson),
..., 270
Mother, 253–54
Mr, 154–55
Beatrice, 341, 343; as wife of Richard, 343n
Elizabeth, 268, 327
Katherine, 65, 73
Peter, son of Richard, 187–88
Richard, 264n, 268, 276, 280–81, 333, 336, 347, 371
Robert, 327, 338
Robson,
..., 253–54
Mother, 253–55, 285, 288–90
Alice, 286–90
Margaret, daughter of Ranulf, 234n
Ralph, 24, 234, 244, 294–95, 298–300, 307–11, 337, 353, 355, 360–61
Ranulf, 234
Robynson *see* Robinson
Roper, Simon, 156, 234, 242–43
Rosse, Walter, 18
Rount, Robert, 149
Route (Rowte, Rowtt, Rowtte), Robert, 67, 67n, 136–37, 365
Rowce, Elizabeth, wife of William, 333
Rowson, Henry, 147–48
Rowston, 109n

Rowte *see* Route
Rowth (Rowthe), William, 138, 145, 150, 164
Rowtt, Rowtte *see* Route
Rushbe (Rischbe, Ruschbe, Rushebe, Russebye, Russhby, Russhebye),
Anne, 352n
Dorothy, 306n
Leonard, 217, 251, 268–69, 284, 294–97, 306, 308–309, 311, 349, 371n
William, 279, 331, 345, 352, 355
Rushurth, Harry, son of Thomas, 352
Russebye, Russhby, Russhebye *see* Rushbe
Rychardson *see* Richardson
Rychmonde *see* Richmond
Rycroft, John, 364
Rydlay, Thomas, 20
Rygald *see* Rigald
Ryggs *see* Riggs
Rykard, Alice, 162

Sadler,
John, 47–48, 51, 55
Sir Ralph, 9n
Richard, 119
St Poll (Sampall, Sampoull, Sayntpolle, Sempull, St Paule, St Pole),
Mr, 154, 177, 221, 229
George, 170, 170n
Jacob or James, son of Thomas, 154n
Thomasina, daughter of George, 154n
Saleby, rector of, *see* Dudding, Reginald
Salisbury, diocese, bishop of, *see* Jewel, John
Sall, Robert, 314
Salmon (Salman, Salmone),
Margery, 313
Robert, 293–94, 332
Thomas, 350
Saltfleet Haven (Saltfleethaven), 2, 23, 26, 164, 236, 236n, 237, 343, 354
St Catherine's chantry, 9n
Saltfleetby All Saints (Saltfletby), 7n, 72, 83, 83n
Saltmarsh (Saltmars, Saltmers),
..., 191–92, 196, 202, 225, 235, 316–17, 319, 338, 345, 345n, 359, 362
..., wife of, 23, 225–27
Robert, 296, 312, 314, 319, 338n
Same, Edward, 240, 240n
Sampall, Sampoull *see* St Poll
Sampson, Thomas, 277

Sanderson (Sandeson, Saunderson,
    Sawnderson),
  Henry, 92n
  Robert, son of Henry, 92
  Thomas, 177
  William, 326
Sands, Margaret, 258
Sausthorpe (Sawthrop), church, 132
Sawayghe, Richard, 306
  Sawer, ..., 156
Sawnderson *see* Sanderson
Saxilby, 19, 334n
  churchwardens' accounts, 1n, 4, 24,
    25n
Sayntpolle *see* St Poll
Scamblesby (Skamelsbe), 362
Scopholm *see* Skupholme
Scot *see* Scott
Scothern, 170n
Scott (Scot, Scotte),
  Agnes, 244, 253, 255–59, 261–63, 289
  Anne, 254, 261
  John, 110
  Margaret, 254
  Thomas, *alias* Thomas Stickney, abbot
    of Revesby, 43n
Scotter, 318n
Seamer, ..., 258
Segura, Spain, 340n
  Sellby, ..., 232
Sempull *see* St Poll
Serbe, John, 307
  Seresby, Mother, 289
Seymour, Jane, queen of England, 125n
Shadworth, ..., 250
Shellton, John, 187
Sheperd *see* Shepperd
Shepley, William, 311n
Shepperd (Sheperd),
  Richard, 327
  Robert, 338
Shorton, Robert, prebendary, 3, 3n
Sidens, Mr, 295
Simcote (Simcott, Symcot, Symcote,
    Symcots),
  Mr, 318, 348
  George, 337
  George, son of William, 333
  Susan, 348n
  Susan, daughter of Mr, 350
  Susan, daughter of William, 352
  William, 348n
Singingman, William, 111–12, 116
Sixhills, priory, 303n

  prior of, 304
Skamelsbe *see* Scamblesby
Skelton,
  Elizabeth, 297–98, 304
  John, 311n
  Richard, 311n
  Stephen, 297n
  William, 292, 296
Skenrall, Harry, 329
Skepholme *see* Skupholme
Skidbrooke (Skidbrouke), 336
Skipwith (Skypwith),
  Mr, 170, 176
  Alice, wife of Sir William, 237n
  John, 237
  John, son of Sir William and Alice,
    237n
  Katherine, 189n
  Mary, 133n
  Sir William, 177, 177n, 183, 187, 237n,
    340, 340n
Skorell *see* Skurrall
Skupholme (Scopholm, Skepholme,
    Skopholm, Skupholm),
  John, 151, 159, 229, 239, 247, 283, 294,
    332, 334
  John, son of John, 151n
Skurrall (Skorell, Skurall, Skurralle,
    Skurrell),
  Agnes, wife of Henry, 309n
  Annas, wife of Harry, 352
  Dorothy, daughter of Henry, 309n
  Harry, 299, 309–10, 337–39, 344
  John, son of Henry, 309n
Skynner, Thomas, 304
Skypwith *see* Skipwith
Slea, River, 6
Smetthe *see* Smith
Smilay, Christopher, 366
Smith (Smetthe, Smyth, Smythe),
  Mr, 300, 302, 323, 327
  Christopher, 79n
  Hugh, 347
  John, 58, 77, 119, 127, 146, 176, 211,
    214, 224, 236, 266–67, 269
  Luke, 26, 362
  Margaret, 189
  Margaret, wife of John, 206
  Martin, 237, 253, 261, 288
  R., 101
  Richard, 78–79, 85, 123, 130, 183,
    189–90, 195–96, 224–25,
    227–28, 234–35, 242–43, 260

Robert, 45, 45n, 53, 61, 76, 78, 83, 86, 100, 102, 111, 125–26, 365
Thomas, 55–56, 234, 259, 268–69, 271, 273, 280, 291, 315, 318, 333, 335, 371
Walter, 337
William, 83, 83n, 84, 87–88, 93–95, 100, 102, 108–109, 111, 117–18, 123, 125–26, 132–33, 137, 139
Smithson (Smythson),
..., 263, 329, 336
Martin, 259
Robert, 322, 344
William, 254
Smyth, Smythe *see* Smith
Smythson *see* Smithson
Snarford, 170n
Snarforth, Alice, 313
Soirbe (Soyrbe), John, 298, 298n, 314
Somercotes, North, 7n, 115, 283n, 305n
Somercotes, North or South, (Somarcokes), parsons of, 168n
Somerscales (Somerskaills, Somerskells),
George, 224, 237–38, 277
Janet, 352
Joan, 355
John, 333
William, 211, 213–15, 225, 282, 291, 297, 304, 327, 369–70
Somerset, duke of, 10n
Somerskaills, Somerskells *see* Somerscales
Sorby (Sorbe),
Janet, 289
John, 318
South (Sowth, Sowthe),
John, 333, 335, 339, 351, 353, 371
William, 342
Southampton, earl of, *see* Fitzwilliam, William
Sowth, Sowthe *see* South
Soyrbe *see* Soirbe
Spain,
Philip II of, 6n
wine from, 318n
Spalding (Spaldyng, Spaldynge, Spallyng, Spawlling),
..., 196
Alice, wife of John, 14243
John, 159, 226, 272, 276–77, 297, 368, 370
Richard, 334
Robert, son of John, 187–88
Stephen, 333, 339, 346, 349, 371

Spaldwyn, John, 218, 220–21, 225, 369
Spaldyng, Spaldynge, Spallyng, Spawlling *see* Spalding
Spedle *see* Spendle
Spellysbe, George, 187
Spencer,
Mistress, 174
Agnes, wife of Thomas, 98–99
Isabel, wife of Richard, 130, 206
Janet, wife of John, 181
John, 69–70, 74, 89, 129, 129n, 130, 133, 137, 215, 365–66
Richard, 53, 53n, 60, 62, 86, 125, 148–49, 155, 304, 367
Robert, 27, 38, 38n, 39, 59, 67, 69, 74n, 81, 85, 88, 94, 142, 159, 164, 176, 178, 197, 211, 213–14, 218, 231, 240, 247, 264, 365, 367–69
Robert, son of Robert, 197
Thomas, 16, 16n, 33, 33n, 40, 52, 58, 61, 74n, 78–79, 87, 98, 134–35, 138, 161, 163, 177, 179, 186–87, 192, 206, 367–68
Thomas, the younger, 181
Spendle (Spedle),
Janet, 179
Janet, wife of John, 182
Spenethorne *see* Spenythorne
Spenlow (Spenlay, Spenlof, Spenlowe),
John, 159, 211, 211n, 213–14, 266, 271, 368–69
Thomas, 206
Spenythorne (Spenethorne, Spenythorn),
Thomas, 81, 85, 151, 154–55, 162–63, 367
Spilsby (Spilesby), 278
Spillesby (Spilesby, Spilsby, Spyllesbe, Spyllesby, Spylsby),
Beatrice, wife of Gregory, 99
George, 4, 81, 81n, 98, 103–104, 110–11, 118–19, 124, 126–27, 134, 172, 178, 185, 188, 216, 367, 369
Squyrall, Henry, 236
Stainby, 342n
Stainfield, priory, prioress of, *see* Bessby, Elizabeth
Stefnson, Robert, 365
Stenigot, 340n
Stewton (Steuton), 39n, 40, 192, 202–203
parson of, 47n
Stickney, Thomas, *alias* Thomas Scotte, abbot of Revesby, 43n
Stoke by Clare, Suffolk, college, 3n

Stoker,
    Joanna, 304n
    Marion, 263
    Stephen, 168
    Walter, 304, 356, 356n
Storre, James, 307, 314
Story,
    ..., 253, 256, 261–62
    Mother, 259
    Cuthbert, 223, 223n
    Emott, wife of Cuthbert, 216, 216n
    Isabel, 256–57, 259, 261–62
    James, 210, 353
    Janet, 254–59, 261–63, 290
    Richard, 349
Stowte, Richard, 337
Stubbs, Ralph, 348–49
Stut (Stute, Stutt, Stutte), Roger, 25, 297,
    297n, 326, 332–33, 339, 353, 371
Sudbury, Thomas, vicar of Louth St
    James, 162n
Suffolk, duke of, 138, 177n
Sutterton, churchwardens of, 39n
Sutton, George, 127, 197, 201, 277, 368–69
Swarby, 240n
Swelynge, Richard, 321
Swetyng,
    Robert, 27–28, 339, 339n, 361, 361n,
        362
    William, 313
Swillington, Thomas, 80n
Swineshead (Swynshed, Swynsted), 39n
    abbey, 13n
Swyne,
    Agnes, wife of John, 216
    John, 192, 273, 277, 369
Swynshed, Swynsted see Swineshead
Syll (Cyll),
    ..., 60, 237
    Agnes, 240
    Richard, 41, 41n, 85, 144
Symcot, Symcote, Symcots see Simcote
Sympson (Symson),
    ..., 234, 242, 275, 296
    George, 26–27, 233, 271
    Robert, 234, 266, 352
Sysson,
    Elizabeth, wife of John, 47
    John, 60
Syver, John, 203

Tace (Tacye),
    ..., 66, 85, 93–94, 100
    John, 67, 67n, 69, 74, 85, 101

Tailer, Tailler, Taillor, Tailor see Taylor
Talke (Talkes, Talks, Tauk, Taulx),
    Alice, 91–92, 107
    John, 48, 56, 73, 83–84
Taller,
    Anne, 357
    Isabel, widow, 358
    Joanna, wife of William, 292
Tanner, ..., 326
Tathwell, 283n
Tattershall, 6, 260
    college, 3n
Tauk, Taulx see Talke
Taylor (Tailer, Tailler, Taillor, Tailor,
        Taller, Tayleor, Tayler, Tayleyor,
        Tayllyer, Taylyor),
    Mr, 183, 336
    Alexander, 367n
    Alexander, son of Robert, 33n
    Joanna, 296n
    John, 107, 117, 342
    Richard, 80
    Thomas, 8, 8n, 137, 137n, 172, 183n,
        224, 364–65
    William, 146, 204, 212, 296, 368, 369n
Temple (Tempell),
    ..., 253
    Thomas, 275
Tenant (Tenand),
    Janet, wife of John, 181
    John, 140, 151–52, 159, 179
Tetney, 221n
    Thame, Oxfordshire, abbey, abbot of,
        see King, Robert
    Than, Annes, wife of Robert, 181
    Theddlethorpe St Helen
        (Theddlethorpe, Theddylthorpe),
        2, 7n, 9, 83, 83n, 308, 341
Theker, Roger, 278
Thew,
    Mrs, 249
    John, 304, 304n
    Simon, 154, 264, 273, 278, 278n, 370
    Thimelby see Thymolby
    Thissilton, Janet, 258
Thomas,
    Bedle, 317
    Godfrey, 278
    John, 366
Thomasson, Elizabeth, 313
Thomlinson (Thomlynson, Thomplinson,
        Tomlinson),
    Mother, 253–54
    Agnes, 258

Alice, 253, 257–59, 261–63
Thomson (Tompson, Tomson),
 ..., 367
 George, vicar of Louth St James, 36n
 Isabel, 358
 John, 56, 364
 Margaret, 203
 Thomas, 334, 343
Thorndicke (Thorndik),
 Nicholas, 240, 243, 308
 William, son of Nicholas, 241
Thorneley,
 Isabel, wife of John, 206
 Isabel, wife of Robert, 206n
Thornton Abbey, 20, 79n, 241n
Thornton College, 20
Thorpe, John, 67n
Thorpe Hall, 37n, 72n, 191n
Thymolby (Thimelby, Thymelbe, Thymolbe),
 Janet, 296–97
 Joanna, 297n
 Margaret, 55, 57
Todd (Todds, Tods),
 ..., 252–55, 257–59, 261–63, 287–90
 Hugh, 272
 Isabel, sister of Margaret, 285
 Margaret, 261, 285–86
 Robert, 145
Tomlinson *see* Thomlinson
Tompson, Tomson *see* Thomson
 Tonke, Alice, 179
Topcliff (Topclyff, Topclyffe, Topclyp, Toplif),
 ..., 218
 Mr, 278, 296
 Richard, 240
 William, 213
Toplis, John, 292
Torrington, East or West, (Turrington), 317
Totte, Harry, 330
Tottery, Harry, 273
Tours, France, 145n
Toye, Nicholas, 309, 323
Treigolde, Robert, 366
Trusthorpe, 7n, 121n
Tunis, Tunisia, 162n
Tupholme, abbey, 4n, 99n
Turkey,
 people of, 161, 162n
 pirates of, 161n
Turner, ..., 253–54
Turrington *see* Torrington, East or West

Tyburn, Middlesex, 3, 47n, 80n
Tyler (Tylar, Tyllar),
 George, 59–60, 66, 68, 77, 79, 87–89, 131, 139
 John, 251
 Thomas, 19, 190–91
Tynckeler, Matthew, 50
Tyrwhitt (Tyrwhit),
 Mr, 318
 Marmaduke, 318n

Unsant, Jok, *alias* John Wilson, 116n
Upton,
 Hammond, 284
 Janet, wife of Nicholas, 137
 Nicholas, 44, 44n, 49, 49n, 50, 57, 61, 66, 74, 85, 87–88, 93–95, 100, 102–103, 108–112, 116–19, 123–27, 131, 133, 137, 143, 150–51, 155–57, 163–65, 169, 171–72, 174–75
Utterby, 7n

Verley, Henry, 270
Voragine, Jacobus de, 86n

Wade (Waday, Wady, Wayd, Wayde),
 ..., 176, 178, 191–92, 234, 253–54, 259, 261–63
 Alice, 258–59, 261–63
 Isabel, 65
 James, 288
 Janet, 261–62
 Robert, 253–54, 259, 262–63
Wadsley, John, 363
Wady *see* Wade
Wailis *see* Wallace
Waite (Wait, Wat, Wate, Wayte),
 ..., 50
 Isabel, 306
 Isabel, wife of Roger, 311n
 John, 350
 Roger, 300–301, 303, 327, 359
 Thomas, 44
Wake,
 ..., 252
 John, 39n, 209
 Thomas, 27, 271, 326
 William, 37
Walker (Walkar),
 ..., 252, 258, 261–62
 Agnes, wife of Richard, 91–92
 Alice, wife of William, 33n, 48, 56

Anne, wife of William, 79
Gyleane, 310
Janet, 256–59, 261–63
Julie, 306, 306n
Richard, 104, 120, 136, 142, 154, 333, 368
William, 48n, 70, 79, 90, 97–99, 107, 115, 122, 130, 137, 149, 155, 162, 169, 365
Wallays *see* Wallis
Walle, Robert, 178
Wallis (Wailis, Wallays, Walles, Walleys),
Alexander, 33n, 40
Anne, 303n
James, prior of Sixhills, 304n
John, son of Robert, 136
Robert, 16
Walmesgate, 237n
Wardall (Wardale, Wardayll, Wardell, Wardyll),
Mother, 278
Widow, 362
Agnes, wife of Matthew, 314
Margaret, wife of Matthew, 148–49, 149n, 358
Matthew, 104, 104n, 177, 179, 264, 276, 301, 326–27, 347, 350, 368–71
Thomas, 146, 204, 210, 281, 284, 358, 358n, 360, 368–70
Warde, Janet, 341
Wardell *see* Wardall
Wardyll *see* Wardall
Wat, Wate *see* Waite
Wath (Wathe, Wayth),
…, 138–39, 144
John, 144, 144n, 145, 150, 156–57, 165, 170–71, 173, 176, 183–85, 187, 191–92, 196, 201, 203, 207–209, 211–12, 219–21, 229, 233, 238, 242, 244, 246, 252, 271, 277
Roger, 301, 327
Watson,
Agnes, 343
John, 19, 279
Margaret, 334
Richard, 123, 130
Robert, son of Richard, 122
Thomas, 227, 242–43, 313
William, 358
Watterhouse (Watterhous), Oliver, 316, 339
Watts, John, 188
Wayd, Wayde *see* Wade

Wayrd, Richard, 292
Wayte *see* Waite
Wayth *see* Wath
Weest *see* West
Weikeley *see* Wheatley
Welborn,
John, 68
Peter, 321
Welebe, Welloby *see* Willoughby
Wells, Thomas, 358
Welton, 183
parsons of, 168n
Welton le Wold, 23
Wenstable, Thomas, 274
Wentforth,
Janet, 224
Robert, 142–43, 148, 155
West (Weest),
Margaret, wife of William, 121–22, 130
Robert, 41–42, 50, 68, 95, 223, 340, 371
William, 40, 40n, 45, 75, 79, 101, 127, 140, 167–68, 168n, 173, 297, 366–68
Westerby (Westabye, Westerbe),
…, 234
Robert, 200, 200n, 204, 212, 232–33, 273–74
Westmells (Westmeles, Westmelles, Westmels, Westmold, Westmols),
Robert, 36, 48, 55, 65, 73, 84, 92, 99, 107, 115, 122, 130, 136, 142, 148, 154, 162, 168, 173, 179, 181, 188
Wethecall *see* Withcall
Wether, Richard, 143
Weytlay, Weyttley *see* Wheatley
Whale,
Annes, 179
Annes, wife of Robert, 181
Whallay, Robert, 75–76, 313
Wheatley (Weikeley, Weytlay, Weyttley, Wheatle, Wheteley, Whetely, Whetley),
Mr, 276
Mrs, 275
John, 241, 241n, 243, 260, 271
Katherine, 55
White (Whet, Whett, Whit, Whyt, Whyte, Wyte),
…, 256, 258, 261–63
family of, 11
Mr, 301, 348, 350, 353

Allyn, 253
  Cecily, wife of John, 35–36
  Elizabeth, 256
  Ellen, 256–59, 261–63
  John, 37, 48, 53, 62, 73, 85, 87, 92, 99, 101–102, 107, 112, 115, 118, 122, 125, 132, 134, 136, 142–43, 145, 148–49, 162–63, 168, 173, 179, 181, 188
  Judith, wife of Richard, 347
  Julian, 48
  Philip, 62
  Richard, 363
  Robert, 73, 99, 107
  Susan, 349
  Thomas, 257, 314
  William, 19, 56–57, 172, 175, 177, 200, 212, 215, 221, 224, 232, 237–39, 246–48, 263–64, 270, 276, 279, 283–84, 301, 301n, 302–305, 307, 312, 318–19, 322, 324, 332, 335, 343, 346, 354, 359, 362, 370–71
Whittington (Whittyngton),
  Mr, 271, 302, 356
  Alexander, 271n
Whyt, Whyte *see* White
Wigford, church of St Mary, 109n
Wigtoft, 13n, 18, 20
  churchwardens' accounts, 1n, 5, 244n
Wilkynson, John, 327
Willabie *see* Willoughby
  Wille, Cuthbert, 358, 362
Willerbe *see* Willoughby
William, John, 148
Williams, Henry, prebendary, 3n, 109n, 283n
Williamson (Wyllamson, Wylliamson),
  Mr, senior, 174
  Agnes, 122
  Joan, wife of John, 64n
  Joanna, 83
  John, 48, 55, 64, 64n, 73, 91, 99, 107, 115, 122–23, 136, 142, 154, 162, 173, 188
  John, senior, 168
  Nicholas, 263
Willis *see* Willows
Willoby *see* Willoughby
Willor, …, 352
Willos *see* Willows
Willoughby (Welebe, Welloby, Willabie, Willerbe, Willoby, Willougby,
  Wollarbe, Wollarby, Wollerby, Woloby, Wyllebe, Wyllowbe),
  Lord, 211, 275, 278, 294
  Mr, 165
  Joanna, wife of Thomas, 173n
  Joanna, wife of William, 173
  John, 278
  Katherine, 126n, 211n
  Thomas, 45, 52, 146, 151, 172, 186, 190, 367–68
  Thomas, son of Thomas, 56
  Sir William, Baron Willoughby, 191, 191n
Willows (Willis, Willos, Willowes),
  George, 211n, 272, 343, 370–71
Willyngam (Wylingam, Wyllyngam),
  Isabel, 323, 333, 335, 342, 345, 349, 353, 360
Wilsford, quarry, 6
Wilson (Wylson),
  …, 253, 257–58, 262
  Father, 256, 259, 261–63
  Mr, 202
  Anthony, 326, 329
  Geoffrey, 298, 316
  Joanna, daughter of Thomas, 352n
  John, 59n, 116, 116n
  John, *alias* Jok Unsant, 116n
  Martin, 262
  Miles, 149
  Owtred, 133
Winchester, Hampshire, cathedral, 6n
Windsor, Berkshire, park, 305n
Wingod *see* Wyngod
Winter (Wynter),
  Emott, wife of Robert, 292, 292n
  Robert, 280, 349, 354–55
  Thomas, 9, 350, 357
Witham, River, 6
Withcall (Wethecall), 274
  curate of, 79n
Wodall *see* Wodhall
Woddnyll, …, 179
Wodhall (Wodall), Richard, 172, 181
Wolds, The, 2, 6
Wollarbe, Wollarby, Wollerby, Woloby *see* Willoughby
Wood (A Woode, Woode),
  Father, 252–56, 258–59, 261–63, 274, 285, 288–89
  John, 221n
  Richard, 255
  Walter, 221, 229, 239, 247

Woolerby, Thomas, 131
Woolsby, Richard, 212
    Wordall, Agnes, 318
    Worledge (Worghlege), Peter, 292, 296
Worsley (Worseldy, Worseley, Worsely,
    Worslaw, Worslay, Worslaye,
    Worsler),
  ..., 284
  Agnes, 7n, 265n
  Agnes, wife of William, 269
  George, 199, 211, 215, 221
  George, son of William, 212
  Maud, wife of William, 47
  William, 7, 18n, 69, 69n, 94, 110, 151,
    204, 212, 215, 221, 228–29,
    265–66, 270
Worth, John, 312
Wright (Wryght),
  ..., 325
  Anne, 56, 58
  Beatrice, 286
  Cecilia, wife of Thomas, 358, 358n
  George, 251
  Isabel, 313
  John, 85, 148, 217
  Margaret, 258–59, 261–63, 286
  Margaret, senior, 253
  Richard, 250, 271, 271n, 293, 349
  Robert, 265, 313
Wyatt, Sir Thomas, 246
Wygersley, Margaret, 133n
Wygon, John, 340

Wylingam *see* Willyngam
Wyllamson *see* Williamson
Wyllebe *see* Willoughby
Wylliamson *see* Williamson
Wyllowbe *see* Willoughby
Wylly, Cots, 275
Wyllyngam *see* Willyngam
Wylson *see* Wilson
Wyndell (Wyndkell),
  ..., 289, 330
  Father, 262, 288
  Mother, 287
Wyngod (Wingod),
  Joanne, wife of William, 47–48
  William, 47–48, 50, 56
Wynnyngton, Lawrence, 9n
Wynskall, Thomas, 327
Wynter *see* Winter
Wyte *see* White
Wythell, William, 219
Wytt, William, 273
Wytton, Robert, 92

Ymos *see* Hymas
Ynglych *see* Inglish
Younger, Robert, 61
York, 8n, 88n, 168n
Yorkshire, county, 244n
Young,
  Agnes, 277
  Janet, wife of John, 73

INDEX OF SUBJECTS

Abbeys and priories, 3, 4n, 6n, 13n, 20, 21n, 33n, 43n, 59n, 76n, 79n, 92n, 99n, 117n, 129n, 148n, 171n, 177n, 181n, 241n, 303n, 337n; *see also* Nunneries

Acts of Parliament,
 Act for Maintenance of Artillery and for Debarring of Unlawful Games (1541), 26n
 Act for Mending the Highways (1555), 14, 264, 264n
 Act for the Preservation of Grain (1566), 4n, 345n
 Act to destroy choughs, crows and rooks, 4n, 226n
 Act to Reform Certain Disorders touching Ministers of the Church (1571), 26n
 Dissolution of Colleges Act (1547), 22n
 Subscription (ThirtyNine Articles) Act (1571), 26n
 Vagabonds Act (1530), 22n, 126n

Alms, 4, 13, 23, 30, 183–85, 187, 189–92, 195–96, 200–203, 207–211, 217–20, 225–26, 253, 266n, 270–71, 274–76, 285n, 293, 317n

Altars, 5, 8, 101, 110n, 206, 206n, 235, 237, 239, 242, 260
 cloths of, 25, 74, 85, 116, 134, 137, 143–45, 149, 155, 163, 169–71, 174, 194–95, 227n, 238, 243–46, 259–60, 269, 271, 275, 311, 335, 349
 high, 23–24, 52–53, 92, 99–100, 102–103, 108, 110, 123, 131, 137, 143–45, 150, 155, 157, 163, 166, 169, 171, 174, 185, 191, 207, 237, 245–46, 266, 272, 359
 stone for, 236
 table for, 274
 taking down of, 19, 209, 209n
 towels for, 201, 244
 washing of, 44, 49–50, 56–57, 66, 117

Amercements and fines, 277, 281, 297, 332, 336, 360

Animals and birds,
 bear, *see under* Officials
 bee, 8
 bird, 226n, 232, 232n
 bull, 27, 53, 58, 61–62, 64, 75, 83, 85, 88, 95, 100, 102–103, 108, 111, 125, 132, 138, 144, 150, 156, 164, 169, 173–75, 177–78, 182, 187, 190, 193, 203, 207, 215, 218, 220, 224, 227–28, 231–32, 244, 248, 251, 264, 266, 271–72, 274, 276–82, 292, 296–99, 304–306, 308, 311–12, 314–15, 317–19, 322, 325–26, 328, 330, 332–34, 337, 339–40, 342, 344–46, 348–50, 353, 356–57, 362
 bull, pied, 317
 calf, 102, 110, 132, 317
 cattle, 4n, 27, 53n, 58, 125, 144, 190, 196, 207, 307, 319
 chough, 4n, 226n
 cow, 8, 27, 99, 102, 307, 311, 316–17, 322, 324, 326, 329, 332–33, 336, 339–40, 342, 346, 348
 crow, 4n, 226n, 345
 dog, 208, 232–33, 235, 238, 267; *see also under* Trades and occupations
 dove, 125–26, 220, 234, 272
 eagle, 306
 horse, 28, 77, 87, 94, 101, 126, 133, 151, 157–58, 171, 191, 195, 214, 243, 247–48, 264, 336, 355, 361
  Old English Black, 6n
  packhorse, 6, 6n
 impounding of, 189n
 lamb, 8
 livestock, 2
 management of, 10
 pig, 8
 pigeon. 270
 poultry, 8
 protection of, 175n

INDEX OF SUBJECTS

rook, 4n, 226n
sheep, 12, 58, 170, 349, 359
spider, 85
starling, 226, 226n
swine, 58
vermin, 4, 345n
Annuities and pensions, 22n, 79n, 100n, 148n, 181n, 183n, 184n, 241n, 265n, 303n
Apprentices and apprenticeships, 29, 80n
Archery and butts, 26, 26n, 27, 164, 164n, 208n, 228, 251, 266, 271, 278, 298, 307, 314–15, 329, 344, 354
Armies, 17, 266n
captain, 170n, 354
captain, petty, 33n, 45n, 70n, 74n, 221n
pikeman, 203
soldier, 203, 239, 246, 354
Arms *see* Weapons and Arms
Arrests, 3n, 17
Assizes,
of ale, 45n
of bread, 45n

Badges, for poor folk, 22, 126
Banks, 13n
Baptisms and christenings, 18n; *see also* Books, parish register
Barns, 9, 43n, 86n
Beacons, 26, 354n
fire beacon, 275, 354
Bedehouses *see under* Houses and buildings
Bells, 7, 13n, 19, 36n, 39, 39n, 41–42, 52, 55, 58–61, 66–69, 74, 77–78, 78n, 85–87, 94–95, 109, 116–18, 125–26, 138, 145, 148, 150, 158, 165, 170–71, 183–85, 189, 197, 206, 210–11, 219, 223, 227, 231–32, 236, 241–42, 246, 250, 251n, 252, 260, 265–66, 270, 273, 275, 280, 282, 293, 296–98, 306, 313–14, 319, 321–22, 326–28, 333–34, 340–42, 345–48, 352, 354, 356–57, 361, 363
casting of, 43n
clapper of, 42, 79, 85, 93, 93n, 94, 100, 150, 157, 165, 175, 184, 191, 205, 251, 281–82, 291, 315, 359
collars of, 41–42, 50–51, 58, 101, 126, 158, 171, 175–77, 183–84, 203, 225, 227, 235, 356, 360
damage to, 337
dressing of, 238, 300, 315

frame of, 171, 207
hammer of, 318
handbell, 25, 41n, 110, 117, 334
hanging of, 138, 278
helping of, 220
keeper of, 143, 150, 155, 169, 174, 194
keeping of, 44, 49–50, 56–57, 66, 74, 85, 93, 100, 108, 116, 123, 131, 137, 163, 189, 200–201, 217, 292, 317–18, 322–24, 329–31, 335, 343, 348, 360
knolling of, 269
maintenance of, 1, 41n
mending of, 88, 102, 127, 175–76, 227, 242–43, 267, 269, 272, 275, 343, 353, 360, 362
ringing of, 7, 11, 30, 55, 73, 79, 83, 90, 97, 99, 106, 122, 181, 240, 282, 284, 292–93, 353, 360
rope of, 6, 252, 260, 293n, 337
sale of, 197n
staple of, 58
strings of, 39, 42, 50–51, 58–61, 66–67, 74, 76–78, 86, 94–95, 100, 109, 111, 116–18, 125, 131, 133, 138, 144, 150, 165, 170, 175, 177, 184, 196, 200, 226, 234–35, 242, 252, 269, 275, 279, 293, 298, 309, 315, 331, 343, 349–50, 360–62
surveying of, 276
taking down of, 210, 226
tolling of, 7
trussing of, 89, 175
wedge of, 93, 127
wheel of, 40, 60–61, 86n, 87–88, 94, 102, 125, 150, 164–65, 169–70, 183, 219, 226, 242, 252, 260, 269, 280, 284, 315, 317, 356, 362–63
yoke and yoking of, 52, 61, 102, 280
See also under Trades and occupations
Benefices, 241n
Bequests and legacies, 56, 15, 115, 122, 161, 173n, 183n, 197, 312
to paupers, 33n
Bibles *see under* Books
Birds *see* Animals
Boats *see* Ships and boats
Bonds and obligations, 42, 190–91, 197, 229, 236, 239, 243, 247–48, 277, 281, 283
Books, 24, 87, 150, 166, 170, 203, 226, 241, 252, 259, 274
antiphon, 79, 79n, 87, 94, 101, 279

INDEX OF SUBJECTS

antiphonary, 169, 169n, 170
Apologia pro Ecclesia Anglicana, 359, 359n, 360
bible, 16, 18, 132, 139, 139n, 142, 147, 151, 297, 351
binding of, 79
book for the corporation, 300, 302, 327
book of accounts, 51, 76, 126, 142n, 178, 277, 293, 326
book of admonition about marriages, 295
book of articles made by the archbishop of Canterbury, 26, 295
Book of Common Prayer, 19n, 25n, 200, 200n, 298n
book of Papistry, 25
book of prayers against the Turks, 162n
book of the sewers, 308
breviary, 236n
burning of, 16, 16n, 33n
cartulary, 236n
cause book, 319, 319n
clasps of, 132
collection book, 298
coucher, 236–37
covers of, 102, 132–33
destruction of, 25
dirige book, 23, 235
dressing of, 102, 133
Easter or Tithe Book, 8
gradual, 79, 79n
grail, 170, 237
Homilies, 19, 19n, 202–203, 325, 359n
hymnbook, 279
injunctions, king's, 15, 202
inventory of church goods, 195, 195n, 225
legend book, 86, 86n, 109, 165
liturgical text, 3, 5, 23, 29
making of, 279
manual, 235–36
mass book, 235
mending of, 88, 102, 190
Paraphrases (upon the Epistles), 195, 195n, 295, 297, 351
parish register, 2, 17, 18, 18n, 132, 132n, 134, 138, 156, 158, 170, 175, 187n, 190–91, 196, 200–201, 210, 217, 223n, 226, 232, 234, 280, 282, 291n, 292, 295, 298–99, 314–15, 317, 319, 322–24, 329–31, 335, 343, 345, 348, 351, 353, 360

Postells, 350–51
processioner, 170, 170n
profession, 241
psalm book, 363
psalter, 200, 209, 235, 331
register of poor men's names, 260
religious text, 19
Royal Injunctions (1538), 132n, 133n
Royal Injunctions (1547), 1719
service book, 324
song book, 25, 232, 345
spiritual text, 5
subsidy book, 218
verse book, 170
Boonworks and boon days, 14, 14n, 208, 208n, 242, 272, 308, 311–12, 326, 332, 339, 346, 351, 357
Boundaries, disputes about, 4n
Bowls, 8n
Boxes *see* Chests and boxes
Brewing and breweries, 45n, 340, 340n, 343, 346
Bridges, 13, 13n, 204, 218, 231, 233, 243, 251, 269, 275, 291, 294, 317, 319, 323, 329–30, 336, 344, 354–55, 360
footbridge, 228
repairs of, 4, 293
Buildings *see* Houses and buildings
Bulls, papal, 26
Burials, 7, 9, 30, 64, 72, 83, 90–91, 97–98, 106, 114, 129, 133, 142, 177, 179, 182, 182n, 187, 196, 199, 203, 206, 216, 223–24, 231, 240–41, 250, 260, 263, 265–66, 277–79, 281–82, 284, 292–93, 295–97, 304, 306, 312–14, 321–22, 327–28, 333–34, 340–43, 346–48, 350–52, 357, 359
of paupers, 134, 137
Burning *see* Fires and burning
Butts *see* Archery and butts

Calendars, 25, 298
Candles and candlesticks, 19, 25, 42n, 43n, 44n, 69, 78n, 94, 102, 111, 131, 145, 157, 165, 170–71, 185, 192, 196, 202, 209–10, 219, 224, 226, 235, 243, 252, 260, 270–72, 275, 323, 335
chandelier, 132n
making of, 190
mending of, 68, 72, 85, 100, 116, 139, 185
Paschal candle, 24, 111, 111n

INDEX OF SUBJECTS

percher, 78
scouring of, 42–43, 52–53, 61, 67, 69, 78, 87–88, 95, 103, 110, 112, 118–19, 127, 134, 139, 145, 151, 158, 166, 172, 177, 201
serge, 158, 214, 231, 246
Canopies, 24, 103, 158
Captives *see* prisoners and captives
Carpentry, 41n; *see also under* Trades and occupations
Carts and wagons, 58, 281n
bier, 126, 126n
cart, 6
pageant, 43, 43n, 101, 112
wagon, 6
wain, 171, 281, 307
Castles, 27, 29, 67n, 323, 338–39, 345n, 361n; *see also under* Officials
Cathedrals, 2, 6n, 25n, 88n, 284n, 334n
Chancels *see under* Parts of churches
Chantries, 6n, 8, 8n, 9n, 21n, 37n, 101n, 181, 184n
Chapels, 6n, 8–9, 9n, 38, 40, 40n, 75n, 83n, 129, 136, 156, 161, 161n, 162n, 163, 165, 182, 338n, 362n
chapel royal, 267n
Chapters, 2, 202
Charities, 22, 43n, 161, 244, 271n
Charters, 100n, 300n, 307n
royal, 59n
Chests and boxes, 12, 41n, 51, 268
ark, 305, 311
banner chest, 305
box, 186
chest, 126, 138, 144, 176, 189, 224, 239n, 270, 305, 311, 337
coffer, 125, 146, 151, 224
hutch, 41, 45, 45n, 54, 60, 79n, 97, 146, 151, 162n, 188, 214, 361
locker, 206 207
poor man's box, 15, 15n, 19, 22–23, 126n, 183n, 194, 199, 204–207, 212, 216, 223n, 224, 265, 292, 297, 304–305, 312, 351
pyx, 24, 51, 51n, 103
Chimes, 40–42, 44, 49–50, 59, 61, 66, 76, 88, 94, 118, 126, 138–39, 158, 163, 176, 183, 226, 234–35, 244, 250, 279, 299, 324–25, 329, 345, 355, 361
chime house, 270
hammer of, 102, 299
keeper of, 85, 92, 100, 108, 116, 123, 131, 137, 143, 149, 155, 163, 169, 174, 182, 194, 292
keeping of, 56–57, 66, 74, 189, 200, 210, 217, 227, 231–33, 235, 241, 267, 280, 294, 311, 315, 317–18, 322–24, 329–31, 335, 343, 348, 353, 36
maker of, 325
mending of, 51, 59, 68, 94–95, 102, 125, 133, 144–45, 151, 164, 169–70, 175, 201–202, 209, 218, 228, 235, 243, 259–60, 270, 298, 309
repairs of, 1
rope of, 132, 156, 164, 176
strings of, 76, 101, 201, 242, 316
wheel of, 41, 43, 58, 66, 77, 85, 87, 101, 109, 139, 170, 195, 201, 218, 268, 270, 315
wire of, 323
Chimneys, 110, 124, 126–27
Choirs, 19, 22n, 25, 25n, 36n, 39, 43, 50, 52, 58, 60–62, 72, 75, 78, 78n, 80, 85, 87–88, 93–94, 101, 101n, 103, 110, 112, 117, 117n, 124, 133–34, 139, 144, 158, 166, 169n, 171, 178, 189–90, 192, 200, 210, 210–11, 217–18, 224, 227–28, 235, 245–46, 260, 267n, 279, 295, 305, 308, 311, 318, 335, 340, 343, 345–46, 350, 353, 359–60
door of, 123, 126, 138, 165, 172, 270, 275, 318, 331, 336
Christenings *see* Baptisms
Churchings *see under* Services, religious
Churchyards, 22n, 52, 77, 117, 125, 170, 200, 250–51, 355, 362
dressing of, 269, 284
gates of, 78, 85, 100, 137–38, 144, 155, 157, 176, 218, 234, 279, 294, 318
house in, 7, 306, 326, 329, 331–32, 334, 336, 341, 359
mending of, 177
pale of, 251
school in, 266
stile of, 138, 279
walls of, 125, 184, 187, 299, 323
well in, 158
Citizens, 47n, 104n, 111n
Clergy and religious,
abbot, 8, 43, 43n, 80n, 170n, 191n, 231n
Anabaptists, 18n

INDEX OF SUBJECTS

archbishop, 19n, 25n, 26, 295, 295n, 298, 341n
archdeacon, 212n
bedesman, 29
bishop, 4n, 10, 13n, 21n, 26, 26n, 59n, 80n, 329n, 359n, 365n
bishop, suffragan, 80, 80n, 85, 93, 110, 117, 124, 156, 164, 170, 176
canon, 79n, 241n, 303n
chancellor of bishop, 96n
chaplain, 21, 37, 72, 84, 89n, 99, 107, 115, 154n, 168, 223n, 227n, 241n, 265n
choirmaster, 22n, 25n, 59n
chorister, 13, 22n, 25, 25n, 29
clergy, 3, 3n, 13
cleric, 4
commissary, 72, 72n, 183
curate, 79n, 236
deacon, 11
dean, 2, 25n, 37n, 72n, 139n, 189n, 201, 233
friar, 65n, 80n
keeper of altar of St Peter, 88n
keeper of the church book, 178
minister, 22n
monk, 15n, 76n, 80n, 170n, 191n
nun, 147, 147n, 148n, 149, 155n, 181, 181n, 221n, 303n
organist, 13, 22n, 25n, 59n
parson, 47n, 56, 109–10, 168n
Pope, 26
preacher, 4, 20, 308, 308n
prebendary, 23, 8, 109n, 283n
priest, 3, 11n, 16n, 17n, 48, 48n, 52, 52n, 59n, 80, 88n, 89, 109, 110n, 116, 121–23, 132–33, 142, 154n, 156, 162, 164, 168, 168n, 181–82, 188, 192
priest, chantry, 37n, 101n, 184n
prior, 223n, 304n
proctor, 33, 45, 53, 62, 70, 81, 90, 97, 104, 112, 120, 127, 140, 146, 152, 159, 166, 179, 185
rector, 1–2, 8, 80n, 184n, 303n
registrar, bishop's, 86n, 142n
server, 43n
singingman, 16n, 22n, 40n
taxation of, 16n
treasurer of Lincoln cathedral, 88n
vicar, 3, 8, 11n, 15, 24, 36, 36n, 37, 47n, 50, 52n, 65n, 102, 113n, 137–38, 151n, 156, 176n, 178, 184, 209, 212, 212n, 251–52, 271, 295–96,
  298–300, 303n, 305, 308–309, 325, 331, 361–62
Clocks, 44, 58, 139, 176, 196, 242, 250, 268, 270, 274, 310, 325, 330, 345, 361
  axe, hammer of, 310
  collar of, 150
  hammer of, 69
  keeper of, 85, 92, 100, 108, 116, 123, 131, 137, 143, 149, 155, 163, 169, 174, 182, 194, 292
  keeping of, 49–50, 56–57, 66, 74, 189, 200, 210, 217, 227, 231–33, 235, 241, 267, 280, 294, 311, 315, 317–18, 322–24, 329–31, 335, 343, 348, 353, 360
  maintenance of, 41n
  mending of, 51, 59, 94–95, 109, 133, 144, 150–51, 191, 195, 201–202, 225, 228, 252, 271, 273, 295, 336, 350, 355, 361
  painting of, 298
  repairs of, 1
  rope of, 164, 275
  strings of, 61, 88, 109, 124, 134
  watch of, 150
  wheel of, 273, 355
  wire of, 323
  See also under Trades and occupations
Cloth, 138, 237–38, 291n, 335
  arras, 39, 39n
  banner, 214, 224, 250–51
  buckram, 67, 108–109, 134, 238, 245
  camlet, 245, 245n
  canvas, 67, 94, 103, 237, 244–45, 270n, 326
  corporax, 117, 244
  cross cloth, 19, 89, 93, 235
  flock, 354, 354n
  gold, 171
  harden cloth, 326, 355
  hemp, 101
  kerchief, 122
  linen, 52, 110n, 112, 117n, 125, 132, 171n, 231, 234, 244–45, 267, 270n, 325, 331, 338
  mending of, 134, 171
  napery, 92
  of altars, 25, 74, 85, 116, 134, 137, 143–45, 149, 155, 163, 169–71, 174, 194–95, 227n, 238, 243–46, 259–60, 269, 271, 275, 311, 335, 349
  painted, 24, 238
  painting of, 260

INDEX OF SUBJECTS 409

passion cloth, 25, 335
ribbon, 67, 134, 145
rood cloth, 271
russel, 235, 245, 245n, 260, 347
sarsenet, 89
satin, 65n, 103
say, 109, 109n
serge, 172
silk, 36n, 44, 52, 67, 103, 110n, 158,
    171n, 238, 245, 270
silk, Spanish, 238
tablecloth, 315
towel, 110, 201, 244
veil cloth, 304
velvet, 36n, 65n, 145, 169, 235, 340
washing of, 108, 116, 123, 131, 137, 143,
    149, 155, 163, 16970, 174, 189,
    194, 202, 217, 227n, 243, 260,
    269, 271, 275, 299–300, 310–11,
    315, 317–18, 322–23, 325, 329,
    335, 343, 348, 353, 360
woollen, 2, 270n
worsted, 238
See also under Altars
Clothes and vestments, 3, 22n, 29, 45,
    45n, 91n, 158, 199, 246, 305, 311,
    340, 342
    alb, 45, 52, 66, 76, 80, 85, 102, 112,
        118, 125, 138, 175–76, 231, 236,
        243, 269–70, 305, 311
    amice, 102, 175n, 243, 246
    belt, 354n
    coat, 26, 348, 354, 356
    coif, 342n
    cope, 44, 44n, 80, 85, 93, 108, 131,
        133–34, 139, 169, 184, 246, 260,
        270, 305, 311, 342, 342n
    corslet, 26, 244n, 356
    doublet, 65n
    girdle, 26, 58, 66, 75, 88, 110, 126, 150,
        157, 244n, 354
    gown, 272
    hallowing of, 110
    Herod's clothes, 67, 67n
    hood, 175
    jack, 270
    jacket, 270n
    maker of, 156
    making of, 144–45
    mending of, 52, 66, 77–78, 108–109,
        131, 133–34, 157, 184, 260
    robe, 141n
    rochet, 52, 268, 271
    shirt, 237n
    shoes, 308

    stole, 171
    suit, 235
    surplice, 52n, 110, 132, 156, 171,
        202–203, 209, 211, 236–37, 243,
        251–52, 267–71, 279, 294–96,
        299–300, 308–311, 315, 325, 331,
        338, 349
    towel, 270–71
    veil, 19, 95, 151
    washing of, 74, 85
Coffers *see under* Chests and boxes
Coffins, 126n, 279
    Collections, gatherings and offerings,
        14–16, 30, 185, 291, 320, 322,
        328, 333–34, 346, 349, 351, 357
    Colleges, 3n, 20
Commemorations, 7
Communions, 110n, 201n
    cup of, 25, 351, 356
Corporations, 10, 21n, 28–30, 59n, 93n,
    300, 300n
    accounts of, 304
    book of, 300, 302, 327
    charter of, 100n
    creation of, 22
    meeting room for, 294n
    See also under Officials
Cottages *see under* Houses and buildings
Councils, 226
Courts,
    dean's court, 233
    King's Bench, 247n
    Lincoln Consistory Court, 7n
    manorial, 10, 10n, 12, 29, 36n, 129n,
        329n, 365n
    of piepowder, 39n
    Prebendal Court, 7n
    Star Chamber, 53n
    See also under Officials
Crime and offences, criminal cases, 10
Crops, 4
    corn, 77n, 138, 343, 349
    hay, 306, 309, 316, 325, 329, 336, 340
    management of, 10
    peas, 269n
    protection of, 175n, 226n
    straw, 317, 336
    winter, 17
Crosses, in the marketplace, 124
Cry *see* Hue and cry

Dams, 144
    Debts and debtors, 10, 39n, 199, 212,
        215, 221, 229, 248, 303, 359

Depositions, 16, 22n, 76n, 116n, 139n, 142n, 154n, 244n
Dikes and diking, 12, 14, 51, 116, 116n, 119, 125, 131, 175, 175n, 189–92, 19697, 200, 202–203, 217, 232, 251, 283, 293, 296, 300, 307, 309, 314, 316–17, 319, 322, 326, 330, 336, 340, 344–45, 362
Diseases *see under* Illness and sickness
Ditches, 13n, 116n, 175n
Drains *see* Sewers
Drink *see* Food and drink
Dung, muck and mud,
  dirt, 94
  dung, 293–94
  muck, 93, 270
  mud, 295
  sod, 27, 228, 266, 271, 307, 314, 316n, 329, 354

Enclosure and enclosing, 201n, 238, 308
  bill of, 201
  enclosure survey, 8
  enclosing of the churchyard, 201
Escapes, 339n, 361n
  of prisoners, 27
Excommunications, 26
Executions, 47n, 80n, 88n, 116n, 246n
Executors, 223, 250

Fairs, 29, 39n, 93, 93n, 265, 295n, 307, 312, 314, 317, 324
  steward of, 39n
Farms, 14n
Festivals *see under* Services, religious
  Felons and felony, 27
Fences,
  mending of, 66
  pale, 251
Fens and fenlands, 5
Feretories *see under* Shrines
Fines *see* Amercements
Fires and burning, 12n, 28, 61, 164, 239, 239n, 354
  burning of books, 16, 16n, 33n
  Easter fire, 260n
  fire, 260, 272, 309
  fire beacon, 26
  fire beacon, 275
  fire brigade, 12, 28
  scathe fire, 28, 96, 103, 214
Floods and flooding *see under* Weather
Flowers and plants,
  flower, 100, 334
  hemp, 201
  peasecod, 269
  weed, 66
Food and drink,
  ale, 5, 23, 45n, 125, 233, 236, 278
  beer, 45n
  bread, 5, 23, 45n, 124n, 125, 184, 226–27, 232–34, 236, 266
  bread, holy, 124
  breakfast, 171, 177
  butter, 238
  dinner, 21, 184, 187, 189
  drink, 13n, 38, 39, 43, 144, 184, 227–28, 232, 266, 314
  honey, 8
  malmsey, 228, 228n
  meat, 13, 27, 38–39, 43, 61, 67, 77, 87, 94, 102, 125, 131, 144, 173, 187, 190, 211, 219, 227–28, 233–34, 236, 243, 245–46, 251, 266, 271, 273, 275, 278–80, 307, 309–310, 314–17, 319, 336–37, 349–50, 354–56, 361
  milk, 8
  sack, 318, 318n
  sugar, 318
  venison, 127
  wine, 5, 86n, 125, 170, 176, 183, 226–27, 228n, 232–34, 237, 294, 316, 318n, 330
Forests *see* Woods and forests
Frankincense and incense, 24, 85n, 139, 237
Fraternities, 162n
Fugitives, 361n
Funerals, 7
Furnaces *see* Ovens and furnaces

Games and sports,
  archery *see* Archery and butts
  tennis, 208n
Gardens, 8
Garths *see under* Parts of churches
Gates, 13, 53n, 61, 61n, 66, 78, 87, 100–101, 111, 125, 132, 144, 150, 217, 232, 246, 264, 269, 273, 296, 307, 319, 329, 336, 343–44, 354–55
  hanging of, 293, 296, 349, 354
  making of, 294, 309
  mending of, 86, 172n, 176, 218, 232, 245, 273, 279, 295, 325, 345

of church, 9, 209, 234, 242, 251, 259, 294–95, 298, 325, 331, 361
of churchyard, 78, 85, 100, 137–38, 144, 155–57, 176, 218, 234, 279, 294, 318
Gatherings *see* Collections
Girdles *see under* Clothes and vestments
Glazing, 196, 203, 233, 246, 252, 294; *see also under* Trades and occupations
Graves,
    covering of, 42n, 78, 252, 269, 271, 274–76, 284, 296, 298–300, 307–11, 315, 317–18, 323–24, 330–32, 337, 343–45, 349–50, 355–56, 360, 362
    laying down of, 270
    mending of, 309
Guilds, 4, 6n, 13, 28, 184, 202n
    Corpus Christi guild, 12n, 22, 96, 112, 212, 215
    Holy Trinity guild, 8, 11–12, 21–22, 22n, 29, 36, 43n, 73, 84, 89n, 96, 111n, 122, 136, 154, 168, 183n, 192, 265n
    officials of, 33n
    Palmers' guild, 11, 13, 29
    St George's guild, 61n
    St Mary's guild (Lady guild), 7n, 11, 11n, 12, 21–22, 22n, 29, 33n, 36n, 37, 37n, 41n, 45n, 48, 48n, 53, 64n, 65, 65n, 72n, 73, 78n, 80, 89n, 92, 96, 100n, 107, 111n, 112, 115, 122, 134n, 139n, 143, 154, 162, 170n, 173, 182, 183n, 188, 192, 214, 223n, 227n, 241n
    St Peter's guild, 12n, 22, 96, 112
    suppression of, 22, 30
    See also under Officials
Gutters, 13n, 117n, 175
    runnel, 117, 117n

Handcuffs *see* Manacles
Hangings, suicide, 348–49
Harbours *see* Ports and harbours
Hedges and hedging, 49, 51, 109, 114, 116, 124, 131, 138, 154, 158, 164, 169, 175, 177, 186, 190, 195, 197, 199–201, 203, 207, 215, 219, 227, 232–34, 242–43, 246, 251, 272, 293, 296–97, 307, 309, 311, 316, 318–19, 322–23, 325, 330, 332, 338, 342–45, 348, 353, 359–60, 362
Hides and skins, 51, 66, 74, 83, 86–87, 94, 101–102, 110, 132–33, 151, 157–58, 170, 243, 267, 277, 281, 291, 297, 305–306, 312, 334, 349
Highways *see* Roads
Hospitals, 20n
    leper, 64n
Houses and buildings, 8, 38, 124, 145, 145n, 164, 172, 176, 231–32, 275, 306, 318
    almshouse, 22
    bedehouse, 12, 22, 126n, 202
    burning of, 28, 214
    cattleshed, 9
    chime house, 270, 314, 319, 331, 336, 355
    clergy house, 314n
    cottage, 11n, 100n, 150
    dwelling house, 83n
    house in churchyard, 7, 306, 326, 329, 331–32, 334, 336, 341, 359
    lodge, 52, 74, 77, 79, 86–87, 90, 97, 102, 108–110, 116–17, 119, 124–27, 139, 171, 209–210, 355
    plague house, 241
    poorhouse, 9, 64n, 202n
    schoolhouse, 22n, 103, 176, 183, 187, 189, 196, 233, 266–67
    workhouse, 334
Hue and cry, 27, 339n, 361

Illness and sickness, 145, 227
    disease, 225n, 236n
    epidemic, 23, 164n
    plague, 23, 66n, 133, 133n, 145, 145n, 164, 183, 241
    relief of sick people, 23
    sickness, 196, 227, 236, 254, 258, 269, 278, 287
    See also under Hospitals
Images, 25, 144, 195
    making of, 268
    of St George, 18, 133
    of St George with the dragon, 18, 18n
    of the Virgin, 197n
    painting of, 268
    sale of, 19
    taking down of, 133n
Implements *see* Tools and implements
Incense *see* Frankincense
Indentures, 71, 93, 139, 190, 283n
Indictments, 110
Injunctions, 139n; *see also under* Books
Ink, 30
Inns and taverns, 29, 175, 178

INDEX OF SUBJECTS

Jewels and jewellery, 43n, 59n, 96n
   bead, 44, 64, 69, 96, 99
   coral, 64, 69, 99
   gaud, 64, 64n
   pearl, 44
   ring, gold, 45

Lamps *see* Lights and lamps
Leases, 305
Legacies *see* Bequests
Lepers and leprosy, 64n
Letters, 126, 138, 278, 340
   of attorney, 93
Libraries, 11, 294
Licences, 21
   for lands to be given for the
      maintenance of chantry, 37n
   to beg, 126n
Lights and lamps, 22, 43n, 132n
   lamp light, 162, 162n, 173, 204
   lantern, 66, 78, 144, 226, 243, 323
   Lenten light, 238
   Plough light, 12n, 43, 70, 72, 79, 96,
      104, 118–19, 146, 151, 158–59,
      166, 186, 190, 204, 211, 215, 221,
      224, 231, 264–65, 282, 297, 304
   St Michael light, 112
   sepulchre light, 24, 104, 244, 275, 280,
      335
Loans, 12, 276
Lofts *see under* Parts of churches

Madness and lunacy, carrying mad women
   out of town, 218
Manacles and handcuffs, 27, 108
Manors, 4n, 10, 189n, 300n, 305, 305n,
   347; *see also under* Courts
Maps, 117, 117n
Markets and marketplaces, 5, 89, 17, 29,
   59, 59n, 83n, 94, 124–25, 156n,
   208n, 210, 210n, 217, 227, 242, 295,
   359n
   corn-market, 16
   sheep-market, 12
   See also under Officials
Marriages, 295n
   book of admonition about, 295
Marshes and marshlands, 2, 5, 13n, 29,
   175n
Meadows, 14
Metals,
   brass, 205, 211, 215, 221, 229
   copper, 8n, 74, 235
   gold, 45, 171, 238, 245
   iron, 12n, 28, 38, 40, 41n, 52, 58n,
      59–61, 61n, 66, 75, 78, 85,
      87–88, 95–96, 100–103, 109, 111,
      117, 119, 125–26, 131–33, 138–39,
      144, 150–51, 157–58, 163, 165,
      170–71, 183–84, 190, 196, 205,
      209, 214, 219–20, 224, 227, 232,
      239, 242–43, 260, 268–70, 273,
      279–80, 282, 291, 293, 296–97,
      299, 305, 310–11, 315, 317–18,
      325–26, 331, 333, 336, 345, 351,
      354–55, 361
   latten, 144, 150, 164–65, 185, 246
   lead, 38, 41–43, 43n, 44–45, 49–50,
      52–53, 58–60, 64, 67, 72, 75–79,
      81, 88, 90, 94, 97, 101, 110,
      112, 119, 124–25, 132–33, 139,
      144–45, 150–52, 156–57, 165,
      171n, 173, 175, 185, 200–201,
      203, 207–208, 212, 215, 217, 221,
      227–29, 233, 235, 237–38, 241,
      244, 252, 267, 270, 273, 279–80,
      292, 296, 307–308, 315, 317–18,
      322–24, 329–31, 335–36, 340,
      343, 346, 348–49, 353, 355, 360
   osmund, 58
   pewter, 76
   silver, 29, 43, 43n, 44, 64, 66, 69, 85,
      94, 124, 134, 139, 150, 162n, 163,
      166, 172, 174, 177, 184, 187, 213n,
      214, 297, 305, 311, 340, 346,
      351, 356
   solder, 38–39, 41–42, 60, 62, 68, 76,
      79, 81, 87–88, 90, 97, 101–102,
      109–110, 117, 125, 157, 163, 171,
      176, 184, 220, 242, 307, 309,
      329–30, 343–44, 355, 361–62
   tin, 305–306
Mills, 217, 228, 233, 243, 245, 329n, 345,
   354, 362
   water, 329n
Minerals and natural resources,
   boulder, 207
   chalk, 338, 344
   charcoal, 40n, 151, 158, 165, 172, 177,
      360
   clay, 86, 102, 125, 183, 187, 267,
      336–37
   coal, 17, 33n, 40, 40n, 50, 53, 59, 61,
      69, 76, 78–79, 85, 87, 89, 93,
      95, 108, 111–12, 117–19, 124,
      126–27, 133–34, 138–39, 145,
      184–85, 191, 291n
   coral, 44

freestone, 118, 131
glass, 38–39, 43n, 60, 62, 67–68,
    87–88, 95, 102–103, 108,
    117–18, 125–26, 139, 144–45,
    150, 156–58, 165, 170–71, 176,
    187, 190–92, 196, 203, 219–20,
    242, 271, 293–94, 329–31, 349,
    360–63
grease, 50, 52, 67
gum, 139n
ivory, 157n
leather, 2, 51, 58, 60, 66, 68, 74, 126,
    132, 218, 270n, 356, 360
lime, 19, 38–40, 43, 59–62, 66, 68,
    76–79, 87–89, 95, 102–103, 109,
    111, 118–19, 124–26, 139, 144,
    150, 156–58, 164, 169, 171–72,
    175, 183–85, 190–91, 206, 220,
    228, 232, 234, 268, 294, 299,
    308–309, 323, 328, 330, 337–38,
    344, 349–50, 356, 362
oil, 75n, 134n, 187n
reed, 260
resin, 139n
sand, 75–76, 117, 175, 183, 228, 234,
    236, 242, 267, 323, 328, 337–38
stone, 6, 9, 13, 13n, 19, 23, 38–39, 39n,
    43, 61–62, 66, 70, 78, 85, 87–88,
    93, 95, 102, 104, 111, 127, 132,
    134, 140, 150–52, 156–57, 159,
    166, 172, 178, 187, 193, 200,
    202, 204–205, 208n, 210, 224,
    228–29, 234, 236, 239, 242,
    244, 251, 267, 274, 310, 323–24,
    328–30, 337–39, 344, 362
straw, 67, 77, 85n, 86, 267
tar, 269
timber, 9, 24, 28, 4041, 61, 7678, 81,
    87, 90, 97, 109, 138, 171, 251,
    260, 294, 305, 319, 349
wax, 19, 24, 78–79, 102, 132n, 144–45,
    159, 190, 207, 214, 238, 244–45,
    260, 270–71, 275, 279–80, 305,
    311, 324, 347
wood, 9, 38–40, 53, 59–62, 67, 75–76,
    78–79, 87, 92n, 101, 103, 117, 119,
    124, 132–33, 150, 154, 157–58,
    171, 185, 187, 201, 217, 224, 234,
    239, 239n, 241, 244–45, 251,
    260, 269–70, 272, 275–77, 279,
    291, 294, 299, 305–309, 315,
    324, 331, 335–36, 338, 343, 345,
    354–55, 359
Miracles, paintings of, 19

Mowing, 309
Muck and mud *see* Dung
Music and songs,
    chanting, 111n
    music, 169n
    polyphony, 111n
    singing, 343
    See also under Books; Schools; Trades
        and occupations
Musters, 170n, 176, 176n, 266

Nunneries, 65n

Obligations *see* Bonds
Occupations *see* Trades and occupations
Offerings *see* Collections
Officials,
    admiral, lord, 17, 124, 124n
    alderman, 11, 11n, 33n, 45n, 53, 80,
        122n
    alderman of guild, 89n, 111n
    alderman, deputy, 48n
    assistant of corporation, 11, 59n, 100n,
        112n, 240n, 300n, 304n, 327, 334
    assistant of school, 282, 301–303
    attorney, 111n
    attorney of the Court of
        Augmentations, 21
    auditor, 59n, 183n
    bailiff, 4, 10–11, 11n, 27, 70n, 304n,
        329n
    beadle, 266, 266n, 267–68, 270, 272n,
        293–96, 298–99, 308–309, 314,
        317
    burgess, 11, 122n
    chamberlain of guild, 33n, 41n, 45n,
        111n
    chancellor, 336
    clerk of the market, 164, 244
    clerk, parish, 3, 178
    collector of tax, 284
    commissioners, 201, 228, 237, 337
    commissioner, royal, 25
    commissioner for chantries, 21n
    commissioner of inquisition *post*
        mortem, 21n
    commissioner of sewers, 175n, 318n
    commissioner of subsidy, 14n, 33n
    constable, 4, 10, 59n, 145, 145n, 176,
        191–92, 195, 234, 266n, 273,
        278, 284, 328–29, 338
    constable of castle, 307n
    coroner, 349
    councillor, 11, 11n

INDEX OF SUBJECTS

councillor at law, 303n
dikereeve, 4, 14
gentleman of the Privy Chamber, 189n
jailer, 317
justice, 195, 201
justice of assize, 297
justice of peace (JP), 177n, 340n
justice of sewers, 175, 316, 330
keeper of bears (bearward), 150, 150n, 164
keeper of the wood at Louth Park, 70n
lieutenant, 225
mayor, 11, 11n, 21n, 278, 278n, 296n
member of Parliament (MP), 21n, 76n, 170n, 177n, 191n, 211n, 278n, 301n, 318n, 340n, 342n
merchant of the Staple of Calais, 6n, 21, 94n, 240n
organ builder, king's, 12
overseer of works, 96
ploughman, 43n
privy seal, lord, 17, 126, 126n
reeve, 10, 45n
registrar, bishop's, 16
schoolmaster, 22
sheriff, 307n, 318n, 340n
steward of bishop, 76n, 189n
steward of court, 365
steward of fair, 39n
steward of manor, 10, 36n, 129n
surveyor of the boon-days, 311
surveyor of the highways, 14, 265, 272, 277, 297, 312, 319, 326, 332–33, 339, 346, 350–51, 357
surveyor, crown, 21n
town crier, 42n
treasurer of Lincoln, 8
usher to the grammar school, 265n
vicegerent in spirituals, 15
warden of corporation, 11, 21n, 59n, 100n, 112n, 204n, 240n, 300n, 303n, 304n, 305n, 326–28, 334–35, 342, 348, 353
warden of school, 282, 282n, 301, 301n, 302–303, 326
See also Citizens
Old age and aged persons, 276, 281
Orchards, 8
Organs, 12, 42, 42n, 44, 66, 75, 77–78, 78n, 79–80, 87, 208, 220, 224, 308, 349, 360
blower of, 143, 149, 155, 163, 169, 174, 182, 189, 194
blowing of, 44n, 85, 92, 100, 108, 116, 123, 131, 137, 200, 218, 227, 227n, 232–33, 235, 238, 241, 250, 267, 292, 308, 335, 343, 348, 353, 360
case of, 304
mending of, 100, 151, 309
regal, 80n
Ornaments and furniture, 3
ampoule, 75, 75n, 103
aspergillum, 157n
banner, 108
basin, 19, 134
button, 44
canopy, 238, 246
case, corporax, 246
censer, 23, 25, 85, 87, 95, 110, 110n, 150, 235, 334
chalice, 25, 44n, 200, 214, 281, 281n, 282, 291, 297, 305, 311, 340, 346, 353
chrismatory, 145, 187, 187n, 246
church furniture, 5, 20, 23
cross, 58, 60, 74, 93–94, 124, 144, 150, 162n, 163–64, 166, 169, 175, 185, 187, 192n, 235, 237, 244, 246, 260, 276–77, 309, 362
crucifix, 44
cruet, 25, 86, 246
cup, communion, 25, 351, 356
curtain, 101
font, 88, 96, 172, 325, 325n
frame, 298
hassock, 218, 233
hearse, 238
lectern, 19, 132, 208, 224, 279
mat, 202, 218, 308, 345
nat, 323
paten, 25, 281, 281n, 282, 291, 297, 305, 311, 353
pax, 157–58, 237
pew, 11, 11n, 207, 207n, 211, 246
phial, 134, 134n
plate, 68, 190, 213, 213n
pulpit, 19, 19n, 88, 202, 208
pyx, 102, 175n, 214, 246, 266–67, 359n
removal of church fittings, 25
riddel, 203
rood, 19, 24, 243–45, 260, 335, 362
rood figures, 24, 89n
sale of church fittings, 25
seat, 108, 318
sepulchre, 238–39, 244, 246, 250, 260, 264, 271–72, 278
silverware, 29
sprinkle, 86
sprinkle, holy water, 279

INDEX OF SUBJECTS

staff, 93, 260
stock, holy water, 19
stool, 61, 79, 85, 119, 124, 127, 208, 224, 227, 246, 271, 279, 317–18, 332, 360
stoup, holy water, 86n
strinkle, 157, 157n, 176, 190, 237, 269, 275
tabernacle, 25, 26n, 175n, 359
table, 19, 24, 95, 118, 210, 298
table, altar, 274
table, communion, 19, 209n, 210n, 315, 351
taper, 79, 104, 119
thurible, 85n
trestle, 68
trough, 87
vat, 138, 205
vat, holy water, 23–24, 50–51, 101, 155, 157–58, 236–37, 242, 335
vial, 158, 163
See also Candles and candlesticks; Lights and lamps; Torches
Outlaws and outlawries, 27
Ovens and furnaces,
  furnaces, 77, 77n
  oven, 151, 158, 165

Pageants, 43, 43n, 101, 112
Paint and paintings, 19, 246, 251, 260, 268, 335, 361–62
  of clocks, 298
  of glass, 39n
  of scripture, 26
  portraits, 162n
  wall painting, 19, 24, 190n
Pales *see under* Fences
Paper, 40, 69, 86–87, 133, 156, 175, 189, 195–96, 200, 202–203, 209, 220, 226, 241, 251, 260, 278, 293, 310, 331, 345, 362
Parchments, 40n, 76, 166, 170, 241, 267, 279, 281–82, 291, 291n, 297, 305–306, 345n
Pardons, table for, 118
Parsonages, 283n
Parts of churches,
  aisle, 75–76, 85, 87, 89, 9395, 109, 118, 211, 218, 323
  bellhouse chamber, 76, 79, 126, 207, 337; door of, 279, 325
  buttress, 111
  ceiling, 235, 264
  chamber, 269–70

  chamber, clerk's, 77, 117, 126, 144, 172, 187
  chancels, 133, 338n
  clockhouse, 184, 315, 361; door of, 50, 59, 86, 93, 279
  door, 58–59, 68, 75–77, 86–88, 95, 101, 111, 116–17, 132–33, 137–38, 172, 184, 187, 189, 196, 209, 220, 228, 270, 307, 336, 345; *see also under* Parts of churches, bellhouse chamber, clockhouse, and steeple
  galilee, 41, 41n
  gallery, 52, 78, 118, 124–25, 133, 138, 183, 185, 220
  garth, 40, 61, 66
  lead house, 323
  library, 294
  loft, bell, 94
  loft, rood, 12, 19, 24n, 25–26, 26n, 42n, 95, 126, 144, 192n, 207, 239, 239n, 245, 299, 299n, 305, 311, 319, 359, 361–62
  porch, 7, 46, 54, 57, 72, 83, 90, 109, 129, 142, 157, 184, 187, 294n, 310, 313, 337, 358
  revestry, 117, 188–89
  roof, 41, 43, 74n, 171n
  sacristy, 109, 117n
  screen, rood, 18, 24n, 42n, 299n
  sepulchre house, 24
  spire, 1, 6, 8n, 12, 30, 36n, 39n, 44n, 56n, 67n, 68n, 75n, 81n, 84n, 122n, 144n
  stall, 52, 59–61, 75, 75n, 77–78, 87, 102–103, 112, 119, 119n, 122, 132, 139, 150, 154, 156–58, 164–65, 172, 190, 196, 208, 210, 217–19, 227, 252, 269, 295, 309
  steeple, 1, 7, 13, 39–41, 60, 66, 68, 76–79, 85, 87, 93–96, 110, 112, 118–19, 125, 132–34, 137, 144, 165, 171, 175, 177, 183, 190–91, 267–68, 274, 311, 323, 330–31, 249, 353, 355, 360; door of, 86, 138, 144, 150, 158, 171, 271, 274–75, 279, 337
  steps, 85
  stile, 60, 87, 103, 117, 138, 150, 202, 234, 246, 270, 279
  treasure house, 116n
  vestry, 4, 96n, 117n, 349
  walls, 24, 59, 66, 94, 109–10, 144, 156, 164, 175, 187, 210, 234, 244, 259, 299, 323–24, 328, 350, 356

windows, 38, 43n, 51, 60–61, 67, 76–78, 85, 87–89, 93–95, 102–103, 108, 112, 117–18, 125–26, 133, 138–39, 144–45, 150, 156–58, 165, 170–71, 176, 187, 190–92, 196, 203, 208–209, 211, 219–20, 226, 233, 237, 242, 252, 271, 280, 293–94, 308, 323, 329–30, 330n, 331, 349–50, 360–63

    See also Chantries; Chapels; Choirs; Gates; Gutters

Pasture, 318
Paupers *see* Poverty and paupers
Paving and pavements, 12, 85, 109, 158, 197
Pensions *see* Annuities
Petitions and supplications, 126
Portraits *see* Paint and paintings
Pinfolds, 189n
Pirates and piracy, 161n
Pits, 204, 208, 252, 279, 338
    saw, 208n
Plants *see* Flowers and plants
Plays, 39, 39n, 43n
Ploughs, 359
    Poor *see* Poverty and paupers
Ports and harbours,
    haven, 2, 29
    inlet, 2
    port, 29
Poverty and paupers, 3n, 4, 13, 23, 23n, 30, 183, 183n, 184–85, 187, 189, 234, 252n, 285n, 293, 339
    badges for poor folk, 22, 126
    bequests to, 33n, 291n, 292, 302n
    burials of paupers, 133–34, 137
    gatherers for, 239
    lodge for, 52
    names of poor men, 260
    poor child, 220
    poor folk, 271, 334
    poor gentleman, 138
    poor man, 110, 226, 253, 271, 273, 278
    poor people, 254
    poor woman, 196
    relief of, 236–37, 269, 273–74, 283
    See also under Houses and buildings
Prayers and praying, 7, 15
    Lord's Prayer, 25, 298n
    See also under Books
Prebends, 283n
Presentments, 233
Priories *see* Abbeys

Prisoners and captives, 10, 27n, 162n, 164, 176, 177n, 210, 251, 264, 273, 317, 323–24, 325n, 347n
    confinement of, 67n
    restraining of, 108n
    transporting of, 27, 29
Processions, 42n, 125, 359n
Proclamations, 233
    royal, 220
Pumps, 176–77
Punishments,
    gallows, 64n, 92n
    hanging, 17
    hung, drawn and quartered, 3n
    imprisonment, 126n
    pillory, 27n
    stocks, 27n
Purses, 156

Qualifications, bachelor of law, 80
Quarries and quarrying, 6, 26, 208, 208n, 251, 278, 315, 329, 337n, 338–39, 359, 359n
Quittances, 183, 329

Rebellions and rebels, 129n, 246n
    Lincolnshire Rising, 3, 3n, 13n, 1416, 16n, 17, 21n, 22n, 29, 33n, 40n, 43n, 45n, 52n, 59n, 67n, 68n, 70n, 74n, 76n, 80n, 81n, 86n, 92n, 96n, 104n, 110n, 111n, 113n, 114n, 116n, 117n, 126n, 139n, 142n, 154n, 170n, 177n, 181n, 195n, 221n, 231n, 244n, 320n
    Northern Rebellion (1569), 26, 244n, 354n, 356n, 359n
    Pilgrimage of Grace, 88n
Relics, 44n, 206n
Rents and services,
    fee farm, 300, 327
    landlaw, 329
    See also Boon-works
Rivers and watercourses,
    river, 2, 6, 77n
    stream, 13n
Roads and highways,
    Act for Mending the Highways (1555), 14, 264, 264n
    amendment of, 265
    carriageway, 306n
    causeway, 12, 13n
    cleaning of, 42n, 116
    highway, 169, 212, 221, 229, 233, 239, 251, 328–29, 332

INDEX OF SUBJECTS 417

lane, 343
maintenance of, 14, 14n, 212n
mending of, 94, 144, 156, 169, 218, 233, 251
repairs of, 4, 12, 69n, 212, 221, 229, 239
street, 116, 330
surveyors of, 265
way, 132, 144, 156
See also under Officials
Royalty,
accession of Edward VI, 5
birth of Edward VI, 5, 125
death of Henry VIII, 56
excommunication of Elizabeth I, 26
marriage of Queen Mary, 6, 6n
proclamation of Queen Mary, 6, 233
See also under Chapels; Charters
Ruin and decay, 336–37, 350, 356

Sacraments, 79, 104, 116, 119, 175, 201n, 238
Saints, 66n
relics of, 44n
Sawing, 42, 50–51, 60–61, 75, 87, 138, 293, 310
Scaffolds and scaffolding, 39n, 95–96, 117n
Scholars, 227
Schools, 266, 282
grammar, 9, 13, 20, 20n, 21, 21n, 22n, 29–30, 59n, 64n, 100n, 112, 173n, 209n, 300, 300n, 338n
petty school, 21, 21n, 266
song school, 21, 29, 103, 108, 117n, 125, 187, 233n, 266n
See also under Houses and buildings; Officials; Trades and occupations
Scripture, 298
paintings of, 26, 362
ten commandments, 25, 298, 298n
Seas, 2, 13n, 24
Sermons, 19n, 20, 113n, 350n
Services, religious, 343, 348, 360
churching, 282, 282n
dirge, 6
harvest festival, 42n 269
mass, 17n, 74, 74n, 87, 95n, 117n, 124n, 133, 148n
month's mind, 36n
morrow mass, 86
obit, 6n, 36n, 64n, 174, 179
requiem, 36n, 148n

See also under Books
Sewers and drains,
cleansing of, 12, 219
drain, 4, 59n, 196, 308
keeping of, 307, 314
mending of, 228, 246
scouring of, 165, 169–71, 176, 191
sewer, 13, 87, 116n, 131, 134, 156, 163–65, 169–71, 174–76, 191, 219, 228, 246, 298, 307–308, 314, 318
See also under Officials
Ships and boats, vessel, 2
Shops, 43n, 104n, 142n
Shrines, 19, 132n
feretory, 44, 44n, 64, 93, 103, 111, 163, 183, 189
Sickness *see* Illness and sickness
Singing and songs *see under* Books; Music and songs; Schools; Trades and occupations
Skins *see* Hides and skins
Soap, 237
Sports *see* Games and sports
Springs, 10, 93n
Statues, 18, 61n
Stiles *see under* Churchyards; Parts of churches
Stipends *see* Wages and stipends
Storms *see under* Weather
Strangers, 342
Strays, 189n, 208n, 317, 362
Subsidies *see* Taxes
Suicides, 348–49
Summons, 132n
Supplications *see* Petitions
Sureties, 42, 212, 221, 229, 239, 281, 284
Surplices *see under* Clothes and vestments
Surveys, of enclosure, 8
Suspensions, 201
Synods, 295n
Tapestries, 39n

Taverns *see* Inns
Taxes and subsidies, 2, 131, 284, 316, 329
aid for the emperor against the Turks, 161
clerical subsidy, 3
First Fruit and Tenths, 16n
Lay Subsidy (1524/25), 33n
Peter's Pence, 24n
subsidy, 176, 218n
See also under Officials
Terriers, glebe, 78
Testaments *see* Wills and testaments

INDEX OF SUBJECTS

Thatch and thatching, 28, 42, 67n, 77, 110, 116–17, 117n, 125–26, 171, 184, 209–10, 266–67, 336
Theology and theologians, 16, 16n
Threads and yarn, 44, 44n, 52, 67, 108–109, 131, 144–45, 157n, 176–77, 268, 325
  crewl, 108
  packthread, 94, 246, 299
Tithes, 8, 65n
  of bees, gardens, honey, lambs, milk, orchards, pigs, poultry and wool, 8
Tools and implements,
  anchor, 361
  axle tree, 118, 139, 201, 325
  band, 156
  bar, 87, 94, 273, 344, 354, 360, 363
  bar, iron, 38, 60, 139, 144, 150, 170–71, 196, 219–20, 293, 361
  barrel, 59, 270
  barrow, 210
  basket, 124, 124n
  beam, 86n
  bellows, 42, 58, 76, 79n, 124, 304
  besom, 60
  board, 103
  board, thack, 109
  bobbin, 157n
  bolt, 60, 171n, 225, 251n, 268, 294, 308, 310, 325, 336, 361
  bolt, iron, 101, 126, 138
  bowstring, 266
  brick, 236, 338
  bridle, 214
  broom, 60
  brush, 86n, 164
  bucket, holy water, 235
  chain, 62, 87, 132, 176, 235, 268, 279
  clapboard, 59, 266, 279
  clapper, *see under* Bells
  clasp, 86, 132, 157, 220, 238, 252, 268
  clog, 74
  cord, 176, 238, 260, 271, 355
  cotterell, 171, 171n, 361
  cradle, 268
  cramp, 252
  crook, 103, 220, 227, 343, 354
  crossette, 335n
  crowbar, 214n
  cruck, 329
  cruet, 335n
  fetters, 337
  flake, 131
  flitch, 323, 323n
  forelock, 171, 171n
  gavelock, 214, 214n, 220, 297, 305, 311, 333, 339, 346, 351
  gimmer, 77, 227, 251n
  glue, 86, 86n, 349
  grate, 60, 69, 87, 100, 138, 150, 202, 226, 234, 242, 260, 299
  gudgeon, 86, 86n, 94, 252, 267, 269–70
  hammer, 42, 69, 102, 318; *see also under* Bells; Chimes; Clocks
  harness, 318
  hasp, 61, 61n, 88, 138, 234, 251, 259
  hinge, 77n
  hook, 12n, 111, 214, 227, 279–80, 293, 336
  hook, fire, 293
  hook, iron, 28, 96, 103, 109, 117
  hoop, 41, 77, 78n, 132n, 251, 307, 361
  horn, 299, 360
  inkle, 88, 245–46
  key, 41, 51–52, 60, 66, 69, 86, 88, 103, 108, 111, 116, 116n, 119, 123, 126, 132, 137, 144, 146, 151, 158, 170, 172, 187, 189, 196, 209, 220, 225, 228, 267–68, 270–71, 279, 325, 345, 350, 354–55, 361
  kit, 268
  ladder, 12n, 68, 85, 96, 137, 165, 203, 245, 268, 305, 307, 311, 330, 362
  lath, 108, 332
  lock, 19, 51, 58–60, 66, 69, 74, 76, 87–88, 93, 95, 102–103, 108, 111, 118, 125, 132, 137–38, 144, 155–56, 171–72, 187, 209, 218, 220, 233–34, 238, 243, 251, 260, 270–71, 275, 279, 307–308, 318, 325, 337, 339, 345, 355, 360
  mortar, 203
  mould, 297
  nail, 38, 43, 52–53, 59–61, 67–68, 75–78, 88, 93–95, 102–103, 108–109, 111–12, 117, 119, 124–26, 132–33, 138–39, 144–45, 150, 155–57, 164–65, 169–71, 175, 177, 183–84, 187, 189–90, 201–202, 210, 217, 219–20, 226–27, 232, 235, 237, 242, 244–46, 251–52, 260, 267–70, 272, 274–75, 279, 293, 293n, 295–96, 298–99, 309n, 311, 317–18, 324–26, 331–32, 337, 343, 349–50, 355–56, 361–62
  nail, lath, 315
  nail, penny, 310, 315

napkin, 203
net, 345
padlock, 325
pane, 297
pick, 220, 225, 232, 234, 244, 251, 267, 282, 291, 297, 305, 307, 310–11, 333, 339, 346, 351
piercer, 78, 78n
pike, 273
pin, 87, 93, 157n, 268
pitch, 102
plank, 62, 78, 175, 217, 219, 260, 270, 291, 294, 299, 309–10, 319, 325, 343, 345, 349, 360, 362
plaster, 267, 331, 355
pole, 279–80
post, 273, 349
pulley, 75, 268, 330
rail, 93, 116, 217, 219–20, 237, 273–74, 279, 349, 359
ring, 111
ring, curtain, 101, 245, 260
ring, iron, 111
rochet, 116
rope, 2n, 6, 43, 51, 85n, 117, 117n, 132, 138, 156, 164, 176, 183, 209, 218–19, 232, 244, 252, 260, 267, 274–75, 280, 295, 310, 331, 336–37, 350, 355, 361
rossel, 38, 68, 102–103, 309, 329
sallet, 294
sarking board, 74, 74n, 75
scaffold, 196, 330, 362
shovel, 226
skep, 227
sleeper, 294, 332
sneck, 85, 117
spar, 177, 267, 271, 310, 331, 336, 349
spindle, 86n
splint, 294
spout, 13, 40, 52, 76, 87, 119, 165, 338
spring, 102, 318
spur, 217
staff, 164, 218, 250, 354, 356
stake, 267, 319, 323, 355
stanchion, 138
stang, 50
staple, 61, 68, 85–88, 138, 226–27, 234, 251, 259, 279, 294, 318, 337, 360–61
stay, 69, 85, 219, 317, 362
stirrup, 361
stob, 227, 227n
stock, 244, 246
stoop, 217, 273, 307

stooth, 86, 86n
string, 39, 236; *see also under* Bells; Chimes; Clocks
taper, 132n
tile, 58, 77, 206, 236, 337–38
trace, 293, 293n
trestle, 102, 233, 310, 349
trough, 124, 209, 242–43
trundle, 132, 202, 318, 331
tub, 78n
vartiwell, 77, 77n, 245, 307, 343–44, 354
wedge, 337, 361
wheel, 184, 200, 209, 225, 232; *see also under* Bells; Chimes; Clocks
wick, 271
wire, 59, 76, 95, 111, 126, 138, 144–45, 158, 183, 196, 226–27, 234, 251, 323
wiver, 331, 331n
Torches, 51, 58, 61–62, 87, 184
   link, 52, 52n
Towers, 13
Trades and occupations,
   actor, *see* player
   barber, 89–90, 172, 367, 369
   barker, 2, 364
   bell founder, 337
   bellman, 42n, 49, 52–53, 56–57, 61, 66, 74, 78, 95, 112, 116, 118–19, 123, 126–27, 131–34, 137, 143, 150, 155, 163–64, 174–76, 178, 182–83, 208, 250n, 251, 271, 294–97, 318, 330, 337, 343–44, 348, 350, 353, 355–56, 360
   blacksmith, 273
   bricklayer, 328
   butcher, 37, 40n, 45n, 53, 72, 72n, 74, 113, 291, 333, 335, 364–67, 371
   capper, 365–66
   cardmaker, 96–97, 144, 368
   carpenter, 29, 36n, 59n, 116n, 140, 250, 366
   carver, 18n, 366
   chapman, 275
   clerk, 1, 47n, 51, 76, 95, 101, 118, 126, 134, 137–38, 145, 156–57, 165, 176, 185, 189, 191, 227, 237, 241, 243, 253, 270, 303, 331, 336, 338, 340, 341n, 346, 365
   clerk, parish, 41, 41n, 44, 49–50, 56–57, 66, 74, 151
   clocksmith, 58, 61, 94, 191, 355
   composer, 25n

constable, 171
cooper, 78
corviser, 177, 365–66
cowherd, 75n, 311n
dog whipper, 208n, 227n, 232–33, 235, 238, 267
draper, 2, 8n, 16n, 33, 38n, 104, 104n, 135, 283n, 364–68
dyer, 91n
embroiderer, 77–78
finer, 58
fletcher, 123, 365
fossor, 176, 176n
fuller, 2, 62n, 112, 366, 368
gilder, 95–96
glazier, 29, 38, 60–61, 76, 78, 87, 93, 102, 119, 125, 133, 150, 308, 317, 323, 330–31, 349, 355, 360
glover, 2, 45, 45n, 53, 81n, 183n, 356n, 358, 366–67
goldsmith, 139n, 179, 181–82, 188, 334, 364, 366
harper, 313
husbandman, 37, 39n, 73n, 92, 121n, 135, 140, 151, 266, 366, 368
ironmonger, 47n
labourer, 13, 18, 40, 87, 93, 133–34, 138, 156, 164, 175, 217–18, 228, 232, 266, 269, 309, 330, 354, 361–62
litster, 91, 91n, 92, 114–15, 364
maid, 278
mason, 29, 44, 44n, 50, 59–62, 66, 68, 76, 87, 103, 267–68, 293, 361
mercer, 2, 9n, 36, 36n, 37, 43n, 45, 59n, 62, 72n, 96n, 97, 100n, 104, 119–20, 140, 172n, 275n, 364–68
merchant, 4, 6, 6n, 7, 29, 37–38, 41n, 48, 55, 64n, 83n, 99n, 143, 149, 364–65
merchant of the Staple of Calais, 29n, 37n, 40n, 65n
miller, 53, 53n, 62, 62n, 122, 365–67
musician, 22n
neatherd, 75, 75n, 95, 307, 311, 316, 319, 329, 336, 344, 360
organ maker, 80n
organ player, 270
painter, 24, 66, 195–96
pavior, 241n
pewterer, 19
pinder, 189–90, 195–96
piper, 358
player, 39, 39n, 190, 225, 225n

plumber, 29, 41–43, 51–53, 60, 67, 75–79, 88, 101, 109–110, 117, 119, 163, 218, 296–97, 299, 306–309, 322–23, 325, 331, 336, 343–44, 355, 360
rider, 126
roper, 36, 59n, 309, 349, 362, 365
saddler, 91–92, 122, 159n, 364, 367
sawyer, 42, 59n, 61, 87, 150, 156, 190, 251
schoolmaster, 13, 20–21, 22n, 112, 117n, 119, 241n, 265n, 347n
scrivener, 268
servant, 4n, 24, 38–39, 41–42, 52, 60–62, 66, 68–69, 77, 79, 80n, 87–88, 92n, 93, 110, 118, 125, 132–33, 137–38, 144, 150, 157, 161n, 163, 165, 171, 174, 176–77, 190, 201, 267, 273, 296, 307, 322–23, 339, 348–49, 355
shearman, 69n, 104, 104n, 358n, 368
shoemaker, 2, 16n, 36–37, 40n, 92, 104, 104n, 177n, 244n, 346n, 364, 365n, 367–68
shopkeeper, 6
singingman, 68n, 89, 94, 100n, 110–11, 111n, 112, 116, 139, 145
skinner, 166
smith, 1, 27–28, 40, 40n, 41–43, 50, 52, 59, 66, 68, 68n, 69, 74n, 85, 87–88, 94, 108, 117, 119, 127, 137–38, 144–45, 148, 165, 169–71, 175–76, 184, 209, 212, 214, 217, 220, 242, 268–70, 273, 293–95, 298, 325, 361–62, 366
swineherd, 307, 314, 316–19, 322, 329–30, 336, 344–45, 354, 360
tailor, 33, 33n, 43, 45, 53, 64n, 106n, 135, 142n, 260, 364–67, 367n, 368
tanner, 2, 45, 45n, 291n, 297, 358n, 366–67, 371
thatcher, 110, 125, 267
tiler, 236n, 324, 337–38, 350, 355–56
tinker, 60, 134, 139n
tradesman, 4, 6
walker, 62, 92
weaver, 2, 53, 69n, 73n, 101n, 140, 223n, 227n, 364–68
wheelwright, 129
woolpacker, 168n
workman, 88
wright, 36, 39n, 76–77, 108, 187, 232,

INDEX OF SUBJECTS

267, 273, 294, 299, 310, 331, 349, 355, 362, 365
yeoman, 16n, 36n, 37n, 40n, 41n, 110, 110n, 159n, 172n, 188n, 192n, 204n, 211n, 221n, 239n, 246n, 273n, 282n, 311n, 329n, 365–66
Trees, 119, 144, 227, 251, 280, 293–94, 310
  ash, 93n, 169n
  elm, 139n
  hazel, 41n
  willow, 41n, 86n, 171, 252, 280, 307, 312, 340, 343, 359
Trespasses, of cattle, 4n
Troughs, 40, 161
Turnpikes, 354–55

Universities, 48n

Vicarages, 23, 9n, 40
Visitations, 15–16, 16n, 116, 226, 336

Wafers, 51n
Wages and stipends, 3, 4n, 13, 22, 22n, 27, 43n, 50, 59–60, 67, 77, 87, 94–96, 101n, 102, 111–12, 116–19, 119n, 121n, 125, 131, 134, 142n, 144, 154n, 156–57, 181n, 187, 190, 202–203, 208–11, 219, 223n, 224, 227–28, 231–36, 238, 241, 241n, 242–43, 245–46, 250–51, 265n, 266–67, 270–71, 273–75, 279–80, 284, 293–300, 307–311, 314–19, 323–25, 329–31, 336–37, 343–45, 349–50, 353–56, 360–61
Wagons see Carts and wagons
  Wainscot, 51, 51n, 5, 60, 101, 138
Walls and walling, 13n, 74, 86, 266, 336; see also under Churchyards; Paint and paintings; Parts of churches
War and military, equipment, 4; see also Weapons and arms
Washing see under Altars; see also Whitewashing
Watercourses see Rivers and watercourses
Weapons and arms, 354n
  Almain rivet, 244, 244n, 294
  armour, 26, 26n, 244n, 325n, 354n
  arrow, 27n
  bow, 27n, 139n, 244n
  bowstring, 266
  bullet, 26
  caliver, 244n
  coat of plate, 26
  corslet, 26, 244n, 356
  dagger, 244n
  gorget, 244, 244n
  gun, 26, 354–55
  gunpowder, 26, 354, 356
  harness, 26, 203, 325, 329, 350, 354–56, 363
  longbow, 27n
  matches, 354
  musket, 26n, 354n
  pike, 26
  sallet, 244, 354, 354n
  splint, 244
  sword, 18n, 95, 215, 244n
Weather,
  flooding, 2, 175n, 360, 362
  rain, 362n
  snow, 145
  storm, 266n, 362
  wind, 151, 355, 362n
  wind, great, 118–19
Weathercocks and weathervanes, 8n, 39n, 67, 67n, 68
Webs, of spiders, 85, 89, 93
Wells, 158, 217–18, 227, 234n, 268, 273, 295, 323
  holy, 308n
Whitewashing, 19, 19n, 24, 190n, 191, 210, 244; see also Washing
Widows, 36–37, 44–45, 48, 53, 89, 94n, 121–22, 122n, 123, 129, 142–43, 156, 197, 231, 301n, 306n, 308n, 352, 358
Wills and testaments, 3n, 7n, 8, 8n, 33n, 36n, 37n, 47n, 65n, 83n, 86, 93, 100n, 115n, 122n, 137, 172n, 183, 223n, 277n, 283n, 291n, 302n
Woods and forests, 70n, 85, 227, 316
  coppice, 334
Wool and woollen goods, 2, 8, 96n, 270n
Writs, 132n, 247n
  of *latitat*, 247

Yarn *see* Threads and yarn